The GREAT AGE of DISCOVERY

By the same author:

Conquest by Man

The GREAT AGE of DISCOVERY

by PAUL HERRMANN

Translated by Arnold J. Pomerans

HARPER & BROTHERS

Publishers : New York

THE GREAT AGE OF DISCOVERY

This book was first published in Germany under the title *Zeigt mir Adams Testament.*

This book is published in England under the title of *The World Unveiled*

Library of Congress catalog card number: 57-11783

DEDICATED TO

MY WEDNESDAY EVENING

CIRCLE OF FRIENDS

IN GRATITUDE

CONTENTS

PART ONE

HELP US, HOLY MOTHER OF GUADALUPE!

PART TWO

THE EARTH IS A SPHERE

PART FOUR

THE EMPIRE OF THE FOUR CORNERS OF THE WORLD

PART FIVE

GUAIAC, THE 'FRENCH DISEASE' AND THE WELSERS

PART SIX

THE TEMPTING SOUTH SEA

PART SEVEN

THE CALL OF THE DESERT

ILLUSTRATIONS IN THE TEXT

A section of pictures will be found following page 174

MAPS

ACKNOWLEDGEMENTS

Permission to reproduce the illustrations in the text of this book was kindly given as follows: Nos. 32 and 33 by Ullstein Bilderdienst, Berlin; No. 16 by Verlag Sebastian Lux, Murnau, from Orion: *Weisse Kulturbringer in Altamerika*, October 1953; No. 42 by Essener Verlagsanstalt, Essen, from Baumann-Thurnwald-Westermann: *Völkerkunde von Afrika*; all others from archives.

ACKNOWLEDGEMENTS

[illegible]

PART ONE

HELP US, HOLY MOTHER OF GUADALUPE!

A little boy with a big jug of beer · The 'Book of Chronicles' · Widow Petrejus does not hold with black magic · Anthonius Koberger and Dr. Hartmann Schedel · Albrecht Dürer's studio covers the news · Columbus makes a pilgrimage · The Indians are coming! · Intelligence agents are at work, and dangerous news is abroad · Of the blessings of poverty and of buried cultures · How sure is the Admiral of himself? . The Porta dell' Olivella in Genoa · A bank official turns sailor · Shipwreck and rescue in Portugal · A wool-carder's son learns Latin and enters society · Of sea-beans, bamboo and driftwood · What lies behind the waters? · Paolo Toscanelli, the specialist on East Asia · Columbus is wrong about the circumference of the earth · The 'Trade'-secret of the Portuguese · What did Columbus know about the Vikings? · Emigration to Spain · The Admiral, the fleet and the men · Columbus forges the log · Of longitude and latitude · The cruel Sargasso Sea · Flocks of birds show the way · Help us, Holy Mother of Guadalupe! · 'Tierra! Tierra!' · The landing on San Salvador · The legend of the noble savage · The white gods · Where is the Great Khan of Tartary? · Pleasant dreams in a hammock · In search of gold · Brown men with smoking mouths · Shipwreck and return · The pilgrimage continued · The swineherd Pizarro and the nobleman Hernando Cortés look on · Two kings divide the world between themselves · Further voyages and the end of Columbus · The scope of his discoveries.

I

23rd December 1493

THE winter is hard this year. For weeks the venerable city of Nuremberg has lain under a soft coverlet of snow. How gay the great old houses look under their peaks of snow; how contentedly they pull these cosy nightcaps down over their heads. The upper storeys, jutting like chins far into the street, are adorned with glittering unkempt beards: a curtain of icicles, here glowing like threads of silver, there lightly powdered by the snow crystals carried by yesterday's north wind.

Today the air is still. Peace reigns over the town. Tomorrow Christmas will be celebrated. Little candles will be burning everywhere; oxen and asses, those silent creatures who witnessed Our Lord's nativity, will be given their Christmas portions of hay and clover. At this time tomorrow, hymns of praise will be sung by the priests in the churches of St. Lorenz and St. Sebaldus, the silver voice of the bell of Our Lady will ring out above the town, the church of the Holy Ghost will add its chimes, and in the resounding peal of all the bells the Christ-child will enter the city.

Blessed be Jesus Christ, Amen.

Let us follow this lad who is clenching two huge measures of ale in his tiny fists. His pious eagerness for the morrow, the birthday of the Christ-child, makes him tremble as if with cold. He is making for Anthony Koberger's house in the 'Latin Quarter' of Nuremberg where live the goldsmith Dürer, father of the great Albrecht, the scribe Neudorfer, the painter Wolgemuth and Hartmann Schedel, the physician and world chronicler.

He is a real child, this twelve-year-old boy. He has no inkling that some twenty years later he will be one of the great in the hierarchy of black magicians of the printing press and that, in our time, works that originated in the workshop of Johann Petrejus in Nuremberg will be worth their weight in gold.

Yet on this Christmas Eve, in the year of Our Lord 1493, he is but a little boy fetching beer, anxious and cold. Nevertheless, he does it gladly, for inside Koberger's big house festivities have already begun.

And what a momentous day it is! The *magnum opus*, the *Register of the book of chronicles and histories, with figures and illustrations from the beginning of the world unto our times* by Hartmann Schedel, *doctor medicinae,* is finished at last and is being printed today. Yesterday the prime went into the press, the big two-page map of Germany, with seas, rivers, mountains and cities clearly depicted. Here there was Lundea, in Anglia, which today we call London, there Antwerf, in Flandria, Hamburg, Lübick, Dantzig, Melbing, in German lands, and Riga high up towards 'Midnight'. And in the south there were the old names of Lyons, Geneva, Berne, Munich, Vienna, Ofen, Belgrade, Wardein, Sibenburg and Constantinople: all the great cities of the world.

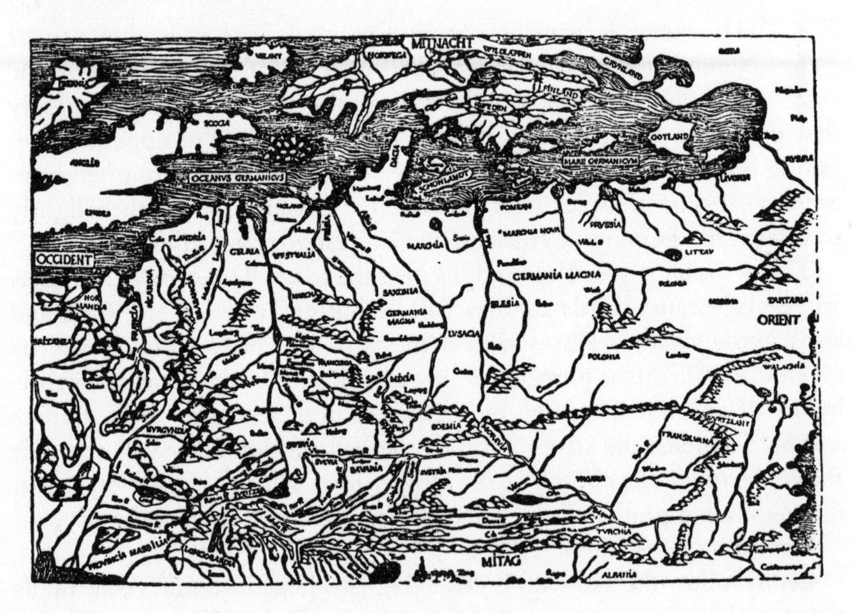

I. Map of Central Europe.

Now the second forme of these two pages was lying under the press: page cclxxxvi with a great hymn of praise to Germania and the German nation and the very last page with the *impressum*, or as we call it today, the copyright imprint.

Our little lad Johannes Peter, later to be known as Petrejus, most honourable citizen of the free city of Nuremberg, had, that morning of the 23rd December 1493, been allowed near the forme to give some small assistance. He had watched the master compositor joining together the individual letters of the *impressum*. Its text—the outcome of days of consultations between Hartmann Schedel the author, Anthonius Koberger the publisher, Georg Alten the translator from the Latin, the 'honourable and wise' Sebaldus Schreyer and Sebastian Kammermaister, financiers of the whole venture, and the two painters and illustrators Michael Wolgemuth and Wilhelm Pleydenwurth—he knew by heart:

Within these pages has been gathered together, most diligently and carefully, the book of Chronicles and Histories worthy of recall from the beginning of the world unto our times, written by men highly skilled in Latin; and brought into German by Georgius Alten, sometime scribe at Nuremberg, which book, after much consultation and sometimes, though never without cause, selection, was printed by the honourable and meritorious Anthony Koberger, in Nuremberg, on the suggestion and at the behest of the honourable and wise Sebaldus Schreyer and Sebastian Kammermaister, burghers of the town, and with the co-operation of Michael Wolgemuth and Wilhelm Pleydenwurth, painters and fellow burghers, who have embellished it with figures. On the xxiij day of the month of December after the birth of Christ our Saviour in the year M.cccc.xciij.

Our young friend, Johannes Petrejus, had helped the finisher to place paper and board under the forme so that each letter stood out clear and beautiful. He had held the inkpot for the master as he inked the sentence, he had seen with what measured stroke the master of the press worked the lever turning the giant wooden screw that brought the heavy platen onto the printing forme. These processes had greatly excited his interest. In his excitement he knew that he stood on the threshold of a new age. But he did not suspect how dangerous the printing press that he was now serving would become one day. There were days, he had to admit, when his mother's anxious forebodings about this new black magic would fill him with disquiet. She had so often been right in the past. He could not then foresee how true her presentiments would become, for in his diligent strivings to help the progress of this new art—some decades later he was to be the first to replace the wooden screw by one made of brass that would function more easily and more smoothly—he would merely contribute to making the written word supreme, thus sending forth into the old world of nature this new creature, the printing, reading, scientific man.

Indeed, how could he have suspected it on such a night as this? The principal himself was there to watch the printing of the last two pages: Herr Anthonius Koberger, owner of the greatest printing works in the world, with some twenty master compositors, all learned gentlemen, and with more than a hundred workers. In Frankfurt, Venice, Hamburg, Ulm, Augsburg, Basle, Erfurt, Vienna, Lyons, and in another six great cities of Europe, he owned bookshops in which there sat book-keepers, booksellers and forwarding agents. Now, if Anthonius Koberger himself were there, an honest and honourable man, then surely little Johannes's mother must be wrong. No Koberger dealt in things that were dishonest.

Now he is in front of Koberger's house. Out in the street he can hear the sharp clatter of the presses followed by a great thump as the forme is being withdrawn for re-inking. Click—clack—click it goes, as if there were bones inside it rattling in rhythm.

The boy feels his flesh creep, then he pushes against the doors with all his might. Slowly they swing back and at once he is bathed in that strange smell of ink, oil and lead which pervades every printing works and which no one who has once breathed it can ever forget.

Hartmann Schedel's Nuremberg *World Chronicle*, a huge folio, comprising many hundreds of pages, and weighing some fourteen pounds, is the greatest incunabulum in the world. Anton Koberger had every right to be proud of the fact that this gigantic work, with its two thousand woodcuts, had come from *his* publishing house, from *his* printing works. For there was no more convincing evidence of the rapid progress made by the black art of printing in the span of but fifty years. In later centuries, only radio and television, two other means of publication, two other technical possibilities for abolishing the barrier of distance, were to develop with equal speed. This is very significant. For such things generally announce the birth of a new epoch after a long period of quiescence. And just as radio and television are undoubtedly the means of expression of that new chapter of history which began with the Second World War, so the technical achievement of Koberger's *World Chronicle* also was the sign of a new age.

It is true that in many respects this *World Chronicle* was but old wine in a new bottle. In spirit, this gigantic book, whose printing Anton Koberger completed on the 23rd December 1493, still largely belongs to the Middle Ages. On one of the last pages he implores his readers, 'exalted rulers, prelates, emperors and kings, dukes, lords and servants', to remember that the end is nigh. 'Open your eyes, unstop your ears, and remember times past and future: so that the sleep of death come not upon you unawares, nor yet the sudden stroke of changing Fortune hurt you!' This is the conventional prophecy of doom pervading the end of the fifteenth century, and known to us from innumerable similar expressions: the day of judgement draweth nigh; repent, O ye children of men! And just as conventionally, Koberger's *Chronicle* includes a dance of death. The first of these gruesome illustrations appeared in 1421 as a fresco on the walls of the Cimetière des Innocents, in Paris, and ever since the wild dance of Death, the great leveller, with his victims, has been reproduced countless times, according to the conceptions of the Middle Ages.

Now the dance of death contained in the Nuremberg *World Chronicle* is by far the most gruesome example of these works of art. This page, drawn by Albrecht Dürer and cut in wood in his workshops, is no longer innocently naïve; it is intellectual and full of brooding irony. Death himself has stepped into the background—he is leaning on the left side of the picture and has been reduced to the role of a despised piper playing for the dancers. A male and female skeleton, so realistically drawn that you could hear their bones chatter, occupy the foreground. The sensual delight of this dance is so real that it seems as if the wild cries uttered by the dancers grant no rest to the other poor souls: putrefying corpses are rising out of their graves towards the tempting rhythms. Soon the virgin on the right of the picture will partake of the delights. On a body which once was beautiful there now hang decayed breasts, and entrails from the burst belly trail around thighs recently caressed by lusting hands.

1. *The dance of death from Schedel's* World Chronicle.

It is terrible to behold, and it is meant to be so. There is intention in this page, an evil intention. In it there speaks the diseased delight in horror, a lascivious, perverse delight. This is not mere speculation on the part of the publisher. The theme of Dürer's page belongs to the Middle Ages, and anyone wishing to publish an illustrated world history in Koberger's times had perforce to include a dance of death also. But the way in which it has been done is modern; so much so that with different technical means it might well be the product of the tortured art of our own uncertain days.

The *way* in which Koberger has illustrated his work is another sign of modernity. Of course several printed books had been illustrated before the Nuremberg *World Chronicle*. There was the famous *Golden Throne*, a book printed by Albrecht Pfister in Hamburg in 1470. It contained twenty-five pictures, but these pictures were actually nothing but two woodcuts, repeated again and again with different captions. The same procedure had been used by Peter Schöffer of Mainz, when he published his *Saxon Chronicles* in 1492. He had commissioned a painter to make woodcuts of four pictures of cities and of a few drawings of knights, ladies and bishops. And this sufficed him from the beginning of the world up to his own days. Neither he nor his readers were in the least disturbed by the fact that Halberstadt looked just the same as Rome, Hamburg like Salzwedel, or Münster like Hildesheim. It is difficult for us to understand this. Evidently illustration in his time had merely symbolical value.

Not even Koberger broke with this habit completely in his *World Chronicle*. Even in this, his prize exhibit, the same picture serves for emperors, kings and church dignitaries belonging to quite different times and countries. Moreover we are astonished to find that the illustration representing Mainz turns up in other places as Naples, Aquileia, Bologna and Lyons. Judging by his intentions, however, this is only an expedient. And it is just this which is unique and new. For a very large proportion of the illustrations of cities shown in the Nuremberg *World Chronicle* are authentic. Koberger had sent Michael Wolgemuth and Wilhelm Pleydenwurth, Dürer's great teachers and colleagues, on a long tour of central Europe, so that he could obtain genuine, realistic pictures of cities for his giant work. The illustrations of Nuremberg, Augsburg, Munich, Vienna, Strasbourg and Magdeburg are genuine. At the end of the fifteenth century they really looked as they are shown in the *World Chronicle*. And this is especially interesting in the case of Magdeburg because, some hundred and fifty years later, it was completely destroyed by Tilly, so that it is from Koberger's *Chronicle* alone that we know how it looked.

Photographs, television, the cinema, have made us all so picture-conscious that it is impossible for us to realize just how great was Koberger's break with the past. For previously, the real had been thought far less interesting than the spectacular. Here reality emerges—probably for the first time in the West—as valuable and interesting in its own right. And up to now, reality, simply because it is real, has on the whole retained this position of esteem.

Thus, we find a mixture of medieval and modern tendencies in this great work of Koberger. It came about when, for one historic second, time was balancing on the razor's edge. For shortly after this 23rd of December 1493, Nuremberg too was to learn that one Cristobál Colon, Admiral of His Most Christian Majesty, the King of Spain, had discovered new lands beyond the oceans.

2

24th June 1493

While Anton Koberger's printing presses were working busily in Nuremberg, the centre of geographical sciences in Europe, a strange train of pilgrims was setting forth from the royal camp in Barcelona.

Royal servants, clad in red, white and gold costumes, resplendent in the coats of arms of Aragon and Castile, were walking proudly in front.

Following them came penitent monks, wearing rough cowls, their heads bared to the scorching sun, burning candles in their hands. Behind the richly dressed, nimble courtiers, the monks appeared insignificant kill-joys, save for the fact that they must continually straighten their wax candles, drooping in the melting heat of the sun, thus providing a constant source of laughter for the gaping crowds lining the streets.

And then a hush falls over the astonished people. They crane their necks, stand on tip-toe in anticipation. Here they come! There are five of them, clad like the monks but without candles. Their sharp-featured brown faces with their beak-like noses are framed by their tossing raven-black hair, which despite the restraining influence of the monks, is tied up with coloured bands and decked with strange, multi-coloured feathers.

They are Indians!—people from beyond the Ocean, subjects of the Great Khan of Asia! Even in their monkish garbs they look strange and threatening, and when one of the spectators crosses himself and pronounces the conventional, fervent prayer of the people of Estremadura, 'Help us, Holy Mother of Guadalupe!', those around him join in immediately. A murmur runs along the crowd-lined street. This sound accompanies the Indians wherever they go. It surprises them and they discover, when they ask its meaning, that the Holy Virgin of Guadalupe affords special protection to warriors. They are highly interested, for they too are warriors. In their homeland across the great sea all men bear arms.

Not many years later, their compatriots and brothers in Mexico and Peru will erect roughly carved statues of the great Helpbringer everywhere; new Guadalupes will be created. The old gods have been unable to withstand the foreigners—perhaps the white woman will help. If she takes pity on the victorious white men, how much more merciful will she not be to the subjected and enslaved!

This happened five hundred years ago. But today, wherever there are Indians in South America, the same low, fervent murmurs can be heard; here whispered threateningly, there shouted loudly in despairing defiance, 'Help us, Holy Mother of Guadalupe!'

Our train of pilgrims is proceeding to an old Gothic cloister built in one of the valleys running across the Sierra of Guadalupe, to the beautiful statue of the Virgin of Guadalupe which, as the legend goes, was carved by St. Luke himself. The peasants, beggars and mountebanks, the aged and infirm, the whores and nobles, standing on both sides of the road, know exactly who is coming now. He is one of the great of this world, asking for absolution from his sins. He is the Admiral, the conqueror of the ocean, who has found land beyond the infinite flood.

Was it witchcraft or the grace of the Almighty which had guided this stranger, who, it is said, is half Jew and half Moor? Or, if this is all a trick of the devil, how did he manage to save his ships when they slid down over the curvature of the spherical earth into the bottomless pit? What exhortations did he use, so that the forces of the earth allowed him to climb up the curved ocean-mountain on his return voyage to Spain, against all the laws of nature?

While the festive procession was winding slowly and with difficulty through the mountains of Estremadura, dusty, secretive riders were galloping along the roads near the Atlantic. In the middle of March 1493, Don Luis de la Cerda, Duke of Medinaceli, Spanish grandee, merchant prince and ship-owner, had learned, through his private spies in Lisbon, that Columbus had returned, having found there all that he had hoped for. And barely eight days later, in the last week of March, an agent's report was received by the chief of the secret service of the Signoria in Florence, in which it said that, on the order of the King of Spain, some young men in three little caravels had discovered a large inhabited island on the western side of the ocean. Iron was unknown there, but there was an abundance of gold, cotton, and spices.

It is clear that this report struck Florence like lightning. Although the rich city on the Arno was not so immediately interested in sea-trade as were Genoa or Naples, like all other large Italian cities it lived on the importation of African gold, Oriental spices and delicacies, and on banking and stock-exchange transactions. This particularly profitable activity would be severely damaged if what the Spanish agents reported was true. Business with Africa and the Orient had become so difficult and so hazardous since the occupation of Constantinople by the Turks, that trade was automatically compelled to look towards the newly discovered western countries. There is no doubt that the Italians were alive to the challenges and threats of these new Spanish discoveries, but not even the shrewdest Italian banker and ship-owner was in a position to assess the full extent of the consequences. Nobody could have foreseen that his town was to become so impoverished that, but a few generations later, it would no longer be able to replace its dilapidated old houses, churches, and fortifications by modern buildings, and that its flourishing community life would remain at a standstill. Because of Columbus's great discovery, we of today can walk through the same old streets of Venice, Pavia, Florence, Ravenna or Siena, in Rothenburg, Nordlingen, Augsburg and Nuremberg, as did our forefathers some five hundred years before us: people live, love and die in the same houses as they did of old, worship in the same churches, peer over the same parapets and battlements, where some twenty generations before their ancestors grimly lowered the visors of their steel caps before the enemy. Time seems to have stood still here. Just as Pompeii and Herculaneum were once buried by Vesuvius, another kind of burial took place here, unique in cultural history. The fact is that immediately after the discovery of America, trade shifted suddenly from the

Mediterranean shores and from the cities of upper Germany towards Spain and Portugal. The quays of Italian ports became deserted, the granaries remained empty. Time seemed to have stopped.

It was of course impossible for the Italian contemporaries of Columbus to foresee all this. Yet they could not help being disturbed and anxious, and while their German business colleagues beyond the Alps continued to live unperturbed, just as if nothing had happened, great interest and curiosity were aroused in Italy by any news coming from Spain. On the 9th April 1493, the Italian merchant Hannibale Zenaro who lived in Barcelona, sent his brother in Milan a full report about the discoveries of Columbus. Scarcely two weeks passed before a copy of this letter was on the desk of the Duke Ercole d'Este. At the same time Rome received a copy of the famous report of his voyage which Columbus had submitted to their Spanish Majesties. More details of this report will be given later. At the end of April 1493, the Duke of Milan, Ludovico il Moro, was informed of the content of this report by his ambassador in Rome. And on the 25th April 1493, the town clerk of Siena noted that 'from many written reports sent by compatriots in Spain and from oral reports of many other reliable witnesses', he had learned that a certain Cristoforo Colombo had discovered new islands west of the ocean, full of gold and spices; 'and the people there believe that our people are gods', he added. At the beginning of May 1493, this report of Columbus appeared in Rome as a special broadsheet; this pamphlet designed for a wide circulation might well have been the forerunner of the newspapers of today. In 1494 it was reprinted in Antwerp, Basle and Paris.

2. *The* Santa Maria, *Columbus's flagship.*

Strange and inexplicable as it seems, the shrewd merchants from the great commercial cities of southern Germany had obviously learned little of the excitement of their Italian partners and business friends. This is confirmed by the documentary evidence in our possession. On the 14th July

1493, Dr. Hieronymus Münzer of Nuremberg, on the orders of the German Emperor Maximilian, wrote to King John II of Portugal a long and urgent letter, reading as follows:

> ... Maximilian, the invincible King, who on his mother's side is himself of Portuguese descent, desires to request your Majesty, through this my clumsy letter, to search out the eastern lands of rich Cathay. As Aristotle asserts at the end of the second book on the Heavens and the Earth, and Seneca in the fifth book of his Natural History, and Petrus Alliacus, the most learned cardinal of his age, and many other illustrious men also, so I too contend that the beginning of the inhabited east of the earth lies very close to the end of the inhabited west. Proofs thereof are the elephants, which abound in both places, as also the reeds from the foreshores of the east, which are carried by storms to the shores of the Azores. There are countless and even conclusive proofs, from which we can clearly deduce that the sea in the direction of eastern Cathay can be crossed in a very few days....
>
> You have means and riches in abundance, you have very experienced seamen, who themselves would gladly attain immortality and glory, but what glory will you yourself not gain, if you manage to acquaint the west with the inhabited east, and what profit will this not bring to your trade? You will make the islands of the ocean a treasure trove, and awe-struck Kings will submit to your rule!

Obviously this letter would never have been written had the discoveries of Columbus been known in Nuremberg in midsummer 1493, or had the people truly been convinced that the Italian had actually reached the eastern coasts of Asia. Even four years later, in 1497, when Bartholomäus Kistler of Strasbourg printed in German Columbus's report to their Spanish Majesties, the title-page says 'A very pretty reading of some islands discovered, but a little while ago, by the King of Hispania, and telling of the great many wonderful things which are in the selfsame islands'.

Did the learned German pedants not wish to believe the son of an Italian wool-carder? He maintained that he had been to Cathay, that wonderful land of which, two hundred years before, the Venetian Marco Polo had given such enthusiastic reports. Columbus, they argued, might well have discovered very many islands, far across the sea, but did they truly belong to Cathay?

Not only the German geographers, but other people too questioned the truth of the report. Columbus himself appeared to be quite certain of his case. But was he in fact?

True, in Barcelona, at the royal camp, honours were piled upon him. From now on he was to be known as 'Admiral of the Oceans', Viceroy and Governor of all Indian islands, and during the festive reception given in his honour he had sat next to their Majesties. He was made a noble and owned a coat of arms granted him by the King himself, and in his luggage he carried the official letters patent that confirmed him and his descendants 'for now and evermore' in all his high offices.

He had accepted all these honours gladly, but a worm was gnawing at his conscience. On the strenuous, penitent march to the great Merciful Lady of Guadalupe, he was constantly assailed by a doubt which was to torture him throughout his life: was it really Cathay that he had found? Cathay: that meant gold, in abundance. But the island Cipangu, of which Marco Polo reported that it lay before the land of the Great Khan in the eastern sea, was equally full of gold and precious stones. True, he had returned with much gold from his voyage, so much that the rulers themselves were convinced. Yet if you looked at it carefully, it was but a meagre amount and he could not get rid of his doubts. In fact all the later voyages of Columbus were one single frantic search, an effort to prove his hopes, contentions and pretences of having truly been to China or India.

3. Columbus's coat of arms.

Help us, Holy Mother of Guadalupe!

In Talavera de la Reina, west of Madrid, Columbus and his procession are crossing the Tagus. The road winding upwards is hardly more than a mule path along the Sierra de Estremadura. The sun is burning mercilessly from a June sky. The mountain ranges are a greyish-brown in this harsh light, like the petrified waves of a stony sea. Merciless, unrelenting, strange and evil! How far is God!

And yet, God has visibly guided and led him, Cristoforo Colombo, the poor wool-carder from 'Genova la Superba', the rich and mighty Genoa, whose inhabitants always thought themselves superior to all other Italians.

While the Admiral is panting slowly up the mountain, step by step and with beating pulse, his thoughts wander back to his lovely Italian home, to his happy childhood and youth, to his beginnings many, many years ago.

There was Genoa and his father's house near the Porta dell' Olivella, the eastern gate of the city. There was his father, Domenico Colombo, a volatile Genoese wool-carder by trade, and at the same time gatekeeper of the Olivella. But the eighty-four Genoese pounds which he received as his yearly wage did not go far, and the income from his own work was but little. Hunger was common in the Colombos' house, and although Domenico was much esteemed, he never managed to make anything like a fortune. Apart from his weaver's business, he later opened a cheese shop, and at the same time he tried his luck in the wine trade, but he always made promises which he could not keep; time and again he would order goods for which he could not pay. There were debts—in short, nothing seemed to go well with Cristoforo's father.

Thus Cristoforo Colombo, born in 1451, grew up the son of a fairly honourable, but humble family. He only learned to read and write late, but he understood a little of wool-weaving, and the many-sided business activities of his father allowed him early on to become acquainted with all kinds of trades and branches of business. But he did not know Latin, and therefore he lacked the entry to any kind of more academic education and all higher knowledge; in fact, he did not even know Italian properly. Obviously, when a young man, he had only spoken the Genoese dialect which is almost incomprehensible over the rest of Italy. All this made his start in life rather difficult, but already at the age of nineteen (on the 31st October 1470) he was standing surety for a debt of forty-eight Genoese pounds which his father had contracted. Cristoforo Colombo seems to have understood a little of business, and to have earned money when still quite a young man.

A little later we find him employed by the Centurione, a Genoese banking house: no doubt he must have impressed his employers favourably as an astute young fellow. It is owing to his work for the Centurione that Columbus went to sea. Obviously, like every boy who grows up near the sea, he often went out in fishing-boats for a sail. Perhaps he even watched the cartographers here and there brooding over their 'portolani', that new kind of sea map which became fashionable at that time. For Genoa was the seat of a famous school of cartographers, which supplied all seafaring cities of Italy with maps and which was regularly consulted by Portugal whenever a new expedition to Africa was being prepared. It is also possible that between 1470 and 1472 he was hired to serve on one of the many trading sailers. But the first evidence we have of a sea voyage is for 1475, when he went to Chios in the service of the Centurione. In the early summer of 1476, as we know, he set out again in a great Genoese convoy, which was supposed to bring mastic from the Mediterranean to Lisbon, but in the middle of August the convoy was attacked off the south coast of Portugal, not far from Cape St. Vincent and Lagos, by a strong Portuguese-French fleet, and was destroyed.

This experience brought great changes in his life. His ship was sunk and he was slightly injured. Clinging to a spar, he was carried ashore in the neighbourhood of Lagos. Some weeks later, he went to Lisbon. This lovely city on the shores of the Tagus was at that time the most interesting place in the world for merchants and seafarers. The royal merchant fleets arrived there each year from distant Africa, their holds full of valuables and the strangest things: heavy cases of iron, thick bags full of sharp Malagua pepper, giant bundles of elephant tusks and ever-new hordes of anxiously grinning black slaves. Fat-bellied cogs from Hamburg and London anchored next to the slim Portuguese caravels; the goods were being stacked in the Placa do Comercio. Thick crowds of men forced their way through the narrow streets and alleys: bright-eyed Moors, fair-haired Icelanders, proud, silent Castilians, fat Greeks, shining black Negro princes from the Gold Coast, quick-witted Italians, well-fed weavers from Flanders, elegant Frenchmen.

It may have been the beginning of 1477 when Cristoforo Colombo arrived in Lisbon. The blue-eyed, red-haired stalwart from Genoa did not understand one word of Portuguese, and yet he soon felt at home in this strange city. There had always been a strong Genoese colony in Lisbon: bankers, captains, astronomers and cartographers. He had many acquaintances among them, surely someone would help him to get on his feet again.

And this is what happened. Soon Columbus was clad according to his rank, soon he earned enough, and perhaps had sufficient leisure to learn Portuguese, Spanish and Latin. Latin above all! Unless you knew that language of science, the language of all textbooks, it was impossible to become a navigator or an astronomer. And that was a necessity here. Cristoforo Colombo had learnt much in the school of cartographers in Genoa to stand him in good stead now. With tremendous zeal he threw himself into his studies and was soon to be proficient enough in the use of cartographer's tools to satisfy even the high demands of Lisbon.

But naturally the Genoese firebrand had too much wanderlust in him to spend his life bent over maps. After some time he returned once again to the Centurione, which had a branch in Lisbon. In 1478 the business house sent its former employee to Madeira to buy sugar. Meanwhile, the young Genoese had made the acquaintance of Felipa Perestrello de Moniz, the daughter of Bartolomeo Perestrello, who had died some years before and who had been the Governor of Porto Santo, a little island in Madeira. A brother of Felipa had been Governor of the island since 1473. Having such excellent connections with Madeira, Columbus must certainly have appeared useful to the Centurione. Probably Columbus and Dona Felipa were married shortly before the beginning of this voyage. The young lady could hardly have had any money; her dowry must have consisted chiefly of her social connections and the nautical maps and memoranda of her late father.

We do not know whether the story of being shipwrecked off the Portuguese coast is in fact true. Recently doubt has been thrown upon it with very good reason, and it is quite possible that Columbus came to Lisbon as a commercial traveller. But his marriage with a lady who, although by no means wealthy, nevertheless belonged to the Portuguese nobility, is well supported. There can be little doubt that the young seafarer and merchant made great strides forward in these years of his Portuguese apprenticeship.

3

For the last few days the *leste* has been blowing from Africa, a dry hot desert wind. The sun is hidden behind a brownish mist; everything is covered with red dust. It grates between the teeth, makes the eyes burn and gets in even through closed windows. Africa is over four hundred miles away, the wide ocean stretches far between but this does not improve matters in the least. It is as if one crouched before the open grate of a baker's oven. No, it is much worse! For this desert wind makes one unbearably irritable and nervous. Knives will be drawn before night in the taverns of La Vilha, below in the harbour.

The *leste* here in Porto Santo is very rare in the middle of August, but when it does blow, it is a sign that the weather will change. Very soon, perhaps even tomorrow, the wind will blow from the west, from the far immeasurable ocean. Then Neptune's horses will come riding in, with waving manes, neck to neck. Heavy breakers will thunder against the rock so that their primordial roar can be heard through the length and breadth of the island. Foam will froth up high like a church tower and the salt spray will be borne by the wind, high up even to the mountain tops of the little island.

This is how Bartolomeo Perestrello, who had succeeded his father as Governor of Porto Santo, had explained matters to his brother-in-law, unexpectedly arrived from Lisbon. His young wife led him delightedly to the favourite places of her childhood, and told many things to her husband, who listened intently.

And then the west wind blew stormily. Columbus was no navigator yet. This voyage was the first time he had been on the high seas, out of sight of land. Moved and shuddering, he looked down over the raging sea from the high cliffs of La Vilha. May God have mercy on the souls of those at sea!

Two days later everything was quiet again. There was hardly any surf left. Daybreak saw Columbus at the shore—carefully he looked for the places where small beaches protruded beyond the rocks. He had to see for himself those strange things cast ashore that his wife had played with during her childhood. 'Sea-beans' she had said floated in after such storms, and light-yellow reeds or pieces of wood closed below, looking like pewter grass, but strong and big like jugs: things which were unknown to his world and which must have come from far away.

Columbus was as if struck by lightning when Dona Felipa had told him this. Only recently he had read about such pieces of wood or reeds in Ptolemy's great work on the preparation of geographical maps, which had become an essential manual for every cartographer. The famous man of letters of antiquity had said that they did not grow in Africa, but in Asia and probably in India.

Dom Bartolomeo confirmed his sister's account. Indeed, he said, such strange pieces of wood could be found occasionally in Porto Santo, and he got up and took a yellow reed, thick like a small barrel with knots or brownish bands, from the big old chest. Columbus trembled with excitement as he looked at the bamboo stem. If such things were of interest to his brother-in-law, Bartolomeo continued, here was something similar which must certainly also have come from far and which must have been carved by strange men. He pointed to a longish piece of carved driftwood, cut so crudely that it was at once obvious that it could not have been fashioned with iron.

The next day Columbus was up with the dawn and down on the beach. And sure enough he found *Favas do Mar*, sea-beans, with a dark-brown sheen like chestnuts, but somewhat bigger. He had never seen such things before—they must certainly have come from most distant shores. But he was quite certain that nothing like them had been mentioned by Ptolemy.

Well, nothing like it *could* have been mentioned by Ptolemy. For the *Favas do Mar* are the seeds of the *Entada adans*, or the *Entada gigas*, a kind of climbing leguminosae, which is found, above all, in tropical America. It is one of those plants that look like a serpent, and which make the layman think that God, when creating snakes, had these plants as His models. Usually the *Entada adans* winds bizarrely along trees, and bunches up into repulsive knots. But this snake-like plant, this boa constrictor of chlorophyll and cellulose, does not care a bit if it has to creep for yards along the earth in the vague hope of finding another tree. And this unpleasant creature leaves behind as its seed the 'sea-bean', a most cleverly designed water-craft, kept afloat by air-filled space, and protected by hard shells which are very difficult to break. Only sun and a little bit of moist earth are needed by this devilish thing in order, as it were, to be hatched out and to follow the creeping, suffocating activity of its primordial destiny.

Of all this Ptolemy, and consequently Columbus, had known nothing. But we need no great imagination to picture how astonished the discoverer must have been when he found these sea-beans, and how he crammed his pockets full with them.

And if anyone should ask when he first conceived his great plan, we shall have to answer: here on the beach of Porto Santo, here in the old alleys of La Vilha, here in the Governor of the island's mansion. Only one proof for all these conclusions exists: it is certain that Bartolomeo Perestrello had shown his Italian brother-in-law a piece of driftwood carved by human hands, but without the use of iron, and cast ashore by the storm. But this is all that tradition tells us. Of course we may assume as certain that Columbus did indeed hear of and see these sea-beans and bamboo stems. It is likely also that it was here, in Porto Santo, that he thought of India for the first time, and of the possibility of sailing there straight across the Atlantic Ocean. However there is no *proof* of this assumption, for there is absolutely no documentary evidence confirming it in black and white. Only the time when all this happened is certain. It was midsummer 1479, more precisely in August of that year. For on the 25th August, Columbus appeared as a witness before the court of Funchal, and from the record of his evidence it emerges that he intended to return to Lisbon the next day.

It is natural that people have always been puzzled about what gave the great Genoese sailor his idea that Asia must lie behind the ocean, and that it could be more simply reached by sailing west than by rounding Africa. It is possible that the idea came to him as we have assumed, but it is also possible that he got it from his brother Bartolomeo, who had settled in Lisbon as a cartographer in the autumn of 1480, and who was naturally very familiar with the nautical and geographical problems of his time. Perhaps this brilliant notion even goes back to Paolo Toscanelli, a Florentine physician, who, in 1474, had advised the Portuguese king, Alphonso V, to sail for India on a direct course, straight across the Atlantic Ocean.

Paolo Pozzi di Toscanelli was, at the time he gave this weighty advice to the crowned head of Portugal, no longer a young man. He was close on eighty years old, had seen and experienced much, and was certain of his case and the wisdom of his age. Since he had been close to the Papal Court, almost a generation earlier, he had had the opportunity of talking about the Great Khan and his lands with a Nestorian legate, who had been sent 'from the northern parts of upper India' to Pope Eugenius IV (1431–1447). These conversations confirmed what Marco Polo had once reported. At the same time as this otherwise unknown Christian ambassador arrived, another traveller from Asia came to Italy: the Venetian Nicolo Conti, who had lived in the Far East for twenty-five years and, apart from making the acquaintance of India and China, had also been to the Sunda Islands. His report was so interesting that the papal private secretary, Bracciolini, was ordered to make an official record of it. And when Toscanelli was still a young man, in 1424, a third traveller from Asia, the Florentine merchant Bartolomeo, after disappearing for twenty-four years, returned again to his home town on the Arno. Our physician who was so interested in geography had questioned him also, most thoroughly.

Thus Toscanelli must undoubtedly have been an important expert on eastern Asia, and since the theory of the spherical shape of the Earth had at this time become the common property of all learned men, it is not strange that his comment on the first African expedition of his contemporary, Prince Henry of Portugal, was that he had gone the long way round, although in fact Henry's earlier expeditions probably did not have the Indian Ocean as their objective. *Buscar el levante por el poniente*, we must look for 'the east in the west', and reach India by a direct voyage, straight across the Atlantic.

Our Florentine doctor was not a man to hide his light under a bushel. He discussed his convictions endlessly with every possible scientist of his time, among them a Portuguese priest who had lived in Rome about the middle of the fifteenth century and who was soon to be appointed Father Confessor to Alphonso V of Portugal. For that reason, Toscanelli was not

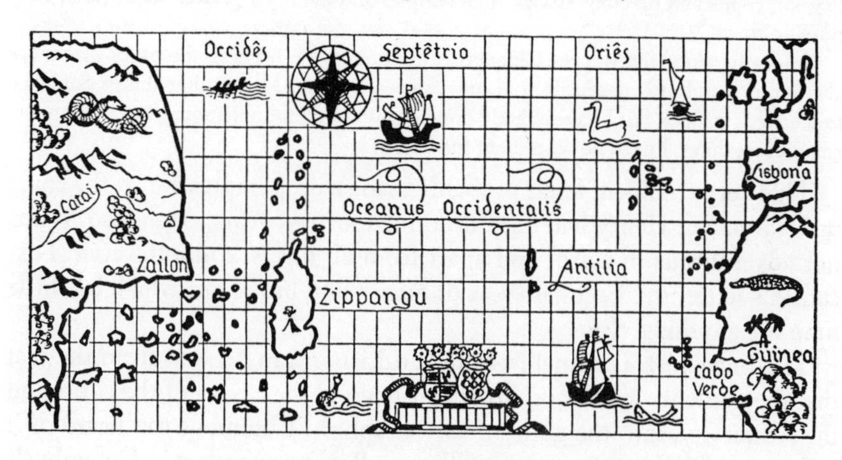

II. A reconstruction of Toscanelli's map of 1474.

particularly surprised when in the spring of 1474 he received a long letter from this priest, asking for his expert opinion on the idea of seeking India west of the Atlantic Ocean. This request resulted in the magnificent letter which Toscanelli wrote to his old friend in Lisbon on the 25th June 1474:

I have been pleased to learn that you entertain such good relations with your noble and magnanimous sovereign. I have often spoken of the shortest way to India, the home of spices, for the direct path across the ocean is quicker than that which you seek through Guinea. You inform me now that the King would like once more to hear my comments and have a clear picture of how it is possible to take this path.

Although I am of the opinion that this should be demonstrated with the help of a globe of the earth, as it facilitates comprehension, I will explain the course by means of a map which is similar to a nautical chart. I am enclosing a map which I have drawn myself and which includes the west of the inhabited world from Ireland to Guinea, as well as all islands which lie on the way. Opposite to these islands in the west is the beginning of India, with the islands and places which you could visit beyond the Equator. I have also noted the distances and number of miles to be covered before reaching those lands which produce so many kinds of spices, delicacies, precious stones and jewels.

Do not be surprised by the fact that I have called 'western' those regions of the earth from which spices come, although it is commonly said that they are in the east. Vertical lines running from the top to the bottom of the map give the distances from east to west. The horizontal lines show the distances from south to north. I have moreover included in my map many places in Indian countries for which you could make, if unforeseen events, such as storms or adverse winds, should arise....

On my map there are twenty-six sections from Lisbon sailing due west, of which each one is 250 miles wide—i.e. one-third of the circumference of the earth—up to the glorious great city of Quinsai. Its size is 100 miles or 25 leagues and it contains ten marble bridges. Its name means 'The City of the Heavens'. It is found in the province of Mangi, not far from the land of Cathay, in which the king usually resides.

From the island of Antilia, which you call the 'Island of the Seven Cities', to Cipangu there are ten divisions, in other words 2,500 miles or 625 leagues. Cipangu is very rich in gold, pearls and precious stones. The temples and the royal palaces are covered with pure gold.

Naturally, since the way to Cipangu is unknown, the ways to the other places are also unknown, but it is certain that one can reach them. Many other things could be said on this subject, but I have already done so by word of mouth and, since you understand everything, I need not comment further....

This very confident letter probably made a deep impression at the court in Lisbon. But Henry had been dead for fourteen years, Alphonso V was not adventurous in spirit, and apart from all this, six months after Toscanelli's letter, the Castilian War of Succession broke out which left little time for anything else.

The impact of Toscanelli's letter on Lisbon can be seen from the fact that the contents were soon broadcast beyond the circles of the court and the Admiralty, into the guild of cartographers. Columbus too heard of it and, some decades ago, a copy of Toscanelli's expert report in Columbus's own handwriting was discovered.

It seems as if the idea of an Atlantic voyage was somehow present in the air at that time, so that anyone adventurous enough could, in a manner of speaking, simply reach out and take it—as was done for example by the Flemish captain, van Olmen, who, admittedly without result, in 1486 sailed from the Azores to the west, or by the Nuremberg patrician Hieronymus Münzer, whose imploring letter to the King of Portugal, written in 1493, we have already quoted. Perhaps other people too had had this thought, had reflected upon it and had uttered it. But only Cristoforo Colombo from Genoa absorbed it and made it his own, and he alone carried it into practice.

What is certain is that Columbus had studied all the available historical and geographical literature very carefully. In the first place, there were Marco Polo's reports, Pliny's *Natural History*, d'Ailly's *Imago mundi* and the *Historia rerum ubique gestarum* of Aeneas Sylvius. All these works began by describing Asia, the land of the Great Khan, as unbelievably rich in people, in the products of their diligence and in natural treasures. And, furthermore, they all said that it would not be far to Asia straight across the Atlantic Ocean from the west coast of Europe. If only one could get a fair picture of the circumference of the earth, then everything else would be straightforward.

Now the circumference of the earth could be calculated without any difficulty, once one knew the distance from one degree to the next. Eratosthenes, some two hundred years before Christ, had estimated this distance almost correctly to be 59·5 nautical miles. However, Columbus did not rely on Eratosthenes, but on the Arabs, who estimated the distance between the degrees of longitude to be less. On top of this the Genoese, in his calculations, did not use the Arabic, but the much shorter Italian mile and thus he assumed that the distance from degree to degree along the Equator was only 45 nautical miles.

These calculations led Columbus to the erroneous conclusion that the circumference of the earth was a quarter less than antiquity had taught. Not satisfied with this he also moved the coastline of Asia much further east. According to his estimates the inhabited part of Eurasia had an extension of some 285°, and since he wanted to start his voyage to the west from the Canary Islands, the distance to the Asiatic coast was only 66°.

Even this figure was too high for Columbus, and he reduced his estimate by a further 10 per cent, so that his final calculations gave the distance between the Canaries and Japan, at the Equator where the degrees of longitude are furthest apart, as about 60°. Since a degree of longitude at about 30° N. was, according to his assumption, only forty miles distant from the next, he believed that he should cross the ocean at this latitude and that by covering about 2,400 nautical miles he would be able to reach eastern Asia. This meant sailing for about three weeks at a speed of four nautical miles per hour.

This was quite possible. The fast Portuguese caravels could maintain such speeds even over longer distances without any difficulties, and voyages lasting some three weeks out of sight of land did not appear impossible to seafarers at the end of the fifteenth century. We know from a mandate given to the above-named Flemish captain and discoverer van Olmen in the year 1486, by the King of Portugal, that his command over the fleet destined for the western ocean was to last for forty days. Since this expedition started from the Azores, this could only mean that people undertook to sail for forty days without sight of land—just about as much time as was necessary under favourable circumstances to go from the east African coast to India with the trade winds. But it was clear to Columbus that, without a solid theoretical foundation to his proposal, he would never be in a position to convince any of the court officials in Lisbon. We must now examine the reasons which prompted the Crown of Portugal to reject the offer and plan of the Genoese captain.

Six years had passed since the late summer of 1479 during which, as we assume, a first presentiment of his future great plan came to Columbus. For six years he had gathered material, partly in Lisbon, partly in Madeira, which he visited on repeated occasions, but he no longer spent his time sitting behind his writing-desk. From 1483 to 1484 he was at sea again, and possibly the voyage which led him to the Guinea coast of Africa became the second great turning-point of his life.

The geographers of antiquity had taught that the zone around the

III. Winds and currents in the Atlantic Ocean.

Equator was a fiery band girdling the earth and so hot that it was uninhabitable. Columbus had found this statement in many a venerable, thick folio, just as we can still read it today in old books. And now he had a proof that the ancients had been mistaken. Day after day the fleet which was meant to bring reinforcements for the recently built Portuguese fort of São Jorge da Mina—Elmina as it is called today—was sailing along on the port tack carried by a pleasantly cool north-east wind. True, it was very hot. But the heat was by no means unbearable, and there could be no longer any reason for believing that the sun would burn out all life in these parts.

This was an important discovery, and the fact that the great writers of antiquity had been mistaken made a profound impression on Columbus, as can be seen from the fact that in his own copy of the *Historia rerum* of Aeneas Sylvius he made the following irate marginal corrections: 'The hot zone is by no means uninhabitable; on the contrary it is richly peopled and is crossed by the Portuguese without any difficulties. Fort Mina of our gracious King of Portugal is also situated in this zone.'

Another thing which impressed Columbus was the wind. Oddly enough, nothing had ever been said about this strange phenomenon of the North-East Trade, though this regular stream of air directed towards the equatorial zone had been observed by many an old ocean navigator. But this was surely only a lacuna in tradition itself. Seamen could not have helped noticing this phenomenon, and there can be no doubt that from the time of the Phoenicians up to the Portuguese navigators at the end of the Middle Ages, every Atlantic captain counted on the existence of the Trades in calculating his sailing course. It is certain that the Portuguese expeditions returning from Africa must have reported this in detail, but these reports were filed away in the archives of the crown as 'top secret'. Therefore, it would be a mistake to come to the conclusion that Columbus knew nothing of the Trades just because his crew of Spaniards became alarmed when the same wind blew them day after day on their way to America.

For one thing, Columbus had certainly become acquainted with the trade winds some ten years before his famous voyage of discovery. It is true he did not know how far across the Atlantic this wind continued to blow. But since the ocean, according to his calculations, was not so very wide, it seemed very likely that the Trade would accompany him to the opposite shore of the great ocean. We must stress that this hypothesis is not supported by any kind of documentary evidence, but there is no doubt that this voyage to Elmina, this very personal encounter with the Trade and the inhabitability of the hot zone, gave Columbus a last impetus to submit his plans to the Crown of Portugal.

4

Had Columbus any right to believe that the King of Portugal and his experts, the *Junta dos Mathemáticos*, would be as eager and enthusiastic about his project as he himself was? It was about this time that the Portuguese captain and explorer Diego Cão was advancing far down the

South African coast. His aim, on orders from Lisbon, was probably to circumnavigate Africa: in the meantime it must have become clear to the *Junta dos Mathemáticos* that the black continent neither stretched as far as the South Pole nor was joined on to Asia. In a manner of speaking, the sea-route to India was now within reach of the Portuguese Admiralty. And since Henry the Navigator had agreed with the Pope, some decades before, that all lands discovered beyond Cape Bojador would belong to Portugal, there could be no political difficulties. It did look as if the sea-route to India lay unquestionably within Portuguese dominion.

It was at this very moment that Columbus arrived on the scene. His behaviour was anything but modest. '*Para buscar el levante por el poniente*', in order to reach India from the west, he did not ask for one ship only, but demanded a whole fleet. He could quite justifiably have been sent packing by the court. Why should they have deemed it necessary to spend a single cruzado, a single farthing, on so uncertain a project, if they were reasonably confident that they were about to reach India by the already explored path around Africa? Even so Columbus was treated with tact. The Italian explorer was referred to the experts, to the *Junta dos Mathemáticos*.

It is not known what objections this body of experts made when Columbus submitted his plans to them in 1485. In all probability they did not agree with his estimates of the distance, and quoted either Ptolemy, who had calculated the approximate distance between Europe and the eastern borders of Asia to be about 12,000 miles, or Toscanelli, who had said the distance was more than 5,600 miles. Even in the case of Toscanelli's mere 5,600 miles, these distances represented more than fifty days at sea. If the Junta, as probably happened, based its calculations on the twelve thousand miles of Ptolemy, this led to more than a hundred days at sea, a span of time which would have frightened even a nautical college made up of youthful, daring seamen, let alone one of learned professors.

Since Columbus was ready to stake his own life on the idea he put forward, we must assume that he had good reasons for his rather forcible corrections to the calculations of the leading geographical lights, both of antiquity and of his own day. It would certainly be wrong to believe that the Genoese was just an adventurer, although the discovery of new lands had at that time become a kind of profession. Despite many economic difficulties Columbus was by no means reduced to gamble all on one throw of the dice, and the demands which he made to both the Portuguese Crown and later the Spanish before his journeys were so exorbitant that only a man quite certain of his case could have had the nerve to make them. What was it that had made the son of a small Genoese wool-carder so certain? Mere megalomania, which is so often the cause of boastful decisions, and—we must admit it—even of some successful undertakings, could hardly have been the reason. When Columbus went to sea, in the year 1492, he was after all a man of forty-one years of age, mature and reasonable and no longer a youthful daredevil. To contradict authorities such as Ptolemy, Marinus and Paolo Toscanelli, to struggle for years with Portuguese and Spanish committees of scientists, and finally to take on the undoubtedly deeply felt personal responsibility for the life of all those men who were to accompany him on his expedition—all this supposes more than conceit. It is for this reason that until very recent times it has been assumed time and again that Columbus had known for *certain* that land could be found in the West across the Atlantic. In research work on Columbus, the question whether the explorer had been to Iceland in 1477, as his son Ferdinand maintained, has always been of considerable importance. For there he would surely have heard of Vinland, that fertile land of grapes which the Greenland Vikings had discovered beyond the ocean. The American Samuel Eliot Morison and those Scandinavian geographers who agree with him are of the opinion that this journey had in fact taken place, and that Columbus's many conflicting reports about Iceland are not so important that we should reject the possibility of his voyage there because of them. Other scholars, mainly English, and in Germany particularly the geographer Richard Hennig, emphatically disagree with this idea, and, basing their opinion on plausible reasons, are convinced that Columbus never travelled further than the north of England. But we need not delay over this point. We are justified in assuming that at the end of the fifteenth century the sagas about Vinland were known far and wide, and were on the lips of every seaman. Thus Columbus hardly needed to go to Iceland to know for certain that land had been discovered in the western ocean.

He probably learnt even more than that. In the middle of the fourteenth century an expedition from Scandinavia sent reconnaissance units, which most likely penetrated sufficiently deep into America to realize that this country was no mere island but in fact a huge continent. The headquarters of this expedition were probably located on Newport or Rhode Island, and thus certainly within reach of the Norsemen from Greenland. It is true that we have no written evidence to the effect that the above-mentioned reconnaissance units, which we might assume went as far as the Great Lakes, ever rejoined either the Vinlandian forward base or the home base in Greenland. However, the contrary cannot be proved either, and knowing at what speed such news customarily spread amongst the natives, we may well assume that the members of the Scandinavian headquarters in Newport, who were on very good terms with their Indian neighbours, were by no means badly informed about the fate of those of their comrades who were operating 1,250 miles further west, even if they never saw them again.

And even if none of this should have happened, if at the time of Columbus nothing was known of the Vinland tradition, it was by no means unknown in Europe that there were extensive lands west of the northern ocean. It was not only Bishop Adam of Bremen who had heard and reported on this; many other high dignitaries of the Church, above all the Pope himself, were equally well-informed, and what is more at first hand. Since at the time there was a very brisk traffic between central Europe and the far north, we may justifiably assume that a great number of leading merchant houses, seamen and shippers had learned about it too. Finally we

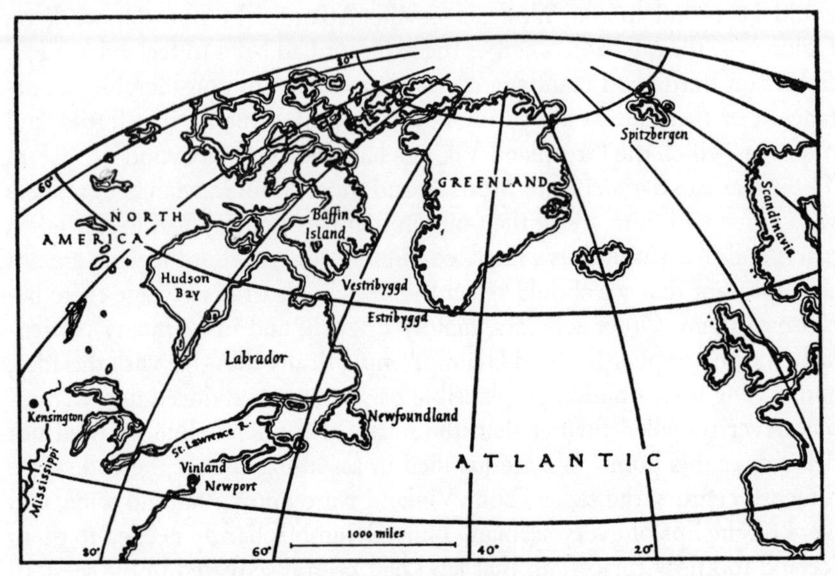

IV. The North Atlantic.

must not forget that, a few years before Columbus, a big Portuguese-Norwegian expedition had set out under the joint command of the German captains Pining and Pothorst and of the Portuguese explorer João Cortereal. This voyage of discovery had taken place in 1473. We may well assume that it went to north-eastern America, and that they reached their destination, seeing that Cortereal was given the post of Governor of the island of Torceira in the Azores as a reward for the discovery of Cape Cod. There can hardly be any doubt that Columbus had heard of this undertaking and its results, but since this report of the expedition, just like all other news about lands lying in the high north-west, only spoke of rather bare, hard regions, at best of gigantic forests with wild-growing vine, it was of no special interest to central Europe. It could only have been the most northern part of the East Asiatic coast, and not those lands of which Marco Polo had told. From all this we may draw the conclusion that the Norsemen's discoveries were not given all the attention they deserved.

5

As we have already mentioned, the *Junta dos Mathemáticos*, that committee of experts set up by the Portuguese Crown, rejected Columbus's plan. This happened in all probability at the beginning of the year 1485, and probably in so polite a form that Columbus had no reason to leave Portugal because of it. But his great plan at that time had so much become a part of himself that he could no longer bear to live in the country which had rejected it. So, in the summer of 1485, he left Portugal for Spain.

For reasons unknown to us, Columbus first went to Palos on the Rio Tinto. His five-year-old son, Diego, who after the recent death of Dona Felipa, his mother, had to be found a home, was received by the Franciscans of the La Rabida monastery near Palos. At the gates of the monastery, our explorer met Brother Antonio de Marchena, custodian of the Franciscan district of Seville, who happened to be visiting La Rabida. Brother Antonio was an astronomer of high repute. His mind teeming with ideas, Columbus is sure to have told the friendly Franciscan of his plans. The other was at once interested, then he became fascinated, and finally convinced; on his advice, and with his help, Columbus penned a memorandum to Don Enrique de Guzmán, the richest dignitary of Spain.

This memorandum was an immediate success. In Spain they knew only too well that Portugal was quite obviously on the way to finding the sea-route to India. It can be imagined how lively an interest Spain must have taken in a man who had just arrived from Lisbon, and who claimed that he knew of a very much shorter route to India and China. And so it was that Guzmán declared himself ready to put three or four caravels at the immediate disposal of the Portuguese-Genoese immigrant. But suddenly there arose complications in foreign affairs. Guzmán was forced to interrupt his negotiations with Columbus. His place was taken by Don Luis de la Cerda, Duke of Medinaceli. Cerda, for his part, was also quite willing to give Columbus the ships he required, but thinking it essential to inform the Crown of his plans, he told Queen Isabella of Castile of his intentions. Isabella became highly interested. She decided to take a personal interest in the expedition and had Columbus summoned to appear before her. In April 1486 the future 'Admiral of the Oceans' was introduced to the Spanish royal couple in the Alcazar of Cordoba. This decisive first meeting with Their Spanish Majesties turned out to be a great success for Columbus. His plan was submitted to the Queen's counsellors and his name immediately placed on the list of salaries of the privy purse. All he had to do now was to wait a little.

This waiting was to last six long years, six torturing, painful years, during which it often looked as if Columbus would be able to start at any moment for the West, only for his departure to be postponed once more. Later Columbus spoke bitterly of those years when his opponents believed that they could make jokes at his expense, treating him as a foreign upstart. The major obstacle was not so much the spherical form of the earth, but still the question of the distance between Europe and the east coast of Asia. Doing just what the *Junta dos Mathemáticos* in Portugal had done, the committee of Spanish experts, meeting by the order of Queen Isabella under the presidency of Fernando de Talavera, Prior of El Prado and father confessor to Her Majesty, reported that the distances calculated by Columbus were much too small and that his plan was impracticable. At the same time, however, Talavera must have been deeply impressed by Columbus himself. The council adjourned without drafting a conclusive report.

Nothing more happened in the summer of 1486, and it appears it was not until four and a half years later, towards the end of 1490, that this report was finally presented: it was decisively negative, justifiably enough in one respect at least, since the theory of Columbus about the narrow width of the ocean was certainly wrong. However, the Crown did not endorse the attitude of its experts. Their Majesties informed Columbus that they would discuss his enterprise once the wars against Granada and the Moors were over.

For Columbus this evasive attitude of the Crown was unbearable. In the meantime he had once again tried to get into contact with Portugal and was even thinking of starting negotiations with France and England. In any case he wished to leave Spain. At the beginning of 1492, immediately after the expulsion of the Moors from Granada, he approached Isabella and Ferdinand again, only to be told this time that his project would not be carried out.

While Columbus, depressed and embittered after his long fruitless wait, saddled his mule and rode off towards Cordoba, a man who knew and esteemed him had obtained an audience with Isabella. He was Luis de Santángel, the Lord Privy Purse. He pointed out to the Queen that after all the risk to the Crown was not so great and also stated his readiness, if necessary, to take on himself the cost of finding and equipping a fleet.

The miracle had happened! Santángel managed to convince the Queen. A messenger on horseback was sent racing after Columbus, reaching him ten miles away on the bridge across the Pinos. Columbus reined up and returned to Court. True, the two million maravedís (about five thousand pounds sterling), the cost of the enterprise, were not yet fully at his disposal. Columbus was asked to provide 250,000 maravedís himself, and Santángel for his part agreed to contribute the same amount. But everything was now settled in principle. In the middle of April 1492, the Spanish Crown drew up the decisive contracts with Cristobal Colon: the small son of a wool-carder from Genoa was given an hereditary title, he was appointed 'Admiral of the Oceans', Viceroy and Governor-General of all the lands and islands discovered by him, and finally he obtained a tax-free share of 10% in all the treasures which would reach Spain from 'across'. This was all settled on the 12th May 1492.

Ten days later the 'Admiral of the Oceans' arrived in Palos. He wished to begin his voyage here, where he first set foot on Spanish soil seven years before. It may sound strange that this small harbour, which compared with Seville or Cadiz was so insignificant and remote, was chosen as point of departure for such an important voyage. However, there were very good reasons for this. First of all, it was Palos with its surrounding country which more than other parts had already supplied the captains and crews for the previous Spanish voyages to Africa. Thus the little town's population of born sailors was used to the idea of distant voyages, and at the same time it owned a fleet of highly seaworthy caravels. In fact the Crown had an eye on these and acted rather high-handedly in the matter. The town of Palos, which had fallen into disfavour with Their Spanish Majesties for some reason or other, was simply ordered to put two caravels at the Admiral's disposal. We can easily imagine how reluctantly this was done, and that the *Niña*, a caravel of sixty tons belonging to Juan Niño from Moguer, near Palos, and the *Pinta*, a ship of equal size, which belonged to Cristobal Quintero of Palos, were not exactly the best ships to be found in the small port.

In fact the two ships were very small—at most sixty feet long and twenty feet wide. We must not be deceived by the tonnages of the Middle Ages. Though we are told that the *Niña* and the *Pinta* were of sixty tons each, we must not take it that this was either a measure of the water displacement or of their capacity. Not until the seventeenth century was the tonnage of a ship calculated by means of a formula based on the length, breadth and depth of a craft. Before that time tonnage referred simply to the number of tuns of wine which could be placed below deck.

As his flagship, Columbus chartered the *Santa Maria*. A vessel of some eighty tons, she was considerably larger than the *Niña* and the *Pinta*, and being a wide-bellied, broadly built, full-rigged ship, was also an excellent transport vessel, but under sail very much slower than the two elegant caravels. She was a trading ship which happened to have put into port at Palos. Her owner and master, Juan de la Cosa, took part in Columbus's voyage as second-in-command. The owner of the *Niña*, Juan Niño, also sailed with them. He was captain of his ship, while Cristóbal Quintero, the owner of the *Pinta*, was hired as an able-bodied seaman. The pilot of the *Pinta* was Francisco Pinzón, a seaman from Palos, whose elder brother, Martin Alonzo Pinzón, joined the same ship as captain. The other officers, as well as the crews, on the expedition came almost without exception from Palos and the country around. Apart from Columbus, only four other non-Spaniards took part in this journey to India.

This contradicts the fable we occasionally meet, that Columbus's sailors had been convicts press-ganged into service at sea. There can be no question that this story is completely unfounded, and the fact that these ninety men came from the same region and were often related to one another can be counted as one of the factors which contributed to the success of the enterprise.

Of the appearance of the three ships we know practically nothing. All the pictures which exist are inexact and most likely the products of some artist's creative fancy. Nor do we know very much about the fitting out of the Indian fleet. But we may assume that Columbus had taken very special care about such an essential condition for the success of his voyage. He himself had sailed before the mast as a seaman, and on his journeys to Madeira and Africa between 1478 and 1484 he had learnt the special importance of adequate equipment, particularly in tropical regions. And just as he was past master in the practical art of navigation and the steering of great ships, so he also knew from his personal experience of seamen what supplies were necessary for a long voyage in southern latitudes, and what kind of articles were needed for trading with the natives. It is said that Columbus's expedition had enough supplies to allow for one year's absence from Europe and that he had provided per day and per man one pint of wine, one pound of biscuits, eleven ounces of meat or fish, and in addition, onions, vegetables, cheese, etc. Since the Admiral had counted on a voyage of only three weeks, the great care and consideration he gave to the task are obvious.

Thus the summer of 1492 passed. At the beginning of August the three ships were reported seaworthy to the 'Admiral of the Oceans', and on the 3rd of August 1492, half an hour before sunrise, at about 5.45, the *Santa Maria*, the *Pinta* and the *Niña* weighed anchor.

6

The Canary Islands were the first port of call, as the last Spanish outposts in the ocean. It was Columbus's conviction that they were situated at the same latitude as Cipangu-Japan, which he hoped to discover by sailing with the north-easterly winds prevailing in these regions at this time of year.

The voyage to the Canaries was completed reasonably quickly, and at dawn on the 9th August, Gran Canaria, the central island, was sighted. Here there was another short pause before starting on the great voyage. The *Pinta*, whose rudder had come unshipped, had to be repaired, and the lateen sails of the *Niña*, which had proved impracticable in directly following winds, were replaced by square sails. Thus Columbus must have known for certain that he would have to tack but little and that he could count largely on easterly winds. Finally, water and firewood were taken on board, and what gaps there were in the supplies of provisions were made good by means of fresh food. All these preparations lasted until the 5th September 1492. Early that day Columbus heard Mass for the last time in the Church of the Ascension in Las Palmas, and then put out to sea; four days later, at dusk, on Sunday the 9th September, land faded out of sight. For thirty-four days they were to see nothing but sea and sky.

That Sunday, when passing Ferro, the most westerly of the Canary Islands, Columbus had already made up his mind not to inform his crew of the real distance they covered each day, as one means of preserving their morale. He had let it be known that land would be sighted after about 750 sea-miles. We may certainly assume that he himself allowed for a large margin of error and did not completely trust his own calculations. In any case he thought it best to give out as small a daily reckoning as possible, and thus to keep a certain 'reserve' in hand which could be used in case of mutiny. Every captain of his day who undertook a long crossing had to reckon with the possibility of such incidents. The fact that at the very beginning of the expedition Columbus had to take safety measures of this kind, shows how clearly he had understood the vital problem of his voyage. It was a psychological one: how to keep control over a crowd of ignorant, superstitious, badly fed, overworked and badly quartered men.

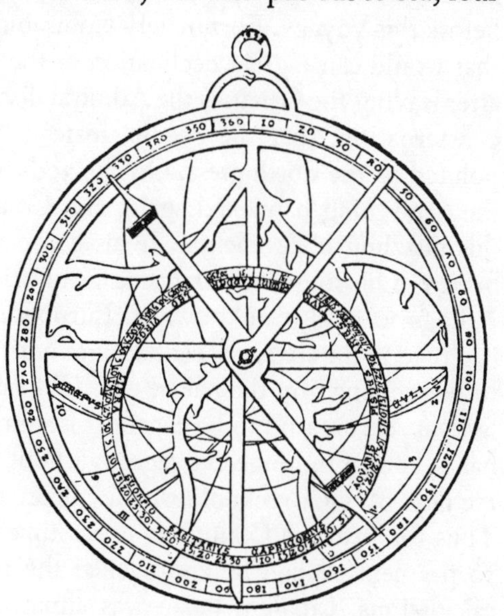

4. *Astrolabe of the year 1468 belonging to Joh. Regiomontanus.*

His task was made easier through the inadequacy of the nautical instruments of his time. The sextant was not yet in existence, the astrolabe was difficult to use—in any case Columbus probably did not understand it—the simple ship's quadrant, which the Admiral had taken with him, failed, of course, when it came to finding a star through the small sight on a tossing and pitching ship, and thus, just as a thousand years before

Columbus's journey and for a long time after it, they had to rely on the daily reckoning; this meant the recording of the compass readings on the map and a daily estimate of the distance covered. With such useful instruments as a properly functioning compass and a log, indicating the speed of the ship, this is a very simple matter. Columbus had none of these means at his disposal. True, the compass had been known and used for six generations, but the phenomenon of magnetic variation had hardly been investigated at that time, even though it had been observed a century before this voyage. Fortunately Columbus had not many regions to cross that would cause great declination of the needle, though only a few days after leaving the Canaries the Admiral discovered, to his astonishment and consternation, that the needle, instead of pointing to the North Star, pointed to the north-west. On the 30th September, far out in the ocean, the same thing happened again, and Columbus was deeply disturbed by this puzzling phenomenon. If his compass should fail, he would be deprived of his most important means of orientation.

Logs were also unknown in Europe in Columbus's time. They were invented in the sixteenth century and until that time the speed of a ship had to be reckoned by the naked eye. Old salts, who have spent their whole lives at sea, are said to be capable of estimating the speed of a ship within half a knot. On longer voyages, without any means of checking the correctness of such reckonings, this direct method is found unsatisfactory. Thus for instance Columbus overestimated the speed of his flagship by 10 per cent. When he approached the regions where, according to his calculations, Cipangu-Japan was situated, he must have done a lot of worrying in secret. He must surely have known that here, in the calculating of the ship's speed, was one of the weakest points of his navigation. Last but not least, there was no means of measuring with any accuracy the course of time itself. In those days, on board any sizeable ship, there was found an *ampolleta*, a sandglass which had to be turned every thirty minutes. This was the responsibility of a cabin boy. We need little imagination to realize that such a timekeeper was not always as reliable as he might have been, and occasionally Columbus made a note in his diary about his fears that the boy might be neglecting his duty. What is more, it was inevitable that the running of the sand from the upper to the lower section would be severely disturbed by the tossing and pitching of the ship. In such circumstances there could be no question of obtaining anything like even an approximate reckoning. But since other means were unknown, and particularly since astronomical navigation was not then the business of seamen but of mathematicians, there was little that could be done to improve matters.

But as we have already stated, Columbus's voyage was not a problem of navigation in the proper sense of the word, especially as he was very fortunate in that the trade winds extended quite far to the north. Modern sailing manuals recommend, for early autumn east–west voyages from north Europe to the U.S.A., a course which lies in the latitude of 20° N. Columbus kept between 6° and 10° further to the north, but nevertheless stayed within the Trades almost all the time.

His fleet was hurrying along towards the west, sails billowing in the constantly following wind. For the Admiral, this great speed allowing him to cover distances of 150–170 nautical miles each day was most gladdening, but not so to his crew, who became more and more restless, thinking that no other wind ever blew at all in these latitudes. On the 22nd December when the India fleet had been tacking against unfavourable winds for two days, Columbus noted with satisfaction: 'This contrary wind has been a great help to me, because my crew had become very anxious, thinking that, with this favourable wind blowing all the while, they would never be able to return to Spain, and great unrest prevailed on board.' This proves on the one hand that some of Columbus's fleet—apart from himself—may never have heard of the trade winds, and on the other that the restlessness of the crew was already a marked sign of the growing fear of the sailors. Admittedly, at that time they had been sailing for about eight days through the Sargasso Sea, that *mare pigrum* of antiquity, of which it was said that its sticky weeds would not let go of any ship that its green arms had embraced. Naturally the sight of these vast meadows of *Sargassum bacciferum*, or gulf-weed, must have been most frightening, though actually the plants only grow to a height of eighteen inches and generally are but weak structures that bend and sway and become intertwined. In the centre of the Sargasso Sea, a region of about the size of Europe, these masses of weed appear nevertheless to be so matted that they can present a danger to small vessels. At any rate this is the opinion of the Danish botanist G. Foster who, in the twenties of this century, went on an exploratory expedition into the Sargasso Sea and reported that large sections of this meadow of seaweed were so dense that one could walk on them. If this is true, then we can imagine how disturbing it must have been for Columbus's sailors when, for almost two weeks, they sailed along the borders of this uncanny prairie. And when at night this immensity was glowing from horizon to horizon with the blue-green and yellow phosphorescence of innumerable fishes and molluscs, the sight must have been particularly terrifying. The Admiral tried to pacify his crew. Columbus ordered soundings to be made at more frequent intervals, and the depths plumbed were found to be 200 fathoms and sometimes even more. Nevertheless, the fear remained that some day they would be stuck in one of these floating meadows. This was very nerve-racking, and it is no wonder that the forecastle began to grumble.

Disappointed hopes added to the trouble. After Columbus had pointed out that the weeds had not impeded the rapid progress of the ship, he had also expressed the belief that so much greenery must needs indicate the immediate vicinity of land. When, on top of this, they had observed the passage of great flocks of seabirds, it looked as if his hopes were indeed well-founded and about to be proved correct. But day after day went by without even a trace of land on the horizon. It was assumed that the groups of islands that appeared on the cosmographers' charts of these regions had been missed. Francisco Pinzón, the pilot of the *Pinta*, was so convinced of this, that on the evening of the 25th September he approached close to the *Santa Maria* and suggested to Columbus that they alter course in search of the islands, but Columbus declined to do so. There was no time to lose; his aim was India.

While they were still arguing over this, Francisco's older brother Martin Pinzón suddenly sprang up with a shout of glee.

'Tierra, tierra!—Land, land!' he shouted across to Columbus from the stern of the ship, pointing to the south-west. And indeed everyone could make out the faint dark strip, stretching across the distant horizon. At the sight of it Columbus threw himself upon his knees to intone the *Gloria in excelsis*, while the crew of his three ships joined in this hymn of thanksgiving with joyous hearts.

All night long the ships stood to the south-west. Next day at dawn, as the morning glowed and glittered across the sea, there was no longer any sign of land. Disappointment was deep and general, but Columbus himself was the least affected. According to his secret reckoning, he had only completed two-thirds of his voyage. If land was sighted here, it could only be an island, an island furthermore where they would have to drop anchor, which to him only meant delay and loss of time. His urge was to press on towards the west, towards his goal.

During the six days between the 25th September and the 1st October 1492, the winds were changeable, restless, as if Neptune had not yet decided where to send the three slowly drifting ships. There was little work on board. The crew had time to reflect and brood over their thoughts. Counting on their fingers they realized that almost three weeks had gone by since they had their last sight of land. Three weeks? Had not the Admiral told them that they would not have to sail for more than three weeks? The grumbles of the crew soon turned into menaces. Hard words were exchanged, and in their minds they started to contemplate what would happen if the Admiral were thrown overboard one dark night; in short, open mutiny was about to break out. Of course Columbus was aware of all this and he could well imagine what was brewing. When some officers, in the name of the crew, asked him to turn back, he rebuked them gruffly: Let them reflect well what would happen if they returned to Spain without having accomplished anything, and without him, their Admiral.

Of course, they could murder him if they chose, but then the gallows would be waiting for them. If, on the other hand, they persevered, they would all become fabulously rich and each one of them was assured of the King's bounty. India was not far away. They only had to hold on for another few days.

Once more Columbus managed to pacify his crew. His luck might even hold on the next occasion, but that would be the very last time: either they would throw him overboard or force him to return. Something *must* happen in the next few days, he *must* find land. He had just gone over the secret reckoning again. They had covered 707 miles to this day, the 1st October 1492. The next three or four days would have to prove him right. Of course he too was restless, nervous and irritable. But surely God had not led him so miraculously, only to forsake him now. He could not possibly be wrong.

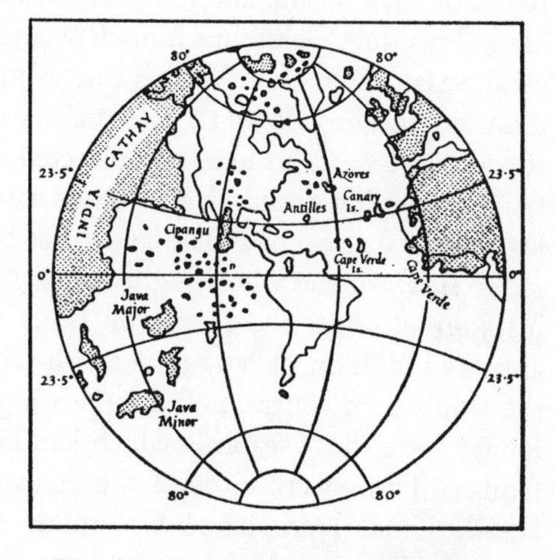

V. Sketch contrasting Columbus's notions with the real geographical conditions.

Nevertheless, the order was given for every inch of sail to be set in order to make the most of the steady wind that blew full force from the east. The ships raced wildly towards the west with a foaming wake and across a swirling sea. They covered 182 miles in a day's reckoning—almost eight nautical miles per hour and not much less than the speed of an average tramp ship of our days. Meanwhile the forecastle had more time for reflection and brooding. Rumours were starting up anew. But again large flocks of birds were seen passing overhead—Columbus knew only too well that this did not necessarily mean anything, that they were only seabirds crossing the ocean on quite unknown courses, but the crew had no inkling of this. They thought land must be near, and once more calmed down.

Thus the 6th October arrived. The *Pinta* drew close to the flagship, and through cupped hands Pinzón shouted his advice that Columbus ought to alter course to the south-west. Naturally Pinzón had kept his own reckoning. He knew just as well as Columbus that the 750 miles, the supposed distance between the Canaries and Japan, had long been covered. He had no doubt that they had missed Cipangu and were approaching the shores of Asia. The Admiral reflected on this and, recalling once more what Marco Polo had said of the position of China in relation to Japan, he decided to continue on his westerly course, though he must have known perfectly clearly the significance of Pinzón's intervention. What was happening on the *Pinta* was the beginnings of mutiny in which even captain and officers were joining. It was high time that they sighted land.

And lo!—the desired land seemed to materialize. In the small hours of the morning of the 7th October a signal came thundering from the *Niña* sailing in front: Land in sight! On the Admiral's ship, too, they had seen the dark strip on the horizon, but no one had dared to raise the shout of land. This time Columbus himself seemed to be much more sceptical than on the 25th September. We have no reports of *Gloria in excelsis*, nor of the Admiral kneeling down to give praise to God. He stood on deck, looking towards the west, his blue eyes directed to the wide ocean and to that dark faint strip lying ahead. A few hours later, he knew that it had not been land. But he also knew that land must be close by. '*Toda la noche oyeron pasar pájaros*', the whole night we could hear birds passing, he wrote in his journal. And the flocks of birds which since early morning had appeared high on the sky on a south-westerly course, at a sharp angle to the ship's own course, and disappearing behind the horizon in front, no longer were those seabirds which had been seen towards the end of September. These were birds of the fields and therefore land must be close ahead. Land, land, land! Columbus changed his course in a south-westerly direction. Pinzón must have noticed this with great satisfaction: the Admiral was agreeing with him after all!

Yet four days later things again began to look critical on the *Pinta*. The crew was refusing to go on. Pinzón, strengthened in his position by the change of course ordered by the Admiral, pointed out to his crew the birds which had flown all night across the ocean and were making for the south-west. He too knew that land could not be far. Thus he managed to keep order aboard his ship. After all, Pinzón was looked upon by his crew as one of themselves. Like them he was a man from Palos, and not only had they known him for years but many of them were his kinsfolk.

But things did not look nearly so favourable on the flagship, which had caught the spark of rebellion. Columbus was a foreigner, one of those cursed Italian *dagoes* who seemed to have pushed their way to the front of Christian navigation and who were beginning to impose themselves in Spain. What was worse, he had come into the country from hated Portugal. There, they had ignored him with his obstinacy and crazy ideas. Should he be allowed to do with Spanish sailors as he pleased? The most vociferous were the Basques and Galicians from north-western Spain. Amongst these men from Castile and Aragon, they felt as much like strangers as Columbus himself. By what right did he deem himself better or cleverer than they?

Columbus had had time to prepare himself to face mutiny. Should he fail to pacify his crew and should it come to the point, his position would be desperate. It was now too late for strictness, for draconian measures, for keel-hauling or stringing offenders up to the mainyard. The forecastle was quite right, he was, and always would be, a stranger, and if force had to be met by force, he was certain to come off worst. Thus he wrote in his journal:

> Today the crew complained about the insufferable length of the voyage and said that they could not stand it any longer, but the Admiral encouraged them as best he could, pointing out the great rewards that were awaiting them. Their complaints and grievances were all the more unreasonable, since they now were within reach of India. It was useless to rebel. The expedition had started for India, and he neither would, nor could, rest until he had found it with the help of our Lord.

Other reports on this critical 10th October added that Columbus had promised his crew that he would return home if his fleet did not discover land within two or three days, and later authorities have said, concerning the events of these first days of October 1492, that Columbus himself had been uncertain and had looked upon these two or three days' grace as a divine test of the value of his enterprise. What really happened on board the three ships is far from clear, but what is certain is that Columbus once more had his way—admittedly for the very last time. At all costs land must be found.

And once again a miracle happened in this story so full of miracles. As the *Niña* was racing ahead under full sail towards the south-west, someone on board spotted a drifting object floating on the waves. It was fished out of the water and lo! it was found to be a green branch with blossom on it; it looked like a Castilian dog rose. Then the *Pinta* made similar catches: a board, a reed, a green shore plant and a staff quite obviously carved by human hands. Immediately the rebellious murmurs ceased. Even the most stupid cabin boy could now see that land must be close at hand.

Thus the 10th October passed and the 11th came and went after a windy day on a rough sea. Towards evening Columbus made a short speech to his crew, in which he pointed out God's goodness to them and admonished the night-watch to special vigilance. Then as always the *Salve Regina* was chanted and the new watch reported for duty, but those off duty did not sleep. Gradually most of them came up on deck, all eyes turning to the west and staring hopefully. Although land was close by the Admiral left the sails unfurled and the squadron raced towards the west at great speed. The moon would rise at 11 o'clock and with its help sailing would be safer. If they came upon a reef when sailing at high speed in such a sea and wind—may God have mercy on them! In this atmosphere of mounting excitement which not even Columbus could withstand, the shouts of 'Lumbra! Tierra! A light! Land!', coming suddenly from able-bodied seaman Pedro Ysquierdo, had the effect of an electric shock. Columbus too had seen the light, and two or three others who stood with him on top of the castle, but the light did not appear again. They must have been mistaken.

Tension was growing. The stiff trade wind continued to blow. The ships pursued their race towards the west at seven or eight knots. About two o'clock the moon stood high in the sky, and while, directly behind the fleet, the sea to the east and the foaming wake receded into darkness, everything in front was clear and silvery. Snow-white were the crests of the waves, and like a diamond-studded robe the watery spray lapped over the bow. The faster *Pinta* was a few miles in front of the flagship, with Rodrigo de Triana from Palos in the crow's-nest, when suddenly far ahead he had a glimpse in the moonlight of a brilliant white surface that looked like a sand-dune. And here it was, and there again with a darker strip in between. In the tossing and pitching of the ship Triana let pass a good deal of time. He did not wish to make a false report, and apart from that he was afraid of the Pinzóns and of the scoffing of his comrades. Still he would very much have liked to earn the silken jerkin which Columbus had promised to whoever first sighted land. What is more, he might even get a share of the annual rent of 10,000 maravedís which the Captain would receive as his reward from the Crown. Rodrigo de Triana went on staring into the darkness with great concentration—he was right: through the glitter and shine in front of him the dark strip was growing clearer, no doubt that it was land.

'*Tierra, tierra!*' he roared, at the top of his voice.

Pinzón on the quarter-deck quickly peered forward. The fellow was right!

'Fire the signal gun,' he yelled to the forecastle.

A tongue of flame licked round the mouth of the gun, the dull thud of the report rumbled over the sea, reaching the flagship now some way behind.

The crew jumped to their feet and swarmed up the rigging. They noticed that the *Pinta* had already reduced sail and was slowing down. The *Santa Maria* caught up and shot past, so close through the lee that the yards seemed to touch, and when Columbus hailed across: 'Señor Martin, have you seen land?' the answer roared back from many throats, 'Sir, the reward has been won!' The land was now but six sea-miles ahead. All three ships were making directly for it. In less than an hour they would be close in. Columbus ordered all sails, except the main, to be furled, and the small fleet laid-to for the night. Dawn broke at about 4.30. There before their eyes stretched a coral island covered with green trees, heavy breakers rolling towards its brightly shining beach. They would have to sail past the south of the island and try to drop anchor on the lee-side.

The great objective had been reached. These reefs tallied exactly with the descriptions made to Columbus of the approaches to the shores of India. He was overcome with feelings of happiness and gratitude. So he had been right after all and God had granted him victory! Perhaps his first thought was for the great treasures now within easy reach, the bars of gold, the jewels and pearls, the bales of silk, the abundant stores of spices and delicacies spoken of by Marco Polo, but he must also have remembered that, without the help of God, he could never have wrested from Arabs and Mamelukes the monopoly of entry to the Far East. He, the ambassador of the Christian Church, had triumphed over the infidels, despite tremendous difficulties. It was only much later that the truth about this country was discovered, that in fact it was neither Asia nor Cipangu, and that the letter which Columbus carried, addressed by the King of Spain to the Great Khan, could never have reached its addressee, and that Luis de Torres, the learned Jew, but a convert to Christianity, whom Columbus had brought along because he spoke not only Hebrew but also Arabic and other Oriental languages as well, would never be called upon to display his talents as an interpreter. It is well known that Columbus was convinced that he had landed on the eastern shores of Asia. He had in fact discovered San Salvador, one of the Bahama Islands, now known as Watling's Island and called Guanahani by the natives.

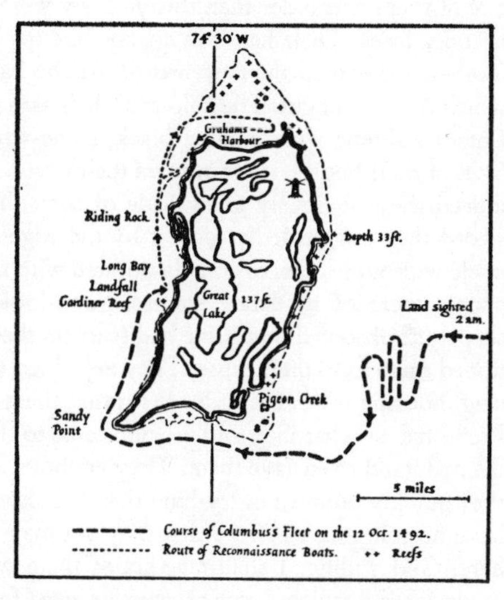

VI. San Salvador or Watling's Island.

On Friday, 12th October 1492, soon after sunrise and after he had found a suitable place for dropping anchor, Columbus took possession of the foreign shore with due Spanish ceremony. In the first boat, holding the Royal Standard, stood Columbus himself; behind him, under the banners of the India expedition, came the captains of the *Pinta* and the *Niña*, surrounded by an armed company. Columbus was the first to go ashore. He threw himself on his knees, kissed the earth, praised God with tears of joy and christened the island San Salvador.

He then called the two captains and Rodrigo de Escobedo, notary of his fleet, and also Rodrigo Sanchez from Segovia. After assembling all those who had landed with him, and in the presence of many natives who had foregathered there he solemnly took possession of the island in the name of Their Catholic Majesties. . . . Then the Christians proclaimed him Admiral and Viceroy and took an oath of obedience to him as the representative of Their Majesties. . . .

The ceremony was concluded with a *Salve Regina*. The Indians, Tainos, who belonged to the language group of the Arawaks and who had been watching the strange big ships since early morning, approached shyly but most anxiously. They appeared to be primitive but friendly people and they were quite overcome when Columbus made them a present of red caps and glass beads.

They went about unclad as when they were born; the women too were completely naked, although I only saw one young girl. In fact only young people were there, no one of them was older than thirty. They were well built, pleasant to look at and with friendly faces. Their hair was coarse, like the tails of horses; they let it fall over their foreheads down to their eyebrows. At the back of their heads they had a long crop which they never cut. The colour of their skin was the same as that of the natives of the Canaries. Some were painted black, some white, some red. Some put paint on their faces or their bodies, some only on their noses. They carried practically no weapons and indeed they obviously knew little of such things. When they were shown a drawn sword they unguardedly took it by the edge and hurt themselves. Their lances were made without iron, occasionally pointed with the tooth of a fish or a similar object. The people were of moderate stature, good-looking, and their limbs were strong and shapely. I observed that some had scars on their bodies and, by means of signs, I questioned them as to their cause. They explained that people had come across the sea from neighbouring islands in order to capture them, and that they had defended themselves. I reflected on what they told me, and came to the conclusion that people had come from the mainland to enslave them. They are bound to be excellent servants for I found that they quickly imitated everything that was shown them. Since it would appear that they have no religion, I believe that they yet may become good Christians. When leaving here, God willing, I shall take six of them with me for Your Majesties so that they might learn Spanish. I saw no animals apart from parrots.

The Spaniards also noted, almost from the very outset, that the Indians looked upon their bearded and white-skinned guests as men from Heaven. Elsewhere,[1] we have told in detail of the legends, so widespread in Mexico and Peru, of a bearded white god who would one day come from the east, and of the prophecies in both these regions, so remote from each other, of the return of this god and his sons in the distant future. In subsequent chapters we shall have to return once more to this subject, but here we merely wish to note that legends of this kind seem to have been prevalent even amongst the primitive Tainos, long since extinct. Columbus reported that on two occasions the *Indios* had actually greeted him as God and the Son of Heaven; similarly, he more than once observed that he had frequently come across Indians nearly as white as Spaniards, and certainly lighter-skinned than the natives of the Canary Islands. If we recall that the Bahamas and the West Indian Islands lie full in the path of the north-easterly trades, and that thus it is more than likely that many ships were carried from the Old to the New World, then the appearance of white Indians in these regions will not strike one as particularly strange. However, Columbus no more than made a note of the fact. This is very understandable if we realize that it is unlikely that Columbus reflected on

[1] Paul Herrmann, *Conquest by Man* (Harper & Brothers, 1955).

whether white people had been there before him. After all he was convinced that he was in Asia and that many Europeans had preceded him there. Only Cortés and Pizarro, who knew that the New World was a continent situated between Europe and the Far East, could find such things remarkable.

It is interesting also to note that here, in this report of Columbus, we have the foundation of that legend of a blissfully happy and innocent existence, unspoilt by culture and civilization, which afterwards was to become the sentimental yearning of *Retournons à la nature*! Later we shall

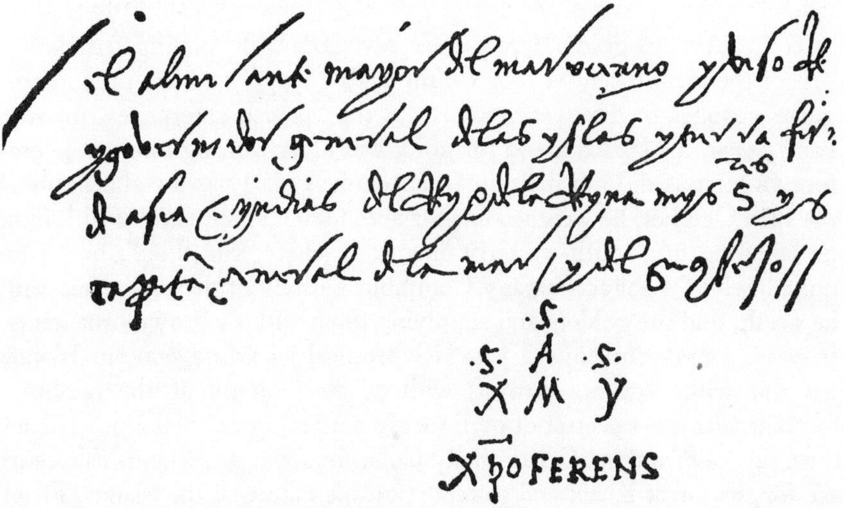

5. *Specimen of Columbus's writing and signature.*

hear the same laudatory accounts from Cook and his companions. Before the time of Columbus, it was not customary to be lyrical about savages and their way of life, although the Portuguese voyages along the shores of southern Africa must have offered more ample opportunities for doing so. Like so many other things, this attitude seems to be connected with the general *fin de siècle* dissatisfaction prevalent in Europe at the time. Only people completely discontented with the decadent state of society could have looked upon the primitive Tainos as innocent children of God. A mere nine months later, Columbus himself was to be sharply disillusioned. When, on his second voyage to America, he landed on Santa Maria de Guadalupe, he discovered quite unequivocal signs of cannibalism. And when members of his crew freed a number of castrated Arawak boys, who had been captured by the Caribs of Guadalupe and were being fattened for the pot, when young slave girls who had broken out from their cages came swimming across to the flagship, girls who were kept by the Caribs for the sole purpose of producing babies, because these babies were considered to be special delicacies, then Columbus must have realized that the alleged natural innocence of the 'noble savages' was rather a misconception.

However interesting all this might be for the Old World, Columbus soon found out that there were no treasures of any value in Guanahani. 'It looked to us as if the island were poor in everything', Columbus remarked in one of his reports and elsewhere he added with full emphasis:

> It was particularly important for me to learn whether any gold existed among them; some wore small golden bars through their noses. From their signs I learnt that in an island to the south there lived a king, owning whole vessels of gold. . . . The gold, which the natives wear in their noses, comes from this island. But I do not wish to lose any time in searching for it for I must endeavour to reach Cipangu quickly.

Gold! Always gold! Here we see revealed, with unmitigated clarity, one of the main incentives for Columbus's voyage. Just as in the Portuguese voyages of discovery, so also in the Spanish enterprises, the *auri sacra fames*, the cursed greed for gold, was a very strong motive. Therefore Columbus did not dally in Guanahani. As early as the afternoon of the 14th October, he weighed anchor and, taking seven natives with him, he sailed on in a south-westerly direction, where, said the Tainos, who quite likely did not accompany Columbus entirely of their own free will, he would find the golden land supplying them with their own ornaments. It was a wonderful voyage past rich tropical island vegetation. Islands covered with flowers, glowing with all the colours of the rainbow, fragrant with the sweetest of perfumes, emerged one after the other from the clear, calm waters. Occasionally Columbus sent messengers ashore to ask for the Great Khan, and to report on the nature of the islands. From one of these missions, his sailors returned with the report that the savages had beds that looked like mats of cotton and which they called *hamacas*.

> They are made with a kind of slipknot. The cords do not run criss-cross but are joined together along their lengths in so loose a manner that a hand can be placed between them. . . . These *hamacas* have a length of five and a half feet and their two ends consist of many loops of these cords. . . . With these they are attached to the posts of the huts so that they hang freely above the ground and swing in the air. . . . One can sleep peacefully in them.

This news seems to have interested Columbus. Since he was a practical man he might well have realized that this would solve the problem of finding a way for sailors on board ship to sleep and rest. In any case, the Spaniards were the first to introduce hammocks on their ships, and thousands of honest seamen will have given grateful thanks to their great colleague, Columbus, even though they did not know him, many, many times in their lives when after a long watch they could stretch out in one of these. A little later the Portuguese also introduced the use of hammocks in their ships. According to the German navigator and merchant Hans Mayr, who reported the fact in 1505, the Portuguese had come across them in India: a net of palm fibres fastened to a post and offering space for one man. Thus the discovery of the hammock seems to have been made on two independent occasions.

But of course Columbus was not satisfied with mere historical glory and his disappointment was mounting slowly. The land of gold continued to elude him. He still placed great hopes on Cuba, which the natives had described to him as an island already opened up to trade, and he wrote in his journal:

> This island can be nothing but Cipangu. All I have to do is simply to look for the gold and spices. In any event I shall have to search out Quinsay to deliver the royal letter to the Great Khan.

However, the Admiral of the Spanish Crown must have begun to have some slight doubt as to whether these islands were in fact connected with Cipangu. Yet, when a few days later, on the 28th October, he dropped anchor before Cuba, he had lost all his doubts. The rainy season had just finished so that tropical nature was glowing in all its glory. Columbus never tired of praising the incomparable magic of this region. 'The scent of the flowers and trees is glorious beyond all description. The song of birds and the chirping of crickets may be heard all night. The air is soft and balmy, being neither hot nor cold. Here would I like to live for ever', he wrote in his diary, and full of the joy of discovery he believed that he could see mastic in all the forests, banks of pearls in the sea, and gold in the metallic sheen of the river-beds. No doubt, this was Cipangu! Or if not Cipangu, then it must be India. He was sure now that he had finally reached his great objective.

6. *Tobacco drinking.*

But the gold of which he had dreamt, the heavy bars and great nuggets of gold lying about everywhere, the trinkets which had no value for the natives because they were so common; all this could not be found. This dream of *El Dorado* which he had chased across the great ocean from distant Spain remained a dream. The Indians now told him that the great king who owned all the gold did not reside on the island of Cuba, but on *Cibao*. Again Columbus interpreted this place-name as Cipangu and sailed on. On the 2nd November he sent two men ashore with orders to discover more about the nature of these regions. Four days later the messengers returned, and in his entry for the 6th November Columbus reported in detail what had happened to them:

My messengers reported that after a march of about twelve miles they had discovered a village with about one thousand inhabitants. The natives had received them ceremoniously, had lodged them in the most beautiful houses, carried them in their arms, kissed their hands and feet and, in short, had tried to make it clear to them in every possible way that it was known the white men had descended from the gods. Some fifty men and women had asked for permission to return with them to the Heaven of the eternal gods. My two messengers reported that they had encountered many men and women carrying some sort of cylinder in which sweetly smelling herbs were glowing. These they supposed were dried herb stalks covered by an equally dry but broader leaf. The people sucked the other end of the cylinder and, as it were, drank in the smoke. Although this apparently intoxicated them it also seemed to protect them from fatigue. The natives said that they called these cylinders *tabacos*.

The report of the two messengers, which, according to Columbus's diary, gave information concerning the character of the area, the nature of the trees growing there, its spices and delicacies, said nothing of gold. And after all, the latter had been the whole purpose of the voyage. No doubt the Spanish Majesties would be very pleased to learn that their new lands were so fertile and full of a host of good things. But what Spain needed, and needed desperately, at this moment was gold, and nothing but gold, for when the Moors and Jews were expelled they had taken their capital with them. Yet gold was precisely what could not be found.

Columbus's crew seemed to sense the mounting restlessness of the Admiral. Disappointment spread, and on the 21st November, Martin Alonzo Pinzón, Columbus's immediate subordinate, deserted together with the *Pinta* in order to discover the land of gold off his own bat. Good weather alone remained faithful to Columbus. Despite the fact that tornadoes are so common in these latitudes, he continued to sail day after day under the same smiling sky and with the same soft breezes. At the beginning of December he reached Haiti, of which the natives on board could only speak with shy wonder and slight horror. They called the inhabitants of the island Caribs and said they were cannibals. Once again Columbus made a mistake. He misunderstood his native guides and misinterpreted the term *caniba* which they applied to the inhabitants of Haiti (and from which the word cannibal was later derived) as the customary appellation of the subjects of the Great Khan.

But the Great Khan remained just as elusive as Cipangu and Quinsay. Through the carelessness of the helmsman they even foundered. The *Santa Maria* struck a sandbank and could no longer put to sea. Therefore the sailors brought everything ashore that could be of any importance and since the *Niña*, the smallest of the craft, was not large enough to hold all of them, a part of the crew stayed behind in a fort, quickly built from the wreckage of the *Santa Maria*, while Columbus sailed on. Relations with the natives were good. The *cacique*, as the Indians called their ruler, seemed to be well disposed towards the strangers, and food and supplies of all kinds sufficient for a whole year were stored in the fort so that, as far as was humanly possible to predict, nothing untoward could happen. Furthermore Haiti seemed to be much richer in gold than the previous islands. During the short time they stayed there after the shipwreck, while the fort was being constructed, they gathered quite a handsome treasure of gold

VII. Columbus's own sketch of the north coast of Haiti.

through exchanges with the natives. Thus gold had been discovered, true not very much, but enough to cover the costs of the *empresa de las Indias*.

Shortly after the shipwreck, Pinzón returned with somewhat feeble excuses for his absence. His unauthorized search for the gold-land had been fruitless, and the Admiral could justly assume that his self-willed subordinate would avoid any future escapades. But who could guarantee that one day he would not slip off again in order to get back to Spain before Columbus? This thought left the Admiral no peace. Having had to wait for so many years before finally managing to reach the object of his dreams, it was not pleasant to think that another might anticipate him in tasting of the glories of these new discoveries. Thus in the middle of January 1493 he decided to return to Spain.

This decision must have been a difficult one to make. For a full twelve weeks now he had sailed up and down what he assumed to be the shores of Asia without finding either Cipangu or the Great Khan. No dignitaries, loaded with gold and clad in brocade, had awaited him, but only poverty-stricken, naked savages. Nowhere had he found those thickly populated cities Marco Polo had spoken of so eloquently. Not a single spice of trading importance had been discovered, but only poor substitutes for cinnamon and pepper. True, he had discovered gold on Haiti and a regular working would certainly prove rewarding. But how could he prove to Their Catholic Majesties that he had really been to the shores of Cathay, the lands of the Great Khan? Certainly Columbus could not have had happy thoughts in his mind when on the night of the 15th–16th January 1493 he left Haiti on his voyage home to Spain.

As we have seen, the crossing from the Canaries to the Bahama Islands was not so much a feat of nautical skill as a test of moral courage, but the voyage home made the highest demands on the navigational ability of the Admiral, his captains and pilots. No obliging trade wind blew the ships across the breadths of the oceans: rather Columbus had to use his wits to get out of the zone of the Trades and find traces of westerly winds. As far as Bermuda he sailed a northerly course, on the starboard tack against easterly winds. When two weeks after his departure he had the west wind behind him, it was a wicked winter wind bringing squalls, storms, hurricanes, icy showers and a wild sea. The two caravels ploughed their way

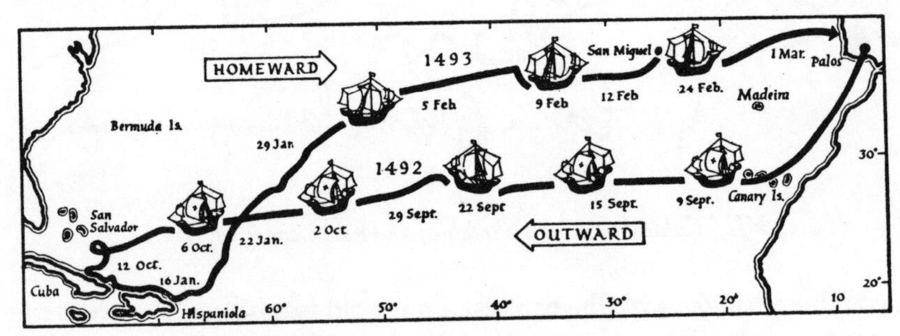

VIII. Columbus's route on his first voyage to America.

to the east, pitching so much that the bow was continually swamped by the foaming breakers, and the rudder, more than two-thirds out of the sea, was practically useless.

On the 12th February the weather became still worse. For a long time disaster threatened the tiny ships. The wind blew fiercely all day long and kept changing its direction from west to south-west; as a result there were extraordinarily strong heavy cross-seas. Columbus had taken in all sails, and so the steadying and lifting force of the wind was denied the ships which laboured heavily along, creaking in all their seams. When after twenty-four hours the storm abated somewhat, the sails were unfurled once more; but the wind rose again with full force from the south-west on the afternoon of the 13th February. Because of the mighty swell from the west, heavy cross-seas broke across the ships. During that night, Columbus's ship, the *Niña*, lost sight of the *Pinta*. The *Niña*, lacking adequate ballast and in constant danger of capsizing, fought its way towards the east. For hours, Columbus himself lost all hope, no longer able to believe that things could end well. Full of forebodings of his fate, he threw a tightly sealed little barrel overboard containing a short report on his voyage. He then summoned his crew to appear before him, and they drew lots twice to decide who should make a pilgrimage to the Holy Virgin of Guadalupe in the mountains of Estremadura if they got safely back to Spain. And each time the lot fell to Columbus. So passed the 14th February. Towards evening the storm abated, the sea slowly grew calmer and by night the danger had passed. A quiet day followed, and on the evening of the 15th February 1493 land could just be made out ahead. Columbus immediately came to the correct conclusion that this could only be one of the Azores islands. In fact it was Santa Maria, the most southerly of them.

Now the worst was over. The nautical feat demanded of Columbus's skill had been successfully performed. He had discovered the way home. Some unpleasant weeks followed in the power of the Portuguese who owned the Azores and who treated the homeward-bound voyager, allegedly from Asia, with none too friendly a spirit because in their opinion Columbus had gone illegally to Guinea. But in the end, they let him go and allowed him to sail. On the 14th March 1493, after a total absence of seven and a half months, Columbus re-entered Palos harbour. The *Pinta*, too, arrived on the same evening. After it had been driven off its course by the storm, at the end of February it had sighted the Galician coast of northern Spain, and had finally sailed along the coast as far as Palos. Pinzón had already made haste to inform Their Catholic Majesties of the discovery of new lands and of his own happy return from Galicia. But Ferdinand and Isabella understood only too well the significance of his haste. Pinzón was not summoned to the court. He had to stay on board his ship and, deeply wounded by the royal disfavour, he stole back to Palos. He could not bear this dashing of his hopes. He fell ill on board ship, handed over command to his brother, and died soon after reaching Palos.

There is no need to stress that Columbus's return was the occasion for a magnificent reception, and for a great number of feasts and banquets. The Royal Court, at that time in Barcelona, showered every possible distinction on the courageous discoverer, who, accompanied by a number of *Indios*, and surrounded by all kinds of strange objects from the New World, had presented himself to Their Catholic Majesties. Columbus made good use of their favourable attitude to him to praise the beauties of the new land, its immense riches, the wonders of the tropics, their fertility and their glory. True, when he had first set sail he had promised to find the Indian islands of Cipangu, so rich in spices, and also the kingdoms of Japan and Cathay, the great Chinese Empire with its innumerable canals, its marble bridges and its golden palaces, so wondrously described by Marco Polo. He had obviously failed to do so and a few doubting and questioning voices were raised amid the general jubilation. Columbus himself could not have expected otherwise. Thus in the final sentences of the report of his voyage written for the Spanish King, he protected himself in advance against all attacks in that he depicted himself—and this must in fact have been his real attitude—as God's tool, whose 'voyage, albeit apparently executed with so much levity, will resound to the glory of Christianity'. Yet despite all doubts, the idea that these newly discovered lands could be parts of a previously unknown continent was naturally not even considered, and very soon a start was made to prepare a large armada to conquer the land in the west.

During the preparations for this, Columbus, fulfilling his vow, started on his pilgrimage to the Madonna of Guadalupe. From Barcelona he first made for Madrid and from there to the Sierra de Estremadura. No itinerary of the Admiral's pilgrimage exists and thus we do not know in detail what paths Columbus used. But it is not impossible that he travelled by way of Trujillo and that Francisco, the fourteen-year-old son of the swineherd Pizarro, gazed in wonder as the mighty man's train of pilgrims went past along the road. A few decades later this self-same Francisco Pizarro was to overrun the gigantic land of the Incas and would himself take the place of Inca, the Son of the Sun. And to the south-west, in the little town of Medellin, which Columbus might have passed through some days later, another young boy might well have stood by the roadside to see the Admiral: Fernando Cortés, who would one day conquer Mexico and win the fabulous Kingdom of the Aztecs for the Crown of Spain.

Columbus's train of pilgrims was a magnificent spectacle, and excited much interest. On the one hand there were the officers of the Crown who accompanied the Admiral and who were destined to hold high offices in the new lands beyond the ocean. Then there were the six *Indios* who had been baptized at the Spanish Royal Court and who were about to return to their compatriots as true believers in Christ. Finally there was Don Cristobal Colón himself, Grandee of Spain, Admiral of the Oceans and Viceroy of the lands discovered by him: a greying, ruddy-complexioned, serious man of commanding presence. It was well known during that summer of 1493, when he rode through Spain in the guise of a pilgrim, that he had been closeted for many days with Their Majesties and that he had been honoured and distinguished by them as no other seaman had been before him. Dark rumours had reached them from near-by Portugal of the despair of King John on receiving the news of Columbus's safe return. According to these rumours he had exclaimed: 'Was I completely stricken with blindness? Why did I let this man go?'

The Portuguese King had not let matters rest there; he had immediately taken steps to gain something from the discoveries of Columbus for himself. Even before Columbus had arrived in Barcelona, the Spanish ambassador in Lisbon had reported to the Court that Portugal was equipping a fleet, whose aim was the new lands beyond the ocean. This had to be prevented, first of all by diplomatic means and since, according to the ideas on international law current at the end of the Middle Ages, the Pope alone could dispose of all those lands not yet belonging to Christian rulers, His Holiness was immediately approached by Spain. Pope Alexander VI, a born Spaniard himself, was deeply indebted to Spain and the Spanish Crown and thus as early as the beginning of May 1493, the Vatican decreed that the newly discovered islands or continents found by the *dilectus filius Christophorus Colón* all belonged to the Spanish Crown. It is true that in certain respects this contradicted previous Papal decisions, and in particular the bull *Aeterni regis* of 1481, according to which Portugal had the right to lay claim to all lands lying south and west of the Canaries. Naturally, Portugal did not hesitate to insist on this right with great force. Thereupon Spain sent a delegation to the Pope, and at the end of June 1493 the Papal Court, in the famous bull *Inter caetera*, decreed that a line drawn from the North to the South Pole, one hundred miles west of the Azores, was to be the border between the Spanish and the Portuguese spheres of control.

Undoubtedly this decision of Alexander VI was based on the reports Columbus had given of his voyages. The longitude of 38° W. lies very close to this demarcation line and divides the climate of the old world and that of America. At this point the temperature changed, the Trades set in with full force, the compass deviated to the north-west, different constellations appeared in the skies, giant meadows of floating seaweeds covered the ocean, in short, as Columbus reported of his third voyage, it looked 'as if a hill had been left behind on the horizon'. Seamen might have understood this, but landlubbers could not make much sense of it, and they might have found a commentary by Las Casas easier to understand. In his reports about America he tells us that there are neither lice nor fleas there and then continues:

> Usually ships and people going to sea are crawling with these little animals; on one's first voyage they always cause much trouble and much distress. What is remarkable in the voyage to India is the fact that lice are hatched as far as the Canary Islands, and as far as one hundred miles west or as far as the longitude of the Azores. But then they die and as soon as the first islands of America are entered no one has any lice.

For people from the Mediterranean, where flies and other insects even today are a plague, such statements must naturally have caused much surprise. We do not know whether the formal Spanish diplomats who persuaded Alexander VI to decree this line of demarcation of 38° W. had spoken of this. If this were the case, then lice and flies played a part in creating the world-famous division between the Spanish and Portuguese spheres of control.

During the weeks and months of these diplomatic negotiations, preparations had been completed by Juan de Fonseca, nephew of the Archbiship of Seville, for Columbus's second voyage across the ocean. In five months, this capable merchant and organizer had managed to collect and to equip fully a fleet of seventeen ships. On the 25th September 1493 he was ready. Seventeen ships bedecked with flags and banners and with twelve hundred Spaniards on board left Cadiz sailing south-west.

Full of hopes for the future, Columbus had given some thought to developing the new lands agriculturally: he took with him cattle, sheep, pigs, horses, seeds of European grain and sugar-cane, all presents from the Old to the New World, which would make successful colonization possible. All these were to flourish beyond expectation in the new lands. On the 2nd October the armada arrived in Gran Canaria, and between the 7th and 10th October it started on its ocean crossing. Sailing before the north-east Trade it reached the West Indian islands as early as the 4th November. In order to make full use of the Trade Columbus had

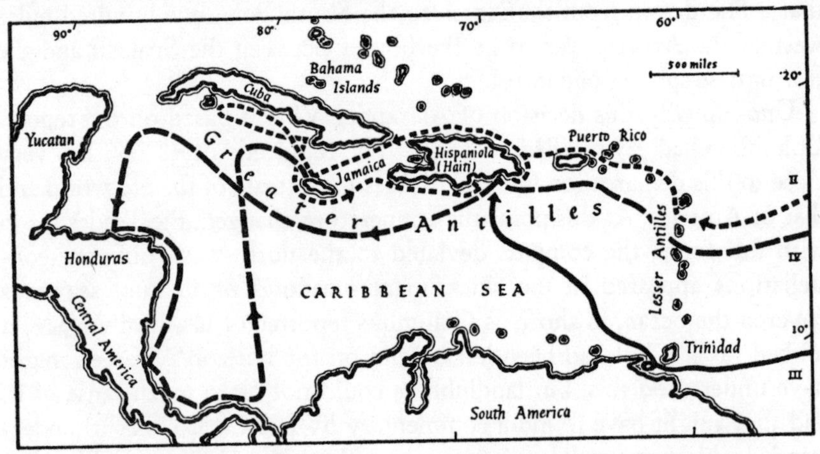

IX. The routes of Columbus's second, third and fourth voyages.

this time set a more southerly course. On the 22nd November the fleet anchored off Haiti; not one year had elapsed since Columbus had bidden farewell to the first Spanish settlement on the island, the Feste Natividad. But instead of the flourishing community he had expected to find, he was faced with ruins and desolation. Cruelties and bloodshed had so aroused the natives against their white oppressors that they had used the occasion of a Spanish reconnaissance expedition into the interior to avenge themselves. Columbus was so disappointed at discovering the remains of murder and arson, instead of the expected bars of gold, that he ordered the settlement's well to be dug up, thinking it to be the secret cache for the treasures that those he had left behind had surely collected. Nothing could be found and it was decided to establish a new settlement in a more favourable position. This settlement, christened Isabella by Columbus, in honour of the Queen, looked like a real fortress. It was placed under the command of his brother Diego, and he himself returned on board ship in order finally to spy out the fabulous Cipangu.

But both Cipangu and Ophir, suspected to lie in the interior of Haiti, proved to be nothing but foolish deceptions. Many hopes collapsed here. Moreover, those who accompanied Columbus on the second voyage were mainly of the type that had never been used to work, and who thought that one had merely to come to foreign lands to find riches unlimited. They had come for gold. They had thought they would be able to fill their pockets with little effort and return to their comfortable homes as gentlemen of great wealth. But reality had failed them. Thus it was that many more disillusioned people returned from this second voyage, begun under such promising auspices, than had done so from the first. On the 11th June 1496, Columbus returned once again to Cadiz surrounded by the evidence of his discoveries: gold, natives and tropical showpieces. But this time his reception was considerably cooler than it had been on his first return, for once again he had come back without what was expected of him; without mountains of gold. True, he could still manage to allay the disfavour with which he was openly met, but it took two full years for him to obtain the means for his third voyage in 1498. Again he discovered many new lands, but even this third expedition did not grant him the satisfaction of reaching his aim: Cipangu. Still, he managed to discover the El Dorado, which the natives had spoken about, in the gold-fields of Cibao on the island of Haiti. Nuggets of gold, the size of hens' eggs, were found in large quantities, and this discovery was a high measure of recompense for the terrible losses of men and property caused by the collapse of Isabella, the settlement which had taken the place of Port Natividad on Haiti. A fever, originating in the nearby lowlands, had wiped out people by the score, and this opportunity had been used by criminal elements for robbing, plundering, and outrages of all kinds. Columbus checked the smouldering rebellion, but in doing so he was forced to take repressive measures against some sons of the Spanish

X. The town of Isabella in Haiti.

nobility, and so it did not take long for him to be decried at home as a slave-driver, a bloodthirsty monster and high-handed tyrant. Thus, while Columbus was still busy establishing order the command arrived from Spain that Columbus must answer for his crimes before Their Majesties. He started on the return voyage in chains. Although, once in Spain, the prosecution was soon dropped, his good relationship with the Spanish Crown was finished for ever. And in 1502—perhaps more in order to be rid of him than because great store was set by his fourth voyage—the King agreed to his plan for a final effort to find the route to East India, which the Portuguese had just succeeded in reaching via Africa.

Steering west along the north coast of Honduras, Columbus this time went beyond the regions he had previously discovered as far as the isthmus of Panama. Here he learned of a great ocean a few days' journey from this shore. He also learned of the unique culture of the Mayas in Yucatan. This news revived his old expectations, which had become shaky when he had heard of the unknown sea beyond the shores. Nowhere could he discover a western passage, so Columbus was in fact led to believe he was facing the continent in which he had hoped to discover Marco Polo's wonderland. He was also told of Ciguare, the mythical gold-land in the north-west, where men and women went about in shining gold ornaments, and which today is believed to have been Mexico. He himself had the satisfaction once again of finding gold, but the bad state of the ships which the Spaniards had given this troublesome fellow forced him to interrupt his journey and to start on the voyage back.

By the time they reached Jamaica, the vessels had begun to leak so much that there could be no question of continuing. Cut off from all contact with the Spanish colony, Columbus and the rest of his crew had to waste almost a whole year before the governor of Haiti, appointed by the Crown, decided to do something for the shipwrecked company, of whose condition he had long been informed. After a long absence, Columbus returned once again to Spain in the autumn of 1504, only to find his patron Isabella of Castile on her deathbed. Columbus's great resilience had been broken by the vexations and humiliations showered on him. For two years he continued the fight for his rights, and for the restitution of the favours bestowed on him. Then he gave up. He died on Ascension Day, in the year of Our Lord 1506, and with him passed away one of the greatest men who had ever worked for Spain. For it was owing to Columbus that the Spanish King could boast, not many years later, that the sun never set on his domain.

The consequences of his discoveries had, as we know, been unpredictable. The most immediate consequence was the decline of Turkish power in Europe, though the terrible storming of Vienna by the Turks in the second half of the seventeenth century was to reveal the full extent of the dangers to Europe from this quarter. The centre of the world had shifted to the northern and western shores of Europe, where it would remain for centuries. Through Columbus's courageous discoveries the Atlantic Ocean had become an 'inland sea'.

All that remains is to ask how the news brought by Columbus spread through Europe and what effects it had. The first question cannot be answered satisfactorily. It would appear that the Latin world was the first to learn about Columbus, and that north of the Alps more time passed before his discoveries were known.

Since at first all knowledge of the exploits of Columbus was based on his own reports, it is easy to understand why it was generally believed that the Admiral had in fact gone to India. Thus the circumference of the earth had to be considerably smaller than Ptolemy had taught. Once again the ancients, those much admired masters of thought and knowledge, had quite obviously been in error. But as early as the autumn of 1493 doubts were voiced whether the new land beyond the ocean in the west was in fact India. And on the 1st November 1493 Peter Martyr in a letter to Cardinal Sforza coined the term 'New World' in speaking of Columbus as the *repertor ille Novi Orbis*. True, he was not completely certain, for he admitted that these might be previously unknown islands lying off Asia. It was only when Magellán sailed round the world that the truth was known. But still, Peter Martyr had invented the expression 'New World'; only in 1583 did the name America, derived from the Christian name of Amerigo Vespucci, another great Italian seafarer, come into common use.

7. Title-page of a broadsheet on Columbus's landing, which appeared in Florence in 1493

Our second question regarding the effects that the discovery of the New World had on the Old is even more difficult to answer. To understand these effects we shall have to return to the documents of the time.[1] They are imbued with the deep despair felt by thoughtful men towards the end of the fifteenth century. Their forefathers having made a magnificent start into the world at the times of the crusades, everything seemed now to be

[1] See also *Conquest by Man* (Harper & Brothers),

stagnation. The Church of Christ had become divided, the Turks had brought devastation to the whole of the Balkans, and had advanced up to the gates of Vienna. Catholicism was rotting in the morass of cynicism, and not only God and religion were affected but also science, faith in the Emperor, respect for money—the very foundations of society. On the one hand, heresy was rife, questioning the Pope and his authority; on the other, the rise of nationalism was undermining the unity of feudal Christendom. The Emperor of the Holy Roman Empire, successor to Charlemagne, and temporal Lord of the West, not only had to fight against the kings of France and England but his own lords and nobles had risen up against him. And traditional values and institutions, which existed on earth by the grace of God, were now confronted with a fresh enemy, capitalism, which was mercilessly to unhinge the whole frame of the world. How could an epoch such as the Middle Ages, based as it was on an unyielding belief in absolute values, in authority, spiritual and temporal, come to terms with this general upheaval of its most cherished unquestioned tenets? It could not, and despondency set in. A deep *malaise* had gripped the world, a feeling that *this* age was inferior to *earlier* epochs had become widespread: and then a poor sailor from Genoa, a humble citizen, discovered, thanks only to his unshakeable tenacity, a new land in which the white man, so sick and doubting of himself, was treated as a god.

The spiritual consequences are clear. The discovery of America must have had the same immediate effect on that self-doubting generation as would arise if contemporaries of *ours* were to land on some far-distant star, there to be greeted as gods. The Reformation and Counter-Reformation, the opulence of the Baroque period, indeed even the French Revolution of 1789, are the expression of the significance of Columbus's discovery for the old world: the European recovered his self-respect; a start towards new shores and a new day had been made. Admittedly this tonic effect quite often turned into arrogance, and at the very beginning of this new age there appeared the poisonous germ of megalomania whose terrible consequences we have all felt, are still feeling and will continue to feel.

PART TWO

THE EARTH IS A SPHERE

Curses on pepper! · Pepper-currency · Ulrich von Hutten sticks to his homespuns · Of cattle and spices · The inflationary legend of King Midas · The 'Black Friday' of 1499 · 'No call for spices' · Stock-taking with Widow Pithan · The Pope declares a Holy Cold War · The taste of port, and how Portugal received its name · Page meets nobleman · Vasco da Gama discovers the sea-route to East India · Is scurvy infectious? · The Vikings and $C_6H_8O_6$ *· Of ships that are sewn together · Christian Indians · The Rajah of Calicut grants an audience · Saints with long teeth and many arms · Return to Portugal · Of the 'cauchemar de la victoire' and of the disadvantages of being a victor · Lodovico Varthema, the King of Adventurers · A 'sobresalente' is given an honourable discharge · 160 per cent profit in the spice trade · Francisco Serrão deserts to the Moluccas, Fernão de Magalhães emigrates to Spain · Of an unemployed bank director, and why the New World is called America · Where is the passage to India? · Of the tragic mockery of fate · In Rio de Janeiro there are many beautiful girls · The secret charts are misleading: great disappointments on the River Plate · The Admiral provokes a mutiny · Genius or madman? · Of the right to disobey misguided superiors · Magellán finds the passage, but rats cost one ducat each · Recipe for a stew of old leather · Landing on the Philippines, and Magellán's death · Drinking arrack in Borneo · The 'Ilhas das Especierias' · Of ugly women and jealous husbands · Return to Spain · A day is missing from the calendar.*

I

THANKS be to God for pepper!

People in Lisbon had lived by the pepper trade for the last quarter of a century. Each new expedition, sent by the Crown to Africa, brought back shiploads of this precious spice to Portugal. While the quays of Venice were becoming deserted, merchandise from all over the earth was arriving at Lisbon. Those merchants who had begun to deal in the pepper business at the beginning of the seventies, when the profits from the Africa trade were granted to John, the Crown Prince, had long since become wealthy. For pepper was the ideal trade. It was worth its weight in silver. Customs duties, rents and taxes, even court fines, were paid in pepper. It bought ground and land, paid off mortgages, could buy burghership and coats of arms. The most beautiful women, the noblest horses, the most brilliant jewels, precious carpets, rare furs: all of these could be had for pepper.

Since that time the price of pepper has fallen steadily. In 1473, when John himself began to participate in this great business, this hot spice had still been so costly that only the great of the land could afford it, but, in the year of Our Lord 1498, even ordinary people could pepper their Sunday or holiday chicken. They too could enjoy the fashionable supper dish of a mixture of sugar and pepper, toasted on bread.

True, this was nothing but a fad and many voices were raised against this preference for Oriental spices and delicacies. Ulrich von Hutten, the famous German classicist, was one of the loudest objectors, and very significantly the fighting slogans of this intellectual landowner, 'expropriated' by the course of events, are noticeably tempered by national and anti-capitalist resentments. 'After Pliny's times, the old Germans fed themselves on oatmeal', he wrote in one place. 'Now it has become the fashion to live on products from overseas. This has brought riches to the Fuggers[1] and their clique, and so long as we remain slaves to our stomachs, they alone in all Germany will have riches and live in palaces.' Elsewhere he asserted: 'I wish to mention the life of my grandfather, Lorenz Hutten, as a glowing example of a simple life. He was a rich man and held the highest offices in both the civil and military services. But pepper, ginger,

[1] Fuggers: old merchant family in Augsburg, raised to the nobility and attaining great riches in the sixteenth century; bankers of Kaiser and Pope, patrons of the arts. (A.J.P.)

saffron and other foreign spices never crossed his threshold, and he only wore coats of German wool.'

How familiar all this sounds! And at the same time how fatuous and threadbare. How often have we heard such diatribes, and how futile they have always been! In any case, as far as the importation of tropical spices was concerned, Hutten's pamphlets were completely without effect. The need for seasoning was very real. Europe in the Middle Ages did not produce enough fodder to maintain its livestock through the winter, and so, in all countries, a great slaughter was made in autumn. After the gargantuan feasts given on such occasions, the left-overs were smoked and pickled. Admittedly, at the courts of the great, the first ice-cellars had already been constructed, but the mass of the population, right up to the end of the seventeenth century, ate pickled and smoked meat during three-quarters of the year. Fresh meat was obtainable only during the summer and early autumn and so, to make this monotonous diet more palatable, oriental spices and condiments were used in ever-increasing quantities until, in the words of a contemporary song, dishes were so spiced that people's mouths smelled like an apothecary's store, and hot vapours escaped from their lips like steam.

Since the time of the crusades, the most sought-after of these spices, imported from the east, had been pepper, that strange fruit of the *piper nigrum*. For a long time Europeans believed that its shrivelled appearance was due to roasting over a slow fire. Only towards the end of the Middle Ages was it learnt that this hot, devilish object had been neither roasted nor treated in any other mysterious way. If the shell was left on, when the berries were being dried in the sun, the result was black pepper; if the shell was removed before drying, a mild, white pepper was obtained. In the main, the latter variety was sent to Asia, and to China in particular, which at that time consumed even more pepper than today, while the black pepper was exported to Europe. For centuries, Alexandria in Egypt and also Venice had been the main centres of the pepper trade.

Then, suddenly, Lisbon had stepped to the forefront and had become the leading port for this profitable business. With ever-increasing imports, the price of pepper had dropped and it was no longer possible to get rich as quickly as during the golden decades of this admired 'capital of Europe'. However, with the fall in the price of pepper there occurred a corresponding rise in consumption. Since even burghers and artisans had a share in the riches of the Orient, demand had increased by leaps and bounds. Merchants from Portugal, Spain and France, from Germany, from the Netherlands and the Scandinavian countries, all of whom had once been the customers of the rich Italians, now came to Lisbon. The Alpine passes, which, but a few years previously, had been crowded with the covered wagons of the merchants from upper Germany on their long path to

Genoa, Venice and Milan, were deserted. The silver, from the Fuggers' mines in Silesia and Hungary or extracted from mines in the Tyrol and Carinthia, and also their copper for casting gun barrels, now flowed in an endless stream to Portugal. Whole shiploads of the finest Flemish lace were arriving from Antwerp; innumerable bags of corn and thick bales of the finest leather from the Baltic lands of the Prussians, Estonians and Lithuanians, while the Norwegians and Swedes paid in furs. Arctic and silver-fox skins, polar-bear skins, walrus tusks—all luxuries which once not even the Court of the Crown had been able to afford—had now become quite common in Lisbon.

8. Pepper harvest.

Was this expansion of trade not wonderful! Was this not progress! Even the ordinary citizen of Portugal shared in the great successes of civilization, in the economic prosperity and the general advance.

Admittedly, in Portugal people did little but congratulate themselves on their luck. But in Venice it was a different story. Portugal was cutting away the basis of its prosperity. The Venetians were angry. At first they limited themselves to mere propaganda. They declared with emphasis and authority that the months'-long transport of valuable spices in the damp holds of the ocean-going caravels spoilt the aroma and made the Oriental delicacies unpalatable for the true gourmet. When this did not have the desired effect, they tried to incite the Sultan of Egypt. In October of 1502, they sent one of their best brains, one Benedetto Sanudo, to Cairo, to point out to the Sultan that he would be the worst hit if Portugal was allowed to monopolize the spice trade. The Sultan was asked to persuade the Indian Rajahs to sell nothing to the Portuguese, since otherwise all the precious money, which hitherto had gone into his exchequer, would go to them instead. The Venetians themselves would have no option but to buy in Lisbon instead of Alexandria—which was in fact what happened from 1515 onwards. But the Sultan declined. At that moment he could do nothing. Then, according to rumours current at the time, Venice sent artillery officers and experts to strengthen the defences of the Indian Rajahs. It is not certain that these rumours were correct, yet it is not impossible, for trade with Egypt and India was the very basis of the economic existence of Venice, and when one is driven into a corner all means are legitimate.

The economic situation was an urgent reason why the Italian merchant-republics had to use all means at their disposal to stem the advancing tide of the Portuguese. Italy stood by no means alone. Spain and France were also worried by this new prosperity of Portugal. Diplomatic relations became strained and no effort was spared to make things as difficult as possible for the upstart power. But since, as far back as 1481, the Pope had granted Portugal sovereignty over all the lands lying south and west of the Canaries, very little could be done. At least in that respect Portugal was quite safe.

Unfortunately, the situation at home was not all calm sailing. Many merchants had gained great wealth from the pepper trade, and the State and the Crown, who had a share in every bag of spice sold, had done very well also. And yet severe crises kept recurring, for the boundless, sudden influx of highly priced spices had the same consequences in Portugal as the flood of gold that came upon Spain after the discovery of America. Food prices, which were governed by the harvests and by the demand of the population, did not fluctuate with the dropping prices of gold and spices, and since on top of all this sailors and adventurers were converging in their thousands on the Iberian peninsula, bread, meat and butter became dearer and dearer. Wages and manufacturing costs also increased, and in the first half of the sixteenth century, many articles essential for life had risen in price by as much as 250 per cent.

At the time nobody could say how it had happened. Capitalism was still in its cradle. Neither Pope nor Emperor could do anything to stop the tragedy. Only fifty years later an unknown figure, the lawyer and political theoretician, Jean Bodin, concluded in his *Discours sur les causes de l'extrême cherté qui est aujourd'hui en France*, published at Paris in 1568, that the terrible increase in general prices was caused by the surfeit of gold and silver. Jean Bodin's theory was completely correct. When he was born at the beginning of the sixteenth century, the total amount of precious metals in Europe was about seven thousand tons, with a value of between 150 million pounds to 250 million pounds; at the end of the century in the vaults of the merchants, in the carters' huts and the palaces of kings, this had increased to about 23,000 tons of silver and 750 tons of gold with a value of 600 to 750 million pounds. The old fable of King Midas, in whose hands everything changed to gold, had become a reality in the West during the sixteenth century. A single convoy arriving in Seville carried a load of gold worth three million ducats, and the Duke of Albuquerque had forty solid silver ladders made so that his servants might fetch down the twelve hundred silver bowls and the fourteen hundred silver plates from the high shelves, whenever he gave a banquet. But gold cannot be eaten and silver does not quench thirst. Thus the prices of foodstuffs climbed to dizzy heights. Deeply worried, people took note of this puzzling phenomenon which characteristically made its first appearance on the Iberian peninsula. They explained it through the increase in population, bad harvests, wars and finally through the evil of usury. The prophetic admonition of the German poet Freidank, some 250 years earlier: 'God has created three estates: knights, peasants and clerics. The fourth was the devil's own work, which is called the estate of usury,' was now on everyone's lips.

Even the great 'pepperbags', as the merchants were suddenly called, were anxious, for every time one of the still larger royal Portuguese armadas returned, utter confusion reigned in the spice market. This happened first in 1460, when the fleet brought back *malaguetta* from Africa, those highly prized 'corns of paradise' which had previously been imported from Alexandria through Venice. In 1485 it happened a second time when Diego Cão arrived on the Tagus, his ships laden with pepper.

Nobody in Lisbon had expected this. Fully convinced that the demand would increase and that prices would rise, the spice merchants had been confident. Great cargoes of spices had been bought on speculation and then, quite contrary to all expectation, tens of thousands of quintals of pepper and 'corns of paradise' were suddenly piling up in the docks. The import firms had to settle, and since prices at the mere news of the arrival of the fleet had fallen by half, bankruptcy followed on bankruptcy.

Curses on pepper! Curses on the pepperbags! Curses and death and hellfire to the usurers!

Such slumps had already struck Lisbon twice before, but they had been forgotten in the course of the years and, compared with the events of the 10th July 1499, the black Friday of this year, they appeared almost benign. Early that morning the caravel *Berrio*, commanded by Nicolão Coelho and belonging to Vasco da Gama's India fleet, arrived in Lisbon. Since his departure two years ago, nothing had been heard of the Admiral's fleet. Now one of the four ships which had once sailed out of harbour, had returned manned by a handful of emaciated sailors covered with ulcerous scabs, its holds full of spice. The other ships which were bound to arrive within the next few days were equally laden.

In a matter of hours, the news was all over the town. The spice merchants paled and closed their offices at noon. They were finished, every man jack of them, each firm, each business. The fact that of the one hundred and fifty sailors who had left with Vasco da Gama only fifty had returned, that many families would that night put out the lights, cover up their mirrors, leave their windows and doors open, so that the souls of the dead could return for the last time to their wives and children, was not considered of prime importance. But that wholesale importers were closing their stores, that they could no longer meet their commitments and were bankrupt was very serious news indeed!

This collapse of prosperity spread through the whole of Europe. 'There is no demand whatever for spices, since everyone is expecting news from Portugal,' could be read in the business reports of the great Ravensburger Gesellschaft, one of the most famous Upper-German trading combines of the time. And reporting on the Stock Exchange of Frankfurt-am-Main, the correspondent of the Ravensburger wrote to his head office: 'Nobody dares to have any large dealings in spices, for all are afraid of shipments that might arrive from Calicut.'

Not only the large firms but grocers also were affected. There was far less specialization in those days than we have today, and an average trader's store at the beginning of the sixteenth century had as wide a range of articles as an American drug store. The widow Pithan in the middle of the sixteenth century, as we know from a yearly inventory, had supplies of the following goods in her store in Frankfurt: rice, currants, wine, pepper, nutmeg and all other spices, cotton, linen, paper, alum, sandalwood, dye-woods, pigments, gold, silver, copper, tin, lead, leather, tobacco, sugar, saffron, wax, tartar and also fabrics from Epinal, Augsburg and Brabant. Equally diverse and confusing was the shop of Hans von Ringen, 'Spicy Hans' as he was called, in Frankfurt-am-Main in 1516. It seems clear that shops selling and stocking such a wide range of goods were affected by any fluctuations in the prices, and that their customers had to bear the brunt.

And thus the cry was raised time after time: Curses on pepper! At the Royal Court in Portugal, too, the gravity of the situation could be read on the courtiers' faces. It was not so much the lamentable condition of the subjects that troubled them, as the realization that the exploitation of the discovery of the sea-route to East India was by no means an unmixed blessing, and that now it was impossible to go back to the more stable economy of former times. 'As ye sow, so also shall ye reap', and the Portuguese economy could not pay for the harvest. Portugal, at that time, had only a million inhabitants and it was manifest that alone it could not manage to carry the great political burden brought back by Vasco da Gama in his weather-beaten ships. This little country, having subjected half the world, had made enemies not only of the Indian Sultans but also of the Arabs and the Egyptian Mamelukes, in whose hands the Oriental spice trade was concentrated. For this reason the Crown, soon after the return of its most successful Admiral, sent out shrewd negotiators to Germany to contact the Fuggers and the Welsers,[1] who up to that time had been interested in Italy. Portugal, which had quite suddenly become the

[1] Another powerful patrician family of Augsburg merchants (A.J.P.).

economic fulcrum of the world, was desperately in need of a blood transfusion and required the reviving injection of big capital, and this was in the hands of the German bankers.

But this borrowing of strange blood was not to have the expected effects. For even before it came about, before international high finance had gained a firm footing in Portugal, news arrived that the rich and mighty land of Egypt was in its death throes, and thus a completely new situation, whose consequences were unpredictable, had arisen. For almost five centuries the West had done everything in its power to dislodge the land on the Nile from its position of middleman in trade with the Orient. Nothing had helped, neither the Papal bulls of excommunication nor yet the blockade of Egypt by the fleets of the orders of knighthood. Cairo and Alexandria had continued to be the trading centres for spices and delicacies. First tentatively and hesitantly, then in ever-larger numbers, European ships, heavily armed merchantmen from Venice, high-built caravels from Catalonia, fast Genoese galleys had sailed into their ports. Certain conditions had been imposed: the 'foreigners' had to hand over the tillers and yards of their ships to the Egyptian harbour-masters so that they were immobilized. Their ships' crews were allotted berths with others of their own nation. They were forced to buy all their goods in stipulated quantities and at fixed prices from the Sultan's stores, but they were not plagued by import duties or taxes, excepting in the case of precious metals, and here the import duty was small. The profits from this skilful exploitation of the monopoly had been tremendous. It had increased steadily up to the middle of the fifteenth century, when the Sultan of Egypt was suddenly confronted by two enemies, more terrible and insurmountable than all political conditions.

The two enemies were called sugar and cotton. These were the only two trading products that Egypt produced herself and from which the land derived its proper living. Neither really belonged to the Nile. Sugar-cane came from India, where it had been cultivated since time immemorial, and cotton from the tropics. Both need much sun and moist soil. Thus in Egypt they prospered wonderfully well, and it seemed as if the alluvial land near the Nile had been prepared specially for these plants. As early as the ninth century, people had known how to refine sugar, and almost at the same time it was discovered how to work the extremely delicate white fibres covering the seed of the cotton plant. About A.D. 1000 the first shipments of Egyptian sugar arrived in Venice and the rich were delighted with the taste of the granular powder. The crusades spread its fame quickly through Europe, and next to the fine cotton fabrics, sugar was soon to become one of the chief exports of Egypt. But until the seventeenth century it remained so expensive that it could only be bought from the apothecary by the half-ounce, so that in northern Europe syrup or honey continued to be the chief means of sweetening. One whole pig was the bartering price for a pound of sugar.

For some centuries the Sultans managed to keep the cultivation of sugar-cane and the technical processing of cotton secret. But from 1300 onwards, both plants were grown along the shores of the Mediterranean. The plantations in Madeira and the Canaries were to become extremely vast, and the Nuremberg *World Chronicle* of 1493 stated triumphantly:

> There is found amongst other fruits so much sugar that all Europe is beyond measure endowed with it. The name of the island is Madeira, whence cometh Madeira sugar.

When Europe itself began to produce sugar and cotton, the demand for Egypto-Indian granulated sugar and for Melis (Malta) sugar fell rapidly. Europe began buying Canary sugar from Madeira and the Canaries, and also the cheaper Cassonage sugar which came in great barrels from Brazil. Yet even this, the cheapest sugar available in 1620, cost some thirty guilders per hundredweight, and this was a fortune.

The same thing happened with cotton. Although cotton from the farms in Apulia, Sicily, Crete, Greece, Spain and Malta was considered less valuable, it was also much cheaper and so presented the Egyptian exporters with a deadly threat. The purchase of Indian cotton and its re-sale to Western firms became quite impossible for Egypt, because of the cost involved. Hence these two commodities, which had so long been the wealth of Egypt, became its ruin.

Meanwhile, the Portuguese, during their voyages to Africa, had managed to lay hands on a sizeable quantity of spices and other products at the very source of their production. As a result the merchants no longer needed the Mameluke Sultans for obtaining even ivory. The Portuguese trading-houses in Lisbon could supply all their requirements. The Egyptian purse remained empty, her harbours deserted and, as early as the beginning of the sixteenth century, the magnificent capital cities of Alexandria and Cairo had become nothing but ghostly shadows of their former glory. Once again the political centre had shifted, and until the building of the Suez Canal, Egypt's influence on Europe was to decline rapidly.

The clever rulers at the Portuguese Court very quickly realized that Egypt's economic rôle had fallen to them. They understood that they would have to control India, that they would have to occupy Malacca and Aden, and that they would have to secure, not only West Africa, but the whole wide stretch of the East African shore. They were terrified by the task facing them, a task far too great for their resources. The present that Vasco da Gama had brought back from his great voyage had proved to be as deceptive as the Trojan Horse.

2

Once the land- and sea-power of Carthage had been shattered, Roman fleets began to range throughout the Mediterranean. They called the granite promontory jutting out into the sea and protecting the wide basin formed by the river Douro 'the hot harbour', *Portus Cale.* Later the Iberians called it Portocale; and Portocale was the name of this town even when it flourished under the Goths and the Vandals, who during the fifth century descended on the land like locusts. The Moors, who ruled it three centuries later, still retained the old name. From the Minho and the coves of the Galician coast in the far north to the Tagus in the south, it is the only great harbour, and for long the old settlement was to be the 'capital' of the whole rocky province on the western ocean.

The 25th October 1147 saw the end of this, for on that day Christian crusaders stormed Lisbon and freed it from the rule of the Moors. They called the whole country after the name of the harbour where they had first dropped anchor. From now on it was called Portugal and the ancient Portus Cale on the Douro, the river of wine and happiness, would henceforth bear the modest name of Oporto, the harbour.

Gourmets the world over will feel their hearts beat faster at the mention of Oporto. Pure port wine, not that brownish-coloured liquid which commonly bears this name, but light purple in hue, similar in taste to old Burgundy, only with more body and of more mature sweetness, is a true gift of God. Very rarely is it exported, and to drink it one must go to Oporto where since olden times it has been sold in the side-streets near the São Martinho da Cedofeite, the famous church of Theodomir, King of the Suevi. Whoever comes from Oporto is proud of the world-wide fame of his old city, but the fact that the Douro must take second place to the Tagus, that the name of Lisbon is mentioned before that of Oporto, that the former has become the capital and that Portus Cale has thus fallen back, all this wounds their pride, and ever since that 25th October 1147, this *leal e invicta cidade*, the 'loyal and invincible city' on the Douro, has been a rival of the more fortunate Lisbon.

In 1480, the year when Fernão de Magalhães, later to be known as Fernando Magellán, the first man to sail round the world, was born, the discord between the two cities was naturally more pronounced than it is today. Those who, like Magalhães, a *fidalgo de cota de armas*, were not of the highest Lisbon nobility counted but little at the Court. They were looked upon with the same distrust which they, in turn, felt for the smooth and polished courtiers. This was one of the reasons why Fernão de Magalhães later turned traitor to Portugal.

The region of Alentejo, according to modern reckoning one hour by car from Lisbon, had a different history. This fertile and spacious province on the Bay of Sines would only later join the kingdom ruled by Lisbon. Here there was no venerable tradition, no rivalry with the brilliant city on the Tagus. Here there were no noblemen of the fourth rank; here mighty barons ruled like kings. It was a young land, a kind of colony. Those who, like the da Gamas, went to Court from here did not bear grudges; they came without disfavour and suspicion. If they were of the higher nobility, they were gladly received in the spacious halls and the shady archways of the Royal Palace, where today stands the Praça do Comércio, Commerce Square. They were not long in joining in with the proud cry: *Quem nao tem visto Lisboa, nao tem visto cousa boa*' (Who has not seen Lisbon has not seen beauty). They quickly believed in the legend that Ulysses, the great Greek seafarer, was the founder of the settlement of Olisipo, Lisbon.

When Fernão de Magalhães was born, Vasco da Gama, the third son of the knight commander of Sines and Cercal, was already sailing in one of the countless Portuguese caravels. In 1480, Vasco was just 11 years old and still a child, though big enough to fetch cannonballs hot from the furnace. Portugal was setting the example of sending its children to sea, an example to be followed by England some three hundred years later. Those who want to become seamen cannot get to sea early enough. That Vasco, the son of the commander and captain Estevão da Gama, was to follow in his father's footsteps, had long since been decided. His father belonged to the old school of seamen drilled by the Infante, Prince Henry, called the 'Navigator' although he had never been to sea. Estevão had led many a voyage to Africa, and was an experienced sailor and, when Bartolomé Diaz returned from the Cape of Good Hope in 1487, the King appointed Captain da Gama as commander of the next fleet of discovery. Ten years later, in 1498, this fleet finally put to sea. Its commander was not Estevão the father, but Vasco the son.

During this period, when expedition after expedition set sail from Portugal in a never-ending stream, Fernão de Magelhães served as page to the Queen. He knew that his presence at the Court was of great importance for his father. Now his future was assured. It was a great honour to carry the Queen's colours; but while his companions, older than himself, were given commands on the caravels of His Majesty, or a commission in Fort Elmina on the Gold Coast, or in the infantry in the fortifications on the Azores, Fernão had to stay behind in Lisbon—he was too young.

As yet he had no idea of what destiny held in store for him. When in the middle of January 1497 Vasco da Gama, during an official audience of King Manuel, received his appointment of Admiral of the India Fleets, Fernão de Magalhães must certainly have witnessed this festive ceremony. But there was nothing to connect the tall, glittering cavalier from the nobility of Sines and Circal, the brave captain who despite his mere twenty-seven years was already a seaman tested in a thousand battles, with the slightly built, olive-skinned page of the Queen with his piercing black eyes and abundant black hair. But fate had already decreed that these two radically different men were to be brothers and comrades. Magalhães was to become the heir to his more fortunate predecessor, their names must both be mentioned in the same breath: Vasco da Gama and Fernão de Magalhães!

When the news of Columbus's successful return from his first voyage reached Lisbon, there was much concern lest Spain might be fortunate enough to achieve in one stroke the goal that Portugal had sought incessantly for decades. True, it was in Portugal itself that people had first begun to doubt whether Columbus had in fact been to the western shores of Asia, but nobody could be certain, and there was reason enough for anxiety. Whoever controlled the sea-route to India was lord of the earth. Prince Henry's nautical academy in Portugal had realized this at a time when in the rest of Europe horizons did not stretch much further than the church tower of the neighbouring town. Germany was in a parlous state of political confusion and dismemberment. France was constantly at war with England. In Italy there were internecine struggles which hampered the efficiency of even such great seaports as Genoa, Naples, and Venice. Spain had for long been occupied with its struggle against the Moors—and it was Portugal alone which, for one and a half centuries, had enjoyed set frontiers and internal stability. This small country on the western coast of the Iberian peninsula had taken full advantage of its start over the other powers, and when Bartolomé Diaz sailed round the Cape of Good Hope in 1487, he had accomplished the great aim of almost the whole of the fifteenth century: he had opened up the sea-route to East Asia and shown beyond doubt that to the east of the Black Continent there was the sea and not mainland as the ancients had thought.

This achievement of the Portuguese was even greater than that of the following years, when the new route was exploited, for it was made in the face of incessant struggles for every foot of unknown land, for every mile of new sea. It was a unique joint venture on the part of countless brave seamen whose names and deeds have been far too rarely recorded by history. Their original driving force was always the pure spirit of discovery. Even today, it is by no means all plain sailing to navigate a ship down the west coast of Africa. The South-east Trade, the strong Benguela currents, together with the tremendous breakers, which, however weak the wind, are thrown against the shore, make this part of the sea not very safe even for large ships—it requires real courage and skill to sail in these parts.

Portugal was not lacking in these qualities at that time. No matter how many were drowned, how many died of scurvy and other diseases, no matter how many ships returned from afar bringing back nothing more than the knowledge of ever-new deserted coasts, during these eight decades from the beginning of the sea enterprises, Portugal was never in want for heroes. And finally they succeeded: the sea-route to East India, sought out so systematically, was found.

It was first discovered by Diaz in 1487. But it needed eleven more years before the final objective was reached. This last stage, consisting of the nearly eight hundred sea-miles from Diaz's turning point on the east coast of Africa up to the Arabs' sphere of control and then the final leap to India, was carefully prepared. As early as the end of the 'eighties, a Portuguese mission had left for East Africa with orders to investigate the shore more closely by using the land-route, and to consider the possibility of voyages to India. The expedition, guided by Arab traders, reached Sofala, beyond the Zambesi. By establishing contacts via the Arabs with merchants along the western shore of India, favourable ground had been prepared for later Portuguese enterprises. The towns of Cannanore, Calicut and Goa appeared likely to be receptive to Portuguese traders, and they were in fact to become the chief Portuguese bases in India. Reports received in Portugal from these expeditions, together with information from other reliable sources, confirmed Bartolomé Diaz's views that the gates of India were open and that they could be reached on the sea-route. A fleet of ships was built and equipped as soon as possible and placed under the command of Vasco da Gama. The Portuguese navy had searched out the best man to be found for this task. True, the India-Admiral was still very young, but he had proved his worth during many great voyages, and particularly as a commander of the fleet. And this was decisive here. Of course only an experienced sailor could be given command of the India fleet, but even more important he had to have unquestioned authority. After all, the small Portuguese ships were expected to be at sea for months without seeing land, or in any case longer than any before them. This fact, together with the conditions on board sea-going ships of the time, demanded uncommon strength of character from the commander. The unyielding, yet diplomatic, Vasco was just the right man for the job. If anybody were to succeed it would be Vasco, and the expedition *had* to succeed, whatever the price in lives or material. Columbus had just left on his third voyage to America, and the gold that so far had eluded him might be found at any moment. Thus it was time Portugal took the last decisive step, particularly since one thing had by now become quite clear to the western neighbours of the proud Spaniards: it was not India that Columbus had discovered.

3

The candles cast a dim light. The man kneeling on the altar steps apart from the rest of the congregation turned his head. A warm, red light filtered through the high Gothic windows down into the chapel of Our Lady of Bethlehem. Dawn was breaking on the morning of the 8th July 1497. The monks of the hermitage of Rastello near Lisbon, today called Belem, began to intone the *Salve Regina*; the vigils were at an end.

The lonely man below the altar was struggling through the most difficult hour of his life. It was not too late to turn back. He could still have jumped on his horse and returned his command to Their Majesties in the Palace. He would have been an outcast until his death, both he and his family, if he had done so. He would have had to sit in his country estate, inactive, despised, forgotten. What tortured him was not fear for his own life—he had risked that often enough all these years in the service of the King—but fear for the lives of his crew. The one hundred and fifty souls given into his care, would he be able to return them all, safe and sound? There was scurvy, that strange, terrible disease of sailors for which there was no medicine and no cure. There were battles to be fought with the Arabs; there were the Indian Sultans on whose attitude everything depended. How many people might have to die for his sake!

For his sake? If he returned the commission somebody else would receive it. The sea-route to India was so near discovery that there was no way back, not even for the King. Even if he, Vasco da Gama, had ridden post-haste to Their Majesties to implore them not to put him to the test, they could not have stopped the ships from sailing. If it was God's will that the ships must sail this route, then there was no more skilled guide than he. If he refused, his crime before God and history would be made blacker with the lives of those whom his experience might have saved.

Manuel the King, too, must have slept badly that night of Saturday, 8th July 1497. Had he not been the King, he would have gone to the quayside in Rastello to watch his fleet depart. It bore the might and the glory of the Portuguese Crown on board. If it should fail in reaching its distant aim in the Orient, then Spain would have conquered. Then all that had happened since Henry the Navigator would have been mere futility. But if Vasco da Gama should discover the sea-route to East India then Portugal would confront the most tremendous task of its history. Were its land, its people, its peasants and nobles strong enough for the task? Were they able enough? Were they the chosen or the victims of God?

On the morning of the 8th July 1497, the sun having hardly risen above the horizon, Manuel called his Father Confessor and before a number of witnesses he made a solemn vow. In the place of the old hermitage in Rastello, he would erect a great cloister, which would be the burial place for him and his successors. Immediately after Vasco da Gama's return in 1499 he laid the foundation stone of the Convento dos Jeronymos do Belem, that glorious monastery built by the master Joano de Castilho high above the town where, twenty years later, Manuel was to find eternal sleep. Thus one of the great moments in history was preserved in this magnificent building—a reminder of that night when, nearly five hundred years ago, the fate of the West lay for one fleeting second in the hands of the King of Portugal.

Only the guards had remained on board the four ships of the India fleet. Despite the triple wine ration issued that night, it was quiet on deck. Occasionally the rattle of chains, of the twelve criminals sentenced to death, could be heard from below deck. Vasco da Gama was taking them to India as reinforcements for particularly dangerous contingencies. Nothing else disturbed the stillness of that soft night. Silently the guards stared across to the lights of Rastello, dejectedly they listened to the noises from the nearby land.

The last night! Would they ever see Portugal again?

During the first light of dawn the pipings of the boatswains could be heard from the flagship, the caravel *Gabriel*. Pedro d'Alemquer, Vasco da Gama's chief pilot, had gone for a last tour of inspection of the *Raphael*, commanded by Paulo da Gama, the Admiral's elder brother. When the boat made fast to the gangway of the *Raphael*, the guards reported that all was well. In the still night the water could be heard lapping rhythmically against the sides of the ships. They went on to the *Berrio*, the small caravel under the command of Nicolão Coelho, Knight of the Blood Royal. It could only carry fifty tons, while the newly built *Gabriel* and *Raphael* could each carry one hundred and twenty. 'May God have mercy on those in the *Berrio*!' thought Martin Alonso, the interpreter for Bantu languages, who was following the first pilot's final tour of inspection by the sound. He knew from his own experience the dangers facing these flat-bottomed, fast little ships of the Portuguese navy. He shuddered as he remembered his own long captivity in the jungle of the Congo after his little caravel had foundered. That was how he had come to learn Bantu languages and why he was travelling in comfort on the Admiral's ship. Fortune was indeed smiling upon him.

Now they had left the *Berrio*. The sound of the oars dipping into the water could be heard from the *Gabriel*.

'Now the madman is even paddling to the old supply barge,' somebody whispered into Martin Alonso's ear. He was startled. It was not wise to open one's mouth too wide on the Admiral's ship. In the light of the stars he could see that it was Diego Diaz, the famous Bartolomé Diaz's younger brother, who was standing next to him and who was going along to India as private secretary.

The supply ship, a massive object of two hundred tons, commanded by an old comrade of Vasco da Gama, and due to be sunk in Mossel Bay beyond the Cape of Good Hope, piped the chief pilot on and off, and now the oars could be heard as the boat returned to the Admiral's ship.

It was high time. The procession was emerging from the chapel of Our Dear Lady into the first rays of the rising sun. Slowly the train made its way to the harbour. Each of the hundred men who had been allowed to accompany the Admiral to the vigils, carried a candle in his hand.

Boats were launched from all the ships to receive the men on board. They quickly climbed up the rope ladders onto their ships as the mainsails were hauled up the mast to the sound of drums and shrill pipes. Anchor chains rattled and clumsily the four ships started moving down the Tagus towards the sea on an ebbing tide. The morning breeze soughed in the canvas. The sun had risen, and the turrets of S. Julião and Cascães grew smaller and smaller; soon even the mighty cliffs of Cape Espichel were nothing more than a thin black line on the horizon.

Three weeks later, on the 25th July, they sighted the Cape Verde Islands. The fleet took water and firewood on board as well as fresh meat, fruit and some vegetables, and after a stop of eight days they put to sea again. Warned by the experience of their predecessors, Vasco's armada kept far from the African shore, so that it crossed the Atlantic calms at their narrowest point—much closer to South America than to Africa. The days passed uneventfully. The favourable wind continued and although occasionally there were periods of calm, when the sails hung idle from the yards, the wind soon returned to fill the bellying sails.

Then something exciting happened:

> On the 22nd August while sailing from the south towards the west we discovered many birds looking like herons, and as night fell they made for the south-west very vigorously in the manner of birds that are flying shorewards. . . .

This is written in the *Roteira da viagem de Vasco da Gama*, the diary of a simple sailor serving on the *Raphael*. Since Vasco da Gama and his crew were experienced sailors, they knew, of course, what these flocks of birds meant and that land could not be far away to the south-west. On the same day the Admiral calculated that his distance from Africa was more than eight hundred leagues. Even if his reckoning was wrong, one thing is certain: the Portuguese must have come very close indeed to the shores of Brazil, and it was pure accident that they did not come within sight of it.

Long and difficult days of sailing in the Atlantic calms followed, and at the beginning of November 1497, the African coast came into sight approximately in the region of Saint Helena Bay, somewhat north of the

Cape of Good Hope. Here the weather deteriorated owing to the effect of Arctic currents which brought snow, hail and icy rain. The fleet had now been at sea without sight of land for three months, and this, coupled with the unpleasant change in climate, decided Vasco da Gama to order a

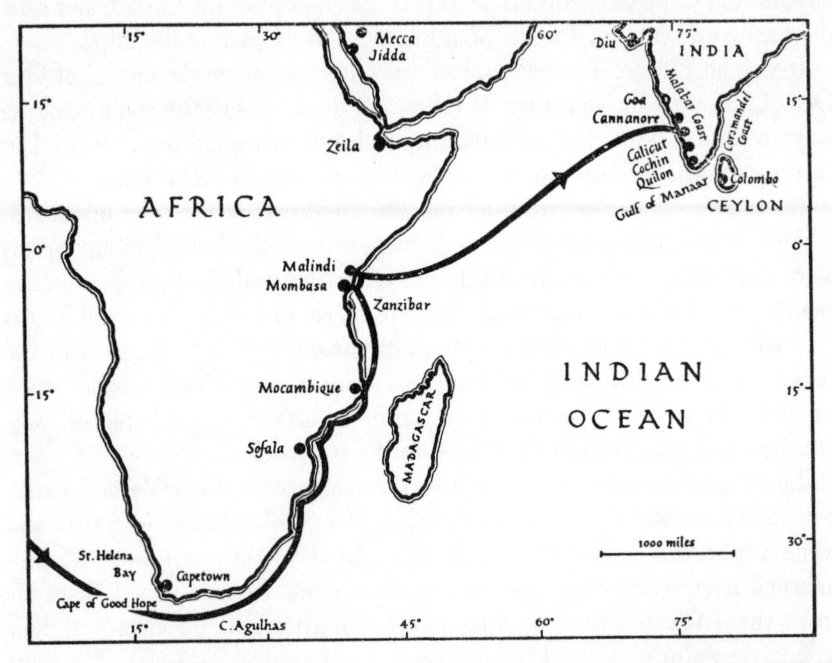

XI. Route of Vasco da Gama's first voyage to India.

few days of rest ashore. Here they met natives for the first time but the encounter was most disappointing. In the *Roteira* we can read the following:

> In this land there live people of brown colour who gain their livelihood from hunting whales, sea-lions, gazelles and from cultivating plants. They use skins for their clothing and the men wear sheaths of leather and shells over their genitals. Their weapons are made of horn hardened by fire, and they have many dogs which look just like Portuguese dogs. These also can bark. When we had gone ashore we caught one of the natives of small stature. We took him along to the ship and the commander gave him food and had him dressed in beautiful clothes, and then put him ashore again. Next day forty or fifty of them arrived, and the Admiral showed them many kinds of goods to find out if similar things existed in their country: jewels, gold, cloves, cinnamon, and such like. But they understood nothing and behaved like people who had never seen such things.

Vasco had used this time of rest to determine the height of the sun, since this could not be done on board with any degree of accuracy. To his great joy he realized that he was only thirty leagues north of the Cape and that his course had been correct. The dangerous Guinea coast had been avoided and the Cape was not far away. Nevertheless almost three weeks were to pass before they could sail round it. Gales of unprecedented fury were impeding their progress. But on Wednesday, 22nd November 1497, towards noon, they rounded the Cape and altered course northwards.

Soon after, Vasco weighed anchor in Mossel Bay, in the same place where ten years previously Bartolomé Diaz had landed. He did not do this entirely by choice. True, in order to take legal possession of the new country with Papal assent, the India-Admiral had to erect a wooden cross, and an armorial post bearing the insignia of the Portuguese Crown. But the real reason was much more serious and gave extreme cause for worry. For weeks now the crew had shown signs of fatigue and weakness. The complexions of the weather-beaten, sunburnt old salts had turned a greenish-yellow; their eyes were surrounded by dark rings, some complained of aches in their limbs, while others found that their gums had turned blue and had swollen painfully.

Vasco da Gama knew immediately what this meant, and what dreaded guest had appeared on his armada. He had experienced enough of this and he knew the extreme speed with which these symptoms spread and became worse. The swelling gums would begin to bleed; they would then grow across the teeth so that it would be impossible to chew the ship's biscuits. The stricken men would begin to stink like rotting corpses and bluish, stone-hard ulcers would appear on their skin. Their tortured blood would stream out of their noses and mouths, and then they would swell up with water to die in agony.

The causes of this disease, called scurvy, were unknown until twenty years ago. The fact that it was due to a daily deficiency of 0·05 grammes of $C_6H_8O_6$, ascorbic acid, was only discovered in 1933 and 1934 by English, German and Swiss chemists. Until then, medical science and the seafarers of all nations were completely groping in the dark. As late as 1907, that famous German encyclopaedia, *Meyers Grosses Konversationslexikon*, had the following entry under scurvy: 'It is to be assumed that this is an infection whose undiscovered agent can only act in a greatly weakened organism.' And in agreement with medical opinion the world over, Meyer advised: 'If there is cause to fear an epidemic outbreak of scurvy, great care must be taken for cleanliness, warm clothing, airing of rooms, exercise and fresh air, adequate meals and a suitable choice and diversity of food.' When we read this today it appears quite ridiculous, particularly since, beginning with the Vikings almost 1,500 years ago, all seamen stressed the importance of having onions, radishes, oranges, lemons and raw sauerkraut on board. They knew from experience that fresh food, and vegetables in particular, worked wonders with this strange disease. Thus it must have been fairly clear that scurvy was a deficiency disease due to bad nutrition during long voyages, and that it could not possibly be infectious or epidemic. On the other hand, it had been observed very early on that by no means all the members of a ship's crew became victims to scurvy, even though they lived under the same conditions as their sick comrades. And modern science has shown that animals such as rats and rabbits can do without ascorbic acid and not suffer any bad effects.

XII. Map of Moçambique, dated 1612.

The reasons for this are not yet finally explained, and thus we can understand why scurvy was for so long held to be an infection. For after all, pestilency, leprosy, typhus and cholera did not attack everybody. Many were immune to these scourges of God, just as today also, influenza, cancer, tuberculosis or infantile paralysis only attack some individuals and not all of us. Why this is so and what factors are involved we do not know. Thus we are no wiser than our parents. True, we know that ascorbic acid—or Vitamin C as we call it—is a miraculous cure against scurvy. But the particular effect of this vitamin on the cell organism has not been completely elucidated.

Vasco da Gama did what he could in Mossel Bay. He used every effort to obtain fresh food from the Hottentots, and the *Roteira* reports that many seals were killed as well: '. . . gigantic creatures with mighty fangs, and so thick a skin, that no spear, however vigorously thrown, could hurt them.' Penguins too were hunted, 'birds as large as ducks, but unable to fly, and braying like asses'. But these measures were inadequate for a crew brought so low by scurvy. As the Portuguese continued their voyage, lack of drinking water began to make itself felt since northerly winds had delayed the fleet for far too long, and, at the end of January 1498, it had again become necessary to interrupt the voyage for a long rest. Thus Vasco sailed up the Quelimane branch of the river Zambesi, where he called a halt for a full month.

The first task there was the digging of graves. A considerable number of Portuguese sailors had been unable to withstand the strain of such a long voyage: thirty men had died and most of the others were stricken with scurvy. The last few days before landing had made particularly heavy demands on the crew. There had been high seas, the wind had been unfavourable and the constant tacking, involving as it did a continual shifting of sails, had been very strenuous work. Furthermore the rigging of the ships had been severely damaged and the keels covered with barnacles, algae, shells, seaweed and other organisms, severely obstructing the free sailing of the ships.

On the other hand there was the comforting thought that the greater part of the distance had already been covered, for when one day two natives approached the ships, the Portuguese were delighted to discover that they were wearing turbans bearing the green emblems of pilgrims to Mecca. Thus the sphere of Arab control could no longer be far off. At the beginning of 1498, in the harbour of Mozambique, Fernão Martins, the interpreter for Arabic languages, managed to enter into conversation with native merchants. They proved to be Moors.

> They said that Prester John did not live far from there, that he owned many cities along the ocean and that the inhabitants of these places were merchants with many large ships. John himself was said to be living far in the interior of his country and could only be reached by camel. The Moors brought with them two Indian Christians. These and many other things were told us by the self-same Moors, which made us so happy that we wept with joy.

A little later the first dhows were encountered in the harbour of Mozambique, Arab freighters returning from India. This is what the *Roteira* has to say about them:

> These ships are large and have no deck. The planks are not nailed together but are sewn up with fibres. The sails consist of mats of palm fibre and the seamen have Genoese magnetic needles for determining direction, and also quadrants and charts of the sea.

Ships that were sewn together: this sounds fabulous but it is the pure truth. Over a century and a half before this, the Dominican Jordanus Catalani, Bishop of Colombo, today known as Quilon on the coast of southern India, had reported the same thing. In 1330 in a letter to the members of his order in Italy, he had related that although the ships sailing between India and Africa were very large, they did not consist of any iron whatsoever, being sewn 'with a thread manufactured from a certain plant'. Because these vessels did not have a covering deck they shipped much water and the sailors had to stand by the pumps continuously.

This sounds like an Oriental seaman's yarn of the type told by Sinbad the Sailor, but such sewn-up ships exist even today. They can be seen in their masses at the quays of Zanzibar, and anyone who has skirted the long coast-line of Sumatra has encountered them in every harbour from Meulaboh in the north down to Telok Betong in the Straits of Sunda. *Ntepe* is the name given to these vessels; they are open boats of about forty tons with a low prow, a high stern and tremendously large three-cornered lateen sails, and they are really 'sewn-up'. For everything, ribs, keel, planks and washboard, is tied together, knotted and spliced with unbreakable water-tight coir, a kind of thread made from the fibre of the coconut. These ships ply up and down between Africa and India just as in olden times: more than 2,800 miles of sea, and it makes one's flesh creep to encounter one of them on the open sea.

Naturally the Portuguese were most keenly interested in these strange vessels. If such primitive objects could stand a voyage to India, then their own caravels, the fruit of much experience and study, should prove well up to the task before them. The fact that the Arab sailing ships to India looked so clumsy and bad was most encouraging for the Portuguese. If ever it was to come to an argument, the caravels were infinitely superior to them in speed, manœuvrability and armament, and even here, so far down south, the Arabs left no doubt about their hostile attitude. At first Vasco da Gama believed this enmity to arise from religious motives; for it broke out openly when three inhabitants from the Christian oasis of Habesh in Abyssinia discovered images of the Archangel Gabriel on the Admiral's ship and reverently knelt before them in the presence of the Mohammedans. Soon, however, it emerged that the assumed ideological causes of Arab enmity were in fact of a marked mercantile nature: the Arab trade with India was being threatened. Their monopoly could only be saved if they managed to destroy the Portuguese armada with one stroke. Force could not avail them here, and therefore the sheiks tried to shipwreck the Portuguese fleet by supplying them with treacherous pilots. Their plan misfired at the last moment, but Vasco da Gama thought it best to sail on towards the north.

But even in Mombasa, their next port of call, things were no different.

The impending arrival of the 'Giaours', these accursed Christian dogs, had long been reported and the Portuguese had great difficulty in repulsing a nocturnal attack on their fleet. Here, in Mombasa, they were probably in the most critical situation of their whole voyage. More than a quarter of the crew had died and the remainder were sluggish invalids, stricken with fever and scurvy. The Admiral himself was affected by the superhuman exertions of the voyage, and he needed every last shred of his personal influence to repair the moral damage to his crew. We are told that at this time he turned his hand everywhere to simple sailors' work and that frequently he remained on deck for two consecutive watches. And the impossible was achieved: with great luck the Portuguese escaped the Arabs and finally reached the high sea unmolested. In the middle of April, fresh food was found in Melinde (Malindi, in Kenya), for the Arab ruler of the town was friendly, firstly because of hereditary enmity against the ruler of Mombasa, and also because a large India fleet manned by Thomaeans from the coast of Malabar was lying in the harbour.

This report in the *Roteira* has frequently been contested. It has been thought that these 'Thomaeans' could only have been Buddhists whose religious customs were in fact similar to those of many Western Christians. But according to the investigations of the German geographer Richard Hennig, a flourishing Thomaean community of Christians existed in early India, so that there is no reason for doubting the quite definite statements in the *Roteira*. The Portuguese had learnt of this some days before landing: 'On Easter day the Moors whom we had caught told us that four Christian ships from India lay at anchor in the harbour of the said city of Malindi. . . .' And when Vasco da Gama himself weighed anchor, these Thomaeans streamed across to the Portuguese ships. The *Roteira* tells:

> Here we found four ships of Indian Christians. When the latter approached the ship of Paulo da Gama, on which the Admiral happened to be, they were shown an altarpiece on which was depicted the Mother of God with Jesus Christ in her arms at the foot of the Cross, together with the Apostles. And when they saw this self-same altarpiece, the Indians threw themselves to the ground. During our entire stay they came in order to say their prayers and they brought cloves, pepper and other things which they offered up.

In these circumstances their stay in Malindi was rather pleasant, and finally, for a large sum of gold, they managed to acquire a *moallen*, a pilot, who promised to steer their fleet safely across the Indian Ocean.

4

On the 24th April 1498 the last and happiest part of the voyage was started. Those ill with scurvy had fully recovered because of the abundant supplies of fresh victuals and vegetables, and for three weeks a favourable wind drove the ships onwards at speed. What interested the Portuguese most on this last stretch was, according to the reports of those taking part in the voyage, the pilot Ahmed Ibn, the son of Maiad, who had come aboard at Malindi and who was alleged to have been a Thomaean from the coast of Malabar. His navigational prowess was remarkable—he understood Genoese needles, as the then latest achievements of direction-finding, magnetic needles, were called, as well as quadrants and nautical charts. This was most surprising since, despite their size, the Arab and

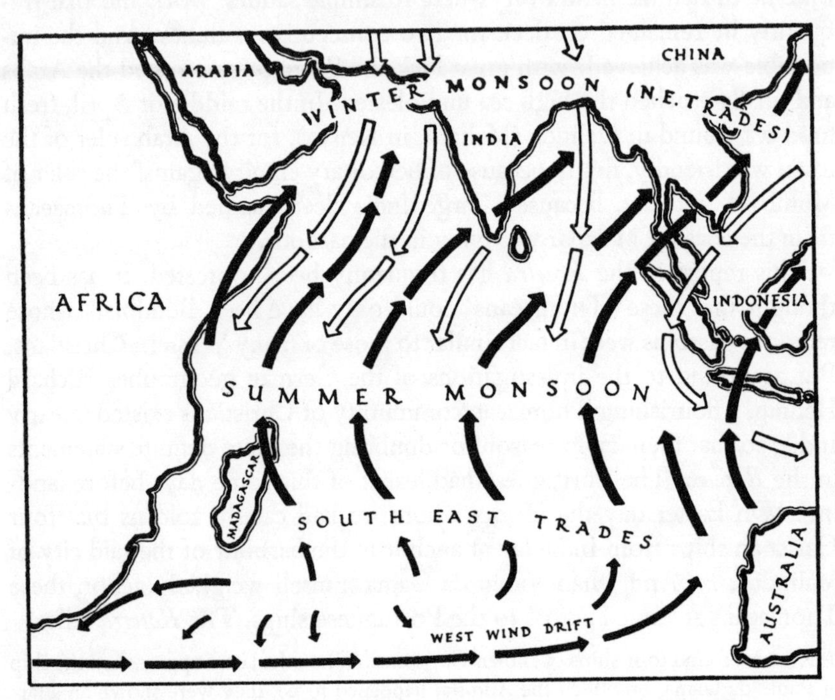

XIII. Winter and summer monsoons in the Indian Ocean.

Indian dhows which the Portuguese had seen appeared to be miserable and manifestly unseaworthy vessels. They reeled clumsily across the sea with the wind on the quarter; tacking was quite out of the question for them and they were far less manœuvrable than the Portuguese caravels. It was a wonder that they did not fall to pieces whenever the sea got a little rough, yet year after year they would cross hundreds of leagues undamaged. Admittedly weather conditions were quite extraordinary. The Indian pilot asserted that, while during that time of the year there would never be anything but the even south-westerly wind that had driven the Portuguese armada before it for a whole three weeks, some months later a north-easterly would prevail for just as long and just as evenly. It was for this reason, he said, that voyages to Arabia and Africa were usually made in winter, but to India only at the beginning of summer. Thus he had no hesitation in predicting a happy crossing.

In this the *moallen* was proved to be entirely right; understandably enough, seeing that he had never experienced anything else. Generation after generation of seamen had set sail in early summer to go from Africa to India, to return in the autumn. As early as 1500 B.C., East Africa had known all kinds of merchandise of Indian origin, and had been equally well acquainted with these distant shores, so that when, at the time of Christ's birth, the Roman Admirals were busy compiling their charts for a voyage from Egypt to India, they could learn many details from the Arab seamen. Thus in one of the sailing manuals of antiquity we can read that the coast of India is near whenever great shoals of sea-snakes are encountered. This information was still fully valid in the sixteenth century. In 1505 a powerful Portuguese fleet sailing to India was accompanied by some merchant sailors equipped by the Augsburg House of Welser. Balthasar Sprenger, an employee of the Welsers, had been sent along to India with these ships. He noted in his diary that when approaching the foreign shore 'many crabs and snakes were seen to infest the waters near the ships', and his colleague Giovanni Empoli, who had travelled to India as early as 1503 as representative of some North Italian merchant houses, confirmed this:

> Then we saw the sea full of snakes and in such masses that I cannot find words for it. They were slender and relatively long and swam with their heads above the water. The last signs are red crabs which are not very large. When all these signs appeared, we knew that we were close to shore, at a distance of about seventy leagues!

We can see that this is ancient knowledge indeed, handed down from father to son for thousands of years, and that with the help of the Indian pilot Vasco da Gama's task was quickly accomplished. The armada had weighed anchor on the 24th April at Malindi, and towards the evening of the 20th May, the ships reached the docks of Calicut: the sea-route to India had been conquered by Portugal! True, the reception in Calicut was not exactly friendly; it was a portent of the fierce battles which the Portuguese would have to wage for their colonial possessions in India. And it is probably due to the tact of the Admiral alone that he could return home unharmed.

Vasco went to work very carefully; he put one of the criminals in his care into a dinghy and let him paddle to the harbour. This strange newcomer succeeded in reaching the quay and was shown to the foreign quarters where, as he reported on his return to the Admiral's ship, he had encountered two Moorish sailors from Tunis who had addressed him in fluent Castilian with the usual obscene greetings common to sailors the whole world over. This undoubtedly restored the spiritual equilibrium of the poor devil, who, lost and forlorn in the busy back streets of Calicut, was suddenly confronted by what must have been a wild-looking horde of Dravidian navvies, and who could not have felt too sure of his life. This first unexpected greeting was followed by a longer conversation in which the two Moorish sailors made it quite clear that they considered the Portuguese as unfair competition whose speedy departure to hell they would only welcome.

Vasco da Gama had known from the very start of the voyage that neither the Mohammedan Sultans of India, nor yet the native princes, the Rajahs, would welcome the arrival of the Portuguese fleet. The Arabs had for centuries had the trading monopoly of the whole range of commodities that could be found in the bazaars of Calicut: precious stones from Ceylon, pearls from the Gulf of Manar, cloves from the Moluccas, nutmeg from the Banda Sea, camphor from Borneo, and pepper from Sumatra and the Malabar Coast. It was easy to foresee that they would not view the arrival of uninvited competitors, armed to the teeth, with too friendly an eye.

At first things did not go too badly. Vasco da Gama, who had not received any specific diplomatic instructions from the King, and who could, at will, present himself either as a merchant or as a special ambassador of the Crown, showed himself in the full splendour of his might, and sent word to the Samudrin Rajah of Calicut, the 'Ruler of the Sea', that he intended to call on him as the representative of the King of Portugal. Audience was granted by the Rajah, and on the 28th May 1498 the Portuguese ceremoniously entered the royal palace. The reception by the crowd was not unfriendly and the *Roteira* tells with obvious pleasure:

> The said city of Calicut is Christian. Its Christians are people of brown colour. Some of them wear long beards and long hair, others again cut their hair short, and yet others shave their heads and wear only a tuft on the crown thus showing that they are Christians.

Yet when the Portuguese visited a 'church' in Calicut, they were very astonished indeed:

> A great many saints were drawn on the walls of the church; they had haloes, but the manner of their representation was strange, for their teeth were so large that they protruded a whole inch beyond their lips and every saint had four or five arms.

Their astonishment was increased even further, when the Portuguese discovered that the path of their train was lined by armed men, ostentatiously bearing naked swords. This looked far from Christian hospitality. But nothing untoward befell them; they arrived unharmed at the palace and the audience with the betel-nut-chewing Samudrin passed with mutual assurances of friendship. An amusing report of this visit from the pen of one of Vasco da Gama's escorts has been preserved. It reads as follows:

> We found the King sitting on a chair. He was of a dark brown colour and was dressed in some white garment from the waist to the knees. The rest of him was naked. A long cord, on which were strung several magnificent gold rings with large rubies,

was attached to his apparel. On his left arm, above the elbow, he wore an armband consisting of three bangles joined together. They were richly set with precious stones; the middle one, which was larger than the two others, was embellished with large stones, which must have been of considerable value. Another big brilliant stone, a diamond the size of a thumb, also hung from this central bangle. About his neck the King wore a double string of pearls which reached down to the waist, each pearl the size of a hazelnut. Over this he had a thin, round golden chain, with a jewel in the shape of a heart, surrounded by large pearls and covered with a great mass of rubies; in the middle of it was a stone as large as a bean, which, judging by its sparkle, was extremely

9. Calicut in India.

valuable and which was called emerald. When later we asked about this precious stone and also about the armband and a further pearl which the King had fastened to his hair, we learnt that these three pieces were part of the Crown Jewels of the Kings of Calicut. The King had long black hair, brushed towards the top and knotted at the crown. About the knot a chain of pearls was wound, similar to the one he wore about the neck. It ended in a pear-shaped pearl, larger than all the others and most certainly of great value. His ears were pierced and from them hung many golden ear-rings, richly embellished with pearls. Close to the King there stood a little boy, clad completely in silk. He carried a red sunshade braided with gold and jewels and with a knob in the middle, a hand's span in width and made of the same materials. Every one of the ribs of the sunshade was made of pure gold also! He also bore a short sword, one ell in length, with a handle made of gold and precious stones and fitted with pendants of pearls. On the other side a page held a copious golden basin, into which the King would spit. Also next to his chair, there stood a high Brahman, who, from time to time, would hand the King a green leaf enveloping other objects. The leaf was the size of an orange leaf and the King would chew at it continuously and then spit into the basin. When one leaf was chewed up the King would start on a fresh one. He enjoyed only the juice of the leaf and the lime and other finely cut substances which were wrapped in it. The whole thing is the size of a chestnut. This mixture of leaf and spices stains the mouth and the teeth red. They all followed this custom day after day, and it made their breath very pleasant.

Thus the audience was apparently a success, and the Rajah's Chamberlain announced that he would make a preliminary inspection of the gifts sent by the King of Portugal.

But that evening, when from the decks of their ships the Portuguese sailors tried to talk with the Arabs in the little boats swarming around them, angry shouts were raised: 'A curse on the lot of you! What the devil do you want here? What ill wind has blown you to these shores!' And the Arabs jeered derisively when the Portuguese told them that they were really looking for the Indian Christians and were only buying spices incidentally. Vasco himself had made this point in his opening address to the ruler of Calicut; it was not the search for gold that had brought them there, for they had more than enough gold at home. They were there, at the command of their King, for the sole purpose of establishing ties of friendship with the Christian Indians, whom they had sought in vain for the last sixty years. The King had heard this, perhaps with astonishment, but in any case with a great show of friendliness. It was the Arab sailors who, that evening, gave the first warning. When the Chamberlain appeared next morning, the Portuguese could see at once that even at Court the wind had obviously changed overnight.

For when the Minister inspected the presents chosen by Vasco for the King, scarlet capes, sugar, oil, honey, striped cottons, washing-bowls, corals and hats, he laughed derisively about the trash that the King of Portugal, reputed to be so rich and mighty, had had the impertinence to send to the King of Calicut. Even the poorest pilgrim to Mecca would have spent more, and in any case gold alone was a present fitting for the Samudrin. 'After he had left, Moorish merchants arrived who all spoke with contempt of the presents which the commander desired to send to the King.'

The attitude of the Indians was based on sound reasons. India was poor in gold, and yet its imports of spices from the Moluccas had to be paid for in precious metals. In consequence, it was extremely important for the Rajah to obtain gold or silver. Other goods were useless to him, and the Portuguese, like the Romans before them, soon realized that bartering with the Orient was out of the question.

Nor did the disappointed laughter of the Minister remain without a royal echo. During the next day's audience the Portuguese, with the Admiral at their head, were suddenly taken prisoner, and it required all Vasco's diplomacy to extricate himself and his companions from a position which could easily have become desperate. By taking hostages, the Portuguese made a counter-move which gave them some freedom of movement and enabled them to load their ships with spices; but Vasco da Gama quickly realized that, for the moment at least, Arab influence in India was too strong, and he decided to return home. During the last few days before the return voyage, the Portuguese contented themselves with recording much geographical and economic information which would be of use during possible future visits.

From this selfsame land of Calicut, called High India, come the spices eaten throughout the realm of Portugal, and likewise in all the countries of the world. Similarly many precious stones of all kinds come from the same city. Calicut herself only produces the following spices: much ginger and pepper and cinnamon, although the latter is not as fine as that which comes from an island called Cillao (Ceylon). This island is an eight days' journey from Calicut. All this cinnamon goes to the said city of Calicut or to an island which is called Meleca (Malacca) whence they send cloves to Calicut. From here, ships from Mecca fetch the spices and carry them to a city called Judea (Jidda) which is fifty days' sailing with a favourable wind. There they unload and pay their duty to the Great Sultan. Then the spices are loaded into small ships which carry them across the Red Sea to another place close to Sinai called Tuuz (Suez). Here too they pay duty. At Tuuz the spices are loaded onto camels, hired by the merchants for four crusados each, which carry them to Cairo, a journey of ten days, and there they pay duty again. Once again the spices are loaded on ships which go down a river called the Nile, which comes down from the land of Prester John. They travel for two days down this river till they come to a place called Roxete (Rosetta, on the western Nile Delta). Here they pay duty once more and again transfer their cargo onto camels and, after yet another day's journey, they reach Alexandria, which is a seaport. Thither come Venetian and Genoese galleys to fetch the spices. . . .

So runs the *Roteira*, which was extremely well-informed. It must have become clear to the Portuguese during their stay in Calicut that the real riches of the Orient could only be found much further east—in Malacca and the Spice Islands (the Moluccas). Vasco da Gama dared not undertake this extra voyage with his weak fleet. Thus, on the 29th August 1498, sails were unfurled on the three Portuguese ships, and an off-shore wind carried them out of the reach of the swarm of heavily armed boats which, at the last moment, were trying to attack the foreigners.

The journey back was very slow. It was too early for the north-east monsoon to help their passage to Africa, and, in addition, da Gama took a western course too soon. The wind varied between absolute calm and stiff breezes from every possible direction, driving the Portuguese ships up and down the Indian Ocean. There was another outbreak of scurvy, that horrible lingering death, against which there was no help. The crews were at the end of their strength. Discipline disappeared completely, outbreaks of mutiny were frequent, and even the unshakeable Vasco was on the point of returning to India, no matter what ill might befall them there. But at last a favourable wind sprang up and, shortly before reaching the African shore, despite the sickness among them, the Portuguese managed to beat off an attack by Arab pirates. Finally they reached Malindi where, even on the voyage out, they had been received in amity.

The Portuguese stayed in Malindi for only five days; they were all eager to return home after so long and eventful a voyage. Yet there was to be one more tragedy. The losses from scurvy and fever on the return voyage from India to Africa had been so numerous that there was not sufficient crew to man all three ships, the supply ship having been destroyed previously in Mossel Bay during the voyage out. It would have been foolhardy to attempt the difficult voyage around the Cape with such a reduced crew, and therefore Vasco ordered the *Raphael* to be set on fire. On the 17th January 1499, towards evening, the last smouldering remains of the proud ship sank into the sea. Vasco could not bear to take leave of the figurehead, a very impressive statue of St. Raphael, for it was under the protection of this saint that he had managed to reach his objective. Thus he had the figurehead of the *Raphael* salvaged and brought into his cabin. It was to accompany him on all his journeys like a talisman.

And St. Raphael did his duty. After an extremely quick and happy voyage without any further incidents, the two remaining ships of the India fleet dropped anchor in their home harbour on the Tagus on the 10th July 1499. The commander himself was not on board. He had disembarked at Terceira, an island in the Azores, with his brother, the captain of the *Gabriel*, who was dying. Thus death had taken its toll even among the captains—a fact which bears conclusive testimony to the superhuman exertions demanded from all who took part in the enterprise.

The Admiral only returned to Portugal at the beginning of September 1499. He was given a tremendous reception and was officially appointed Admiral of the Indian Ocean, and the King bestowed upon him, his children and brothers the title of Dom, an honour reserved for the Titulados, a very limited section of the old nobility. Finally Manuel of Portugal granted him the hereditary suzerainty over Sines and Cercal, his home towns. This was particularly dear to the Admiral's heart, and he was moved to tears when on Christmas Day 1499 he held the documents of investiture in his hands.

But the price of pepper in Lisbon had dropped to rock-bottom. Bills of exchange and letters of credit of a great number of leading import houses could no longer be honoured. No one would invest even one crusado in the spice market. Curses on pepper! Curses on the pepper-bags! Hell fire on the usurers!

5

25th March 1505

Twenty-two caravels were lying at anchor in the Tagus, twenty-two heavily armed, large ocean-going ships, carrying hundreds of experienced sailors, artisans of all kinds, sailmakers and carpenters and 1,500 soldiers armed to the teeth. Their commander was Admiral Francisco d'Almeida, Viceroy of India, and not Vasco da Gama. This may sound odd, but it is not safe for a relatively young dynasty to allow one man to become too powerful. In fact, Portugal was a family concern. Whoever wore the crown was also the managing director. Thus it was logical that the captains and admirals who, when all was said and done, all set sail for the glittering Far East under the King's orders and at *his* risk, could not be allowed to become too powerful. This was the reason why Diego Cão, who between 1485 and 1486 almost reached the Cape of Good Hope, was relieved of his command, why Bartolomé Diaz was no longer called upon after he had rounded the southern tip of Africa in 1488, and why Vasco da Gama, who had twice been to India, was not automatically put in command once more.

However, Vasco da Gama was allowed to test the equipment of the fleet, and since he did so with commendable zeal, the King some years later appointed him Duke of Vidigueira: but this was by no means done out of generosity. Only when the experienced Admiral intimated that he might place his skill at the disposal of other states—Vasco da Gama must have been thinking of Spain or France—did Manuel of Portugal consent to soothe his former commander's wounded vanity.

Thus did Francisco d'Almeida become the commander of the greatest fleet that Portugal had so far sent to India. In the cathedral of Lisbon he proudly received from the King's own hand the banner of white damask with the Cross embroidered on it, under whose sign he was expected to spread death and destruction among Arabs and Indians alike. Behind him there knelt 1,500 volunteers, soldiers carefully selected and tested in every possible way. All of them had now confessed their sins, received the sacrament and sworn an oath of loyalty to Christ, and to their King. They rose as one man and to the sound of the city bells and the salutes from the fleet's guns they marched down to the harbour.

A crew of 1,500 men! Yet only one of them was to be hallmarked by history and glorified by geography. His name was Fernão de Magalhães. He was twenty-four years old, a native of Oporto and had been page to the Queen. Now he was a simple *sobresalente*, an unknown volunteer.

With swelling sails, the armada put to sea. Since the Orient was unwilling to buy any European wares, it was carrying ballast, and—a jinx. For this voyage was by no means an exploratory or trading venture, like the previous Portuguese voyages, but an expedition with a clearly defined military aim: the East African shore was to be made safe and the Indian coast was to be brought firmly into Portuguese hands. They were haunted not by the '*cauchemar* of coalitions', that nightmare which later disturbed Bismarck so that he would start from sleep gasping for breath, but the *cauchemar de la victoire*, the nightmare of victory. No doubt the discovery of a sea-route to India had been a great deed, but now they were being forced to proceed along the trail they had blazed, despite the fact that it was proving a tremendous drain on Portuguese resources and was claiming many, many victims, and even though the wisest heads at the Court of Portugal were beginning to realize that the country was heading for disaster.

Now it was too late to go back. In the middle of March 1506, the Portuguese fleet, fully prepared for battle, lay at anchor in the harbour of Cannanore, a city somewhat north of Calicut. Everything seemed to be peaceful ashore. Fishing boats were proceeding about their business, Arab trading vessels at the quays of the great harbour were being loaded and unloaded—and yet, in some way, the atmosphere was tense. The guards on the Portuguese ships could feel it in their every nerve. And when, shortly after the quick tropical nightfall, something was heard splashing at the bow of the Admiral's ship, the Portuguese peasant boy who was staring through the darkness at the sparse lights ashore, knew instinctively that it was no shark but a man swimming in the water. And yet how could it be a man, in the dark of night, utterly alone in a sea infested with bloodthirsty fish? As quick as lightning a rope was flung over the side of the ship. A low whistle informed the mate at the helm. The barefooted watch ran silently on deck and pulled the man, who had now grasped the rope, on board.

There on the ship stood one of the most reckless adventurers of all time. His name was Lodovico Varthema, a native of Bologna in Italy a born globe-trotter and vagabond. 'Because my head was too thick and not made for studying books, I have tried to see the world with my own eyes. I believe that the report of one single eye-witness is worth more than all accounts based on hearsay,' he declared. A little later he was sitting in the cabin of the chief armaments officer on the Admiral's ship, a glass of the best port wine before him, and Francisco d'Almeida himself was awakened to hear the story of this extraordinary adventurer.

Chance had led this man to Egypt. But chance had let him go again, and one day he had appeared in Damascus. His gazelle-like Syrian paramour conjugated the verb 'to love' with him for so long that he could speak Arabic fluently. Foreign languages are always useful, and it did not take long before the commander of the Mameluke guards, the bodyguard of the Sultan, noticed this tall young stranger. Tired of his Arabian mistress, Lodovico Varthema joined the Syrian guard and, a few months later, he and his comrades were ordered to escort a caravan to Mecca. Thus he was the first European to enter the Holy City of Islam. With his own eyes he saw the Caaba, the holy black meteor!

Francisco d'Almeida lifted his heavy head with quickened interest. Mecca! The Holy City of the Muslims! And when this odd vagabond reported that in 1503, during his stay in the 'Rome of Islam' and during Vasco da Gama's second voyage to India, neither spice nor silk had been known there, the Admiral asked his private secretary, who was recording the interview, to repeat that sentence.

Varthema told how he had sailed up and down the Indian Ocean from Diu, on the coast of India, to Zeila near Jibuti, and to Dhufar, an Arab port, how he had gone to Aden, to Hormuz on the Persian Gulf, to Herat and Shiraz, and how from there he had come to Cannanore and Calicut.

'And then?' the Admiral asked. Lodovico Varthema had so many astonishing things to report that the night seemed to fly past. In 1505 he had been to East India, to Ceylon and the incredibly rich Bengal; at Pegu in Burma he had bartered corals for rubies; in Malacca he had been served with shark's fins and rotten eggs on giant Chinese junks; in Sumatra, which Ibn Batuta and Marco Polo had still called Little Java, and whose real name was now being mentioned for the first time, he had come across its subtle perfumes, intoxicating scents and precious incense—and finally he had sailed to the Spice Islands, the Moluccas.

Francisco d'Almeida had been on duty on the bridge since entering the harbour. He had managed to go below to sleep but had been rudely awakened. During Varthema's narrative, he kept on dozing off with his chin sinking onto his chest, but when Varthema mentioned the Spice Islands he soon became wide awake. Marco Polo had told of them but had never seen these happy islands himself. This was important information and although the Portuguese was almost sick with fatigue he cross-examined the Italian vagabond closely about the *Ilhas das Especierias*.

The rest seemed less important to the Portuguese officer. He knew himself only too well that he would have to fight for his very life. His chin sank back onto his chest again when Varthema continued. The diplomatic measures taken by the Sultan of Egypt, the Italian said, having been unsuccessful, and the Pope being unable to exert any pressure on Portugal, and moreover since the Western Christians paid little attention to the Sultan's threat of destroying Jerusalem and the Holy Places of Christianity with fire and sword, all the powers damaged by the expansion of Portuguese trade had jointly decided to destroy the advancing armada of the Crown of Portugal in one fell swoop. This conspiracy included not only the Indian Rajahs, and particularly the Rajah of Calicut, the Sultan of Egypt, but also the Venetians who had sent cannon-makers and gunners to Calicut.

Much of this was known to Francisco d'Almeida. He had heard of the threatening letters which the Sultan of the Mamelukes had sent to the King of Portugal in 1502, and two years later to the Pope. The fact that this fellow who had just swum out to his ship from Cannanore also knew it, added some credibility to the rest of his reports. When Varthema had claimed that he had been to the Spice Islands himself, he might well have been spinning a yarn, though an interesting one. But the Admiral sat up at once when he was told that the Portuguese fleet would be attacked at dawn by the two hundred ships of the Rajah of Calicut, which, being greatly superior in number, might well destroy it. It was this that made this tramp of the oceans, this noble vagabond, a very important person.

Almeida ordered all his men to their battle stations. When on the morning of the 16th March 1506, the Arabs did in fact attack, they were received by overwhelming salvos from every available gun. The Portuguese fleet consisted of only eleven caravels but because of their technical superiority they proved to be more than a match for the two hundred Arab vessels. The battle was won. It cost the Portuguese eighty dead and two hundred wounded, a tremendous loss, but it brought them the possession of the shores of India. Yet it was this very victory which decided that Spain, not Portugal, would be the ruler of the world.

For amongst the two hundred wounded was the 'unknown soldier', Fernão de Magalhães. History had conceived the strange notion of giving the palm for the first man to sail round the world to this insignificant outsider. Many historical events may be explained away by subsequent generations, but not this! There is no reason why Magalhães was chosen, since dozens of other captains would have done equally well.

Fernão de Magalhães was wounded seriously enough for him to be sent back home. In midsummer 1507, he arrived in Lisbon on the same ship as Lodovico Varthema. He had, of course, questioned the Italian very closely during the long voyage. Lodovico was only too delighted to satisfy the curiosity of this gawky young volunteer and he talked incessantly, and what he said did not fall on barren soil. When, some twelve years later, Magalhães finally started on his great voyage around the world, he was fulfilling a desire that Lodovico Varthema had once planted in him.

Yet it was not only this confused kaleidoscope of exotic countries that had tempted him, there was another more serious and very concrete reason. When Magalhães landed in Lisbon he saw three well-known ships moored to the quays: the *Rafael*, the *Leonhard*, and the *Hieronymus*. These three ships, all traders, had gone out with the fleet of Francisco d'Almeida, but although they had been under his command, they did not belong to the Crown of Portugal; they were owned by the mighty German Welser family, who had equipped the ships and also undertaken to maintain the crew for eighteen months. Of course, Magalhães knew the two German merchants who had gone along to India with hese ships: Balthasar Sprenger from Vils on the Lech, who was later to write a faithful little book about his sea-voyage on the *Leonhard*, and the *scriva da feytoria*, the clerk Hans Mayr from Augsburg, who had sailed on the *Rafael*.

A few days later he met the two Germans, bursting with rage. Balthasar Sprenger told him that he and the cargo of his ships were being detained in

Lisbon. After the terrible slump in the pepper and spice market following the return of Vasco da Gama's fleet, the Crown had held up the two German trading ships to prevent them selling their cargo of spices either in Portugal or in Antwerp or Frankfurt, thus allowing the Portuguese to make the best of a bad situation. Had he, Balthasar Sprenger, loaded much spice? Well of course he had! The well-fed German, whose face was becoming more and more contorted with fury, told Magalhães of his successes. He had twelve thousand quintals of pepper on board. Of this the Crown was to have an agreed 30 per cent, leaving eight thousand four hundred quintals. Since the price of pepper was twenty crusados per quintal, the eight thousand four hundred quintals which were his by right would have sold for 168,000 crusados. Furthermore he had been thinking of buying direct from the Moluccas! Naturally he would deal in cloves, and he exhorted his new Portuguese friend to listen. On the *Ilhas das Especierias* one hundredweight of cloves cost two ducats, in Calicut as much as fifty and in London more than two hundred ducats. This was real business, against which everything else was insignificant.

Magalhães was breathless with excitement. Quickly he calculated what profit the German merchants would make on selling their pepper. Almeida's fleet had not touched on the Moluccas, and had bought its cargo from middlemen. What profits could be made by buying directly from the Moluccas themselves! And since Magalhães came from Oporto and was as poor as a church mouse, he was to remember these things, just as he was to remember Lodovico Varthema's colourful tales.

No evidence tells us of the date and day of week on which Balthasar Sprenger or Hans Mayr met Magalhães in Lisbon, but it is probable that this meeting really did take place. In any case, it is certain that Magalhães knew of the gigantic profits to be made in the spice trade. Of course, it is not likely he knew all the above details, which have been compiled from the account books of the Welsers, nor were mercantile considerations by any means the sole motives for his tremendous deed. But there is no doubt that they must have had a part in it. The *auri sacra fames*, the cursed greed for gold and possessions, is admitted to be one of the most heavy hereditary burdens which Adam and Eve have handed down to us. Magalhães, too, must have had his share of it.

6

His great idea had to wait for some years before it could be put into action. For the time being Fernão de Magalhães was still only one of the many wounded colonial soldiers, waiting at Lisbon for further orders. He had to wait till the summer of 1508 before he was finally transferred to the fleet of López de Sequeira, which was to make a reconnaissance trip to Malacca.

This was a matter requiring some diplomacy. The large city of the *aurea chersonesus*, the golden peninsula in the Far East, could not simply be overrun. The Sultan would have to be tricked, and, to do so, Sequeira was to appear before him as a trader and merchant. The Portuguese Admiralty had provided him with its best men, and it was a great honour for Magalhães to be included. In all such expeditions, the possibility of clashes between those in command of the ships and the specially chosen individualists that made up the crew had always to be faced. The leaders of commando enterprises are confronted with a unique situation. While their men must be as sternly disciplined as in other units, the personality of the individual must not be broken, but must be given adequate opportunities for proving its worth. This is an almost insoluble problem. López de Sequeira, for one, was not able to solve it; nor was Fernão de Magalhães, the pig-headed *sobresalente* from the district of Oporto, capable of playing the role of subordinate assigned to him. When some years later he was sent back to Portugal he took back with him the reputation of being obstinate and irascible. Magalhães had by then discovered that survivors of commando raids are seldom promoted. This was a further cause for his subsequent departure from his native country.

The fleet of López de Sequeira reached India at the beginning of April 1509 and dropped anchor in Calicut. Four months later, in September, the Portuguese were lying off Malacca. Wherever they looked along the quay of the great harbour, there were ships. Here there were gigantic Chinese junks with tremendous sails made of matting, their hulls built high out of the water, there Malayan *praus* and the deep south-sea outriggers, and there again Arab dhows whose lateen sails stood out in sweeping and elegant grandeur against the turquoise-coloured sky. Here there was constant activity, a veritable ant-hill of life and movement, an incessant bartering and bargaining, a babel of all the languages of the eastern world. For Malacca, a settlement founded by Malaya in 1280, not far from the Singapore of today, was a real international harbour, just like Calicut, Alexandria and Lisbon. True, not all ships going to or from the east and west passed there. It was only in late autumn and winter that, because of wind conditions, sea traffic passed through the Straits of Malacca; the normal sea-route to and from China was through the Sunda Straits and past the Philippines. Nevertheless, spice-traders were bound to make use of Malacca, and since their trade was carried out mostly by barter, one could find every type of merchandise there: African slaves, who in China were considered to be most desirable merchandise, gigantic stacks of cinnamon, cloves and pepper, tremendous vessels of Japanese *saké*, carefully packed crates of the finest of Chinese porcelain, sandalwood from the island of Timor, sealed leather bags of precious stones from Ceylon, cashmere from Bengal, finely chiselled and supple swords from Damascus, precious Siamese carved ivory and long-limbed Circassian concubines. Everything of value in the world was marketed here.

Of course the impending arrival of the Portuguese fleet had long been reported to the Sultan of Malacca. Naturally, everyone in the glittering palace, close to the mosque on the hills surrounding the city, knew only too well that these strangers and their dazzling white sails out there in the harbour were no merchants like the quiet, polite and smiling captains of the junks from China, Siam and Japan. The secret service had long ago presented detailed reports on the bloody butcheries which these infidel dogs had perpetrated in India. Even in Malacca they knew only too well the meaning of the long bronze-coloured smooth barrels with black gaping mouths pointing overboard from the foreign ships. They had nothing to oppose all this, excepting guile. If they could manage to split up the Portuguese armada, to entice the crew ashore and to overpower each ship individually—only then might the danger be averted.

For this reason Sequeira and his crew were received with a great show of cordiality and politeness when their boats arrived in the harbour, and they were more than surprised when a few days later arrows came whistling through the air, when the decks of the ships were teeming with brown devils and when the land commando was mown down, man after man. Magalhães, who had been suspicious from the very start, had warned the Admiral. Now from the high castle of the flagship he could see how his comrades in the harbour were shedding their life's blood under the slashing blows of Malayan creeses. Together with some other soldiers, he leapt into a dinghy, paddled to the quay and, fighting his way through, managed to rescue the last survivor of the landing party, his friend Francisco Serrão.

This was a heavy defeat for the Portuguese. Not only had they lost more than a third of their crew and all their boats, but they had also completely lost face in the whole of the East. At the same time this catastrophe proved the turning point in the life of the former page and minor nobleman. He had distinguished himself and so, two years later, in 1511, having been made an officer after six years' service, he himself stood on the deck of a ship sent by Portugal for the final conquest of Malacca. This time they were successful. After some weeks of hard battles with changing fortunes, the greatest harbour of the Far East became Portuguese.

Once again Magalhães had emerged covered with glory. But he was not one to blow his own trumpet; he was not interested in selling himself. On the contrary, on quite a few occasions he had bitter quarrels with his superiors, and when, during a shipwreck, he sided with the crew, facing the raging of the storm in their company while the *capitães e fidalgos*, the captains and noblemen, took to the boats, he was done for. His name did not appear on the list of those who, some months later, were sent from the Far East to pay homage to the Pope in the Vatican. He was not there when the Pope offered solemn thanksgiving on behalf of the Iberian maritime power, *urbi et orbi*, before God and the whole world, when Tristão da Cunha led panthers and leopards in a grandiose march of victory, when pearls, rubies and turquoises of unprecedented beauty fell from da Cunha's hands into the golden vessels held out to him by the Pope's attendants; he did not hear the jubilations of the Romans when the gigantic Indian elephant, which had been brought across the sea alive, bent his knee three times before the Holy Father.

Nor was he there when Francisco Serrão, his old friend, took possession of the Spice Islands. For he was deliberately excluded from the three Portuguese men-of-war which, after the conquest of Malacca, were ordered to take possession of the *Ilhas das Especierias*, those islands in the Molucca Sea so rich in spices: Tidore, Ternate, Amboina and Banda. While he must have moved heaven and earth to be allowed to accompany his comrade Serrão, like every other soldier he must have known that he must never tempt fate. Thus he bade farewell to Serrão with a heavy heart, a farewell which was to be their last.

This old friend, a happy-go-lucky son of Andalusia, was to turn his back on all the confusion of the West. After suffering shipwreck, he chose to remain in Amboina, where he married the little brown daughter of the brown chief. The ruling king, living on an island many miles away, appointed our Portuguese Robinson Crusoe his Grand Vizier; and thenceforth the former captain of His Majesty the King of Portugal was never again to have the slightest wish to change his paradisaical *dolce far niente* in the Moluccas for a soldier's uniform, to be rudely reprimanded and to carry his own skin to the market for those fat gentlemen who were always to be found where there was no shooting and where easy money could be made.

Just as a modern Crusoe will generally not renounce his desire for books and whisky, so Francisco Serrão felt impelled to write letters to his comrade Magalhães and looked forward to the replies. Whenever any boat left from Amboina for Malacca, its light-brown, bare-footed captain would be handed a humble package, wrapped in wax cloth, and some months later an India veteran, idling away his time in Lisbon, would find in it the same wonderful excitement which the adventurer Varthema had communicated to him many years earlier. 'It is richer, bigger and infinitely more beautiful than that discovered by da Gama,' the former *grumete*, the sailor who had managed to work his way up to viceroy, wrote, continuing to speak with enthusiastic, almost poetic, turns of phrase of the paradise over which he ruled. He did not suspect that he would one day pay for these delights with his life, and that in 1521 he was to die in agony from a tropical poison. Even today it is not known whether his death was caused by natives or by his own compatriots, envious of his independence, and obviously disapproving of Serrão's friendship with the traitor Magalhães.

When Magalhães was sent back home from India in 1512 he felt no longer at home in Lisbon. He was deeply disturbed when he, like every other soldier, was faced with the fact that the world had not stood still while he had been risking his skin on foreign soil. Lisbon, once a little city, had long since become an important harbour. In Rastello, a mighty cathedral had taken the place of the little Chapel to Our Dear Lady; splendid churches and spacious palaces had been built, and the quayside was thronged with ships. All the dialects of the world could be heard in its streets and alleys. People of all colours and from all lands crowded into the exchanges, into the agencies, into the brokers' and shipping masters' offices. Old friends had either left or had died in distant lands, or else they had grown rich and fat and no longer wished to know the home-comers. To be away had often been bitter enough, but to return and find that one had actually been written off was even harder to bear.

Those who, like Magalhães, came from Oporto, and who were suspicious and wide-awake from the start, were not willing to listen to the customary babblings that only fate was to blame and that it was stupid not to forget their resentment. All that meant nothing to Magalhães. He saw only too well what was going on. He and his comrades who had risked their lives and health for Portugal, whose bodies were covered with scars and whose deeds alone had enabled the stay-at-homes to indulge in their happy games of dice, the joyous clinking of glasses and their fat businesses, had now become superfluous, useless and a nuisance. Since Magalhães himself was of noble birth, he for one was relatively well off. As a *fidalgo escudeiro* he received a monthly pension of 1,850 reis (about 18*s*.) and furthermore, because he had once been a royal page, he still belonged to the household of the Crown, and was thus spared the humiliation of having to go begging in the back-streets of the harbours of Belem and Rastello as other officers were forced to do.

Thus passed a long, painful year. A new expeditionary force was set up in the summer of 1513, and Magalhães went along to Morocco with the infantry. This was dangerous folly. The old sailor knew nothing of land battles, and the inevitable happened: he was wounded in the left knee during hand-to-hand fighting and became unfit for further service at the front. In 1515, his opponents took the opportunity to get rid of this upstart officer, who had neither friends nor connections of importance, and who, in addition, came from Oporto. They sent him home once and for all.

A few months later Magalhães limped into the audience chamber of the royal palace in Lisbon. The King and he had been acquainted for many years and they disliked each other with equal intensity. The gauche young nobleman asked the King for a new commission, but he did not beseech — he demanded. Manuel refused his request brusquely. Equally brusquely Magalhães was rebuffed when he demanded an increase in his pension of two hundred reis. He was told he was no better than a beggar. But this was not to be Manuel's lucky day. When Magalhães finally asked whether the King would allow him to serve in some other country where, since he was thirty-five years old, he might still hope for some advancement in his fortunes, the fat, flat-footed monarch told him irately that it was a matter of supreme indifference to him how the captain intended to spend his future.

This was a final slap in the face. Magalhães, used to receiving the worst, did not bat an eyelid, but he knew now that his decision was made. The great historic moment had arrived. He settled his affairs and some twelve months later, on the 20th October 1517, the unwanted Portuguese officer crossed the border into Spain, a grandiose plan in his pocket.

7

This grandiose plan was based on an equally grandiose error. Later on, when the Spanish fleet led by Magalhães was groping its way along the coast of South America with great difficulty in its search for a passage to the Sea of Cathay, the Admiral was to realize this only too well, for he was then to live through the most difficult hours of his life. But that time had not yet come, and for the moment everything looked fascinatingly and illusively logical.

It had long been known that Columbus, contrary to his own firm belief, had neither landed on the shores of India, nor of China. Even after his first voyage loudly doubting voices had made themselves heard in Portugal, Italy, Germany, England and France. When it was learnt that, during his third voyage, Columbus had made his crew swear solemnly that they were all convinced of having reached Asia, the scepticism became general. No, the new land could not possibly have been Cathay. But then what was it? A group of islands? A continent?

In 1497 the Genoese Captain Giovanni Caboto, sailing under the English flag, discovered land high up in the north, the Newfoundland and Labrador of today. This new land, he thought, must be very large indeed, for from it mighty rivers poured into the ocean. But more could not be discovered. Thick pack-ice forced the English expedition to return. Apparently those icebound, deserted regions were directly connected with the Arctic. At that very time, but hundreds of miles away, Columbus had also dropped anchor near the shores of what was obviously another very large country. For the first time he had reached the coast of America, and not merely the islands before it. He investigated this region from the Orinoco to Honduras. He was still quite certain that this tremendous stretch of shore belonged to Asia. But when he returned to Spain in 1504, they knew better. For deep in the south also, land had been discovered. The Portuguese Admiral Cabral, on the way to India, had touched upon shores south of the Equator. Two landmarks noticed by Cabral and christened by him with their modern names, viz. the harbour Porto Seguro and Monte Pascoal at about 16° S., make it clear where the Portuguese had landed and that they had discovered Brazil.

For the cartographers everything was still uncertain. True, it had been said since olden times that the western ocean was full of large islands, so that the quite independent landings from the high north to the deep south were not surprising. But then something quite unexpected happened. A former bank official appeared on the scene and, taking stock of all previous discoveries, including quite a few of his own, he declared to an astonished world: 'So far men have sailed along these shores for upwards of 600 miles, and seeing that the end is still nowhere in sight, I am firmly convinced that what we have here is no mere island but an entire continent.'

The name of this former bank official was Amerigo Vespucci. He came from a very respectable, if somewhat unusual, patrician family of Florence. One of its members, a shining light in the field of jurisprudence, had the following inscription carved on his gravestone by his fellow-citizens: 'Here lies a man who should either have lived for ever, or who should never have seen the light of day'. While this was meant with due deference, it yet shows clearly that this dignitary *utriusque juris* did not quite fit into the narrow burghers' life of the rich city on the Arno. Later the eccentricity of the Vespuccis was to express itself in a more harmless form, for instance in their choice of names for their male descendants. Amerigo's father was called Anastasius, a name that had not been used for decades and which, to say the least, was uncommon. The son's full name was Almerigo, an Italian form of the old and equally unusual Germanic 'Almerich'.

At the beginning of 1496, Almerigo Vespucci, manager of the Medici bank's branch in Seville, was faced with a situation in which he, a man of forty-five years of age, was suddenly without a job. Since he had private means, the closing of this branch of the bank was not a great catastrophe for him. It meant freedom; and he made the widest possible use of it. He put to sea and sailed for the newly discovered lands in the Western Ocean. His ships left from Cadiz at the beginning of 1497, and when he finally returned to the west five years later, he had discovered that these new lands were tremendously wide and that, at least as far as where Rio de Janeiro is today, a tremendous region of fertile soil and defiant rocks barred the way to the west. Amerigo Vespucci realized that this could not possibly be an island, but that it was a gigantic continent. Thus, when the German geographer Waldseemüller called it after Vespucci's Christian name: Almerichland, the name stuck.

Columbus had in fact discovered a new continent. But since the earth is a sphere, more water was bound to be behind those strange lands, an infinite ocean of water. The Portuguese on the Moluccas had already reported that the size of the waves suggested the existence of huge masses of water extending to the east. While Portugal, still lacking sufficient ships and soldiers, had not yet officially annexed the Moluccas, the self-exiled Portuguese in Amboina and Ternate, above all Francisco Serrão of whom we have already heard, continued to speak of this gigantic ocean.

Anyone who discovered a passage through this new continent was likely to reach the Moluccas before the Portuguese, who had to make the long voyage round Africa. But who could tell if there was a passage? For all one knew, the new continent of America might stretch as far south as the uninhabitable frozen regions of the Antarctic, and up to the Arctic in the north.

Spain diligently sent expedition after expedition in order to clear up this doubt. By 1510 it was known that no passage existed as far as 33° N., i.e. up to the region of modern Charleston. As far as the eye could see there was land, unbroken stretches of shore, impenetrable mountain ranges. The report sent by Vásquez de Ayllon, Minister of the Government of Santo Domingo, to the Colonial Office of the Spanish Empire in Seville about his voyage of exploration to the north that year, was most discouraging.

Then came the year 1513, with further sensational news: the sea, assumed to exist beyond the strange continent, had at last been discovered. The Spanish conquistador, Nuñes de Balboa, had seen this ocean with his own eyes after having marched for three terrible weeks through the jungles of Central America. Soon afterwards he was to be beheaded as a mutineer, but his reports were such that there could no longer be any doubts. The ocean separating America from Cathay, India and the Moluccas had ceased to be a mere scientific theory, it had become a reality.

If there was an ocean then there must be a passage, for it was unthinkable that the American barrier should stretch from pole to pole without any break. This conclusion seemed so obvious that even the avaricious and deeply sceptical Charles V—later elected Emperor of the Holy Roman Empire, thanks mainly to the Fuggers—subscribed to it. At this propitious moment there suddenly appeared before him a Portuguese exile by the name of Magalhães, a rather insignificant officer who, after seeing service abroad, had been dismissed, and who confidently asserted that he knew where this passage could be found. All he needed for sailing round the world was a few ships.

This passage, as imagined by Fernando Magellán—we shall henceforth call him by his Spanish name—was of course non-existent, and was created artificially four centuries later, on the 15th August 1914, when the first ship passed through the Panama Canal to reach the Pacific from the Atlantic Ocean in a matter of a few hours. Actually, the Spaniards themselves had had the thought of breaking through the isthmus of Panama and making the passage which Nature herself had barred, but in 1551 the bigot Philip II forbade his people, on pain of death, to harbour such sinful thoughts, which ran counter to the divine order. Thus the idea fell into oblivion until Alexander von Humboldt revived it in 1829.

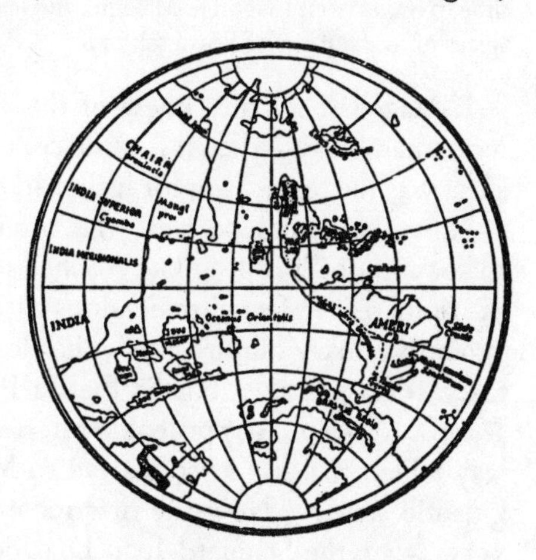

XIV. Johannes W. Schöner's globe.

Fortunately, Magellán was unable to look into the future and he was absolutely certain that he knew the way. The great German historian, Leopold von Ranke, once said of Columbus's discovery that never had a greater error produced greater consequences, and this applies equally as much to the discoveries made by our stubborn young nobleman from the district of Oporto.

But how did this error arise? On what did Magellán base his conviction that there was a passage, that he knew where it could be found, and that he could promise to sail round the world in one single voyage? Historians have long tried to answer this question. They first believed that Martin Behaim, the chief cartographer of the Crown of Portugal, who originally came from Nuremberg, had left a map, after his death in 1507, on which the passage was marked, but they could find no convincing proof of this. Then they thought about the famous globe, still extant, fashioned in 1515 by Johannes Schöner of Nuremberg, on which a passage is actually marked, though in quite the wrong place. It was conjectured that the map and the globe had been kept in the *Tesoria* at Lisbon, the secret royal archive, and that Magellán had had access to them. Finally they discovered an old German broadsheet, the *Copia der Newen Zeytung auss Presill Landt* printed in 1507 by Erhart Öglin at Augsburg. In it was the report that a Portuguese ship had discovered a deep channel cutting into the land at about 40° S., and had travelled along it for two full days without reaching its end, but had then been driven away by storms. It was made clear that this tremendous passage was bound to lead to the western ocean and that it would not be too difficult to reach Malacca through it.

And when they had reached the said regions, namely 40° S., they discovered the land of Presill (Brazil), having a *cabo*, that is to say a point or a place which stretches out into the sea. And they sailed around the said *cabo*. . . . And when they had rounded the *cabo*, as is reported, and sailed or travelled towards the north-west, the weather became so bad and the wind so strong that they could not sail or travel further. . . . The *peloto*, that is to say, the guide or leader of the ship, was a fairly good friend of mine. He spoke to me and expressed the opinion that from the said *cabo dye Pressil*, that is the beginning of the land of Brazil, it was a distance of six hundred miles toward Malaqua. He also thought that through this *viagio*, that is to say, way or voyage, it would take a short time to travel from Lisbon to Malaqua and back again, which would help to bring much spices unto the King of Portugal. . . .

If Magellán actually knew of this astonishing report—and this seems more than likely—then it is quite conceivable that this old German broadsheet was the real reason for his wish to sail round the world.

Now the actual passage, the Strait of Magellán, is found at about 52° S. and no European had reached it before the year 1520. However, at 35° S. there is in fact a tremendous gap in the South American continent, a gigantic estuary hundreds of miles long, that could well have been mistaken for a passage. This is the La Plata Estuary, and the report in the *Newe Zeytung* of 1507 probably referred to the Plate River—the *viagio*, the way which was supposed to lead to Malacca in so short a time, being its gigantic estuary. Now the first record we have of the Plate River is in 1515, when the Spaniard Juan Díaz de Solís reached it in his own search for a passage through the continent. At first he was certain that he had found the *paso*, but his hopes were soon dashed when he discovered that the broad channel was nothing but the mouth of a river. As the German broadsheet apparently spoke of La Plata some eight years earlier, it looks as if a Portuguese ship had reached it long before the Spaniards. Since, in 1504, Manuel of Portugal had forbidden on pain of death the publication of any information about navigation, so that foreigners could not derive benefit from Portuguese discoveries, it is not impossible that this earlier voyage had been kept a secret. In any case the River Plate itself was not marked on any old maps; hence Magellán's error, but also his confidence in his enterprise.

Apart from Columbus, Magellán is always the most widely quoted example of the fact that tremendous successes are sometimes the result of mistakes. Ingenuous people conclude from this that it makes very little difference whether the motives of an action are objectively correct or not, it is action alone which counts. Supporters of this thesis conveniently overlook how relative are truth and error in our world. At a simple level, it is easy enough to separate them but, seen in the prism of a great personality, they intermingle and the difference between them is so finely graded that truth may arise from error and error may give birth to truth. We know that faith can move even mountains, and here the faith of one brave man, so to speak, broke a passage through the Cambrian formation of Patagonia, the hardest rock on earth. It was because of this faith alone that what had been a stupid error was turned into an accomplished fact, even though this *paso*, this passage, did not open up where his burning faith had seen it. Ironically enough, Magellán discovered it at the southernmost tip of the gigantic American continent, so that he might just as quickly have gone round Cape Horn. But the discovery of the passage had to come when it did for, as we shall see, if it had been put off by as little as one day, Magellán would probably have had to turn back.

Naturally considerations of this kind were never part of Magellán's way of thinking. They are retrospective in the fullest meaning of the word, and anyone reflecting thus in his presence would not have been allowed to pursue such thoughts for long. Magellán was a man of purpose, of reason and cool calculation, who left nothing to accident, to mere intuitions or to inspiration. He was concerned with realities alone. Everything that he did was most carefully planned down to the last detail. When he crossed the border into Spain in 1517, he already had some good connections there, which he inteded to use to better his fortunes. About a year later he married Beatrix de Barbosa, daughter of the Director of the Arsenal of Spain—no shining beauty but endowed with 600,000 maravedís. She not only brought him a dowry of money but also Spanish citizenship and direct connections with the *Domus Indica*, the famous India Office in Seville, for naturally Diego de Barbosa, his father-in-law, was in good standing with the officials there.

When Magellán knocked at the door, he was no longer an unknown name. All the same, he found it difficult at first to arouse interest, but in the end the India Office accepted his project. The counsellors submitted the plan to Charles V, and the Emperor looked favourably upon Magellán's plans. Even though he was normally not in the habit of giving Conquistadors anything but his imperial blessing, he made a grant of 6,454,209 maravedís (about six to seven thousand pounds) to the Portuguese discoverer. True, a considerable share of the cost was left to private financiers, namely the Dutch shipper de Haro and his friends, while the Emperor made sure of the lion's share of possible discoveries for himself. This procedure had often proved successful. If private circles were prepared to gamble their money on such risky enterprises, the Crown was quite prepared to accept it. For after all the Crown would have to incur a great deal of expenditure in later years. Time after time the State had had to intervene when its subjects had come to a dead end. Nobody could blame Charles if he kept a cool head in face of such daring enterprises, and it was remarkable enough that the Emperor had declared himself ready, on behalf of Spain, to share in financing the expedition.

On the 22nd of March 1518, the decisive agreement was signed in

Valladolid: Charles V undertook to provide five ships and all supplies for two years. He appointed Magellán *adelantado* and *gobernador*, and gave him a salary as well as a share in the profits of the voyage. Magellán, for his part, was to discover 'in the realm of the oceans belonging to us, islands, continents and rich spices'. One has to admit that all risks in this undertaking were borne by the Crown and the private financiers; if Magellán had discovered nothing then the invested capital would have been lost. This would have meant a great deal to a business-minded ruler such as Charles V who was constantly hard pressed for money. It must also be remembered that he was besieged daily with similar projects and that he, more than anyone else, must have been sick and tired of grandiose plans. Therefore if he pledged himself to give financial aid to this particular expedition, it could only have been because he was convinced by the unshakeable faith and determination of this ugly, limping, former Portuguese officer. Magellán despite his awkward manners had managed to force Charles V, a pessimist by inclination and vocation, to do his will. Thus His Imperial Majesty confirmed:

It is our will that in recognition of the efforts and costs of this voyage, from the net profit you bring back, and after due deduction for the cost of the fleet has been made, you will be allowed to retain a fifth part as a reward. So that your voyage be ensured, and so that you may fulfil your plan, I promise you five ships: two of a hundred and thirty tons each, two of ninety and one of sixty tons, with crews, supplies and armaments sufficient for two years and for two hundred and thirty-four heads, including captains, officers and sailors of the fleet.

This I promise you and you have my royal word that I will protect you, as I hereby give the signature of my name.

Valladolid, on the 22nd March, 1518. I
the King.

True, another year was to pass before the crew had been hired and the ships equipped. Although the Crown had shown itself astonishingly magnanimous in signing the agreements it suddenly began to quibble. The five sailing ships which it had agreed to supply turned out to be very old and unseaworthy, and Magellán had to overhaul them completely. Stefan Zweig, some years ago, when writing his fine book on Magellán, looked up the accounts for equipping this fleet and there, among other things, were the following items needed for making the best of what appears to have been a very bad job indeed:

175,098 maravedís for the wood for beams and planks.
104,244 maravedís wages for the work of the carpenters.
6,790 maravedís wages for the sawing of the planks.
142,532 maravedís for the iron-work of the ship.
129,539 maravedís wages for the caulking of the ship.
149,076 maravedís for obtaining 173 pieces of canvas.
324,170 maravedís for 221 hundredweights of cables, splices and hemp.

These figures show clearly that the ships of the Crown of Spain were by no means in the best possible condition. Apparently, they lacked both top-masts and yards; in any case Magellán allotted a further 37,437 maravedís to this purpose. Pumps and rudders were missing, the hulks were completely rotten and not even anchors were provided—quite obviously, Charles V's counsellors must have chosen indiscriminately from the ships' graveyards, so as to fulfil the contract with the least possible cost to the Crown.

The rest of the equipment, as the accounts show, was also extremely poor and the human material quite pitiful. It consisted of thirty-seven Portuguese, some thirty Italians and nineteen Frenchmen. In addition there were Flemings, Basques, Germans, Greeks, Englishmen, Negroes, Malays and above all, Spaniards. Many of them were desperadoes and criminals who hoped to regain freedom and whiten their reputations by taking part in this expedition. Most of them had never seen the sea, and had no idea of navigation. It is most surprising that any of them ever got back alive from this expedition. While the de Haros of Antwerp had done their best, it cannot be said that the Spanish Crown ever fully overcame its proverbial stinginess. When all is said and done, it did no more than protect Magellán against attacks by the Portuguese. This was necessary enough, for when Lisbon heard of the reasons for Magellán's alliance with Spain, and when it discovered that he could not be bought off by money or honours, Portugal had recourse to the gangster methods of the Renaissance, which, in accordance with the general *mores* of the time, were quite permissible even for the State and the Crown. However they did not manage to get Magellán out of the way, and on the 10th August 1519, the Molucca fleet, flying the flag of Spain at its masthead and next to it Magellán's coat-of-arms, *argent, three bars checky, sable and gules*, set sail from Seville down the Guadalquivir.

Even before the departure, unpleasant incidents had taken place with the other captains and this made clear Magellán's very difficult position, despite his official protection. The captains of the four other ships were all pure-blooded Spaniards, some of them even noblemen, and they were very unwilling to take orders from a Portuguese; the Captain-General was finally forced to intervene physically to keep discipline and nip the incipient mutiny in the bud. With his own hand he placed the captain of the *San Antonio*, Vice-Admiral Cartagena, in irons and left no doubt in the mind of the whole fleet that there was only one person who was giving the orders. It can easily be imagined what effect this had on a crew thrown together from almost all the nations of Europe, and what energy Magellán needed to exert his authority over them.

Magellán achieved the impossible and the first stages of the voyage were accomplished without incident. At the end of November 1519 the fleet reached the shores of Brazil, near what is today called Recife or Pernambuco, and on the 13th December, after a voyage of eleven weeks, it dropped anchor in the bay of Rio de Janeiro. The tired seamen were as happy as if they had been in paradise. Actually they had made an unauthorized landing. The instructions of the King expressly forbade them to set foot on land within the Portuguese sphere of control, but since their cousins from Lisbon had not yet founded a settlement there, and since that enchantingly beautiful bay still belonged to no one, the Spaniards could quite happily send their boats ashore. Magellán's crew tasted the strange fruits, the 'large round pine-cones' which the brown-skinned natives called *ananas* (pineapple) and which were so extraordinarily sweet and tasty; the batata, a farinaceous fruit resembling the chestnut, and finally the sugar cane which at that time was still very rare, even though it was being cultivated all over North Africa and in many places in Spain and Italy. Other things, such as chickens, geese and parrots, were equally in demand, but naturally very high on the scale of delight came the young girls of Rio de Janeiro! 'They wear', as all the diaries of the voyage report, 'no other clothes than their hair, and in exchange for a knife or an axe, we could obtain two or even three of these daughters of Eve, so perfect and well-shaped in every possible way.' This may sound very ungentlemanly and mercenary; and the majority of that bunch of near scoundrels that formed Magellán's crew must at first have thought of nothing but their lust. Yet if we read between the lines of their reports we see that even these rough men were deeply touched by the natural nobility that has always been so characteristic of the girls and women of this most beautiful of all harbours.

Magellán was terribly impatient to be off again. He had determined, by means of the astrolabe, that they were at about 24° S. The passage was supposed to be at 40° S. Thus only 16° of latitude separated him from his objective. He tried to hurry up preparations for departure, but after an eleven weeks' voyage, algae, barnacles and weeds had attached themselves to the ships and had to be persuaded to leave, the sails had to be resewn and trimmed and ends spliced – in short, two weeks had to go by before the fleet was again reported seaworthy. On the 26th December, Magellán started on what he assumed to be the final and decisive stage of his voyage. Since the wind was favourable, he ordered every available inch of sail to be set and at high speed the armada raced towards the south. After only fourteen days of sailing it had covered some twelve hundred miles of coastline. With much joy the Admiral noticed that the shore at starboard was slowly receding towards the west. At the Lobos islands, shortly before reaching the Montevideo of today, the strange coast had made way for a bay, almost at right angles. Simultaneously there opened up the full width of the gigantic estuary formed by the River Plate. Anyone reaching here and firmly believing that he had found the road to the *Mar del Sur*, to the South Sea, would find his heart beating faster in his excitement. Soon the whole fleet knew that they had reached the *paso*, and in view of the gigantic waters which stretched endlessly towards the west, everybody, including the rebellious Spanish captain, was clearly convinced that within another few days they would be making their way to the rich Cathay and the golden Cipangu.

Oddly enough not a single one of Magellán's crew of two hundred and seventy seems to have had the common sense to throw a mug overboard and to taste the water. He would have discovered that, even far outside the La Plata estuary, it was still sweet, for he would have tasted fresh river-water. Even the yellowish colour of the sea raised no doubts in them, so sure were they of their cause. Thus two weeks passed during which sailing operations became more and more difficult; men were sent in the long-boats to explore, and finally the truth was known that there was no passage. The gigantic bay was the mouth of a tremendous river and the route to Asia over the southern ocean was no nearer.

Magellán must have been sick to death when he realized this, and when, on the 2nd of February 1520, from the bridge of his ship he gave the order to set off again, dozens of pairs of eyes must have stared at him with ill-concealed hostility. But not a muscle moved in his face; the sails went up and, before a fresh northerly wind, the armada continued its course to the south. The Admiral still had one loophole through which he could hope to save himself for the time being. The old reports had said that the passage opened at about 40° S., but so far he had only reached 35° S., and many miles still separated him from his objective or from the complete collapse of all his hopes. Was the Captain-General then really so certain, so full of faith and confidence as his contemporaries believed? Or had he some doubts from the very start?

In the India Office at Seville the experts were shaking their heads when they checked Magellán's supply accounts: 21,383 pounds of ships' biscuits, 480 pounds of oil, 570 pounds of pickled meat, 1,120 pounds of cheese, 200 barrels of sardines, 238 dozen dried fish in bundles, and 1,700 pounds of dried fish in barrels. He had taken all these on board. In addition there was a tremendous cargo of beans, peas, lentils, flour, rice, sugar, garlic, onions, raisins, currants, figs, capers, salt, honey, etc. This was far, far more than was customary, this was enough to nourish his whole fleet for two full years! Why did this foreigner, this captain from Portugal, need so many provisions? What was in his mind? And people started to whisper and murmur in the India Office. But what could be done against the Emperor's favourite, against the son-in-law of the Director of the Arsenal? So nothing was said, and Magellán alone on board knew how well his enterprise was supplied with provisions.

Had the Admiral left himself a way for escape here? It is certain that his supplies were sufficient for two years. It is also certain that Magellán kept the extent of his provisions secret, for had he told his sailors that they would have to reckon with a two years' voyage, he would have had to press-gang and drag them aboard ship by force. Such things *had* to be kept secret, and anyone in Magellán's position would have done likewise. While the Captain-General might well have suspected that he was setting out on a long voyage, we would be wrong to infer from this that he was bluffing all the way.

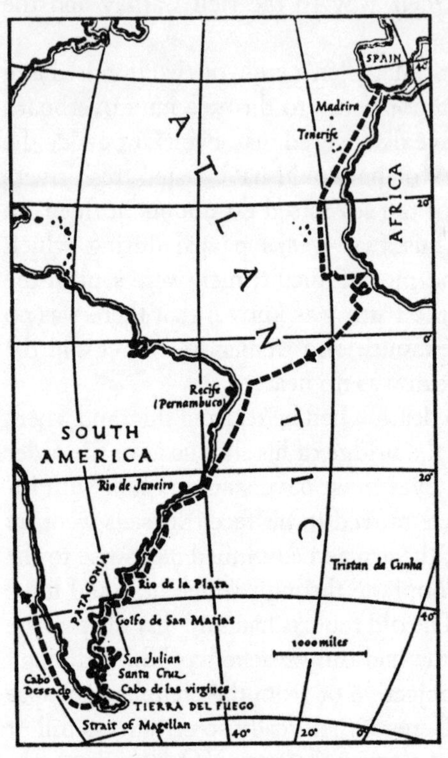

XV. Magellán's voyage to South America.

On the 24th February 1520, three weeks after the hasty departure from La Plata, Magellán had sailed down the coast as far as the *Golfo de San Matias*. He was making rather slow progress, probably because he examined every bay and recess carefully. His officers and crew were beginning to abandon all hope of success. Then suddenly, just after the Punta Vermeja, the entry to the Bay of Saint Matthew, had been rounded, no moreland could be seen from the crow's nest. During the next twelve sailing hours hopes ran high once more.

By the evening of this 24th February 1520, Magellán was to know that even this last hope had been in vain. There was no passage, but only a large bay. His face not showing a trace of his emotion, the Admiral went down to his cabin, realizing that from now on he was his own prisoner. Should he call his captains and tell them he had been wrong all along about the *paso*? No, they would clap him in irons, they would break every bone in his body, if he told them that.

That night Magellán must have decided to sail on, come what may, and at whatever cost. Possibly he might have to forfeit his own life, perhaps it would cost the lives of the whole expedition. What of it! It was not the spirit of adventure alone which was driving the Admiral to continue his voyage at any price; he must have continued to hold fast to his belief in a passage, even though the secret maps had proved inaccurate.

We know nothing of what happened on that fateful night. Even if in our inner eye we can see the Captain-General pacing up and down in his narrow cabin, we may be wrong. It is equally possible that Fernando Magellán slept soundly for eight hours that night, and that he was completely untouched by the tremendous scope of his decision. It must be granted that geniuses and maniacs live in a different spiritual climate from that of the ordinary man, and that it is difficult to draw a dividing line between them.

Thus the voyage continued, until on the 31st March 1520, as the anchors were rattling down from the bows of the Spanish ships in the bay of Port San Julián, Magellán informed his crew that he intended to pass the winter there. At the same time he ordered that the daily rations should be cut by one-half. This was an open challenge and two days later, as the Captain-General had expected, mutiny broke out.

Detailed reports of the events of this mutiny have been preserved for us in the journal of Antonio Pigafetta, a young nobleman from Vicenza, in Italy, who had left his respectable wealthy family to see the world. It was customary in those days for the sons of noble houses to make an educative tour, via Rome and Paris to the Imperial Court, in order to see something of the world. This young Italian nobleman appeared one day in the train of the Papal Protonotary at the Royal camp of Charles V in Barcelona, and hardly had he heard of Magellán and his secret expedition, than he made an immediate appeal to Charles V to be allowed to participate in this magnificent enterprise.

No one seeing the bust of the youthful Charles V, modelled by Konrad Meit in 1517, which portrays him as having been an open-minded, inquiring young man, can doubt that an equally adventurous and eager youth such as Antonio Pigafetta almost immediately obtained the favour he was seeking. Antonio Pigafetta soon held a magnificent sealed document which, in many complicated, courtly turns of phrase, appointed him Magellán's private secretary, in which capacity he was to join the expedition.

It is thus that our callow youth found himself in the midst of that throng of professional adventurers, clerks, unscrupulous business men and old salts. Never in his home had they spoken of money and profits, nor had it been suggested that different ways of behaviour existed from those practised in his own circle. In short he knew little of the real world in which cunning and strength reigned supreme. His race had long since forgotten that it was because of these very qualities that primitive man had managed to survive and lord it over the rest of the creation, and that the ideal of a gentleman could only exist when man had become supreme, and his supremacy unthreatened.

Many others in the place of Antonio Pigafetta would have quickly run away or would have returned to their Papal Protonotary and continued on their journey to Paris, but the young Italian patrician was made of sterner stuff. Though he frequently had to bite his lip, he remained on board, and took part in the whole voyage from the first to the last day. He was one of the few survivors who managed to get back and the only one who made any written reports during the voyage. Since he knew that he was a greenhorn, he kept away from difficult, complicated things. He noticed the sparks of dissatisfaction between Magellán and his captains, just as everybody else on board had noticed them, but he knew that he was too inexperienced to fathom clearly the complicated situation of intrigue and slander, mutiny and plot, and so he kept silent and restricted himself to facts, to immediate events. These, however, he recorded with photographic fidelity.

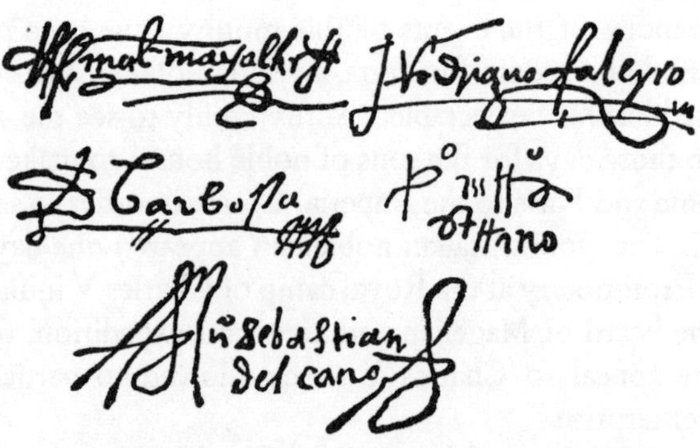

10. Seamen and soldiers found writing difficult, as can clearly be seen from the signatures of Magellán's officers.

For five months we stayed in the harbour, which we called the harbour of San Julian. Here much dissatisfaction and distrust rose up against Magellán. Immediately after we had dropped anchor in this harbour, Magellán gave orders for dwellings to be erected on land. He also ordered the daily rations to be cut so that they would last for a longer period of time. The crews and also the captains objected to both these commands. The dissatisfied demanded to return home. Magellán refused even to discuss the matter and, when his crew persisted, he had some of the worst offenders arrested and punished. But this only exasperated the men. On the 1st April, 1520, when Magellán had ordered us all to go ashore and to attend Mass, the captains Juan de Cartagena, Luis de Mendoza and Gaspar de Quesada did not appear. Open mutiny broke out not long after. Juan de Cartagena was the ringleader. In the night between the 1st and 2nd April, he went on board the *San Antonio* and took prisoner its captain, who had remained faithful to Magellán, and disarmed the crew. On the morning of the 2nd April, the mutineers had three ships in their power, the captain of the *Victoria* having sided with them also. Magellán, apart from his own ship, the *Trinidad*, only had the *Santiago* under captain Serrano on his side. Through a ruse the Admiral managed to take possession of the *Victoria*, then he placed his three ships at the exit of the harbour. During the night, the *San Antonio*, whose crew was on the side of the mutineers, broke anchor and drifted close to the flagship. The *San Antonio* was quickly taken, particularly since the crew immediately declared themselves in favour of Magellán. As a result, Juan de Cartagena and the *Concepción*, his ship, had to submit to Magellán. Their punishment was speedy. At first the ringleaders were put in irons. Captain Mendoza, of the *Victoria*, had been killed in the unexpected attack which had given Magellán possession of the ship. Juan de Cartagena and a chaplain who had joined the mutiny were marooned and left to their fate. The crews who had participated in the mutiny were pardoned....

These then are the facts that Pigafetta witnessed and described. As we have seen he tells us nothing of the psychological factors, how the anger of the captains rose to boiling point, how Magellán saw which way the wind was blowing, and how he waited for the crucial moment when fate was to offer him success. Justice, when it is purely concerned with establishing guilt and passing sentence, has no need for an elaborate setting. Courts-martial require only the post to which the offender is tied and the sandheap to receive his body. But whenever it is not only a question of avenging and judging, but of influencing, of stressing the terrible sanctity of law, justice requires an experienced stage-manager and effective scenery.

Magellán knew only too well that he would require a suitable stage for his plan, and that he would have to wait for the sparks to become flames before quenching them once and for all. The harbour of San Julián supplied the ideal setting for the drama: heavy storm clouds, threatening rocks and icy desolation made a fitting theatre for the dénouement of that clash of wills. Two of the ringleaders were marooned. Nothing has ever been heard of them. The third ringleader, captain Gaspar de Quesada, was beheaded. Because he was a particularly capable and trusted officer of the Spanish Crown his execution had to be turned into a spectacle. The record of the court as preserved by the *escribanos*, the official recorders, is many pages long. The judgement, expressed in the formal verbiage of the Spanish homeland, was a foregone conclusion. The execution itself seemed to have been rehearsed: a semi-circle of rocks rising as in an amphitheatre, a semi-circle of motionless men and officers, black clouds from a threatening sky. In the centre of the stage the executioner's block. In front of it, the grim lord of life and death—the Admiral himself, his greying hair falling deep over his forehead, a short-legged, lame man with eyes flashing nervously over the whole scene. Cold shudders ran down the spines of the spectators, but not from the icy wind. The 'old man' had thought out some fiendish refinement. For next to the block where Gaspar de Quesada was to lay his head, stood Luis de Molino, his own servant and foster-brother. Magellán had promised to pardon him on condition that he took the life of his master. And Molino had accepted the devilish order. The head of Quesada fell under the sharp, heavy axe, the smashed vertebrae crunched gruesomely, the red flame of his blood gushed out like a torrent from the open pipe of his throat, and the bestial yells of Luis de Molino re-echoed from the rocks.

Pigafetta, the private secretary and confidant of Magellán, stood at his side, along with the other high-ranking officers of the fleet. He viewed the dissenting captains as common mutineers, but were they so in fact?

Magellán knew better than that. Despite his fanaticism, he was an honourable and just man at heart, and he must have known that at root his opponents were no mutineers at all. In the first place he, as an old soldier, must have been impressed by the fact that their enterprise was planned and carried out with military precision. To checkmate him by means of a lightning attack against the *San Antonio*, was a masterly piece of strategy. There was no doubt, they were able fellows. Furthermore, the King had expressly confirmed them in their offices of inspectors, treasurers and accountants of his enterprise. When, for the sake of the expedition, he had to push them completely into the background, they had an undoubted right to resist. He had excluded them completely, he had been *forced* to take the measures he did. The fact that they drew their swords in order to defend the property of their King against what they considered a maniac, could not be considered a crime.

Magellán was faced with a difficult decision. Nobody knows how he fought his way through it, since not a single line from his or anybody else's hand concerning this dilemma has come down to us. We can only refer to the general picture of the man that history has preserved, which leads us to assume that he himself was deeply aware of the tragedy of his situation. He, a Portuguese nobleman, who had been forced to emigrate from his native land in order to carry through his great plan and so had been dubbed a turncoat, and who for this reason alone was bound to do his utmost to obtain his goal, was opposed by Spanish nobles who had sworn a holy oath to their King and whose sense of duty forced them to rise up against an Admiral whom they considered an irresponsible foreigner. By human standards, the scales were equally balanced.

But this turncoat, this stranger, this maniac, was no longer himself. So long as there was still the slightest possibility of discovering the passage, so long as his ships were not impeded in their voyage towards the south by the same thick barrier of ice which, twenty years previously, had barred the way to Giovanni Caboto in the north-west, he would remain a prisoner to his task. What others considered their sworn duty *had* to be treated as mutiny and punished accordingly. This he did with well-nigh diabolic cunning, planning every detail and calculating the result of every action. A few hours after the outbreak of the mutiny, Magellán had regained complete control over his fleet.

8

As an old sailor Magellán knew the enemy that would face him during the winter months. This enemy was not hunger, but idleness. Not so many years had passed since the Admiral himself had been a simple sailor below deck. He had had experience of what happens when hundreds of men are herded together in a cramped space, lounging about without anything to do, forever retelling the same old jokes and stories which everyone has grown heartily sick of. He knew it would lead to friction and finally to mutiny—mutiny from below. The danger was particularly great on that uninhabited, desolate coast swept by continuous storms, where winters were dark and long. Thus he hounded his men until they dropped with fatigue; for almost five whole months he hunted them as the pack hunts the stag. Trees were felled, beams and planks were cut and sails renewed, ballast was restowed. Slipways were built, gigantic winches heaved the ships ashore, the keels were repaired and rotten places in the hull made good; everybody was busy carpentering, hammering, drilling, caulking, sweeping, scrubbing and painting, as if the fleet were due to sail the very next day.

Magellán's men swore like troopers at their Admiral's 'occupational therapy'. But they did not rise up against him, they remained healthy, and above all their ships were seaworthy once again.

Magellán's own position was difficult, too. He did not know what the future held. He had allowed it to be known that he would sail south, skirting the coast, as far as 75° S., when, if the passage should still elude them, he would turn east and make for the Moluccas on the usual route. While this was a concession to his captains it was also a sign of Magellán's own uncertainty, and thus another challenge. But there was no mutiny, for fear still held his men by the throat.

Nor was there mutiny when Magellán, in his impatience, pressed on much too early. At the end of May 1520, he sent the corvette, *Santiago*, out into the darkness and the storms with orders to reconnoitre to the south. Captain Serrano left without protest. Weeks passed by without any news and then, one day, two men weakened by hunger staggered down the hills to the harbour of San Julián. They were sailors from the *Santiago* and they brought bad tidings: their ship had foundered, and the survivors were waiting a few days' journey further south, in a deplorable plight.

A strange event came to break the tension caused by all these misfortunes. One day, a strange man-like being was seen skulking on the slopes surrounding San Julián. To the relatively small-sized Spaniards, it appeared larger than life. They especially noted the enormous size of its feet and called it *Patagon*, 'big feet', and the land in which these giants lived, Patagonia.

The gawky fellow who had appeared from nowhere was in a good mood, for he danced and sang. Pigafetta, who had not found anything

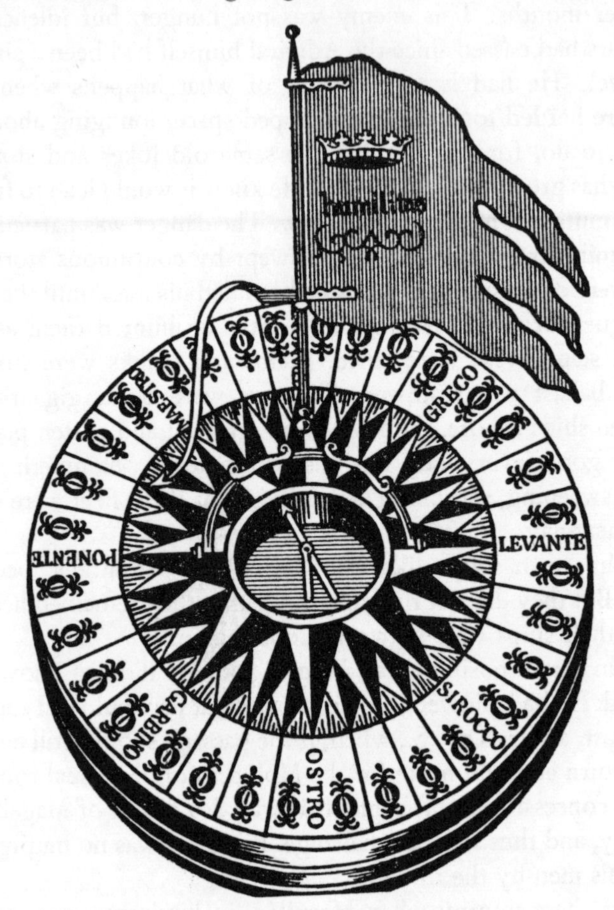

11. Magellán's compass.

worthy to report in his diary for a long time exploited this scene like a born journalist. He missed nothing. He noticed the red and yellow circles which the savage had painted around his eyes, as his tribal colours. He added that this strange being was clad in the skins of some unknown animal, skilfully joined together. We know now it was the fur of the guanaco, which Patagonians still wear to this day. In a light-hearted vein he told how the Admiral ordered one of the sailors to dance and sing, and to throw sand over himself, just as the savage had done. To the great amusement of his comrades the sailor proved to be so skilful that the native seemed to understand the strangers wished him no harm and he approached them peacefully.

He was quite happy to be brought to the small island to which the captain and his companions had repaired in the meanwhile. The Patagonian seemed glad to see us and kept on pointing to the sky, obviously to express his conviction that we had come from there. The fellow was so tremendously large that our heads reached up to his waist at most. The captain gave orders for him to be given food and drink, and amongst other things he made him a present of a small mirror. When the giant saw himself in it, he was so frightened that he stumbled backwards suddenly, knocking down four of our sailors, who by chance were standing close behind him.

No Spaniard had ever seen such primitive people and when, attracted by the noise, some more Patagonians, including some female giants, appeared, the Spaniards were overjoyed. They would gladly have caught one of these tremendous fellows and taken him to Spain. To see him devouring live rats, swallowing half a loaf of bread in a few bites and handling the mirror and the little bells with which he had been presented was a spectacle they fain would have shared with those back home. But not even the toughest of the sailors dared to touch him. Then he was shown some handcuffs and was made to understand that they were a beautiful, jingling ornament. The unsuspecting savage fell into the trap, the steel snapped close; the giant was defenceless and caught, and he was dragged to one of the ships where soon he perished like an animal.

Magellán had received express orders from the India Office to bring back specimens of all men, animals and plants, which he discovered on his journey. However, he heartily disliked unnecessary violence or cruelty, and had not harmed one hair of the natives in the bay of Rio de Janeiro. He was deeply troubled that one of these poor souls had perished now, and he felt that evil and death hung over the harbour of San Julián. They must sail away from it at all costs.

They finally did so at the end of August 1520. Magellán's fleet was now reduced to four ships. It proved to be no pleasure cruise, since it was still the season for the sudden spring squalls which whip over the sea from the highlands and which even now can endanger shipping. Here and there ice floes were drifting in the water, the days were still short and the dark stormy nights interminably long. The loss of the *Santiago* was felt to be a tragedy. She had been the smallest ship of the fleet, but also the most agile and the one with the least draught. Whenever reconnaissance work had to be done, whenever the dark uncanny fiords had to be explored, the small corvette had been called upon, but now Magellán had to use one of his large, heavy ships for this purpose. After two days he had had enough of it. The Captain-General called a halt in the mouth of a river discovered by the *Santiago* shortly before she went down, and on the 26th August he set up winter quarters for another two months.

Fate here played him a shabby trick. For only two days' voyage further south lay the *paso*, the cherished passage, between walls of gneiss and granite. It was a mere stone's throw in comparison with the distance they had covered, but Magellán did not even send out a boat. His intuition, which so far had led him over all obstacles, had deserted him. His confidence had died, and hopelessness and despair seemed to paralyse him.

XVI. Map of the Strait of Magellán (1586).

But still he forced himself to carry on. On the 18th October 1520, they set off again and, after a short voyage, the fleet passed a large, deep bay, south of a projecting headland.

It was the 21st October, the day of the Eleven Thousand Virgins, and they had reached 52° S. The weather was uncertain, with scattered squalls and a choppy sea. The bay looked like all the other bays they had explored in vain, and thus neither pilots nor captains saw any reason to investigate it further. Magellán too must have been doubtful and undecided. More than a year had passed since he had left Seville, more than half his supplies had gone. Even under the most favourable circumstances he would have to continue sailing for many a month. Time was running out, every day was precious. Then he gave the decisive order. The *San Antonio* and the *Concepción* were sent off with orders to return in five days' time, at the latest. This was the maximum that Magellán was willing to risk. The two ships, driven by a fresh breeze, soon disappeared behind the cape. They were hardly out of sight when a hurricane hit the bay. The *Trinidad*, Magellán's flagship, and the *Victoria* just managed to take refuge in the roadstead, but the other ships were already too deeply engaged in the strait. The storm must have hit them full on and there could be no doubt that they must be considered lost.

Once again Pigafetta faithfully recorded the events of these days. But he wrote not one word about the *dramatis personae*, the active and suffering witnesses of this tragedy. Events were more important to him than people; and he noted laconically:

> The two ships had been driven further into the bay by the sudden storms. Those on board feared certain shipwreck on the rocky shores, when suddenly they noticed that the bay opened up on the other side also. They followed this new passage and came to a further bay and thence into yet a third one. They then turned back to carry this promising news to Magellán as speedily as possible. They were under way for two days. We had taken it for granted, since we could not see them, that they had foundered in the storm. When we saw smoke rising from the shores we thought that this was a signal lit by the survivors to attract our attention. Then both ships came towards us from the bay with billowing sails and flying flags. Cannons roared and shouts of joy could be heard. . . .

We can imagine, but not describe, what this moment must have meant for Magellán. True, he was not yet certain that the long channel would lead to the *Mar del Sur*, and that in this grey, rocky wilderness there lay the passage to the sunny shores of that South Sea which Balboa had discovered a few years before. But no other breach had led so far inland as this. Could it be *the* passage? The crews and the captains of the other ships insisted that it was, since the water was salt, and since the effects of the tides were felt so strongly. Magellán sent a longboat on reconnaissance.

Then came the order for the ships to follow. The sails were unfurled and the anchors weighed. The breeze filled out the sails and the four ships slowly gathered way, threading the narrow channel into which the longboat had disappeared. Desolate, rocky cliffs threatened them from either side. There was no sign of life, human or animal, but at night innumerable fires could be seen everywhere. They called this strange, uncanny land the *Tierra del Fuego*, the land of fire. They did not know that in this *estrecho*, this strait, their ships were not only crossing from ocean to ocean, but were also passing from one age to another. They had voyaged back hundreds of thousands of years, to a time when men did not yet know how to make a fire and had to guard a flame jealously day and night, lest it should go out for ever, for the tribes that lived there—people of European origin according to Otto Menghin's recent statements—still lived in the early Stone Ages. Like their early blood relatives in Spain and North Africa, they made red and black tracings of their hands on the walls of deep caves and caverns, and like them also, they scratched geometric figures, artistic maze-like designs and the tracks of the animals they hunted, into the hard rock. They were, however, even more primitive than the early Europeans. They knew the usefulness of fire, and used it in their daily lives, but they had to tend and feed it carefully so that it did not go out. And thus, in that bleak wilderness, where the night wind whistled over the weather-beaten rocks, thousands of ghost-like, fiery eyes glowed on the heights. It was an eerie journey.

The eastern entrance revealed nothing of what lay in wait for the expedition. At first gentle green slopes ran down to the beaches but as soon as the first bends in the narrow channel had been rounded, the mountains on each side seemed to rise to immeasurable heights, enclosing the passage within walls of naked rock some 6,000 feet high. The sea, as if resenting this restriction of its domain, boiled and seethed angrily around needle-sharp rocks. To add to these dangers impenetrable mists would blanket out visibility. Countless ships of all nations have found their end here. It is a miracle and a tribute to Magellán's nautical skill that he conquered this distance of 375 miles without losing one ship.

The pilot of the *San Antonio*, Estevão Gómez, a relative of the Admiral, lost his nerve. He pointed out to Magellán that most of the food had decayed and that they were threatened by starvation; the condition of the ships, too, gave much cause for anxiety. Under these circumstances he thought it was wrong to sail on to the Moluccas. They could return to Spain very honourably now, and a second expedition would then make for the Moluccas without any danger. But Magellán remained unmoved. He ordered the voyage to continue and in a secret proclamation to the captains, he threatened anyone informing the crew of the shortage of supplies with death. They would continue even if they had to eat the leather covering the yards.

This was too much for Estevão Gómez. Sincerely worried about the unseaworthy condition of the ships and the lack of stores, he plotted with the crew of the *San Antonio* to overpower their captain and turn back for Spain. Five months later, while his comrades were lying at anchor in the Philippines, in the opposite half of the world, the *San Antonio* entered Seville with some dozen deserters on board. Their escape had been carried out secretly in one of the many southward inlets of Admiralty Sound, which the *Concepción* and the *San Antonio* had been sent to investigate. They had turned tail at the very moment that the Admiral's longboat returned, the sailors in it waving and cheering: the South Sea had been sighted! The *estrecho* had in fact led them to the other ocean; Magellán had been right!

Magellán, looking rather emaciated, his hair having turned grey during the last few months, stood on the castle of the *Trinidad* as the glad tidings were jubilantly announced. Suddenly the sailors stopped shouting and looked at each other, embarrassed. The man up there had covered his face with his hands and tears were streaming from between his fingers. He turned away sobbing. The sailors could not understand: their Admiral, who had seemed to be made of iron, was sobbing like a baby, *por alegría*, out of joy, out of deep happiness and gratitude.

Then came the news of the disappearance of the *San Antonio*. Magellán was deeply affected. Fate had dealt him many blows, but this was by far the worst. The *San Antonio*, his largest ship, had been carrying the greatest proportion of the provisions. Search parties were sent out, but could find nothing: neither dead, nor débris. Since the weather had been fine, there was only one possible conclusion: the *San Antonio* had deserted. Magellán would not believe this. But Andrea de San Martín, the astronomer and astrologer of the fleet, confirmed it. It was written in the horoscope, the stars had said so and stars did not lie!

Perhaps this was Fate's last warning to Magellán. Had Estevão Gómez been right in his advice to be contented with the discovery of the passage? True, Charles V had been promised in writing that the western sea-route to the Moluccas would be followed to its precious end, but the ships were not much good now and their provisions were inadequate. To redeem his pledge Magellán had to gamble with the lives of them all.

He hesitated. Then he had it made known to all his captains:

'Fernando de Magellán, Knight of the Order of St. Jacob, Captain-General of the fleet sent out by His Majesty to discover the Moluccas, to Captains, Pilots, Mates, Boatswains:

'I know that my intention to continue our enterprise makes you fear that you may be exposed to the gravest dangers, without any hope of success. You believe that we have too little time for the completion of this voyage.

'I have never rejected any opinion unheard, never despised any advice; matters have always been discussed in the open, and, during all our discussions, each one of you has been able to voice his opinions freely. But after what happened in the harbour of San Julián, I deemed it more advisable to hear your opinions individually than to call a meeting.

'Therefore I ask you to put down in writing anything that you consider of value for the safety of this fleet and for the service of His Majesty. I require you particularly not to give counsel that runs counter to the intentions of the King our Sovereign, and to the oath which you have sworn to me. In the name of the King, and as your Admiral, I order you to inform me of everything that you consider might contribute to a good voyage, and that you put down your reasons in writing, without keeping anything from me. I shall then let you have my own opinion and my decision.'

This order of the day was a master stroke of diplomacy. Magellán really was at a loss what to do; he was thinking of the return voyage and what the India Office would say. The *San Antonio* would have arrived first with the news of the events in San Julián, and the deserters would doubtless have complained of the Admiral's fanatical severity. This had to be countered, not when they returned, but here and now. His officers might well smile sceptically as they read that Magellán had never rejected any advice and had always discussed things in the open. They knew that this was untrue. But written evidence is permanent and those who, like the Admiral, were thinking they might have to face a military court did well to furnish themselves with an excuse. He himself could not let them know how bad things really were, hence his conclusion: 'I shall then let you have my own opinion and my decision.'

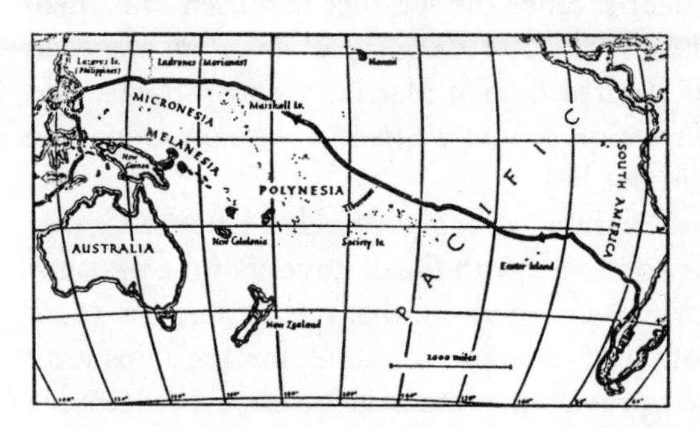

XVII. Magellán's crossing of the Pacific Ocean.

Turns of phrase of this kind are not well suited to evoke confidence, let alone to reawaken lost faith. Thus the officers sent a reply cloaked in yeas and nays, in ifs and buts. All of them were thinking of San Julían. They were not surprised when on the 28th November 1520, they received the signal from the flagship: 'Set sail! Follow me!'

After thirty more days, the *Cabo Deseado*, 'the Cape of Hope', at the Pacific end of the Straits of Magellán disappeared from sight. The fleet sailed westwards with a fresh breeze. They were now entering hell itself. At first they were sailing through a world of brilliance and beauty. The sun shone gloriously. Light summer clouds floated merrily across a silken blue sky and the ships danced along over the white crests of the waves. The Spaniards christened this new ocean, so pleasantly different from the furious might of the Atlantic, *El Pacifico.*

Months passed and still the same wind blew, still the same waves followed the ship, still the same clouds crossed the skies—and over them the same sun poured down its blinding, scorching rays.

This was worse than purgatory. As the miles and days went by, the Spaniards seemed to be getting ever deeper into Satanic regions. The single sip of water which was their daily ration, and for which they longed avariciously for twenty-four hours a day, stank like the pestilence. They had to hold their noses when they drank it. The ship's biscuits were alive with long, fat maggots, which had so riddled the hard chunks as to turn them into repulsive dust, and to top it all hundreds of rats had left their droppings over all the stores. The men had to force themselves to eat, even though they were ravenous. The meat, above all, had gone so rotten that it glowed in the dark and the sailors preferred to hunt the rats and eat them instead. When skinned and cleaned they did not taste too bad. The price for a roasted rat rose from a few maravedís to a whole golden ducat. But since it was not always possible to catch the beasts, which the fear of death had endowed with wings, the leather covers were taken off the yards, soaked in seawater, boiled and devoured.

We know all this and many other details from Pigafetta, who concluded his report as follows:

> In three months and twenty days we covered almost four thousand leagues. At night, five brilliant stars could be seen in the western sky arranged like a cross. Nowhere could we see land apart from two little uninhabited islands on which there was nothing but trees and birds. It was not possible to anchor near them. The water round them was teeming with sharks. We therefore called them the 'Unhappy Islands'. They are two hundred leagues apart, the first is at 15° S. and the next at 9° S.
>
> We continued sailing in a north-westerly direction until we came to the Equator. After we had crossed it, we turned west, keeping to a course between west and north-west. We continued constantly westwards for two hundred leagues and then we changed course again and sailed towards the south-west until we reached 13° N. When we had sailed some seventy leagues along this latitude we discovered a little island at 12° N....

Even the most hellish times must come to an end. Their journey through Hades had now lasted a full 110 days. Fate had led them through the clusters of Polynesian islands without their seeing more than a few cliffs and reefs. Finally on the 6th March 1521, thick cumulus clouds could be seen above the horizon. We know today that these are caused by convection currents rising from sand and naked rock glowing in the heat of the sun, and never from forest and sea. These bulging masses of cumuli towering high in the sky usually indicate that large sand surfaces or rocky islands lie below them. Magellán's Spaniards did not know that Polynesian sailors had kept a look out for such clouds on their long journeys across the ocean since time immemorial. Consequently the Spaniards had no idea what they meant, and when the look-out in the crow's-nest reported land, the whole ship was taken by surprise. Even the sufferers from scurvy, covered with sores, dragged themselves on deck. Land, land, land!

The fine, delicate lines on the horizon, discovered at dusk on 6th March 1521, proved next morning to be fertile islands rich in coconut palms and banana groves, like magic gardens planted in the sea. While fresh food and fresh water were uppermost in all their minds, a punitive expedition had first to be sent ashore. The natives, who swarmed round Magellán's fleet in their canoes, were stealing everything that was not battened down and had even managed to remove the longboat fastened to the stern of the *Victoria*.

The Spaniards took rather 'Platonic' revenge by calling these groups of islands the Ladrones, 'The Islands of Thieves'.

About a week later, on the 16th March, the fleet discovered land once more. Magellán's heart beat faster for, according to his calculations, these new islands could be nothing but the Moluccas, the fabulous *Ilhas das Especierias*. He approached the shore very carefully and dropped anchor off an uninhabited island. There might well be long established Portuguese outposts there, and he had no wish to be attacked by them or even by the natives, since all his three ships were nothing but floating hospitals, and those of the crew who were not suffering from scurvy had become so weakened by hunger that they could not possibly hold a crossbow.

But nothing happened. The natives, who crossed over from the neighbouring islands, were good-natured and friendly. Much to Magellán's relief, they knew nothing of the Portuguese. On the other hand, the natives had little understanding of Malay—it was obviously not their mother-tongue. These islands were not then the Moluccas. The Admiral rushed below deck to fetch the ship's quadrant. He sighted the sun. The pilot, next to him, read off the degree and Magellán had to admit to himself that none of the calculations he had made at sea had been right. He was a full 10° too far to the north, and thus the islands before him must be uncharted territory.

He could do nothing for a time. The most important thing was for the sick to recuperate. The officers and men threw themselves on the delicious, strange fruits that the natives brought them by the boat-load: bananas and coconuts, which received high praise from Pigafetta. Furthermore, there was no lack of pigs and chickens; and the natives even had a kind of wine: palm wine, the fermented juice of the coconut palm. All these delicacies could be had in abundance for a few little bells or a mirror. But the most beautiful thing was the water, pure, fresh, cool spring water which, as the spoiled patrician's son Pigafetta reports, was held in greater esteem by the sailors than even the most precious wines at home. And in all these fresh fruits and vegetables, in the new wine and the meat, was hidden some strange medicine. The Spaniards not only filled their bellies, they became healthy again. Stinking, festering boils disappeared, loose gums became firm and ulcers cleared up, water which had caused all the limbs to swell up hideously, drained away from the body, and the dizziness which had troubled them continually ceased. In short, almost overnight, they had become as newborn, and it is characteristic of Magellán that he christened these islands the Lazarus Islands, after the parable in the Gospel. This name, like that of the Ladrones, has today fallen into disuse. While the latter were renamed the Marianas, after a Spanish Queen, the Lazarus Islands are now known as the Philippines after Crown Prince Felipe, who later became Philip II of Spain.

Hardly a week later, the crew having fully recovered by now, Magellán sailed across to Cebu, chief island of the Philippines. He wanted to lay in an ample supply of food for the rest of his voyage to the Moluccas and, after some initial difficulties, all went extremely well. The Sultan of Cebu pledged his brotherhood with Magellán and took an oath of fidelity to the King of Spain. He even gave the ships' chaplains an opportunity to satisfy

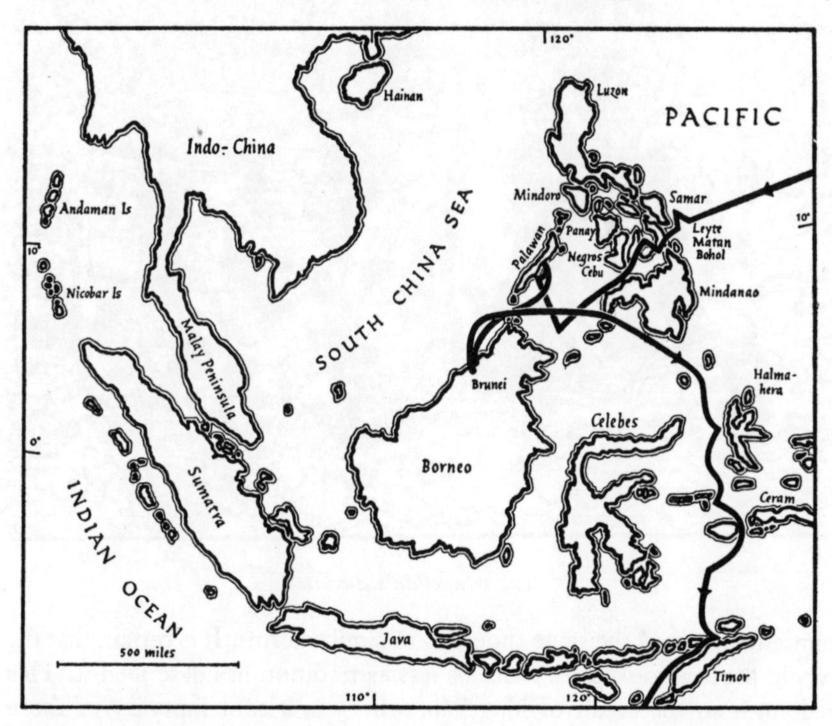

XVIII. A wild-goose chase between the Ilhas das Especierias, the Spice Islands.

their great zeal by arranging a mass baptism in which 800 men and women became converted to Christianity. Naturally—and how could it be otherwise?—the friendship of the natives and their desire for conversion was due to their recognition of the technical superiority of the strangers. The sound of cannon is an argument that is difficult to counter. But no naked force was used. Magellán let it be known expressly that those who did not wish to be baptized had no need to do so and that no harm would befall them. Naturally, Christians would be treated better.

> Then, as if with one mouth, they all declared that they wanted to become Christians, not from fear and not from servility but of their own free wills. They put themselves completely in the hands of the Admiral, so that he might deal with them as he would with his own men.

This is no cynical allusion to later times and to quite a different style of re-education. The words quoted are by Stefan Zweig, and Pigafetta

12. Magellán's death.

himself expressed the same thoughts in similar terms. It is certain that the whole process took place more or less as tradition has described it. This redounds to the credit of Magellán, who was a contemporary of those bloody conquerors, Cortés and Pizarro. Although he too could be harsh and severe, he was always intelligent and humane when dealing with the vanquished.

Magellán was undoubtedly a firmly convinced Catholic, and it is certain that such scenes of religious conversion satisfied him deeply, but it was not these alone that made him feel the terrible weeks and months behind them had not been in vain. Since the islands he had discovered were completely unknown in Europe and were frequently visited by Indian and Chinese merchants, he knew that his great objective, the Spice Islands, lay immediately before him. In his westward voyage across parts of the world that had never been navigated before, he had crossed the same longitude that the Portuguese had approached two years earlier sailing east. We can imagine the triumph felt when he realized this. The spherical shape of the earth, previously a mere theory, had now been finally proved.

He was not to survive to enjoy recognition for this supreme achievement. The chieftain of the neighbouring island of Matan refused to recognize the stranger and to follow the example of the Sultan of Cebu. Magellán led a punitive expedition, but suddenly found his fifty poorly armed sailors ambushed by an army of 1,500. Mortally wounded by a poisonous arrow the commander ordered a retreat. This turned into a headlong flight and Magellán's body had to be left behind. Deeply moved, Pigafetta noted:

They had killed our mirror, our light, our succour and faithful guide. Even when they had wounded him, he kept turning to the shore to see whether we had reached the boats safely.

Elsewhere he wrote the following epitaph:

His main virtues were constancy and perseverance even in the most difficult situations. Thus, for instance, he bore hunger better than all the rest of us. He was well versed in the art of reading nautical maps and he understood navigation better than all the pilots. The best proof of his wonderful intuition is the fact that he circumnavigated the world—for he had as good as completed his aim when he died—no man having preceded him in this.

These few words sum up everything that can be said to the glory of this unique man: he had forged the passage that Columbus had hoped for; he had proved what the Genoese mariner had believed and suspected, that the earth was round. What tremendous force was radiated by this conqueror of the earth is shown by a report of the English geographer Crawfurd, when he wrote that the name of Magellán was held in great honour in the Philippines, and that, even so long after as the middle of the last century, the Matanese were held in general disfavour for having killed so worthy and deserving a man.

The death of the Admiral seemed to seal the fate of the whole expedition. During their stay in Cebu, twenty-five officers were butchered at a banquet given by the Sultan. A hundred and fourteen men of the two hundred and seventy who had originally left Spain were left, but only a handful of these were to reach Europe some eighteen months later. That they survived at all after endless months of the most terrible privations was only possible because Magellán's personality was still felt, and because the few survivors of his voyage had become his spiritual heirs through continuous contact with him. In their honour, we wish to relate their further history very briefly.

A few days after Magellán's death, his fleet weighed anchor, but constant changes of course were necessary among that treacherous maze of islands. It was soon seen that there were not sufficient sailors to man all three remaining ships, and the decision was taken to put fire to the oldest of them, the *Concepción*. The men on the *Trinidad* and *Victoria* stared silently at the burning ship. Gaspar de Quesada had once been its captair and he had been executed for his part in the conspiracy so merciless' stamped out in San Julián. Was it an accident that the *Concepción* too !

to go down, or had the arm of the Admiral reached out once more from the beyond? When the burning pitch of the caulking poured bloodily into the sea, ghastly memories were conjured up, and no one on board could find sleep that night.

The *Concepción* sank before the island of Bohol in the Philippines, some four days' journey away from the Moluccas. But instead of sailing to the south-west the Spaniards cruised about aimlessly. Soon they were faced by the old enemy: hunger, and finally they reached the point when they thought that their end had come. They dropped anchor off an unknown island that had suddenly appeared. Both crew and officers intended to land there to await death with stoic, Spanish grandeur.

Juan Campos, an ordinary rifleman, jumped into a boat and rowed ashore to return a few hours later, his boat packed to the brim with provisions. A good-natured chieftain had given him the most necessary foodstuffs. He even gave the Spaniards a pilot to guide them to Borneo. After a few days' rest, they sailed on and, towards the end of June, they arrived in the harbour of Brunei on Borneo which was already in the Portuguese sphere of influence.

Pigafetta tells us that they were received with a sumptuous banquet. Thirty different dishes were placed before them by the Sultan and the rice-wine, a drink as clear as water which the natives called arrack, was flowing in streams. But despite the friendly reception the Spaniards remained on their guard, for when the Sultan of Brunei's navy next day tried to approach the ships of the Spaniards, it was welcomed with a salute of fire. The gun ports were opened and the cannons poured a hail of lead and stones down on the natives. The Spaniards thought it best to leave this treacherous place as quickly as possible, and in order not to waste any time, they hacked through the ropes and left the anchors behind.

Terrible weeks followed. The Spaniards drifted up and down between the islands. Once again hunger was to descend upon them. Since they did not dare to land, thay attacked all junks they encountered, robbing them of provisions, spices, gold and men. One of the captured Malays came from Ternate. He knew the route there and told that Francisco Serrão, Magellán's old friend and comrade, had died in the meantime. The Spaniards forced him to become their pilot. On the 6th November 1521, five mountainous islands crowned by volcanoes were sighted. The expedition had reached its goal: the Moluccas!

This is how Pigafetta described the delights of these islands:

> Cloves, sago, ginger, coconuts, rice, almonds, bananas, sweet and sour pomegranates, sugar-cane, nut and sesame-oil, cucumbers, pumpkins and pineapples—an extraordinarily refreshing fruit about the size of our water melons—could be found here, as well as a peachlike fruit called guava, and many other edible plants. Furthermore there were goats and poultry in abundance, and honey, gathered by bees the size

of ants in hollow trees, was plentiful. White and coloured parrots flocked in the trees; the red ones were most sought after, not because they were edible, as one might have supposed, but because they were the quickest to learn to speak.

These were not the only things that interested our reporter. He listed in detail the price of fabrics and utensils, and of an abundance of other articles including gold and jewels.

Furthermore, for each island he gave the exact geographical position and the best course to approach it, and his information was to be of great value to the cartographers of his time. Pigafetta also commented about the women of the Moluccas; contrary to all later European experience he denied them any beauty and declared, moreover, that the men were so jealous that it seemed 'that they were possessed by the devil'. Reading between the lines, the reader might well conclude that our reporter had received a telling rebuff, which, in fact, turned out to be for the best, since later on he stated that on all these islands 'the venereal plague was more widespread than anywhere else in the world'. This was due to the 'lechery which these poor heathens practise'. But in addition to rich foods, parrots and ugly women, there was a whole host of other remarkable things: for example, a tree whose leaves, as soon as they fell to the ground, began to crawl as if they were alive. Pigafetta relates quite seriously:

> On each side of the leaf they have some sort of organs, which look like two short pointed feet, yet if they are cut off, neither blood nor sap drips from the wound. I preserved one of these leaves in a bowl for eight days; but when I tried to touch it, it began to run about in the bowl. I fail to understand what these leaves live on. I assume it is on air. Similarly there are certain birds, which according to the description of the natives, are much like our own jackdaws. These birds fly out to sea where they are swallowed alive by whales. Once inside the stomach of the whale, the bird attacks the heart of the fish and begins to consume it. Naturally the whale dies and is carried ashore by the wind and waves, and is then cut open by the Indians. They discover the bird alive, still busily swallowing the heart of the whale.

He shows more sense when he says that the Portuguese had deliberately invented the legend 'that here the sea was so shallow and the darkness and fog so impenetrable that sailing was impossible', because it was a way of 'keeping other people away' from the Moluccas.

On the whole, however, Pigafetta repeats everything he is told without showing the suspicion of a doubt. The magic of the tropics had made him only too willing to believe in even the most incredible things, though, now and again, he states that he considers the natives' stories as fairy-tales. He did not believe when they told him that not far to the north of these regions, in the Bay of China, there were birds large enough to carry off grown men and even the largest of animals, or that on one of the small Molucca islands there lived dwarfs hardly two feet high, yet whose ears were so big that they could comfortably lie down on one while covering themselves with the other. In contrast to his normal gullibility, he found it difficult to believe that in Java widows were burnt alive.

Thus his diary is a mixture of truth and falsehood: a judgement which we can apply equally well to travel stories of our own day. The fictitious parts need not detract too much from the value of the whole, provided only they are colourful and entertaining and provided the author is careful to arrive at the truth in the body of his report. How difficult it is to maintain one's balance when writing about the tropics, is known by all who have been there. We cannot blame Pigafetta; his diary is one of the most readable of travel reports. He considered the main importance of a travel report to lie in the descriptions of people and social conditions of the countries he visited. We get a clear impression that when he was giving information of a political or mercantile nature, he was merely fulfilling a task which did not interest him greatly. It is unfortunate that we have not the space here to include additional lengthy quotations from his diary; but these passages may perhaps serve to give a taste of the natural narrative talents of this 'roving reporter' as we would call him today.

Their visit to the Moluccas was on the whole successful. They achieved their objective of trading profitably, and the *Victoria* and the *Trinidad* were soon filled to the hatches with precious spices. In the end the sailors removed even their trousers, shirts and coats in order to acquire as much treasure as possible, and on the 21st December 1521, St. Thomas's Day, the homeward journey began.

The return voyage, like that from Spain to South America, did not take place under a lucky star. The *Trinidad* began to leak and the *Victoria* left her behind for repair. Later the crew of the *Trinidad* tried to return to Spain through the Strait of Magellán, but they were delayed so much by storms that in the end they had to abandon the idea and make for the west again. All the men on board, from the captain down to the last cabin-boy, were so completely exhausted from their exertions that the Portuguese had little difficulty in capturing Magellán's former flagship. In order to demoralize the desperately sick crew even further, the Portuguese interned them in the most unhealthy harbour place possible. Only three or four of them managed to reach Spain many years later. This too can be ascribed to the mockery of Fate, for the commander of the *Trinidad* was Magellán's former armaments officer, Gómez de Espinosa, one of the few who had remained faithful to the Admiral in the fatal hours in San Julián. It was his dagger that had been plunged between the ribs of Luis de Mendoza, the rebellious captain of the *Victoria.* Now he himself had become captain of the flagship, and she was dragging him down with her. The other captain, however, the rebellious Basque Sebastián del Cano, had merely been a simple sailor, and this fact had saved his life. Now he was standing on the bridge, captain of the *Victoria.* Destiny, instead of destroying him for doubting of the possibility of sailing round the world, covered him with the full glory that, by right, belonged to Magellán. *Primus cirumdedisti me*! is the motto inscribed over the globe of the world, which Charles V ordered to be set into del Cano's coat of arms, and not into the real hero's. However it must not be thought that the *Victoria* had had an easy time of it. Its captain must surely have been a good second to Magellán in hardness and toughness. After three and a half months the ship reached the Cape of Good Hope. The supplies were either completely finished or completely rotten. The sick begged to be set ashore in Mozambique, but as that was a Portuguese settlement, del Cano refused. Pigafetta noted:

> Since most sailors valued their honour more than their life, we decided to risk everything in returning to Spain, no matter what dangers might befall us.

That the *Victoria* finally struggled back to Spain was entirely due to the courage of its captain. Forty-seven white men and thirteen natives had started the voyage to Spain on his ship: only fifteen Europeans and three natives were to reach the goal. All the others had died and, in accordance with the custom, their bodies were committed to the deep. Pigafetta relates the following particular:

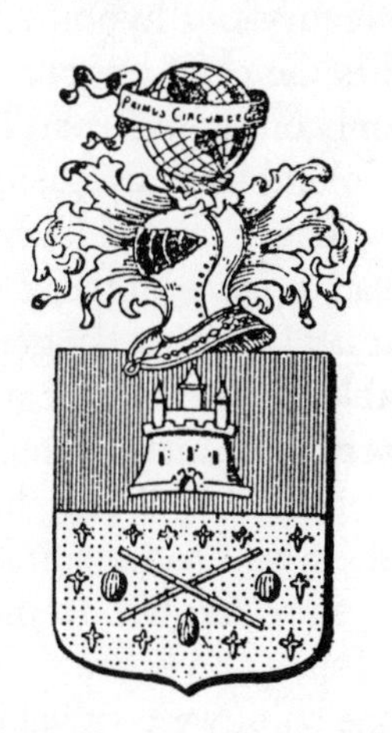

13. Juan Sebastian del Cano's coat of arms.

> The bodies of Christians went down with their faces upwards, while the Indians sank with their faces averted. If God in his mercy had not finally granted us favourable weather we should all have perished of hunger.

On the 6th September 1522, almost three years after the departure of the fleet, the *Victoria*, more a wreck than a ship, finally arrived at the coast of Spain. The survivors of this first voyage around the world went barefooted to the nearest holy shrine to give thanks for their happy salvation. Their mood however was not happy. The losses had been too terrible, the memories of the horrors they had suffered during the voyage too gruesome. To cap it all, they were shaken by one seemingly inexplicable fact. According to their most reliable logbook, they had landed on the 6th December, but to the whole of Spain and the rest of the Christian world, it was the 7th. God seemed to have been so incensed by these impudent voyagers that he had struck out a whole day from their lives. To make matters worse it was quickly realized that all feast days had been celebrated wrongly during the voyage, and that none of the holy commands of the Christian religion, such as not to eat meat on Friday, and to keep the Sabbath as a day of rest, had been observed.

Only weeks later, after diligent astronomical studies, did Pigafetta manage to find the solution to that riddle which the Arabs had already answered two hundred years earlier. When one sails round the earth towards the east, the sun rises four minutes earlier with each new degree of longitude. Three hundred and sixty degrees of longitude means a total of 1,440 minutes, or a whole day. If, on the other hand, one sails towards the west, the sun rises four minutes later with each degree of longitude so that after circumnavigating the world a whole day is lost. This proved the century-old hypothesis that the earth was spherical, and perhaps therein lies the chief importance of Magellán's expedition. In this respect, it has only one counterpart in the whole history of the conquest of earth by man: Columbus's voyage to America.

Magellán's achievement proved to be of little other value. It is true he had discovered the southern passage through the American continent, but it lay in such a dangerous zone that its value for sea-traffic was questionable. The need for a sea-route across America in the middle latitudes remained unanswered and was to remain so until the building of the Panama Canal four hundred years later. Magellán's circumnavigation of the world had a quite different significance from the point of view of the Spanish Crown. In the first place, it appeared that the six hundredweight of spices on board the *Victoria*, despite the losses caused by water entering the hold, were valuable enough to cover all costs. Furthermore, Magellán had brought incontrovertible proof that the Moluccas lay in that part of the earth which Papal decree had adjudged to Spain. Thus the economic monopoly of the Portuguese was broken and the daring voyage of a single man marked the beginning of a new chapter in the history of the world. The period of Spanish hegemony had started.

PART THREE

THE WHITE GODS CONQUER MEXICO

Of the weakness of numbers · Of dragons that can neigh · Quetzalcoatl, the 'White Saviour' · The Cross as the religious symbol of the Indians · Baptism, Confession and Holy Communion in Aztec Lands · Montezuma's address from the throne · Cortés falls off the wall of a young ladies' boarding school · Marriage or gaol · Doña Marina, Princess and Saint · The 'Votan' legend of the Mayas · Science says 'No' · Do 'solar' gods have fair hair and blue eyes? · The dogma of 'Convergence' · Short discourse on wheeled toys and ancient Indian highways · Of the cotton chromosomes · Of women, gold and other trifles · Of the usefulness of Latin for committing arson · Of man-eating gods · The conquest of Popocatepetl · Entry into Tenochtitlan · Chocolatl, tobacco and other sights in the great city · Albrecht Dürer pronounces on Mexican art · Of the tribute exacted by the Aztec occupational power, and of the 'Fifth Column' · The floating gardens of Itztapalapan · The Babylonian turrets, and the temples of Mexico · Secret incursion into the Emperor's treasury · Cortés pulls a fast one on his men, and Montezuma is captured · Riot in Tenochtitlan · The Emperor's death, the mass rising and the 'noche triste' · The strange prophecy of Crossbowman Botello · The mountain-fleet of the Spaniards · Cortés's articles of war · Siege and conquest of Tenochtitlan · The treasure is gone · Of Mexico City's descent to hell, and of the results of miscegenation · Expedition to the Pacific · Where is the passage? · Cortés's death.

I

IT was unbearably hot, and yet the calendar only read the 25th March 1519. At home in Spain, spring would now be in full blossom; the trees, the meadows and the fields decked with flowers and fresh leaves, and gentle breezes would be blowing from the mountains across the fertile plains.

Here it was like an oven. The sun, like a disc of molten lead, seemed to bear down on the earth from the dusty sky. The outlines of the land were distorted by currents of hot air rising from the scorching sand and from the mangrove swamps. The eleven ships of Hernando Cortés were at anchor in the mouth of the Tabasco, known today by the name of the Grijalva River in the Bay of Campeche, only a few degrees north of the Equator and always hot and feverish.

The monotonous rumble of drums could be heard from inland, penetrating in some mysterious way the thickly-matted jungle. The rolls on the drums were punctuated by shrill yells that seemed to issue from the throats of some strange beings, suffering the torments of hell. The Spaniards were to learn that these sounds were produced by conch shells which the Indians used like trumpets when their armies were advancing to battle.

Hernando Cortés was at the head of six hundred and sixty-three intrepid adventurers. They had come to these foreign shores to seek their fortune, but as they slipped on their thickly padded buff-coats and chain-mail, protection against the enemy's arrows, and tightened the straps of their helmets, they knew they would have to give battle and wondered whether it was worth it after all. They had a premonition that the New World would prove difficult to conquer, and they were right.

They were facing ten thousand disciplined Indian fighters, who not only scorned death but even sought it gladly. Yet, although the Spaniards were hopelessly outnumbered, other factors were operating on their side which were to turn the scales in their favour.

Since horses were unknown in America, the Indians obviously had no cavalry. The natives of Haiti and the Antilles had simply gaped when the strangers had jumped on their horses and had started to gallop, but here in Yucatan, when the sixteen mounted troopers which formed Cortés's cavalry came thundering along, the harness on the horses glittering and jingling, their lances at the ready, the Indians were filled with horror. They thought that horse and rider were one being, a kind of centaur. (When Pizarro landed in Peru, some years later, the natives believed exactly the same thing about *his* cavalry.) And when one of the riders fell from his horse, the *indios* were convinced that this strange being had split into two. Why were they subject to this hysterical fear, which had not occurred elsewhere?

Gunpowder, too, was unknown to the Indians, and naturally they had never seen cannons or muskets. They were seized by wild panic when their best fighters were mown down, row after row, by the inexplicable thunder and lightning coming from so far away. Despite all this, it is difficult to explain the fact that the Spaniards were victorious at the first skirmish, and that they later managed to conquer a state that was larger and richer than Spain. The reasons for this were largely irrational, and although most of them have been lost with time, we are certain of two: one was called Quetzalcoatl and was a god; the other was called Marina and was a very beautiful, clever and lovable woman.

14. *Quetzalcoatl—from the Codex Magliabecchiano in Florence.*

From the reports of Columbus, we know that a strange legend was told and believed along the eastern shore of the new continent. Once upon a time, the legend went, a host of white gods had come across the ocean from the East. It was not known where they had come from or what became of them, but in 1492, when the Spaniards landed on the Antilles, they were received and hailed as 'white gods'. And later Magellán reported from the southernmost point of the New World that, there too, he and his crew had been taken for gods. So far the belief had remained little more than a myth to which only lip-service was paid, but when Cortés started on his campaign of conquest, it was soon obvious that the Aztecs still revered the leader of that host of unknown white strangers. They spoke of him as a fair, blue-eyed and bearded god, and had called him Quetzalcoatl, after the glowing plumage of the quetzal bird. Cortés was told that a few centuries before—it has since been discovered that it must have been during the eleventh or twelfth centuries—this stranger had suddenly appeared in Mexico from the wide regions of the East. He appeared clad in a garment of coarse black cloth, with a round neckline; his cloak had short broad sleeves and hung open in front. Cortés did not recognize the description: it did not resemble a priest's cassock such as he was familiar with, but such a style of dress had existed in early Europe and was worn as late as the sixteenth century in the part of Greenland settled by the Vikings.

Cortés was very surprised and greatly affected to learn from the *indios* that this unknown god had proclaimed a new religion and new moral laws.

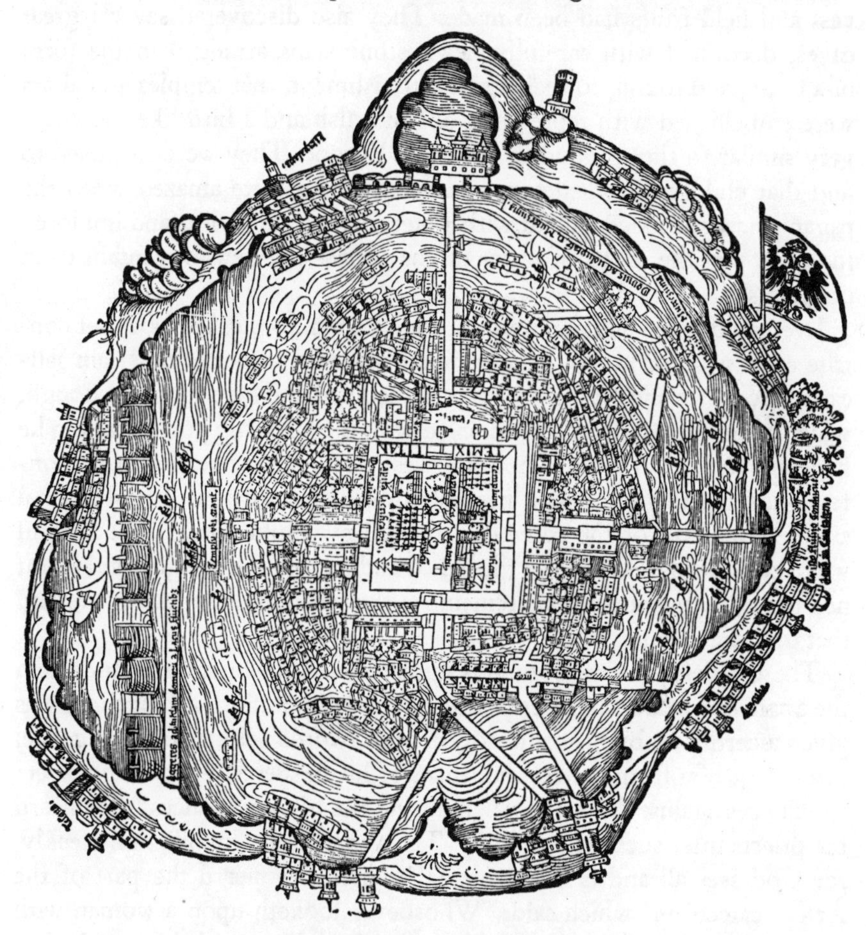

15. *Town plan of Mexico.*

He had apparently been gracious and kind, enlightened and of great wisdom. Whenever there had been talk of war, he had stopped up his ears, because he hated bloodshed and violence so strongly. For a long time the Indians had remained faithful to Quetzalcoatl, 'the god through whom we live, the all-present, the invisible, the only god of complete perfection and purity'. Even now, no other offerings than flowers and fruit were made to him on the huge pyramid temple of Cholula, where stood his altar under the sign of the Cross, while the war god Huitzilopochtli demanded living beings for sacrifice. Their forefathers, however, had risen up in rebellion against Quetzalcoatl and he had fled East before the bloody deeds of

Huitzilopochtli, from Tabasco across the infinite ocean into Tlapallan, the land of dreams; but before leaving he had prophesied that his angry white brothers would one day return to Mexico to conquer the land.

A little later the Spaniards found stone crosses at which offerings of harvest and field fruits had been made. They also discovered several great caves, decorated with carefully hewn stone slabs arranged in the form of a cross, and found, to their great astonishment, that temples and altars were embellished with representations of a fish and a bird like the dove, very similar to those found in Christian Europe. They were surprised to find that children in Mexico were baptized, and were amazed when the pagan priest sprinkled a child with water, moistened its lips and implored the gods that the drops of water might cleanse the newborn infant from original sin.

Even confession and communion were known to the Aztecs. After contrite confession of his sins, the penitent was told to perform certain self-castigation rites and was then declared absolved and given idols of dough, which he ate and so became reconciled with the heavenly powers whom he had offended. 'Oh God, Thou knowest', ran the Aztec prayer of confession, 'that this poor man has failed, not wantonly but from original sin.' At the end of the ceremony the priest would dismiss the faithful with these words: 'Clothe ye the naked and feed ye the hungry, and count not the cost to yourselves. Remember that their flesh is like yours and that they are men like you.'

These beliefs presented obvious similarities with Christianity, and when the Spaniards heard that after penitence and communion each penitent was given a certificate by his confessor, in other words a Letter of Indulgence, protecting him from the consequences of his misdeeds, even with respect to offences against the State; when during the 'divine services' they heard the priests utter such sentences as: 'Thou shalt suffer humiliation meekly, for God sees all and is thy avenger!' when they heard the part of the Aztec 'catechism' which said: 'Whosoever looketh upon a woman with too much curiosity has already committed adultery with his eyes', then they could no longer avoid the conclusion that the *indios* must believe them to be the successors of an unknown Christian saint and missionary, who had somehow come to the New World.

Almost at the same time that Cortés realized this, a meeting was being held at the Court of Montezuma II, the last of the Aztec Emperors. He had summoned all his dignitaries, both spiritual and secular, and the heads of all the noble families in his realm to his gigantic residence, whose supporting pillars rose out of a lake. Bluntly he informed them of what his spies had discovered about the strange foreigners who had recently approached the shore of Mexico in large 'floating houses', whose glittering sails gave them the appearance of great swans.

The Aztec leaders were deeply impressed. Only recently had their poets sung the following lines which had instantly achieved great popularity:

> Alas! Woe the unhappy times!
> Our country's doom is sealed.
> The starlight is spent
> And the fair city of flowers and wisdom
> Will perish.

Then the spies' report was read to the assembled company of lords, barons, generals and priests, who all knew the traditional sayings predicting the return of Quetzalcoatl in the year One Reed and, since according to the Aztec calendar with its period of fifty-two years, the year One Reed had just returned, they were all depressed, dejected and full of evil premonitions. They knew only too well that the Emperor's spy service was utterly reliable and that the accuracy of its reports was unquestionable. The spies had submitted drawings to bear out their reports, skilfully depicting the foreigners' ships with their gleaming white sails, and also the strange four-footed dragon gods used by the enemy. The spies had also shown the long pipes with their round, threatening mouths which spewed forth lightning that could kill at a great distance, the glittering cuirasses, the ominously lowered visors, the lances, crossbows and swords: in short, these sketches performed the same task that was to be fulfilled five hundred years later by television, of making distant things, so to speak, present.

At last the Emperor's spokesmen stood up. Montezuma II, who had ascended to the throne seventeen years before, in 1502, wished the following to be known:

'Beloved brethren! Dear friends! You all know that our forefathers did not come from this land in which we dwell, but that they were led to this country by some mighty prince from far distant shores. This prince left this country, accompanied by a few of his followers, but returned after an interval to find that our ancestors, his subjects, had built new cities, had taken unto themselves wives from among the daughters of this land and had made their homes in this country. Therefore they had no wish to leave their homes and their new country and return with him, and since they no longer wanted him as their lord, he departed unattended, declaring that he would yield for the time being, but would return one day with a great host, or would send another in his place, to claim his due. You all know that we have long awaited him. From all that we have just heard of the foreign general and of the emperor on whose orders he has crossed the sea to find us, coming from his own land where the sun rises and where the prince of our ancestors had once returned, I am persuaded that he is the great lord whom we have awaited, especially as he let it be known that he himself has always known about us. Though our forefathers rejected and denied their lord, we wish to honour him and give praise and thanks to the gods, that at long last he, whom we have so long awaited, has appeared. Thus I pray you to respect him as our own hereditary lord. . . .'

Cortés naturally knew nothing of this meeting. He was just an ordinary Spanish nobleman bent on conquest and developing trade with foreign lands. He was thirty-four years old and most of his life had been filled with daring escapades, amorous intrigues, and other diversions befitting a knight. He came of an excellent family, owning a small landed estate near Medellín in the district of Estremadura, which was quite sufficient for their needs. His father, Martín Cortés de Monroy, had been a captain in the infantry and would often tell of his experiences to the family gathered around the fireplace.

At first, Martín Cortés had little hope that his son would follow in his footsteps. He was a delicate child who seemed to be better fitted for the rôle of priest or courtier. When on his seventeenth birthday Hernando Cortés asked his father's permission to become a soldier, Captain Martín Cortés was both surprised and relieved. He had not seen his son since that day, three years earlier, when he had sent him to a College in Salamanca in the hope that they would make a good lawyer of him. Now the boy stood before him: a head taller than himself, broad as a tree-trunk, slim in the hips like a blade from Toledo; in short, the very picture of a man. True, Hernando's account of himself was somewhat less satisfactory. He knew Latin fairly well, his prose style was adequate, and he could manage to string verses together, but it seemed that he had learnt very little else, and his academic record consisted mainly of pranks and escapades.

Thus Martín Cortés welcomed his son's wish to become a soldier and his son did not let him down. It seems that Hernando Cortés took to his new vocation from the start; in addition to acquiring the necessary skills of riding, fencing and shooting, he studied the history of Rome and the art of war and generalship. When Columbus started on his fourth voyage to America in 1502, Hernando Cortés was honoured by being asked to accompany the expedition. This was what he had been longing for, but in this hour when fortune seemed to smile on him, Cortés experienced the fickleness of this classic turncoat: a few days before the departure of the fleet he slipped off the garden wall of the most fashionable boarding school for young ladies of noble birth in Madrid, where he was having a most gallant affair. Thus, when Columbus weighed anchor, he was in hospital with a thickly-bandaged broken leg.

It was only two years later, in 1504, that the young man, now nineteen years old, managed to get 'across' to the other side. For seven years he led the life of a *hacendado*, then, in 1511, he became private secretary to Don Diego de Velásquez who, during Columbus's second expedition (1493–1496) had acquired a considerable fortune in Haiti and had later been appointed Governor of Cuba. Since Cortés was an excellent soldier, Velásquez overlooked many of his faults. But when his private secretary seduced the beautiful Doña Catalina Suárez, one of the four daughters of Don Diego Suárez, Velásquez exploded. He had his young colleague locked up in prison and only let him out when Cortés agreed to go to the altar with Doña Catalina.

Now as Cortés was standing on the quarterdeck of his flagship, the *Capitana*, he felt well pleased with himself. As he looked back over his past life he could feel that not a single hour had been empty or wasted. True the last years spent as a Cuban *hacendado*, in charge of a large farm and as councillor of the small town of Baracoa, had been a little boring, but that was now past history as he had been fortunate enough to escape from it. When Velásquez first heard the rumours that there was land west of Cuba, and when the first expeditions returned bringing confirmation of them, Don Diego remembered the restless gallant who had once been his secretary. He quickly appointed him chief of the new expedition which was to explore the unknown shores and to bring back as much gold as possible.

It is most probable that, until the evening after the battle on the Tabasco, Hernando Cortés had envisaged no other future for himself. It was then that an unexpected turn of events was to force the leader of the enterprise out of his complacency into the limelight of history. History used as her agent a quite unknown Indian woman who, flashing like a meteor into the annals of history, at the point when two very different cultures were meeting in head-on collision, was later to disappear into obscurity just as abruptly.

Twenty young girls and women had been sent by the chieftains of Tabasco and the neighbouring regions with friendly greetings to the victorious foreign general. Experience had taught that this was the surest way of pacifying even the wildest of men. If only Quetzalcoatl, the 'God of the temperate air', might grant that the violent young foreigner might also become more temperate through this gift! This prayer was granted. A few days later the sails were furled on the ships of the white gods, and soon the swans' wings disappeared below the horizon. The chiefs rubbed their hands with relief; they had been right again. In their gratitude Quetzalcoatl was given a particularly beautiful offering.

The wise priests, however, were wrong for, on the contrary, by means of their gift they turned an ordinary young Spanish nobleman into a conqueror who was going to unhinge their world.

When Cortés examined the young ladies who were sent on board his ship, he noticed, amongst the shy, tearful Indian women, a light-brown, commanding young girl who seemed to come from different stock. The interpreter soon learned that, unlike her companions, she was a mere slave and that she was not from Yucatan but from Mexico where her father had been prince of the province of Coatzalcualco, on the south-eastern borders of the Mexican empire, and also general of the Mexican army in Painalla, the capital of the district. Her name, it appeared, was Malitzin Tenepal.

When, fifty years later, the knight Bernal Díaz del Castillo, *regidor* of the city of Guatemala in Nova Hispania and an old friend and comrade-in-arms of Hernando Cortés, wrote his memoirs, he had this to say about that strange brown girl: 'She was a noble lady, used to ruling land and people and this could plainly be seen. . . .' This observation must stand to Bernal Díaz's credit. Although himself of humble origin, he could recognize true nobility, and had been impressed by the strange slave-girl. We may safely conclude that Hernando Cortés himself could not have failed to be deeply touched by her.

The day after their arrival on board the twenty Indian women were baptized by the priest, Bartolomeo de Olmedo. Bernal Díaz tells us that 'with the help of the interpreter, Bartolomeo de Olmedo delivered a sermon in which he told them of the glories of our holy religion and of the evil of their own idolatry. The woman of whom I have already spoken was christened Marina.' Thus the beautiful young Indian girl, who was to become Cortés's partner in life for six decisive years, became known to posterity as Doña Marina. Bernal Díaz is the main source of our information concerning her. She had been sold into slavery after her father's death and her mother's almost immediate remarriage, and had thus reached the Court of the Prince of Tabasco. There she had learnt the Maya dialect, so that she could speak it as fluently as her Aztec mother tongue. This fact must have drawn Cortés's attention to the young girl. He could make himself understood to the Mayas through interpreters, but the strange Aztec sounds, which could now and then be heard here on the borders of the Mexican empire, had defeated all efforts at comprehension. Hence Marina now had an important rôle to play, and she must have done more than merely interpret. She gave Cortés information concerning the nature of Aztec government. She confirmed and explained the mysterious stories about El Dorado, and spoke of the tense relations that existed between the Aztecs and their allies in Cempoalla, Tlaxcala, Texcoco and Cholula. Cortés was later able to exploit these rifts in the Aztec alliance of states, and so conquer a whole empire.

This might smack of hatred and treason, of revenge and resentment, but such could hardly have been the case. Obviously Marina must have loved Hernando Cortés deeply, and since she had grown up in a theocratic world, she must *perforce* have looked upon the Conquistadors as God's ambassadors and upon their enterprise as a kind of crusade. In any case she believed firmly in the missionary ideal of the conquest, and became a sincere Christian. It seems that, despite all their faults, the rule of the returning white gods would be more beneficial to her people than the rule of Huitzilopochtli and his priests. So convinced of this was she, that in 1525 she went, accompanied by Cortés, to Coatzalcualco to visit her mother. The princess was terrified when she finally recognized her daughter, for she thought she would now be called to account for her former inhuman behaviour, and both Spaniards and Indians were fully of the opinion that she had deserved whatever punishment she would receive. Marina, contrary to all expectation, went up to her mother and embraced her tenderly. Then she turned to the crowd and said in accents poignant with emotion: 'My mother did not know what she was doing when she sold me. Since that time I have been instructed in the Christian faith and am infinitely happier than I have ever been!' This scene of reunion and love was so moving, and touched the hearts of all so deeply, that even fifty years later Bernal Díaz, the tough, mercenary soldier still swore: 'Y todo esto que dijo, se lo oí muy certificamente y se lo juro, amén!'

Marina acted as translator for her own people, just as she had done for the Spaniards, and again added her own wise comments and explanations. Although she often had to admit failure, she tried invariably to alleviate unnecessary severity, to see that justice was administered fairly, to prevent senseless cruelty, and there is no doubt that she saved much of Mexico. This position of mediator between the two peoples gave her enormous influence and, two generations later, Bernal Díaz del Castillo had to confess: 'Her power in New Spain was very great. She could bend the Indians fully to her will and thus she was of the greatest importance to us, for only through her influence, and with the help of God, could many things be managed. Without her, we should never have been able to understand the Mexican tongue and we should never have accomplished as much as we did.'

The *indios* seem to have respected her more than even the Mother of God, whose image the Spaniards took everywhere with them, placing it on all their altars. When that lovely young woman herself bore a child, who was called Martín Cortés, she became, and has ever remained, an object of almost religious veneration for her compatriots. The mercenaries, buccaneers and pirates of Cortés's army, great noblemen and simple soldiers from the common people, paid the foreign woman due reverence by giving her the noble Spanish title of Doña and calling her Doña Marina.

But what of Cortés himself? The Aztec woman is mentioned but once in his letters as 'another interpreter who is in my train'. This may sound extremely petty and ungrateful, but he had named her child after his own father, thus setting a great precedent. While it was later to become quite fashionable for members of the high Spanish nobility to marry Aztec princesses (today there is a Spanish family boasting the Emperor Montezuma among its forebears) there could be no question of such a union for

Cortés, particularly since Marina was rightly considered to be booty and a slave-girl, and by no means the princess she really was. But nevertheless, when Cortés accepted the son she had given him into his family by calling him after his own father, he showed her great honour, and we must therefore conclude that he esteemed and greatly loved his dark-skinned mistress.

Marina had risen from obscurity on to the stage of history, and after a brief period of fame she returned into oblivion. In 1525 she was married to a Castilian knight, Juan Xamarillo, and Cortés heaped valuable presents on the couple; the deeds of that marriage are still preserved, but after this date we have no further information concerning Marina.

History pulled down the curtain on her but even today she is still remembered in the folklore and songs of the *indios* for her love and self-sacrifice. The songs and ballads about her preserve the gentle radiance and calm that once emanated from her. The miracle of her appearance on the scene of history, just when the fate of two colliding worlds was placed in her hands, is unforgotten.

2

It is very doubtful whether Marina continued to look upon Cortés as the reincarnation of Quetzalcoatl. Yet she must have believed that the cruasading idea of the Conquistadors was in keeping with the spirit of that religious teacher. Thus one may well assume that she told her beloved Cortés about Quetzalcoatl, and that, quite apart from Aztec traditions, she probably told him about the folklore of the Mayas, which has since become famous as the 'Votan'-legend of the natives of Yucatan. This legend, which, to quote the German Americanist Hans-Dietrich Disselhoff, is considered by orthodox investigators to be nothing but 'a modern fable based on fancy', states that once upon a time tall, fair-haired, blue-eyed men had landed from great ships, which had glistened like the scales of a serpent's skin and, when these ships had approached the shore, it was as if huge, sparkling snakes were crawling across the sea. These unknown men wore strange clothes and had ornaments resembling coiled serpents around their foreheads. Now, the Holy Serpent had been one of the most ancient godheads revered by the Mayas of Yucatan. When these fair-skinned serpent-crowned beings arrived in their glistening-scaly ships, it was generally believed that the foreigners were sons of the Holy Serpent and were gods themselves. These 'White Gods' had later settled in Yucatan, but the noblest among them had gone on to neighbouring Mexico.

This 'Votan' legend of the Yucatan *indios* is probably based on the fact that the weather-god of one of their tribes had long been known as Votan. Historians, basing their hypotheses on the assumption that the Mayas had migrated from the jungles of Guatemala to their new home in Yucatan, only in the year A.D. 1000, have stated that the origins of this strange legend can be dated fairly accurately, but the appearance of the legend coincides rather significantly with the time when the Vikings from Greenland discovered America, and colonized part of the shore of Massachusetts. More recent research tends to prove that the date A.D. 1000 can no longer be considered acceptable, and that the Mayas probably migrated to Yucatan as early as the fifth and sixth centuries A.D.

In her recent book, entitled *Lost Worlds*, the American writer Ann Terry White has some interesting remarks to make concerning the 'Votan' legend. Her descriptions of the landing of the god are highly reminiscent of the traditional dragon-prowed ships of the Vikings, lined with the embossed shields of the crew, which in the sun would make the ships sparkle like scaly reptiles.

All this could hardly have been of any importance to Cortés, who certainly knew nothing of the Vikings and was not likely to have been especially interested in the fact that white men had reached the shores of the New World as early as five hundred years before him. But it is all the more interesting for us today since it has long been asserted, even by recent historians, that the whole Quetzalcoatl tradition is nothing but a Christian embellishment of ancient Indian sagas, nothing but 'the invention of the white man who cannot bear to be left out of anything', as Hans-Dietrich Disselhoff puts it in his very instructive work on ancient American cultures. Now it seems to be an established fact that in the original Indian sagas, which were current long before the appearance of the Aztecs, Quetzalcoatl was *not* described as a white god. Apparently this embellishment was added later on, and thus we may well suspect that the myth of Quetzalcoatl was nothing but propaganda on the part of the Conquistadors, for the sole purpose of facilitating their seizure of power in Mexico.

But is this rather cynical interpretation really justified? Why did not those Spaniards, who soon after the conquest of the Aztec Empire began to record the sagas and religions of this exotic country, in fact describe the 'White Saviour' as they themselves undoubtedly imagined him to be, i.e. with dark hair and brown eyes? When a conquering power, superior in arms and civilization, wishes to impose its religion on subjected peoples, then the god or gods of this religion will invariably be conceived in the conqueror's own image. This, however, the Spaniards did not do, seeing that Quetzalcoatl was no olive-skinned, dark-eyed and dark-haired replica of the Conquistadors, but quite the opposite, having fair hair and blue eyes. Were not the conquered people of the New World bound to have said: 'You Spaniards look quite different from our "God of Light", in whose name you have come and in whose name we have received you. You cannot possibly be his sons!'?

If we assume that the myth of Quetzalcoatl was the invention of the Spaniards, then we can only say that they proceeded in the most stupidly clumsy manner possible. Their 'invention' was so badly thought out that its inner contradiction must perforce have moved the Indians to disbelief. Obviously the assumption that the myth of the white gods had been inserted into the folk-lore of the New World from motives of Christian zeal is untenable. Once this rather obvious conclusion is admitted, then it follows that the legend of the White Saviour must have been Indian in origin, and that white men did in fact reach Yucatan and Mexico some time during the Middle Ages, and that possibly they were Vikings sailing to America.

We have dwelt on this subject at such length in order to arrive at those results which expert investigators have discovered in the last decades from logical arguments. To sum up these results: it is unquestionable that some form of contact between the Old and the New Worlds had taken place at an early date in the Christian era, though we have very little evidence to prove this conclusion outright.

It must, in all fairness, be stated that most contemporary historians, specializing in this period, reject such hypotheses out of hand, just as they once derided the Catholic investigator, Carl Maria Kaufmann, who, some thirty years ago, was the first to deal with these strange events in his book *Amerika und das Urchristentum*. The Americanist, Walter Krickeberg, may be taken as representative of this attitude:

> The striking parallels with Christian beliefs, found in the American sagas, belong to the common fund of myths inherited by the cultures of the Old and New Worlds. Such parallels exist in other spheres as well, and their explanation must be left to future investigations.

Thus these historians do not really believe in the possibility that direct cultural contacts were made, preferring to base their opinions on the traditional concept of *convergence*, a unique similarity between certain cultural phenomena which, as the German ethnologist Hans Plischke has recently stated, is explained by the fact that 'since all humanity has basically the same psychological make-up, it must, when faced by the same phenomena and the same necessities, arrive at the same or a similar solution'.

By adopting this concept we have done nothing but replace one unknown quantity by another, for the concept of 'convergence' is no more than a working hypothesis, an unproved premise based on nothing but the comparatively great diffusion of cultural patterns in the Old World. When we realize (as, for example, through reading such a work as Ruth Benedict's *Patterns of Culture*) what diametrically opposed cultural trends do exist and that fraud, deceit and murder, which since time immemorial have been considered to be morally wrong by the Old World, are elsewhere considered morally acceptable, and that in other cultures power and the worship of power, which we value so highly, are considered to be foolish and ridiculous, then we must perforce be somewhat sceptical as regards the above assertion that all humanity thinks along the same lines.

Americanists, aware that the primitive religions of the Old World also had deified the Sun, Moon and stars, believed that they could apply this knowledge to the New World. While there can be no question that in ancient America stellar gods had played an important rôle, and that the white 'gods' who appeared were taken for the anthropomorphosis of the great miracle of the Sun, as is seen in the myths and legends of many Indian peoples, Americanists have little justification in maintaining that the God of Light, Quetzalcoatl, is of solar origin, and is in fact the personification of the Sun, which rises out of the eastern ocean, travels calmly over the earth to sink in the west, and that the white skin of Quetzalcoatl, his benevolence and gentleness and the offerings of flowers and fruits, are all due to this.

If this were indeed the case, how can we explain his blue eyes, his long beard, the signs of the cross on his clothing, original sin, baptism, confession, communion, his 'clothe ye the naked and feed ye the poor!'?—but our Americanists do not ask such questions. These are part of the 'common fund belonging to the Old World and the New, the explanation of which must be left to future investigators'!

This, to say the least, is a most surprising example of dogmatic faith, and has much in common with the position of the American writer, D. G. Brinton, who in his work *American Hero-Myths*, published in 1882, wrote the following:

> By sight and light we see and learn. Nothing, therefore, is more natural than to attribute to the light-god the early progress in the arts of domestic and social life. Thus light came to be personified as the embodiment of culture and knowledge, of wisdom, and of peace and prosperity which are necessary for the growth of learning. The fair complexion of these heroes is nothing but a reference to the white light of the dawn. Their ample hair and beard are the rays of the sun that flow from his radiant visage. Their loose and large robes typify the enfolding of the firmament by the light and the winds.

This sounds quite reasonable, at least for inhabitants of temperate zones who welcome the Sun as a friend, but of course this attitude does not apply in the case of people living in tropical climates. Moreover the theory is some eighty years old and dates back to a period when serious archaeological research was non-existent in America, i.e. long before the series of magnificent discoveries made at the beginning of our century. These finds of rock-paintings, sculptures, jade carvings, pottery, reliefs on temple walls, coloured drawings and religious books, originating from Mexico and Yucatan, which, without exception, show faces with long, well-groomed beards, proved conclusively that these are no representations of mystical and mythical 'solar' beings but of the most mortal of men. Great numbers of these finds are exhibited in the American Museum of National History in New York, in the Musée de l'Homme in Paris and in the collections of the National Geographical Society in Washington.

Parallel finds were also made in Peru of realistic sculptures, ceramics, etc., showing *men* with long beards beautifully curled and groomed. Brinton's theory that these strange bearded white heroes were derived from

16. Negroid and European faces taken from ancient Indian wall-paintings in Chitzen Itza.

the Sun is far from the truth, and our credulity is strained considerably when it is asserted that coloured people, who had never seen a white man, could, by accident, have gratuitously imagined beards, white skins and fair hair. If this were so, we might well ask where are the 'white gods' of Africa, for such discoveries would have been most appropriate there. Similarly, where in Northern Europe do we find 'black gods' symbolizing the long winter night, whose effect must indeed have been terrifyingly real to the primitive inhabitants of those regions?

Now it might be asserted that these rock carvings, sculptures and reliefs simply depicted bearded people, for bearded men were occasionally found even amongst the Indians and Chinese, and that therefore the theory of their solar origin is unfounded and unnecessary. In this case the natives of those regions are assumed to have singled out, for their statues and paintings, anomalies and surprising deviations from the normal clean-shaven Indian condition.

However, this lame point was refuted by the discoveries made by the Americans, A. Morris, E. H. Morris and J. Charlot, some twenty years ago, in the war temple of Chitzen Itza of Yucatan. They found a number of more or less well-preserved frescoes dating from the tenth or eleventh century A.D., showing a sea-battle between warriors of a dark race and those of a light-skinned, obviously fair race. These frescoes have nothing mythical about them at all, but, on the contrary, they depict scenes of battle, torture, and death on the sacrificial stone so realistically that they can well compare with modern photo-reportage.

It is generally believed that these wall paintings of Chitzen Itza are authentic representations of the battles between the Mayas and the Toltecs,

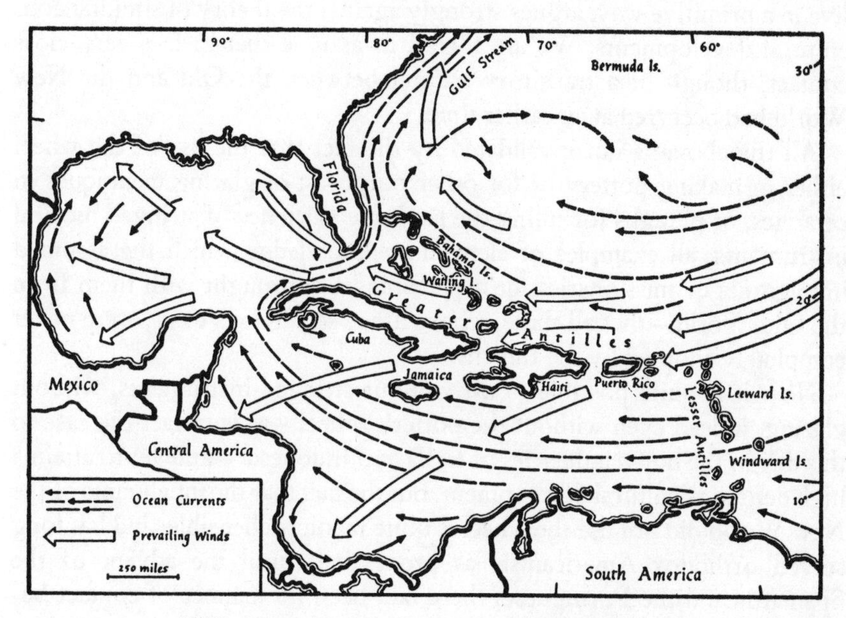

XIX. Winds and currents in the Atlantic Ocean.

the pre-Aztec peoples to whom Quetzalcoatl had originally appeared. We shall refrain from giving our opinion on this point since discussion is still in progress, but we do wish to stress that the many parallels found between the Old and the New World apply almost exclusively to those regions of America which are exposed to the drift of wind and ocean currents from Europe, and that any water-craft, including Alain Bombard's inflatable rubber-dinghy, cannot fail to reach Central America once it is caught up by these currents.

In whatever way we judge and assess the significance of this fact, we must admit that it was more than a strange coincidence which made Cortés land at that point in Central America where culture was most highly developed. Nowhere else did such a well-organized and administered state exist with villages and hamlets, with noblemen, priests and army; in short, a ready-made empire which, once it had passed into Spanish hands, could be ruled just like Europe. The Spaniards accepted all this without much questioning or surprise. They never thought of asking themselves what would have happened had they entered America at the points where the vast northern prairies or the jungles of the Orinoco and Amazon rivers reach the sea. They never realized that here they would have been sucked up like a shower in a desert, and that the success of their enterprise depended on their finding a country whose civilization had developed along similar lines to their own. The fact that they managed to discover such a land, while in the rest of the huge American continent man continued to live in a primitive way, argues strongly against the theory of simultaneous cultural developments. We are forced to assume that in fact very close contact, though of a transitory nature, between the Old and the New World had occurred at an earlier time.

All the above is not invalidated by the fact that the use of the wheel either in making pottery or for other purposes, of glazing techniques in ceramics, of ploughs for tilling the land, the existence of stringed musical instruments, all examples of elementary knowledge which the assumed immigrants or missionaries must perforce have brought with them from the Old World—that all these, whose use is so obvious to us, were never completely adopted by the Indians.

Now it is quite possible to do without stringed instruments, without glazing, indeed even without the potter's wheel—as is in fact the case to this day in the home industries of India and Indonesia—and yet to attain a high degree of cultural development, but the fact that the inhabitants of the New World did not use the wheel is quite incomprehensible, and has long served orthodox Americanists as proof that, until the advent of the Spaniards and the Portuguese, there had been no manner of contact between the two worlds. While it can easily be proved that there was a widespread use of revolving objects such as spindles, drills rotated by a bow, tops, bull-roarers, etc., in the American cultures, and although heavy stones used for building purposes in Peru show the marks of the rounded tree-trunks used for their transportation, the question whether Indian architects habitually used some kind of roller in moving the gigantic slabs with which they built their sacred buildings and castles, has remained unanswered. The solution of this problem is of major importance, for archaeology shows that before inventing the wheel and applying it in the form of vehicles, man first used rollers.

In any event not even the argument of the wheel can be used to prove the absence of any prior contact with the Old World. Some years ago, the American archaeologist, Gordon F. Ekholm, discovered that children's toys on wheels, fabulous little creatures that could be pushed or pulled along, had been known in Central America.

Strangely enough, this knowledge was never applied to transport and industry, though it would have been the obvious thing to do so. True, draught animals were not known in the New World (the horse, for example, was only introduced into America by the Conquistadors), and the idea of training dogs to pull carts, as their Eskimo cousins had done with their sleigh-dogs in Greenland and Canada, might simply not have occurred to the Indians, nor that of harnessing men to pull the royal palanquin along in ceremonial processions. But on the other hand, as Ekholm has pointed out, excellent roads had existed since ancient times. In northern Yucatan, between Cobá and Yaxuna, there exist to this day well-preserved remains of the old Maya road, stretching for more than sixty miles. These roads are fully ten yards wide and, with their excellent surfaces, they are in no way inferior to modern highways.

Be that as it may, today it is certain that the Indians were as well acquainted with the principle of the wheel as we Europeans, and that they simply failed to apply their knowledge. A parallel example is given by the world of Islam which almost exclusively used beasts of burden. This strange failure to apply the principle of the wheel must be left unexplained. Gordon F. Ekholm believes that it was due to a conservative adherence to old customs, which was in fact a marked characteristic of the Indians, and thus the cause of the lack of technical development in pre-Columbian America. This explanation still leaves the question of this tradition-bound inertia unanswered, just as is the question why Europe had to wait for the Renaissance before making great strides in the development of technology. We shall have to be content with simply noting such odd facts, and leaving it at that.

It may appear that we have strayed too far from our path, that all this has little bearing on the history of discoveries. Yet all forms of history—political, philosophic, military, economic, or artistic—are, after all, nothing but aspects of cultural history, and for this reason the above diversion was made. At this point the author begs the reader to follow him on yet another bypath, and to ponder on a book written in 1947 by three American botanists, which, since it bore the forbidding title *The Evolution of Gossypium and the Differentiation of the Cultivated Cottons*, did not become a best-seller.

At first glance this publication is pretty heavy going, for it deals with the number and nature of the chromosomes in the cotton seed. The book states that all cottons of the Old World have thirteen *large* chromosomes, while the wild cotton of the New World—as is seen from countless specimens found in Central America—has thirteen *small* chromosomes. Thus it seems certain that two similar, yet clearly distinct types of cotton have existed from earliest times.

But the three American investigators discovered more than this. When they investigated the seeds of the cotton *cultivated* by the ancient American peoples, long before Columbus and the appearance of Europeans, they discovered that there were twenty-six chromosomes in the domesticated variety—thirteen large and thirteen small. Thus the two wild-growing types of both the Old and the New Worlds must have been crossed. But how had the seeds come from the Old World into the New? Across the Bering Straits, during the ancient migrations, when the original inhabitants of this New Continent had streamed into their new home? C. O. Sauer, who has dealt with this question, considers this impossible. The climate of these sub-arctic regions has always been so severe that the delicate warmth-loving cotton-seed could not possibly have survived transportation across the Bering Straits. It must have entered America via the tropical or subtropical zones, i.e. the West Indies or Mexico.

Strange as it may seem, our scientists are most unwilling to admit that the distance of some sixteen hundred miles between the Canaries and Central America is more easily bridged with the help of the Trades and ocean currents than the distance of some ten thousand miles separating Asia from America *against* the Trades, and also, for most of the way, against the currents. Consequently they busied themselves searching for the Old World type of cotton, viz. cotton with thirteen large chromosomes, in Melanesia, Micronesia, New Guinea and the Polynesian Islands. Alas, it was nowhere to be found, and only types with twenty-six chromosomes were discovered. Neither here nor on the path across the Pacific could there have taken place the import into America of Old World cotton. Only one route remained: across the Atlantic and thence to the Pacific.

Could birds have been responsible for carrying the seed? Birds do not eat cotton seeds. Could storms have blown them across the gigantic ocean? It is improbable, and furthermore cotton immediately loses its germinating powers once it is exposed to moist air. For this same reason ocean currents could not have been the carrying agents. What is the real answer to such an awkward problem?

Very few scientists have drawn the obvious conclusion. We do not wish to rush in where angels fear to tread, but we could not resist broaching these problems, merely to show that, despite the diversity of fabric, the essences of all things are deeply related.

3

From the day when the Spaniards had sailed out of the mouth of the Tabasco at the end of March, Bernal Díaz del Castillo had scarcely had a chance to sleep. Cortés had kept the young man up in the crow's-nest practically without interruption. The strong country lad of twenty-two, who came from Medina del Campo in the province of León, in the very heart of old Castile, had been in these strange regions once before. It was hardly a year since he had sailed under Juan de Grijalva—nephew of Diego

Velásquez—along the coast of Yucatan, through the Bay of Campeche as far as the modern Vera Cruz in Mexico.

Bernal Díaz was anything but happy crouching up there on the mast. Neither he nor Cortés could guess that he, a mere peasant lad, would one day be called *Capitán General de la Nueva España y Costa del Sur*, and would be addressed as *Señor* and *Regidor* of the city of Guatemala, nor yet that one day he would write a book of his memoirs. Now, at the beginning of April 1519, all he did was to curse and bewail his fate while perched up on high. Every so often the captain on the quarter-deck would ask if he could see anything, but what was he meant to see? To port he could see nothing but marshes and sand, while to starboard there was an infinite expanse of water without a single ship or island. How irritating it was that he could not remember the outlines of the land of Montezuma where he had been but a year ago. If only he could catch another glimpse of those high snowy peaks, the *sierra nevada*, or the wide lagoon of Alvarado, he would know where he was.

Bernal Díaz de Castillo was a simple man and he could not have known that, on his fourth voyage, Columbus had encountered Aztec craft on the high seas off the coast of Honduras: strangely shaped boats with crews of brown men, dressed in coloured cottons, possessing copper tools and queer weapons, who, when asked where they came from, had pointed to the West. Nor did Bernal Díaz know of the confidential report made by Grijalva on his return to his uncle Diego Velásquez. This was a rather sketchy and confused document, for Grijalva had no interpreter with him, and conversation and trading with the *indios* of the coast of Mexico had proved difficult. Nevertheless the Spaniards had gleaned that somewhere, far to the west on a lofty plateau, there was a vast city, completely surrounded by water and ruled by a king possessing immeasurable treasures of gold and jewels. This was why Cortés gave Bernal no peace up in the crow's-nest, but kept on asking if the look-out had anything to report.

Days passed in this vain search until, early on Maundy Thursday, a light was seen glimmering high up and far away on the port side. A little later, the sun rising from its ocean bed lit up the snow-covered peaks of a range of mountains, and excitement soon ran through the eleven Spanish ships. A few hours after they anchored in the vicinity of what is today Vera Cruz, and the curtain went up on one of the most momentous dramas of all time.

The first scenes were played at breathtaking pace. Hardly thirty minutes had elapsed from the order to drop anchor, when two large war canoes filled with Indians appeared. They made fast to the *Capitana*, the flagship, and a dozen Indians climbed up the rope-ladders on board, asking to see the *tlatoan*, the commander, to whom they showed great respect and whose pleasure they inquired.

They were following the express orders of Montezuma, the 'angry lord', Emperor of Mexico, who had been priest before becoming emperor. For many long years he had sat poring over faded picture-writings in the gloomy cell of his cloister, telling of Quetzalcoatl and the future return of the white gods. He knew the old legend, and had watched the whites. For years their every movement near his empire had been reported to him, for

17. Cortés receives gifts from the inhabitants of Tlaxcala.

wherever the Spaniards went, thousands of dark eyes watched them. Montezuma had given orders that all the strangers' wishes must be fulfilled. Should they demand gold in exchange for the glittering glass beads which they carried with them, and which the Aztecs believed to be jade, then gold they should have. Should they demand women or other less precious substances: turkeys, stags, rabbits, bread and the like, their wishes should be met without question. Perhaps in this way they could be pacified, these avenging sons of the white saviour, and would return to their own land.

Montezuma was no appeaser, and it would be wrong to look upon him in this light. He was not yet quite certain whether the strangers were in fact sent by Quetzalcoatl, but even if this were so, the terrible war god Huitzipochtli would unleash a slaughter in the heavens with terrible repercussions on earth. Thus, while the strangers must be shown every courtesy and respect, they must be persuaded to leave again. He knew that he could count on his guards, who had sworn their priest-king loyalty unto death, on his armies and on his people. The white men were few and could be crushed at a blow, but to take arms against Quetzalcoatl would be a great sin.

Thus Montezuma was in a quandary, and hesitated just at the crucial moment. Instead of trusting to his arms, he sent the Spaniards valuable offerings, and so enticed them to lay their hands on this El Dorado whatever the cost.

Maurice Collis in his recent *Cortés and Montezumá* tells us that Montezuma's final decision was brought about by a most remarkable coincidence. According to the old prophecies, Quetzalcoatl, returning from the East, would land in the year 'One Reed'. This year recurred, according to the peculiar Aztec calendar, every fifty-two years and it can be imagined with what anxiety the Aztec high priests had during the past centuries watched the fateful year approach, and how relieved they had been as it passed. The angry lord Quetzalcoatl had not shown himself in the years 1363, 1415, nor yet in 1467, and once again the year One Reed was drawing nigh. Now there were portents of the coming disaster. In 1517 the first 'floating houses with the wings of swans' had appeared over the horizon: this had been the expedition led by Hernandez de Cordoba which discovered Yucatan and went as far as the Bay of Campeche. The white gods had returned in the early summer of 1518. This time the 'floating houses' had anchored just off the shores of Mexico, and Montezuma's scouts could observe the strangers from very close quarters. 'They had white skins, long beards and long hair', they reported to their king. But the strangers had not stayed for long. A few weeks later their swans' wings disappeared in the eastern ocean.

When Cortés arrived, the Aztec calendar read One Reed. The king and the priests were deeply anxious. In the temples throughout the land monks searched their holy books for guidance. It was clearly stated that Quetzalcoatl would return on the day 'Nine Wind'.

Cortés, who dropped anchor on Maundy Thursday of the year 1519, must certainly have intended to go ashore that same day, but since the visit of the Indians was so protracted, he decided to land the morning of Good Friday. Cortés, Christ's ambassador, set foot for the first time on the soil of this New World on the day of Christ's death.

By postponing his landing Cortés had fulfilled the old prophecy, for the 22nd April 1519, according to the Aztec calendar, was the day Nine Wind in the year One Reed. The Aztec 'scriptures' were 'to come to pass', down to the last brush stroke of the holy pictures. On Good Friday, good Catholics wear black and so Cortés was clad in a black doublet when he landed. Quetzalcoatl had also been depicted in black in the holy books of the Aztecs. The white stranger wore a low, black hat—that fashionable headgear which can be seen in many early sixteenth-century paintings of nobles—and Quetzalcoatl also had worn a similar hat. Quetzalcoatl had sailed away from the region of Tabasco towards his divine home in the East, and these white strangers came from the East and had landed in the self-same spot, Tabasco! There had only been a handful of them, but with their firebreathing dragons, their thunderbolts and lightning they had managed to overpower ten thousand of their opponents. Only gods could have done that!

Montezuma's spy service needed twenty-four hours to cover the distance between the shore and the residence of their king and so, at about the same time that Cortés stepped onto the shores of Mexico, Montezuma received the news that the white gods had returned. At once he despatched fast messengers to the governor, ordering him to discover whether in fact these strangers were connected with Quetzalcoatl in any way. Thus on the first day of Easter 1519, two days after the landing in Vera Cruz, the Lord Teutlile, Montezuma's governor for the border provinces, a man specially devoted and faithful to the emperor, paid his respects to Cortés. Bernal Díaz del Castillo has given us a very full description of this decisive scene:

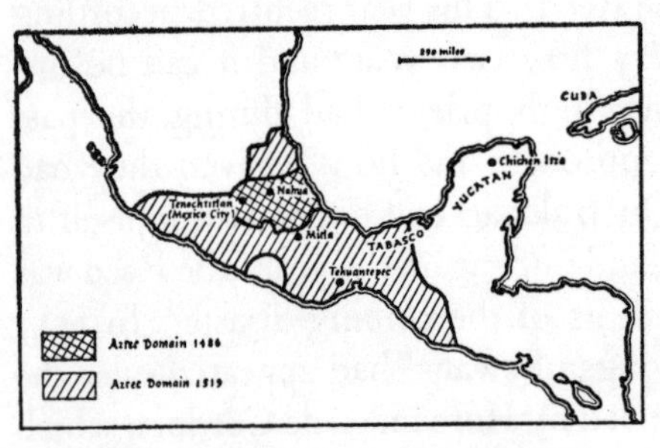

XX. The Empire of the Aztecs.

On Easter Day, the Lord Teutlile appeared in person. Cortés welcomed him, embraced him, and invited him to the divine service, about to begin. Father Bartolomeo de Olmedo and Brother Juan Díaz were celebrating mass. Afterwards the governor and the noblest in his train sat down to eat with Cortés and his officers.

After dinner, Cortés, with the assistance of Doña Marina, conversed with Teutlile, telling him that we were Christians and servants of the greatest ruler on earth, the Emperor Charles, and that we had come on his orders to this land of whose existence and of that of its ruler, King Montezuma, he had always known. Thus Cortés appeared in the name of His Majesty with the earnest desire to become the friend of Montezuma. He asked the governor to show him the way to his lord and master, so that he could pay his respects and proclaim unto him the message of the Emperor.

Teutlile replied proudly: 'Before you ask an audience of my king, you would do well to inspect the presents I have brought and tell me which of them you have need of.'

Thereupon he opened a wickerwork case containing a quantity of golden objects of excellent workmanship, and handed Cortés twenty bales of white cotton, together with featherwork-embroideries and other precious things, the details of which I cannot rightly recall after so many years, and also food, particularly chickens, dried fish and fruit.

Cortés accepted all these gifts with gracious dignity, and in exchange he presented the governor with polished glass beads and other objects from Spain. He then requested him to let it be known in his province that the inhabitants should call at the ships, since we had brought many beautiful and useful things with us which we would trade for gold.

Teutlile accepted the presents, declaring that his lord and master, who was a mighty ruler, would be glad to receive the message and presents from the great white emperor. He would speedily have the presents conveyed and ask for his king's orders.

The Indian governor had with him some extremely skilful artists and he ordered these to depict the face, bearing and dress of the Captain-General, of all officers and also of some of the soldiers, the appearance of ships and horses, of cannon and cannon-balls, and even of our two dogs: in short, of all the people and things that he had seen on his visit. These drawings also were conveyed to King Montezuma.

To give him some idea of our power, Cortés ordered the guns to be charged with a great quantity of powder and told Alvarado and the other horsemen to hang bells on all their horses' bridles, and then to mount and gallop past Montezuma's ambassador.

After the cavalcade, the guns were fired. The stone balls made a tremendous noise and echoed as they whistled over the sands. The Indians were terribly startled and the artists were ordered to perpetuate this event also in their pictures.

One of the Spaniards was wearing a helmet, gilded in parts. Teutlile, who noticed this, remarked that their ancestors had worn similar helmets, and that one of them was preserved as a memento in the temple of their war god. Cortés replied that he would very much like to see it and presented Teutlile with the Spanish helmet, and in doing so expressed the desire for a helmet-full of gold grains which he would fain have sent to his lord and emperor.

Teutlile then took his leave of Cortés and hastened to the Court of Montezuma to report and hand him the presents of the Spaniards and show the pictures his artists had drawn. The King was highly astonished at all he had seen and heard, and when he saw the helmet, he, too, recognized the similarity with that in the temple of the war god and he no longer doubted that we belonged to that people who, according to their ancient lore, would one day come and rule over them.

About a week passed before Teutlile appeared again. This time he brought another chief with him, and more than a hundred heavily laden carriers. Cortés received the two noblemen in the friendliest way possible and invited them to be seated next to him. After long speeches of welcome had been made on both sides the two Aztecs displayed their presents:

A round disc of gold, on which were depicted symbols of the Sun and Stars, weighing more than six hundred ounces, a similar disc in silver, the size of a wagon-wheel, showing the Moon and weighing over three hundred ounces, a bracelet fashioned of seven pieces of gold which had one hundred and eighty-three small emeralds and two hundred and thirty-two precious stones similar to rubies suspended from it, twenty-six little golden bells with ten beautiful pearls; eight other golden bracelets; a spherical mirror the size of a man's fist made of marcasite and set with gold of the finest workmanship, a truly princely gift; a quantity of golden and silver ornaments; a great many golden figures representing dogs, lions, monkeys, frogs and other animals; a number of golden medals; a number of jewels in settings which were more valuable than the jewels themselves....

After the two chiefs had handed Cortés these treasures, one of them declared that King Montezuma was highly delighted with the news of the arrival of such great heroes in his lands. It was his wish to make the acquaintance of the great emperor of whom he had already heard, but, because of the great distances between them, he would for the meantime have to be content with making him a valuable present. The King's spokesman added that Montezuma would be delighted to place at our disposal everything we might need during our stay in his land. However, he would prefer not to meet Cortés personally since this was unnecessary and would cause far too many great difficulties.

Montezuma's ambassadors were delighted with the wine served them during the meal and declared that such nectar was unknown in Mexico. The Spanish cuisine, too, met with their full approval: the White Gods knew how to live! However, Lord Teutlile had not come to feast, but had a mission to fulfil at this banquet. He had to discover whether the Whites were indeed gods, and, as his contribution to the feast, he had brought some Aztec delicacies to the table. The Spaniards were highly interested, but when they discovered that the beautifully arranged baskets containing turkeys, fish, maize, fruit, shellfish and baked snakes were dripping with blood—human blood, as Lord Teutlile explained to the foreign gods—they turned aside from this fare with revulsion and horror. The Aztec governor had expected this reception, for Quetzalcoatl had declared the eating of human flesh to be sinful and abhorrent. Yet Teutlile wished to be quite certain. He told Cortés that he had brought in his train a slave to be used as sacrifice. Should the white god but lift his little finger, the slave's heart would be offered him within the instant.

Cortés-Quetzalcoatl was outraged. He had noticed that one of the Indians had been watching him very closely, and he asked whether he was the one destined for the slaughter. Teutlile confirmed this. The man's interest in Cortés was quite understandable, for he had been told that he would serve as nourishment for the returning Lord Quetzalcoatl. Although this was a great honour for him, he must naturally have asked himself whether the sacrifice would be performed in the customary manner of tearing out the heart while it was still beating or whether, in honour of the White God, a much more painful sacrificial rite would be substituted.

Cortés's reaction told Teutlile all he wanted to know. The strangers were in fact the sons of Quetzalcoatl, and he understood only too well why Montezuma was trying his utmost to keep them from Tenochtitlan. The White God would take a terrible revenge, and surely the other gods would not allow him to return without making some resistance. There would be massacre on earth and in heaven. Clearly it was a solemn duty to avert this disaster. Perhaps it would be possible to persuade Quetzalcoatl to return once more to his heavenly paradise. Consequently Lord Teutlile added his own dissuading comments to the message of his royal master.

Cortés was not in the least put off by this refusal of the Emperor. Smilingly he called across to his adjutants: 'This Montezuma seems to be quite an unapproachable gentleman. We shall have to saddle our horses and hunt the old fox out in his lair.' Those addressed dutifully smiled back, but at heart they were deeply upset. They remembered a strange scene that had taken place one Sunday in Cuba half a year ago, shortly before their departure, when Diego Velásquez had gone to mass in the company of Hernando Cortés, his Captain-General. A mountebank by the name of Cervantes, who had been standing by the roadside, had called out to the governor: 'Hey, cousin Diego, what are you thinking of? I know your Captain-General only too well! He is aiming high—just you look out! That one will make off with your whole fleet, he's as obstinate

18. Spaniards in battle against the Indians.

as a mule!' At the time nobody had paid any attention to him, but here on foreign shores, at the foot of the snow-capped mountains beyond which lay the rich capital of Mexico, his words took on new importance. Obviously it would be impossible to restrain Cortés now, for if Montezuma made presents worth a King's ransom of his own free will, what would he not yield up if prodded a little? They had found the land of gold, which Columbus had searched for in vain all his life.

Cortés, too, must have remembered that scene when he noticed the hesitancy of his officers and instinctively he knew that some decisive action was necessary. Suddenly the memory of a Latin exercise which he had been forced to read when a student in Salamanca, flashed through his mind. It was a passage from Sextus Aurelius Victor, one of the consuls of

Rome who had also written a history of the Roman Emperors. He had told the story how, in the year A.D. 363, the Emperor Julian during a similar moment of hesitation, at the beginning of the war with Persia, had simply ordered all the ships to be burned, thus to impress on all his men that there was no going back.

The Captain-General smiled at the thought that a classical education was proving of some value after all. Now he knew what steps to take to force his men to accept his decisions. When some months later Cortés had to stamp out a mutiny, he realized that the time for action had come. The Captain-General had the ships of his fleet dragged into the shallow waters, just before the fortification he had constructed in Vera Cruz, and ordered torches to be tossed on to the tinder-dry wood. The ships burned down to the water-line and then were submerged in the mud. No air could get at them, and they lie there to this day, preserved as in a museum—the weapons, tableware, and other objects still in the cabins. Recently a beginning was made to raise the caravels, the mummified witnesses of a hasty action obviously decided on the spur of the moment.

Immediately afterwards, on the 16th August 1519, the Spaniards began their march on Tenochtitlan, the residence of Montezuma. They were entering upon no small undertaking, for although they would be able to exploit the lack of inner unity of the Aztec empire—originally it had been developed from the forcible welding together of many small towns and tribes carried out by Montezuma's great-grandfather against the wishes of most of its thirty-eight provinces—they were sallying forth to give battle to a highly civilized power with a well trained army on its own ground. The Spaniards, fortunately for them, had superior weapons, for by technical standards the Aztecs lived in the Stone Age, iron being completely unknown to them. When they needed a hard cutting surface, the Aztecs made use of obsidian, a volcanic substance resembling black glass which could be polished and cut until it was sharp as a razor; still, their *maquahuitls*, swords covered with obsidian, were only dangerous during the first few blows, for they quickly became blunted and ineffective and, in any case, they were little use against the armour of the Spaniards. On the other hand the Aztecs' complete scorn of death made them dangerous opponents. Their indifference to death was not only the result of the martial spirit pervading the whole people, but was also based on a religious attitude.

Like the ancient Germans, Greeks and Romans, the Aztecs too worshipped a great number of gods. These deities were endowed with many magical powers and could cause earthquakes and rain, floods and long droughts—but the victory of the daytime gods over the powers of night and darkness was by no means certain. As the Mexican anthropologist Alonso Caso puts it in his book, *The Religion of the Aztecs*, the light-bringing gods were reborn from the womb of the old Earth Goddess with the dawn of each new-born day, to die again each evening and illuminate the dead underworld with their light. When, with the light of the golden morning, they emerged once more from *mictlan*, the land of the dead, they would constantly have to fight for their existence with their Brothers, the stars, and their big Sister, the Moon. Armed with the rays of the Sun, the 'Serpent of Fire', they had to put the night to flight. Whenever they were successful their victory meant a new day of life for men.

These notions seem to have been of more recent origin. In earliest times, the ritual sacrifice of flowers and fruit had probably been more important, but a ghastly event, of which we know no details, was perhaps the reason why the customary offerings were felt to have become insufficient and ineffective. According to a legend recounted in the holy writings of the Aztecs, which has its parallel in the Bible, the Sun once remained motionless on its course, but had halted on the night, not the day side of the world, and for three whole days, it had remained invisible. The Aztec culture, which accepted superstition and magic, is not likely to have reached the conclusion that a volcanic eruption had completely hidden the light of the Sun by its ashes, but there are modern reports which prove that this is indeed a very possible explanation. The Aztecs believed that the Sun had become involved in a struggle for life or death and that his reappearance was only due to the happy outcome of this struggle. It was the duty of all humanity, they concluded, to help the Sun and all the good spirits in their struggle to return and to live, so that this terrifying blackness should not recur. If the statues of the gods were given human blood, if they were offered beating hearts, torn from living bodies, then the power of the sacrificed passed into them and helped them in their struggle.

Just as the Aztecs, Mayas and other Indian tribes believed they could fortify and increase their own courage and wisdom by absorbing the flesh and blood of their prisoners, they thought that the power of the gods also could be increased by human sacrifice. To be a victim and be offered to the gods was a pious deed and a high honour, for the souls of those so sacrificed and those of fallen warriors were certain to pass into the beyond. They would accompany the Sun to its zenith, and at night would sparkle in the eternal heavens like stars. All other mortals, however, would descend to *mictlan*, the underworld. Thus by their own consent men were slaughtered in their thousands. Nevertheless the fear remained that this was insufficient and that the supernatural powers would lose their might, and thus the Aztecs had to look beyond their own people for victims to the debilitated gods. The Aztec 'empire' was built on this metaphysical fear, for its warriors were not promoted according to the number of enemies they had killed but by the number they had captured. Times of peace, with their inadequate number of offered-up hearts, meant periods of great danger, and so their peculiar beliefs forced the Aztecs to wage war incessantly.

Bishop Zumarraga, one of the first spiritual High Dignitaries of Mexico, reported sacrifices of more than twenty thousand men a year. Perhaps this figure is exaggerated to make the venerable gentleman's own achievements shine all the brighter, but it is quite certain that wars were often waged for the express purpose of capturing people and that ghastly massacres of prisoners usually followed the successful termination of hostilities. If we stress the horrible decimations caused by the Spaniards, it must be remembered that they had witnessed even more horrifying cruelties, and that the thought of freeing the world of such bloody monsters as the Aztec priests must have weighed heavily with them. We are told that 136,000 skulls, thickly crusted with blood, were discovered in the great temple of Tenochtitlan. To the Spaniards this was the acme of horror and barbarity, and people with such beliefs had no right to live.

The Aztecs considered that life was pain and torture and that death alone was delivery. It is obvious that people with such a credo would supply the material for an irresistible army. In fact, not a single Spaniard would have remained alive had the Aztecs, so to speak, meant business. Compared with their numbers and their willingness to embrace death, the superior weapons of the Spaniards would have been as naught. Cannons had to be cleaned, charged, levelled and fired, and these operations could take anything up to thirty minutes; the rate of firing of their blunderbusses was hardly more rapid. The Spaniards' fire-arms had more of a moral than an actual effect, and this could not last for ever. Even though the Spaniards' crossbows, whose bolts would cut clean through Aztec shields and armour —thus taking their toll much more quickly than blunderbusses and cannons—proved to be most effective, and although the long lances of the Spanish cavalry proved their worth to such an extent that Cortés later equipped his infantry with them, the Spaniards' victory was the result of nothing but the enemy's internal dissensions.

The head of the Aztec army was the King-cum-High-Priest, the Aztec state being based on the priesthood and the army. As in all more primitive societies, the state stood high above any personal rights and claims, and as in ancient Egypt, rigid regimentation deliberately suppressed all individuality and only the arts allowed a certain scope for personal enterprise. There was a strong tendency towards the stereotyped, the ostentatious, the exaggerated in official art, but there also existed other forms of art which created such wonderful things that even the gold-hungry Spanish mercenaries treasured them more for their artistry than for their gold. They would have agreed with Albrecht Dürer who had said, after inspecting a collection of Mexican art treasures in Brussels in 1520: 'They are all very precious indeed. All my life long I have seen nothing that so gladdened my heart as these wonderful artistic things produced by the subtle genius of men in foreign lands.'

Although the Aztec empire was technically backward, artistically and administratively it could bear comparison with quite advanced cultures. The Aztecs used excellent maps, their postal services were as highly developed as they were in the China of Marco Polo, a legal code existed and was applied without regard for rank or person, their astronomers produced remarkably accurate calendars and their technicians magnificent roads and noble bridges. Drawing and sculpture were highly esteemed, though painting seems to have been rather neglected. By contrast, the pictures they made with featherwork were very impressive, and the Spaniards admiringly reported of the existence of feather paintings that could compare favourably with the great European masterpieces of art.

This then was the state which Cortés and his handful of Spaniards wanted to conquer. True, it had reached a stage in its historical development where progress had come to a standstill, it was an empire held together by means of fear, terror and cruelty, and, in fact, many Aztecs were longing for a more humane form of government. Cortés was aware of this and indeed he counted upon the existence of a fifth column in Montezuma's empire. To someone paging through one of the old Aztec tribute rolls, which chance has preserved, it immediately becomes clear that the cruelty of Aztec despotism must automatically have provoked resistance. In it are shown in detail the fields which certain districts had to till for the occupying power, the number of young men who had to be sent to Temixtitan as recruits, and how many sacrificial slaves had to be supplied yearly. This meant that the chiefs of villages had to go man-hunting to pay their taxes, as we should say. In addition the number of concubines to be supplied, the number of snakes to serve as fodder in the zoo of the Aztec emperor, the amounts of cocoa and *octli*, the intoxicating drink, of honey and cigars, of resin and timber, copper implements, jewels, gold and silver, the yellow and white 'excrement of the gods', as the Aztecs were wont to call these two precious metals, which had to be produced, are all listed in detail.

It required tremendous courage, bordering on madness, and relentless daring, to attack such a power and, though their main incentive was the prospect of unlimited wealth, we must admit that the Spaniards were also inspired by that same fervour that once had proved a source of strength for the Crusaders. Spain had only just been delivered from the Moors and now the Cross had to be carried beyond the oceans. There is no doubt but that this incentive, too, had immense significance for Cortés and his men.

4

In his advance on Tenochtitlan, Cortés saw to it that the route passed Cempoalan, the capital city of the Totonacs which had been recently conquered by the Aztecs, and also through the free state of Tlaxcala which did not owe allegiance to Montezuma. Their route roughly followed the modern railway line running from Vera Cruz to Mexico City, and when the Spaniards reached the foot of Orizaba, a mountain more than 18,000 feet high, they found themselves below those snow-capped peaks which they had seen in the distance from the sea. They were now on the high plateau of Mexico, some eight thousand feet above sea level, and thus had completed one half of the two hundred and eighty miles journey separating them from Montezuma's capital. Since the states to the east of the capital were either independent or had but recently been annexed, there was no serious resistance, particularly as Montezuma had decided to let the strangers approach him.

This enemy was burdened with all kinds of spiritual excess luggage. Not only had Cortés given express instructions that the Indians were not to be harmed, but he insisted that they were to be treated in a humane way, thus converting them to Christianity, the religion of love. In his orders there was not the slightest hint of colonization or war. When war eventually did break out it was the unexpected result of successes beyond all hopes.

The five hundred and fifty men led by Cortés on that march to Tenochtitlan were full of every kind of doubt and fear. Although they were armed with forty crossbows, sixteen blunderbusses, fifteen horses, ten heavy and four light cannon, and were thus well prepared by European standards, once they came to Cempoalan with its thirty thousand inhabitants they became more than anxious, for they realized that if the brown people of that thickly populated city, built not of flimsy huts as they expected but of thick-walled houses, chose to rise up against them, they would simply be swept away. But here the Spaniards obtained their first glimpses of ancient Mexican culture, and it was the material and artistic wealth which they encountered at every step that finally decided them.

Cortés must have realized that he could not afford to antagonize these masses, and loath as he was to pass sentences of death, yet anyone caught stealing even as little as a turkey was summarily executed. For the same reason he restrained the ferocity of his Indian allies, who naturally were considerably more aggressive than the Spaniards. When for example a group of Aztec bailiffs from the treasury in Mexico appeared in Cempoalan to collect unpaid taxes just after the Spaniards had entered the town, Cortés had them returned to Montezuma unharmed, much to the surprise of the taxpayers of Cempoalan.

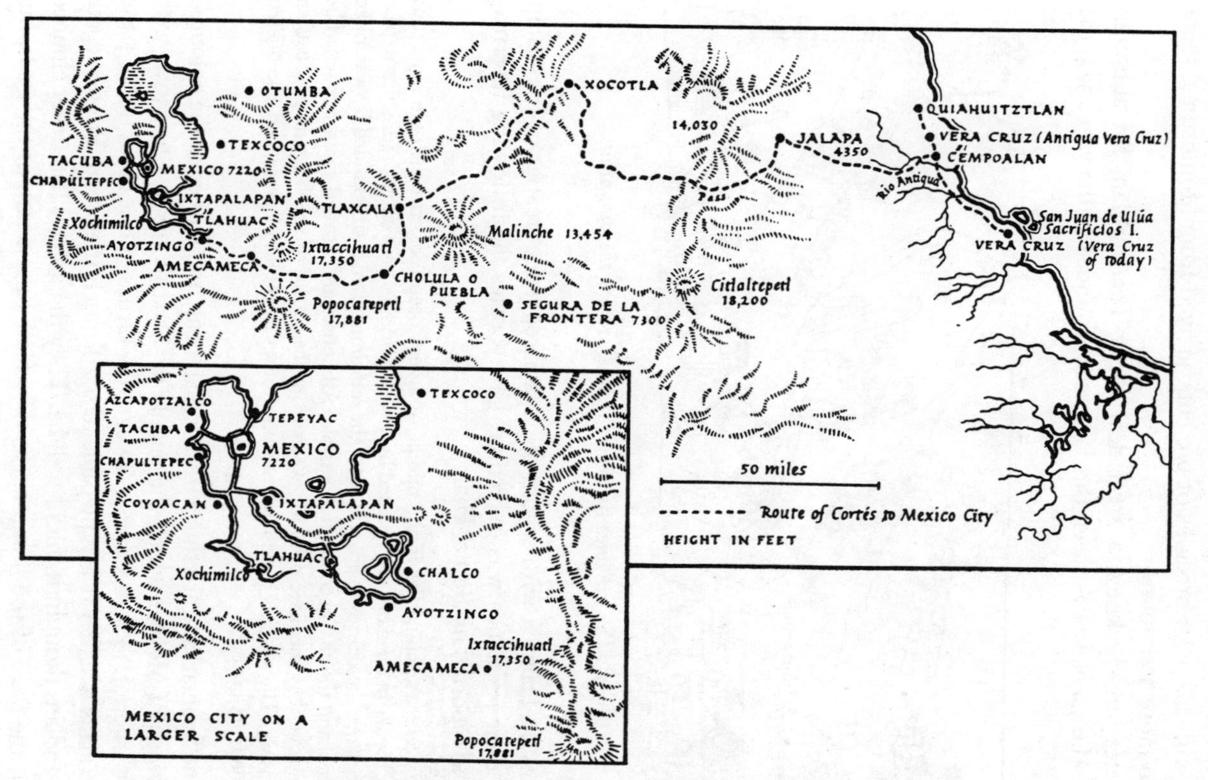

XXI. *Map of the Spanish Conquista of Mexico.*

This made the Spaniards' path much easier. Hard battles awaited the Spaniards in the town of Cholula, but their victories put to flight not so much the enemy as the Spaniards' own fears, and when a further mission, laden with the most precious of presents, arrived from Montezuma, there was no more hesitation.

Cortés already knew a great deal about Tenochtitlan, for although Doña Marina had never seen this large city, founded in the year 1324, the

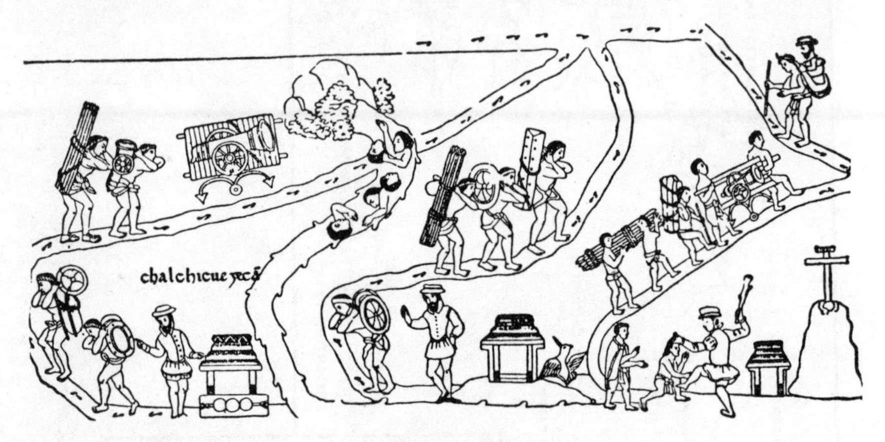

19. The advance of the Spaniards across the mountains.

princes of Tlaxcala with whom the Spaniards made treaties of friendship once their resistance was overcome, gave Cortés the following information, as reported by Bernal Díaz:

> Montezuma's capital lies in the middle of a very deep lake, in which are numerous dams. Breaks in the dams are spanned by wooden bridges high enough for ships to pass under. Once these bridges are removed, the remaining dam is surrounded by water like an island and the city becomes inaccessible. All houses are fortified against attack. The whole town has adequate drinking water from the source of the Chapultepec, half an hour away. The water is conducted to some houses by means of pipes, and also offered for sale from boats.

The Spaniards heard this with astonishment, and looked at the coloured drawings of Mexico which the people of Tlaxcala fetched to show, with great interest. Then Captain Diego de Ordas thought of asking the Tlaxcalans whether it was possible to see Tenochtitlan from Popocatepetl. The Indians thought it might well be. They themselves had never climbed up to the peak of the mountain as they feared the wrath of the gods, but since Mexico City lay at the foot of Popocatepetl, it should be possible to see it from the peak.

Thus it came about that this volcano of 17,887 feet was first climbed, and that the de Ordas family have since had a volcano inscribed in their coat of arms. Some Indians went along as bearers as far as half way up but then there occurred one of the regular eruptions of the volcano—particularly active at that time. When the Indians saw ashes and burning lava thrown up from the seething mouth, they threw down their packs and raced downhill. Diego de Ordas continued almost to the peak; below him he could see the blue lake of Mexico, the great city with its gigantic buildings, its glittering pyramids, its long dams and the tremendous aqueduct running right across the lake.

Neither Cortés nor any of his men had ever seen an active volcano, moreover none of them had ever had the thought of climbing a mountain. This fashion was to develop much later. Diego de Ordas dutifully reported that the crater had 'a diameter of about a quarter of an hour's walk', but this is all that has been recorded of this first ascent. The sight of Tenochtitlan was much, much more important. Soon Cortés and his men, after days of hard marching, were standing at the entrance of the broad valley in which Tenochtitlan was situated. Hardly three weeks ago disaster had nearly overtaken them in the great city of Cholula, the 'Rome' of ancient Mexico. The Indians of Cholula, though nothing but subject allies of the Aztecs, had tried to corner and finish off the strangers in their narrow streets, but their plan had miscarried. Cortés overpowered the princes, priests and generals of the city and then, when it was without leaders, he attacked with such ferocity that after a few hours the great city was in his hands.

When he heard of this, Montezuma immediately sent a host of ambassadors to welcome Cortés into Mexico. Everybody, including the chiefs of Tlaxcala, the princess of Cholula and even Doña Marina cautioned the Captain-General that Montezuma wanted to entice the strangers into his city, then, under a show of friendliness and peaceful intentions, to attack them after the example of Cholula. Cortés himself knew only too well the dangers lurking in a city of lagoons and how desperate a venture it was to march into the capital city of the Aztecs. But now there was no going back—he was too deep in the land of the enemy. Vera Cruz and its small fort were two hundred and eighty miles away, and he could count on no help or assistance on the way back to it. If he turned back now his army would not get very far. The brown devils would throw themselves in their thousands on him and his soldiers. Sharpshooters would snipe at them from every house, rocks would rain down on them from every mountain ledge, every pass would have to be cleared with blood. It could not be done. The order for the day must be: Forward!

In the early hours of 8th November 1519, three months after the beginning of their march, the Spaniards stood on the south-east banks of the Lake of Mexico, at the foot of the long, broad causeway leading to Tenochtitlan. They spent the night in a gigantic palace, gloriously furnished with ceilings of sweet-smelling cedar-wood and costly tapestries that outdid in splendour all the palaces of Spain. They had seen the wonderful floating gardens which Cuitlahuac, Montezuma's brother, had planted with the aid of the famous gardeners of Tabasco: miracles of scent and colour, such as the West had never known.

Floating gardens—in fact they were gardens originally laid on closely woven wickerwork floats, similar to those in southern China, Kashmir and Burma. In a manner of speaking, Cuitlahuac had anticipated the modern science of hydroponics, discovering that plants could bud, blossom and bear fruit without soil, if only their roots were in water. Following an ancient tradition of the valley of Mexico, he had created floral floats in the Lake of Itztapalapan. Soon roots sprouted from the thin layers of humus on the wickerwork and anchored them to the bottom, thus turning them into artificial islands, those *chinampas*, known from ancient times, even long before the Aztecs marched into Mexico. Today, just as five hundred years ago, lovers glide in narrow gondolas along the canals separating the well-tended gardens, but instead of the sacrificial pyres burning on the altars, the *teocallis*, those gigantic, truncated pyramids of ancient Mexico, today neon lights from the surrounding skyscrapers spread their glow across these gardens; instead of throbbing drumbeats on human skin, the drone of huge aeroplanes can be heard, and instead of the shrill sounds of the Aztec conch shells we now have the jangle of electric guitars and the tearful wail of jazz trumpets emerging from countless portable radios.

When the sun appeared over the eastern mountains, the temples and castles of Montezuma, and the tall houses of Tenochtitlan rising from the blue waters, were within easy reach of the Spaniards. The brilliant light reflected by the white stucco of the buildings seemed to welcome the strangers.

The holy places of the Aztecs, like the famous temple-towers of Ur and Babylon, were built in the shape of truncated pyramids, on top of which stood the sacrificial altars to the gods. Whereas the pyramids of Egypt, including even the ancient terraced pyramids of the Pharaohs Zoser and Seneferu, were built as royal tombs, the pyramids of the New World served the gods and life. A certain doubt was cast on the latter assertion at the 30th International Congress of Americanists, held in autumn, 1952. Previously it had been believed that the pyramids of the Aztecs and Mayas had not been intended as the graves of kings and high priests, but at this congress the Mexican archaeologist, Dr Ruz L'Huillier, made the startling announcement that he had discovered the grave of a Maya prince in one of the pyramid temples investigated by him in Palenque. Further excavations have proved that the pyramids of the New World were intended for use as tombs as well as temples.

Naturally on that morning of the 8th November 1519, the Spaniards made no such reflections. Only a few miles separated them from the fabulous buildings of Tenochtitlan, glittering in the early sun. The eighteen-year-old Bernal Díaz del Castillo was struck spellbound by their beauty: 'When we saw this miracle, we did not know what to say, or even whether the things we beheld before us were real. There lay the great city, and we were not even four hundred men strong.'

The Spaniards' hearts were beating excitedly as they advanced in battle formation along the dam leading from the mainland to the city. The causeway was crammed with people and on both sides of it the lake was covered with canoes, so crowded that they were near to sinking. The Indians had come in their thousands to witness the entry of the white gods and the Spaniards could hear them murmuring words that sounded like '*Teules*, *Teules*', the Spanish version for the Aztec plural of *teotl*, god. We can see how attentively Cortés watched every detail from the report he sent to his Emperor one year later, on the 30th October 1520.

Half a mile before the city, there begins a paved road leading on to the dam from the left. At this point is built a strong castle called Xoloc, surrounded by a wall the height of two men, and fortified by turrets, a keep and two other towers. This castle has but two gates, people entering by one and leaving by the other.

Shortly before reaching the city, we crossed a wooden drawbridge, spanning a gap in the dam ten feet in width. Even inside the city there are many such drawbridges, so that the different parts of the town can be better defended.

Once across the bridge, I was met by the mighty lord Montezuma. . . . He walked in the middle of the street between his brother and his nephew, the princes of Ixtapalapan and Texcoco. . . . All three were dressed in the same way, excepting that the lord Montezuma was wearing shoes, the others going barefoot, albeit the general custom in those parts was to be shod. I approached him on horseback and dismounted as soon as I drew near him, stepping forward to embrace him, but those next to him signalled me not to touch him. . . .

The Spaniards had marched across the dam with mixed feelings and had looked at the many drawbridges with suspicion, for they knew that once they were inside the city their fate lay in Montezuma's hands.

Montezuma was wearing a *tilmatli*, the customary square cloak made of coloured cotton and richly set with jewels. His shoes had soles of gold and even the laces which wound about his ankles were gold-plated. His mien was serious but not downhearted, and his whole bearing was that of a mighty ruler, conscious of his great dignity.

Montezuma must have been about fifty years old. His body, though slightly built, was well proportioned. The colour of his skin was rather lighter than that of the majority of the Indians. His hair was not very long, reaching just over his ears, and his dark beard was well trimmed though rather sparse. His face was oval in shape and his eyes were gay and mild in character. His whole being gave the impression of benevolence, but promised severity if the need arose. He was well groomed and very clean, and used to bathe every afternoon. He had many daughters of the nobility as his concubines, and two princesses as his legitimate wives. He would visit them secretly, so that only a few servants knew of it. He would discard his raiment after wearing it for no more than two or three days. The two hundred captains of his bodyguard lived in the halls next to his own. Not everyone could address him, this privilege being reserved for a very few, and when his subjects were admitted to audience they had to take off their valuable blankets, serving them as cloaks, and their sandals, before approaching him, their eyes cast down, it being forbidden to look him in the face. They would bow reverently three times repeating all the time: 'Lord, my lord, my great lord!'

The Spaniards were much interested in that strange city, and noted that, while the houses of the poorer people were simple structures of reeds and clay, the nobility lived in magnificent stone mansions. The *azoteas*, the flat roofs, were all fitted with turrets and embrasures. Every house, though embellished with flowers and surrounded by garden terraces, was fortified; even the palace which Montezuma allotted the Spaniards for their quarters was such a fortification. It had been the residence of his father, Axayacatl, and had been built some fifty years earlier near the modern site of the cathedral in Mexico City. Cortés inspected the building very quickly and placed his guns so that they covered the gates and all the approaches, and established a rota of guards and watches. The Spaniards knew that only time would tell if the peace was genuine; in the meantime, while they were in a besieged fortification, they were not powerless and to make this clear, they fired a few salvoes from their guns. Their fire pierced the dark of night, and their report rolled like thunder over town and lake.

Otherwise, the night passed peacefully. The Spaniards had eaten well and were looking forward to breakfast consisting of tasty *chocolatl* (a frothy chocolate drink flavoured with vanilla, considered to be an aphrodisiac) and the dried tobacco leaf, with which the Spaniards were already familiar from their stay on the Antilles. The Aztecs 'drank' it from golden tubes, the forerunners of our pipes. The Spaniards were very chary of eating meat. During their advance on Tenochtitlan, they had often encountered small wooden cages containing men and women being fattened up for the next great feast. This generally took place on religious occasions only, but the palace in which they lived was holy territory, and the Tlaxcalans had told them often enough that Montezuma quite often ate of the flesh of small children for breakfast. After breakfast the Spaniards diverted themselves in the broad courts of the gigantic palace. They climbed on to the roofs and looked down with astonishment on the streets teeming with people, but they did not venture outside. Cortés had forbidden them on pain of death to leave their quarters.

Bernal Díaz was allowed out once, to join Cortés and a small group of Spaniards on an official tour of Tenochtitlan. The report he has given of this tour is colourful and interesting, pride of place going to the great market of Tlatelolco situated in the west of the city, at the foot of the gigantic temple pyramid of Huitzlipochtli. This is how Díaz described it:

We beheld with astonishment that mighty square, the many wares exhibited, the teeming mass of people and the order which prevailed everywhere.

Everything deserving our attention was pointed out to us by the noble lords from the court of Montezuma, who were accompanying us. The market was divided up according to the goods sold. We inspected gold and silver work, jewels, beautiful materials, other luxuries, and men and women slaves who were sold in great numbers, just as the Negroes from Guinea are sold in the Portuguese slave market.

Then there were less valuable wares: cotton, textiles, yarn and cocoa, in short, all the products of New Spain could be found. I was constantly reminded of the fair in Medina del Campo, my birthplace, where every different type of merchandise has its special street. In one place there were textiles and fabrics, ropes and shoes, in another cooked sweet roots; here, skins of tigers, lions, jackals, otters and other animals, there, fruit, cakes, honey and other delicacies. Yet another section was taken up by the carpenters who were offering tables, chairs, cribs and other articles for sale; the potters came next, followed by the merchants selling paper, tobacco, sweet-smelling ointments and powders. Even human excrement was being sold from boats since, according to the Mexicans, leather could not be properly tanned without it. However fantastic and unpleasant this may appear, it is nevertheless true, and to gather this valuable substance structures of reed and grass were erected in all the streets to hide those making use of them from the glances of the passers-by. In addition, instruments of copper, brass and tin, and cups and jugs of painted wood were displayed. We saw traders selling gold just as it came from the mines, packed in tubes fashioned from the bones of geese. In short, there were so many things that I cannot describe them all....

Continuing their tour, the Spaniards passed steam baths with most artfully contrived hot-water conduits. They had their hair cut and their beards trimmed in public hairdressing saloons, they inspected botanical gardens and the zoo with its many cages of wild animals, they visited jewellers and feather workers, and met the couriers of the imperial post and the sergeants of police. They were greatly impressed by all these things. They tasted of the dishes of the market kitchens, where they were given turkey and a tasty drink called *octli* or *pulque*, a milky-looking wine made from the agave. *Chocolatl* was sold everywhere in the streets.

The Spaniards made but this one excursion into the town, and for the rest of their stay they remained in their quarters. They examined everything in the halls and rooms of the tremendous building and with the practised hand of old soldiers, they lifted the tapestries, and knocked against the walls to see if by chance a hollow echo would reveal some secrets hidden between the apparently solid walls. Soon their efforts were to be rewarded; one of the walls, when tapped, betrayed a cavity behind it. The Spaniards were not long in discovering that a door had been blocked up recently. Cortés was called, and Alonso Yannez, the carpenter who had discovered the hollow space, was ordered to break it open. The Spaniards entered, to find themselves in Montezuma's private treasure house. They were dazzled and covered their eyes with their hands: a long, lofty hall opened before them, shining and glittering with all the colours of the rainbow. Here there lay heaps of precious stones and beautiful jewellery, while bars of gold and silver and bales of rich materials were stacked high up to the ceiling. Bernal Díaz was allowed to enter and was overcome by the sight. 'I did not think, being the young boy I was then,' he wrote many decades later, 'that the whole world contained such riches.'

They walled the door up again and took an oath of absolute silence, but the thought of those treasures would not let them rest. They had but to stretch out a hand to become wealthy beyond measure, and yet, being prisoners, they could not move. The treasures were worthless as long as they were surrounded by hundreds of thousands of Aztecs. They brooded over their situation and since they were the children of their age, they soon had the Machiavellian idea of overpowering Montezuma. He was the head of that centralized state, being King, high priest, and war lord of Mexico in one person. He was the head of the feathered Aztec serpent, and once that head was cut off, all that would remain would be the soulless empty skin, easy to deal with.

Four captains and twelve subalterns approached Cortés and discovered their chief had had similar thoughts. They decided on a trick to overpower Montezuma and planned its execution for the morrow. They spent the night sending fervent prayers to God and the saints to help them in their treachery.

Events began to move the next morning, the 14th November 1519. The wily Cortés not only trumped Montezuma but his own people too. He politely suggested to the Aztec that he move into the Spaniards' headquarters. The Emperor refused and long speeches of invitation and refusal followed. Finally the officers accompanying Cortés intervened. They threatened Montezuma bluntly with death if he did not accept the 'invitation' of his friend Cortés. The Emperor had no choice. He stepped into his litter and, together with all his women and servants, he went into Spanish captivity.

Cortés smiled to himself for the action had been unavoidable. The Aztecs had only to pull down some of the bridges for the Spanish headquarters to become completely isolated, and it was obvious that they could not have held out for long without water and food. Thus while the taking hostage of the Mexican priest-king had been a political necessity, Cortés was delighted to have managed it that his men, and not he himself, had threatened Montezuma with death. The Emperor would now trust him *alone*, unwittingly making him the sole ruler over that gigantic empire. Cortés had foreseen that the Aztec dignitaries would never forget that their king had preferred captivity to death, and that Montezuma would be forced to destroy his own leaders. Montezuma, still hoping that the strangers would leave one day, and that he might again become the leader of his people, was loath to carry out the bloody deed himself, and preferred to deliver his friends of yesterday into the hand of the Spaniards, just as

Cortés had foreseen he would. This treachery was carried out a few days later, and with one stroke Cortés had made further resistance to the Spaniards impossible.

At the earliest possible opportunity he made his noble prisoner take an oath of loyalty to the Emperor Charles V and offer the distant overlord all his treasure. Once again the walled-up door was opened and, for three whole days, Montezuma's attendants dragged the treasures from their dark hiding-place into the Spanish headquarters, where they were divided up among the soldiers.

But our Conquistadors were not allowed time to contemplate their wealth, for the news soon reached Cortés that Diego de Velásquez had finally decided to punish his former private secretary for his desertion. Cortés was informed that nineteen ships, carrying nine hundred soldiers, twenty cannon, eighty horsemen, a hundred and twenty crossbowmen and seventy musketeers had anchored off the coast of Mexico. Cortés did not wait and, although things were far from settled in Tenochtitlan, he set out for Vera Cruz in the first week of May 1520, with a company of two hundred and sixty chosen men. He reached the coast by a series of forced marches, and there, in a midnight battle, fought on Whit Monday of the year 1520 under tropical rain, he managed to defeat a punitive force almost five times his own strength, many soldiers of the enemy suddenly deserting to his side. Thus Cortés returned to Tenochtitlan at the head of an army of a thousand infantrymen, ninety-six mounted soldiers, eighty crossbowmen and the same number of musketeers.

This was a considerable force and Cortés was soon to need it all. The Aztec secret service was functioning as before, and Montezuma was told why Cortés had left for the coast in such a hurried manner. During the absence of the Captain-General there were bloody disputes in Tenochtitlan and though everything was peaceful on the 24th June 1520, when the Spanish army marched into Mexico for the second time, it was an uneasy peace, the peace before the storm. Not a soul came out to meet the victorious commander; the streets were empty and echoed to the steps of the Spaniards. To divert the attention of his men, Cortés ordered the band to strike up, but the piercing sound of the horns merely resembled a death cry, the shrill flutes sounded anxious, and the great drums were soon overshadowed by the evil throbbing beat of the blood-encrusted kettledrums standing on the temple pyramids. Cold shivers ran down the backs of the Spaniards.

What had happened? Possibly Montezuma had meanwhile made contact with the priests of the Huitzlipochtli temple, on the site of which Cortés had ceremoniously erected a church. If this had indeed been the case, then the Aztec priests had been much shrewder than the other leaders. They must have inveigled Montezuma into believing that they were still faithful to him, thus preventing the King from going over to the Spaniards completely. In fact, Montezuma was to tell Cortés that if he so much as lifted his royal finger, the whole country would rise up against the invader. Cortés was not deceived, but his guards were ordered to sleep in their boots, sword in hand. If the Aztecs did rise up, it would of course have meant the end of the Spaniards. Fortunately Cortés knew these threats were idle and that, whatever the outcome, Montezuma for one would be the loser.

20. Drawing of a Spaniard on horseback.

In fact the last thing Montezuma wanted was to fight, and he was no doubt sincere when he sent a messenger to assure Cortés of his friendship. But his rule and authority had been broken—his people heeded their King no longer.

The Spaniards reached their headquarters unmolested, but next morning the storm broke. The streets and squares, so empty the day before, were now teeming with armed Indians; arrows whizzed into the Spanish headquarters from the *azoteas*, the turreted roofs of the neighbouring houses. Some Indians foaming at the mouths like madmen tried to set fire to the palace of Axayacatl. The mass uprising, the national upsurge of the Aztecs against the foreigners which Cortés and Montezuma had tried to prevent, had at last begun.

5

The situation looked very bleak for the Spaniards. They could hold out for some days in their headquarters, for there were fair stocks of food and water and enough ammunition for the crossbows, the muskets and the cannon, but it was more than twelve days' marching from Tenochtitlan to the coast, and they would have to fight every inch of the way against countless hordes of brown devils.

Cortés himself believed that the anger of the people would soon be exhausted, and that although there would be battles they would not be very serious. He based his belief on the fact that with few exceptions the leaders of the Aztecs were in his power, so that large-scale attacks could not be properly organized. He also doubted the resolution of the Aztec soldiers, thinking they would not risk their skins for so inhuman a regime. If only the Spaniards could hit back and show that they were not afraid then the howling mob outside would change their tune. Thus he decided to make a sortie.

The following day, the 22nd June 1520, after first having cannonaded the town, the Spaniards sallied forth from their headquarters and met with apparent success. Yet the decisive victory which the Captain-General had expected did not materialize, for the Aztecs soon reassembled, and there was no doubt that it was *they* who were masters of the field. To add to the dismay of the Spaniards, there was now much greater order in the enemy ranks. Officers of the Aztec army, wearing copper armour plates on their chests, red headbands in their hair and epaulettes awarded them by the Emperor, had taken over the command, supported by the priests. Each unit carried its own banner, and high above that sea of colour there waved the Aztec national flag: the feathered eagle grasping a coiling serpent in its talons. It seemed that the whole population, as well as the regular soldiery, had taken up arms. The Spaniards, anxious as they were to reach the comparative safety of their camp, were much impressed by their opponents' absolute contempt for death. The Aztecs clung to the Spanish horses, trying to dislodge the riders from their saddles; armed only with their primitive wooden spears they rushed against guns and muskets, and fought with fanatical courage.

Towards evening, Cortés sounded the retreat. The Spaniards managed with difficulty to make their way back to their quarters. The second night passed without incident. The Aztecs did not like to fight in the dark, but they kept up the siege. Cortés could see that the position was desperate. His easy successes during the advance into Mexico had made him overconfident, but since he was not sitting in the generals' quarters far behind the front, but actively participating in the action, it was not too late to take steps to remedy the situation.

He still had one trump card left—the Emperor Montezuma. Cortés knew only too well that this card was no longer very valuable, but he had little choice in the matter. His noble captive was placed on the turrets of the headquarters in full regalia, the white and blue *tilmatli*, the Emperor's cloak, the *xiuhuitzolli*, the 'headband of turquoise mosaic', as the Mexican crown was called, and the golden sceptre, and forced to plead with the multitude. As Montezuma began to speak, a hush fell over the crowd, for they were still in the grip of a century-old tradition and they bowed their foreheads to the ground. This obeisance seemed to reassure the unhappy Montezuma who was playing the rôle of monarch for the last time. But soon the crowd, incited by the officers and priests, began to murmur, and as their anger mounted, stones and arrows were loosed against him. Hit many times, Montezuma sank to the ground. He was not fatally injured but his heart was broken. He tore off all his finery, and crouched in a corner of his palace. A few days later he was dead.

The last hope of Cortés had collapsed. Now there was no alternative but to fight for every inch of the dams leading to the mainland. This is how the Captain-General reported this stage of the adventure to Charles V:

I reflected on the grave danger in which we stood, on the great losses that the enemy had caused us day after day, and I was in great anxiety lest the last stone dam should be destroyed like all the others. Had this been the case we should all have died of hunger. My men begged me to make a sortie from the city, as many of their comrades were wounded and no longer fit for battle. I decided to comply with their wishes in the following manner.

I had as much gold and gems as we could carry away packed in sacks, and entrusted these to a number of officers, admonishing them, in Your Majesty's name, to do everything in their power to take these treasures with them. I also gave them a horse and some foot-soldiers as support.... The rest of the gold I distributed among the Spanish soldiery....

When we came to the remains of the first bridge, destroyed by the Indians, we set up the emergency bridge which I had previously ordered to be constructed, and we met with little resistance while doing so. However, a few Aztec guards on watch raised such a clamour that before we had reached the next bridge, a great crowd of Mexicans had collected and began to attack us on all sides, from boats as well as from the land.

With five horsemen and a hundred foot-soldiers I hurriedly crossed the ditches between the last three bridges, leaving the foot-soldiers there as an advance guard, as I myself hastened to the rear-guard which was now on the third and last bridge, where it was waging a violent battle and suffering heavy losses. A great number of Spaniards had lost their lives, and so had almost all the Tlaxcalans, our allies. Many women also, who had been serving the Spaniards, were killed. Many horses, all the gold, treasure, clothes and a quantity of other things which we had wanted to bring away with us were lost, including all our cannon.

Those who were still living rallied and began to advance. I covered them with five horsemen and seventy foot-soldiers. Step by step we advanced, fighting every inch of the way until we reached the town of Tacuba, lying a little in front of the end of the dam.... The lake lay on both sides of our route and the enemy could attack us from their boats without suffering damage themselves. Those of the enemy who attacked us from the land were repulsed and quickly hastened back to the water. Thus their losses were small except for those crushed to death in the congestion. With much trouble and anguish I managed to lead the rear-guard to the above-named town....

On the night of the 30th June 1520, at the point where the short dam, running across the lake to the west, reached the mainland near Tacuba, Cortés called his famous *noche triste*, his first halt, and then collapsed under a cedar tree that is still standing there today. Completely exhausted physically, bleeding from many wounds, facing the collapse of his whole enterprise, and bearing the heavy responsibility for the death of hundreds of brave Spanish soldiers, he covered his face with his hands and wept. Perhaps nothing else so much gained him the unquestioning loyalty and devotion of his old guard as this moment of his spiritual breakdown. Those simple soldiers were deeply touched when they saw that their leader, the unapproachable Captain-General, had burst into tears for his fallen comrades and was showing simple human feelings just as they had.

The enemy attacks had taken a heavy toll. Four hundred and fifty Spaniards were missing, eighty horses and all the cannon had been lost, almost the complete booty of gold and jewels and some three thousand men of the auxiliary troops from Tlaxcala were in the hands of the Aztecs. If the Aztecs had immediately followed up their success, then not a Spaniard would have lived to tell the tale.

The Spaniards made their way to the coast along byways, but this only delayed the inevitable from happening: on the 8th July 1520, the exhausted Spaniards were met near Otumba by the entire Aztec army, determined to prevent the hated Spaniards from escaping and to destroy them utterly. At this point the 'White Gods' rose to their old heights. The Captain-General knew that the Aztecs would consider the battle lost once their national flag was wrested from them. He peered over the heads of the howling masses of the enemy, and there in the distance floated the Mexican banner in all its glory. In the bright sunlight he could clearly see the feathered eagle with the serpent in its talons. One of the Aztec generals was bearing the emblem on a standard fastened to his back. Almost automatically Cortés dug his spurs into his horse, and followed only by the youthful ensign Juan Salamanca de Ontiveros, whose cream-coloured mare was almost as fast as the stallion of his commander, he started on his ride of death right across the thick masses of the *indios*. The improbable happened: the Indian general fell after a short struggle. In wild triumph, Cortés raised the Aztec national banner towards his men, and in utter confusion the Indians took to flight. Cortés, who had felt himself to be the messenger of Christ, was now quite convinced that he owed his victory to God the Son, and the Aztecs felt certain that Quetzalcoatl had at last vanquished the other gods, and that to continue the struggle now was useless. Cortés-Quetzalcoatl could not be conquered by any human means. Bernal Díaz says of this moment that 'it was as if we had no wounds, no hunger, no thirst, and no fatigue from the work of war'. A few days later Cortés and the remainder of his men reached the land of Tlaxcala.

Luckily the Tlaxcalans kept faith with their Spanish allies. They knew what had happened in Mexico, but they also knew of the battle of Otumba. Their bards and balladiers were already singing of the courageous charge of the Captain-General, of the death of the Aztec commander and of the bravery of Juan Salamanca de Ontiveros. The *indios* whispered that the owner of the holy banner of Tenochtitlan must indeed be invincible.

The people of Tlaxcala knew even more than this. Throughout the length and breadth of the land, they were telling of the strange prophecy made by an Italian crossbowman named Botello belonging to Cortés's army. At the time, only those in Cortés's closest confidence were told of this prophecy but now it was on everyone's lips. The officers went so far as to say that it was in fact this ordinary soldier who had been responsible for the successful escape from Tenochtitlan, on the night of the 30th June 1520. He had prophesied that no one would be saved if the departure were delayed beyond that date. He had also added that it would make no difference to him personally, since both he and his brother would fall anyway, but if the Captain-General were to follow his prophetic advice, he would soon become a mighty ruler.

The Tlaxcalans pondered over this, and when investigations were made, it was found that both Botello and his brother had fallen during the *noche triste*. This made a deep impression; obviously the gods were on the strangers' side. On top of all this there were the advantages to be drawn from alliance with the Europeans against the Aztecs. One of the Elders speaking in the Great Council, held to decide what attitude to adopt towards the Spaniards, pointed out these benefits, and his speech met with warm approval:

> If you go back even more than a hundred years, do you remember a time when Tlaxcala was as rich and mighty as it has been since the days when the white strangers first came to us? Never before have we had gold, fabrics and salt, for formerly we could not obtain these things. Wherever our warriors go in the company of the strangers, they are held in high repute. Even if many of them have recently fallen in Mexico, had not our ancestors of yore declared that men would come from the East to subject us?

Considerations of this kind must have weighed heavily with the people of Tlaxcala. This was very fortunate indeed for Cortés, for it meant that he could soon reform his army, and this was essential if he were to vindicate himself in Spain. Velásquez must long ago have told the India Office how uncivilly Cortés had treated him, and that his independent action against the Aztecs was a breach of His Imperial Majesty's express orders.

If only Velásquez could be kept in ignorance! Cortés despatched a fast messenger to Vera Cruz with orders to the governor, whom he himself had appointed, not to allow any ships to leave for Cuba, and to send him post-haste the crews of any ships that might land. As ever, the Captain-General was full of grandiose plans. With ceaseless energy he busied himself with reorganizing his army for the conquest of Mexico, and in fact he managed to persuade his men to return there. As he wrote in a letter to the Emperor during these critical days, he was more than ever convinced of the truth of his old motto, that fortune smiled on the brave alone. In any case, he had no choice in the matter, for should the Indians notice that his faith in his cause and its ultimate success were weakened, he would never be able to reach the coast.

Fortune did continue to smile on the brave. A number of ships had arrived at Vera Cruz full of Spanish mercenaries and adventurers, armed to the teeth and determined to get rich quickly in the Mexican 'gold rush'. Cortés quickly enrolled them in his army and soon found himself before Tenochtitlan at the head of five hundred and fifty men, including eighty crossbowmen, forty horsemen and nine cannon. Shortly before moving in to the attack, he received unexpected reinforcements from Haiti, so that his strength was increased to almost eight hundred men, including eighty-four horsemen and a hundred and ninety-four crossbowmen.

In addition to this considerable fighting force the Spaniards had a fleet. Before beginning his second march, Cortés had ordered thirteen brigantines to be built in Tlaxcala, far away from Mexico. When they were ready, they were dismantled and carried in sections by Indian porters as far as Texcoco, some sixty miles away, where the lake begins. There they were reassembled and launched on the 28th April 1521, the second day of Pentecost. The launchings were celebrated by High Mass followed by a parade. As the flags went up on the ships, Cortés had the order of the day read:

No one, under grave penalties, may dishonour the name of Our Lord Jesus Christ, of His Blessed Maker, of the Holy Apostles and of the Saints;

No one may ill-treat a single one of our allies, who are accompanying us only for our sake, or deprive them of their booty be it gold or anything else;

No one may leave his quarters by night or day to go to a camp belonging to our allies;

Every soldier must take good care of his arms and keep them ready for battle;

No one, under grave penalty, may gamble for arms or horses;

No one may sleep unarmed or barefoot, unless, in exceptional cases of illness or injury, permission has been granted.

Apart from this, the general rules of war were read out once again, according to which all those who fell asleep during watches were threatened with death; the same punishment to be meted out to those who left their posts without their captain's permission, who abandoned their comrades during battles, or ran away.

The soldiers knew why Cortés had these things announced; the final battle was about to begin. On the 30th May the Spaniards surrounded Mexico and cut off its supply of drinking water. The thirteen brigantines patrolled the lake constantly. The siege lasted for seventy-five days, until the 13th August. In a series of desperate battles, the Aztecs lost over two hundred thousand soldiers, the Spaniards more than a hundred. When Tenochtitlan finally surrendered on the 13th August, it was a heap of smouldering ashes. Cortés had made several offers of peace to Montezuma's successor, young King Guatemotzin, the 'Swooping Eagle', but the priests of the Huitzilopochtli Temple had forced their rejection. It has often been asked why these offers were not accepted, since even the most fanatical adherents of Huitzilopochtli could see that the cause of the old gods was lost. The Spaniards advancing from three sides along the dams, and cutting off the fourth side, the lake of Tenochtitlan, with their brigantines, were inexorably drawing nearer yard by yard, and it was only a question of days before they would be storming the holy city. But, as Maurice Collis has pointed out, such rational questions really miss the point. The Aztecs believed implicitly in magic and astrology, and events in the heavenly vault gave the priests new hope and courage. For them Quetzalcoatl was represented by the planet Venus, which every 584 days is in conjunction with the Sun, so that the light of the 'White God' becomes invisible immediately after sunset. What conclusion could be more

21. The siege of Mexico.

obvious to the Aztecs than that the disappearance of this planet signified the overthrow of his human image returned to earth? The Indian auxiliaries had their astrologers too, whose interpretation agreed with that of the Aztecs, and thus Cortés lost his Indian allies, all of whom laid down their arms and disappeared into the mountains. This strengthened the hand of the priests of Huitzilopochtli, and of course they refused Cortés's offers of peace. The fighting became increasingly bitter. Whenever a Spaniard was captured, he was mercilessly sacrificed—some seventy in all suffered this fate. Cortés and his men were horrified when, day after day, they had to listen to the bloodcurdling screams of their unfortunate comrades, whose hearts were torn out of their living bodies by the priests, while the Spaniards were powerless to help them in their agony.

In the end the Spaniards had to fight their way right up to Guatemotzin's palace, built in isolation on the lake. The King knew that all was lost, and, towards nightfall, he tried to escape with his family across the lake in fifty large canoes. But Cortés's brigantines were faster. Captain García

Columbus landing on Guanahani (San Salvador). Seventeenth-century etching.

Indian hammock. The hammock was discovered twice: in India and in America.

Fernando Magellán, the first circumnavigator of the world and discoverer of the Strait of Magellán.

Vasco da Gama, discoverer of the sea route to East India.

Christopher Columbus. This picture may not resemble him. No reliable pictures exist either of Columbus or of his fleet.

'My sails are wings, glory my reward' was part of the inscription surrounding this picture of the *Victoria,* Magellán's flagship.

An Arab dhow. These boats with their lateen sails continue to cross the Indian Ocean to this day. (*Paul Popper*)

The bearded god Quetzalcoatl. Pre-Columbian sculpture in jade.

Chitzen Itza temple-pyramid in Yucatan. Like the ancient Egyptians the Mayas and Aztecs built gigantic pyramids. (*Laenderpress*)

The 'Temple of the Three Windows' in Machu Pichu, Peru. These Cyclopean structures of the Incas continue to evoke admiration and astonishment. (*Laenderpress*)

Pizarro becoming reconciled with Almagro; both are taking an oath of friendship.

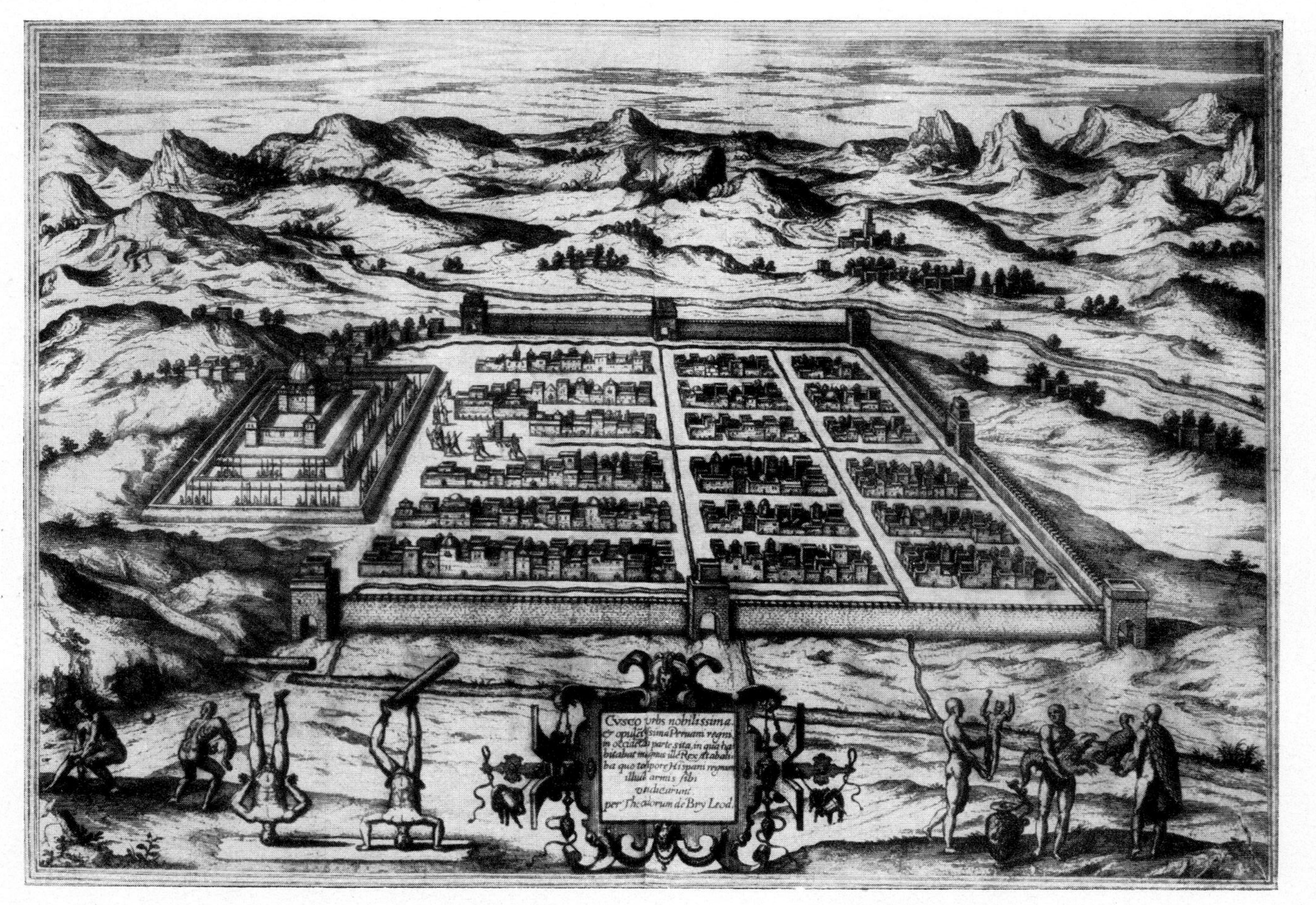

Plan of Cuzco, the old capital of Peru. This arrangement of rectangular blocks was quite unknown to Europe in the Middle Ages.

Polynesian outriggers. It was with boats of this kind that the 'Vikings of the South Sea' crossed the oceans.

Six hundred giant stone faces stare far across the sea from Easter Island. (*Paul Popper*)

'Moai kavakava' is the name given to this and other similar wood-carvings on Easter Island. They are meant to represent the spirits of the dead. (*Helfritz*)

African slave caravan. Fettered by means of heavy logs around their necks, these most miserable of men were dragged through the whole of Africa.

Egyptian 'Pointed Tombs' is how Dr. Oliver Dapper described these pyramids in the Land of the Nile, in about 1760.

Elephants on the banks of Lake Chad. This is how Gustav Nachtigal saw this sweet-water lake.

Timbuktu on the Niger. This modern photograph explains why this town in the sand was for so long called Queen of the Desert. (*Laenderpress*)

A noble Targui. Slender fingers and noble hands are holding the burnous in place. (*Bourdelon*)

Ghardaia in the Sahara. The market and the town with a minaret in the background. (*Paul Popper*)

Jungle telegraph. The electrifying sound of the drums can be heard many miles away.

One of the three mosques in Timbuktu, at the edge of the town. The donkeys are carrying clay, the chief building material. (*Laenderpress*)

The Victoria Falls in Southern Rhodesia. 'Thundering Smoke' is what the natives call this natural wonder. (*Laenderpress*)

Canoes of the natives of the Congo. The natives negotiate their boats with extreme skill past the dangerous rapids. (*Ullstein*)

The Ripon Falls of Lake Victoria. (*Paul Popper*)

Gustav Nachtigal. (*Ullstein*)

James Cook.

Adolf Overweg.

David Livingstone.

Holquín was the first to overtake the royal fugitives; he ordered them to stop, and when this order was disregarded he let loose a hail of crossbow and musket fire. Guatemotzin rose up in his canoe and in stentorian tones addressed his enemies:

'Do not shoot. I am the King of Mexico. Do not touch my wife and children nor anything I have with me, take me alone to Cortés.' His request was granted. Cortés gazed closely at the man who had offered him such tough resistance. Guatemotzin was an imposing figure; lighter-skinned then his compatriots, he had a friendly, oval face with large expressive eyes, and despite his mere twenty-three years, he already had the dignity of his position.

Now that the war was over, the Spaniards could amble through the city. They clambered up on the blood-crusted pyramid of Huitzilopochtli, and turned away in horror when they recognized the heads of many an old comrade ranged on the beams of the altar chamber. They walked through Guatemotzin's palace, still strewn with corpses. The banks of the lake, streets and houses, markets and gardens, all were covered with the dead. Bernal Díaz reported fifty years later:

> The fetid stench caused Guatemotzin to request Cortés that the inhabitants of Mexico be allowed to leave the city. As soon as permission was granted, long rows of men, women and children began creeping across the dams. For three days and three nights the evacuation continued and the plight of those who had survived the fighting was so terrible that we were moved to great pity. When at last the city seemed empty, Cortés sent in a party of men to report on conditions there. There were dead everywhere — the only living creatures left in the city were a few, poor people, too old and infirm to drag themselves across the dams. The streets and squares seemed to have been ploughed up, for the starving inhabitants had searched every inch of ground for roots; they had even stripped the bark off the trees, so great was their hunger. There was no fresh water left and yet, in those days of terrible want, no one had eaten the flesh of Mexicans but only that of the enemy. Truly no other people on earth has had to suffer hunger, thirst and the horrors of war like the people of this city.

Cortés's first order to Guatemotzin, whom he had confirmed as the ruler of Mexico, was that the three mile long pipe-line, supplying Tenochtitlan with drinking water, should be repaired as quickly as possible. Secondly he charged the Aztec to have the many dead burned and to see that order was restored in the city. When both these things had been done, the Spaniards started searching for loot. What they found did not satisfy their expectations, and so they decided to torture Guatemotzin until he betrayed his secret treasure house. His feet were soaked in oil and then roasted over a slow fire. The Aztec's lips remained sealed and he suffered this ghastly agony without a cry. Cortés himself had been loath to descend to these means, but he had no choice. He was well acquainted with the Imperial Court of Spain, and knew that if he protested he would be arraigned on suspicion of having made a secret pact with Guatemotzin, and of having kept the treasure for himself. Finally, in 1524, during his campaign against Honduras, Cortés had the 'Swooping Eagle' beheaded, on the grounds that he had been preparing a conspiracy against the power of Spain.

Once victory was finally assured, the Captain-General began the task of rebuilding the badly destroyed city. It rose, completely changed in character, but as beautiful as ever. The lake which surrounded Tenochtitlan was drained by the Spaniards as a precautionary measure against possible attacks, and the ground regained was levelled by using the debris of the old fortifications. When this had been done Cortés sent for architects and masons to build a cathedral on the foundations of the temple of Huitzilopochtli. This cathedral is the largest in the whole American continent and the square before it is the second largest in the whole world, being just a fraction smaller than the Red Square in Moscow. The largest bull-fighting arena in the world, the largest theatre on American soil and the widest triumphal arch ever constructed in the New World were added to the gigantic buildings of the *conquista* in the ensuing centuries.

This taste for the exaggerated and the colossal was an offshoot of the megalomania cultivated by Montezuma and taken over by Cortés. It can still be seen very clearly in the Mexico City of today. Nothing is sufficient unto itself, everything must be bigger, taller, more imposing, more gigantic, more tremendous than anything else in the world. It is as if a curse lay over the city.

And in fact a curse does lie on it. Mexico City is built on mud, not on solid rock and, as long as this mud was kept moist by the waters of the drained lake it could support the weight of the gigantic buildings. But when the lagoon was allowed to dry up the mud became desiccated, and it caved in. Mexico City began to sink; at first it sank by some eight inches a year, then eleven, and now by some twenty-three inches—a descent into the inferno that cannot be arrested.

If only the lake could be restored, then perhaps the curse of the Aztecs might be lifted. If only one of the rivers gushing down from the mountains could be diverted into the subsoil of the sinking city, to moisten and so strengthen the mud foundation! Thousands of deeply sunk wells drain off the underground rivers, and façades continue to tilt, towers to lean, gaping rents appear in domes—the whole town with its glittering skyscrapers of glass and steel, its towering churches and noble palaces, is inexorably sinking into the depths. This is the visible punishment for the White Gods' crime of allowing the lake to flow away.

The curse of the Aztecs is expressed in yet another way—through miscegenation. Through an increase in the birthrate of the red race, the level of European blood is becoming lower and lower. It seems that the sinking city is an ironical symbol of this. Already there is proud talk of 'Indo-

American countries', and Aztec, the ancestral language, is again spoken in the land once ruled by Huitzilopochtli.

Be that as it may, Mexico City is a fabulous place and Cortés could rightly be proud of the fact that he had recreated it with its beautiful baroque gables, dreamy gardens, resplendent gateways and bubbling fountains. But these acts of peace did him little good. The proverbial ingratitude of the House of Habsburg towards its faithful servants was to be his lot as well. He fared little better than Columbus.

Not long after Cortés had raised Tenochtitlan from its ashes and once more made it a worthy capital city for Mexico, the order for his arrest arrived in Vera Cruz. This was no easy matter, for who would have dared to arrest the victorious commander, surrounded as he was by soldiers faithful to him unto death? Thus nothing came of this and an imperial repeal arrived a little later with the solemn confirmation of Cortés as Governor of New Spain. Nevertheless the Captain-General thought it advisable to make personal contact with his Spanish homeland. But before doing so, there still remained a number of ventures he wished to carry out. Thus he wrote, in a letter to Charles V, dated the 15th May 1522:

> Whereas now for some considerable time I have had reports of the ocean beyond, I diligently made inquiries whether one could reach its shores by land.
>
> I learned that the ocean beyond could be reached by a journey lasting twelve to fourteen days. It was obvious to me that the discovery of the said ocean would serve Your Imperial Majesty's needs well, seeing that it is sure to contain many islands rich in gold, pearls, precious stones and valuable spices and also in other wonderful and rare things.
>
> Therefore I dispatched four Spaniards, two on one, and two on another route. After I had instructed them in their duties and given them some friendly Indians to serve as guides, they set out on their way with orders from me not to return ere they had reached the ocean and ere they had declared both land and ocean part of Your Imperial Majesty's domain.
>
> Two of these Spaniards travelled a hundred and thirty miles to the ocean without any impediment and through glorious lands, and there on the shores they erected a number of crosses as tokens. The other two were away a little longer seeing that they had to travel a hundred and fifty miles before reaching the ocean. They too took possession of the shore there.

These expeditions to the coast of the Pacific paved the way for the discovery of California, the southern tip of which was reached as early as 1533, though only in 1539 was it realized that it was not an island. About the same time Cortés sent expeditions to the east in the direction of Florida. These enterprises had the object of 'advancing as far as the cod fish', for the existence of a strait stretching to the South Sea was held to be certain.

In May 1528, twenty-four years after he had left Spain, Cortés stepped ashore on the soil of his homeland. He was received by the Emperor with all graciousness, but the governorship of Mexico was not returned to him. Charles V thought it advisable to vest nothing but military power in the hands of so domineering a man and thus to force him to satisfy his urge for action outside Mexico. Cortés could obviously see the intention behind this action and it is certain that he was deeply hurt and offended, though he never protested. After some time spent in looking after his estate, he set off on further military enterprises which took him as far as California. His object was to find a passage across to the Pacific Ocean, a hope that had haunted him for years. On one occasion he even sold his wife's jewels to equip an expedition to seek out this passage. In an age interested only in material values, this persistent devotion to an idea gives us a clue to the vision and greatness of a man, whom ignorant writers have seen fit to brand as a cruel criminal.

His personality cannot be assessed by the ordinary bourgeois yardstick, for no truly great man fits into the limited scale of that petty measure, either in greatness or in depravity. He was nineteen years old when he came to the New World, wilful, born and trained to rule, and during the first few years in his new home he did not perhaps reveal the lighter side of himself. Las Casas's complaint that Cortés's wealth was acquired at the cost of many Indian lives is perhaps well justified. But when, in November 1518, he weighed anchor off Cuba and started on his voyage towards the West, the onus and the responsibility fell on the shoulders of a man worthy of their magnitude. Cortés had always possessed the magic power, common to all great commanders, of being able to take a band of ruffians and turn them into a disciplined, devoted company. In the last analysis, however, Cortés remains an inexplicable, uninterpretable historical phenomenon.

In 1540 Cortés once again landed in Spain where he remained for seven years, a highly esteemed but a powerless man. He had just decided to return to Mexico when he fell ill with dysentery and died in Seville on Friday, 2nd December, 1547, at the age of sixty-three.

It was he above all others who had made Spain great, yet it is doubtful whether he had rendered a real service to his motherland. The nation was much too small, too poor and too divided to be able to cope with the tremendous lands which Columbus, Cortés and other courageous individuals had won for it. Spain, during this period, constantly produced individuals for whom Europe was too small, who needed the whole globe to work out their destinies, and the State had no option but to place its protective hand on the new continents annexed to it, appointing for their administration the best people at its disposal. The Spaniards could not settle their new possessions as the Roman State had done and as the British Empire was to do later, and so they had no alternative but to rule by force. That this policy was bound to come to grief was clear to far-sighted observers even of the time, although they could not possibly have suspected the enormity of the fall that lay in wait for Spain.

PART FOUR

THE EMPIRE OF THE FOUR CORNERS OF THE WORLD

A stowaway discovers the South Sea · Why the Great Khan of the Tartars could not help the Indians · Francisco Pizarro, the swineherd, takes French leave · 'Ferdinand the Mad', Pizarro and Almagro found a discovery business · Pedro de Candia lands in Tumbez · Pizarro tricks his partners · Huayna Capac, the reigning Inca, learns of the arrival of the white men and makes his will · Pizarro's march to Cajamarca · Of fearful horses · The capture of Atahualpa · The puzzle of Tiahuanaco · Where did the Incas come from, and who are they? . Viracocha, the bearded white god · Christian influences in the 'Empire of the Four Corners of the World' · Fair-haired Inca princesses and other 'White Indians' · Road-building, Exchequers and District Commands · The 'writing' of the Incas · The Incas as sailors · Balsa rafts · Did the Indians discover Polynesia? · Gold in the prison-cell of the royal captive · Reports about Cuzco · The murder of Atahualpa · 'El Dorado' in the Amazon jungles · The desertion of Captain Orellana · The Amazons · Was the Archbishop of Lima a liar? · Modern legends of the Amazons · The curse of the Incas · Murder of Pizarro and Almagro · Spain dies from indigestion · Bolivar, the last victim.

I

HOW thrilling to live on Haiti! How much gayer life was here than in staid old Spain across the ocean! True, in Spain he, Nuñez de Balboa, would not have had to skulk behind crates while waiting for that idiot of a watch on the *Santa Barbara* to turn his steps towards the quarterdeck. At home he would by now have been captain or perhaps even a colonel, but in any event no stowaway. Here he was nothing but a bankrupt planter to whom nobody would lend a brass farthing. He was played out for the time being; tomorrow morning they would come to lock him in the debtors' prison, and his debts were such that sitting there for two generations would not be sufficient to pay them off. There was nothing for it, he had to get away!

His was no gentlemanly leave-taking, he had to admit, half amused and half angry. It was a disgrace that after thirty-five years of his adventurous existence on earth, things had now come to this pass. But, the devil take it, there was no point in complaining. He was still young and with luck he might yet accomplish great things.

Ah! the lad up there was finally moving to the other side of the ship. The long-awaited moment had come at last. Slowly Balboa climbed up the rope hanging from the forecastle of the *Santa Barbara* into the water. One of the hatchways on the upper deck was open and this was obviously his best way in. Now he was level with the gallery; he silently prayed that there was no one in it. He stood for a moment listening at the hatch, and then he leapt. There was a slight thud as the hatch closed behind the fugitive.

It is thanks to the fact that nobody on the *Santa Barbara* had yet returned from shore leave that Peru was discovered by Europeans. However surprising this may sound, it is an established fact. Somehow it seems a fitting beginning for so unusual a story as the conquest of a well-organized state by an army of a hundred and seventy-one badly-armed Europeans, led by a man who could neither read nor write and never even learned to sign his own name.

This is how the story started: The lawyer Enciso from Haiti had, at the beginning of the year 1510, decided to go into partnership with Don Pedro Ojeda, to whom the Crown had granted comprehensive trading licences covering the northern coast of what is today Colombia. To this end he chartered a ship, hired men, bought supplies and made a voyage to Uraba in Colombia, the operational base previously established by Ojeda. It was this voyage that Nuñez de Balboa had joined albeit as a stowaway. This did not worry him overmuch, nor was Don Enciso particularly upset when after two days' sailing Nuñez de Balboa made a sudden appearance from the hold. This happened at the very moment when Enciso had begun to regret the whole enterprise, those two days having been more than sufficient to give him the worst possible opinion of his crew and of his own ability to lead such a motley gang of unsavoury desperadoes.

Nuñez de Balboa seemed to be ideally suited for just such a task as this. He was tall and tough as nails, though a bit of a windbag, and he hated the dull monotony of a quiet bourgeois life like the plague. Enciso was glad to receive him, and thus Balboa was suddenly promoted from stowaway to leader of the expedition. Later he was even appointed mayor of the newly founded town of Darien over the head of Enciso who returned to Spain in high dudgeon at this affront. The sudden rise in his fortunes, from bankrupt ne'er-do-well to mayor, and finally even to Governor and Captain-General, worked wonders for Balboa. The former braggart and show-off became a mature leader, fervently admired by his men, and, despite fever and the poisoned arrows of the natives, he managed to roam through the length and breadth of the country.

Balboa made systematic contact with the Indian tribes, and since he did everything in his power to prevent injustice and violence, he soon managed to gain the confidence of the natives. They supplied the labour force, gathered and washed gold for the white men and provided them with food. When at last the Spanish Captain-General married Careta, the daughter of an Indian chief, peace was fully established.

It was this friendly relationship that enabled Balboa to uncover the greatest secret of the New World. The Indians told him that not far away in the west there lay a vast 'Blue Ocean' never beheld by European eyes. Balboa was all ears; he was not simply a prospector, a professional gold-digger and unscrupulous adventurer. True, he was pleased when the Indians added that further towards the West there was more gold to be found, but the news of the ocean excited him just as much as the reports of gold-bedecked *indios*, with their palaces and castles set amid gigantic parks and long palm avenues. He knew at once what this meant, for the problem of where Columbus had actually been had never been solved. The unknown ocean, a very short distance to the West, supplied the final proof that it had not been Asia, but a new Continent that the great Genoese seafarer had discovered.

Balboa was restless with impatience. That very night he jumped on a horse and galloped through the spacious town of Darien towards the haciendas outside, to the brothels and taverns. When morning dawned, he had gathered a body of a hundred and ninety men, terribly drunk but ready for adventure. In addition he had collected a few hundred *indios* as bearers and a pack of a dozen slavering bloodhounds. The Indians of those regions were no longer afraid of horses, but they were terrified of the half-savage man-hunting dogs. Whoever goes exploring the dark unknown jungle does well to take a few dogs along!

It was a cursed and devilish enterprise and it lasted only three weeks, but each week saw the death of forty men. By the time they had passed through the land of the rich Indian overlords with its temples full of grotesque masks and its well-defended castles, only sixty-nine out of the original hundred and ninety were left. Their march had taken them through bogs in which lurked alligators and poisonous snakes, across precipitous mountains, and all the way they had to run the gauntlet of arrows and spears launched by an invisible enemy. Nature proved just as hostile as the Indians: scorpions, huge ants and spiders, leeches and clouds of mosquitoes made life almost unbearable. The men were in a pitiable state and, as they crossed the oppressive, damp jungle regions, their faces and hands were swollen from the innumerable bites and some of them were shivering and sweating with fever. As the fever gained hold of them they became mad and delirious and would strike out blindly at their comrades, who had no choice but to tie them up and leave them to their fate. Eventually an insurmountable rock-face forced the expedition to retrace their steps and seek another way round. Instead of the tied-up madmen, they found their remains, either crawling alive with ants or else their bones picked clean. After that a dagger was thrust between the ribs of those attacked by shivers and fever, for in that jungle hell murder was an act of mercy.

Ponquiaco, the son of one of the mighty chiefs of the regions they were crossing, joined the strangers. He led them on to a mountain from which they could see the 'Blue Ocean'. Balboa advanced the last few dozen yards by himself. Crouching on his hands and knees he tore his way through the thickly matted undergrowth, and at 11 a.m. on the 22nd September 1513, he had his first glimpse of a gigantic sea, with tremendous foaming breakers. This was the peak of his life. He could not foresee that some months later he would be beheaded as rebel, but he did know that henceforth he would be immortal, as only Columbus and Alexander before him. Three days later he stood on the shore of the new ocean and wearing helmet, armour, and glittering thigh pieces, he waded chest high into the water, sword in hand. Covered by the foaming spray, he called his comrades to witness that he took possession of the new ocean and all the bordering lands and kingdoms for and on behalf of the Spanish Crown.

This trip across the Darien Isthmus to the Pacific Ocean had by no means been Balboa's first enterprise. Since his arrival in the New World, he had time and again made smaller or larger marches into Central America. It was in 1511, during one of the earliest of these expeditions, of which Francisco Pizarro was a member, that, according to Prescott, Balboa had first heard of Peru. One day while weighing out gold with a native, the latter had thumped his fist on the scale and shouted at Balboa: 'If you love gold so much and are prepared to stake your life for it, then I know of a land where people eat and drink out of golden vessels, and where gold is as cheap as iron is in your land.'

The conquest of Peru, of whose riches and greatness the Spaniards were soon to learn more, was still a long way off, but their main fear, that the Great Khan of the Tartars might come to the assistance of the Indians, had been allayed by Balboa's discovery of an ocean which separated America from Asia, thus making Tartar intervention improbable. It was not difficult to find some one willing to undertake the long march to Peru. Francisco Pizarro, an ordinary mercenary in Balboa's army, saw his opportunity.

This illegitimate son of the small landed nobleman, Colonel Gonzalo Pizarro, first saw the light of day at Trujillo in Spain in the year 1475. No festivities greeted his birth and indeed no one ever dreamed that the son of a slut of a servant-girl would ever become more than a swineherd. His first few years of life passed by quite unheroically—Pizarro did in fact become a swineherd, and is said to have run away to Seville because one of his pigs had escaped and he feared his father's wrath. Towards the end of the fifteenth century, Seville had become the employment exchange for the riff-raff of Europe, waiting to go to America. Although it might be said that, even then, Pizarro was carrying the baton of Captain-General of the Crown of Aragon and Castile in his knapsack, no one paid much attention to the raw country lad, and it was only some twelve years later, when he had become a citizen of Panama and the owner of vast tracts of land, that he came within striking distance of his destiny.

Pizarro had a very close companion, named Diego de Almagro, a man with an exceptional talent for organizing, though, like Pizarro himself, tainted with bastardy. It is instructive to compare the traditional portraits of these two men. Pizarro is the taller, but by far the more sinister-looking. The peasant face of Almagro—his father had been a common labourer in some insignificant hamlet in Spain—reveals only too well the violent temper and the gross, cruel nature of its owner, though basically it is not an evil face. Pizarro's expression, on the other hand, while betraying the utter depravity of his character, shows a certain fiendish majesty and impressive strength, which even today fascinates those who behold his image. Of all the Conquistadors he cuts the most colourful figure, veering, as he did, between mean cunning and heroism, unspeakable cruelty and self-sacrifice, cold calculation and irresponsible intrepidity. Unfortunately we have no portrait of the third partner, Father Hernando de Luque, curate in Panama, who played such a large rôle in the story of the conquest of Peru. It was through his personal influence that the whole enterprise was started, though later Pizarro was to push him completely into the background.

This pack of rogues met towards the end of 1521 and planned to conquer and exploit the great, rich land of *Birú*, of which, by now, more detailed news had reached Panama. But even the citizens of Panama, used as they were to fantastic schemes and people, were somewhat startled when they heard of the founding of that new firm. Father Ferdinand, who had invested twenty-thousand gold pesos in the 'firm', was christened 'Ferdinand the Mad', and his two partners fared no better. For weeks they were the butt of jokes made at their expense by the *caballeros* of the region, and all three of them found it best to avoid being seen in Panama.

The first expeditions, which took place between 1524 and 1526, were complete failures. Only about one-third of the men engaged managed to get back each time—the others died from poisoned arrows, hunger and exposure. It became increasingly difficult to recruit men for another attempt, though Pizarro and Almagro—who were both over fifty years old at the time—remained unmoved and utterly convinced that one day they would not only discover, but also conquer, the fabulous gold-land of *Birú*. So certain were they of this, that in the spring of 1526 they drew up a regular agreement about the division of the land. Father Luque, too, was a party to this contract, and his two partners undertook to give him a third of all the lands, gold, silver, jewels, and other profits of the venture. Since neither Almagro nor Pizarro could write his own signature, two honourable citizens of Panama signed this ridiculous document on behalf of the two illiterates.

The hope of discovering Peru may well have been shared by many other adventurers in Panama, for to find Peru was after all not so impossibly difficult; but the idea of following the example of Cortés in Mexico and of conquering the place was utterly preposterous. All reports of the kingdom of the Incas stressed its high level of administration and culture. It was said that the frontiers of this state, in addition to the protection afforded by almost insurmountable mountains, were defended by tens of thousands of well-disciplined soldiers. An excellent system of roads, together with a highly efficient intelligence service, connected every point of this gigantic empire with the capital of the Inca Emperor. It was learned that every single position of the defence system was strengthened by tremendous fortifications, that there were huge storehouses of food in the capital and adequate supplies of water, so that siege tactics would be pointless. Even taking into consideration the superior weapons of the Spaniards, it was presumptuous to hope for success, however slight, against the forces that this state could muster.

These arguments were like water off a duck's back to Pizarro, and it is this iron resolution and persistence of his, at a time when the world was writing him off as a madman, that makes him such a remarkable person. Despite the unsavoury elements of his character, this fanaticism places him amongst the few men remembered by history. The final success of his plan was nothing but the confirmation of his personality, which never rose to greater heights than during those long years of stubborn preparation. Only in 1531 did he finally set sail for Peru with a hundred and eighty men and twenty-seven horses on board. In the meantime, a number of episodes had taken place which we shall not pass over in silence, since they cast a significant light on Pizarro's character.

The Governor of Panama, Pedro de los Ríos, perturbed by the fact that only invalids, cripples and dying men returned from expeditions led by Pizarro, ordered the old mercenary to cease from all such activity. This action roused Pizarro's ire more than anything else, for when in 1528 the Governor's order to return arrived during a reconnaisance expedition to Peru, Pizarro seized his sword out of its sheath and before the assembled crew drew a line on the sand and said: 'Comrades, there to the south lies our way of suffering. We shall end it in *Birú* but we shall be rich for life.' Then he turned to the north and thundered: 'There lies the path to a life of inactivity and poverty in Panamá. The choice is yours!' As he said this, he crossed the line he had drawn, and thirteen of his crew followed him. It was these outcasts who were later to become the lords of Peru.

During the summer of 1528, Pizarro turned up one day at the Imperial Court in Toledo in Spain, having decided to make a personal report to the Emperor about the coastal towns of Peru which he had seen, and to ask for financial support. He had chosen his moment well for Cortés happened to be in Spain at the same time. To bear out his reports, Pizarro presented the Court with gold and silver, some llamas and also some fine fabrics, closely resembling silk, though in fact made from vicuna wool, at the time unknown in Europe. Pizarro took with him the knight Pedro de Candía, son of a noble family of Crete, whom he had earlier sent to Tumbez, a port in Peru situated a few degrees south. Prescott has reported Candía's landing in Peru at length:

> He was sent on shore, dressed in complete mail, as became a good knight, with his sword by his side, and his arquebuse on his shoulder. The Indians were even more dazzled by his appearance than by Molina's, as the sun fell brightly on his polished armour and glanced from his military weapons. They had heard much of the formidable arquebuse from their townsmen who had come in the vessel, and they besought Candia 'to let it speak to them'. He accordingly set up a wooden board as a target, and, taking deliberate aim, fired off the musket. The flash of the powder and the startling report of the piece, as the board, struck by the ball, was shivered into splinters, filled the natives with dismay. Some fell on the ground, covering their faces with their hands, and others

approached the cavalier with feelings of awe, which were gradually dispelled by the assurance they received from the smiling expression of his countenance.

They then showed him the same hospitable attentions which they had paid to Molina; and his description of the marvels of the place, on his return, fell nothing short of his predecessor's. The fortress, which was surrounded by a triple row of wall, was strongly garrisoned. The temple he described as literally tapestried with plates of gold and silver. Adjoining this structure was a sort of convent appropriated to the Inca's destined brides, who manifested great curiosity to see him. Whether this was gratified is not clear; but Candia described the gardens of the convent, which he entered, as glowing with imitations of fruits and vegetables all in pure gold and silver. He had seen a number of artisans at work, whose sole business seemed to be to furnish these gorgeous decorations for the religious houses.

Pizarro received an enthusiastic reception at Court, seeing that his news came so soon after Cortés's reports on the wonders of Mexico, and the one-time swineherd did not find it too difficult to gain the favour of Their Majesties. Pizarro, greatly to his discredit, behaved like one of his former charges and spoke not a word about Almagro, his partner, who had fought for the common cause no less vigorously than Pizarro himself. It seemed quite sufficient to Pizarro that Their Majesties should appoint Almagro Governor of some god-forsaken spot in Peru, while he himself was appointed Captain-General of Peru. Not a word about Almagro, but the thirteen faithful, who had stood by Pizarro, were all made *hidalgos* by an agreement between Pizarro and the Spanish Crown, dated July 1529. 'In return,' the Spanish historian Gómara reports, 'Pizarro promised great treasures and lands. To be able to hire men he boasted of far greater riches than were known to him, yet all he said was nothing compared with the reality to be discovered.'

This shabby treatment was more than the basically good-hearted Diego de Almagro could take. He rightly felt that he had been done down, and his simple peasant mind could never forget this. Pizarro, despite the disloyalty of his action, had behaved shrewdly in Spain. He knew that two equal rulers would never be able to conquer a new land, and thus Almagro had to play second fiddle to him. Pizarro did not know that his cunning and double-dealing was later to cost him his own life.

2

Thus was played the prologue to the great drama of Peru. It cost thousands and thousands of human lives. The protagonists—Pizarro, Atahualpa, the ruler of the Incas, his brother Huascar, and Almagro—were all to shed their blood before the fall of the curtain.

It seems that the two Inca Kings were the only ones to know in advance that they had lost the game and would die. Just as Cortés's arrival in

Mexico had been heralded by dreadful portents, so comets had flashed across the skies of Peru, earthquakes had shaken the mountains, and fiery, blood-red rings had surrounded the friendly moon. The soothsayers and wise men were agreed that death and destruction were near. Sadly they gazed at the pictures of the dance of death in their old holy texts, for just as in the West at the end of the Middle Ages, in Peru, too, there seems to have prevailed a sad and hopeless mood of dejection, an obsession with the theme of death.

When in 1527 the then reigning Inca, Huayna Capac, had learnt of the arrival of white men in Tumbez, he had been petrified with horror. In his account of the Inca Empire, written not long after the conquest of Peru and submitted for verification and correction to forty-two leading Incas, Pedro Sarmiento de Gamboa states the following:

> When the Inca ruler learned of this he was so filled with fear and sadness that he locked himself in his chamber and did not emerge from it before nightfall. Other fast messengers, sent by his governors at the coast, arrived to report that the foreigners had forced their way into the houses and palaces, and had plundered them and taken away all the treasure. No force had prevailed against them, and even when they had been directed to the houses in which the Incas kept wild beasts, they had emerged unharmed. The King was beside himself with astonishment when he heard their story and made the messengers repeat it. They said: 'Inca, there is no more to report, except that the lions and other wild beasts that you kept in cages there, crawled before the strangers and waved their tails as if they were tame.' Then the King ordered the messengers to repeat a second time what had happened, for he still could not believe that such things could be true.

Some years later Huayna Capac in his official testament, drawn up as he lay dying, ordered his people not to oppose the will of heaven, and summoning the heads of the *Ayllus*, the leading families of his empire, he spoke as follows:

> Many years ago my father, the Sun, revealed to me that after the reign of twelve of his royal children there would appear a strange people, never before seen in these regions, who would conquer and subject this empire and many others as well. I believe that he must have been referring to those strangers who have but recently been sighted at sea close to our coast. They are said to be a powerful race, superior to us in every way. Now we know that with me the number of twelve Incas has been fulfilled and therefore I say unto you: A few years after my home-going, that powerful people will appear and fulfil the prophecies of our father, the Sun; they will conquer and govern our empire. I order you to obey and serve them, for they are superior to you in every way, their laws are better than ours, their arms invincible.
>
> Peace be unto you—I am now going to my father the Sun who has called me....

How strangely history has repeated itself here! The same scene whereby, some years earlier, the last Emperor of the Aztecs, in a surprisingly similar document, had submitted to the white invaders, was now being re-enacted many thousands of miles to the south in the Empire of the Incas.

This is, of course, neither accident nor falsification of history. Montezuma's abdication and Huayna Capac's political testament are both historically authentic. Just as Montezuma believed that he was right to capitulate, so also the last Inca of the undivided empire of *Birú* knew that his and his people's hour had come.

So far it has proved impossible to discover the sources from which both these Indian rulers obtained their fatal knowledge. We have nothing but circumstantial evidence, but all of it tends to show that the early Americans were more or less cognizant of the superior power of the whites – just as people in Europe had always dreamed of a strange new continent lying to the west.

Naturally, Huayna Capac's order not to offer resistance to the strangers paralysed the Incas. In addition the great empire was divided by civil war. Departing from ancient customs, Huayna Capac, twelfth Inca Emperor, had divided his realm between his two sons, Atahualpa and Huascar. The two brothers began to fight for supremacy shortly after the death of their father, just at the moment when Pizarro began his attack, and indeed without this great stroke of luck Pizarro could never have subdued Peru. As it was he could take full advantage of the terrible internecine slaughter that almost paralysed the country.

At the beginning of January 1531, the Captain-General finally set sail from Panama with a fleet of three ships, sighting the coast of Ecuador thirteen days later. After landing in the Bay of San Mateo, one degree north of the Equator, he decided to begin at once with the conquest of the Inca Empire. Soon the Spaniards were marching in their heavy armour and thickly padded tunics against the rich town of Coaque. Then they stormed Tumbez, Almagro's future seat, the very town that had received the Spaniards so peacefully four years earlier. Once again the loot surpassed even the greedy desperadoes' expectations.

These first engagements in the vicinity of the coast had proved difficult enough. The land was barren and the Spaniards had to cross gigantic sand-dunes, endless deserts and completely bare mountains. Not even when they had conquered the Western Cordillera did their difficulties cease. As is well known the Andes reach a considerable height, and even the lowest passes can be as high as 16,500 feet. Once over the mountains, one comes to the Puna, a high plateau scorched by the sun during the day, but bitterly cold at night. Apart from occasional rough patches of grass the Puna is completely bare.

Pizarro had thought it better to leave the less reliable of his men at the coast, and had started on his journey with a devoted army of a hundred and two infantry, seventeen crossbowmen, sixty-three horsemen and three musketeers. His first objective was Cajamarca, the residence of Atahualpa. The Spaniards passed through many narrow passes and canyons, where a handful of courageous men could have held up a whole army, but owing to the civil war none of the many Inca fortifications in the High Cordillera was manned at the time. Everywhere Pizarro was received amicably and supplied with provisions, and so the Spaniards were allowed to proceed unchallenged over the high mountain passes until one day they stood before Cajamarca.

All this did not take place by accident. Pizarro was just as well informed of the internal political situation in Peru as Atahualpa of the approach of the Spaniards. In Cajamarca they had long deliberated whether an army should not be sent out to meet the strangers and destroy them in the mountains, but Atahualpa had just defeated his brother Huascar decisively, and so felt strong enough to entice this new enemy into the interior of the country.

22. *Inca Huascar being captured by Atahualpa's generals.*

On 15th November 1532, the Spaniards marched into Cajamarca. On the other side of the valley they could see the tents of the Inca camp, the glittering spear points, the threatening glint of armour and fifty thousand battle-tested soldiers, recently returned from the civil war. Perhaps Pizarro realized the foolhardiness of his undertaking, but now there was no going back before a decisive victory had been won on the high plateau of Peru. He had to conquer by fair means or foul, and conquer he did! His victory was a massacre the like of which cannot be imagined, and a betrayal of innocent people that only a Pizarro could have planned.

After entering the completely deserted city, Pizarro halted his forces on the *plaza*. In the late afternoon of 15th November 1532, his half-brother, the legitimate Hernando de Pizarro, educated at the Spanish Court and thus qualified to appear even before an Inca, rode over to Atahualpa and invited him to visit his 'brother' Pizarro in Cajamarca. Atahualpa did not move a muscle while he received this message; he did not even raise his head when Hernando appeared before him. Finally one of the Inca counsellors explained curtly that the King was observing one of his holy fasts, and that he would visit the Spaniard in Cajamarca the following day. One of the cavalry officers accompanying Hernando, who had in the meantime been displaying his equestrian prowess, suddenly galloped right across the square towards the Inca as if he intended to ride him down, and checking his horse close to the King, addressed him courteously. The officer knew what a deep impression these unknown animals made on the Incas and had hoped in this way to produce a reaction in the King. But Atahualpa remained silent and unaffected. A few of his noblemen who had retreated in panic before the snorting 'monster' were beheaded that very evening for their cowardice.

This first meeting had made a very strong impression on the Spaniards. They spent the night in prayers and sharpening their swords, for they were surrounded by the enemy's army. The odds were that next day would see the end of them all, but Pizarro, remembering the capture of Montezuma by Cortés, had planned a similar stratagem. When on the next day Atahualpa, accompanied by his leading nobles, priests and guards, came to visit the Spaniards, he found a deserted camp. Not a Spaniard was to be seen anywhere. In astonishment, the King asked where the strangers were, and he was given to understand that they were probably so terrified of such an exalted ruler that they had gone into hiding. 'In truth,' commented Pedro Pizarro, cousin of the Governor, 'most of us were shaking with terror.' Then the chaplain, Vicente Valverde, stepped forward and delivered a speech on the Christian religion, God, the Pope and the Emperor, which was translated into *Quechua*, the language of the Incas, by a Spanish-speaking Indian. This speech ended with the demand that Atahualpa renounce his power in favour of Charles V and his gods in favour of Christ. Atahualpa listened patiently for a long time, then he sharply rejected the proposal. Seizing the breviary out of the priest's hands, he put it to his ear, but when it did not start speaking as he had expected, he threw it to the ground in rage. What Pizarro had so fervently hoped for had now happened; the Inca had given him grounds for provocation: the holy Christian religion had been offended. With the battle cry 'St. James and at them!' he rushed out of his hiding-place with twenty heavily armed men and overcame the ruler.

At once the thunder of the cannon sounded; trumpets blared, and the foot-soldiers and cavalry rushed out from their hiding places. When the Indians saw the horses galloping towards them, they did not know where to fly for refuge, and were trampled down by the onrush of the cavalry. The horsemen rode down the fleeing enemy and the foot soldiers came up to finish them off. Four thousand Indians were killed in the space of half an hour.

This half-hour, this horrible mass-murder of unarmed Indians, saw the collapse of the Inca empire. It is advisable to halt the story at this point in order to cast a brief glance at the internal politics of that great empire. Only thus will it become clear how military victory was the least of the difficulties that Pizarro had to face.

3

If it is ever your fortune, or your fate, to travel on the La Paz–Guaqui line in South America, you will find that at one point the train begins a seemingly endless climb. Slowly it toils upwards until at 12,550 feet it arrives at TIAHUANACO—FORJADOR DE CIVILIZACIONES, as the station name board proudly informs you. The traveller unaccustomed to such heights finds his heart beating more rapidly than usual, and he is strangely excited as if by alcohol. He wonders if anyone can live, in this 'forge of civilization', amid such desolation.

As soon as the train pulls into the station, tiny children dash alongside yelling '*monolos, monolos*'. They are selling small replicas of the strange monolithic statues that can be seen lining the shores of Lake Titicaca in the distance.

When, sixty years ago, the Austrian engineer Arthur Posnansky came to Lake Titicaca and to Tiahuanaco, he was held spellbound by these giant statues and thought them at least eighteen thousand years old. The 'Sun-Temple' of Tiahuanaco, the *Kalasassaya*, whose gigantic ruins lie quite near to the railway track, impressed him especially and he thought that here must be the cradle of mankind, the birthplace of all cultures. Present-day archaeologists afford his theories scant respect. They consider that Tiahuanaco is only two thousand years old at the most, thus placing the beginnings of its culture at approximately the same time as the birth of Christ. However, the impact made by the gigantic temple, the richly sculptured sun-portal, hewn out of a gigantic block of andesite, the tremendous stone pillars—ten feet high, six and a half feet deep and up to sixteen and a half feet wide, and the huge slabs of the altar, whose fragments still measure twenty feet in length, thirteen feet in width and five feet broad—is such, that it is easy to understand why Posnansky believed that an unknown people with a highly developed artistic and technological culture had once lived in these regions.

It is incredible that those buildings, whose magnificence survives even in their fragments, should have been erected by primitive natives using only chisels and axes of stone, which had to be resharpened after every stroke. Yet the pillars and slabs of the sun-temple are mathematically exact, clean-cut and accurately jointed.

The slabs used to build the temple weigh a hundred tons and more, and must have been transported from the quarries on the other shore of Lake Titicaca on rafts. The gigantic blocks must have been dragged into position by human hands alone, for the people of Tiahuanaco had no wagons or draught-animals, and were ignorant of the use of pulleys.

A vast necropolis, covering a hundred and ten acres, surrounds the lake, and fragments of urns and human bones can be seen everywhere. Human

XXII. The coast of Peru.

skulls, discoloured and brittle with age, were found in Cuzco, to the south-west, with strange holes, each the size of a florin, in different parts of the skull. Had these been injuries, received in battle, they would have led to immediate death, but seeing that the edges of these holes are regular and clean and look as if a modern surgeon had trepanned them with a bone-saw, they cannot possibly have been the results of battle-wounds. What a breath-taking discovery! The most difficult trepanations must have been performed two thousand years ago, by surgeons using stone files and obsidian scalpels, and yet so expertly that a modern brain surgeon could not do better. It sounds incredible, but it is true!

In La Paz can be seen an ancient tourniquet, used quite recently by

Peruvian doctors in the course of a surgical operation, during which the patient, suffering from severe anaemia, lost hardly any blood. This was remarkable enough, but the skull operations presented an even greater problem. They were apparently performed on living subjects and must have been successful since definite formations of new bone tissue could clearly be seen on the skulls. This not only proves that the patient survived the operation but also that he continued to live for some years afterwards.

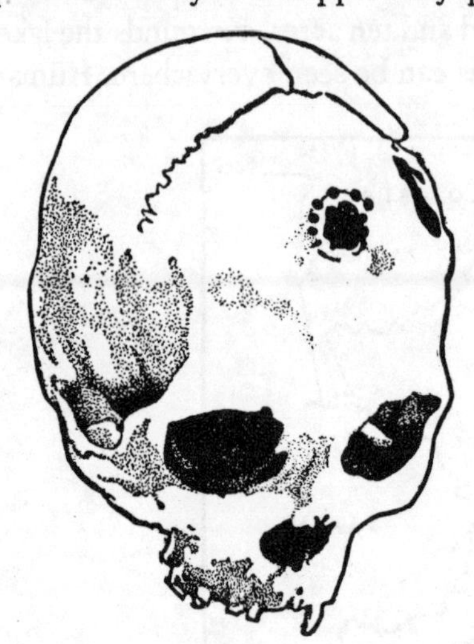

23. Trepanning of a skull.

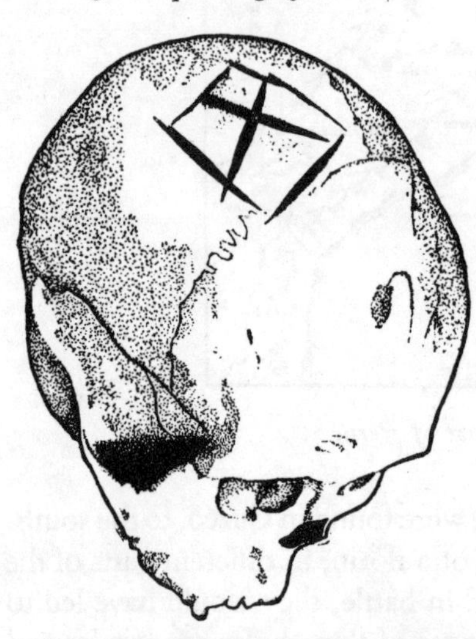

24. Rectangular and diagonal incisions made by means of a tumi.

There is no written evidence of these miracles; all that is left are the skulls, hundreds of skulls, from almost every part of Peru and Bolivia. Many of them have these new bone formations, but by no means all of them. Were it not for the fact that, until a few centuries ago, similar operations were performed in the Polynesian islands in the South Pacific, it might reasonably have been believed that the trepanations of South America had not served a medical, but some other kind of purpose.

Yet this was not the case, and since such difficult surgical operations, like the huge buildings mentioned earlier on, presuppose a high level of skill and experience, archaeologists have made a constant search for the origins of the Tiahuanaco culture. Although some believe that the people of Tiahuanaco belonged to the Aymará group of Indians, who continue to live in the Cordillera highlands to this day, this hypothesis cannot be proved, nor would it explain why the Tiahuanaco culture should suddenly have appeared, 'ready-made', and without a trace of intermediate stages of development..

It is this lack of evidence of any earlier and less advanced stages in the Tiahuanaco culture which has led archaeologists to seek for proof of possible cultural influences from outside. The great champion of this theory is Thor Heyerdahl, the Norwegian ethnologist who, in his writings on the subject, refers to the famous 'Viracocha Legend', still so current in many parts of South America, where the inhabitants refer to white men simply as 'Viracocha'.

Who and what was Viracocha? According to Heyerdahl, this legend is obviously a South American parallel to the Quetzalcoatl Myth of the Mayas and Aztecs. Viracocha, too, was a white god, old and bearded, and had appeared in the land long before the arrival of the Incas. He too had brought a cross with him, and had placed it upon a mountain. He had preached, baptized, listened to confession, imposed penances on sinners and had granted them absolution from their sins. He founded the city of Cuzco, taught crafts and all forms of higher morality, and then withdrew to the Sun-Island on Lake Titicaca where, the story goes, he established his capital. Later he quarrelled with Chief Cari from the valley of Coquimbo. Cari vanquished Viracocha, killing most of his white men, but sparing the women and children. The White Saviour himself escaped miraculously, and followed by some of his closest disciples, he turned to the Western Ocean where, sitting on his magic cloak, he had disappeared across the waves. But before leaving he had preached for all the world to hear that when in the far distant future the time was ripe, he would send his messengers, 'bearded white men'.

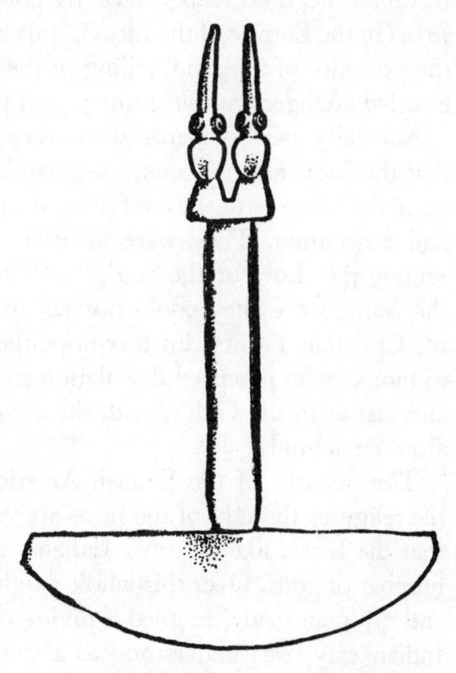

25. The tumi, *by means of which the Incas carried out skull operations.*

Heyerdahl quotes as his source Cieza de León's *Crónica del Perú*, written in 1553. Cieza de León was a comrade-in-arms of Pizarro, but his *Crónica*, as Americanists emphasize, is nothing but second-hand information. Viracocha, they stress, did not belong to the Inca pantheon and de León's tales were nothing but superstitious Inca myths. Nevertheless Pizarro's men were astonished. Only recently Mayas and Aztecs had hailed Cortés and his men as the long-awaited 'White Gods', and now the Spaniards were being treated in the same way in Peru! The Incas, too, must have *known* of the existence of light-skinned, fair-haired people. Thus white messengers *must* somehow have reached America from the world of the Whites, at some period in the past.

Cieza de León himself did not draw this conclusion, but he could not ignore the fact that when in 1527 his men, amongst whom were many blue-eyed and fair-haired descendants of the Goths and Vandals, entered Peru, they were greeted with shy reverence by the *indios*. As the Swiss traveller, Siegfried Huber, recently pointed out in his book, *Im Reich der Inka* (In the Empire of the Incas), 'this behaviour can only be explained by the existence of a legend, telling of the visit of some fair-haired and fair-bearded strangers to the country, and prophesying their return'.

Naturally the Spaniards were very interested when they discovered that the Incas not only confessed regularly to a high priest, sworn to observe the 'secrecy of the confessional', but that they also knew of penance and absolution. They were amazed to find in Cuzco an idol representing the 'Lord of the Sun', the 'Son of the Sun', and the 'Brother of the Sun', since they could not fail to notice the striking analogy with the Christian Trinity. Furthermore, the Inca religion had different orders of monks who practised flagellation and observed regular and strict fasts, and just as in the Old World, there were many saintly hermits living in absolute solitude.

The remarks of the Finnish Americanist, Rafael Karsten, concerning the religious thought of the Incas are very interesting. He has emphasized that the Incas, like all other Indians, were in fact polytheists revering a number of gods. Over this whole pantheon of gods, who were, in a sense, entirely man-made, reigned a divine overlord who, in a completely un-Indian way, was understood as a spiritual, incorporeal being: God the Creator, Viracocha. The Incas had learned of the existence of this supreme deity from the Tiahuanaco culture. Viracocha stood high over the Sun and was 'the eternal lord, symbol of the world and its unchanging foundation . . . the Son of the Sun . . . the creator of the world. . . .' of one of the oldest of Inca prayers.

This is a very significant discovery. It makes it likely that Viracocha, like Quetzalcoatl, had in fact been a white Christian missionary coming from the West. This theory is backed up by the fact that, at the time of the Spanish conquest, many Peruvian nobles had fair hair and white skins. Particularly the *Coyas*, the 'Beloved Women', as the female dependants of the leading Inca nobles were called, frequently bore a striking resemblance to European women. This is very surprising, since the Incas belong to the same ethnological group as the Quechua Indians, one of the tribes that had probably come from northern Peru, but of whose ultimate origin we know nothing. However, Rafael Karsten has pointed out that anthropologically 'they are one of the exotic races which come closest in type to the white race'. Spanish tradition confirms this for, as Siegfried Huber has recently reported in his *Relación del descubrimiento y conquista de los reinos del Peru*, Pedro Pizarro, cousin of the conqueror, was amazed to see Indians closely resembling white men, who, in their own opinion, were superior in mind and beauty to their darker-skinned compatriots.

> The people of the kingdom of Peru were light-skinned, their hair being similar in colour to ripe wheat. The lords and ladies were fairer still, like Spaniards. In this country I met an Indian woman with her child, both so light-skinned that they hardly differed from white people. It is said of them there that they are the children of gods.

Since Pedro Pizarro's *Relación* is not easily come by we wish also to cite the Spanish text:

> *Esta gente del reino del Peru era blanca, de color trigueño, y entre los señores y señoras eran más blancos como españoles. Yo vide en esta tierra una muger india y un niño que de blancos y rubios casi no vian. Estos decían ellos que eran hijos de los ídolos.*

This sounds highly improbable and is usually dismissed as an exaggeration, but in the preceding chapter of this book we have already mentioned that the coloured wall-paintings in Chitzen Itzá quite obviously represented a white people in battle with dark-skinned enemies. The evidence *need* not necessarily be deceptive, and if one bears in mind the fact that marriage between close relatives had long been the custom at the court of the Inca Kings as a measure of keeping the royal blood pure and unpolluted, it is quite possible that at the time of the Conquista the Peruvian nobility could boast many white-skinned members. But even if we agree to accept the weighty circumstantial evidence that European elements had indeed been introduced into the American aristocracy, it is by no means certain where these elements came from. They could have come from Asia just like the Mongoloid elements among the American natives, in which case the numerous Indo-European splinter groups in North-East Asia would be their early relatives. On the other hand, they could have come to America across the Atlantic Ocean. This may sound far-fetched, but in fact the ocean, with its favourable winds and currents, presented a much smaller barrier. The colonization of Madagascar and the Malayan peninsula is an argument in favour of this hypothesis that is difficult to refute.

Furthermore, 'white' Indians seem to exist to this very day. In 1926 the American ethnologist Harris, who had studied the Indians of the San Blas region, reported that their hair was straw-coloured and their complexion almost white. The English explorer, Colonel Fawcett, F.R.G.S., who died in 1925 during his last expedition to the jungles of South America, has given us an account of the journeys he made in those regions between 1906 and 1921 in his posthumously published book, *Exploration Fawcett*. In this book he tells how he and other explorers had frequently come across white Indians: 'People with red hair and blue eyes like a *Gringo*'. Such reports have always been dismissed with the assertion that their authors had come across cases of albinos, but this explanation seems to be far-fetched. Fawcett, for one, when describing a blue-eyed red-haired Indian belonging to the Maxubi, a wild Indian tribe in Amazonia, mentions quite emphatically that he was not an albino.

Still more explicit is one of Fawcett's authorities, the French manager of the rubber plantation Santa Rosa on the Abuna, a tributary of the Rio Madeira. Fawcett recounts how, during his first expedition, in 1906–7, the Frenchman had told him:

> There are white Indians on the Acre. My brother went up the Tahuamanu on a launch, and one day, well up river, was told that white Indians were near. He didn't believe it and scoffed at the men who told him, but nevertheless went out in a canoe, and found unmistakable signs of Indians. The next thing he knew, he and his men were being attacked by big, well-built, handsome savages, pure white, with red hair and blue eyes. They fought like devils.... People say these white Indians don't exist, and, when it's proved they do, that they are half-breed mixtures of Spanish and Indian. That's what people say who never saw them, but those who have seen them think differently!

Since Fawcett, who had travelled continuously in Amazonia between 1906 and 1914, and returned to his explorations immediately after the first World War, later to be entrusted with the task of establishing the border between Peru, Bolivia and Brazil, was a scientifically trained man, quite at home among the Indians, it is difficult to ignore the testimony of such a witness and when one bears in mind the reports of Pedro Pizarro, it takes on extra significance.

The older Americanists, who used to dwell upon the mongoloid characteristics of the Indians, gave little credence to Pedro Pizarro. But since the average Indian squaw, by all other accounts, was no great beauty, the gallant Spanish nobility of the times of Charles V and Philip II must either have had quite different aesthetic ideals from ours—a possibility that Spanish art at once refutes—or else we are forced to take Pedro Pizarro's description of the *Coyas* very seriously. In any case it is certain that the haughty and proud Grandees of Aragon and Castile married Inca princesses in great numbers, presented them at Court as their equals, and that two generations later, in 1603, a request for remission of tax signed by five hundred and sixty-seven descendants of ancient Inca families was handed to the Crown of Spain.

If we had similar evidence concerning the Etruscans or that unknown equestrian people, the Hyksos of Egypt, it would in all probability be considered perfectly credible, but the Incas are surrounded by an aura of doubt and uncertainty. This can be explained by the fact that from the very outset the Inca state had something inherently iridescent, dualistic and vague in it. Though the Quechua Indians brought a highly developed culture with them into Peru, the Aymará had a considerable hand in their later political and artistic achievements. The Incas were always ready to assimilate other elements from earlier civilizations into their culture, if only they found them congenial.

We have already mentioned the Tiahuanaco culture but there was also the Chavin culture—its earliest traces date back to about 800 B.C.—which took its name from the ancient place of pilgrimage Chavin de Huantar. Like the Tiahuanaco culture, with its inexplicably advanced medical and technical knowledge, it, too, suddenly emerged in a fully-fledged state. The wonderful temples of this epoch, lasting about a thousand years, the glorious ceramics, and irrigation systems won deep admiration from the Spaniards. Finally there was the Chimu culture, the youngest of the three, thrown up by an Indian tribe originating in the valley of Trujillo in the north of the country, who extended their influence from Tumbez to Lima during the second half of the fifteenth century. Shortly before the Spaniards appeared on the scene, this tribe had been subjected and absorbed by the Incas, thus giving rise to another foreign element within the Inca culture.

XXIII. The Empire of the Incas.

Peru, when conquered by the Spaniards, stretched from Southern Colombia to Central Chile, i.e. in addition to the modern Peru, it counted within its borders Ecuador, Bolivia and northern Chile. The ocean in the west and the Andes in the east formed its natural boundaries. Thus the Inca empire was tremendously long and narrow. This fact explains why great importance was paid to good communications, culminating in the building of tremendous roads, incomparably superior to the famous military roads of the Romans, which, in their magnificence, can only be compared with the giant construction of the Great Wall of China. One of the roads starting from the capital Cuzco ran straight north across Abancay, Andahuylas and Ayacucho as far as Cajamarca and thence via Quito, the capital of Ecuador, up to Pasto in South Colombia; a total length of about 1,250 miles. The main road to the south went past Lake Titicaca and the valley of the Desaguadero to Chuquisaca in southern Bolivia, and thence as far as Tucumán in the Argentine. The coastal towns between Tumbez, in the north, and Nasca, in the south, were also connected by imperial roads which in turn were joined by the high mountain passes.

All these roads, which are up to eight yards wide, contain sections passing through difficult mountainous country or deserts. Modern engineers are full of praise and admiration for the technical achievements of the old Indian road builders. The German Americanist Hans Dietrich Disselhoff in his recent *Geschichte der altamerikanischen Kulturen* (History of Ancient American Cultures) quotes this impressive passage from Cieza de León's History:

> Huayna Capac ordered the construction of a road, larger and wider than any his father had travelled on. . . . Thus was built the proudest and most noteworthy road the world has ever seen. It ran from Cuzco to Quito and joined the road leading to Chile. This road, leading across deep valleys and high mountains, across mountain peaks, through sodden marshes, across hard rock and alongside raging rivers, is without parallel. For long stretches it was cobbled, elsewhere it was hewn out of mountain precipices, and ran across far-distant ranges. Along rivers it was banked, and its path was cleared across fields of snow. Along the entire length of it were situated inns, storehouses, sun temples and postal stations. Did Alexander or any of the other mighty kings who ruled the world build such a road or construct such buildings? . . .

It must be admitted that these roads were not as a rule suitable for wagons, although some even stretches serve as carriageways to this day. Despite their great achievements in many fields, the Incas were ignorant of the wheel. Thus, when building their roads, they did not have to make them suitable for wagons; consequently they constructed their mountain roads, wherever necessary, in terraces. Similarly their bridges did not have to carry wheeled traffic and are constructed with an ease which leaves modern travellers gasping for breath. Most of these were suspension bridges, built of tremendous osier cables, and were capable of bearing the weight of a whole herd of llamas.

Bridges and roads with their *tambos*, caravanserais, were inspected by officials employed for this express purpose. Villages were given the task of maintaining the roads, bridges, *tambos* and postal stations in their areas in good order.

A precaution which all authoritarian systems of government must adopt is the creation of depots for food supplies and military stores. Naturally this is not done out of neighbourly love but from political considerations. The police and army must, under all circumstances, be kept ready and equipped for action, and though the totalitarian state has small concern for its subjects as individuals, it does try to avert the consequences of a bad harvest. It was because of these considerations that the Inca paid great attention to public economy. In his *Historia del nuevo mundo*, Bernabé de Cobo wrote of the food magazines that existed in Peru during the time of the Conquista:

> The supplies stored in these granaries consisted of everything that the people had delivered in tribute, viz. great quantities of maize, dried potatoes, and other vegetables, the dried meat of llamas, stags, and *vicuñas*, great quantities of the most diverse materials such as wool, cotton, feathers, etc.
>
> There were also weapons for equipping the army, whenever it moved from one part of the country to another. Furthermore, there was a great quantity of all those things which had been paid as taxes to the ruler; among them red seashells transported from Tumbez to Cuzco, more than three hundred miles, to be fashioned into small pearls looking like coral.

26. Inca Tupac Yupanqui receiving anaccount from one of his officials.

In addition to the maintenance of roads and an adequate level of food supplies, totalitarian governments also pay great attention to a rapid information service. The Incas introduced a magnificent postal relay-system with fresh runners at every mile or so, so that messages could be delivered as quickly as possible. The Inca post is reputed to have needed ten days for a message from Quito to reach Cuzco, thus covering a distance of over a hundred miles per day. These figures must be approximately correct; in any case there is no doubt that these *chasqui*, the postal relays of the Incas, were capable of a speed far greater than that of the mounted post which the Spaniards later introduced.

In view of this, it is all the more remarkable that the Peruvians did not produce a serviceable system of written communication. Despite the many ways of communication offered by their Quipu-'writing', consisting as it did of knots in multicoloured threads, tightly intertwined, this method served essentially for statistical and numerical purposes. It was an eminently suitable system for recording the strength of troops, herds, the amount of taxes, tribute, etc., but not for transmitting other kinds of messages. For 'telegraphic' purposes the Incas had to use the primitive method of smoke-signals. This deficiency is particularly striking in view of what was otherwise so high a level of civilization, and one is inclined to assume that the ruling circles were unwilling to give their subjects a means of communication that might later on prove dangerous. In any case, private needs—and the possibility of written communication must be considered as such—were of secondary importance to the Inca state, which also explains why they did not use money.

The economic system of the Incas seems to have been based on agrarian communism, not in the modern but in a strict theocratic-hierarchical sense. The cultivation of the soil was a religious task undertaken every year even by the Emperor himself, the Son of the Sun, who owned two-thirds of all the land, the remaining third being the property of the village communities. Although this division did not apply equally to all parts of Peru, nowhere was there privately-owned property. To till the soil and to provide for a good harvest by systematic cultivation and extensive irrigation was not only a duty incumbent on every citizen but also an article of religious faith. The natural consequence of this was to knit the village communities closely together. These village clans were the real core of the Inca empire, and quite often the central power was confronted by rebellious agricultural and village communities. Nevertheless the Incas never succumbed to the temptation of abolishing the traditional forms of communal life. As a rule they contented themselves with appointing the village chiefs and judges to official positions and gaining their favour by means of presents and other signs of esteem. All village communities were closely watched by the *tucui-ricuc*, which literally translated means *see-all*, a group of supervisors invested with extraordinary powers. It must be stressed that justice was administered with draconian severity, and it is significant that offences against the state were punished with incomparably greater severity than offences of a private nature. The guilty were sentenced to be flogged or, in case of more severe offences, to penal labour. If a village failed to fulfil its quota, collective fines were imposed on it through increased taxes. Sometimes whole village communities were forcibly re-

27. *The Inca tilling the land.*

settled as a punitive measure or for political reasons—for instance in order to safeguard a newly-conquered province by means of 'loyal peasants'. Indeed, there is nothing new under the sun!

Nevertheless one would not be completely justified in calling the Inca rule a dictatorship, for to brand a form of government as totalitarian implies a faith in the rights and dignity of the individual, and it is extremely doubtful whether such feelings ever existed in the Inca state with its traditionally rigid agrarian clan society.

28. Inca warrior with catapult, shield and club.

It goes without saying that in such a hierarchical 'ant-state' particular emphasis was placed on taxation and the army. Nobility, officers and priests, and men below the ages of twenty-five and above fifty were exempted from taxes. Everybody else was taxed in that a fixed quota of labour or production was imposed upon him. Magazines, i.e. places containing *quipus*, the telling strings, by whose knots the tax assessments could be told, were located in every provincial capital. In smaller places and in the villages, travelling officials of the treasury saw to it that the quotas were punctiliously fulfilled. In view of the tremendous treasures found in the magazines of the Inca, the Peruvian system of taxation must obviously have worked very successfully.

The Incas had a very efficient system of conscription in which the Spaniards were greatly interested. The men of each village, between the ages of twenty-five and fifty, were organized in 'Fifties' and 'Hundreds' under their own officers. Five 'Hundreds', corresponding perhaps to a modern battalion, and a thousand 'hundreds', perhaps equal to a division, were the tactical units of the Inca army, whose full strength was about two hundred thousand men. During times of conscription, armies seemed to rise up from nowhere, and naturally drill and tactics were equally highly organized. Pizarro's secretary, Francisco de Xérez, gives some interesting details about the army of the Incas in his *Verdadera Relación de la Conquista del Perú.*

Of the battle order of the Indians we can say the following: the advance guard is made up of slingers using smooth pebbles about the size of an egg and able to kill men even at a great distance. The slingers bear shields made of thin but highly resistant boards, and also wear a kind of thickly-padded jerkin as armour. The slingers are followed by the actual army: warriors with cudgels and battle axes; the cudgels are nine feet long and as thick as the lance of a captain. The head of the cudgel is about the size of a man's fist and covered with metal barbs. The battle axes of the Indians are about the same size; the bronze or copper blade is similar in width to our halberds. Many of the chiefs have cudgels and battle axes made of gold and silver; in the hands of the Indians both weapons are highly dangerous. This section is followed by another using lances similar to javelins that are thrown by catapults. Finally the rear guard consists of pike-men whose lances are some thirty feet long. Atahualpa's army was divided into a number of sections, all carrying their own flag. It consisted, without exception, of tall, battle-tested young men, a thousand of whom would no doubt have sufficed to conquer every town of this country, even if it had twenty thousand inhabitants or more.

It is alleged that the Incas, like all other Indians, achieved far less at sea than they did on land. This strikes one as odd when one realizes that the coast-line of the Inca Empire was many thousands of miles long. Now the Spaniards of the Conquista stated quite the opposite, and unanimously declared the Incas to have been great navigators. Apparently doubts were first cast on their navigational prowess by the German-French writer Adalbert von Chamisso. Between 1815 and 1818 he participated as scientific expert in the world cruise of the Russian brig *Rurik*, and soon after his return he published a brilliant report on his experiences, which makes fascinating reading even today. Here we find the glib assertion: 'No American people was ever a people of sailors.' Since his work was one of the great best-sellers of the nineteenth century, his declaration, which obviously did not correspond with the facts, was given credence by a great many people. This apparent contradiction with the assertions of the Spaniards is relatively simple to explain. The seafaring people of the Old World always built their boats on the pattern of the canoe, using a hollowed-out tree-trunk. Whenever one of the sailors of the Old World encountered natives using rafts he would scoff at them, forgetting that his own nautical ancestors had once started with similar rafts. It seemed impossible that people could travel for thousands of miles on one of these objects with absolute safety. Chamisso, too, must have been forcibly struck by this.

This is only one of the many instances of technology striking man with blindness. True, a raft is not particularly comfortable, but if it is kept in the direction of the wind and the waves by means of a drag anchor it is much safer than a boat washed by every heavy breaker.

The proof for this assertion was recently brought home by the French physician, Doctor Alain Bombard, who crossed the Atlantic on an inflatable rubber raft, thus confirming the theories put forward some years previously by the Norwegian explorer Thor Heyerdahl. As is now well known, Heyerdahl wanted to prove that Polynesia must have been settled from America. He did not merely prove this theoretically from his desk, but, following the example of the ancient Indians, he constructed the large rigged raft which he called *Kon-Tiki*, and entrusting himself and his comrades to the mercy of the Trade Winds and ocean currents, he landed some three months later on a small Polynesian island.

At first sight these rafts look gawky, clumsy and fragile. Nevertheless, even in olden times very long voyages were made on them, and there are many reports telling us that Indian balsa rafts, carrying women and children on board, often stayed out at sea for weeks on end. Not merely the islands close to the shore, but even the Galapagos Islands, almost five hundred miles from the mainland, came within the sphere of interest of the Incas. Certain finds made by Thor Heyerdahl during one of his recent expeditions to these islands seem to corroborate the theory of an early contact between these isolated islands and Peru. Thus, the story that the Inca Tupac Yupanqui (1470–95), Atahualpa's grandfather, discovered a series of islands far out in the ocean is likely to be more than a mere legend. Although there is no proof that the islands reached by Tupac Yupanqui and his fleet of four hundred balsa rafts were in fact the Galapagos Islands, on one of the most easterly of the Polynesian islands people still tell of a great sailor, Tupa by name, who once arrived with his fleet of rafts at the island. Thus, there seems some basis for the assumption that, during his year-long wandering at sea, Tupac Yupanqui did in fact reach Polynesia. Despite the improbability of this theory, it must be remembered that rumours of fertile islands lying to the West were rife throughout the entire length of the South American coast at the time of the Conquista, and that the Spaniards themselves put to sea in search of them.

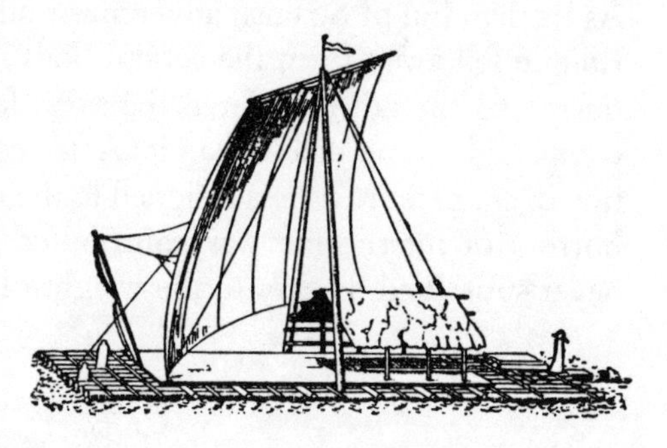

29. A balsa raft.

Although these balsa rafts fulfilled their purpose excellently well they must, with all due respect, be considered rather primitive constructions, and in view of the otherwise high level of Inca culture this cannot fail to arouse our surprise. Such anomalies existed, however, in other forms as well. We have already mentioned that the wheel, and with it wheeled traffic, was completely unknown. The temples (which still have engineers marvelling how the giant slabs were cut, transported, hoisted into position and made to fit together so closely that, although no mortar was used, it is impossible to insert the blade of a knife between them) are covered by roofs of the most primitive kind. To add to our bewilderment and uncertainty of what to believe, we are told that the Incas knew the secret of a mysterious plant-juice which could 'soften' even the hardest of rocks and make it malleable. Brian Fawcett, the son of that famous explorer who met his death in the jungles of South America, has repeatedly mentioned this plant-juice in his books and articles.

Another striking peculiarity about the Incas is that, despite their great political acumen, they made the isolated and almost inaccessible town of Cuzco the capital of their empire. Only when the province of Quito in the north and the coastal regions at the foot of the Western Cordillera had been added, was the traditional centre of government brushed aside—a symbol of the waning of the central authority. By the time that Atahualpa chose the centrally placed city of Cajamarca as his capital, it was too late. As the handful of Spanish adventurers advanced, the outer regions of the Empire fell away from the central body, until finally even that was conquered. Although it suffered the same fate, the Inca Empire proved incomparably more stable than its Aztec counterpart, with its conglomeration of states more or less resigned to their subjection, and though here the horrors of internecine war contributed to its own downfall, the Incas never submitted meekly to the weight of the Spanish yoke.

4

We take up the story again at the point where Pizarro had just delivered his knock-out blow. Atahualpa was in his power and his Inca guards fleeing over the mountains. While the Spaniards were deliberating their next move, Atahualpa took matters into his own hands, and had his brother Huascar murdered. He was afraid that the Spaniards might enter in league with the priesthood and with the vanquished forces of his captured brother, thus ousting Atahualpa from his position of sole ruler.

As he watched the Spaniards making division of their loot, Atahualpa was struck by their obsession with gold. The events deriving from his psychological insight read like a tale from the *Thousand and One Nights*.

> He asked [reports Francisco de Xérez] to be led before Pizarro and offered to fill the room in which he was captured with gold as high as he could reach with his fingertips, if the Spaniard would give him his freedom in return. Pizarro then asked how much time he would need for this and Atahualpa replied: 'two months'. The Governor accepted this offer and told Atahualpa that if he kept his promise he need fear nothing. Thereupon the King immediately sent messengers to his generals ordering them to send at once two thousand Incas laden with gold.

Day after day, a fantastic rain of gold poured into the Spanish camp. Hordes of Indians arrived, all carrying urns, pots and other vessels of pure gold. The heap grew bigger and bigger, but the two months were almost up, and still a considerable space remained to be filled. Then, at the request of the King, Pizarro sent three Spaniards into Cuzco with orders to strip the main temple, *Coricancha*, the Court of Gold, of its golden panelling and to bring it to Pizarro.

These three Spanish mercenaries were the first white men to enter Cuzco. The report they made on their return must be counted as one of the most amazing documents in the history of discovery. The extract quoted is from the version published in Lisbon in 1609 by Garcilasso de la Vega:

> The capital of the Incas is a large city lying in a wide valley, hemmed in on all sides by mountains. This valley is extremely fertile and is blessed with an excellent climate throughout the year, for there are no great variations in temperature. Despite the plentiful supply of water for irrigation provided by the mountain rivers, the air is so dry that meat remains fresh a very long time. The region is almost completely free of vermin, mosquitoes being extremely rare. The city, divided into four parts according to the cardinal points, has some twenty thousand inhabitants. Close to the main street there are two underground water-conduits which are so old that no one knows anything of their origin. The nobles' houses and palaces, the description of which I shall reserve for later, are adorned with magnificent ornaments. The fortress is undoubtedly the most striking building in the town and appears to have been the work of magicians and demons rather than of human architects. It was built of stones so gigantic in size that we could not understand how they had been fetched from a distance of ten to fifteen marching hours along steep and perilous roads, for the Indians had neither wagons nor beasts of burden and must have moved these tremendous weights themselves. They had neither steel nor iron to cleave the rocks, nor tools to shape them. They knew not the use of lime or mortar and yet these huge slabs are fitted together so closely that it is not possible to insert even the blade of a knife between them. Cranes and pulleys are unknown to the Indians, and thus we cannot explain how they moved these tremendous blocks measuring some thirty-eight feet long, eighteen feet wide and two feet thick. The Indians themselves did not esteem this castle most, but preferred the King's temple, dedicated to the Sun. In it were stored up treasures passing all imagination, its very walls being covered with gold from top to bottom. In it was a magnificent altar on which stood a massive image of the Sun, fashioned of pure gold. The face of the god was adorned with flames, extending from one wall to the next, in the same way that our painters often represent the Sun. The whole temple contained just this one idol, since the Incas have but one god, the Sun. On both sides of the Sun were ranged the mummified bodies of the Inca kings, so artfully embalmed that they seemed to be alive. They were seated on golden thrones set on golden daises. Never have we beheld such a wondrous sight.

The remainder of the report made by the three Spaniards of their visit to Cuzco runs in the same vein, and reading between the lines we are conscious that despite their greed for gold, they felt some shame at the sacrilege they were committing, for naturally everything was razed to the ground. The golden statue of the Sun and the panelling of the walls were torn down and put into the melting pot. When the Spaniards finally shared out their loot, it was found that they had gathered some thirteen hundred and twenty-five pounds of gold in bars. In such quantities, however, the precious metal lost most of its value. Those who wanted to pay debts would hang a whole host of golden urns, pots and other objects round the necks of their Indian slaves and, thus equipped, set forth to visit their creditors. If the latter protested at the amount offered in payment, they would be silenced by the immediate addition of further pieces. According to contemporary reports, the Spaniards were exceedingly careless in reckoning up the number of gold bars melted down from the loot, so that the total proceeds of this large-scale robbery probably amounted to almost double the estimated figure of 1,326,500 gold pesos (about ten million pounds). This flood of gold brought many disadvantages in its wake. Since there was no iron, horseshoes were made of silver. Francisco de Xérez tells us the fantastic prices asked for the most essential things: a horse, costing 600 pesos in Spain, was priced at 2,500 pesos in Peru; a bottle of wine could not be bought for under sixty pesos and a coat for less than a hundred and twenty. By the scale of values current in Spain, the meanest of Pizarro's mercenaries were rich men, for they received a minimum of four thousand four hundred gold pesos and a hundred and eighty-one pieces of silver for their part in the conquest, but in Peru they were little better than beggars.

Atahualpa fulfilled his promise shortly before the two months elapsed: his prison, a room seventeen feet wide and twenty-two feet long, was filled with gold to the required height. Needless to say, Pizarro did not keep his side of the bargain, but treated Atahualpa as the Inca had treated his brother: he had him killed. It is significant to note that the only two officers who retained some sense of honour, Hernando Pizarro, half-brother of the General, and the cavalry officer de Soto, were first removed from the scene. As soon as this was done, in August 1533, Atahualpa was murdered. His behaviour when facing death was admirable, and as the chief assassin's private secretary admits, 'he died with much courage, showing no signs of fear....'

Another contemporary report from the hand of one less dependent on Pizarro states:

> Quite apart from their sin before God, the murderers deprived our sovereign the Emperor, and the Spanish nation itself, of countless treasures that this prince might still have given them. Moreover, none of Atahualpa's subjects would have risen up against us, as happened after his death. What is more, it was generally known that the Governor had pledged his word for the safety of Atahualpa.

'Atahualpa could have given the Conquistadors still much more,' and the realization of this was to haunt the murderers. In addition, it slowly came home to Pizarro that in removing the King, he had also removed the whole basis of authority in the country, and that without Atahualpa's help he could do very little with such a centralized state. History has rarely shown such an example of political incompetence on both sides. It was clear that Huascar's assassination would be avenged on Atahualpa himself, and that, in turn, the latter's executioners would be called upon to pay the price of their crime. Blood must be answered with more blood. At first, however, things went well for Pizarro. On 15th November 1533, the capital Cuzco was captured. The Spaniards proved so brutal in their triumph, so ruthless in their search for plunder, so wanton in their venery, that a general uprising against them was the speedy result of their success. The massacres which followed were among the most ghastly recorded by history. The cruelty of the Spaniards was paid out with interest in the same coin. We are reluctant, however, to dwell upon the bestialities engendered by these struggles, from which the Spaniards emerged the victors. Their victory was not due to their superior arms, for hand to hand struggles of that type gave them no scope for exploiting their artillery and fire-arms, but must be ascribed to another cause. November is the month for planting in Peru, and Manco, the leader of the rebels, knew only too well that his people would be visited by a far worse enemy than the Spaniards, if the sowing were delayed any longer. He dismissed his army and carried on guerrilla resistance against the invaders with a small band of nobles from desert hide-outs. It was only in 1544 that his enemies managed to destroy him.

While all these things were going on in and around the capital, elsewhere Gonzalo Pizarro, the younger brother of Francisco, was making great discoveries—for the wrong reasons, we might add.

During the conquest of Peru, the Spaniards had heard rumours that the great river which they had crossed on the way to Cuzco and which they had called the Marañon, led to a wooded country in the east, fabulously rich in gold, emeralds and spices. Naturally enough the rapacious Spaniards enquired of the Incas if they knew anything of that country, but although they met with no success from that quarter, they did not let the matter rest there, and soon the whole army was fired with the prospect of new sources of loot. In the late summer of 1537 a panting messenger, bringing news from Captain Luis Daza, arrived in Lima. Daza reported that in his official capacity as commander of Latacunga he had received a delegation from some Indian tribes bringing tribute of the usual gifts, and he had also learnt that far up in the eastern mountains there lay a holy lake whose bed was paved with gold and jewels. Apparently it was the custom in that region, on every important Indian feast-day, to cover the chief with gold dust which he washed off in the lake, and, as he did so, a gigantic golden bowl, filled to the brim with sapphires, diamonds, golden bracelets and emeralds, was emptied into the lake. The name of this chief was El Dorado, the golden one, and if this report were true, then the riches of the Incas were as nothing compared with the boundless wealth to be found there.

The effect of Daza's news on the Spaniards, already light-headed from the thin mountain air and their successes, was electrifying—they swallowed it hook, line and sinker. Gonzalo Pizarro, deeply conscious that he, too, must achieve some measure of personal glory, saw his opportunity, but he had to bide his time before he was able to go in search of El Dorado.

By his vigorous conduct of the operation against the Inca guerrilla leader Manco, he was finally appointed Governor of Quito in 1540. Gonzalo welcomed this appointment joyfully, since it gave him the opportunity to explore the vast jungles lying to the east, of which rumour promised so much. It was said that one-eyed people lived there; that there were powerful states there, led by women; that there were gigantic forests full of cinnamon and other precious spices; and that that way lay the fabulous world of El Dorado.

Gonzalo was so eager to lay his hands on this wealth, and so convinced of its existence, that within the first few weeks of his arrival in Quito, he persuaded three hundred and fifty Spaniards to accompany him on his march to the Kingdom of El Dorado. Four thousand Indian auxiliaries accompanied that well-armed, well-equipped expedition which counted also on its strength two hundred horses, a gigantic herd of pigs and a thousand bloodhounds. This unwieldy force set forth at the beginning of 1541, and from the very beginning its progress was highly dramatic, for it found itself at the epicentre of one of those terrible earthquakes which continue to make life in the volcanic region of the Andes so precarious even today. The earth split asunder before the horrified eyes of the Spaniards, engulfing a whole Indian village.

For weeks they threaded their way through the jungle under torrential rain, sometimes taking a whole day to advance two miles. Although they found that the rumours of the existence of giant cinnamon trees and of other precious spices were correct, the Spaniards realized that such things were quite worthless so far away from all civilization. Bitterly disappointed, Gonzalo was ready to give up and return, when they encountered some jungle Indians who told them that there was a rich, fertile land flowing with gold and emeralds only ten days' journey away.

Thus, seven months after leaving Quito, the expedition finally reached the Napo, one of the tributaries of the upper Amazon. Since it was impossible to ford its broad waters, the Spaniards decided to build a ship, and eight further weeks elapsed before the rough-and-ready craft was ready. On Christmas Day, 1541, Francisco de Orellana, a knight from Trujillo, was given command over the ship and ordered to take sixty men in search of food. The herd of pigs had long since disintegrated: some had frozen to death in the high Andes, and the remainder had either been eaten by delighted alligators in the jungle marshes, or had managed to escape, and so the Spaniards were in serious want of food.

Orellana, who had previously been leading the advance guard of the expedition, finding himself thus elevated to the rôle of independent commander, decided to abandon Gonzalo and his men to their fate and travel down the Napo on his brigantine, the *Victoria*, hoping ultimately to reach the Atlantic Ocean. Of all the adventurous voyages reported in this book, this is surely the most unusual!

Soon after his departure, Orellana met some of the Indian tribes living along the banks of the Napo, wearing heavy wooden pegs in the lobes of

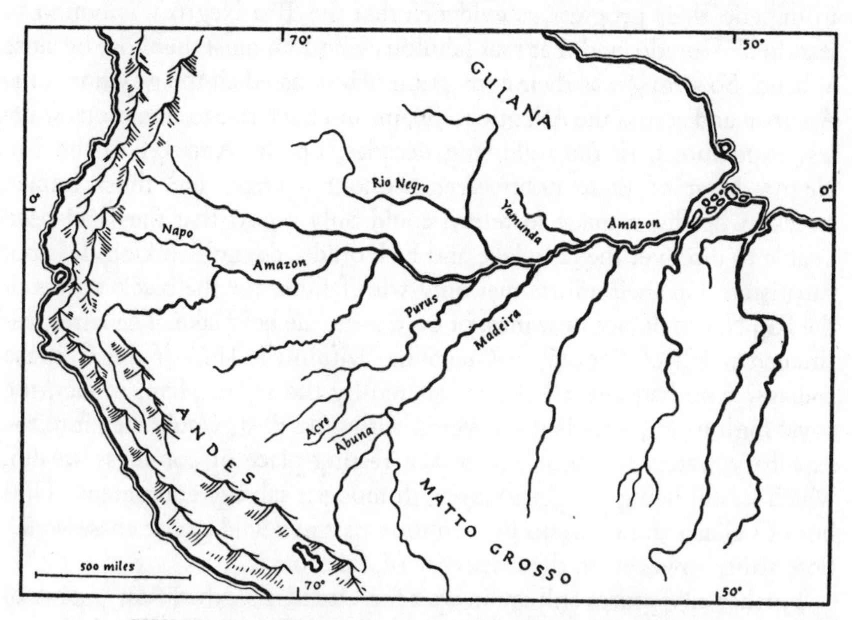

XXIV. The Amazon with its most important tributaries.

their ears. From them the Spaniards learned that the great river was only another ten days' voyage away. Moreover, it was quickly realized that the decision to separate from Pizarro and travel down the Napo had been right, for it would obviously have been impossible for the *Victoria* to sail upstream against the currents strengthened by the rainy season. They had no choice but to go on.

A second brigantine, the *San Pedro*, was quickly constructed, its seams being caulked with *caucho*, the sap of the rubber tree, and the voyage towards the Amazon continued.

Once again the rumours proved to be founded on reality. The river was so wide that its opposite banks could only be seen as a dark line on the horizon. Its waters were far from smooth and placid, and the Spaniards soon found themselves at the mercy of the currents which, even today, make the upper reaches of the Amazon extremely dangerous. They found it difficult to keep to the main stream in the bewildering confusion of creeks, backwaters and islands, but by some miracle Orellana and his men managed each time to find their way back to it. At the Rio Negro their difficulties were increased by an attack from hostile Indians. Poisoned darts and arrows whistled over the decks of the two Spanish ships, and under this covering fire hordes of Indians, screaming madly, attempted to board them. A sudden storm drove the ships through the Indian blockade of canoes, to the comparative safety of the uninhabited forest wilderness.

The Spaniards interpreted the desperate attempts made by the Indians to impede their progress as evidence that the Rio Negro was bound to lead to El Dorado, and that that fabulous kingdom must therefore be close at hand. So strong was their conviction that it lasted all the way down the Amazon and across the Atlantic to Spain, and gave rise to numerous fruitless expeditions, in the following decades, up the Amazon to the Rio Negro. Most of these disappeared without a trace, and those human wrecks who did manage to return could only report that they had been unable to discover the holy lake and El Dorado, the golden king. It is not surprising that their efforts met only with failure, for the black waters of the Rio Negro do not flow into, or even near, the holy lake. The latter was situated north of Bogotá, in Guatavita, within the land of the Chibcha Indians, who had never been conquered by the Incas. Here, in fact, the royal high priest, after being covered with gold dust, would step into the expiatory waters of the lake, the last resting-place of countless wealth, which is still being sought today with modern salvage equipment. Thus both Orellana and Gonzalo Pizarro took part in a wild-goose chase which bore fruit, however, in the discovery of Amazonia.

Further adventures still lay in wait for Orellana's expedition—some of them have remained unexplained to this day. While still sailing down the Napo, many months earlier, the Spaniards had heard that far down the river there was a kingdom peopled by giant women warriors, the *Coniupuara*. Here again the rumours proved correct, that is if Father Gaspar de Carvajal, later to be Archbishop of Lima and one of the two priests who participated in Orellana's voyage, is to be believed. Carvajal maintains, in his very sober report, that when they reached the mouth of the Yamundá they found themselves in the empire of the chieftainess Conori and her female subjects.

Father Carvajal was not a cultured or a particularly saintly man; in fact he was more of a swashbuckler and adventurer than a priest, but he must have had a sufficient fund of general knowledge to know of the existence of stories, current during the Renaissance, of isolated regions inhabited by women only and governed by an Empress or Queen. The location of the Amazon Kingdom was shifted frequently in antiquity, being thought at one time in Asia Minor and later in Southern Russia. Even Northern Europe had its legends of remote islands in the eastern sea, peopled by warrior women. The Crusaders revived the old fable, since they had heard from the Arabs of distant islands or regions populated only by women and ruled by a most bellicose princess. All these legends stated that the Amazon states were visited by men at definite intervals, and that the male children resulting from such visits were returned to the fathers, while the girls remained with the mothers.

We can fairly assume that Father Carvajal knew of these legends which, in his time, were said to refer mainly to islands in the Indian Ocean. When

30. Amazons as depicted by Levinus Hulsius (sixteenth century).

the Amazonian Indians called the great river *amassonas*, the destroyer of boats, he must needs have concluded that they were passing through the land of the Amazons.

In view of the fact that stories of Amazon states have existed in every part of the world, we may well ask whether the assumption that such stories are merely the legendary recollection of earlier matriarchal societies, is an adequate explanation. The problem has never been finally solved. One fact stands out: such fables were almost exclusively applied to islands or other isolated communities, where limited food supplies necessitated some kind of control lest the population should outgrow the food resources. No such stories were ever current in the North American prairies or the great fertile plains of Europe and Asia. We have no reason for branding Gaspar de Carvajal, Archbishop of Lima, as a shameless liar, and despite an understandable degree of exaggeration his reports are probably basically correct. Even to this day rumours of 'arrow-bearing women' are still rife amongst the *indios* of Amazonia, as the Swiss explorer Franz Caspar, who led an expedition into the Matto Grosso in 1949, has reported.

Now Carvajal's report stated in matter-of-fact tones that he had learnt from the hospitable Tupi Indians, who lived in the delta of the Madeira, a river rising in the Matto Grosso in Central Brazil, that the empire of the Amazons ended at the opposite bank of the river. In return for many presents, the Tupi agreed to provide ten warrior-guides who would lead the Spanish ships into that realm. On 24th June 1542, they reached an Amazon village situated deep in the jungle on the banks of the Yamundá, and finally managed to get past it despite the desperate attacks of the surprised women. Tall, light-brown women warriors scrambled on board the ships before the Spaniards could fire a second volley, and the latter had extreme difficulty in repulsing their attack. They were unable to capture any of these long-haired fighters, and were in fact fully occupied in getting away from them.

According to Carvajal, their position was desperate indeed, and they only managed to clear the canals of the Yamundá and reach the Amazon by the wildest feats of courage. The Amazons' darts and arrows had been poisoned, not with the quickly killing *curare*, but with a slow poison, causing paralysis and later death. Alcántara, the first pilot, was the only one of the expedition who had not been wounded in some way.

Night fell on a scene worthy of a vision of Hell. Alcántara, the pilot, was desperately striving to keep his ships from disaster as they raced over the Pauxis rapids. A storm was brewing and heavy tropical rain beat down on the ships. The decks were covered with dead, and the dying uttered bestial screams as the poison slowly took effect, jerking their tormented bodies into fantastic attitudes.

On 11th September 1542, after a voyage of more than two thousand five hundred miles and lasting two hundred and sixty days, Orellana and his men reached the Atlantic. Approximately the same date saw the return of Gonzalo Pizarro to Quito, at the head of nine grievously sick men.

Orellana crossed the Atlantic to Spain to make his report in person to the Crown. He returned a second time to the Amazon in 1545, at the head of five hundred men, in another attempt to discover the land of El Dorado, but this time the jungle claimed its victim and he vanished without leaving a trace.

5

The people of Peru still tell the story that Atahualpa, shortly before his life-thread was cut by Pizarro's hired assassins, uttered a most terrible curse against the foreigners, and the Indians are so convinced of the force of this curse that the women of Casa Blanca, the scene of the execution, wear nothing but black to this day, for here, they say, air, earth and water are accursed. In all probability this curse is a product of popular invention like the famous 'Curse of the Pharaohs' against the desecrators of the Pyramids, though, unlike its Egyptian parallel, all those who had even the slightest connection with the murder of the last Inca did come to a violent end. Although an attempt was made to keep secret the names of the twenty-four jurors who had sentenced Atahualpa to death, it proved unsuccessful, and the Indians searched them out, one by one, and put them to death.

Even then, the Inca vengeance was not satisfied: no sooner had Pizarro created the new capital of Lima, than civil war broke out amongst the whites themselves. In 1538, Almagro, who had nursed a grudge against his former associate for over a year, openly rebelled against Pizarro but was beaten before the gates of Cuzco and later throttled in prison by Pizarro's ruffians. Pizarro himself was to die three years after Almagro, being assassinated in his palace by dissatisfied members of the Almagro clique on the 26th June 1541. Thus began the sequence of revolution and counter-revolution which occupies so much of the South American history, even to this day.

Almagro was one of the first victims of Atahualpa's curse. The second victim was Pizarro, and the third was Spain itself. Spain perished because of its own riches. Instead of extending its industry, attracting labour and exporting its gold, thus establishing a balance between the import of precious metals and social production, Spain passed a law forbidding the export of gold and silver, impeded its own textile industry lest 'the people be tempted to luxurious ways', and finally banished the best workers and most experienced merchants, the Moors and the Jews. As the price of gold fell, the price of bread rose. This was so incomprehensible that the devil was blamed!

The last man to suffer the Inca curse, according to popular South American beliefs, was Bolívar, the great liberator, who was shamefully driven out and banished by the very people he had set free. Shortly before his death, Bolívar remarked bitterly:

'There is no faith in South America. The agreements of its inhabitants are worthless; their constitutions are nothing but inkmarks on paper, their elections battles, their freedom anarchy, and their life a torture.'

Now, when the national hero of five South American states says this about the country to which he owed his life and for which he gladly gave it also, we are almost inclined to believe in the existence and the power of the curse laid by Atahualpa, the last Inca, on country and people alike.

PART FIVE

GUAIAC, THE 'FRENCH DISEASE' AND THE WELSERS

Maximilian's edict against blasphemy, and the 'evil pox' · Fact and Fiction · The origins of syphilis · Astrologers predict the new plague · Guaiac as a remedy · Why did the Welsers go to Venezuela? · Ulrich von Hutten's prescription · Of captains and a letter · Expeditions right through South America · Are the Motilones descendants of German mercenaries? · How Standard Oil protects its fields · German lone wolves traverse the globe · Ulrich Schmiedel and the founding of Buenos Aires · Is it done to eat one's wife?

I

THE sun glared balefully from the leaden sky. The dark air lay thick and heavy between the houses. The Lord Bishop's flag hung limply in the still air. No sound could be heard. The town of Meersburg below the castle gave off a putrid stench. For weeks there had been no rain and the level of the lake had dropped. Its banks were lined with corpses and stinking refuse.

The fields were parched and the wells dry. Drought and famine threatened the land and, hard on their heels, the spectre of the plague.

It was a Saturday in August 1495.

The noise of the workshops had ceased at noon. Usually this was the hour when the town walked and chatted in the main square, but today all was quiet. No one was abroad in the streets.

Suddenly a roll of drums broke the silence. The Lord Bishop's guard were setting out from the castle. They wore wide breeches, steel helmets pulled down over insolent faces, and carried halberds and swords. Six drums beat out the marching rhythm, the boots of thirty-six men clattered on the cobbled street. In the midst of the guard strutted the Lord Bishop's herald. He was young, and this was his first appearance in his official capacity.

Lying on a purple cushion and supported by his outstretched arms was a heavy roll of parchment, and affixed to it the large seal of Maximilian I, Holy Roman Emperor. He was bearing news, important news of the Diet of Worms, which had been in session since March of that year. The whole of Germany was looking to that council with a mixture of hope and fear.

In the main square, the little detachment halted. Trumpets blew a fanfare and then the herald announced Maximilian's edict against blasphemy. Heavy punishments were threatened by Emperor, Electors and the Estates against all who took the name of God or of his son, Jesus Christ, or of Mary, Christ's mother, in vain. Death was the punishment for wilful blasphemy; those offending God's majesty and glory without malice aforethought were to be imprisoned or made to pay heavy fines. The edict continued, saying that God had ever punished such behaviour with:

hunger, earthquakes, pestilence and other plagues. In these days the wickedness of men is being scourged by a severe plague called the evil pox, which formerly was unknown, but in which it is easy to see God's punishment....

The trumpets rang out once again, and the herald held the unrolled parchment high above his head for all to see the seals.

Given and sealed with our royal seal at Worms this seventh day of the month of August in the year fourteen hundred and ninety-five after the birth of Jesus Christ, Our Lord.

Four times the herald waved the edict towards the four cardinal points, and then the guard marched off. Once again silence reigned over the town. It was as if nothing had happened.

But had nothing happened? In fact the arrival of *syphilis* had been officially announced.

Maximilian, a deeply religious man, had long been waging a losing battle against the increasing habit of cursing and swearing. All his previous threats of fines for blasphemy had gone unheeded. Obviously one of his counsellors at the Diet of Worms (which was convoked in 1495 with the intention of establishing internal harmony and a single legal system throughout the country) had had the masterly idea—worthy of modern advertising techniques—of capturing the interest of the public by attributing the new disease, which had been sweeping the country during the past year and causing great anxiety, to the irreligious habits of the people.

In the edict which was to be read aloud in every town and village of Germany the disease was referred to as the 'evil pox', the *malum frantzos*, the 'French disease', though in fact its origins are rather more tangled.

According to popular belief, syphilis first made its appearance during the siege of Naples by Charles VIII of France, i.e. between the 22nd February and the 20th May 1495. All history books repeat this as if it were Gospel, but they are mistaken. There is no mention at all of the outbreak of an epidemic in the chronicles of Naples or in contemporary reports of the siege, nor is any hint given of a new disease. Reports of this strange and previously unknown evil only began *after* the French had left Naples, and as they were marching back to the north.

As the siege of Naples took place in 1495, the year of the Imperial edict, we are drawn to the conclusion that syphilis must have been known north of the Alps before it broke out amongst the French troops in Italy.

Many doctors interested in history have stated that syphilis is European in origin, and that it had long existed in the West, though in latent form. Outbreaks of it had been quite frequent, but as they usually overlapped with periods of plague and pestilence, syphilis had been mistaken for the Black Death, and had never been properly diagnosed. Similarly, these doctors point out, infantile paralysis is always latent in certain regions of Scandinavia, as is typhus in the Balkans and in Mexico.

The exponents of this theory generally quote two documents in support of it, both of which mention the *mal franzose*. The first of these is an Italian manuscript dated 1430, in which this designation is used, the other is a Danish document stating that *in 1483 kom thenne svare franzoske siuge og krankhet ibland kristet folk* (in 1483 this severe French plague and sickness overcame the Christian people). These documents are very interesting, but it is strange that they are the only ones mentioning the disease. It is also odd that neither antiquity, despite its interest in medicine, nor yet the Arabian doctors of the Middle Ages, said a single word about this scourge of God, and that all the contemporaries of the great outbreak, which took place at the end of the fifteenth century, should describe it as a new and previously unknown plague.

These considerations lead us to agree with the old theory, dating back some five hundred years, which speaks of syphilis as a disease of American origin. Las Casas, the great friend of the Indians whom we have already mentioned, in his *Historia de las Indias* states emphatically that this disease was known in America (in an endemic form, as we would say today) long before the appearance of the white man, and he concludes by saying that no one can doubt this. The fact that each Indian dialect has its own expression for syphilis proves that the disease was quite common among the Indians. Further incontrovertible proof has recently been given by the Swedish physician, Professor Folke-Henschen, in his *Die älteste Geschichte der Syphilis in der Beleuchtung neuerer Skelettfunde* (The earliest history of Syphilis in the light of recently discovered skeletons).

As all medical students know, syphilis not only attacks the flesh but also the bone structure of its victims. A sure way of recognizing this vile disease is by the *corona veneris*, a characteristic pathological change in the skull, making the affected parts of the head look as if they had been attacked by worms. The long bones in the arms and legs are similarly damaged. These unmistakable signs have been found in skeletons discovered throughout the length and breadth of the New World, both in North and South America. The age of these skeletons can be dated precisely, and all of them go back to before the time of Columbus. As no discoveries of this type, dating back to the fifteenth century and earlier, have been made in Europe or in Egypt, where the American Elliot Smith examined more than twenty-five thousand skulls without finding a single one showing the marks of syphilis, it seems that the evidence pointing to the American origin of this disease is conclusive.

How then did the pox reach Europe? Through Columbus?

The 'Admiral of the Oceans' made no mention of any striking new disease in his log book, and his men, though exhausted, seem to have been hale and hearty on their return to Spain. Had they become infected in America, the disease would surely have shown itself long before their arrival back in Spain, for syphilis, in the form common during the Renaissance, developed extremely quickly. This was obviously not the case with the crew of the flag-ship.

An old Spanish source, however, states that one of the Pinzóns and many of the crew of the *Pinta* had caught syphilis in America, but we have no further evidence that syphilis was carried back to Europe by the crew of the *Pinta.* There is one fact that can either be interpreted as additional testimony on behalf of this explanation or dismissed as pure coincidence. We quote it without comment: Martín Alonso Pinzón, Captain of the *Pinta*, died soon after his return to Spain.

It must be remembered, however, that Columbus had six Indians on board his flag-ship. In view of the widespread existence of syphilis in the Bahamas and Cuba, it is quite likely that some or all of these men were carriers of *spirochaeta pallida.* As the colour bar and the theory of racial supremacy did not exist in the Old World, it is obvious that these well-proportioned, handsome foreigners did not lack female admirers.

According to Diaz de Isla, a famous Portuguese physician of the time, syphilis broke out in Barcelona in 1493. It could only have been introduced there by the six Indians brought back by Columbus, and perhaps by the infected members of the *Pinta.* The same year saw its arrival in England, where it was known as the *infirmity cumm out of Franche.* By the beginning of summer, 1495, the loathsome disease had become widespread in Germany, where it was known as the *malum frantzos*, the French disease. In this year, the French soldiers, returning from southern Italy, christened this new malady the *mal de Naples*, the Neapolitan disease. For their part, the Italians, like the Germans, sighed about the *mal francese*, the French disease, which they claimed had been brought to Italy by the army of Charles VIII. In 1496, the Poles began to curse about the 'German disease', which had by then overrun their country. By 1499, the Russians were blaming the Poles and by 1512, the inhabitants of the Far East as far as Japan were complaining about the *nambanniassa*, the Portuguese disease. In each case they were referring to the hitherto unknown disease of syphilis.

Only the outbreaks of plague in the Middle Ages, or the great influenza epidemic of 1918, can be compared in severity and swiftness with the first appearance of syphilis. It seems that certain epochs are particularly receptive, both physically and psychologically, to certain maladies.

It is known that Germany at the end of the fifteenth century was in a sense prepared psychologically for the onset of syphilis. Many almanacs had predicted the widespread outbreak of an infectious venereal disease, as much as ten years before syphilis actually arrived there. This is a fact confirmed by so many contemporary reports that it is difficult to dismiss it lightly as pure coincidence.

On the 25th November 1484, Saturn and Jupiter were in conjunction, and though the latter was considered to be a friendly planet, the influence of the former was held to be evil. Moreover since the conjunction took place under Scorpio, the sign governing the sexual organs, it was generally believed that this ominous approach of the two great heavenly bodies would bring a venereal pestilence in its train.

Although we know today how people catch syphilis and how other infections are handed on, we do not know why one person catches such diseases while another does not, even though both are submitted to the same source of infection. We cannot yet explain why some epidemics not only spare certain individuals but even whole regions; why certain diseases are endemic and latent in one area, but appear as devastating epidemics in another. It is possible that unexplained and possibly inexplicable psychological factors play a deciding rôle in such uneven treatment.

Our ancestors were much more strongly affected by such astrological prophecies than we of this scientific age, and they tried to meet the horror of the new disease with confession, fasting and prayer. In the summer of 1506, Albrecht Dürer sent a terrified letter home from Italy:

> Please pay my compliments to our Prior. Prevail upon him to pray fervently for me, that I be saved and particularly from the French [disease], for I know nothing that I fear more, since all about me seem to be afflicted by it. Here many people are eaten up by this sickness until they die of it.

Since prayers and fasting were not always of immediate avail, special patron saints against syphilis were discovered like the otherwise unknown St. Minus, and shrewd publishers, in order to sell more copies of their beautifully illustrated prayers for preservation against syphilis, printed the following at the bottom of the page: 'Whoever carries this prayer on him or says it, is safe from the pox.'

In all probability this spiritual prophylaxis was not very effective, and in Germany the authorities had recourse to the customary *regimina sanitatis*, general hygienic measures observed during all epidemics. Those suffering with the pox were rounded up; the foreigners were escorted across the border, and the local people were locked up in buildings named 'French establishments', which were then isolated by a *cordon sanitaire*. Certain private measures were recommended such as washing out the mouth night and morning and combing the hair thoroughly. Obviously such hygiene was not considered necessary in healthier times!

At first, doctors prescribed no specific treatment for those stricken with syphilis, and were indeed unaware of the way the disease was handed on from person to person. Laymen had their own peculiar and extravagant notions of how it was contracted. The following quotation is from a report made to the Emperor Maximilian by his private secretary, Joseph Grünpeck, who, as a young man, had seen the beaten French soldiers streaming back from Italy across Southern Germany and Alsace.

> Many of those poor fellows were covered from head to foot with vile running sores and looked so repulsive that their own comrades would not go near them. Others

had certain parts of their bodies, namely their foreheads, necks, chests, etc., covered with hard scales like the gnarled lumps found on a tree-trunk. In their pain, the poor devils would tear off these scabs with their fingernails, revealing the purulent flesh underneath. Others had warts and wens in such numbers that they could not be counted, and when these excrescences broke open they gave off a putrid stench that was not to be borne.

People would shrink away in horror from the sufferers and would offer them no help,

for it was considered that any contact whatsoever, whether sharing of quarters, touching their clothes or their bedding, using the same cups or plates, was sufficient to pass on the disease. People even avoided speaking to them because they believed that the very air became infected and therefore dangerous to breathe. No other disease was held to be so easily transmitted as the pox, and even lepers refused to live in the same quarters as the pox-ridden, fearing to become victims of an even more terrible disease than their own!

Although ignorance as to the causes of syphilis was still prevalent at the beginning of the sixteenth century, certain remedies gradually came into common use. One of these remedies was *guaiacum*, the wood of the guaiac-tree, and this explains why syphilis finds itself included in our book. In Germany, in the early sixteenth century, rich man and poor man, nobleman and commoner alike were all afflicted by this loathsome sickness. In fact, the incidence of syphilis was so high, that in 1505 the provincial town of Nordlingen had to beg to be relieved of its contribution to the Swabian Federation, because the 'French' disease had more than doubled the expenses of the burghers for medical treatment. The import of guaiac wood, the staple remedy for the pox, suddenly increased by leaps and bounds.

Guaiac wood is found in Florida, the Antilles, Guiana, Venezuela and Colombia, i.e. those regions from which syphilis was carried to Europe. It has been known by a variety of names including *lignum sanctum*, pox wood, French wood, and even today it is still commonly called *lignum vitae*, the wood of life. It is a very heavy wood with a specific gravity of about 1·5. This means that even very thin shavings of it will not float. It has a very strange, pungent odour and does not burn like other woods, but instead smoulders away leaving a gluey, rubber-like residue.

The Middle Ages had been very fond of the notion that every being, every idea, every object had a counterpart, an opposite, the other side of the medal. Thus God was opposed by the Devil, Good by Evil, and the microscopic by the macroscopic. This strange concept had been taken over by the Renaissance, and so it was believed that America, the source of this new dread disease, must also hold the clue to its cure, and when rumours reached Europe of the wonderful effects of guaiac wood on Indians suffering from the pox, people were only too ready to believe that the antidote had been found.

News of the miraculous healing powers of this wood must have reached the court of the Emperor Charles V of Germany at about the middle of the sixteenth century, for in 1516 the court physician, Nicolaus Poll, was charged to go and investigate the claims made on behalf of the 'wood of life'. Poll published his report in 1517 in the form of a very dry-as-dust little volume. He stated that the Indians in the New World 'commonly used the wood as a cure for syphilis and that three thousand Spaniards had already thrown off the pox with this remedy'. This is either completely false or is based on a misconception, for guaiac wood has no specific effect on syphilis. It is still prescribed today for chronic exanthema, rheumatism and gout, because it contains saponins which stimulate the action of the stomach, intestines and kidneys. Consequently any benefit felt by sufferers from syphilis must have been due to their own wishful thinking or faith in the remedy, and also to the purgative effect of the wood.

It was probably on the basis of this report that Francis I, King of France, sent Captain Jean Belanger to South America in search of guaiac wood, for the King too had become infected. At first, his physicians had been unwilling to tell him the truth, and had treated the sores and ulcers covering the royal body as of no importance and indeed they did disappear for a while. But when they reappeared in a far more horrible form—the secondary stage of syphilis—the doctors had no option but to inform the King that His Royal Highness had become infected with the pox.

According to legend rather than history, the King promptly accused his latest mistress, Madame Ferron, the wife of an eminent Parisian lawyer, of being responsible for his condition. The portrait of Madame Ferron, painted by Leonardo da Vinci, hangs in the Louvre as *La Belle Ferronière*, and it is easy to imagine that such a woman would capture a king's heart. Legend continues that the lawyer Ferron, insanely jealous of his wife's infidelity, had deliberately infected himself with the pox in the Paris stews so as to destroy his wife and her royal lover. He did not live to see his vengeance completed, for the King outlived him by thirty years.

The German classical scholar Ulrich von Hutten, who was also to die of syphilis, was another enthusiastic believer in the virtues of guaiac wood. He published a tract in 1515 entitled *De guaiaci medicina et morbo gallico*, in which he gives detailed advice on how to prepare this infallible treatment. This tract reads just like the leaflets enclosed with modern patent medicines, and one might conclude that the great business houses of the Fuggers and Welsers, who were engaged in the import trade of guaiac wood, had employed von Hutten to sing the praises of this new remedy, and so swell their business. We do not know enough to say whether this was the case, though it is certain that some years later his cousin, Philipp von Hutten, was appointed Governor of the colony founded by the Welsers in Venezuela.

The story of syphilis and guaiac wood provides a rather sinister foretaste of the unholy connections between business and medical science. When Paracelsus, the founder of modern therapeutic chemistry, and one of the greatest doctors of all time, tried to publish his work on syphilis, in which he had stated that the use of guaiac wood was completely futile and had no effect whatsoever on the disease, he met with unexpected resistance, for had the book reached the public, sales of guaiac wood would have dropped considerably. Although Paracelsus had no personal antagonism to the Fuggers and Welsers, it was obviously their influence which lay behind the decision of the Leipzig Medical Faculty to ban his book.

Obviously such sharp practice, capable of suppressing unpleasant opinions, would reward the 'right kind' of publication and von Hutten's tract certainly fitted into that category. It was widely read and quoted as an authoritative work and was printed time and time again. Since the profits to be made from the guaiac trade were truly enormous—its customers were drawn from all ranks of society—there may well have been some financial encouragement behind von Hutten's optimism. It must be stated that no documentary evidence exists to prove or disprove this conjecture, nor have we any proof that it was to exploit the growing demand for guaiac wood that the Welsers decided to form settlements in those parts of the New World where it grows. Perhaps further investigation of the archives of the Spanish branch of the famous firm, and also of the *Welser Codex* in London, will throw more light on the problem. We may, however, safely assert that even if the guaiac trade was not the main reason for establishing these settlements, it certainly was a factor of some importance in the matter.

The reason adduced by the Welsers for wishing to found colonies in the New World was the customary one of going there to prospect for gold. A contract was signed between Hieronymus Sailer, Director of the Welser Company, and the Crown of Spain, in which the Company undertook to proceed to South America with a band of fifty skilled German miners and to found at least two colonies there and to erect three forts.

These colonies were founded in 1528, and although the amount of gold sent back to Spain was not very large, the Welsers did quite good business out of providing the fifty miners, their families and slaves with stores and supplies. However, soon after, it appeared that the Welsers had not placed all their eggs in one basket, for in 1529 a certain Francisco de Ulate, one-time court physician to the Duke of Calabria and to the King of Portugal, arrived in the settlement to supervise the production of some new hush-hush medical preparation. We know of this from the reports of Spanish officials in Venezuela, informing their government of the mysterious activities of the stranger and of a research centre set up in the middle of the jungle. The Spanish Colonial Office acted promptly, for on the 17th February, 1531, they ordered the Welsers to submit samples of their new medicine.

No details are given of what this medicine could have been, but apparently it was an old Indian remedy made by boiling the bark of a certain tree. Since the tree mentioned could not have been the *cinchona*, which at that time grew in Peru alone, we must conclude that de Ulate was engaged in producing a guaiac-ointment. What information we have concerning its manufacture coincides exactly with the details given by von Hutten:

> The drug is prepared in the following way: the wood must be split as finely as possible and then soaked in water for twenty-four hours. It does not matter whether the wood is in the form of splinters, shavings or fine chips. It should be immersed in the proportions of eight pounds of water to one pound of wood. The mixture is then boiled over a slow fire for at least six hours, until half the liquid has been boiled off. The scum forming on the surface is then scooped off and used to anoint sores and ulcers. The fluid left is passed through a sieve and poured into a shallow vessel, while the residue can be boiled up again in another eight pounds of water.
>
> The concoction resulting from the second brew is to be taken with meals, while that from the first must be drunk as a potion. It is the only remedy that can heal us of that terrible disease.

The striking similarity between von Hutten's remedy and the procedure followed by de Ulate, makes it extremely likely that the German merchants were strongly influenced in their decision to found colonies in the New World, by the possibility of making vast profits from the sale of a supposed remedy for a disease prevalent throughout the whole of Europe.

2

Not long after its foundation, the Welser colony in Venezuela underwent a complete change of policy. The reason for this change is not hard to find. In Europe countless thousands of people, including von Hutten, continued to die of the pox, despite the miraculous guaiac cure, and it was becoming increasingly difficult to sell the ointment. Fired by the example of Pizarro, and still believing in the existence of other El Dorados, it was decided to abandon the plantations and mines, with the exception of Coro and Maracaibo, and to try to find out what lay on the other side of the jungle bordering the narrow coastal strip of fertile land. The Governors of the Welser settlements were given a free hand to explore, with the result that during the next ten years, from 1536 to 1546, the wilderness around the Orinoco became one of the best-known areas in the whole of South America.

The Governors of this settlement were not like present-day Foreign Office officials with a steady routine job, but were much more like adventurers in character, unwilling to stay put in one spot, when there was the chance that, by a little exertion and courage, they might discover a new El Dorado and become fabulously wealthy. But the driving force that had led them so far from home was not the prospect of riches alone, as is borne out by a letter written by Philipp von Hutten to 'The Noble and Faithful Bernard von Hutten':

> God knows it was no lust for gold that drove me to undertake this voyage, but quite another yearning that I have had for a long time now. I know I could never have died in peace, if I had not seen India first, and thus I have no regrets, nor do I wish to go back on my undertaking. I beg you not to think ill of me and to greet my dear mother and sister. . . .

The Welsers' colonial agents frequently went beyond their official mandates, and one after the other they would disappear into the jungle on some more or less warlike undertaking, instead of staying in their trading post to look after the Welser profits. Often they would be absent for years and would be written off as dead, only to stagger back one day into the settlement without their men and without having found El Dorado; but far more frequently they would disappear without leaving any trace.

Undoubtedly, the most interesting of the Welser Governors in South America was Nicolaus Federmann who came from a wealthy, respectable family in North Germany. Why he chose that particular career is not known to us, though his imagination was probably struck by hearing about the exploits of Cortés. In 1529, when he was barely twenty-four, he was appointed by the Welsers to lead an expedition to Venezuela. He reached Haiti by the end of the same year, and March of the following year saw him set foot on Venezuelan soil.

Within six months of his arrival there, this confident young man, who had had no previous experience of tropical conditions, started out at the head of one hundred and twenty Spaniards and a hundred Indians on an expedition into the interior, hoping to discover the Orinoco and perhaps also the South Sea seen by Balboa some fifteen years earlier. It was thought at the time that this sea formed a deep bay, cutting far in towards the eastern coast of South America, and that it could be reached without difficulty from Venezuela.

The expedition was doomed to failure before it started. Federmann managed to get as far as the Rio Cojede and the plains near the Rio Portugeza before he was forced to return to Venezuela, his expedition sadly depleted in numbers, and the majority of the survivors suffering from some tropical disease or other. The results of the expedition had, however, not been entirely negative, for Federmann had gained considerable experience of travelling in tropical jungles, and he also knew that next time he would have to travel west and not south. The most valuable result for posterity of Federmann's first expedition was the report composed by the notary accompanying the expedition, a copy of which was submitted to the Spanish government. Federmann had this report translated into German and included it in his *Indianische Historia*, one of the best travel books in any language. Two statements are of particular interest to us. He says that, even in the South American jungle, he and his men were welcomed by the natives as 'Sons of the Sun'. Secondly he reports that in the jungle swamps he had seen with his own eyes pygmies no taller than four or five hands' span. This latter statement has usually been treated as sensationalism, but investigations made during the last fifteen years tend to prove that these areas were in fact inhabited by a tribe of dwarfs.

In 1536, Federmann set out on a second expedition which proved successful. He crossed the Arauca and the Rio Meta and even the Cordillera, by discovering passes some thirteen thousand feet high, and in 1539 he reached Bogotá, the centre of the Chibcha culture. Unfortunately a cruel disappointment awaited him, for he soon realized that he was not the first white man to discover the region, which incidentally was very rich in gold. In Bogotá he met the Conquistador Ximénez de Quesada who had travelled south down the Magdalena River from Colombia, arriving in Bogotá two full years before Federmann. Not many weeks later, one of Pizarro's officers, Sebastián de Benalcázar, who had left Quito in search of El Dorado, appeared on the scene. As one might expect from three such characters they came very near to drawing their swords, but reason prevailed in the end, and they decided to leave it to the Spanish Colonial Office to settle the boundaries between Venezuela, Colombia and Peru. All three of them later returned to Spain. Unfortunately Federmann has left no report of his second expedition, and it is only from other sources that we know he was the first white man to cross the Andes from east to west.

Several other expeditions were made by subsequent Governors but none of them produced any results. The last of them sealed the fate of the Welser settlement in Venezuela; it was led by Philipp von Hutten and by Bartholomäus Welser, the son of the head of the Company, who were both stabbed in the back by envious Spaniards. What with the uncertain profits and the loss of his son, the head of the Welser firm was disgusted with the whole adventure, and in 1555 the colony was handed back to Spain.

The Spanish Colonial Office proved just as unsuccessful with Venezuela as the Welsers had been. The most they could do was to control the narrow coastal strip, for any attempt to penetrate inland via the jungle was met with a hail of poisoned arrows. The situation remains more or less unaltered even today, and the large companies exploiting the oil deposits in Venezuela have had to fight for every square yard they have occupied, and to defend their conquests by continuous warfare against the Motilone Indians, the real masters of the jungle. Extremely little is known about this savage tribe, which has accounted for several luckless ethnologists. The heart of the Motilone country, about seventy-five miles by car from Maracaibo, the oil centre of this rich country, is completely unknown and inaccessible to oil prospectors, although geologists are convinced that it must be extremely rich in deposits of gold, copper and oil. All attempts to oust the Motilone Indians by force, guile or persuasion have failed.

The last person to have risked his life in those regions (and one of the first people to come into actual contact with the Motilone) was the American ethnologist, Robert Holder, sent on a mission by the American Natural History Institute. He carried recommendations from the half-civilized tribes living on the borders of the Motilone territory and was abundantly supplied with presents of knives, tobacco and rolls of canvas. Holder travelled up river by motor-boat at the beginning of 1953, and at first everything went smoothly. The Motilone allowed him to land and deposit his presents on the river bank, but next morning, when the motor was started, a hail of arrows thudded against the sides of the boat. Fortunately Holder, taking no chances with the Motilone, had had the boat armour-plated and the lights covered with bullet-proof glass. When Holder examined some of the arrows which had fallen on deck, he discovered that the Motilone had spent the night unravelling the canvas and using the thread so obtained for tying the knives he had given them to the shafts of their arrows, thus producing a murderous weapon. Occasionally the boat was hit by arrows which must have been fired by some mechanical means, for they obviously came from distances greater than the range of an ordinary bow, or even that of a cross-bow. This seemed to confirm rumours current in Maracaibo that the Motilone had some form of arrow-catapults.

It appears from the above that the Motilone are a very special type of savage tribe; nowhere else in South America do we know of the existence of a tribe using catapults. The use of such a weapon was clearly gleaned from Europeans, but the weapon itself is in keeping with the Motilone's own technical level and with their own resources, since its production demands only wood for the framework and the gut of some animal for the strings.

When the Vikings from Greenland tried to colonize Massachusetts they failed because they did not have adequate stocks of weapons to replace those which had become too blunted for use, or which had fallen into the hands of the enemy. As they could not take a cultural step backwards into the Stone Age and use the materials available, the American colonies had to be abandoned. The Motilone, however, proved themselves wise indeed when they refused to have anything to do with the hand-grenades, rifles, machine-guns and revolvers which they frequently captured, preferring to accept the catapult alone, since it fitted in perfectly with the materials available in their jungle home.

Rumours current in the Christian missions in Maracaibo used to say that the Motilone were white Indians, but no one had ever seen a member of the tribe to confirm or disprove the theory. It was also rumoured that far back in the past, a group of German mercenaries under the command of a Philipp von Hutten or a Nicolaus Federmann, had got lost in the jungle and had in desperation decided to settle there. They then murdered the males of a tribe of Indians and took their places, thus producing the strain of white Indians who, according to rumour, live there to this day.

The large oil companies did not bother with such speculation. When Standard Oil found that its workers at the Santa Ana oilfield were being picked off by Motilone marksmen at distances of more than 300 yards, they abandoned the camp temporarily, only to return with an army of lumberjacks and bull-dozers during the rainy season when the Motilone migrate to the mountain region between Venezuela and Colombia. Working day and night at high speed, a gigantic clearing was made in the jungle and huge electric fences were erected around the oil wells. When the Motilone returned after the rainy season to their old home, they were confronted by an oilfield surrounded by many square miles of open country offering no cover whatsoever, lit up at night by powerful searchlights and guarded by crack riflemen using telescopic sights.

Incredible though this may sound these facts were taken from an article in the German newspaper *Die Welt*, sent by a reporter in Machiques, Venezuela in 1953.

3

About the time of the collapse of the Welser empire in Venezuela, another German happened to be farther south in the same continent, who, after his return to Germany, recounted his experiences in a most interesting book of adventure. His name was Ulrich Schmiedel and he was the second son of the Mayor of Straubing in Bavaria.

Ulrich Schmiedel bears a striking resemblance to Hans Schiltberger who, roughly a hundred and fifty years earlier, in 1394, had taken the field against the heathens as a squire to Knight Lienhard Reichartinger, and in 1427, at the age of fifty, had returned from capture in the Far East. Although one had been a prisoner, a slave first to the Turks and later to the Mongols and the Russians, and the other had retained his freedom and had remained master of his own destiny, what makes them so similar in type is that both represent the specifically German discoverer. Both were lone wolves who went out into the far-distant world without any assistance from the State, entirely on their own initiative and answerable only to themselves.

Engelbert Kämpfer, who explored Japan in the seventeenth century, the theological student Hornemann, who journeyed through the Sahara at the

31. Portrait of Ulrich Schmiedel.

end of the eighteenth, and Ludwig Leichhardt, who crossed Australia in the nineteenth, were also of this type. While all of them were colourful characters, many of these German explorers disappeared without a trace, together with their observations and comments. Those whose memories have survived are but a few: Magister Johannes, pilot and navigator during Admiral Cabral's discovery of Brazil in 1500; Hans Mayr and Balthasar Sprenger, who sailed to India with Francisco d'Almeida and whom we have already met; the sailors Hans Barge and Hans Aleman, who participated in Magellán's voyage, and finally the captains of the Welsers of whom we have just spoken. On a different plane, Ferdinand Cron stepped into the limelight of history at the beginning of the seventeenth century. As Director-General to Philip II of Spain he organized trade between India and China and brought it largely under Spanish control. Five generations later, Felix von Oldenburg played a similar rôle in Portugal. From 1753 onwards he controlled the entire Portuguese trade with India and China, and for ten years he was uncrowned king of Sumatra, Macao, and the Moluccas.

But little is known of all these men. Always they went out alone, independent pioneers and lonely bushrangers. True, on the basis of a statistical report accidentally preserved, we know that of the ninety-four ships that entered the Guadalquivir, roughly a half came from German ports and a third of the passengers came from Hamburg. We may assume that during more favourable seasons this proportion of Germans continued undiminished. But Germany lacked national cohesion, that prerequisite for all great financial, nautical, military and diplomatic achievements so essential for colonization. Admittedly there was no lack of attempts to play at colonial politics. In 1651, the Duke of Kurland acquired bases in Guinea, thirty years later the flag of Brandenburg was flying over Gross-Friedrichsburg, a fort on the Gold Coast, and in 1667 an Oriental Company was founded by the Habsburgs in Vienna. But none of these achievements was really successful. Then, as now, those who went out from Germany were left to their own devices.

This is precisely what happened to Ulrich Schmiedel. He had sailed to South America on a ship, probably financed by the Welsers, one of a fleet of fourteen ships captained by Don Pedro de Mendoza, a chamberlain of Charles V. The ships weighed anchor on the 1st September 1534, and arrived in the estuary of the River Plate the following year. Schmiedel begins his account of his travels with the Land of the Charruas, now known as the Argentine:

> We discovered an Indian settlement containing about two thousand men called *Zechuruass*. As we approached, they took flight and hid themselves with their women and children, but later they became more friendly. These Indians wear no clothes at all, though the women cover their nakedness with a narrow strip of cloth hanging from their navels to their knees. We built a town there, calling it Bonas Ayres, which means 'Good Winds', surrounding it by an earthen wall a spear's length high and three feet wide. Then famine struck the land and the people were in great want. Three Spanish soldiers stole a horse and led it away to eat it in secret, but they were discovered and made to confess and hanged for their crime. That night, while the bodies were hanging from the gallows, other Spaniards crept up to them and cut pieces of flesh from the thighs of the dead men to fill their stomachs, so great was their hunger! Furthermore one Spaniard ate his own brother who had just died.

Today when one hears the song *Buenos Aires, mi tierra querida, Buenos Aires, la perla del Plata!* one may well think back four hundred years to the time when this great city was no more than a miserable fort suffering from famine and in fear of attack from the Indians. Then the food situation had become so desperate that Mendoza was forced to send three hundred men up river in seven rowing boats, to secure provisions of any nature. The Indians defeated the expedition by applying a 'scorched earth' policy, destroying all villages and crops as the invaders approached, and disappearing into the woods with as much as they could carry. One half of

32. Buenos Aires.

the expedition died of hunger and the remainder struggled back to Buenos Aires exhausted and empty-handed. On Schmiedel's advice, the Spaniards changed their policy, trying to win the land they were unable to subject, by friendship.

Although the new policy of offering friendship resulted in the winning over of the Timbos tribe, Mendoza considered the game not worth the candle and decided to cut his losses and return to Spain. Schmiedel, however, stayed behind together with a small nucleus of tougher characters. After repeated skirmishes and unsuccessful raids, the Charruas gave up their resistance to the invaders. Schmiedel has left us full descriptions of these warlike people:

> Their spears are rather short and have points made of flints. They also carry clubs four or five feet long. In addition to the former weapons they all carry ten or twelve pieces of wood about a hand's span in length, to which is attached a large broad tooth taken from some fish. This tooth is very sharp and is used for the following purpose.

At first the Indians fight with the spear and the club, then they throw the club at their enemy's feet so that he falls to the ground. They then leap on him and cut off his head with the fish-tooth knife. When the battle is over, they take the heads they have collected and remove the skin, together with the hair, from the top of the head. They preserve and dry these scalps and tie them to a pole set up before their dwellings, just as in our country a knight or a captain will place a flag in the church.

Divorce was unnecessary among the savage Charruas for once a man had grown tired of his wife he simply cooked her and ate her 'at a great festive banquet like our wedding feasts. An old woman, however, was simply left to work in the fields until she died'!

Although this sounds rather like one of the usual tall stories that abound in early travel books, it must be stated that well-authenticated reports exist, proving that women were treated as no better than cattle. When the King of Nore, one of the chieftains of the Chibcha Indians, paid an official state visit to the Spanish Governor of Colombia he took four wives along with him—two of the unfortunate women, lying flat on the ground, served him as a couch, the third as a pillow and the fourth he had roasted!

Schmiedel had great respect for the military prowess of the Charruas. They built forts and surrounded them with palisades, deep ditches and earthworks. In battle they were absolutely fearless. After a victory they would take all the prisoners and fatten them up for a great victory feast 'as we fatten pigs in Germany'. Like most cannibals, they believed that the strength of the men they ate would pass into their own bodies.

Schmiedel stayed in South America for just under twenty years. During that time, he explored much of the country, going as far afield as Peru, practising a variety of trades including mercenary soldier, ship builder, gold prospector and slave trader. He also had a hand in the founding of the settlements of Asunción and Corpus Christi. Then one day his brother wrote that he was dying and that the family would need Ulrich to look after them.

Thus Schmiedel made his way back home towards the end of July 1552. Of his former comrades only fifty had survived; all had grown old and grey, emaciated and worn out by the terrible deprivations of those years. But still they were proud to have been through it all, as they stressed when Ulrich Schmiedel, their real leader, left them. They knew full well their worth and that it was they, a handful of half-starved men, who in their marches right across the continent up to the Andes and deep down into Peru, had opened the way for the conquest of this large, rich and fertile land. A little of this pride can still be felt in Ulrich Schmiedel's book of adventure. Thus it is not only a German Odyssey, full of anecdotes and amusing tales, but also one of the greatest epics of the new continent—the life-story of one of those brave adventurers to whom the white man owes his supremacy in the world.

PART SIX

THE TEMPTING SOUTH SEA

Of the navigational significance of sauerkraut · The Admiralty orders a vitamin diet · Vegetable patches in the ocean · Portable broth makes perfect glue · James Cook, the middle-brow genius · Princess Purea's tears were real, but did she cry for love? · Tahiti, the 'Temple of Eros' · The passage of Venus of 1769 · Nails—the currency of love · How to grow nail-trees · Where is the 'terra australis'? · Kangaroo soup is delicious · Landing in Batavia and returning to England · The 'Breed of Matang', the blue-eyed Vikings of the South Sea · What has happened to the B blood group in Polynesia? · Edible plants and domestic animals from Indonesia—but not a word of Sanscrit · Who brought the batata? · How did twenty-six chromosomes get into the cotton seed? · Did Viracocha call on Polynesia? · Cook returns to the South Sea · Pressing on to the Antarctic · The secret of the 'Roaring Forties' · The mixed blessings of European contacts · On the art of surf-riding · How do you sail an outrigger? · A short visit to Easter Island · Sergeant Behrens eats potatoes · Where did the Easter Islanders come from? · The mystery of the 'rongo-rongo' tablets · Father Eyraud's 'auto-da-fé' · Who can read Easter Islandese? · Cook resists feminine charms and sticks to his axe · The Melanesians are no beauties · Tacking in the icy South · Return to England and third voyage · Telling time by the chronometer · Discourse on the evil temptations of civilization · Hawaii discovered · The 'British Disease' · Where is the passage to the Atlantic? · 'Beer' from pine-cones · Cook's death · Why the Tchuktches chose the Tsar in preference to King George III

I

GEOGRAPHICAL text-books still assert that exploration of the Pacific was only made possible by the invention of the chronometer and sextant early on in the eighteenth century. While this is true in a sense, it is also false, for it was not thanks to these superior navigational instruments that ships dared to set sail for that unknown ocean, but to two quite different commodities—sauerkraut and concentrated soup. The Pacific presented mariners not so much with a navigational problem as with a problem of diet and nutrition!

This simple fact is proved by the behaviour of Spanish navigators who, right up to the middle of the eighteenth century, restricted themselves to the shortest possible route from their possessions in the New World to the Philippines, and went in fear of any deviation from that course lest their ships be carried into those calms which had nearly proved fatal to Magellán and his men, and which some centuries later nearly drove Jack London frantic during his efforts to sail from Tahiti to Hawaii. It was not the dangers of storms, typhoons or hidden reefs that were feared, but an enemy far more terrible—scurvy.

We have already mentioned this deadly enemy of sailors more than once, in particular during our account of Vasco da Gama's great voyages. Because of it, unknown oceans could not be explored, and even two hundred and fifty years after da Gama it was still taking its dreadful toll of seafarers. Sergeant Carl Friedrich Behrens, a native of Rostock in Mecklenburg, who accompanied the Dutch captain Roggeween on his world tour of 1721 and 1722, has left a vivid description of the horrors let loose when scurvy breaks out on board ship in mid-ocean. We give it here for it applies equally well to most other sailing ships of that period.

> No pen can describe the miseries of life on our ships. Only God knows what we have suffered. Ships reeked of death and the sick, and the stench alone was enough to make you ill. The stricken wailed and lamented unceasingly and their cries would have moved even stones to pity. Some of the afflicted became so thin and emaciated that they looked like walking corpses and death blew them out like so many candles. Others became very fat and were blown up like balloons. These poor devils soon went out of their wits. They were also afflicted with dysentery and passed nothing but blood, except for two or three days before they died when they passed a horrible mess that looked like grey sulphur. This was a sure sign that their hour had come. Others again

were unable to walk and had to slide along the decks on their buttocks. All were overcome by a fearful melancholy. . . . There is no remedy except to eat fresh food, both meat and vegetables. . . . Those who were not seriously ill with scurvy, like myself, were still left very weak and enfeebled. My teeth were loose in my gums, which were swollen up almost as thick as my thumbs, and my body was covered with swellings the size of a hazelnut, red, yellow, green and blue in colour. From this it can be seen that even the healthy were sorely afflicted. . . .

This moving quotation is from Carl Friedrich Behrens's most interesting book, *Der Wohlversuchte Südländer* (The Well-Tried Southerner) which tells of his experiences on Roggeween's ship during its voyage round the world. Countless other reports about the same frightful horrors exist, and it has been calculated that during the first two decades of the seventeenth century more than ten thousand European sailors died of scurvy. It seemed to be not unusual for a ship to return to its home port with scurvy having taken its toll of half the crew. In this connection we may mention some details concerning the English gunship *Eagle*, a ship made famous by the fact that James Cook served on her as an able-bodied seaman. In June 1756, the ship returned to Plymouth, her home port, after a comparatively short voyage. In his reports the captain, Hugh Palliser, stated that during the last month at sea twenty-two men had died of scurvy and a hundred and thirty had fallen grievously ill. A few days later the ship's doctor, the captain himself and four more men also breathed their last.

This impossible state of affairs had continued for centuries, and after a short spell at sea the strength of a ship of the navy would usually be reduced by half owing to this frightful disease. Finally the Admiralty decided to adopt the suggestion of the naval surgeon, Dr. James Lind, who had advised captains to carry as much fresh food as possible, particularly on long voyages.

Lind had been puzzled for years about the causes of scurvy, and eventually came to the conclusion that it was not the result of the climate or the winds, as some people maintained, but of a poor and inadequate diet. Almost at the same time Sir John Pringle, the surgeon and nature healer, was occupied with this problem. At first he thought it must be due to the salt beef, the main item on a sailor's menu, but during the Seven Years' War (1756–63) he noticed that scurvy broke out among the French prisoners detained at Sissinghurst Castle in Kent, even though they were not fed on salt beef. He turned his attention to other possible causes and discovered the answer in the reports of the Medical Officers of Health. Scurvy was also known in the slums of big cities, but when the fruit harvest was good it would disappear as if by magic. Pringle then examined the provision lists for the prisoners at Sissinghurst Castle and found that the cases of scurvy cleared up when the prisoners were given fresh food, e.g. vegetables or fruit, instead of the customary soup.

He had found the answer, but the next problem was to apply his findings to conditions at sea. In the damp, airless holds below deck food soon became rotten and so there was no possibility of loading an adequate supply of vegetables. Then Pringle had a brainwave. He remembered that scurvy was unknown on Scandinavian and North German ships, which always carried hundreds of barrels of uncooked sauerkraut. He then turned to the sages of antiquity and found that both Cato and Pliny had spoken in praise of this food, which, then as now, was a kind of German national dish. Pringle therefore suggested that barrels of sauerkraut be taken on board English ships and given to the sailors.

The result was an immediate storm of protest. All the medical authorities of the day opposed Pringle and declared that sauerkraut contained decaying agents, that it caused flatulence and indigestion. One famous English doctor of the time even went so far as to say that it was poisonous!

Strangely enough, the British Admiralty paid no attention to the detractors of sauerkraut and decided to give it and other antiscorbutics a try. Byron and Wallis's Pacific expedition had already been equipped with supplies to combat scurvy. Pringle's ideas were further put into practice when, in 1767, the Royal Society of London asked the King of England for a grant of two ships and four thousand pounds, so that the passage of Venus across the Sun on the 3rd June 1769, could be observed from the South Sea. The enterprise was, of course, not of a military nature, and the Admiralty was not particularly concerned with disinterested astronomical research, but seeing that France, Sweden and Spain had already equipped ships for similar expeditions and that it might be possible to use this occasion for having a good look round in the Pacific Ocean which had hardly been explored to that date, the Admiralty consented. It was believed by many that somewhere in those unknown expanses of sea must lie a great continent, the *terra australis*, and that it was of the utmost importance to plant the Union Jack there, but of course, officially speaking, the expedition was purely scientific and the Sea Lords bore no responsibility for it. Clearly this was a favourable opportunity for trying out Lind's and Pringle's suggestions on a large scale. If it went wrong, it would not be the Navy but only some mad scientists who would suffer!

The caution of the Admiralty is understandable when one remembers that even as late as the twentieth century scurvy was still considered to be an infectious disease. On the other hand, the authorities must have been very eager to give Pringle's suggestion a try-out, for the importance of fresh fruit and vegetables had long been known. All trading nations of the world were careful to maintain supply stations for ships on long voyages, so that they could take fresh provisions on board. The Swiss geographer, Roland Nitsche, in his recent book *Uralte Wege, ewige Fahrt* (Ancient Routes, Eternal Voyage), in which he shows that the driving force behind the voyages of discovery was nearly always the desire to develop trade, has most aptly named these supply-depots 'Vitamin stations'. The establishing of these stations opened up a new era in colonial politics, for places such as St. Helena, far out in the South Atlantic, Cape Town, Mauritius and Madagascar, which frequently passed from the hands of one nation to another, were not strategic centres but rather strategic vegetable gardens and food depots. While it is true they were defended by fortifications and troops, this was done in the spirit with which a householder puts a fence round his garden. Even so, the cost of such 'fences' always worked out rather high, and so it would be greatly to the Admiralty's advantage if Pringle's scheme did work.

James Cook, the leader of the English expedition of 1767 to the Pacific, was certainly the type of officer who could be counted upon to carry out the orders of his superiors to the letter. This was a matter of some importance to the Sea Lords, for the experiment would have been useless if their orders were not followed precisely.

Pringle was proved completely justified in his belief in antiscorbutics, for Cook returned to England after an absence of over two years with not a single man lost from scurvy! Cook's second voyage was just as conclusive: during an absence of three years and eighteen days only four of his crew died, and not one of them from scurvy. This news was of major importance for seamen, and Cook's detailed report of his voyages was commissioned by the Admiralty for publication. His paper on the treatment of scurvy (in a letter to Sir John Pringle) was published in the *Philosophical Transactions of the Royal Society*.

The report contains nothing to startle us. The fact that it is healthy to eat uncooked cabbage, malt extract, carrot purée, oranges and lemons is known not merely to readers of Gayelord Hauser, and we need waste little time on it. It might be of interest, however, to learn that a kind of meat extract called *Portable Broth* was carried on board an English expedition in 1763. It is generally believed that meat extract was invented by the German chemist Justus von Liebig, but apparently the English had forestalled him! The German scientist Georg Forster, who accompanied Cook on his second voyage, was so struck by this meat extract that he gave a description of it in his report of the voyage:

> Such cakes of broth are sold in London and in all English ports under the name of 'Portable Soup'. They are made of fresh meat, usually beef, bones and offal which are cooked until they become jellified. This jelly is then moulded into small cakes. It greatly resembles glue in colour and consistency and can in fact be used as such. It keeps for many years if protected from moisture and is of great use and value during long sea voyages, when there is always a shortage and want of fresh meat. One or two of these small cakes, when cut up and dissolved in hot water, make an excellent helping of good strong soup. It is sold by the pound and, seeing that it can be made of bones and offal,

it is very cheap. On our ship we had three thousand pounds of this portable soup in metal containers, each one weighing twenty-five pounds.

Clearly this Portable Soup was the forerunner of our modern meat extract cubes. The fact that it could also be used as glue is an advantage that our modern commodity lacks! It is most unlikely that this meat extract had any antiscorbutic value, yet it did contribute to making meals on board ship more tasty, for Cook remarks in his journal that it helped the cooks to prepare a variety of nourishing and pleasant dishes and thus persuaded the crew to eat more vegetables than was their wont.

Cook had prepared the ground for the exploration of the Pacific. It goes without saying that, quite apart from these dietary considerations, he also needed great courage and persistence and great nautical skill.

2

James Cook was a true-born Englishman, a worthy son of Albion, the freest and yet the most conservative country in the world. He came from a poor home, his father having been an agricultural labourer in the small Yorkshire village of Marton-in-Cleveland in the North Riding of Yorkshire. James was the second son of nine children, five of whom died when they were still of tender years. He was born on the 27th October 1728, and even as a child he was particularly bright and gifted. His father took the unusual step for a day-labourer of engaging a tutor for the boy before sending him to a church school. Cook's education lasted in all about five or six years, and so it is unlikely that he was able to progress far beyond the rudiments of reading, writing and arithmetic. At the age of thirteen he was apprenticed to a certain Mr. William Sanderson, a grocer in Staithes, not far from Newcastle, in return for his board and lodging.

At first the boy enjoyed his work; he was level-headed, composed and good at figures and he fitted in well with the life of a busy grocery shop. It is possible that Cook would never have become anything more than a well-to-do tradesman in a small British coastal town, had the sea not been so close at hand. A year and a half later the apprentice who had shown such promise suddenly broke his contract and signed on as cabin-boy on the *Freelove*, a collier of four hundred and fifty tons, plying between Newcastle and London and belonging to the Quaker, John Walker, and his two sons.

Cook soon realized that advancement in his new life depended entirely upon himself. This time he did not quit easily, but stuck to his job, saving every penny and utilizing every spare moment ashore or afloat for studying navigation, astronomy and cartography.

At the end of seven years he was appointed first mate of the *Friendship*, a ship newly built by the firm of John Walker for sailing between England, Norway and the Baltic. His employers were fully satisfied with the young officer and were about to offer him his first ship but Cook, who was by then twenty-seven years old, had other plans for himself. He signed on in the Navy as an Able Seaman, starting his new career on the 25th June 1755, aboard the *Eagle*.

Many people, including his former employers, could not understand this step, but Cook must have known what he was about. The Navy had complained for years of a lack of suitable recruits, and Cook foresaw that it would not be difficult to rise in its ranks. When war broke out between England and France in May 1756, chances of promotion were even greater. It was only two years before Cook rose to the rank of Master and transferred to the *Pembroke*.

The *Pembroke*, together with eighteen other warships, sailed on active service to Canadian waters. Cook made his own particular contribution to the English victories in Canada, for he helped in making the maps that were used in the capture of Quebec in 1759. The Commander of the fleet took note of the very capable young man, and in January 1760, Cook was awarded a gratuity of fifty pounds, a great sum at the time. Soon afterwards Cook began to chart the little-known seas between the coasts of Newfoundland and Nova Scotia and as soon as his work was done in 1761, the Union Jack was planted in those inhospitable regions.

Cook returned to London at the end of October 1762, after an absence of four years. He was now thirty-four years old and wealthy enough to get married. Elizabeth Batts, the twenty-one-year-old daughter of a London merchant, must have found marriage with James Cook rather unexciting, for her taciturn and sober husband with his stubborn jaw, his sharp, straight nose, his deep-set eyes and heavy brows, was very seldom at home.

From the spring of 1763 to the late autumn of 1767, Cook appeared on the Admiralty rolls as 'Mr. James Cook, Engineer and Retinue'. He was paid ten shillings a day, and was sent to continue his charting activities in the Gulf of St. Lawrence close to Newfoundland, in the mouth of the Hudson and off the coast of Labrador. When he submitted his charts, the Admiralty was deeply impressed and called his work 'admirable'. It is not long since Cook's charts were still considered to be the best of these exceptionally difficult regions.

Just at the time when Cook returned, the Admiralty was occupied with the Royal Society's request to supply a ship to sail to the Pacific in order to observe the passage of Venus across the sun. After some hesitation it was decided to promote Cook to the rank of naval lieutenant and to put him in charge of the nautical side of the expedition. He was also instructed to make a systematic survey of the Pacific Ocean.

James Cook fulfilled his task in a masterly manner. Thanks to him the Pacific was explored from east to west and from the Antarctic to the far north. It will be remembered that he was not the first to sail over that gigantic expanse of water. Forty-five years after Magellán had crossed it without sighting more than two barren atolls, Alvaro Mendaña de Neyra

33. A British man-of-war in Cook's time.

had set sail from Callao in Peru to the Pacific. His aim had been to find the rich islands mentioned by the Incas, but, like Magellán, he too had managed to miss the many clusters of islands in the South Seas. After a voyage of eighty days he had finally reached the Solomon Islands deep in Melanesia. He and his crew had lived there among the negroid cannibals for six months before returning to South America. On a second expedition, some thirty years later, Mendaña de Neyra had discovered the Marquesas Islands.

In 1605, Pedro Fernández de Quirós had set sail, only to discover that the South Seas washed round a hitherto unknown continent. Although the chiefs of the Incas had only spoken of islands or groups of islands, people had long been convinced of the existence of an unknown continent which they had called the *terra australis*. It was inconceivable that the greater part of the globe should be covered by water. Like the astronomer Hipparchus, some one hundred and fifty years before the birth of Christ, and Ptolemy three hundred and fifty years later, people were still convinced that land and sea masses were carefully disposed over the surface of the globe to balance similar masses in the opposite hemisphere, and that therefore the great expanse of land in the northern hemisphere must be balanced by a great continent in the southern. Astronomical arguments were produced in support of this hypothesis: it was claimed that the number of fixed stars was proportional to the amount of land on the earth, and that therefore the fixed stars in the southern sky proved that somewhere in the gigantic waters beyond the Equator lay an undiscovered continent.

Quirós was unsuccessful in his search for the *terra australis*. He reached the New Hebrides, and his comrade Torres managed with more luck than judgement to pass through the dangerous strait between New Guinea and Australia now called after his name, but they saw nothing of the great unknown land itself. Cook himself passed through the Torres Strait in 1770.

In 1615 the Dutch made their first entry into the South Seas and one of their ships, the *Eendracht*, landed in Australia, but its captain attached no importance to the event. He contented himself with leaving a plate signed with his name and that of his ship on the foreign shore—this plate was later recovered and is now preserved in a museum in Amsterdam. Between 1642 and 1644 the Dutch sailed right round Australia to reach Tasmania and New Zealand, but as they were chiefly concerned with trade with the East Indies, they gave up any further voyages of discovery. During the 1760's the *Dolphin* under the command of Captain Wallis crossed the Pacific and reached Tahiti, to be followed, a few months later, by the Frenchman, Bougainville, who continued on from Tahiti to the Solomons. The latter islands, discovered by Mendaña in 1567, had been sought for in vain for more than two hundred years. None of these expeditions could afford to remain long in these latitudes because of the danger of scurvy. The Pacific continued to be a *mare incognitum*, an immeasurable, uncharted ocean.

These voyages, however, had made the Pacific a fashionable topic of conversation in Europe, and everyone talked about these Arcadian islands set in an azure sea, about their beautiful women decked in flowers, and the tall athletic men who led a carefree happy existence as hunters and fishermen. The fact that these innocent, unspoilt children of Adam were all cannibals, murderers and head-hunters was not insisted upon, for it did not fit in with the sentimental picture of 'noble savages'.

This legend of an earthly paradise set under the blue skies of the Pacific was due in part to the perennial nostalgia for a Golden Age, and in part to the touching love-story of the Tahitian Princess Purea and Captain Wallis, commander of the British frigate *Dolphin*. Captain Wallis made a full report of the romance to the Admiralty on his return to London and the story of it was soon on everybody's lips. In all probability the gallant captain was greatly mistaken in interpreting the tears shed during the leave-taking audience as evidence that his absence was a cruel blow to the fair lady, and though he was right to weep a little too, he was right for the wrong reasons. It was a common feature of Polynesian customs that whoever set forth on a journey was entitled to a display of sorrow at his departure, and it seems likely that Purea and her entourage were merely being polite after their own fashion!

In London the story of the royal lady's tears was taken at its face value, and certainly it must have provided entertainment in an otherwise routine report, for Captain Wallis thought it necessary also to give detailed descriptions of the young ladies-in-waiting of the Princess. Purea herself was forty-five years old and rather plump, but her lack of physical charms was made up for by her ladies. Reading between the lines of the report, one also gets the impression that the captain, the officers and men of the *Dolphin* had not merely let matters rest there!

As can well be imagined this caused quite a sensation in the august chambers of the British Admiralty, but the vicarious pleasure in the comely maidens of the South Seas was tinged with disappointment that the *terra australis*, which was hoped to be rich in gold and precious jewels, had not been discovered and islands such as had been found were only rich in beautiful young ladies.

Barely eight months after the arrival of the British ship in Tahiti, two French vessels, under the command of Captain Louis Antoine de Bougainville, dropped anchor there. The French reports reached Paris about the same time that Captain Wallis was amusing the Admiralty. The French with true gallantry did not complain that the only jewels to be had—for they too were searching for riches—were beautiful, approachable women! The French captain was positively enchanted by them and called the island, officially annexed for the French Crown, *La Nouvelle Cythère*, thus referring to the island which saw the birth of Venus, the Goddess of Love.

Accounts of Captain Wallis's adventures in the South Seas appeared in many fashionable London newspapers, e.g. the *St. James Chronicle or the British Evening Post* and *The Gazetteer and New Daily Advertiser*, and were quickly followed by similar articles in the French Press. One such article appeared in the *Mercure de France* from the pen of Doctor Commerson, the scientific adviser who sailed with Captain de Bougainville. The learned doctor's delight knew no bounds. 'Tahiti,' he declared, 'is the only place on earth where there are people without vice, where inequality of rank does not exist and where people live without jealousy and discord. These happy people, born under eternally blue skies and fed on the choicest fruits of the earth, are governed by wise old men, the heads of families, rather than by kings, and the whole island knows only one god: the god of love. Every day they make offerings to him, the whole island is his temple, the men are his high priests and the women sacrifice themselves on his altar. *Et quelles femmes, me demanderez-vous? Les rivales des Georgiennes en beauté et les sœurs des grâces, toutes nues!'*

The doctor was no novice and his word could be trusted, for he too worshipped at the same altar. He had taken his Parisian mistress along on the voyage, disguising her as his valet. She played her part so well that nobody suspected that she was other than she appeared to be, but the natives on Tahiti at once penetrated her disguise. A white woman! It was a seven days' wonder for them. They called her *cotu hi haua*, my little gold finger, or *ohu*, jewel of my ear, and composed eulogies to every single part of her body.

The French were highly delighted by the whole affair, and 'Jean-Jacques Rousseau' Commerson's report served them as further evidence for the theory of the natural goodness of man, as proved by the example of primitive peoples. That such a doctrine would have amused and bewildered the inhabitants of Tahiti is proved by the posthumous and ironical memoirs of the Princess Arii Taimai, which were published in Paris in 1901, when they were an immediate success.

When Cook made his appearance in the Pacific it was as an officer in His Majesty's Navy, but his ship was neither a man-o'-war nor one of the large ships of the East India Company. Cook, in a manner typical of his unromantic but strictly practical nature, had realized that the normal type of large vessel with its considerable draught would be of little use to him on this expedition, and that what he most needed was a flat-bottomed broad sailing ship like the collier on which he had started, drawing little water and so able to go close to land even in shallow seas. Such a vessel would have the additional advantage of being spacious enough to hold the extra large stocks of provisions and equipment needed for a very long voyage, such as this would be. Furthermore the crew would have more living-space than in a warship with its rakish lines, and this was most important. On Cook's recommendation the Admiralty bought a four-year-old collier in Whitby, Cook's home port, for the sum of £2,480 10*s*. 11*d*. and put it into service under the name of the *Endeavour*.

The *Endeavour* set sail on the 26th August 1768, at two o'clock in the afternoon, carrying a naval complement of eighty-four, together with fourteen scientists and astronomers. In addition to ten large and twelve small cannon, the *Endeavour* carried supplies for at least eighteen months. The ample holds below deck were filled with gigantic vats containing sauerkraut, containers of 'portable soup', carrot conserve and malt. When the *Endeavour* dropped anchor at Rio de Janeiro the Portuguese Viceroy could not believe that the ship was a unit of the British Navy and not some mere vulgar insignificant trader!

After a few weeks' rest in this magnificent harbour the *Endeavour* set off again towards Cape Horn, which was rounded in the middle of January 1769. Two months later the mountains of Tahiti could be seen rising above the horizon. The first stage of the voyage had been completed.

Cook must also have been pleased that so far he had not a single case of scurvy. His entry for the day when he landed in Royal Bay (Matavay Bay) is most touching:

> 13th April, 1769. . . . At 5 a.m. made sail for the [Royal] Bay and at 7 anchored in thirteen fathoms. At this time we had but very few men upon the sick list, and these had but slight complaints. . . . The sauerkraut, the men at first would not eat it, until I put it into practice—a method I never once knew to fail with seamen—and this was to have some of it dressed every day for the cabin table, and permitted all the officers, without exception, to make use of it, and left to the option of the men either to take as much as they pleased or none at all; but this practice was not continued above a week before I found it necessary to put every one on board to an allowance; for such are the tempers and disposition of seamen in general that whatever you give them out of the common way—although it be ever so much for their good—it will not go down, and you will hear nothing but murmurings against the man that first invented it; but the moment they see their superiors set a value upon it, it becomes the finest stuff in the world and the inventor an honest fellow. . . .

As already mentioned Cook wrote the above after eight months at sea, and the unheard-of sensation that not one sailor had gone sick with scurvy overshadowed all other considerations. Eventually, however, our sober Yorkshireman too felt the urge to record his impressions of that Arcadian isle, though he felt it just as imperative to issue the following order to his crew:

> Rules to be observed by every person in or belonging to His Majesty's Bark the *Endeavour* for the better establishing a regular and uniform trade for provisions, etc., with the inhabitants of George's Island:
>
> 1. To endeavour by every fair means to cultivate a friendship with the natives, and to treat them with all imaginable humanity.
>
> 2. A proper person or persons will be appointed to trade with the natives for all manner of provisions, fruits, and other Productions of the earth; and no officer or seaman or other person belonging to the ship, excepting such as are so appointed, shall trade or offer to trade for any sort of provisions, fruit or other productions of the earth, unless they have my leave to do so.
>
> 3. Every person employed on shore on any duty whatsoever is strictly to attend to the same, and if by neglect he loses any of his arms or working tools, or suffers them to be stolen the full value thereof will be charged against his pay, according to the custom of the Navy in such cases, and he shall receive such further punishment as the nature of the offence may deserve.
>
> 4. The same penalty will be inflicted upon every person who is found to embezzle, trade or offer to trade, with any of the ship's stores of what nature so ever.

5. No sort of iron or anything that is made of iron, or any sort of cloth or other useful or necessary articles, are to be given in exchange for anything but provisions.

J.C.

The above quotation shows the feeling that ran through Cook's mind on reaching Tahiti. His first concern was to establish friendly relations with the natives, for he knew how quickly trouble could arise. When Captain Wallis had landed on those shores there had been sad misunderstandings and an English volley had littered the beach with dead and wounded. Cook was determined to prevent any incident of that kind, and he warned his men that he would punish severely anyone found guilty of antagonizing the inhabitants.

It was also imperative to obtain as much fresh food as possible. Another long voyage lay ahead of them and the fear of scurvy, though greatly reduced by the sauerkraut, had not completely disappeared. Moreover, the men were tired of eating cabbage day after day for nine months on end, and had to be given a change of food.

Whether he was able to enforce sections 4 and 5 of his orders was another matter! Wallis had not been able to cope with this problem and all his efforts to keep the situation in hand had failed miserably. Cook thought the best way to deal with the matter was not to breathe a word of what he had read in Wallis's account.

Wallis had reported the following: the inhabitants of Tahiti were still living in the Stone Age, but knew the value of metals and in particular of iron. They seemed to have an insatiable passion for nails. Wallis had discovered that he could get anything, pigs, bananas, batatas, coconuts, chickens, even dogs, which the natives counted a great delicacy, in exchange for nails!

The ingenuous natives were deeply puzzled and anxious to know the kind of tree that brought forth such fruit, and for this reason they would plant the nails in their gardens and water them with great care in the hope that they would germinate and flourish. Unfortunately they did not sprout but merely went rusty, so the natives devised another scheme to acquire a good supply of nails. One day they appeared on the beach with their wives, sisters and daughters and gestured to the sailors that they could enjoy the ladies' favours for the price of one nail. Overnight the sailors' pockets were filled with nails; they stole them from the stores and pulled them out of the ship's planks, benches and tables. Wallis had to resort to severe measures to save the ship from falling to pieces; but his measures came too late, for the price of provisions had risen phenomenally in the meantime.

Cook wanted to avoid this at all costs but he could not very well put down his fears in black and white, lest he give the sailors ideas, though the crew in all probability were as well informed as he, for three of Wallis's officers were on board the *Endeavour*. His fears were confirmed when soon after dropping anchor a hundredweight of nails disappeared from the stores. Nevertheless he was more successful than Wallis in restraining his men, and the ship came to no harm.

The inhabitants of the South Sea islands were far more backward than the peoples living on the mainland of Asia, for they did not know how to spin or weave, let alone make iron, and clothes such as they wore were extremely makeshift garments consisting of *tapa*, i.e. strips of bark, joined together by fibre. It is not surprising, therefore, that the natives of Tahiti were almost as keen on getting hold of European cloth as they were on acquiring nails, and that they would give almost anything in exchange for hats, trousers and jackets. What they could not obtain through legitimate barter they stole.

This brings us face to face with the many riddles posed by the people of Polynesia. What chiefly puzzled Cook was the appearance of the islanders, and during the first days of his stay in Tahiti he noted the following in his journal:

> They are of various colours: those of the inferior sort, who are obliged to be much exposed to the sun and air, are of a very dark brown; the superiors again, who spend most of their time in their houses under shelter, are not browner than people who are born or reside longer in the West Indies; nay, some of the women are almost as fair as Europeans.

From this it can be seen that Cook explained the difference in colour between the Polynesian nobles and the ordinary peoples of the South Seas by the degree of exposure to the sun. In this he showed that he was very much a product of his time which thought that negroes were not merely dark-skinned but that they were actually burnt black by the sun. Today we are more scientific and know that the amount of pigment in the skin depends on quite other factors.

3

The passage of Venus across the face of the sun—the *raison d'être* of the whole expedition—was due to take place on the 3rd June 1769. Everybody on board, down to the ship's boy, knew the importance of the event and that the next passage of Venus would not occur for another hundred years. Professor Edmund Halley of the Royal Society, the Director of the Greenwich Observatory, had calculated this almost eighty years earlier but he had not been believed, for it seemed unlikely that the passage of Venus could be observed twice in seven years, i.e. in 1762 and 1769, and not again for another century. But Halley had also predicted that the famous comet, which bears his name and which had caused such a sensation during its appearances of 1533, 1607 and 1682, would sail across the sky in 1759, and when it appeared punctually to the very minute foretold by the astronomer, the Royal Society decided to think twice about his calculations concerning the course of Venus. The dust-covered file was taken out of the archives, with the result that in 1762 observers were stationed at different parts of England awaiting the great moment. Unfortunately visibility was bad everywhere and the results were unsatisfying.

Preparations for the passing of 1769 were more elaborate. It was decided to send two observers to the Pacific, two to northern Canada and two to southern Europe. A certain Doctor Bevis, a well-known astro-physicist, to give him his modern appellation, was a member of the organizing committee and he knew just the fellow to lead the expedition to the Pacific, a good sailor, an excellent cartographer and a trained astronomer to boot. 'But what the devil was the man's name?' Then Bevis remembered that at a recent meeting of the Royal Society he had read a report, submitted by Cook, giving details of an eclipse of the sun, which Cook had foretold and later observed. It was not difficult to look up that report, dated 'Newfoundland, 5th August, 1766' and to discover the name of its author.

It took Dr. Bevis some time to find Cook, but the Admiralty welcomed the suggestion, for they were unwilling to put one of the ships of the Royal Navy into the hands of any but their own men. There were no two ways about the matter. Cook, the trained sailor, cartographer and astronomer, was obviously their man. The Royal Society having previously chosen another man, namely Alexander Dalrymple, now made Cook leader of the expedition and awarded him one hundred guineas, together with a further hundred and twenty pounds a year for equipment and supplies. The Navy was much more niggardly. Cook the 'Engineer and Retinue' had received ten shillings a day, but his increase in rank actually brought him a drop in pay for he was henceforth to receive only five shillings.

Nevertheless it was a great honour to be chosen to lead the expedition and the men, too, must have sensed Cook's pride and happiness in his new honours. The great moment arrived, the sky was cloudless and at exactly $9^h 25^m 42^s$ on 3rd June 1769, as Halley had predicted, a small dark point could be observed through the smoked glass of the telescope, moving across the face of the sun. The astronomers were delighted, for it meant that they now had more data for calculating the distance between the sun and the earth, and could give a firm mathematical foundation to their speculations.

Cook's main mission was now completed. He had stood by the telescope and had helped the astronomers to the best of his ability. He had sailed the pinnace round the island, had charted it, and he was anxious now to get away. The *Endeavour* was thoroughly overhauled and everything made shipshape and seaworthy, fresh food and water were taken on board and on the 13th July 1769 they weighed anchor. The next port of call was the group of atolls called the Society Islands. The British flag was hoisted with due ceremony and the waters were sounded and charted. Then the ship sailed southwards in accordance with the Admiralty's secret instructions:

> You are to proceed to the southward in order to make discovery of the continent above-mentioned until you arrive in the latitude of 40°, unless you sooner fall in with it; but not having discovered it, or any evident signs of it, in that run, you are to proceed in search of it to the westward, between the latitude before mentioned and the latitude of 35° until you discover it or fall in with the Eastern side of the land discovered by Tasman and now called New Zealand.

Cook was to explore this island and to return to England on a suitable route. If he succeeded in discovering the continent, he was to pay great attention to the exploration of the largest possible stretch of coast, and to chart bays, harbours and those coastal regions which were important for navigation. He was also to investigate the nature of the land and of its soil, and to classify birds, beasts and fish. Should he discover deposits of minerals or precious stones, he was to bring back samples of them. Furthermore, he was to determine the nature, attitude, customs and approximate number of any natives he might encounter. He was to use every means of befriending them, and in favourable regions to gain their consent to the annexation of the land on behalf of His Britannic Majesty.

This order was quite logical, in view of what was known of the Dutch voyages of discovery in these waters. Abel Tasman, one of the captains of the Dutch fleet, had sailed south-east from Mauritius and had finally reached Tasmania and New Zealand in 1642. It was not known whether these two places were islands or capes of the great *terra australis*.

Cook sailed south from Tahiti and then altered course westwards in the direction of New Zealand. He zealously questioned the natives about the existence of a great continent but could receive no information from them. By the 1st September 1769, he had reached the latitude 40° 22′ South without having discovered the *terra australis*, and so he altered course north. Six weeks later the mountains of New Zealand appeared above the horizon. The question had never been finally resolved whether in fact this land was part of the *terra australis* or if it was an island. Cook's journal gives no indication of his personal feelings; it soberly notes the wind and weather conditions, anchorage and soundings. The next six months were spent in disproving the idea that New Zealand might be part of the great southern continent. By the end of March 1770, Cook might well have set sail for home, for he was convinced that if any new continent did exist, it must lie much further south. On the 31st March he made the following entry in his journal:

> ... and as to a Southern Continent, I do not believe any such thing exists, unless in a high latitude.... Thus I have given my opinion freely and without prejudice, not with

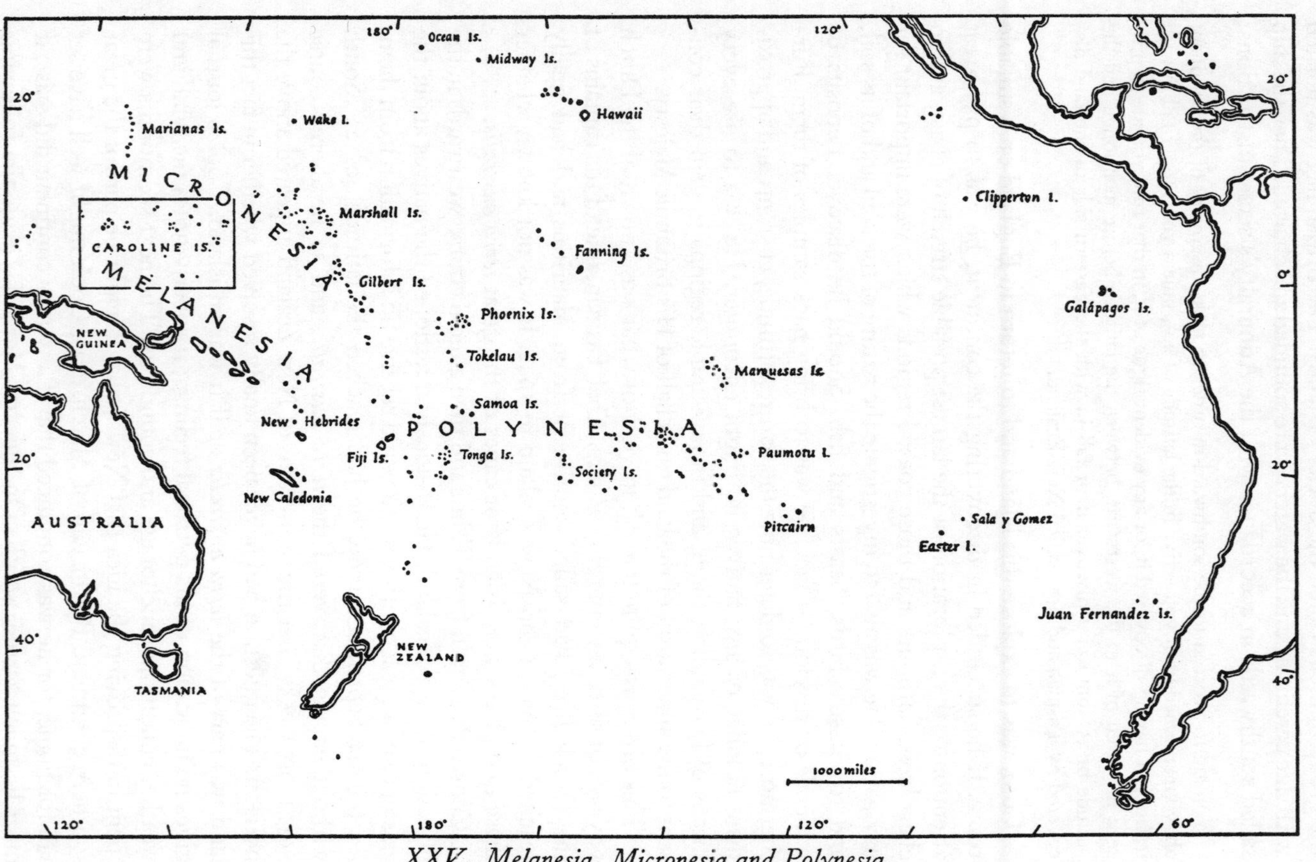

XXV. Melanesia, Micronesia and Polynesia.

any view to discourage any future attempts being made towards discovering the Southern Continent; on the contrary . . . I think it would be a great pity that this thing, which at times has been the object of many ages and nations, should not now be wholly cleared up . . . but in order to ascertain this we must have kept in a higher latitude in the very depth of winter, but the condition of the ship, in every respect, was not thought sufficient for such an undertaking.

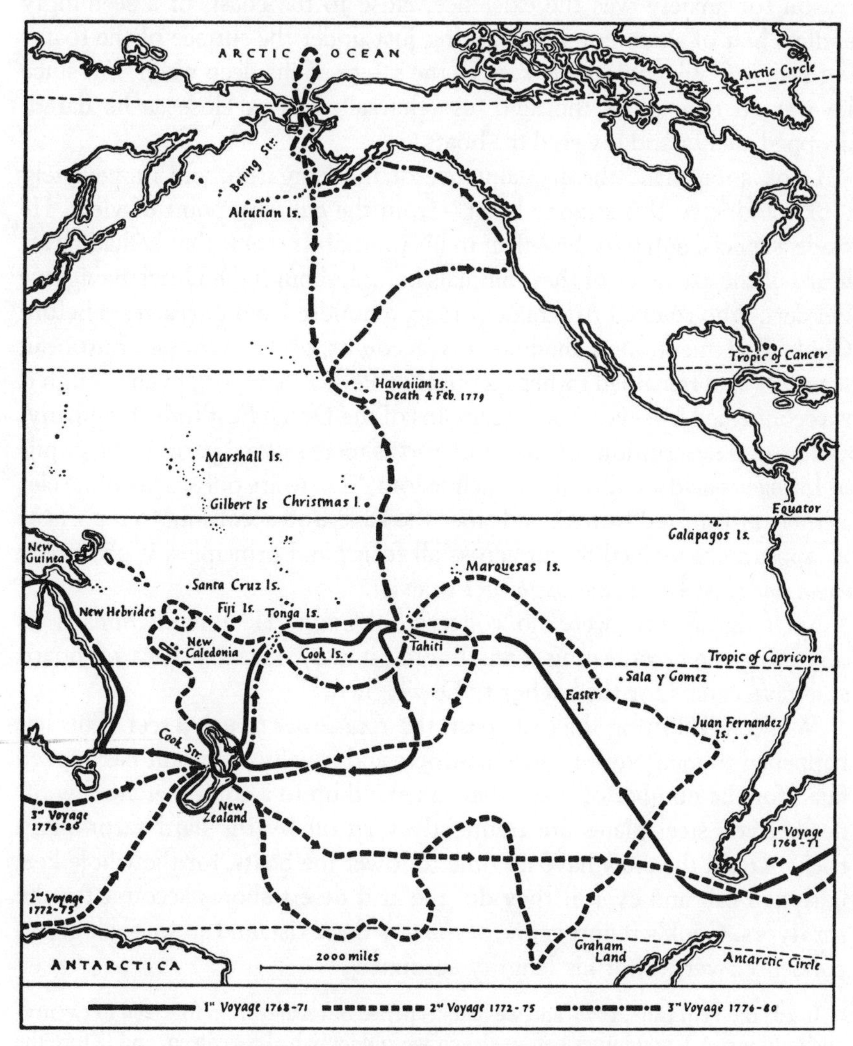

XXVI. *Cook's voyages in the Pacific.*

Although the *Endeavour* had now been away for over two years, the officers were agreed that, before returning, they should first explore the east coast of New Holland, as Australia was then called, or the New Hebrides, and only then sail back to England via the Malayan Archipelago, the Cape of Good Hope and the Atlantic.

The *Endeavour* set off from New Zealand on the 31st March 1770, and two weeks later, on the 18th April, the east coast of Australia was sighted. The country seemed fairly pleasant, despite large stretches of desert; it appeared to be well wooded and to have large expanses of prairie land. The look-out man also spotted some smoke signals, but what gave far more reason for anxiety was the existence, close to the coast, of a seemingly endless belt of sharp coral reefs, lying just under the surface of the foaming water. Cook could have kept to the safety of the deep water, but since he wanted to explore the land also, he sailed in as close as he dared, dropped anchor and lowered the boats.

Cook soon made the acquaintance of the kangaroo, and immediately took a liking to this strange beast—from the culinary point of view. He made a special entry to this effect in his journal. It seems that he had never heard of the existence of these animals before, though the Dutch navigator Pelsaert, who reached Australia in 1640, a hundred and thirty years before Cook, had mentioned them in his accounts of his voyage. European scientists had remained rather sceptical of Pelsaert's report, even though it was confirmed by several other captains of the Dutch East India Company, and treated descriptions of the kangaroo as mere sailors' yarns! The pupils of Linnaeus held stubbornly to their axiom, 'There are only as many species as there are created forms', and since the kangaroo according to reports of its appearance seemed to cut across all forms and principles, it obviously *could not* exist because it *ought not* to exist.

Such discussions were no concern of Cook. He limited himself to observing the beast, eating it and finding it tasty. He went back on board and gave orders for the anchor to be weighed.

While still skirting the east coast, the *Endeavour* struck a reef. This has happened to many unfortunate mariners and usually the result has proved fatal, for the number of boats that can stand up to a coral reef are few indeed. Even steel plates are frequently torn off by the hard razor-sharp rocks. Often the crew have no time to lower the boats, for the whole keel is ripped off, and even if they do, the arid desert shores account for the survivors. Cook's report is one of the few that exist, and so we shall give a condensed version of his lengthy account:

> It was the 11th June, 1770, and we had deepened our water from fourteen to twenty-one fathoms. A few minutes before eleven we suddenly had seventeen, and before the man at the lead could have another cast, the ship struck and stuck fast. Immediately upon this we took in all our sails, hoisted out the boats, and sounded round the ship. Our fears were confirmed: eight miles from the barren coast we had struck a coral reef. All our efforts to heave her off were without success. As we went ashore about the top of high water we not only started water, but threw overboard our guns, iron and stone ballast, casks, hoop staves, oil jars, etc.; many of these last articles lay in the way at coming at heavier. All this time the ship made little or no water. At 11 a.m., being high water as we thought, we tried to heave her off without success, she not being afloat by a

foot or more, notwithstanding by this time we had thrown overboard forty or fifty tons weight.

As the tide fell the ship began to make water as much as two pumps could free; at noon she lay with three or four streaks heel to starboard.... By this time it was 5 p.m. of June 12th; the tide we observed now began to rise, which obliged us to set the third pump to work, as we should have done the fourth also, but could not make it work. At nine the ship righted, and the leak gained upon the pumps considerably. This was an alarming and, I may say, terrible circumstance, and threatened immediate destruction to us. However I resolved to risk all.

Sir Joseph Banks had this to say of the crisis and the crew's behaviour:

No grumbling or growling was to be heard throughout the ship, not even an oath.... I must say for the credit of our people that I believe every man exerted his utmost for the preservation of the ship, contrary to what I have universally heard to be the behaviour of seamen, who, commonly, as soon as a ship is in a desperate situation, begin to plunder and refuse all command. This was no doubt owing to the cool and steady conduct of the officers, who, during the whole time, never gave an order which did not show them to be perfectly composed and unmoved by the circumstances, however dreadful they might appear.

By an extraordinary stroke of good luck the *Endeavour* was not seriously damaged and the leak could be held in check by the pumps until a suitable place to land and repair the damage was found. The bay where they halted for almost two months today bears the name of Cooktown. During the repairs they discovered that they owed the preservation of their ship to the fact that the point of the coral reef which had pierced the planks had broken off and had remained in the hole like a cork.

Once the ship was navigable again, Cook sailed north until the north coast of Australia was reached, then he turned westwards, between the northern tip of Australia and New Guinea, sailing through the Torres Strait to Timor and Java. Here he halted for another rest. According to his calculations it was Tuesday, October 9th, when he landed, though the inhabitants assured him that it was Wednesday, October 10th. So far he had hardly lost any of his men through sickness, but when he set sail three months later, on Boxing Day, 1770, seven members of the crew had died, and there were so many sick below deck that the *Endeavour* resembled a floating hospital. Malaria was the disease which had taken hold of his men and which was thought to be caused by the bad marsh air of the place—hence the name *mal-aria*. In the twenty years alone from 1735 to 1755, before the use of quinine was adopted, malaria claimed almost a million victims among the sailors of all nations. One of the first men to succumb to this scourge was the ship's doctor, Dr. Monkhouse, who died on 5th November. Between this date and the end of February, a further nineteen men died of malaria and most of the crew were affected so that at times there were only a dozen men fit for duty.

In the middle of March 1771, the *Endeavour* sailed into Capetown harbour and some four months later arrived back in England. Of the ninety-four men who had set out three years before on the fourth voyage round the world, only fifty-six returned.

Apart from the excellent view of the passage of Venus the results of the expedition were a little less satisfying: it was not realized that the Australian continent had been discovered. It is true that a great deal had been achieved: it had been established that New Zealand was an island, the exploration of the east coast of Australia had been accomplished, and sauerkraut had been conclusively tested. However, the general public knew little of these things. Although a narrative based on Cook's journal was published in 1773, Cook and his men were expressly forbidden to make known any details of their voyage. The Admiralty even went so far as to confiscate and seal the journals kept by Cook and some of the officers on board the *Endeavour*, and they were not published in their original form until one hundred and twenty years later. Cook was received by the King and gave a full account of his travels to His Majesty. He was then commissioned to the rank of captain and it was realized that Captain Cook's travels were far from over.

4

We have already mentioned that Cook became aware of some of the problems that still puzzle South Sea experts today. The first thing that he found worthy of notice was the colour of the Polynesians, for they were neither black like negroes, yellow like the Chinese nor copper-coloured like the Indians. Many of them, in fact, were sufficiently light-skinned to pass for Europeans. Cook noted this fact in his journal, and similar observations can be found in the diaries kept by two German scientists, Johann Reinhold Forster and his son Georg Forster, who accompanied Cook on his second expedition.

Previously European sailors had only met Indo-Malayan and Mongolian races in the Pacific, and the Polynesian islanders obviously came into a different category, even though they were arbitrarily classified as Malays. To this day we still speak, inaccurately, of a single 'Malayo-Polynesian' race and culture.

Thor Heyerdahl's famous trip on the *Kon-Tiki* has forced new discussion of the problem, and anthropologists and ethnologists have been re-reading the reports of the old discoverers, the first white men to reach the Pacific. All the reports stressed the same thing, i.e. that the Polynesians were tall, well-built, sturdy people and quite different from the rather slightly built Malays; moreover they were not yellow-brown like the latter but light-skinned like Europeans and some were even capable of blushing. All the reports add that their hair had the same fine texture as that of the whites and that it was by no means always black in colour but could range to light brown. Some of the Polynesians had blue eyes and, unlike the Malays and Mongols, the men had beards and were in fact so conscious of this sign of manhood that they spent much care in seeing that it was neat and well-trimmed. This was not known anywhere else in the Pacific. Finally it was reported that their noses were not broad and flat, and their lips not as thick as those of the Malays; in fact in these particular features they looked very much like Europeans. The early discoverers made a distinction, saying that all the above characteristics applied to the 'noble' type of Polynesians, but that another type existed who were not so tall and who had dark, coarse hair, broad noses and protruding lips and dark skins. The reports from all the early discoverers, from Pedro Fernándes de Quirós who arrived in the Pacific in 1595, Carl Friedrich Behrens who touched Easter Island in 1722, Captain Wallis who landed in Tahiti in 1768, right up to Cook and the two Forsters, all agree almost word for word on this question.

The Polynesians themselves were struck by their resemblance to the whites, for one of them who accompanied Cook on his second voyage tried his best to pass for an Englishman. Here is what Georg Forster wrote concerning this fellow:

> Our Tahitian travelling companion, Porea, landed with us dressed in a linen jacket and seaman's trousers. He carried Captain Cook's powder horn and ammunition pouch and wished to be taken for one of us. To this end he spoke not a word of his own language but mumbled all sorts of unintelligible sounds, so that he actually managed to deceive the local people. To be even more convincing he asked us not to call him by his Tahitian name, Porea, but by an English name. . . . At first we could not fathom the purpose of this masquerade but we concluded that he thought he would be more impressive as an English sailor than as a Tahitian noble.

This awareness of the similarity with the white races still exists even today, and a case of it was recorded by Sir Arthur Grimble in his delightful book *A Pattern of Islands* which he wrote after living for many years as the Resident Commissioner on the Gilbert and Ellice Islands in the Pacific:

> The loving-kindness of the . . . Gilbertese race towards Europeans sprang from no feeling of inferiority, but on the contrary, from a most gracious sense of kinship. Their chief ancestral heroes had been, according to tradition, fair-skinned like ourselves. . . . All of these heroic beings, . . . were of the red-complexioned, blue-eyed strain called 'The Company of the Tree, the Breed of Matang'. . . . When white men were first seen in the Gilbert Islands, nearly two hundred years ago, the people said, 'Behold, the Breed of Matang is returned to us. Let us receive them as chiefs and brothers among us, lest the Ancestors be shamed.'

Further evidence of the same kind can be found in the work of the German ethnologist Dr. Bunzendahl, and by now it must have become clear that many authorities are agreed that the light-skinned Polynesians belong to the white race.

Very striking confirmation of this theory—one might go so far as to say proof—was furnished recently by the serologists, i.e. the scientists who investigate the properties of blood serum. As is well known, in 1901 the German biologist Landsteiner discovered that human blood can be divided into three distinct groups with distinct characteristics. He called these groups by the letters O, A and B and discovered that, although the A group predominated in Europe, it became rarer the farther one went east and that the B group became proportionately more predominant. The B group was discovered to be typical of all Asiatic peoples right up to Micronesia and Melanesia, to occur occasionally in the western parts of the great Polynesian triangle but to be completely absent in central Polynesia and the eastern islands. The light-skinned natives of the Pacific have the same blood characteristics as people of central and western Europe.

This surprising statement has been borne out by a large number of subsequent investigations and can no longer be doubted.

At once the fascinating problem was raised as to how Europeans could have reached the distant Pacific. It was clear that, while the Polynesians must undoubtedly be looked upon as members of the white race, they could not have settled in their earthly paradises earlier than the beginning of the Middle Ages.

Our evidence for the above assertion was supplied by James Cook himself. During his first voyage to the Pacific he had taken the priest Tupaia of Tahiti on board the *Endeavour*. Tupaia was an intelligent, adventurous fellow, who wished to see more of the world and so asked the Englishmen if he could accompany them. When Cook landed in New Zealand, he found to his great amazement that his Polynesian passenger had no difficulty in communicating with the cannibal inhabitants of that country. The man from Tahiti and the inhabitants of those remote islands spoke the same language!

Cook had every right to be surprised, for the distance from New Zealand to Tahiti is almost 3,500 miles, i.e. the distance between the northernmost tip of Scandinavia and Lake Chad in Africa, or between Newfoundland and San Francisco. Whereas hundreds of languages existed in the Pacific, so that the natives of one island frequently lacked the means of communicating with those of another, and in Europe a dozen or more vastly different languages existed within half this distance, Chief Tupaia had no trouble in talking with the natives of New Zealand.

Cook later discovered that the same language was spoken, the same traditions observed, the same gods worshipped throughout the entire Polynesian triangle extending between Hawaii, Easter Island and New Zealand, between the latitudes 30° North and 50° South. Although Cook was surprised by such findings, he lacked sufficient historical basis to reach the obvious conclusion that not much time had elapsed since the colonization of the Pacific islands by the Polynesians. Since isolated islands always develop in a very individual manner and since language is never stable, but always subject to perpetual development, a vast range of cultural and linguistic divergences would have been found if these islands had been occupied by these 'Vikings' of the Pacific at the time when the Indo-Germans arrived in the countries between the Indus and the Ganges.

Anthropologists have given these problems much attention in the last few decades. They first investigated Polynesian genealogies, and discovered that noble families could usually trace their descent back to the early Middle Ages, to about the year 400, which, historically speaking, is quite late. It must not be forgotten that the Polynesians had no method of writing in our sense, and that all information and traditions were handed on by word of mouth. There even existed a special group, called the *rongo-rongo* on Mangareva and Easter Island and *orero* on Tahiti, whose job it was to learn all the most important details of tribal succession, religious rites and traditions by heart, thus performing the function of a modern reference library.

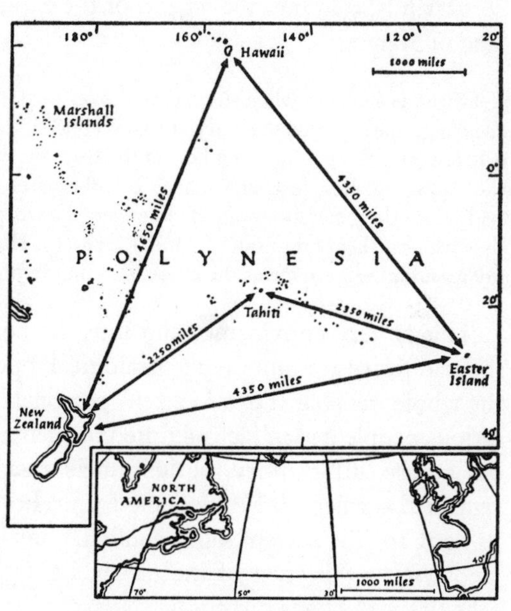

XXVII. The Polynesian triangle.

To us it seems incredible that oral traditions can be considered a reliable basis for historical records, and that facts have been preserved and handed down from generation to generation across the span of close to a thousand years without their becoming distorted by embellishments or misinterpretations. Nevertheless this is the case. Maurata, the last king of Easter Island, when carried off by Peruvian slave-traders in 1862, was able to recite his genealogy as far back as the beginning of the eleventh century. Many noble families on Samoa could trace back their origins to the year A.D. 400, and King Kamakau of Hawaii boasted that he was descended of a line of kings stretching back seventy generations. When one reflects that in 1914 many European royal houses found it difficult to produce a mere thirty-two noble ancestors, one's respect for these princes of the South Seas goes up enormously.

Even quite ordinary folk could reel off a long list of their forebears, and the sanctity of oral tradition is respected in these islands even today, as can be seen from the following quotation from Sir Arthur Grimble. When he was a young colonial official, Nei Tearia, the best story-teller in the Gilbert Islands, told him the legend of the expulsion of man from the happy land of Matang:

> Fifteen years later, when she was well over seventy, I took the script back to her for checking. She repeated the story at that second sitting word for word as she had given it before, and I complimented her on the feat. Her austere face was lit by a smile, but she replied soberly, 'Sir, and shall it be otherwise? Each *karaki* [history] has its own body from the generations of old. These are the words of our grandfathers' fathers, and thus we pass them on to our children's children. How should I change the words that my grandfather gave me as the contents of my mouth?'

This is very convincing, and must be considered sufficient proof that the traditional accounts and genealogical reports of the Polynesians are, on the whole, reliable. Thus it seems reasonable to conclude that this mysterious people had in fact migrated to their new island home in the Pacific during the fifth century, as their ancient sagas related. The problem still remained—where did they come from? Polynesian tradition cannot help us here, for the ancient sagas conflict, some saying that they came from a land lying to the east of the ocean, i.e. from America, and others from exactly the opposite direction.

At this point the philologists lent a hand and found that many Malay and Polynesian words are clearly related:

Malay	*Polynesian*	
mata	mata	eye
ikan	ika	fish
ahi	ahi	fire
lima	rima	hand
manik	manoe	bird

This seemed to indicate that the Polynesians had come from the west, from India perhaps, or Indonesia, but such linguistic similarities are by no means conclusive evidence by themselves, although they do point to a close relationship between Malayan and Polynesian, dating back to very ancient times. The American philologist W. D. Alexander declared, as far back as 1910, that 'the great differences in language and physique between the Polynesians and the present inhabitants of the [Malay] Archipelago, combine with other considerations to prove the immense antiquity of the period when the Polynesians separated from the other branches of the Oceanic race'.

Linguists were divided between the above point of view, and the conviction that there was a single Malayo-Polynesian culture, an offshoot of an 'Austronesian' cultural community. Typical of this point of view is the German anthropologist Professor Hans Nevermann who has stated: 'The Polynesian and Indonesian languages are very closely related, both deriving from a common source, the ancient Austronesian language.'

The question, however, was far from settled, for other philologists pointed out that if a connection did exist between Malay and Polynesian — even if it was of very ancient origin — then Polynesian must have been influenced by an Indo-European dialect. India was occupied by Aryans many thousands of years ago, and it is known that Indonesia adopted Sanscrit as its language at about 350 B.C. Since the Polynesians migrated to their islands as late as the fifth century A.D. their language ought to have contained traces of a Sanscrit influence. Unfortunately for the argument, while such traces can be found in Malay, there are none in Polynesian dialects. Instead, we have evidence of direct links with the languages of Europe, so that the noted linguist, E. Tregear, of New Zealand, could declare in the introduction to his *Maori-Polynesian Comparative Dictionary* that 'the main point against the late arrival of the Maoris from Asia is that many of their words have a more direct connection with the Aryans of Europe, and even with the West of Europe, than with those of Asia'.

It must, in all fairness, be stated that not all linguists agree with Tregear's thesis, though they all agree that no traces of Sanscrit can be found in Polynesian. Two possible conclusions faced linguists, for, as will be remembered, the Polynesians settled in their Pacific islands about the middle of the fifth century A.D., and Indonesian became the common language of Indonesia in 350 B.C. Either the Polynesians emigrated from Indonesia before the advent of Sanscrit (and if this were the case, where did they spend the interim period of seven hundred and fifty years before they emerged again into the light of history?) or they did not come from Indonesia at all.

These questions remain unsettled even to this day, and they are not the only problems facing students of Polynesia. As already mentioned, when Polynesia was discovered by European sailors, the natives were still at the cultural level of the Stone Age. They did not know how to produce metal tools, although there were deposits of iron-sand on the Pacific islands; they had no pottery although there was plenty of clay to be had; they did not know how to weave cloth although wild cotton grew in abundance; they did not know the wheel and had developed no form of building except the most rudimenatry wooden huts. They did not cultivate rice although it is one of the oldest plants cultivated in Asia, chew betel-nut or make palm-wine, and in their art they had no representations of elephants, cows or buffaloes which were common animals in India.

The India of 350 B.C., i.e. about the time when Alexander the Great invaded it, had long left the Stone Age far behind. The Indians knew the use of the wheel and had applied it to carts and carriages, they were expert builders, potters and weavers. They cultivated rice and made palm-wine, and great frescoes depicting cows and elephants covered their walls. If, as many people hold, the Polynesians had originated from somewhere in India, then surely they would have retained at least part of these achievements, and practised these crafts and skills in their new homes. The only answer to this objection is to postulate a complete cultural collapse and to assume that the Polynesians suddenly took several steps backwards to a more primitive level; this is very unlikely, especially with a people who value tradition so highly. Thus we are faced with the unavoidable conclusion that the Polynesians are not of Indian or Indonesian origin.

Zoologists and botanists who made a survey of the flora and fauna of the Polynesian islands have proved that some of the essential edible plants, such as the banana, the sugar-cane, the breadfruit, yam and taro root and all domestic animals, i.e. the pig, dog and chicken, have come to the Pacific from Indonesia, probably from Melanesia via the Fiji Islands. Since these plants and animals are not distributed evenly across the whole oceanic world, one might assume that their appearance is due to later importation, perhaps through successful raids on other islands or through barter. This, however, tells us nothing about the original path followed by the Polynesians.

If they had travelled east from Melanesia, how was it that they were ignorant of the art of making pots? Why was their society patriarchal and not matriarchal like nearly all the other communities in Melanesia? Why did they not chew betel-nut? Why do they not belong to the B-blood group? Why are there no negroes among them, for the Polynesians could not have crossed the 350,000 square miles of the 'Land of Black Islands' overnight! After all, we know that they had migrated from Indonesia before 350 B.C. at the latest, and that they only arrived in the Pacific during the fifth century A.D., thus having had ample time to acquire some of their hosts' customs and to leave behind some evidence of their stay for the anthropologists. Neither of these two things happened, nor is there the slightest proof that any Polynesian people made a longer or shorter visit to New Guinea, to the Admiralty or Solomon Islands, the New Hebrides or to New Caledonia, and furthermore the Polynesians possess none of the typical products of those regions, not even malaria. Although Melanesia is still a malarial area today, this disease is unknown on the Polynesian islands, even though it must be admitted that the climatic conditions under which the *anopheles* mosquito thrives are lacking. All the evidence rules out the possibility that the Polynesians reached their Pacific islands via Melanesia.

It has been suggested that they came from the north via Celebes, the Philippines and then across the Marianas or the Caroline Islands to Micronesia and thence to the Gilbert, Phoenix and Ellice Islands, but this theory is also untenable. Micronesia, 'the world of small islands', consists of a total of 1,458 atolls and islands whose total land surface equals about 1,000 square miles; this land surface, however, is distributed throughout 6,000,000 square miles of ocean and thus it is inconceivable that these islands, scattered in the ocean like a handful of needles in a very large haystack, could have served as a stepping-stone for the Polynesians on their way to the east, for they must have travelled on the most primitive of rafts, crowded with men, women and children, animals and food supplies, without the help of charts and compasses, against the wind and currents, in storms and scorching heat.

Micronesia was only explored by Europeans during the nineteenth century. A single glance at the map will immediately show the reason why. Distances from island to island are so great that modern means of navigation are required to plot the ship's position. Moreover the majority of these atolls are completely barren, consisting only of coral or volcanic rock, on which neither bananas nor breadfruit can grow. We know from Sir Arthur Grimble that it has proved impossible to grow vegetables on the Gilbert and Ellice Islands, even when shiploads of humus have been imported, for the soil would not bind with the pure white coral-sand and the wind simply blew it away. Often water is in short supply and droughts lasting as long as eighteen months have been known.

Consequently it is not surprising that no trace whatsoever of a Polynesian mass excursion across these islands has been found. The Pacific Scientific Congress held in 1949 ruled out the possibility of the Micronesian route. Where then did they come from?

We do not possess the complete answer to this question. Thor Heyerdahl and the *Kon-Tiki* have undoubtedly proved that Polynesia *might* have been colonized from South America, but it has by no means been proved that this was the only route and that Polynesia was settled by people coming from the east *alone*. Heyerdahl himself merely wanted to prove a possibility, a possibility supported, however, by weighty arguments.

One of these arguments had been put forward by Cook. On the 21st October 1769, he noted in his journal that in New Zealand celery was found in 'great plenty', and that they bought some ten pounds of sweet potatoes from the natives. These potatoes were cultivated on a large scale, but at that time of year they were still scarce.

And six weeks later, on Thursday, the 30th November 1769, Cook had to punish Matthew Cox, Henry Stevens and Eman Parreyra, each with twelve lashes, because they had neglected their duty on land and had dug up potatoes in a plantation.

Sweet potatoes in New Zealand! How did they get there? This plant of American origin was to be known in Europe only much later. How then could it have reached New Zealand long before the whites appeared on the scene, for Cook found whole fields of it, carefully cultivated? Later he was to find that the *batata* was common throughout the whole of Polynesia and that it had been cultivated for many generations. At first it was thought that the root vegetable had been carried to Polynesia from America by ocean currents or in the wreckage of ships, but it was found that the sweet potato rots once it comes into contact with salt water.

Thus we are left with the conclusion that the *batata* was carried to Polynesia from America on board ships and that therefore, not so very

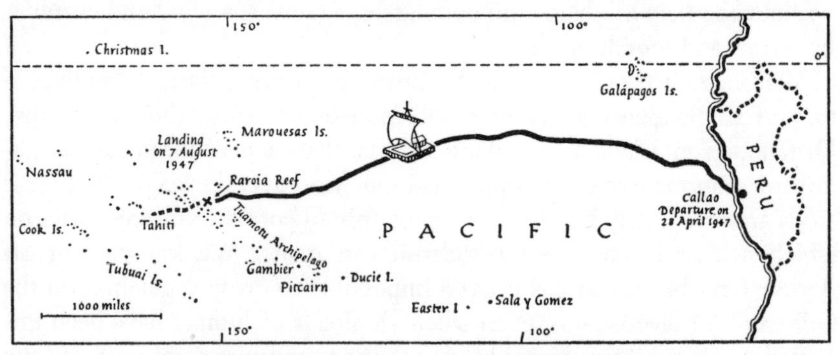

XXVIII. Sketch of the drift of the Kon-Tiki *raft.*

long ago, sailors must have braved the dangers of the tremendous voyage from South America across the Pacific. The men on the *Kon-Tiki* made the same voyage but they had charts, sextants and radio, and they knew beforehand that land did exist somewhere ahead of them in the path of the currents, but the unknown sailors of old had no such equipment, nor the foreknowledge that land existed, and yet they set sail and landed in Polynesia. This conclusion is supported by the fact that the sweet potato is called by the same name, *kumara*, both in Peru and in Polynesia on the other side of the Pacific. This cannot possibly be just coincidence, since there are also other plants which may well have been imported from America, the most important being cotton.

In an earlier chapter we have seen that the cotton plant cultivated by the natives of America, before the arrival of Columbus, was a hybrid, the seed of which had twenty-six chromosomes. When botanists examined the type of cotton growing in Polynesia, they found that the Old World type with thirteen large flat chromosomes did not exist there, and that the only type to be found was the New World variety with twenty-six chromosomes.

That cotton plants already grew in Polynesia before the first Europeans arrived there is quite certain: it could not have been carried there by birds, for birds never touch the cotton seed, nor could it have been carried to

Polynesia by ocean currents, for water quickly kills the life in the seed. We are left with the conclusion that it must have been imported into Polynesia from America by people who travelled in boats.

Convincing though these arguments are, they are only circumstantial evidence. The one piece of factual proof we have that some kind of vessels bridged the vast watery gap between America and the Pacific islands, consists of an old arrow head made from American flint, recently found on Pitcairn island.

The theory that the Polynesian islands were settled by people coming from South America is supported by the fact that many cultural features are common to both sides of the Pacific, and the Norwegian ethnologist, Erland Nordenskjöld, in his most informative work *The Origin of the Indian Civilisations in South America*, which appeared in 1931, has listed forty-nine separate cultural factors common to South America *and* Polynesia. This list covers a striking range of similarities; viz. the most delicate skull and brain operations were performed in both localities; the arithmetical threads of the Incas called the *quipus* corresponded to the knotted threads used by the Polynesians for astronomical calculations and for recording short messages; the people on both sides of the Pacific used conch shells, pan-pipes, feather ornaments, the poncho; they both used the same method to brew an intoxicating drink, they prepared fibre and bark in the same way, their fishing-hooks, nets and paddles showed close resemblances; their calendars had the same peculiarities, etc. The force of such a list as an argument becomes even greater if one has actually compared the objects mentioned side by side. Although we cannot say that there is proof positive that the Polynesians originally came from America, we are justified in stating that some form of contact between the American mainland and the Pacific islands did exist.

If we now turn our attention to the question of winds and currents, we are forced to agree with Thor Heyerdahl that the Polynesians reached their Pacific islands, like the Europeans some thousand years later, from the east, i.e. from America. In fact this was the *only* way for primitive rafts to approach these islands.

The Trades blow, year in, year out, from the west coast of America as far as 160° east, i.e. almost as far as Australia. It is true that sometimes their direction varies slightly, but in the main they blow between the Equator and 30° South, and in consequence all the ocean currents flow in the same direction. These currents travel at an average speed of between one to three miles per hour. Westerly winds are practically non-existent in these parts.

In the regions around Hawaii, i.e. between 20° and 30° North, the Trade blows steadily to the west for six months on end, and even in winter the wind blows in this direction for at least half of every month. The

Marianas and the Carolines are also exposed to the trade winds, but as one approaches the Palau Islands, changeable west winds become more and more frequent. The monsoons appear to be limited to the Philippines, New Guinea and eastern Australia, and during the southern hemisphere's winter a strong north-west monsoon blows bringing heavy rainstorms and even hurricanes in its wake, so that the natives of those areas wait for more settled weather before they go sailing.

The above information makes it extremely unlikely that Polynesia could have been colonized from south-east Asia by people travelling in rudimentary vessels.

Thor Heyerdahl in his book, *American Indians in the Pacific*, on which we have drawn a great deal, has dealt with all these questions in detail, and though he may not have given the final answer there can no longer be any doubt that some kind of primitive craft set sail from America and crossed the Pacific long before the arrival of Europeans.

The last subject which we shall treat in this section is perhaps the most fascinating of all. We have already mentioned the strange 'white' god of the Incas, called Viracocha, who, according to legend, disappeared one day across the western ocean. The name Viracocha is a *Quechua* word, i.e. from the language spoken by the Incas, and is thus of relatively recent date, though the stories of the god may be much older. In all probability he is a figure in the pantheon of Tiahuanaco, the culture which preceded the Incas, where he was referred to as Kon-Tiki, Illa-Tiki or simply Tiki.

Now, strangely enough, the Polynesians also call one of their gods, demi-gods or royal progenitors by the same name. In his book, Heyerdahl has brought a great deal of evidence for this, adding that:

> When we recall that the semi-solar Tici of Peru was remembered over vast territories of the Inca Empire as an early hierarch who left Peru in pre-Inca times on an organised expedition into the East Pacific, it is certainly remarkable to find memories throughout Polynesia of a semi-solar progenitor Tiki, who everywhere began the earliest Polynesian island history.

In all fairness, however, it must be pointed out that the German ethnologist Hans Plischke has recently raised the objection that the significance of the Peruvian Tiki as the *divine* author of all things is not equivalent to the Polynesian Tiki, the human origin, i.e. an ancestor.

As history teaches us, deities are easily transportable. The Olympus of Greece became the Pantheon of Rome, and other religions have spread throughout the world even into areas where the inhabitants were quite unfitted to understand them. Clearly the idea of a holy Peruvian-Polynesian ancestor called Kon-Tiki, who was the beginning of all things, must have been as easy to propagate as the Babylonian-Hebrew notion of a forefather Adam, for the same Kon-Tiki can even be found in Africa among the Bambara of the French Sudan. Madame Georges Magnan of

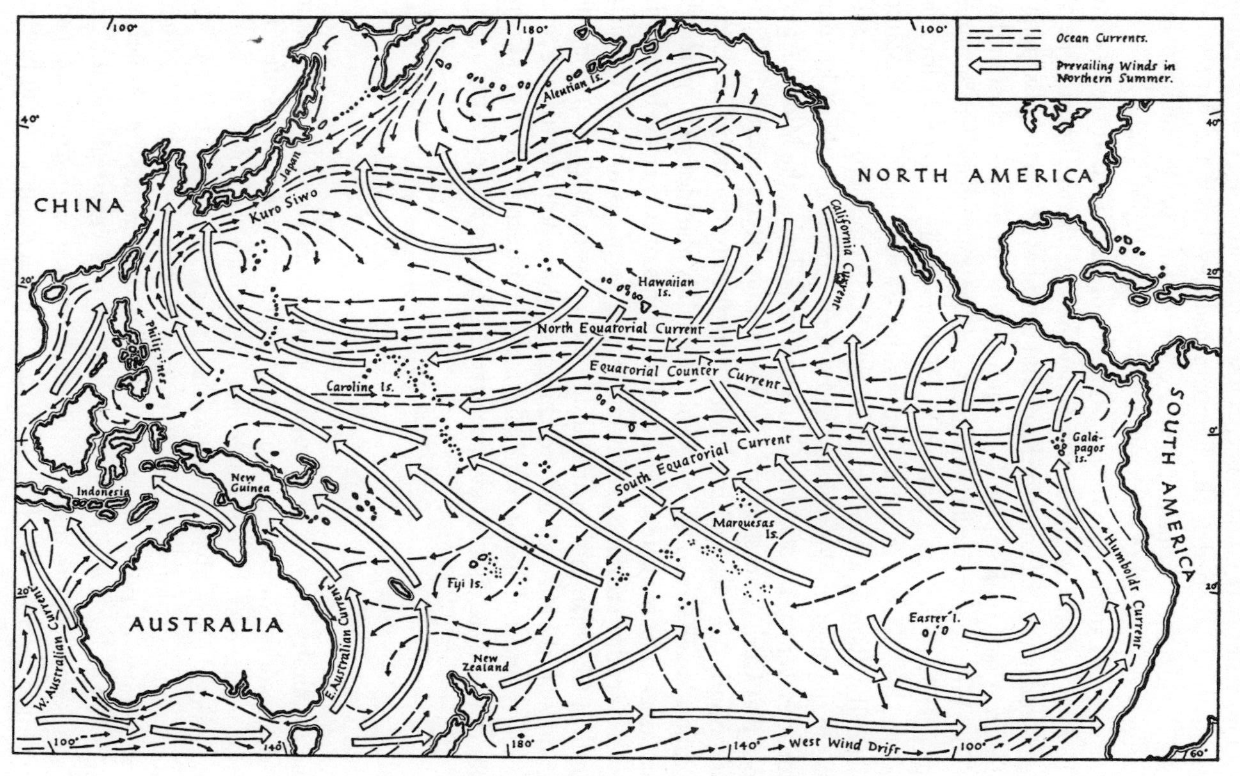

XXIX. *Winds and currents in the Pacific Ocean.*

Sama, near Kayes in French West Africa, has kindly pointed out that the Bambara translate the terms boss, director, lord, master, etc., as Koung-Tighi. This is not pure coincidence, as it would be straining our credibility too much to maintain that the Bambara had developed the expression without any external influence. It is a clear instance of the radiance and persuasiveness attached to the name and the story of Kon-Tiki.

How can we explain the power of the idea of Kon-Tiki? It seems clear that the only explanation lies in the theory that the historical prototype of the demi-god and tribal ancestor Kon-Tiki must have been the disseminator of a great new philosophy. It is but a step to the next conclusion that Kon-Tiki-Viracocha must have been a Christian missionary led by some strange destiny to Peru and Polynesia. Of course there is no proof for this conjecture, but we read in the reports written by such travellers as Marco Polo and Ibn Batuta, a Moslem, how they had come across their compatriots in the most unlikely places, and since we know also that Christian missionaries went as far afield as China and India during the Middle Ages, the idea that Christ's message of love had already been preached in Central and South America and the Pacific, long before the arrival of European sailors, may seem less incredible. Certainly the idea of a merciful, loving father must have impressed the inhabitants of America whose gods were very tawdry creatures, requiring human sacrifices to keep up their strength. If Christian missionaries did in fact cross the ocean between the two continents the effect of their teaching must have been electrifying, and it is small wonder that the name and fame of Viracocha-Kon-Tiki, the saviour of the Incas, should have penetrated even into deepest Africa.

5

The Admiralty showed their confidence in James Cook by asking him to lead a second expedition to the Pacific hardly three months after his return from the first. It is probable that the decision to explore the South Pacific more thoroughly was due to the uneasy situation existing in the North American colonies, and also to the fact that the French had sent out expeditions to those distant waters. The danger that the American colonies might break their ties with England was very real and the Sea Lords hoped perhaps to discover the fabulous *terra australis*, to compensate for their possible loss. It was thought that if it did not extend further south than 30° then it would at least be a fertile continent and might possibly contain natural treasures such as rich deposits of gold, silver or precious stones, which would make England as rich as the conquest of Peru and Mexico had made Spain.

For his second expedition Cook asked for two ships, for he did not wish to take any chances this time. He was given two colliers, the *Drake* of 462 tons and the *Raleigh* of 336 tons. These vessels were renamed the *Resolution*, which became the flagship, and the *Adventure*, which was placed under the command of Captain Furneaux. Once again both ships were laden with enough sauerkraut, lemons and meat-extract to last for two and a half years. In addition to the officers and crew, the German scientist Johann Reinhold Forster and his eighteen-year-old son Georg, two astronomers and the artist W. Hodges accompanied the expedition. Hodges was taken along to make pictorial representations of the voyage. A number of cannons were also fitted to the unwarlike colliers.

Again the comments raised by the appearance of Cook's two ships were anything but admiring. Usually ships of the Royal Navy had an aristocratic look, being built for speed, but here were two ships flying the white ensign, looking for all the world like two broad-bellied merchantmen, and carrying no cannon worth speaking of!

Cook knew exactly what he was about; he was not concerned with questions of appearance; on the contrary, he had the masts of the *Resolution* shortened because he thought they were too high. This meant that the whole rigging had to be altered and, with other alterations to the upper works, that the sailing date had to be postponed until the 13th July 1772.

Cook received the order to sail past Madeira to the Cape of Good Hope and thence to the south, exploring any land he might discover. He was to return across the Pacific to Cape Horn on as southerly a course as possible. This was to be the first circumnavigation of the world from west to east, and the idea of proceeding in that direction was born of Cook's previous experience of those latitudes. He knew that only at about 40° South could he count on constant westerly winds. The Dutch were also aware of this, for Captain Peter Plank of the Dutch East India Company had advised Dutch sailors proceeding to Indonesia not to alter course to the north-east the moment they had rounded the Cape of Good Hope, which course would lead them through the region of the trade winds and possible week-long calms, but to keep south as long as possible. He added that this would cut ten to twelve months off the voyage. Plank was only proved right some sixteen years later when a ship which followed his instructions took a mere six months to sail from Cape Town to Java as against the sixteen to eighteen months required by the old course.

The two ships reached the Cape of Good Hope at the end of October 1772, and stopped to take on further provisions, continuing their voyage three weeks later. At once the great adventure began. The 'Roaring Forties', as the latitudes around 40° South were later to be called, lived up to their future name. Violent gales blew for weeks on end and the temperature dropped so low that Cook noted in his logbook that, although it was now summer in the southern hemisphere, he had met with frost and snow.

During his first expedition Cook had introduced a three-watch system, instead of the usual two, to preserve the strength of the men, and he adopted the same policy this time. The sailors were issued with extra warm clothing and a goodly ration of rum and were therefore in good heart. On the 12th December the first icebergs were sighted, enormous blocks of ice, half a mile in circumference and towering about fifty feet above the surface of the water. Cook made the following entry in his journal:

> It was a flat top, and its sides rose in a perpendicular direction, against which the sea broke exceedingly high. . . . This afforded an agreeable enough sight to the eye, but conveyed to the mind an idea of coldness, much greater than it really was. . . . But the worst was, the ice so clogged the rigging, sails and locks, as to make them exceedingly bad to handle.

Cook was quite right to assume that such masses of ice must have originated from land and were fragments of huge glaciers. He decided to try and find that land despite all the dangers, and thus he continued south, and by the 17th January 1773 he had passed the Antarctic Circle and had reached 67°. The pack-ice was so dense here that he could go no further. He altered course in the direction of New Zealand, for he did not want to be caught in those latitudes with the winter approaching. He had gone further south than any man before him, being only a short distance away from what is known today as Enderby Land in Antarctica proper.

A thick fog blew up on the 8th February, and the *Adventure* was lost to sight and did not reply to signals or even to the cannon. It had been agreed that in the case of separation the ships were to lay by for three days, but even when the fog cleared the *Adventure* was nowhere to be seen. As Cook had already fixed a meeting point in New Zealand he sailed on and landed in Dusky Bay on the south-west tip of New Zealand, after having been at sea for a hundred and ten days. A few days later he was joined by the *Adventure*.

Soon curious natives showed themselves and bartering transactions were quickly under way. The natives were particularly keen on bottles and objects made of iron. As soon as they discovered that the sailors were by no means averse to brown women, they made the most of the situation. Forster reported in his journal:

> As soon as the New Zealanders found this to be the cheapest way of acquiring iron implements, the beach was lined with men, their daughters and sisters. As far as we could tell, they would not make use of their wives for this kind of traffic. It seems that their ideas of chastity are quite different from ours, for an unmarried girl may have as many lovers as she pleases, without in the least losing her reputation.

When Forster noticed that not all the women were willing to be used by the whites he added the following comment:

The natives only lowered themselves to this abominable traffic in their women when the need for iron tools had been created in their midst. It is unfortunate that all our discoveries have involved the deaths of so many innocent people, but this is but little compared with the irreparable damage we have caused by upsetting the moral code. Thus I am concerned lest our arrival in these parts do great harm to its inhabitants.

Captain Furneaux, basing himself on the Admiralty's instructions, wanted to winter in New Zealand, but Cook decided otherwise. He was impatient to discover the South Land and to spend the summer months exploring it at leisure. The two ships set sail at the beginning of June 1773. So far the crews of both ships had enjoyed excellent health, but two weeks later the *Adventure* reported a minor outbreak of scurvy which had caused the death of one man and affected some twenty others. Cook intervened to see that the sick were given sauerkraut, lemons, malt and other antiscorbutic remedies, but sickness had by then gained a hold on the ship.

They were faced by a spell of unfavourable winds. Forster noted in his journal:

We were amazed at the winds which prevailed during the time between our departure from Queen Charlotte's Sound and the moment when the Trade set in. We had expected to have constant westerly winds while we sailed in the latitudes between 50° and 40° South, but we found that in the course of two or three days the wind would veer round and blow from all the points of the compass in turn, though it would occasionally settle and blow with great force from the east. The name Pacific Ocean, in my opinion, can only apply to those waters lying between the two tropics, for only there is the wind constant, and the weather good.

The two ships advanced slowly. They had at least discovered that no land existed in the middle latitudes of the Pacific, and on the 1st August Cook recorded in his logbook that in his opinion if an unknown continent did exist east of New Zealand then it must lie much further south. The only way to test this supposition was by sailing further southwards, but for the moment this was out of the question because the *Adventure*, which by now had many sick on board, had to make for Tahiti as quickly as possible. On the 25th August the two ships dropped anchor in Matavay Bay.

The English sailors were received with a great show of friendliness, for the natives remembered their first visit some four years earlier. Cook was deeply moved when a chief of Tahiti embraced him and wept tears of joy to see him again. To mark his gratitude Cook made the man a particularly valuable gift, for, as he put it, he esteemed this man as if he were his own father. Despite this little show of emotion Cook was still the efficient English officer he had always been. He made a note of the economic situation of Tahiti, which he discovered to have deteriorated in the last four years, and also found room to make an entry about the amazing aquatic skills of the natives. Near the shore the swell was so great that Cook could not remember ever having seen the like of it. No ship could have survived here, and even the best European swimmer would surely have been smashed against the rocks. This very spot was the favourite bathing place of the Tahitians. As the waves rose up they would dive under them, and miraculously appear on the other side. One day they discovered a piece of wreckage in the surf. They dragged it out to sea at once, stood up on it and, driven by the waves and the wind, they rode the surf at a tremendous speed. They derived infinite pleasure from this game, and were just as unperturbed as English children are when they tumble down the hill at Greenwich Park.

The inhabitants of Tahiti were as beautiful as the surroundings in which they lived. Numerous travellers have stressed the fine appearance and courteous nature of the natives. Forster wrote the following after a visit to the Marquesas Islands:

> . . . many of the young people, who had not yet been tattooed, were extraordinarily beautiful and the good proportions of their bodies aroused our admiration. Some of them could have stood next to the masterpieces of antiquity and lost nothing by the comparison. . . . Their features without exception were very agreeable, open and alert, their large black eyes greatly contributing to this effect. Their hair was black, curly and strong, though a few natives had much fairer hair. . . .

Cook reported more or less the same thing of the natives of the Friendly Islands, adding that he had encountered many with European features, some even with Roman noses.

It seems that when the Europeans reached Polynesia, a decline in cultural level had taken place. Forster was nevertheless greatly impressed by the methods of farming practised: crops were grown on irrigated terraces, rising high up the sides of the mountains, as in Indonesia and South America. He also admired their ocean-going vessels:

> No fewer than 159 large war canoes, fifty to ninety feet long, were gathered here. . . . All their canoes are double, i.e. they consist of two canoes connected by fifteen to eighteen strong planks tied amidships. These cross-planks are usually set at a distance of four and a half feet from one another and are twelve to twenty-four feet long. In the latter case they project far beyond the sides of the two boats and give the impression of a deck supported by two canoes. The cross-planks are held in place by two or three rafters fastened lengthways along the outside and middle of the two connected canoes. The bow and the stern curve out of the water, the stern sometimes by as much as twenty feet. . . . These canoes carry a minimum of 144 oarsmen and eight helmsmen, four of whom stand in the stern. . . .

In addition to the crew of 152, the canoes generally carried fifteen to twenty armed men, so that each of them usually had a contingent of 170 to 180 men on board. Clearly such craft would serve to travel great distances and in fact voyages of some 1,250 miles, usually within the Polynesian triangle, were quite frequently made. Forster, whose admiration was often uncritical, nevertheless noticed that these boats were built to sail with a following wind, and that tacking was largely out of the question.

The Austrian explorer Hugo Adolf Bernatzik made the same observation a hundred and fifty years later, and wrote that his outrigger could outstrip the average steamer with only a quarter wind, and that despite its apparent fragility it was far more seaworthy than most European yachts. He added that having experienced squalls and heavy seas on one of these craft, he believed it was quite possible for a mass migration to the Pacific islands to have taken place on them. He continued—and we quote his actual words this time, since it seems incredible that the Polynesians could have crossed against winds, currents and waves in these primitive boats:

It was by no means easy to manœuvre these boats. To alter course the boat had to be turned through 180°, so that the stern became the bow and the heavy tiller had to be moved to the other end of the boat.

This confirms what we have written elsewhere[1] about the sailing powers and techniques of the Polynesians, and is of great importance, as only those who have stood at the helm of a sailing-boat can appreciate. Although geographers, historians, anthropologists, ethnologists, botanists, zoologists and philologists have had their say on the Polynesian problem, the real experts, the sailors themselves, have never been consulted. It is they who should be questioned about the possibility of sailing thousands of miles against winds and currents in one of the primitive Polynesian outriggers!

After spending some weeks in Tahiti, Cook finally set out towards the south. His course took him past the Society and the Friendly Islands, back to New Zealand and thence again towards the South Pole. This time Cook went as far as 71° South and once again his way was blocked by fields of pack-ice.

Once more the flagship lost sight of the *Adventure*; this time the two ships were to be united only in Plymouth harbour. Cook was fully conscious that the success of the expedition now depended on him alone, and the entries for these days in his journal reflect the deep anxiety that such responsibility gave him. On Sunday, 30th January 1774, he wrote:

At four o'clock in the morning, we perceived the clouds, over the horizon to the south, to be of an unusual snow-white brightness, which we knew announced our approach to field-ice. Soon after, it was seen from the top-mast head.... Ninety-seven ice-hills were distinctly seen within the field ... many of them very large, and looking like a ridge of mountains, rising one above another till they were lost in the clouds.... Such mountains of ice as these, were I believe, never seen in the Greenland seas....

... I think there must be some [land] to the south behind this ice; but if there is, it can afford no better retreat for birds, or any other animals, than the ice itself, with which it must be wholly covered. I, who had ambition not only to go farther than anyone had been before, but as far as it was possible for man to go, was not sorry at meeting with this interruption; as it, in some measure, relieved us; at least shortened the dangers and hardships inseparable from the navigation of the southern polar regions. Since, therefore, we could not proceed one inch farther to the south, no other reason need be

[1] Cf. Paul Herrmann, *Conquest by Man* (Harper & Brothers).

assigned for my tacking, and standing back to the north; being at this time in the latitude of 71° 10′ S., longitude 106° 54′ W.

Cook would have been quite justified in returning round Cape Horn to England at this point, for supplies were in a very bad state indeed. The ship's biscuits were alive with maggots—three hundred pounds of them had rotted away completely—and the rest of the food 'could only have been consumed by people in the same plight as we were'. So runs the official entry in the logbook, but the Forsters add a few more details:

Mealtimes were hateful to us, for hardly had the smell of the food reached our nostrils than we were nauseated by the very thought of it. . . . In addition the voyage south was very monotonous; ice, fog, storms, and a rough sea cast a gloom over the ship which was rarely enlivened by a ray of sunshine.

It was no wonder that there were long faces on board when the sailors discovered that the Captain, despite his own illness—an affection of the gall bladder—did not intend to return to England but was making for Easter Island. Chained as he was to his cabin by his illness, Cook, whose agonized groans could often be heard on deck, kept a strong hold on the crew and the passengers. There was only *one* will on the *Resolution* and the thought of mutiny did not so much as enter anyone's head. Even the most stupid realized that Cook himself had no choice in the matter, for somewhere in the gigantic ocean stretches around Easter Island was the last blank space on maps of the southern Pacific. Was the South Land to be found here?

6

The Stratocruiser route from New York to Sydney via Valparaiso was tested by Australian pilots. The flight makes a brief stop at Rapa Nui, i.e. Easter Island, before the last hop to Australia. It is patronized not only by passengers from Chile, Brazil, the Argentine and Peru, but also by North American business men, since it is much shorter than the usual route via Hawaii. The distance between Valparaiso and Rapa Nui is about two thousand sea-miles, or some six flying hours. From there to Pitcairn Island, the scene of the last acts of the drama of the *Bounty*, is another five hours, and the next stop is New Zealand.

To travel along this new route, which was only opened in 1952, is not a very interesting experience, but this applies to all routes across the Pacific, which stretch through empty skies and over deserted waters. In fact the route to Rapa Nui is better than most. For a long time after leaving Valparaiso, one can still see the Aconcagua mountain, towering 23,000 feet above sea level. It is one of the highest peaks of the rugged Cordillera, and the picture of its glittering icc-caps remains imprinted in the traveller's memory for some hundreds of miles. An hour later the Juan Fernandez Islands can be spotted far below. The traveller recalls that Alexander Selkirk, whose experience provided Daniel Defoe with the idea and material for his Robinson Crusoe, was marooned on Masa Tierra, the largest of the three islands, for four years, after a difference of opinion with his captain. But after this nothing much else can be seen. The horizon is bare, and the sea below looks so placid that one would never suspect the regular, delicate markings on the surface of the water to be enormous waves more than thirty-eight feet high.

Some hours later something *can* be seen on the horizon. As the plane approaches it becomes bigger and more distinct, until it can be identified as a gigantic tower of cloud, and below it lies Rapa Nui.

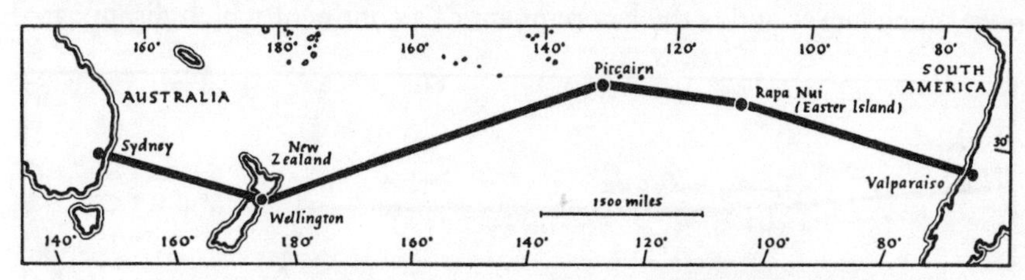

XXX. Route of the trial flight from Valparaiso to Sydney.

These cloud structures build up over all the larger islands of the Pacific, as the hot currents of air rise up from the sun-scorched rock, the glittering coral sand and the steaming lagoons. When the hot air eventually condenses it produces cloud formations, sometimes as much as sixteen thousand feet high, betraying the existence of land at their base. In the past they served Polynesian mariners on their ocean voyages, but today they are pointers for captains of great airliners.

Twenty minutes later, the outlines of volcanoes situated in the north, east and south-west of the island can be clearly seen emerging from the mist. As the plane loses height, it circles the island. We are above Rapa Nui. The first European to set foot on this island did so on Easter Sunday, 1772, and since then it has also been known as Easter Island.

The tourist hotel and the aerodrome grow larger and larger. The plane makes its final circuit and comes in to land. Not far away is the village of Hanga-roa, the only settlement on Easter Island. The passengers are given a folder, published by the Sociedad Amigos de la Isla de Pascua, which identifies the principal buildings and landmarks, and gives some details of the island's history. All around can be seen strange huge rocks, and the passengers read with interest that these are the six hundred giant heads of Rapa Nui.

Easter Island, completely isolated in a measureless ocean, is a chance product of Tertiary volcanic forces. It rises steeply from the ocean floor, almost ten thousand feet below the surface of the water; it is about twelve and a half miles long and its total area amounts to about forty-six square miles. It lies about 2,000 miles from the coast of Chile and about 1,200 miles from the Gamber Islands, the nearest airstrip to the west; about the same distance away from the Marquesas, the Tuamotu Islands and the Tubuai Archipelago in Polynesia. When viewed against the background of these enormous distances, the forty-six square miles of Easter Island are a mere pin-point. Its inhabitants have always been conscious of their isolation and the name they gave to the island was *Tepito re Henua*, the navel of the Earth.

Their legends state that their ancestors came to the island across the great ocean. There is no hint in their oldest legends that Rapa Nui was once much larger and is the last remnant of a continent which disappeared

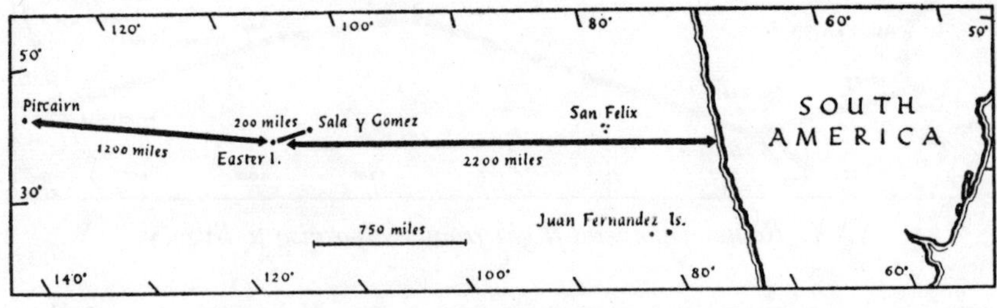

XXXI. Position of Easter Island in the Pacific.

under the surface of the waves, as some people believe, and possibly identical with that mysterious land, ruled by giants, which appeared in a vision to Madame Blavatsky. Even a hundred years before Madame Blavatsky, there had been stories of giants on Easter Island, men so tall that an ordinary mortal could walk beneath the arch of their outstretched legs. These stories were current at the time that Roggeween's reports of his travels were first published. Swift's famous satire *Gulliver's Travels* appeared at the same time, and obviously both became fused in the minds of their contemporaries: Swift's fabulous tale of Brobdingnag, the land of giants, and the no less fabulous report of the Dutch sailor. Cook put an end to these infantile fantasies.

Hörbiger's theory that the world was originally covered with ice received no support from the traditions of this strange island. There was no story of the break-up of a Tertiary moon, which is the basis of Hörbiger's theory, nor of sudden recessions of gigantic water-masses which the original moon had held in place near the Equator, by the force of its attraction. The Easter Islanders knew nothing about volcanoes, although there are more than a dozen of them on the island, and much evidence of them in the form of hot springs. Moreover their language has no expression for a volcano.

Geologists have thoroughly investigated Easter Island, and are quite unanimous in their conclusion that no major terrestrial catastrophe has taken place in this area for hundreds of thousands of years, and that the mineral deposits on Easter Island show no connection with continental formations. This proves beyond the shadow of a doubt that Rapa Nui is not the remnant of a continent which has since disappeared, that its culture is not autochthonous, and that some time in the past the island was colonized by people coming from another land.

This is all that can be stated with certainty about Easter Island; all the rest is surmise, based on more or less convincing circumstantial evidence. However, in 1946, American oceanographers, i.e. scientists who study the formation of the ocean bed, discovered an underwater range of mountains only six hundred miles away from Easter Island, which may possibly be joined, or have been joined, to it. Thus doubt has been cast even on our one certainty! Still, we must leave these questions to the experts and return to some historical facts.

It has long been supposed that the island had already been sighted for the first time 250 years ago. In 1687 a certain Edward Davis saw land from his ship, the *Bachelor's Delight*, at about 27° South. He had no time to land and explore, for he had just attacked and plundered the settlement of Léon in Nicaragua, and was hastening south as fast as he could go, his scuppers running with jewels and his holds filled with bullion. Today it is believed that what he saw were the two small islands, San Felix and San Ambrosio. Since at that time everybody's head was full of stories about a fabulously rich South Land, the two islands, which became known as Davis Land, acquired a halo of mystery and the reputation of being extremely wealthy. Jacob Roggeween was searching for this supposed Pacific El Dorado, and indeed thought his search had come to an end when in 1722 he sighted Easter Island, but when he managed to land he was soon disillusioned. Roggeween's three ships had to lie at anchor close to the island for three whole weeks before he was able to get a boat through the fierce surf, and so he only spent one day there, not much longer than the modern traveller whose plane makes a brief halt on the island to refuel.

On the south-west coast of the island lies Cook's Bay. A liner from Chile visits this every year. In the southern part of the island lies the holy city of Orongo, built underground, the scene of religious celebrations in honour of the divine Bird-Man. It was here that the last queen of the island died at the ripe old age of 114.

The holy mountain *Rano-raraku,* which provided the stone for the gigantic heads that have made Rapa Nui famous throughout the world, is situated in the east of the island. Although these heads are well known through photographs in books and magazines, it is only when one actually sees them, so to speak face to face, as they stare in fixed tranquillity from a hillside or from what is obviously an artificially contrived platform made of stones and covered over with turf, that one can realize their primordial power and true solemnity.

Carl Friedrich Behrens, a warrant officer on Roggeween's ship, has recorded this experience. From the sea, he had espied objects on land looking like gigantic monuments, which, he soon realized, were idols. At night sacrificial fires could be seen glowing round these idols, and by daylight he could make out the natives prostrating themselves before them as if in supplication. On the 8th April the wind dropped sufficiently to enable some of the crew to land:

> Entrusting ourselves into God's hands, we landed with a hundred and fifty men, soldiers as well as seamen. Our Admiral went along in person, together with me. I was the first man of all to set foot on the island. The inhabitants thronged round us in such numbers that we could hardly make our way through them. As some of them made as if to snatch our firearms from us we fired a volley, whereupon they ran away, being greatly frightened. Many of them were killed and many lay wounded. Future generations will tell stories of our deeds. . . . The people were very happy, well-built, strong of limb, and swift of foot, friendly and pleasing in their manners. In colour, they were light brown, almost like Spaniards, yet there were some amongst them who were darker-skinned; others, on the other hand, had fair skins and yet others were reddish in colour, as if burnt by the sun. We found no articles of furniture in their huts, except for red and white blankets which served both as garments and mattresses. When we touched these blankets they felt like silk. In the region in which we found ourselves, there was a village of about twenty houses. The people appeared to carry no weapons, but to rely on their gods or idols, great numbers of which had been erected on the beach. The natives would fall down and worship these images, hewn out of stone and fashioned like the heads of men so artistically that we were much astonished.

Jacob Roggeween also made an entry in the ship's log:

> These statues first caused deep wonder in us, for we could not understand how it was possible that people who lacked both solid timber for scaffolding and also strong ropes, could have erected such idols, well over 30 feet high and correspondingly thick.

Yet even more wonderful things were to be seen on this desert island. Behrens reported that chickens were seen everywhere 'similar to those at home'. It was not difficult to acquire a few hundred of them by barter. Where did they come from? They could not very well have flown there. Moreover there were large fields of potatoes, a vegetable unknown to Behrens, 'tasting almost like bread and used in its stead by the natives', sugar-cane, and much *pisang* (bananas).

Carl Friedrich Behrens's impression of the island was highly favourable, and he concluded his report by saying:

> As regards the food of the people, it seems they obtain all their produce by tilling the soil. The fields were full of growing crops, neatly planted, almost ready for harvesting. . . . The island is very agreeable and it would be very pleasant to spend one's leisure on it. . . . It seems advisable that corn should be sown and vines planted, for these would be of great service when a new voyage is made to discover the South Land.

The prophecy was to be fulfilled to an even greater extent than Behrens imagined. In 1868 the former French officer Jean O. Dutrou-Bornier ordered fruit trees, vines and sugar-cane to be planted, so that today we may wander through large parks and plantations giving four crops a year. Figs, oranges, bananas, lemons, pineapples, *paltas*, *chirimoyas*, papaws, maize, tobacco and coffee now grow in abundance. In fact Easter Island served as a supply and rest station during Admiral Byrd's exploration of the Antarctic.

Fifty years after Roggeween, on Sunday, 13th February 1774, James Cook dropped anchor off Easter Island in the hope that he, too, might be able to barter for fresh provisions. He was to be deeply disappointed, though at first his hopes seemed likely to be fulfilled, for the natives soon paddled out to his ship and handed the sailors a large bunch of bananas as a gift of welcome. Georg Forster made the following entry:

> The joy which the sight of these fruits produced in us can hardly be described. Only people as miserable as we were can have any conception of this. The men, in their happiness, began shouting all at once to the natives in the canoes. . . .

A small expedition was sent ashore next day, only to discover that the island was poor, barren and inhospitable, for the only fresh food they could discover was a few pounds of potatoes and a few scraggy chickens. Cook commented that

> no nation need contend for the honour of the discovery of this island, as there can be few places which afford less convenience for shipping than it does. Here is no safe anchorage, no wood for fuel, nor any fresh water worth taking on board.

Cook's men marched for three days throughout the length and breadth of the island, but the friendly fields mentioned by Behrens seemed to have vanished. They did, however, come across deserted plots showing signs of former cultivation. They discovered the remains of paved roads, the ruins of old harbour installations and of many villages with stone buildings—it seemed as if a terrible catastrophe had befallen the island.

More recent expeditions have confirmed this impression. The stonemasons' workshop, where the giant statues were made, was discovered in the crater of the extinct volcano Rano-raraku. A hundred and fifty figures in all stages of completion and of all sizes, ranging from quite small ones to a colossus seventy feet in length, stand and lie about there, some of them still on the stone rollers on which they were transported, others abandoned on the way to the place of erection, and yet others in the rough state in which they were hewn from the volcanic rock. Near them lay the tools used by the stonemasons: two different kinds of obsidian chisel, and large handy lumps of pumice-stone used for polishing the giant statues. It gave the impression that the workmen had been suddenly forced to interrupt their labours and to escape in headlong flight. Was there a volcanic eruption? If so, nothing is known of it. Perhaps the natives are correct when they tell that five or six generations ago, i.e. in the middle of the eighteenth century, and thus some time during the interval between the visits of Roggeween and Cook, there was a bloody civil war. This is by no means impossible but again there is no proof of it.

Similar gigantic statues to those on Rapa Nui can be found in Bolivia and date back to the Tiahuanaco culture. This type of rock-carving is also found throughout the length of the San Agostín valley in Colombia and also in Guatemala as far as Yucatan. But these regions are thousands of miles away from Easter Island and, despite the many points of similarity, it is by no means certain that any connection exists between the giant heads of the South American continent and those on the remote Pacific island. When we compare the statues carved in stone or wood that are found on the Marquesas Islands, on Pitcairn or on Raïvavaé, the Polynesian islands closest to Rapa Nui, with those of Easter Island we realize that such a connection is far from certain. The Easter Island heads, with their sharply delineated faces, straight noses, thin lips and jutting chins, are unique and have a form found exclusively on this lonely rock island in the middle of the ocean.

The religious impulse which drove the Stone Age men of Easter Island to produce such giant figureheads with their crude tools has long eluded investigations. These ancient sculptors must have possessed a faith like that of our own ancestors who built vast cathedrals in poverty-stricken towns, spending money, goods and the lives of many generations in constructing artistic temples worthy of God the Creator. We do not know exactly how those giant heads were produced and set in position. It is true that after the recent discoveries it is easier to reconstruct the way their stonemasons worked and we have a good idea of the method used to erect the heads, viz. by digging a hole and building a ramp around it, and then lowering the plinth of the idol into the pit, but certain questions still remain unanswered: where did they obtain the ropes, rollers and lifting implements necessary, how did they overcome the sudden slopes and dips in the level of the ground, so typical of Easter Island, and finally where did they obtain the crowds of men necessary for such work?

Roggeween and Behrens had the impression that in 1722 the population of the island numbered several thousands, though present-day anthropologists agree that the total number of inhabitants could never have numbered more than two thousand, and at the time of James Cook, fifteen hundred was a more likely figure. This number of workers would have been quite inadequate for the task of cutting and modelling some six hundred rock statues and then transporting them from the crater of Rano-raraku to their final destination. These statues were not set up at random; it has been discovered that they stand along old roads running from the north, the south and the west of the island, to the holy mountain. Modern technologists have calculated that about forty thousand people were needed to do this work.

These conclusions presuppose a stable government and a large population, yet when Roggeween and Cook visited the island there could have been no question of such a state of affairs. The natives showed scant respect for the stone idols, whereas their erection can only have been the result of deep fervour, nor was there authority enough to order the work or enough men to do it.

The general decline in Polynesian culture which had taken place all over the Pacific applied also to Easter Island. Cook and the other European discoverers encountered an impressive, but a dying culture. The natives proudly told him of a half-legendary king Hotu-Matua, who, driven out of his original kingdom, had reached the island on two boats with three hundred followers on each and supplies of batatas, sugar-cane, yams and bananas, yet these same inhabitants of Easter Island possessed only four or five miserable canoes that were barely strong enough to serve as fishing-boats.

34. European ship. Painting in black and white from the interior of a stone house on Easter Island.

Investigators basing their conclusions on the genealogy of the islanders place Hotu-Matua's arrival on Easter Island in the twelfth or thirteenth century. Although the king arrived with a large number of followers in his train, they seem to have cut all ties with their original home, for even when Roggeween visited the island, the islanders' boats were obviously very poor, unseaworthy craft, made from odd pieces of driftwood and certainly quite incapable of attempting the return journey. Now, as no forests had existed on Rapa Nui since prehistoric times, Hotu-Matua and his men must soon have discovered that they would quickly become prisoners of the island if they could not provide timber for their ships. Thus it is probable that they tried to make contact with the nearest Polynesian islands, though there is no evidence of their doing so. It is also not known whether Hotu-Matua and his followers migrated to this island from the Marquesas, the Tuamotu or the Tubuai Islands. By all accounts they were Polynesians and, judging by their racial and linguistic characteristics, were closely related to their western neighbours, but they told Captain Geiseler, the commander of a German gunboat who put in at the island in 1883, that their ancestors had come from the east, 'sailing constantly towards the sinking sun', from an island group called *maraetoa-hau*, where it was so hot that many died of the heat and plants and fruits dried up. In Geiseler's opinion, this group of islands could only have been the Galapagos Islands. Three years later William E. Thomson, paymaster of the American frigate *Mohican*, which anchored off Rapa Nui from the 19th to 30th December, was told the same story; he too thought the Galapagos Islands the most likely identification.

Such definite statements cannot be ignored, particularly since other evidence exists pointing to links between Easter Island and the mainland of South America. Apart from the unquestionably American batata, there is also the *sapindus saponaria*, a plant which has grown on Easter Island for many centuries and whose original home is tropical America. Both in America and on Easter Island the natives use this plant as an astringent remedy, and also as a kind of soap. The people of Rapa Nui called this plant by the same name as the South American *indios*—on both sides of the ocean it was known as *para para*.

Furthermore, similarities have been discovered between the sand-heaps on which a large proportion of the giant faces of Rapa Nui stood, the 'burial terraces' of central Polynesia and the holy terraced pyramids of South America. Admittedly the latter are on a much larger scale than the *marae*, the burial terraces of Easter Island, but both make use of the same huge carefully chiselled blocks of stone fitting snugly together without the need of cement or mortar. As already mentioned, the same skill in building and handling stone was common in Bolivia and Peru, and we can easily understand that explorers have been struck by the resemblances between the ruins of the Tiahuanaco era in South America and the remains of similar constructions on Easter Island.

But the Easter Islanders were undoubtedly Polynesians! Although Rapa Nui was inhabited prior to the arrival of the light-skinned visitors by an unknown indigenous population possessing negroid and Melanesian characteristics, by the time white discoverers reached the island, Polynesian features predominated. This is clearly stated in Roggeween's reports, and two generations later Cook confirmed that the natives of Easter Island were so like those of the Polynesian islands to the west in colour, stature and language, that it was obvious that they all belonged to one and the same race. A hundred years later, Captain Geiseler also gave it as his opinion that the Easter Islanders were Polynesians. In his official report, dated 1883, he said:

> In appearance, particularly in the shape of their heads, the people are strikingly similar to the Caucasian race. Their eyes are large, and dark brown in colour; their faces are alert and kindly. The men, for the most part, have short beards and moustaches. Their cheekbones are not pronounced and their lips are full, without being thick.

Modern anthropology is in total agreement with these statements. There is no doubt that the inhabitants of Easter Island are Polynesians, and that in racial characteristics, culture and language they are closely related to their western neighbours.

In view of these considerations it is all the more surprising that their development followed such an individual course, and that they were the only people in the Pacific who had a form of 'writing'. The first information about this came not so very long ago. None of the earliest discoverers, Roggeween, Cook, La Pérouse (1786), Kotzebue (1816), Beechey (1826), heard of it, so carefully was the secret of the *rongo-rongo*, the 'speaking' tablets, guarded. Only in 1864 did the natives let out the secret to Father Eugène Eyraud, who went to Easter Island as a missionary. Father Eyraud, a very well-meaning but rather simple soul, was deeply alarmed. He implored the natives to get rid of the wooden tablets, some up to six feet long, scratched on both sides with symbols, which they had brought him. Father Eyraud did not burn them himself, as his colleagues in Central America had done some centuries earlier with Maya manuscripts, but persuaded his flock, who were completely under his influence, to commit the tablets to the flames themselves. Thus during the four years from 1864 to 1868, all but twenty of these tablets were systematically destroyed. Those twenty which survived are distributed in museums throughout the world.

It is difficult to understand why the natives followed Father Eyraud's instructions so willingly. At first it was believed that they must by then have lost the ability to read their tablets, which, as a result, no longer had any meaning or value to them, but this assumption is false, for we have since learned that these 'speaking tablets' were still being studied as late as 1860 and that the last 'king' of Rapa Nui, who was captured by South American slave-traders in 1864, could still read and write. It was also discovered that these tablets were once holy relics, which only a few of the natives were allowed to touch. Shortly after Eyraud's arrival one of the traditional religious tests took place in which the scribes, the *rongo-rongo* men, had to prove before the entire populace that they were still masters of their holy and secret skills. Somehow Father Eugène managed to suppress this ancient ritual which, as the natives believed, had been brought to the island by Hotu-Matua. The result of his interference is that most assertions about Easter Island are based on circumstantial evidence rather than fact.

We do not know how it was that the natives of Rapa Nui, who have never been able to lead the happy, carefree existence of their more fortunate brethren in central Polynesia, came to devise a method for recording their magic formulas, their legends and their myths. In view of the many cultural similarities between Polynesia and South America, some people have suggested that there is a connection between the *amautas*, the noble scribes of the Incas, and the *rongo-rongo* men, despite the fact that the Inca scribes used agave or banana 'paper', while the natives of Rapa Nui used wooden tablets. Of course, it is not possible to prove that this connection existed, and in fact it can be shown that very many of the pictures and symbols used by the Easter Islanders are hieroglyphic representations of objects which had always existed on the island or had been known in central Polynesia. There seem to be only two exceptions to this general rule: one is a stylized hieroglyph of a feline animal, perhaps a kind of puma, and the other obviously represents a frigate bird, an arboreal species unknown on the unwooded Easter Island. These birds, however, were objects of veneration on the Solomon Islands far to the west, and also probably played some rôle in the religion of Peru.

35. *Decoration on a paddle from Easter Island.*

As already stated, all the other symbols appear to have been representations of objects which had been known in Polynesia from the beginning. We are thus forced to the conclusion that these 'Stone Age' natives in this lonely spot in the ocean managed, within a few hundred years, to achieve a cultural feat that had taken all other peoples on earth many thousands. The Easter Island 'writing', as the young German investigator Dr. Thomas S. Barthel recently stated, after many years of research into the problem, was in fact writing true and proper and was used for recording mythological, ritual or magically significant events and formulas.

This discovery explains why there has been a constant search to find a possible link between Easter Island and more developed cultures, but, as no such connection can be proved, we are forced to assume that the *rongo-rongo* men developed their writing in Polynesia themselves. Perhaps this system of recording has something in common with the knotted strings of the Incas, a method found also in ancient China and throughout the whole of Polynesia, according to which the knots on a string or the notches in a stick were given a definite meaning, in the sense that a more or less complicated set of circumstances or ideas was attached to each knot or notch. Possibly Easter Island writing developed from the same system, for it was long believed that even the individual signs on the *rongo-rongo* tablets were nothing but mnemonic symbols.

If this is the case then we must renounce all hope of ever deciphering the messages of the tablets, since it is clearly impossible for us to conjure up the whole sequence of events recalled by each hieroglyph.

Probably less than a hundred years ago the writing on these tablets could have been deciphered and the riddle of the origins of the Polynesians might have been solved, for even King Hotu-Matua was alleged to have had *rongo-rongos* with him when he arrived on the island—the archives of his people consisting of sixty-seven holy tablets. In 1864 Father Eugène Eyraud could still have obtained the answer but he, simple-witted soul that he was, merely looked on complacently as the speaking-tablets were consumed by the flames.

36. Signatures of the Easter Island chieftains.

7

It was not long before Cook realized that little could be gained on Easter Island, and so after only a few days he set sail for the Marquesas, which had not been visited by Europeans since their discovery by Mendaña in 1595. From here he made for Tahiti where he stayed just long enough to take water and provisions on board, and then put to sea once more on a westerly course.

He landed on the Tonga Islands in mid-June 1774, and three weeks later he reached the New Hebrides and afterwards New Caledonia. He and his companions were struck by the great differences between the inhabitants of these western islands and those of Polynesia. The natives were black like negroes, with woolly hair and protruding lips and, unlike their

Polynesian neighbours, they knew little of navigation. Their language also was quite different. It was as if they had reached an entirely different continent.

Cook wrote of the natives of the New Hebrides:

> ... in general, they are the most ugly, ill-proportioned people I ever saw, and in every respect different from any we had met with in this sea. They are a very dark-coloured and rather diminutive race; with long heads, flat faces and monkey countenances.

Cook had reason to be astonished: he had just left a vast region extending between 20° North and 45° South, whose inhabitants all belonged to the same race and where the same language was spoken and the same culture prevailed. The last few days' sailing had taken him almost into a new world.

From New Caledonia, Cook continued on to New Zealand where he took on fresh water, wood and fresh vegetables, and then sailed on a deep southerly course towards Cape Horn. Once again a blank space on the map was filled in, for no ship had ever sailed in the regions between 50° and 55° South before. No land was sighted and it finally became clear to Cook that no *terra australis*, no South Land, did in fact exist.

On the 17th December 1774, after a record voyage of thirty-six days, they sighted Cape Deseado, the western entry to the Strait of Magellán. From here their course skirted the coast; Cook busied himself making soundings, charting and surveying until on the 29th December Cape Horn was rounded. The *Resolution* was now, so to speak, in its home waters: the Atlantic Ocean. Cook made straight for the Cape of Good Hope, the southern tip of Africa. In the middle of January 1775, South Georgia Island was discovered and claimed for the British Crown but Cook had had enough now:

> Besides, I was tired of these high southern latitudes where nothing was to be found but ice and thick fogs. We had now a long hollow swell from the west, a strong indication that there was no land in that direction....

If any land existed at all, it could only be found very far to the south, near the Pole.

> ... The greatest part of this Southern Continent must lie within the polar circle, where the sea is so pestered with ice that the land is inaccessible.

Many decades were to pass before the Antarctic, which Cook had supposed to exist, was first set foot upon by a white man, or presumably by any human being at all.

After long weeks of cruising in icy winds, during which Cook was forced, on more than one occasion, to heave-to in order to clear the rigging of the masses of snow which had collected there, by the method of allowing the sails to flap freely in the wind, the ship sailed into Table Bay, the

1555, calling it by the name of Los Majos. Cook did not believe this story for he noted that had the Spaniards in fact discovered Hawaii they would then have taken on water and provisions there, instead of sending their Philippine-bound ships to Guam much further west. Had they indeed known of Hawaii they would only have needed to alter course slightly to call there, and so would have remained within the Trades all the time. If any doubt still remained about this Spanish claim to have discovered

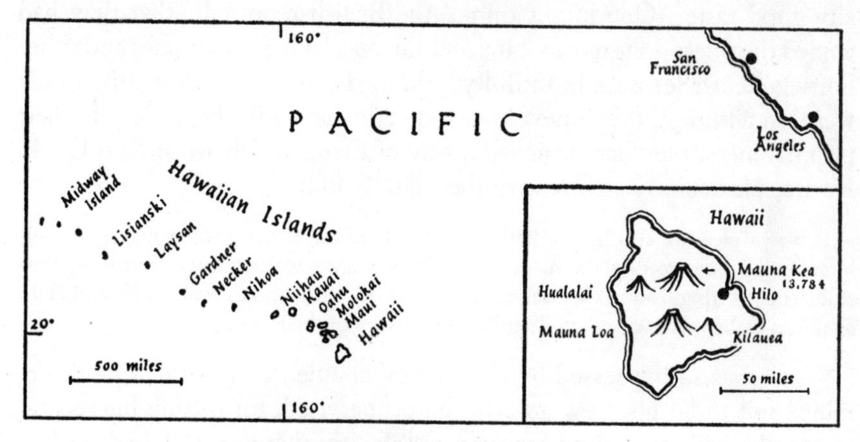

XXXII. Hawaii and the adjacent islands.

Hawaii, 250 years before the arrival of Cook, it must have been dispelled by the behaviour of the natives, who clearly showed that they had never heard of Europeans. Cook noted in his journal:

> In the course of my several voyages, I never before met with the natives of any place so much astonished, as these people were, upon entering a ship. Their eyes were continually flying from object to object . . . strongly marking to us, that, till now, they had never been visited by Europeans, nor been acquainted with any of our commodities except iron; which, however, it was plain, they had only heard of, or had known in some small quantity. . . .

In spite of their primitive condition, the natives bore themselves with natural dignity. They greatly resembled the inhabitants of the other Pacific islands Cook had visited, being light brown in complexion, and they confirmed the impression that they too were Polynesians the moment they began to speak, for they had the same language as the peoples of Tahiti and New Zealand. As soon as the ships arrived, they stole everything that was removable, and when a certain Lieut. Williamson went ashore the next day, the natives crowded round him to such an extent that he ordered his men to fire, and one native was killed. At first, there were no consequences, and wherever Cook appeared he was worshipped like a god. Men and women, even the nobles and the chiefs, would prostrate themselves before him though they did not forget that these strangers had brought death with them. In character they were made of sterner mettle than the frivolous, happy-go-lucky inhabitants of Tahiti.

Cook held them in high esteem for this, despite their cannibalistic habits. Their plantations and fields were carefully laid out and irrigated with great skill, and between them ran banked roads, kept in a good state of order. The paper-mulberry tree, which provided them with cloth, was planted with geometrical precision. Their clothes showed their exceptionally good taste. 'One might think,' the British reported, 'that they had copied the finest designs of China and Europe.' Their calabashes and other household articles were beautifully fashioned and showed how gifted they were. In addition, they knew how to pickle meat—in short, despite their primitiveness, they had achieved a way of living which astonished Cook. He was particularly struck with their family life:

> It was a pleasure to observe with how much affection the women managed their infants, and how readily the men lent their assistance to such a tender office; thus sufficiently distinguishing themselves from those savages who esteem a wife and child as things rather necessary than desirable, or worthy of their notice.

Cook was so impressed by the natives' simple goodness that he determined not to let his crew go ashore unsupervised, for during his second voyage he had realized with shame and disgust that venereal diseases had spread to Tahiti and elsewhere, and that the natives spoke quite freely of the 'British Disease', which the white sailors had brought them. Whether in fact venereal diseases had been imported into the Pacific from Europe, or whether like the batata, cotton and the bottle gourd, it had reached there directly from America, has never been settled, but Cook blamed himself and his lack of supervision for this development, and, conscious of his deep moral responsibility, he noted:

> The order not to permit the crews of the boats to go on shore was issued, that I might do everything to prevent the importation of a fatal disease into this island, which I knew some of our men laboured under, and which, unfortunately, had been already communicated by us to other islands in these seas. With the same view, I ordered all female visitors to be excluded from the ships. . . . Whether these regulations, dictated by humanity, had the desired effect, or no, time only can discover. I had been equally attentive to the same object, when I first visited the Friendly Islands; yet I afterward found, with real concern, that I had not succeeded.

With almost paternal displeasure he added:

> The opportunities and inducements to an intercourse between the sexes are too numerous to be guarded against; and however confident we may be of the health of our men, we are often undeceived too late.

Cook was deeply distressed when, three weeks after issuing this proclamation, an officer and twenty men were forced by sudden storms to spend the night on the island, thus thwarting all his precautions.

When this happened, Cook was just fifty years old. During the last ten years he had not spent long at home, and thus he knew nothing of family life in the real sense of the word—his ship had been his home and his crew his family. All his paternal impulses had been lavished on them, and on the natives. Cook was endowed with a greater measure of brotherly love than the average person on earth, and was later to die on account of it. Love is no mark of genius—Columbus and Magellán had been more brilliant men—but perhaps the world would be much better off if there was less genius and more goodness.

At the beginning of February 1778, the *Resolution* and the *Discovery* left Hawaii, sailing northwards. Six weeks later, at 47° North, the west coast of North America was sighted near the present-day state of Washington, in the region of the Juan de Fuca Strait. Owing to constant storms, Cook had to wait until the end of March before he could land. The place where he went ashore was Nootka Sound on Vancouver Island. The Indian inhabitants, decked in beautiful feathers, soon came out to the ships in their canoes, and trade by barter was quickly under way. It was soon realized that the Indians were already acquainted with iron, and that like the Polynesians they were cannibals.

> . . . the most extraordinary of all the articles which they brought to the ships for sale were human skulls and hands not yet quite stripped of the flesh, which they made our people plainly understand they had eaten. . . .

The Indians were willing to barter everything, including their holy idols and totem-poles, though these would only be given in exchange for brass and copper, while other goods could be had for iron. Brass and copper were so much in demand that, as Cook reported, in the end the sailors got rid of all fittings, containers, candlesticks, and even the buttons off their suits.

At the end of April 1778, after twenty-four days of incessant surveying, Cook set sail again, skirting northwards along the coast. The voyage proved exceptionally dangerous, for the unknown coast was studded with cliffs and sandbanks, swirling currents tossed the ships in all directions, and heavy rainstorms alternated with days of thick fog. The crew were in a ferment and voices were raised condemning the voyage as utter madness. We have a very detailed account of this from the pen of a German sailor, Heinrich Zimmermann, who was hired for the voyage and who published a book about his experiences on his return in 1781. Zimmermann was deeply impressed by Cook's abilities and was genuinely devoted to him. His book tells of this stage of the voyage:

> A great wave of strong opposition had grown up against Cook on both ships, yet the grudges which many bore him were soon overshadowed by a remarkable event. I had often noticed how confidently Cook faced the dangers of the ocean, and how well he

knew them. But apart from this knowledge, he had also a remarkable flair for being able to foresee dangers before they actually happened. I was astonished to perceive that even here, off the shores of America in the midst of constant danger from rocks, shallows and sandbanks, Cook managed to pass his nights in undisturbed sleep. Yet it sometimes happened that he would come storming up on deck in the middle of the night and suddenly order a change of course. It often struck us that he must have received some sign or else had become clairvoyant.

Now on the 24th June—I remember the date exactly—we were sailing along the coast on a very foggy night. Nothing made us suspect any danger lurking in the darkness. Lieutenant Gore, whose watch it was, observed a sudden strong current, and would have sailed on happily, had not Cook suddenly rushed out of his cabin and in

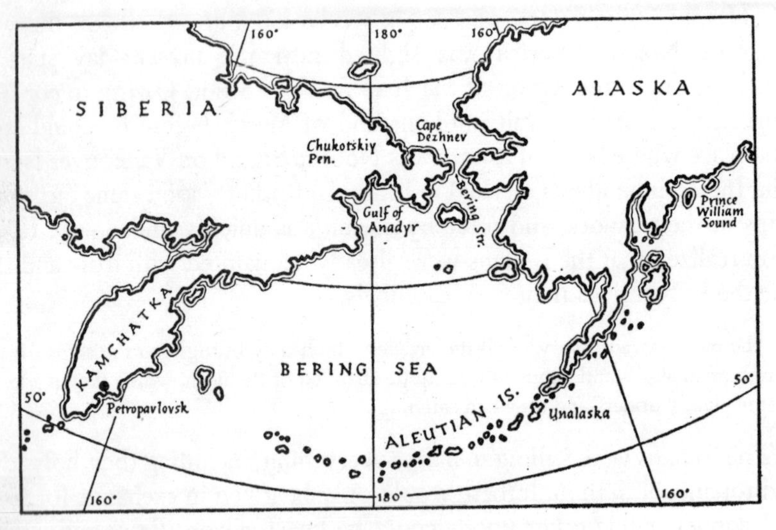

XXXIII. The North Pacific.

great agitation given the order to drop anchor at once. . . . We were all amazed. The sailors stumbled on deck from all parts of the ship, asking what had happened, but no one could answer them for the ships were blanketed round by thick fog. Towards noon of the following day the fog lifted sufficiently for us to see a rock rising steeply out of the sea, barely twenty paces ahead, and that the waters all round us were studded with rocks. There was no doubt but that neither of the ships would have been saved, had not Cook ordered the anchors to be dropped.

We can understand now why Heinrich Zimmermann and his comrades were afterwards filled with an 'almost mystical admiration' for their captain, and it must certainly have made a deep impression upon them that Cook himself did not believe in the existence of a passage to the east, despite the fact that there was the reward of £20,000 for its discovery. Cook's confidence in his own opinion might well have been shaken when in the region of Prince William Sound in Alaska, where the Aleutian Islands meet the continent, the ships came across a deep inlet cut into the land, where in fact a large river empties itself into the ocean. Lieutenant

Gore, Cook's first officer, was certain that here was access to Hudson or Baffin Bay, and he begged Cook to entrust him with the task of exploring the land. He was certain that if he were given twenty men, two longboats and adequate provisions, he could reach England within three months. Cook refused his request, but investigated inlets and bays with special care. Then, pleading the lateness of the season, he followed the Aleutian Archipelago to the west as far as the island of Unalaska.

At the beginning of July, Cook was able to alter course from due north to north-east, and it seemed as if the desired passage had materialized after all, but on the 17th August 1778, the two ships met with ice and could proceed no further.

> Some time before noon we perceived a brightness in the northern horizon, like that reflected from ice, commonly called the blink. It was little noticed, from a supposition that it was improbable we should meet with ice so soon. . . . About an hour after, the sight of a large field of ice left us no longer in doubt about the cause of the brightness of the horizon. At half-past two, we tacked, close to the edge of the ice, in twenty-two fathoms water, being then in the latitude of 70° 41′; not being able to stand on any farther.

As the ice barrier still impeded his ships on the following day, Cook decided to put off his attempt to thrust through to the north-east, and instead to find a more suitable harbour for the winter further south. Not unnaturally he preferred to return to Hawaii, rather than be imprisoned by the ice for seven long months near Petropavlovsk in southern Kamchatka.

At the beginning of 1778 the ships dropped anchor in Neeshaven on Unalaska. There they were overhauled and expeditions were sent out to gather berries and pine-cones. Cook had a brew made of the pine-cones to which he gave the rather ambitious name of 'beer'. Other members of the crew were set to providing fresh meat and fish. The crews of both ships were kept constantly busy, so that they had no time to brood under the desolate grey sky in those wintry surroundings. Under the constant pressure of activity, that old-fashioned, effective 'occupational therapy', nobody had time to become depressed, no one despaired, and, because the diet was rich in vitamins, there was no scurvy.

Nevertheless Cook was only too happy when on the 26th October the ships were ready to leave Unalaska. Some time before this date he had met Russian fishermen and hunters to whom he had handed interim reports addressed to the British Admiralty. He noted that these Russians were quite mad about strong drink. Some natives made occasional appearances, and, much to Cook's great annoyance, amongst them were a number of women whom, of course, his sailors immediately approached, though venereal disease was by no means unknown in those parts. His main reason, however, for wanting to travel south was that winter was drawing dangerously near. Talk about a passage was nothing but a pipe-dream, and even if it did exist it would be so packed with ice that it would have no value at all.

It is odd that Cook made no mention of Russian explorations in eastern Siberia and Alaska. He ordered Corporal Lediard, whom he had sent at the beginning of October to find some Russian hunters thought to be in the vicinity, to tell them that 'we British are the friends and allies of your people', and when some Russian sailors did in fact appear, Cook received them with friendship. However, he wrote not a word about Semion Ivanov Deshnev, that Cossack *hetman* who, as early as 1684, had sailed from the Arctic Ocean on a few hastily assembled boats through the Bering Strait to the Gulf of Anadir in the Pacific Ocean, thus proving that Asia and America were *not* joined, as had previously been believed. Cook only mentions the Dane, Vitus Bering, in passing, while the Russian naval captain, Ivan Fedorov, who in 1732 made the first voyage from Asia to the western coast of America, is completely ignored. These omissions cannot be ascribed to jealousy on Cook's part: in the first place his fame was such that it would not have suffered by competition, and secondly because such pettiness was not in his nature.

On the 19th November 1778, hardly four weeks after leaving Unalaska, land was sighted at 20° North after a pleasantly quick voyage. The land was soon discovered to belong to the Hawaiian Archipelago, and everyone was delighted. Since these islands, including Hawaii itself, had not yet been mapped, Cook investigated their coastlines with typical thoroughness. Only as late as the 17th January 1779 were the anchors of the two British ships finally dropped.

The natives who swarmed around the two ships in their boats knew very well the strangers who had appeared out of the wide ocean on their 'floating islands'. Their brethren on the other islands of the group had long ago told them that these were gods, seafaring gods, dressed in a somewhat unlovely skin of many colours. This skin had the most remarkable holes, into which the strangers would put their hands and bring out the most wonderful things.

The men grinned when they heard this. Their uniforms had been taken for their skins, their ships for floating islands, and they themselves for gods! These natives were just like children! A shy tenderness welled up in these tough sailors, encouraged by the fact that the islanders were the best-looking people they had ever seen. They were tall, slim and well built and looked magnificent in beautiful cloaks of red feathers. Their huts were carefully constructed and artistically decorated.

Heinrich Zimmermann had nothing but admiration for this island. His compatriot, Barthel Lohmann, from Thuringia, who had once been press-ganged by the Dutch and had later been enticed to join Cook's third voyage by the slogans of the London recruiting office, was even more enthusiastic. Zimmermann became suspicious when he noticed Lohmann's ecstatic state of mind, for he knew about the 'South Sea fever' from his own experience in Tahiti, when he had been so overcome by euphoria on beholding the dream island that he had wanted to stay there for ever. A flood of memories rushed back into his mind, of a night spent on that magical island:

> An unprecedented feeling of freedom seemed to be consuming me! What was life on board, that arid, burdensome round of duties, compared with the carefree life that awaited me here! ... I watched the dances from between the trees. The dancers' bodies were lit up by the light of the torches, and in the warm glow they cast a spell of beauty wherever I turned my eyes. The girls swayed in the flickering torch light and their lithe, supple bodies moved in time with the drum-beats. Their arms and hands caressed the air sensuously as if they were in love with it. ... The musicians sat in a small circle and drew music from bamboo sticks of different lengths, which gave out high and low sounds. There were others too ... who sang an enchanted melody with rich harmony; the beauty of it ravished my soul from my body. ... Now the girls were approaching as if they were gliding along, and I felt as if I were in a magic garden that had long been lost, the door of which I had just discovered. ... This was the happiest moment of my life. Here did I want to stay and be happy.

Once bitten, twice shy. ... Zimmermann finally managed to bring his comrade Barthel back to reason, but others were suffering from the same madness. There was talk of storming the arsenal, of open rebellion, of capturing the captain and destroying the boats so that they could not return, but it all came to naught, for the tide of events moved too quickly.

On the evening of the 17th January 1779, Cook withdrew to his cabin. For a long time he had been so taken up with his surveys that his journal had been neglected. A fresh cool breeze blew gently in through the open portholes into his spacious cabin. It had been a lovely day and Cook was pleased with himself, with his men and with the whole world; and conscious of the good work he had accomplished, he wrote:

> At eleven o'clock in the forenoon we anchored in the bay. ... We could not but be struck with the singularity of this scene; and perhaps there were few on board who now lamented our having failed in our endeavours to find a northern passage homeward, last summer. To this disappointment we owed our having it in our power to revisit the *Sandwich Islands*, and to enrich our voyage with a discovery which, though the last, seemed, in many respects, to be the most important that had hitherto been made by Europeans throughout the extent of the Pacific Ocean.

He was not to have a chance to continue his journal. Just a few days before this last entry, he had anxiously noted that it was becoming impossible to keep the women off the ships and that it seemed as if they came for the sole purpose of giving themselves to the sailors. He must have been aware that their weakness for his men, who appeared in the brilliant rôle of heroes, would cause trouble, but probably he did not realize to what extent resentment was smouldering on the island. At first they had been taken for gods, but when it was realized that they treated women in much the same way as mortal men, this ingenuous belief soon faded. Furthermore, when the natives perceived that the strangers were using up all the provisions of the island, they became convinced that the sailors had been driven from their own home by famine and that they were nothing but consuming parasites.

Thus brawls began to be common occurrences, and the British were forced to fire. On the 14th February, the situation had become so threatening that Cook had to intervene. He went ashore in order to pacify the people, but as he was turning round to give orders to his men in the boats, he was stabbed over and over again in the back. His death roused the natives to an even greater pitch of fury, and Cook's body and a number of sailors were literally torn to shreds. Cook's second-in-command, Captain Clerke, commander of the *Discovery*, was on board and managed to save himself and the crew of the boats. It must be counted to his great credit that he restrained the extremely embittered men from taking retaliatory measures.

On the 22nd February 1779, the two British ships left Hawaii. Still following their orders, they tried once again to sail east through the Bering Strait but again the ice presented an impassable barrier. Before they could take refuge in the Russian harbour of St. Peter and St. Paul (Petropavlovsk) on Kamchatka, Captain Clerke died of a lung complaint, contracted before the start of the voyage.

Apart from the many official obituaries that were published when Cook's death became known, there was one which is almost unknown and quite unique. It is to be found in the report sent to St. Petersburg by the governor of Kamchatka, the former Prussian officer, Major Behm. Behm reported that he had had a great diplomatic success. The Tchuktches, inhabitants of eastern Siberia, who had so far successfully resisted Russian domination, had declared their readiness for peace and friendship. They said that they had been visited by two ships, the white crews of which had been so courteous and helpful that they felt they could no longer object to the Russians.

Major Behm reported very correctly, but not entirely without malice, that these two ships could only have been the *Resolution* and the *Discovery*, and certainly not Russian ships. Of course he did not tell this to the Tchuktches. It is thus that the extreme eastern tip of Asia became Russian instead of British!

PART SEVEN

THE CALL OF THE DESERT

'Miller's beast and pastor's child, prosper rarely and often run wild' · What Dr. Olivier Dapper knew of the Niger · The riddle of the okapi · Of the historical significance of make-up · Egyptian mines in South Africa · The Abbé Breuil discovers a white lady · Herodotus is upset by the position of the sun · Only opulent men have corpulent wives · Wonder of wonders: the Niger flows to the east! · Dr. Mungo Park writes a best-seller · A theologian turns explorer · The pleasures of cursing · Water that tastes of goats · A theology student visits Murzuq · A baker's boy runs away to the 'Queen of the Desert' · Leo Africanus tells tall stories · René Caillié and Major Joffre—victors of Timbuktu · Heinrich Barth—the model boy · The jilting · A foreign minister appears—in the nude · The rock-paintings in Tellisarhe and what they mean · Sea-sickness on a camel · Can one drown in the Sahara? · 'Africa blackens' · Kano, the 'London' of the Black Continent · Of the 'Woman with the Big Navel' and the usefulness of a 'Colt' · Strange meeting in the jungle · Vegetarians are stabbed in the back · A Prussian military surgeon becomes a 'hakim' · Dr. Nachtigal and Gerhard Rohlfs · Kufra, the 'Rome of the Desert' · Why date juice must be drunk rather quickly · Gynaecological digression on 'sleeping embryos' · Death by thirst · Slave girls are cheaper than wives · Henri Duveyrier, knight of the desert · Baron d'Haussez is rude to His Majesty's Ambassador · The mysterious Tuareg · Of luxury coaches, bars and swimming-pools in the Sahara · Lt. Vicomte de Foucauld gives a party and is put on probation · A monk in the intelligence service · Princess Dassiné · Père Foucauld in Tamanrasset · The Sahara, tourist paradise of the future · The Hoggar line and highroad through the 'Land of Thirst' · Pros and cons of the Trans-Sahara railway.

I

A delicious smell of apple tart filled the room. The fire sent flickers of light into the dark corners and cast a red glow over the heavy beams across the ceiling. Night was falling, and the house was so peaceful that it seemed you could hear the snowflakes covering the roof with their white mantle. It was Friday night—the hour when Father was planning his Sunday sermon—and you had to be quiet as a mouse. But the boy sitting at the table had not the slightest wish to jump about and play wild games. He was lost in a thick volume open before him—reading and dreaming. He had received the book as a Christmas present from his godfather, and for the last eight days he had done nothing but devour it. It was not new, having been published more than a hundred years earlier, but the book was still as famous as when it had first appeared in 1670. Its author was the learned doctor Olivier Dapper, and it had been published by Jacob van Meurs of Amsterdam. A German translation had soon appeared: *Die Umbständliche und Eigentliche Beschreibung von Afrika Und denen dazu gehörigen Königreichen und Landschaften* ('The Detailed and Proper Description of Africa and the Kingdoms and Lands contained within it'). Since that time many other books on Africa had been written. Antoine François Prévost d'Exiles, who under the name of Abbé Prévost wrote the novel *Manon Lescaut*, had published a many-volumed *History of Voyages* with much information about Africa, a history which to this day remains a wonderful treasure-house for all who have the leisure to dip into it. In 1747, the first volumes of a series of twenty entitled *Allgemeine Historie der Reisen zu Wasser und zu Lande* ('General History of Voyages by Sea and on Land') had appeared in Leipzig. Here, too, the dark continent was described in great detail, but all these books were much too costly for the average man to buy, and so Olivier Dapper's book on Africa held the field for a hundred years and more.

Our lad gazed in wonder at the many pictures in this venerable old tome, and then turned to the maps of the cities, rivers, mountains and deserts of Africa, excitedly studying the written text. He had recently had his twelfth birthday, and he was at an age when boys usually run wild. In fact he used to be no exception to the rule. Only last summer he had built himself a proper Indian wigwam in the garden behind the house, a large, roomy tent of calfskin, just like those of the Sioux and the Apaches in the wide prairies of North America. He had invited his mother and sister and his schoolmates and friends to visit him and they had been most enthusiastic. Obviously the owner of such a magnificent wigwam was an expert Scout and a mighty hunter, and his comrades at once acclaimed him as their Big Chief.

How remote such pastimes seemed to him now! His passion for Indians was dead, forgotten his former enthusiasm for the knightly courage of Juan Ponce de Léon, one of Columbus's officers. The boy had accompanied him in imagination to the wonderful land of Bimini. He too had dropped anchor on Easter Day, 1512, off the coast of Florida and had pored over the map with the Spanish knight in search of Bimini, the source of eternal youth. Then again, he had disguised himself as an Indian medicine-man and had marched for eight years with Cabeza de Vaca across the New World, without meeting another white man until he reached California in 1536. In 1539 he had galloped across the prairies of Georgia and South Carolina with Hernando de Soto, Pizarro's famous cavalry leader, and together they had sailed down the Mississippi, arriving at the Mexican coast in September 1543, after a wild-goose chase lasting four years. He had accompanied the Franciscan missionary Marcos and his negro slave Estevan to the fabulous city of Cibola, capital of the Pueblo Indians, and to the Grand Canyon; he had seen vast herds of buffaloes on the virgin prairies, he had smoked the pipe of peace with the Indian chiefs and had worn eagle feathers in his hair and moccasins on his feet. He had sailed with Jacques Cartier up the St. Lawrence River; he had founded Quebec and Montreal; he had helped to discover Hudson Bay and had met whale hunters and fur traders. He had sailed with Drake, Hawkins and Raleigh and had drifted down the Mississippi with La Salle. In short, he had had a thousand adventures, and an endless chain of wild excitement.

He had found it impossible to fit all these fragments of adventures into a vast canvas—sometimes he had had only the vaguest notion where they had taken place. They had been like the pieces of a jigsaw puzzle, for the great American continent was still an amorphous mass of land, its coast-lines unmapped. How different it was with Africa! Its outlines had been known for a long time. The Black Continent fitted into the map and he could draw its contours with closed eyes. It was true that, apart from the coastal areas, not much was known even of Africa, for not even Dr. Olivier Dapper could fill in the huge gaps, though it was just that which spurred the lad's imagination all the more. Thus it was that the otherwise unruly son of the pastor Friedrich Georg Hornemann, minister of St. Andrea's Church in Hildesheim, was bent over his book as if spellbound.

The boy's father was a little disturbed about his son's passion for adventure. For generations the Hornemanns had been clergymen, and he could not imagine where his son Fritz had acquired this desire to find out about the unknown parts of the world, to travel among the heathen in foreign lands. With a heavy heart the father remembered the old German saying: 'Miller's beast and pastor's child, prosper rarely and often run wild.' But his son was a very serious boy. His teacher had told him that he was far and away the best pupil in the school in geography, and that his wealth of knowledge was astonishing. The Reverend Friedrich Georg Hornemann sighed deeply but let his son be. He knew himself for a very sick man and

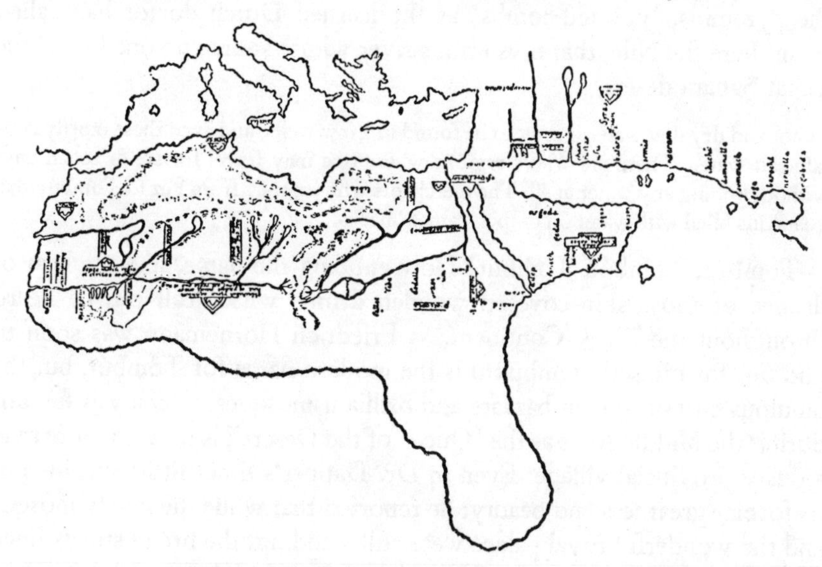

XXXIV. Portolano of Africa, dated 1351.

realizing that his days were numbered, he would have been glad to see his eldest son less wild and more inclined to follow father's footsteps. But God watched over everything; his fate and that of his son were in His hands.

Friedrich Konrad Hornemann's fate was cast on that Christmas Eve of 1784, when his godfather presented him with Olivier Dapper's book on Africa. From the moment he first opened the book till the last day of his short life, the dark continent was to retain its hold on our Fritz. Even as a child he succumbed to the magic charm of Africa. A few years later, having matriculated in the University of Göttingen as a student of theology, he went to call on the famous natural historian and physician Johann Friedrich Blumenbach of Göttingen, to ask for a recommendation to the recently founded Association for Promoting the Discovery of the Interior Parts of Africa, in London. He wanted to become a traveller and explorer.

But at the beginning of 1785, Friedrich Hornemann was only eleven years old, and his visit to Professor Blumenbach a long way off. At school the boy still had to contend with Latin and Pythagoras, but once his lessons were done he would open Olivier Dapper's book and sit breathless with excitement. He would study the map of North Africa, attached to the book, for hours on end. The Mediterranean, the African coast, the Strait of Gibraltar all were marked here. There was Alexandria, the proud old city, which twelve years later was to see him, disguised as an Arab, setting off into the unknown lands of the negroes. Here was Cairo, 'the most noble capital in the world, greater than Rome and Constantinople'; there the pyramids, 'pointed tombs' as the learned Dutch doctor had called them; here the Nile, that mysterious river whose source no one knew; the Great Sahara desert,

> so hot and dry that water is only to be found in a few wells, and even these mostly contain salt water. There are whole regions where one may travel for six or seven days without finding any water at all. The merchants who journey from Fez to Tombút load goatskins filled with water on to their camels' backs.

Tombút, Tombút, Tombút! How enticing the name, like the beat of drums, of those skin-covered wooden drums whose call can be heard throughout the Black Continent, as Friedrich Hornemann was soon to find out for himself. Timbuktu is the modern name for Tombút, but the fabulous city of golden bazaars and brilliant mosques, which was famous during the Middle Ages as the 'Queen of the Desert', is now no more than a dusty provincial village. Even in Dr. Dapper's times little remained of its former greatness and beauty: he reported that while the lovely mosque and the wonderful royal palace were still standing, the broad streets lined with fine houses had completely disappeared, and in their stead there were 'only small huts built of wood and clay and covered with straw'. Yet, he continued, the town was still as wealthy a trading centre as it had ever been.

This line on the map was the Niger, that river of secrets, which Hornemann was later to explore so thoroughly. The boy traced its course down to the sea where it branched out into four mouths: the Gambia, the Senegal, the Rio Grande and the Niger itself. A little inland, the mighty river crossed two large lakes and ran very close to the lower course of the Nile. Might they not be one and the same river?

Not even Dr. Olivier Dapper knew this for certain, although he had once travelled through those regions, and so on his maps he had left the question open, contenting himself with quoting the Arabian geographers of the Middle Ages:

> Amongst the many rivers which cross this region the most famous is the Niger. The Arab topographers claim that the Niger is a branch of the Nile, which first flowed underground to appear again later. Some even state that the Niger and the Nile come from one and the same source: because both have the same kind of fishes in them, and because there are hippopotami in both.

Nowadays this strikes us as rather far-fetched reasoning, yet the sages of antiquity, including the great Ptolemy, had made the same observations, and although Ptolemy had been proved wrong time after time in the course of the centuries, his authority was still unquestioned. Thus the exploration of Africa in modern times began with the riddle of the Niger.

2

Both classical times and the Middle Ages had quite clear ideas about large parts of the Black Continent, and this was very natural, for Africa was separated from Europe only by the Strait of Gibraltar. Its western shores, however, have few good natural harbours, and the extensive coral reefs, gigantic mangrove swamps and the wild Atlantic breakers had prevented all approach to this coast for a long time. Elsewhere, deep belts of desert had made progress into the interior impossible. Nevertheless a great number of voyages of discovery had taken place before the end of the fifteenth century.

The eastern shores were the first to be explored, and the earliest discoverers were the Pharaohs of the Old Kingdom who went there a few thousand years before the birth of Christ, probably to clear up the mystery of the yearly floodings of the Nile. When one realizes that the depth of water in the delta rises from about twenty inches at the end of May to about ten feet in July, and almost twenty-five feet at the beginning of October, it is easy to understand why the ancient Egyptians were eager to find the reason behind the rise and fall of its waters.

Unfortunately we know very little about these early explorations and, as is often the case with early history, we must rely on circumstantial evidence rather than on facts. One almost certain piece of evidence is the fact that Seth, one of the oldest Egyptian gods, who was held to be the patron deity of strangers, was always represented as having the head of an okapi. As is well known, this previously unknown animal was not discovered until 1900, and then in the impenetrable forests of the northern Congo. Its discovery made scientific headlines, for by rights this archaic creature ought not to have existed at all, its nearest relative, the samotherium, having already disappeared from the face of the earth during the Tertiary period. That it still existed was first suspected when the natives of the Congo were heard talking about a giraffe-like animal with horns and stripes on its flanks like a zebra. As the Egyptian god Seth had had an okapi head since the beginnings of the Old Kingdom, the Egyptians must have known of this strange beast since the most ancient of times.

At first this seemed to be out of the question for, as can be proved quite conclusively, the okapi could never have existed north of the Uele, one of the great tributaries of the Congo, for the huge jungle mass comes to an end here, and shade is essential for the okapi's existence. The adjoining region of the Nile swamps, which have never been covered by jungle, would be as insurmountable a barrier for this shy creature as savannahs or deserts. These simple facts rule out the possibility that the okapi could have come as far as the land of the Pharaohs. Are we justified in drawing the conclusion that, three or four thousand years before our era, Egyptian exploratory and trading expeditions had advanced as far as the Congo?

This question must be answered in the affirmative, not only because of the evidence provided by the okapi, but also for the following reason. The ancient Egyptians were probably familiar with the gorilla and certainly with the pygmy tribes of the swamps of the Nile. During Georg Schweinfurth's great expedition of 1870, he came across the pygmy tribe of the Akka, and immediately recalled a passage in Homer which had previously been thought to be purely mythological. At the beginning of Book III of the *Iliad* the great Greek poet wrote:

37. *Battle between pygmies and cranes.*

> When all were drawn up, each company under its own commander, the Trojans advanced with a shouting and a din like that of birds. They filled the air with clamour, like the cranes that fly from the onset of winter and the sudden rains and make for Ocean Stream with raucous cries to bring death and destruction to the Pigmies, launching their wicked onslaught from the morning sky.[1]

Naturally Homer did not witness these alleged fights between the pygmies and the cranes but he must have heard of them and he could *only* have done this in Egypt. Black-skinned pygmies had always been kept as slaves in ancient Egypt to serve as part of the temple ritual. Even Pepi II, a Pharaoh of the sixth dynasty who reigned in the middle of the third millennium B.C., kept black dwarfs at his court, and an inscription of Rameses the Great dating from approximately 1250 B.C. makes it clear that his age knew about the great swamps of the Upper Nile—a region that has only been rediscovered within the last two hundred years.

Thus the ancient Egyptians knew this part of Africa, but in order to have seen the okapi they must have penetrated even further south by 8 to 10° of latitude, i.e. roughly to the watershed between the Congo and the Nile and the volcanic chain north of Lake Kivu. The boundary of the Egyptian sphere of influence must have fallen approximately within this area. Until some time ago, when new evidence came to light, it was thought highly im-

[1] E. V. Rieu's translation (Penguin Classics, 1950).

probable that the Egyptians had crossed the Equator, but when Professor Heinrich Quiring of Berlin made a chemical analysis of cosmetics found in the tomb of an unknown princess of the sixth dynasty, i.e. about 2400 B.C., he discovered that her eyelash-paint contained evident traces of antimony.

Although this might appear to the layman to be completely irrelevant, it was a most important discovery, for it raised the question of where the Pharaohs of the Old Kingdom had obtained this rather rare element. The large Middle East deposits of antimony were only discovered many thousands of years later, and the Egyptian geologists of the time could not have had any knowledge of the deposits in Algeria and Morocco, which were only uncovered long after the decline of Egypt. The problem appeared insoluble, until Professor Quiring remembered that antimony could also be found far to the south in the dark continent, near the lower course of the Zambesi, and that it had been—and still is—mined, together with gold, in Selukwe, Que Que and Gwelo in Mashonaland in Rhodesia.

At once everything fitted into place. The gold-mines of Mashonaland are very ancient and probably had some connection with the Egyptian Pharaohs. In the famous 'Harris Papyrus', that 118-foot-long scroll in which Rameses IV recorded, in 1168 B.C., the great deeds of his father Rameses III, we can read that in 1180 B.C., Rameses the Great sent an expedition of ten thousand men to Punt. Thousands of years earlier, during the Old Kingdom, there had been reports of the Holy Land of Punt. Thus it is known that Sahura, the second Pharaoh of the fifth dynasty, who lived some centuries before the princess with whose make-up we are concerned, imported gold, silver, myrrh and costly woods from there into Egypt. Fifteen hundred years later, Princess Hatshepsut had sent a great expedition to Punt which had returned, after an absence of three years, heavily laden with treasure. At first Punt was thought to have been part of Somaliland, but doubts as to the correctness of this location soon sprang up. It was suggested that the holy land of Punt must have been near the deposits of antimony, i.e. not far from the Zambesi. Numerous mineshafts and galleries, some as much as 320 feet deep, together with smelting works and ovens and also extensive fortifications and palaces, were discovered throughout an area covering thousands of square miles. These finds have not yet been properly examined by expert archaeologists, but even the untrained eye can detect the fact that once upon a time mining and smelting had flourished in that area.

Who, apart from the Pharaohs, could have worked such an extensive mining enterprise?

Until the day that Quiring made his chemical analysis, such ideas had been based on conjecture alone, but with his discovery the pieces of the jigsaw puzzle began to fit together. It must be stated that Quiring's conclusions have not gone unchallenged. It has been pointed out that the distance by sea from the northern part of the Red Sea to the Zambesi is about 5,000 miles. One may well doubt that it was within the power of the ancient Egyptians to have travelled such a vast distance and, in any case, the voyage must have been made through the Strait of Bab-el-Mandeb, and this was only possible during the rather infrequent period when the power of the Sabeans, a rich seafaring people living in South Arabia, was at a low ebb. While the Egyptians might have travelled to the Zambesi by land, along what is nowadays called the 'Cape to Cairo Route', or else have started out up the Nile as far as Mongalla, some 5° north of the Equator, it is unlikely that the Pharaohs penetrated further south than the Equator. More than 1,250 miles of difficult country lay between the Equator and the gold and antimony of Mashonaland. These reasons, it was claimed, were sufficient to disprove Quiring's theory.

The missing proof came to light some years ago, when numerous cave and rock paintings of a fair race were discovered in Rhodesia and other regions of South Africa. At first these were attributed to the Bushmen, but it was soon realized that the polychrome and strikingly vigorous drawings must be much older. Professor Dart, who discovered the South African *Australopithecus*, or the 'Southern Ape', was the first to suggest that these paintings were contemporary with the Stone Age and depicted an invasion by a foreign race of white men coming from the north. Orthodox scientists dismissed Professor Dart as a dreamer and heaped ridicule upon his idea, just as they had done when he had claimed that his ape-man was the missing link. Then in 1929 the German Professor Leo Frobenius spent many months carefully examining the pictures Dart had seen and discovered many more in the process. Frobenius came to the same conclusion as Professor Dart, but again the 'experts' poured scorn on his ideas which clashed with accepted theories. Finally, the greatest living authority on prehistoric rock paintings, the Abbé Breuil, after having made a preliminary survey in 1929, decided to look at this problem more closely. He made countless expeditions between 1942 and 1952 and investigated hundreds of rock and cave paintings. He concluded that both Dart and Frobenius had been correct in their interpretation. The countless paintings of white men obviously belonging to the Mediterranean culture clearly proved that early European influences had in fact reached the south of Africa either by sea or along a route which might have led past the great lakes. To make doubly sure, the Abbé Breuil decided to submit the paintings to radio-carbon tests. The results of the tests proved beyond doubt that the majority of the paintings investigated by Frobenius, Dart and himself were very old indeed, dating back to about 1500 B.C., i.e. to the time of Princess Hatshepsut.

The radio-carbon test is based on the fact that every plant contains a given quantity of radio-active carbon in addition to ordinary carbon. Seeing that all living creatures absorb plant constituents directly or indirectly, radio-active carbon is found in men and animals, particularly in their bones and teeth. While they are alive, this substance is continually replenished, but naturally when they die they no longer absorb further radio-carbon and the amount in their bodies becomes reduced through continuous radiation. After twenty-five thousand years it disappears completely, leaving no trace at all in organic remains. However, up to this point in time, the percentage of radio-active carbon in a body, or in its skeletal remains, can tell us with a high degree of certainty when the body's metabolism had ceased, thus establishing the age of the bones. This method was discovered in 1950 by the American Dr. Willard Libby, and has since become so improved that we can tell from the ashes of old campfires when they were lit. The method also enables us to date prehistoric paintings, when their colours were produced from plant material. Similarly, with it, we can calculate the age of wooden or bone tools, remnants of building timber, wood-paved roads and dikes, and pieces of fabric or leather.

The Abbé Breuil had spent most of the preceding five years below ground in France, Spain, China and the Belgian Congo, examining the pictures on the walls of caves dating from the Ice or Stone Ages. He knew them like the palm of his hand, but these paintings of white men, in distant South Africa, were perhaps the most impressive of all. When he was interviewed by journalists, in 1952, on his return to Europe, he was still breathless with excitement and wonder:

> This is perhaps my greatest scientific triumph. On those walls, in the midst of darkest Africa, I saw the dance of 'white men'. Their skin was white, their hair red and they wore shoes and looked like men of the Mediterranean races. These pictures must have been made by natives to work magic spells, but such pictures are only effective in the natives' opinion if they are exact representations of the object over which they are to have power, and therefore we can take the correctness of the details, painted by those unknown coloured artists, for granted. There is no doubt that those white discoverers of prehistoric times looked just like the men represented in the paintings, dressed in trousers and shoes and decked with jewellery, and that they resembled the pictures of the members of the Mediterranean civilisations of Crete, Egypt and Asia Minor.

We must however be careful that we do not leap to unjustifiable conclusions and realize that we are basing ourselves, so to speak, on circumstantial evidence only. Possibly archaeology will one day give us incontrovertible proof of that tremendous trek through desert, jungle and swamp to the southern regions of Africa, but it is also possible that it will always remain a pure hypothesis, likely to have taken place, but still unproved. However, the glory of the Pharaohs will not be tarnished by the doubt cast upon this feat, for their captains accomplished a far greater exploit that was only to be repeated two thousand years later at the beginning of modern times: the circumnavigation of Africa.

This great voyage took place during the reign of the Pharaoh Necho II (609–594 B.C.) and we know of it from the Greek historian Herodotus, who wrote:

> The shape of Libya [Africa] shows that, save for the part that borders on Asia, it is surrounded on all sides by sea. The first to bring proof of this, as far as I know, was Pharaoh Necho of Egypt. When he ceased the digging of the canal which was to link the Nile with the Red Sea, he equipped an expedition and commanded it to sail round Libya through the Pillars of Hercules [Straits of Gibraltar], back into the Mediterranean, and so return to Egypt. Therefore the Phoenicians left port and sailed out of the Indian Ocean into the southern sea. When autumn fell, they landed, tilled the fields, and waited for the harvest, in whatever part of Libya they happened to be. When they had harvested the corn they sailed on, until, after two years, they sailed through the Pillars of Hercules, and so returned to Egypt again in the third year. They related, which I cannot myself believe, though perhaps some other may, that as they rounded Libya they beheld the sun on their right hand.

The two most significant parts of this passage are the beginning and the end, which refer to the geographical position of Africa. Herodotus appears to have known that this continent was surrounded by the ocean, though subsequent generations, including Ptolemy, the greatest astronomer and geographer of antiquity, thought that the Indian Ocean was an inland sea, that Africa curved towards the east, and that there was a direct bridge of land between Africa and eastern Asia. Ptolemy lived in Alexandria in Egypt at about A.D. 140, in the very country where it had been discovered that it was possible to sail round Africa, but it seems he had no knowledge of that feat, and it was only in 1487, when the Portuguese reached the Cape of Good Hope, that his authority was to be shaken.

This mistake, however, was perhaps less the fault of Ptolemy than of Herodotus himself, who, in the concluding sentence of the passage quoted, states that Necho's expedition had had the sun on the right side during its circumnavigation of Africa. This was bound to appear absurd to people living north of the Equator and even Herodotus, as we can see, was a little ashamed at retelling such nonsense, but as he took his vocation of historian and travel reporter very seriously, he thought it his duty to note down even those things which he himself considered false. This is what he did, adding that he himself knew better. But it is this very comment which suggests that Africa was in fact circumnavigated in very olden times, for if the ships of Necho's expedition sailed in a westerly direction, then, south of the Equator, the Sun must have appeared on the right, i.e. in the north. Thus the very reasons which made ancient geographers dismiss Herodotus's report as ridiculous, confirm its validity.

Admittedly, this voyage took place much too early for its importance to have been appreciated at the time, and we cannot even imagine what

Necho had in mind when he ordered his expedition to set out. Perhaps he was impelled by a disinterested curiosity about the geography of Africa, and though we are apt to consider such a thirst for knowledge more characteristic of modern ages, this must not be ruled out as a possibility. From their own experience, the Egyptians knew much about Africa and

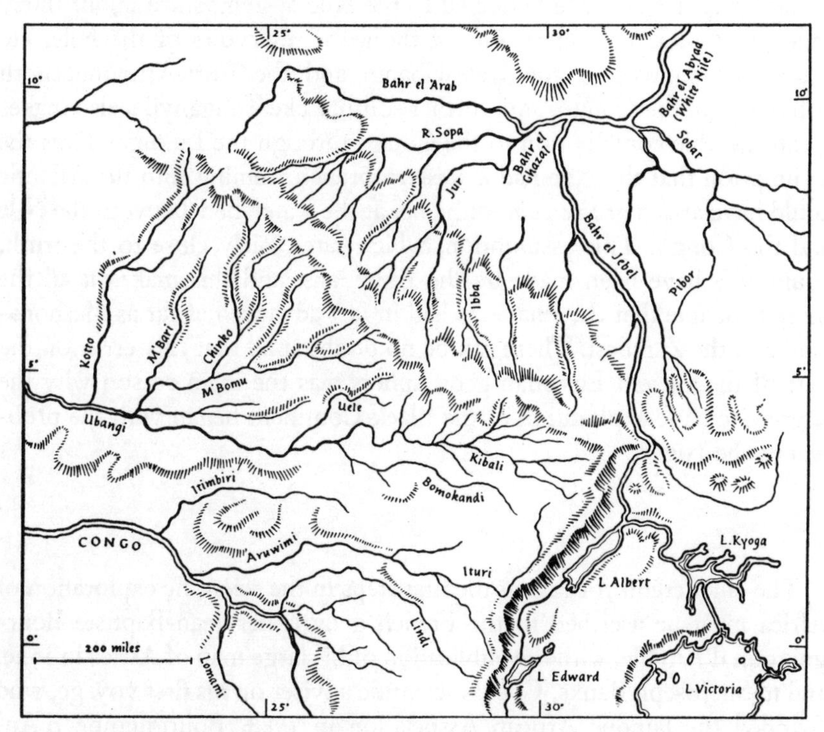

XXXV. The water-shed between the Nile and the Congo.

since, early on in their history, they had heard of a great ocean in the west, they probably wanted to find out as much as there was to be known about their continent. We know for certain that they were deeply interested in the vast lands on their southern borders. This is proved by their belief that the Nile had yet another main branch running from east to west and emptying in the distant western ocean. The Egyptians also thought that this 'other Nile' was responsible for the yearly floods. They imagined that persistent west winds stemmed its flow and drove tremendous masses of water into the river proper at its Mediterranean estuary, thus causing the river to flood its banks. It is clear that the desire to explain this flooding provided a great stimulus for exploration, and there can be no doubt that the Egyptians made attempts to solve the problem even in the very earliest times.

Until comparatively recently the notion of another branch of the Nile running from east to west was shared by most geographers, and the Niger was for long thought to be this other branch. This assumption was finally proved wrong, yet the very fact that it arose must be viewed as further evidence that Egyptian explorers advanced deep into central Africa and far across the Equator to the south. Not the Niger, but the Congo might well have belonged to the Nile system, since about thirty miles west of Lake Albert, one of the great reservoirs of the Nile, are found the sources of the Uele-Ubangi and the Ituri-Aruwimi, both tributaries of the Congo, and, further south, Lake Tanganyika also makes a considerable contribution to the Congo through the Lukuga. Thus the assumption that the Nile had a western branch running into the Atlantic could have arisen *at this point* only, i.e. at the watershed between the Nile and the Congo. This assumption, which came fairly close to the truth, could *only* have been made by the Egyptians, and this makes it all the more probable that the Pharaohs had in fact advanced as far as Mashonaland and the Zambesi. There can be no doubt at all that this error on the part of the ancient Egyptian geographers was the main reason why the later systematic exploration of the Black Continent began with the problem of the Niger.

3

The chief credit for taking the first steps in the scientific exploration of Africa must be ascribed to the French geographer Jean-Baptiste Bourguignon d'Anville, with the publication of his large map of Africa in 1749, and to Sir Joseph Banks, Cook's scientific adviser on his first voyage, who founded the famous African Association in 1788. Bourguignon d'Anville's map demonstrated that real knowledge of Africa was limited to the coastal areas and the Nile Valley, Egypt, Nubia, Abyssinia, Senegambia, around the Cape, and to the regions of the lower Congo and the lower Zambesi, but even in these parts the geographical horizon was very hazy, as can be seen from a glance at d'Anville's map: at once we realize that everything had been pushed towards the north-east; for example, Lake Chad and the area of the Niger had been so far displaced to the top right that the actual distances were cut by almost half. We can now understand why Tripoli, and even Cairo, were considered suitable starting-points for exploring the Niger.

When d'Anville's map of Africa first appeared, Joseph Banks was still a child. Even twenty years later, in 1769, when he joined Cook in his search for the *terra australis*, Africa did not occupy a very great place in his thoughts. This was to change when it became clear that the mysterious South Land did not exist, and that England had to look elsewhere for a substitute to replace the lost American colonies. Thus in 1788, Banks founded the African Association for Promoting the Discovery of the Interior Parts of Africa, and made the following comments, recorded in the *Proceedings*:

... notwithstanding the progress of discovery on the coasts and borders of that vast continent, the map of its interior is still but a wide extended blank on which the geographer ... has traced with a hesitating hand, a few names of unexplored rivers and of uncertain nations.

All this was to be changed by means of systematic explorations of the Black Continent by specially trained scientists. It was clear that the African Association was not indifferent to the 'most important advantage' which would result from the exploration of the unknown regions, the 'extension of trade and the furtherance of British industry'. Yet despite the mercantile stimulus, the Society was first and foremost a scientific association, and it was thanks to its efforts that Africa was so quickly to lose its reputation of being 'The Dark Continent'.

In 1795 the African Association chose the Scottish surgeon and botanist Mungo Park (1771–1806) as one of its first explorers. Park had already won his spurs in India, and on his return to England he had asked Sir Joseph Banks to use his services in Africa. The fact that not one of his four predecessors had returned from the Black Continent did not dismay the confident young man of twenty-four, and at the beginning of 1795 he set out towards the interior from Pisania, a small settlement at the mouth of the River Gambia. His instructions, as he himself has told us, were clear and explicit:

... I was directed, on my arrival in Africa, 'to pass on to the river Niger, either by the way of Bambouk, or by such other route as should be found most convenient — that I should ascertain the course, and, if possible, the rise and termination, of that river — that I should use my utmost exertions to visit the principal towns or cities in its neighbourhood, particularly Tombuctoo and Houssa — and that I should be afterwards at liberty to return to Europe, either by the way of the Gambia, or by such other route, as under all the then existing circumstances of my situation and prospects should appear to me to be most advisable'.

Although his instructions sound quite simple, when Mungo Park tried to join a caravan leaving Pisania for the interior, he met with resistance. The slave-traders, whose 'season' started with the beginning of winter, their merchandise lasting better in the cooler weather than in the heat of summer, were very suspicious of the white traveller and refused to take him along. In the end he had no option but to start out by himself with one horse, two donkeys and provisions for a few days.

The Europeans in Pisania thought they had seen the last of Mungo Park. He himself remained unperturbed, though it is true he was not particularly merry as the entries in his journal during the first stages of his march quite clearly show. After three weeks he met with his first difficulties. On

Christmas Day, 1795, when travelling through the kingdom of Kajaaga on the Senegal, he was stripped of all his possessions and left penniless. In utter despair he sat down under a tree and reflected on his position.

Towards the evening, as I was sitting upon the bentang chewing straws, an old female slave, passing by with a basket upon her head, asked me *if I had got my dinner*. As I thought she only laughed at me, I gave her no answer; but my boy, who was sitting close by, answered for me, and told her that the king's people had robbed me of all my

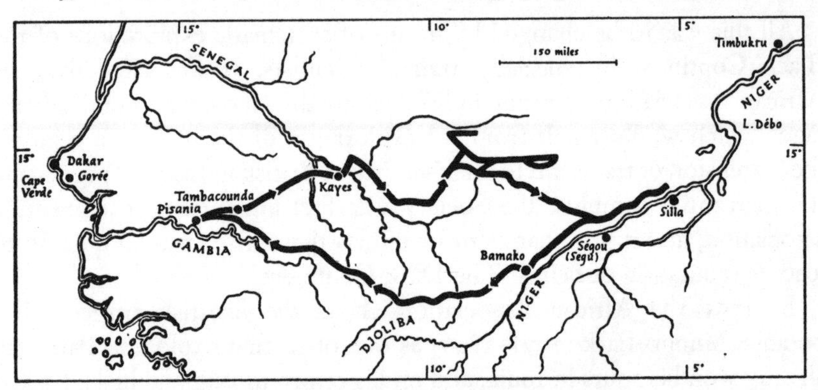

XXXVI. Map of Mungo Park's expedition.

money. On hearing this, the good old woman, with a look of unaffected benevolence, immediately took the basket from her head, and showing me that it contained ground nuts, asked me if I could eat them; being answered in the affirmative, she presented me with a few handfuls, and walked away, before I had time to thank her for this seasonable supply. This trifling circumstance gave me peculiar satisfaction. I reflected with pleasure on the conduct of this poor untutored slave, who, without examining into my character or circumstances, listened implicitly to the dictates of her own heart. Experience had taught her that hunger was painful, and her own distresses made her commiserate those of others.

Despite the hopeless position in which he found himself—without provisions, money, weapons, horse or donkeys—he did not give up, but continued on foot through the dense forests of Senegambia, across deserts, swamps and rugged mountain ranges, covering a distance which today means a few hours in a railway train. He then marched eastwards along the upper Senegal towards the Niger, but on his way was captured by soldiers of Sheik Ali, sovereign of Ludamar, and kept a close prisoner. Even now his courage did not desert him, nor his sense of humour, as can be seen from entries in his journal. He noted that the Arabs were entranced by the unknown but most sensible idea of buttons and buttonholes—perhaps as astonished as we were when we encountered the first zip-fasteners twenty-five years ago—and that they made him operate that magnificent invention time and time again. The ladies at the court of the Arabian ruler were full of the most intimate curiosity, and Mungo Park had to use his wits to get rid of them:

... In the evening (whether from the instigation of others, or impelled by their own ungovernable curiosity, or merely out of frolic, I cannot affirm), a party of them came into my hut, and gave me plainly to understand that the object of their visit was to ascertain, by actual inspection, whether the rite of circumcision extended to the Nazarenes (Christians), as well as to the followers of Mahomet. The reader will easily judge of my surprise at this unexpected declaration; and in order to avoid the proposed scrutiny, I thought it best to treat the business jocularly. I observed to them, that it was not customary in my country to give ocular demonstration in such cases, before so many beautiful women; but that if all of them would retire, except the young lady to whom I pointed (selecting the youngest and handsomest), I would satisfy her curiosity. The ladies enjoyed the jest, and went away laughing heartily; and the young damsel herself to whom I had given the preference (though she did not avail herself of the privilege of inspection), seemed no way displeased at the compliment; for she soon afterwards sent me some meal and milk for my supper.

From the European point of view the Arab ladies were singularly unbeautiful as all of them were inordinately fat, though this was how the Arabs liked their women to be. Just as today chromium-plated motor-cars, bejewelled and mink-coated wives or girl-friends are the accepted social signs of wealth, so in Africa fat wives proved the affluence of their lord and master. This is how Mungo Park describes the standards of feminine beauty in Africa:

The Moors have singular ideas of feminine perfection. The gracefulness of figure and motion, and a countenance enlivened by expression, are by no means essential points in their standard—with them corpulence and beauty appear to be terms nearly synonymous. A woman, of even moderate pretensions, must be one who cannot walk without a slave under each arm to support her; and a perfect beauty is a load for a camel. In consequence of this prevalent taste for unwieldiness of bulk, the Moorish ladies take great pains to acquire it early in life; and for this purpose many of the young girls are compelled, by their mothers, to devour a great quantity of kouskous, and drink a large bowl of camel's milk, every morning. It is of no importance whether the girl has an appetite or not—the kouskous and milk must be swallowed, and obedience is frequently enforced by blows. I have seen a poor girl sit crying, with the bowl at her lips, for more than an hour, and her mother, with a stick in her hand, watching her all the while, and using the stick without mercy, whenever she observed that her daughter was not swallowing. This singular practice, instead of producing indigestion and disease, soon covers the young lady with that degree of plumpness, which, in the eye of a Moor, is perfection itself.

At the beginning of July 1796, Mungo Park seized the opportunity of taking his horse and escaping from the Moors. It seemed an almost hopeless proposition to get away alive without help, money or adequate knowledge of the local language and to cross through regions which offered little more hope of salvation. On the other hand, to have remained with Ali, the Arab king of Ludamar, would have meant certain death for Mungo Park. Thus, like millions of prisoners before and after him, he preferred to risk the adventure of an almost hopeless flight.

The average voyager would have turned west, to the only region where help might have been found, but the young Scot did not even think of capitulation. His instructions were to find and explore the Niger and so he turned east-south-east towards this mysterious river. It was as if he were no longer master of his own will, for he took this path against his better judgement and all hope of salvation, yet the gods smiled upon the blind fool. During the first night of his flight when he was almost dying of thirst, a heavy thunderstorm broke, and he was able to suck the moisture from what scanty clothing the Moors had left him.

By the end of July 1796, Mungo Park found himself in the vicinity of Ségou, today a prominent town in West Africa. From here to the Joliba, the 'Great Water' as the Negroes called the Niger, was but a stone's throw. Although exhausted from his exertions of the last few months, the young Scot was unable to fall asleep that night. Next day, long before daylight, he saddled his horse and as the sun rose he rode down the river banks.

> . . . we rode together through some marshy ground, where, as I was anxiously looking around for the river, one of them called out, *Geo affilli!* ('See the water') and looking forwards, I saw with infinite pleasure the great object of my mission—the long-sought-for majestic Niger, glittering to the morning sun, as broad as the Thames at Westminster, and flowing slowly *to the eastward.* I hastened to the brink, and having drunk of the water, lifted up my fervent thanks in prayer to the Great Ruler of all things, for having thus far crowned my endeavours with success.

The italics in the above passage, which is part of the book he published shortly after his return, are Mungo Park's own. He explained them by continuing:

> The circumstance of the Niger's flowing towards the east, and its collateral points, did not however excite my surprise—for, although I had left Europe in great hesitation on this subject, and rather believed that it ran in the contrary direction, I had made such frequent inquiries during my progress concerning this river, and received from negroes of different nations such clear and decisive assurances that its general course was *towards the rising sun*, as scarce left any doubt in my mind. . . .

His account contains not a single proud or boastful word that *he*, a young man barely twenty-five years old, had finally solved a 2,000-year-old problem that had baffled geographers of all countries and of all times. He had settled that the Niger flows towards the east and could *not* therefore be that mysterious tributary of the Nile thought to empty into the Atlantic; it could *not* be the cause of the yearly floods and it could *not* be the Paradise River which led to the kingdom of Prester John. To make up for the admission that he had slept none too well during the night, Mungo Park adds a very dry and extremely boring description of the town of Ségou. He describes in detail its buildings, population, landing places and canoes, but gives not a word about himself, his own happiness and satisfaction.

Naturally the lone white man caused a great stir amongst the natives, and many councils were held at the Court of King Mansong to decide what to do with him. Finally it was planned to get rid of him at any cost, in order not to cause annoyance to the Arab slave-traders. The Chancellor of the Exchequer dipped deep into the Privy Purse and five thousand cowrie shells, which were legal tender there as in almost all regions of Central Africa, were handed to Mungo Park with the express request that he leave the country at once. Our Scotsman was delighted with this princely gift, which represented about a pound in the money of the time. With a hundred cowrie shells he could buy a day's food for himself and his horse, and so he had nothing to worry about for the next two months. Once more he reflected on whether he should continue or return. Now that he had discovered that the Niger flowed east, his mission was at an end and he could have called a halt to his expedition, particularly since the Arabs presented an ever-growing threat to his safety. The moment of indecision was soon past and Mungo Park turned his horse's head to the east, and to further adventure.

A few days later his horse stumbled and died from exhaustion. He himself was so weak and feverish that he could only drag himself along by sheer will-power. He managed nevertheless to continue a few days longer on a fishing-boat up to the immediate vicinity of Jenné, among the swamps of the middle Niger, but then his effort was spent. The rainy season had begun and the enmity of the Arabs increased daily—it was senseless to continue. In vain he tried to question the natives about the further course of the Niger. They were unable to understand his interest in the river and replied to his questions with their own: were there *no* rivers in his homeland, and was not one river as good as another? When he persisted, he found out that they did know something of the course of the river as far as Timbuktu but that there their knowledge stopped.

At the beginning of August 1796, Mungo Park began to retrace his steps against tremendous difficulties. The rainy season was at its height and the Niger had flooded its banks. For miles he had to wade knee-deep in water across savannahs which had but recently been dry. The natives had by now become almost openly hostile, for the Arab slave-traders were doing all in their power to get rid of this stranger who could only be in Africa for one reason—to intrigue against them and to steal their trade. Time and again the outlook was so black that anyone with less determination than Mungo Park would have given up in sheer despair.

He was to be saved by a pure stroke of luck. The headman of a small African village situated on the banks of the Niger discovered to his utter surprise that the ragged, half-starved white beggar, covered with running sores, was able to write. This village sage had already heard of the existence of white men, for in his youth he had been the slave of an Arab merchant, and he remembered that his master had always spoken of white men in tones of deep respect, as if they were supernatural beings. Thus the natives of the village begged Park to impart one of his magic formulas to them:

. . . when he heard that I was a Christian, he immediately thought of procuring a saphie, and for this purpose brought out his *walha*, or writing-board—assuring me, that he would dress me a supper of rice, if I would write him a saphie to protect him from wicked men. The proposal was of too great consequence to me to be refused. I therefore wrote the board full, from top to bottom, on both sides; and my landlord, to be certain of having the whole force of the charm, washed the writing from the board into a calabash with a little water, and having said a few prayers over it, drank this powerful draught; after which, lest a single word should escape, he licked the board until it was quite dry.

A saphie-writer is a most important personage, to be humoured, fed and helped in every possible way. His glory precedes him like a light, wherever he goes; thus Mungo Park found that life was much smoother for some time, even though the fever which had troubled him at the beginning of his expedition suddenly became so bad that he had to take to his bed. The kind-hearted Negroes took pity on him and cared for him for several months, until he was fit enough to join a caravan travelling westwards. Eight weeks later, in June 1797, he returned to Pisania after an absence of one and a half years. At first nobody recognized him, nor even believed him to be a white man. He had long been given up for lost like all those who had tried to penetrate the African jungle before him. When finally his identity was established as the Dr. Mungo Park who had set out eighteen months earlier, everyone wanted to shake him by the hand and congratulate him.

A few days before Christmas 1797, Mungo Park stepped ashore on British soil. His report to the African Association was published in book form two years later, and was soon translated into most languages. It proved to be an even better best-seller than *Robinson Crusoe*. The simple Scottish surgeon became famous overnight, but though he had no more financial worries, Europe could not hold him for long. He had succumbed to the magic of Africa; his soul was drawn to its immeasurable jungles, its wide plains and its deserts. In 1805, after seven long years of continual petitions, he was sent to Africa by the British Government to chart the course of the Niger. Unfortunately he did not live to accomplish his mission; in 1806, during a fight with hostile tribes, he fell in the rapids near Bussa in northern Nigeria and was drowned.

Mungo Park's great achievements can be summed up as follows: his first journey established the southern limit of the Sahara, and during his second voyage he found a route to the Sudan from the west. Apart from these concrete achievements he was the first man to bring more precise information about the Niger to Europe, though here he contributed to the spreading of a great error. He had found that the Niger flows eastwards, but he could not have known that not far from the place he reached the river makes a vast bend to the south. He had concluded that this mighty river continued to the east and somewhere joined one of the headstreams of the Congo. Vast sums of money and many lives were to be spent in rectifying this mistake.

4

One magical June morning in the year 1795, Johann Friedrich Blumenbach, Professor-in-Ordinary at the University of Göttingen, had been tempted out of his study into the garden. On the desk in his study were the first pages of the manuscript of his new work, his handbook on comparative anatomy and physiology. It was to appear nine years later, in 1804. Blumenbach, who was fifty-five years old at the time, was well aware how much work lay ahead of him, but the sun was so beautiful and the air so fresh that he was reluctant to return to his study. He strolled happily up and down between the box hedges, smelling the flowers and enjoying the sunshine.

At this moment, his maid Anne, a handsome country girl, came into the garden to announce that Friedrich Hornemann, a former student of theology at the University of Göttingen, requested the honour of an interview with the Professor on a matter of some importance.

Hornemann? Hornemann? Blumenbach strained his memory—did he know the name? Yes, indeed he did! He was the pastor's son from Hildesheim, the theology student who had registered for all his courses, and who had obviously studied science and medicine much more diligently than divinity. What on earth could the young man want? Blumenbach told his servant to show Herr Hornemann into his study, and slowly followed her into the house.

A tall, slim young man with clean-cut features, a small head and sparkling blue eyes entered his study. His fine sensitive fingers did not seem to correspond with his determined face and muscular frame. He had the hands of a scholar, of a writer, but his body was taut and sinewy like that of an athlete.

Blumenbach, the founder of comparative anatomy, registered all this automatically, and it took quite some time before he noticed what the young man was saying. A torrent of words was pouring out of the young man's mouth and the Professor had the utmost difficulty in following him. At last he pieced the story together: the young man had come all the way from Hanover to tell his old Professor that theology no longer satisfied him and that he wanted to become an explorer. Would the Professor please write to his old friend Sir Joseph Banks in London, that he knew of a young man ready to explore the Niger, the Sahara and the Nile?

Touched by the obvious sincerity of the young man, and knowing that he was no hot-head whose enthusiasm would wane after a few days, Blumenbach acceded to the young man's request and wrote to Sir Joseph that the young theologian who wanted to go to Africa 'seems to be born for an undertaking of this nature'.

There can be no doubt that Fritz Hornemann, whom we have already met as a child, was well fitted to become an explorer. In 1791, when he was almost nineteen years old, he had gone up to Göttingen, where he had studied theology for eight terms, and was about to take his degree. His father had died several years ago, and his mother was happy that she had been able to keep her eldest son at the University, thus assuring him of an honourable profession. But on the eve of his final examinations, Fritz Hornemann had kicked over the traces and had decided he did not want to be a parson but an explorer. At first his mother had been hurt by his decision, but her love for her son soon helped the wound to heal and she gave him her blessing. He went to see Professor Blumenbach to ask for a recommendation, and two years later in the middle of July 1797, left London via Paris and Marseilles for Cairo, the 'Capital of Africa'.

On the 22nd September 1797, at about the same time that Mungo Park was boarding the ship to bring him back to England, Hornemann arrived in Cairo. In his instructions the African Association had stated that he was to remain in Cairo for some time, and wait for the trading caravan proceeding to the Hausa states on the Niger via Fezzan. The young explorer had been at loggerheads with himself whether he should follow these instructions or not. While still in Paris, he had made the acquaintance of a Turkish grain merchant, resident in Tripoli, who had offered him letters of recommendation so that he could travel to Fezzan unmolested, just as if he were journeying from Paris to Marseilles, but he told him he ought to start from Tripoli, *not* from Cairo. The distance from Tripoli was only a quarter of that from Egypt!

The Turk of course did not know of d'Anville's map, which dated from 1749, nor that in 1790 the African Association had commissioned Major James Rennell to make a new and 'improved' map of Africa, which unfortunately was also rather inaccurate. Hornemann was carrying it in his pack and had studied it so carefully that he remembered every detail on it. According to this map, Cairo was as suitable a starting-point as Tripoli for a journey to Fezzan. Hornemann began to have his doubts about the accuracy of his map when he saw the Turk's obvious surprise at his intention of starting from Cairo, but had not William Young, the secretary of the African Association, made a point of telling him that this map 'had converted conjecture into knowledge'? After a few moments' reflection, Hornemann decided to follow his instructions and remain loyal to the Association. Thus he went to Cairo.

With all the enthusiasm of his twenty-five years, Friedrich Hornemann threw himself into the preparations for this expedition. His Turkish friend in Paris had given the young explorer a whole bundle of letters of recommendation to Arab business friends in Cairo, and they received Hornemann with great kindness. His preparations were almost completed and the young Hornemann was eager to get started when fate struck him a cruel blow: plague broke out in Cairo and the whole town was cordoned off so that no one could leave. This enforced quarantine lasted almost a year.

During this year of idleness, Hornemann had an extraordinary experience. One day, as he was strolling through the bazaars, a man who looked every inch an Arab suddenly uttered a coarse German curse. Hornemann questioned the man and found that, although the fellow had in fact been a Mohammedan for the last ten years, had been to Mecca three times and spoke and wrote Arabic as if it were his mother tongue, his real name was Joseph Freudenberg and he had been born in Cologne on the Rhine. The two Germans were soon deep in conversation, and it was not long before Freudenberg declared his readiness to accompany the young explorer to Murzuq, the capital of Fezzan, as his *dragoman*, his servant and interpreter.

It must have been this chance meeting which suggested to Hornemann that he should make his expedition disguised as an Arab merchant, for the idea only came to him in Cairo. On the 31st August 1798, he wrote to the African Association:

Commonly those who engage in an extraordinary enterprise, consider means yet more extraordinary, as requisite to the success of the undertaking: my opinion, and therewith procedure, will be founded on directly the contrary proposition. The plan which I have chalked out for my journey will be simple and easy to pursue. You shall have it in a single line: 'it is to travel as a Mahometan merchant of the caravan'! I am assured that under such character, I can travel with the same surety as the natives of the country.

Many of the caravan having been to Mecca, are aware that there are numbers of good Mussulmen from various countries who speak not Arabic, and who have different usages and customs; and thus simply attaining a knowledge of certain religious ceremonies and prayers, there is no difficulty in passing generally as a Mahomedan; for to a certain less equivocal criterion of a personal nature, the delicacy of the Mahomedan manners precludes any danger of enquiry.

The above argument was no doubt reasonable enough, provided of course that it was kept secret at all costs, and thus the young explorer hastened to add to his letter:

Pray write, and direct the English Consul at Tripoly, or elsewhere, never to make enquiry of me from the traders of Fezzan, and particularly when conveying any thing from me consigned to you. These people are of a jealous and inquisitive temper, and any inquiries made after me by a Christian might raise a thousand suspicions, and prove even of fatal consequence to me. Nay, should yourselves not hear from me these three years, make no inquiry.

This letter is preserved in the archives of the Royal Geographical Society in London. Its curiosity value lies not only in its content, although this was the first time that an explorer had conceived the idea of dressing and living like a native, but also in the fact that it bears the seal of the First Consul, Napoleon Bonaparte, whose couriers dispatched it to London. The story of how the letter reached London is as follows:

When the outbreak of plague had run its course and the period of quarantine was ended, Freudenberg took steps to find a caravan going to Fezzan, for the original caravan, which Hornemann had wanted to join, had pitched its tents outside plague-stricken Cairo and had of course departed long ago. Eventually Freudenberg made contact with another group of travellers, who were making ready to leave for Fezzan. In a short time he managed to complete all the preparations, but suddenly the French banking house to which Hornemann's letters of credit were addressed refused to let him have any money. They told him that Bonaparte had landed in Egypt and was approaching the gates of Cairo, and that under the circumstances they could not possibly honour a British letter of credit. They had not the slightest intention of exposing themselves to the danger of being closed and of having their capital confiscated for the sole reason that he, a mad German scientist, wanted to set off on some foolhardy scheme. He would have to be patient and wait for a few weeks.

Thus the second caravan also left without the young theologian. Hornemann was by now very angry, for patience had never been his greatest virtue, and as soon as Bonaparte entered the town Hornemann had himself announced. It was fourteen days before Napoleon found time to receive the young explorer who, by now, was beyond himself with fury, but Napoleon managed to bring him to his senses, and gallantly did everything in his power to help the young man; his papers were arranged, money was placed at his disposal, his letters were forwarded to London. On the 5th September 1798, young Hornemann left Cairo on the first part of his travels to the Niger.

By this time Mungo Park's accounts of his journeys had made it clear that the Niger could not possibly be a tributary of the Nile, and that it was vain to hope that the sea-route to India could be shortened by sailing down the Niger and the Nile across Africa. Napoleon knew these facts from his intelligence service and thus he preferred to consider the possibility of building a canal between the lower course of the Nile and the northern end of the Red Sea. Such a canal had once before been built by the Pharaohs of Egypt who had used it for thousands of years. Naturally,

Napoleon did not discuss this project with Hornemann, and so Hornemann entered upon his great adventure quite happily.

The first few days of the ancient caravan route from Cairo to Murzuq, which crossed some of the worst parts of the desert, were sufficient to bring home to Hornemann the many dangers that lay before him. Even in modern times, when distances that took caravans months to cover require only a week by car, we still have to contend with the same enemy—thirst. Hornemann was one of the first white men to see how the Arabs coped with this problem, and he made the following entry in his journal:

> The water collected for the use of the caravans is carried in bags made of goatskins, unripped in the middle, and stripped from the animal as entire as possible; those made at Soudan are the strongest and best; water may be preserved in them for five days, without acquiring a bad taste, the bags of an inferior manufacture give an ill taste, and a smell of the leather, from the second day. To render the skins flexible and lasting, they are greased on the inside with butter, and by the Arabs sometimes with oil, which latter gives quickly a rancid taste, and to any but an Arab, renders the water scarcely fit for drinking.

Hornemann did not have great difficulty in overcoming the discomforts of a desert journey. Usually he kept to the rear of the caravan in order to take a good look round and make a survey of the country, though he had to be extremely careful not to arouse any suspicion. He could keep his curiosity in check while the caravan was crossing monotonous expanses of desert, but found his rôle of ordinary Arab merchant difficult to play when they reached the Siwa Oasis, where, two thousand years earlier, Alexander the Great had consulted the oracle. The next white man to visit the spot had been William George Brown, who had crossed the desert just seven years earlier than Hornemann. Brown had reported that when he had wished to investigate the strange ruins that stood there, he had been driven away by the hostile attitude of the inhabitants. Hornemann too was curious to inspect these ruins at close quarters:

> As we approached the spot destined for our encampment in Vale of Siwah, I descried to the westward some ruins of an extensive building, a few miles distant from the road, and concluded them to be the same as noticed by a late English traveller (Mr. Brown). . . . I accosted some men working in the gardens near, and questioning them as to what they knew of this building, they answered that in former times Siwah was inhabited by infidels. One spokesman, pointing to a building in the centre, said 'tradition tells us, *that edifice* was the hall in which the divan used to assemble; at the time of its construction men were stronger than I am; for those huge stones serving as roof to the fabric, were lifted up and placed there by two men only: there is much gold buried under the walls'. When I then entered into the ruins I was followed by all the people near, and thus prevented examining the place with any accuracy. On a second visit I was not more successful; and when after a few days I returned thither again, some Siwahans directly said to me: 'thou undoubtedly are yet a Christian in thy heart, else why come so often to visit these works of infidels?' In order to maintain the character I had assumed, I was thus necessitated . . . to restrict myself to general observations.

This was by far the wisest course, for the other members of the caravan were beginning to make remarks about the two Germans, whose light skins made them stand out. It was even rumoured that they might be spies of the *giaours*, the infidel dogs. A few days later, as the caravan was about to leave Siwa, the position of the two Germans became critical and it was only the unshakeable equanimity of Hornemann that saved the day. They were just setting out, when the local inhabitants suddenly took up a hostile attitude. The leaders of the caravan and the headman of the village held council together and the situation did not bode well for the two Germans:

During all this time I remained quiet with my baggage, having sent my interpreter to collect intelligence of what was passing. Seeing him return and judging from his manner and haste that he had something of importance to communicate, I ran to meet him. He immediately accosted me with 'Cursed be the moment when I determined upon this journey; we are both unavoidably lost men; they take us for Christians and spies and will assuredly put us to death.' With these words he left me and ran to the baggage where he exchanged his single gun for my double-barrelled one, and armed himself with two braces of pistols. I upbraided him with his want of firmness, told him 'a steady and resolute conduct could alone preserve ourselves and friends; and reminded him that his present behaviour was precisely such as to give weight to the suspicions entertained'. I further urged 'that on his own account he had nothing to fear, having for 12 years been a Mahomedan, and perfectly acquainted with the religion and customs; that myself alone was in danger, and that I hoped to avert it, provided *he* did not intermeddle with my defence'. 'Friend (answered he) you will never hear of danger, but this time you will pay for your temerity.' Perceiving that terror had wholly deprived him of the necessary temper and recollection, I now left him to himself and walked up unarmed, but with a firm and manly step, to this tumultuous assembly. I entered the circle and offered the Mahometan salutation 'Assulam Alekum', but none of the Siwahans returned it. Some of them immediately exclaimed—'You are of the new Christians from Cairo and come to explore our country.' Had I at this time been as well acquainted with Mahometan fanaticism, and the character of the Arabs, as I have been since, I should have deduced my defence from the very terms of the accusation, and stated that I was indeed from Cairo, having fled from the Infidels; as it was, I answered nothing to this general clamour, but sat down and directed my speech to one of the chiefs whose great influence I knew, and who had been often in my tent while at Siwah. 'Tell me, brother (said I), hast thou ever before known 300 armed men to take a journey of three days, in pursuit of two men who dwelt in their midst for ten days, who had eaten and drank with them as friends, and whose tents were open to them all? Thyself has found us praying and reading the Koran; and now thou sayest we are Infidels from Cairo, that is, one of those from whom we fly! Dost thou not know that it is a great sin to tell one of the faithful that he is a Pagan?' I spoke this with an earnest and resolute tone, and many of the congregation seemed won over by it. . . . I was then asked for what purpose we carried Christian papers. I now found that my interpreter had unwarily shown a passport which I had obtained from General Bonaparte with a view not to be detained at the French posts through which I was to pass to the caravan. . . . I answered 'that we did not understand what it contained, but were told that it would allow us to quit Cairo without being molested'. 'This is the book (interrupted my interpreter, who had meanwhile come up) which I understand', and immediately took the Koran. . . . We were ordered, by reading in it, to give proof of our being truly of the religion. Our learning in this respect went far indeed beyond the simple ability of reading. My companion knew the entire Koran by heart, and as for me, I could even then write Arabic, and well too, which with these people was an extraordinary proficiency in learning. We had scarcely given them a sample of our respective talents when the chiefs of our caravan, who to this moment had been silent, loudly took our part, and many of the Siwahans, too, interfered in our favour. In short, the inquiry ended to our complete advantage, though not without the murmuring of some in the multitude who lost the hopes of plunder which the occasion might have afforded.

38. View of Murzuq.

On the 17th November, the caravan finally reached Murzuq, after stopping at the Aujila and Zuila oases. At the time Murzuq was an important trading centre but today the town is of little importance. Trade now follows a different route. Thus while the one-time village of Sebha, less than a hundred miles to the north, now has an aerodrome and is connected with the sea by good roads, the former magnificent capital of Fezzan has fallen into oblivion. Hornemann believed that he had so far covered about half the distance to the Niger. As the caravan routes to the south were infested with robbers, he had to remain in Murzuq for some months, gathering a great deal of important information about such topics as meteorological conditions, local customs and trade. He knew too much about the mercantile leanings of the African Association to omit the latter item.

The commerce in Fezzan is considerable but consists merely of foreign merchandise. From October to February Mourzouk is the great market and place of resort for various great caravans from Cairo, Bengasi, Tripoly, Gadames, Twat and Soudan, and for other smaller troups of traders such as the Tibboes, Rschade, Twaricks and Arabs.

Hornemann gave a list of the goods bought and sold and what regions they came from. He probably smiled to himself when he thought of the interest this part of his letter would arouse in London. A camel-load of English calico, cotton cloth, muslin and silk materials, perfumes, gun-flints, pickaxes, fine wool, soap, sugar, tea, salt, vinegar, pocket-knives, scissors, mirrors and antimony for eye make-up fetched about thirty pounds in Murzuq. If the cargo could be carried safely across the Sahara to the Sudan, it could be sold, after deduction of all expenses, for about a hundred pounds. This represented a clear profit of some 200 per cent and was more than sufficient reason for investigating the route through the great desert most carefully. What is more, this calculation was on the conservative side, and other reports spoke of much higher profits still. For instance, the Englishman William George Brown, who had travelled in 1796 with a large trading caravan from the eastern Sudan right across the desert to Asyut on the lower Nile, had estimated the value of the 'living and dead merchandise' carried by the caravan at about £115,000. The Arab geographers of the Middle Ages went even further than this, and gave almost astronomical figures for the caravans of ten to twelve thousand camels, travelling between Cairo and the upper Nile. Even allowing for those deductions which every merchant incurs in doing business in the Orient, the margin of profit that remained was so great that it could not be rivalled anywhere in the world. We have already emphasized that the profit motive was not the prime consideration of the members of the African Association, but nevertheless they must have been influenced by it to some extent.

5

The same information had already reached Europe three hundred and fifty years earlier, but the man responsible had been neither a geographer nor an explorer. He had not travelled through the desert in order to solve the problem of the Niger, but had endured thirst and discomfort in order to find gold. He did not even do this on his own initiative but on the orders of the Genoese banking house, the Centurione, which, with its branches in Genoa, Caffa in the Crimea, Majorca, Lisbon, Rouen, Antwerp, Bruges and Bristol, had enjoyed a world-wide reputation in the middle of the fifteenth century.

In 1447, the Centurione had approached the most successful prospector of the time, the Genoese Antonio Malfante, for business was in a bad state. Owing to many different factors, such as the rapid flow of precious metals to the Orient, the political upheavals brought by the fifteenth century, i.e. the Hundred Years War between France and England, the incessant strife in Germany and the struggles with the Turks, international monetary arrangements were completely out of gear. Everywhere the value of money was falling and only 'real values' counted, inflationary tendencies were appearing everywhere and European trade relations were maintained with the utmost difficulty by clearing-house arrangements.

This state of affairs was disastrous for the great banking houses. Concern at the situation seems to have been most manifest in highly capitalistic northern Italy. In 1447, Genoa, under the influence of the Centurione, decided to introduce the gold standard. As a logical sequence to this decision, the Centurione suggested to Antonio Malfante in the same year that he should go to the Sahara to determine the true source of the gold which the kings of the Black Continent had put into circulation so generously, and whether there was any chance of taking a direct hand in the sale or production of gold.

Malfante asked for time to think it over, but within a few days of receiving the offer, he accepted and in autumn, 1447, when the summer's heat was over, he sailed across the Mediterranean to Africa. He advanced as far as the Tuat oases in the northern Sahara, and some weeks later he reported by letter that no gold whatever was produced in the great desert. The fact that great quantities of gold were circulating in that region was due to the presence of salt there, which, because it was lacking in large parts of tropical Africa, was precious enough to be bartered for gold. The gold itself came from the south, unattainably far away, and was in firm hands. He added that in spite of his being a Christian and a European he had encountered no hostility in the Tuat oases—surprisingly, it must be added—but he knew that the Arabs engaged in the gold trade watched jealously over their interests and that it would be pointless to establish a branch of the Centurione in Tuat.

Thus the ingenious idea of the Italian banking house came to naught, but the fact that such an expedition could be carried out at all proves that North Africa, despite its impassable deserts, was by no means a completely unknown area. It had been crossed by caravans, at least since the Middle Ages and probably even during classical times, along four great trade routes connecting the south with Egypt and the Mediterranean. The oldest of these, the 'Road of the Oases', was known to the Pharaohs, and recently the French explorer, Frison-Roche, has suggested that Solomon had already used it to transport gold and precious woods for his temple. This 'Road of the Oases' begins in Asyut in upper Egypt, and runs through El Fasher in the Darfur district to Bornu and Lake Chad, where it joins the roads leading to the south. The Arabs later called this route 'The Road of the Forty Days' and used it to fetch ostrich feathers, pepper, ivory, ebony, slaves and gold.

There are three routes from the north, that is from the Mediterranean and Europe. The eastern starts in Tripoli and runs via Murzuq and Bilma to Bornu; the central one starts from Syrtis Minor and leads via Gadamès, Gat and Agadès to Katsina and Kano, and finally the western, east of Tafilalet, connects the route from Fez and Morocco with the salt mines of Taudeni and with the mighty trading metropolis on the Niger, the rich town of Timbuktu.

All these routes are strewn with the bones of men and animals who have fallen on the way. Those who travel through deserts must allow the deserts their toll. In spite of the dangers and difficulties, giant caravans wended their weary way year after year carrying salt to the south and gold to the north. As Islam spread through North Africa and Spain, so the number of the faithful travelling to Mecca increased. These pilgrims used the old caravan routes and we have detailed reports about their excursions across the desert from various sources, including Ali Masudi, an Arab writer of the early tenth century, and Edrisi, the greatest Moorish geographer of the Middle Ages, who engraved a map of the world on a silver plate while at the court of the Norman prince Roger II of Sicily.

It seems that Africa was accessible even at that time to white men, since Ibn Batuta, the great Arab traveller, reported in 1354 when describing his two-year journey to Timbuktu, Gao and Tuat, that white Christians called *Nazareni* were living in the large cities near the Niger and were allowed to be innkeepers. Fifty years later, Anselm d'Ysalguier, the well-known French physician and naturalist from Toulouse, had managed to advance as far as the great trading city of Gao on the Niger during one of his journeys. It is quite certain that the Frenchman was not the only one to have travelled in the Black Continent before the beginning of the later systematic and scientific explorations. Since, however, voyages of discovery were neither of great interest nor of great importance at the time, they were not recorded in the great book of history. Thus we know little about d'Ysalguier's travels. From time to time faded manuscripts, accidentally preserved, are discovered, giving clues to events that we know little or nothing about. Thus, for instance, we have a chance report dating from the 1570's from the hand of the otherwise unknown Florentine merchant Benedetto Dei, in which he tells us—*en passant*!—that in 1470 he travelled to Timbuktu, 'a town in the kingdom of the Berbers'. This is all the more remarkable since the next European report of Timbuktu is dated 1826, and is an account of the journey made by the Scottish explorer Alexander Gordon Laing to the 'Queen of the Sahara'. Until that time Timbuktu had been as inaccessible for Christians as Mecca itself. At the time of Benedetto Dei, things seem to have been much easier, for the Florentine does not give the impression that his journey was in any way surprising. Geographical questions do not seem to have interested him at all, and instead of giving us any information about the route he followed or about travelling conditions, he merely tells us that thick materials from Lombardy were much sought after in Timbuktu. Since Benedetto Dei was by no means reticent in his report about his business successes, we can only conclude from his lack of interest in what would seem to have been a great feat, that Timbuktu was a well-known caravan station at the time, and that it would have been a waste of time to speak of it in greater detail. Our information about these early visits to Africa derives from documents discovered during the last four or five centuries, but in Hornemann's time no one had the slightest inkling that North Africa, and the great desert in particular, had once been frequently visited by white people. Thus the young German explorer was deceived into believing that he was the first white man to arrive in those parts.

Once in Murzuq, he decided to continue to Tripoli in order to write down his experiences and the findings which he had already jotted down in short cryptic phrases. The next part of his expedition would take him to the Niger and to Timbuktu, and it was by no means out of the question that he would meet with death. He felt the need to dispatch his journals as soon as possible so that they should not be lost with him if he were to be killed. He reached Tripoli in the middle of August 1799, and saw to it that his material came into the hands of the British Consul. Even here, under the eyes of the British diplomat and within his sphere of influence, Hornemann continued to play the rôle of the Turkish merchant Musa ben Yussuf so well that the Pasha of Tripoli granted him a passport and letter of recommendation in which he was referred to as one of the Pasha's own men. After the terrible massacre of Christians which had taken place throughout North Africa as a reprisal for the French conquest of Cairo, Hornemann knew only too well that he would have to be doubly careful if he was ever to reach his goal. He realized that he had been too optimistic and rash in the beginning and could now see the real extent of his difficulties. At the beginning of December 1799, before leaving Tripoli, he asked the British consul during a secret visit not to make inquiries about him until three years had passed. Mr. Hooper, the consul, agreed, for he realized that any inquiry might endanger the life of this adventurous young German, a life which would in any case be hanging by a thread during the following months and years. He took leave of this young man firmly convinced that no one was ever to hear from him again.

Mr. Hooper was to be proved right, but before our former theologian was called into the arms of that God whose service he had renounced some years earlier, he was granted his dearest wish: to see Timbuktu, the mysterious Queen of the African desert, and the Niger, that secret Stream of Kings. For all we know Hornemann might even have reached Lake Chad; at least this is what the natives asserted twenty years later when the African Association managed to make detailed inquiries. What really happened to Hornemann will never be known. Probably he died of dysentery in 1801.

Thus the divinity student from Hanover was one of the pioneers preparing the path for those who were to follow later. Perhaps we should add that his times were not yet ripe for the knowledge he had gathered. Merchants were still contented with exploiting a narrow strip of land around the coast. It was the nineteenth century that saw the age of expeditions to the interior—these coincided with the period when the social needs of Europe were making the export of men imperative. It was at this time also that America was truly discovered—before this time it had merely been found. The exploration of Africa, which previously had been a mercantile enticement and a purely scientific problem, had become a pressing necessity. That Friedrich Hornemann had made his exploration before the moment of necessity arose does not detract from his glory. He stands next to Mungo Park as the greatest of the first African explorers, and is a worthy predecessor of those countless travellers whom the African wilderness has called into its darkest reaches.

6

The African Association had had few successes so far. Apart from Mungo Park, none of its explorers had managed to return from Africa. When Hornemann, too, remained silent after the dispatches received from Tripoli, it was realized that he had become yet another victim of the dark continent, and Mungo Park was sent out for the second time to the Niger in 1805. Our Scot was beside himself with joy, and was determined this time to follow the Niger to its mouth. In one of his last letters he wrote: 'I commend myself to the mercy of the Niger with the firm resolution either to discover its mouth or else to perish in the attempt. May the river be my grave if I do not reach the aim of my voyage.' This was strangely prophetic, as was later discovered, for Mungo Park was drowned in the Niger. At the time, England was far too busy to worry about missing explorers in Africa, for its energies were taken up by the struggle against Napoleon. It was only in 1816 that an expedition under the leadership of Major Gray was sent out to make inquiries about Mungo Park.

A member of this expedition, or more precisely one of its reserves, was a strange young man named René Caillié. He was just seventeen years old, and came from the village of Mauzé in the province of Poitou. His father, a baker's assistant, had been sent to prison for some petty larceny which he probably did not commit. This spelt disgrace for honest families, and was probably the reason why young René liked to daydream himself away from the hateful narrow-mindedness of his village. Later, when he was a famous man, he had this to say about his youth:

As soon as I could read and write I was taught a trade. I quickly grew tired of it and spent all my time reading books of travel. I borrowed geographical works and maps. The map of Africa, on which I could see nothing but blank areas, described as unexplored, excited my fantasy more than all the others. This hobby grew into a passion, for the sake of which I gladly renounced everything else.

In fact this seventeen-year-old boy was in the grip of such a passion that we can only call it an obsession. He ran away from home one day without any money or the prospect of help and signed on as a cabin-boy. He deserted his ship in Senegal and hired himself out to a half-breed who was organizing an auxiliary force for Gray's expedition.

This first attempt to become an explorer met with failure. Caillié became so feverish that, to regain his health, he had to be sent back post-haste to France. He stayed in France for about seven years, but in 1824 he was back in Africa. Fired by the ambition to reach Timbuktu and convinced that the 'Queen of the Desert' could never be reached except by posing as an Arab, he began to learn Arabic with fanatical zeal. When he could speak it as well as French, he reported to the authorities and requested help for an expedition to Timbuktu.

Naturally he had no success whatsoever, naturally they laughed at him, and naturally he had not the slightest intention of giving up. He applied to the Governor of the British colony of Sierra Leone, and was given an unexpectedly kind hearing. The English generously gave the young man, obsessed with Africa, a position with a salary of 3,600 francs. They intended to give every chance to this young adventurer, who with his dark hair and dark eyes looked like an Arab, who spoke Arabic fluently and who knew the Koran by heart.

Within a year Caillié managed to save two thousand francs. He wrote triumphantly: 'This is such a large sum of money that with it I shall be able to travel to the ends of the world!' At the same time he read in the newspapers that the Parisian Geographical Society had offered a reward of two thousand francs to the first French explorer to reach Timbuktu and to bring back positive reports from Central Africa.

Caillié did not waste a single day. In the middle of April 1827, he set out by himself with nothing but his savings in his pocket. He started from Kakondy in Sierra Leone on a great voyage through the desert. The journey was a nightmare for the obsessed young man. His means were soon exhausted and fever and scurvy laid him low. At one point he lay by the roadside for days in terrible pain, but he pulled himself along with grim determination and almost a year after his departure, on the 20th April 1828, he reached Timbuktu, having travelled by way of the still-unknown mountainous country of the Futa Jalon Hills and the upper Niger. He was exhausted beyond description, both physically and mentally, and later on confessed:

I longed for nothing more than death. I asked of God, in whom I had placed all my confidence, to let me die confident of a happier life in the beyond.

This complete collapse was probably not only the result of his great exertions, but was almost certainly due also to the terrible disappointment which awaited him in Timbuktu. He learned that he was not the first white man to have entered the city, the Scotsman Alexander Gordon Laing

39. Timbuktu.

having preceded him by two years. Laing had reached Timbuktu by way of the Gadamès and Tuat groups of oases and the Niger. Caillié, who was taken for an escaped Egyptian prisoner of the French, heard this quite by the way. He was also told that that Christian dog had been a spy who had been beaten to death. This tragic story made a deep impression on Caillié. His aspirations, the privations he had borne, the hopes he had cherished—all had come to naught since another had won the race to Timbuktu. True the poor devil had not tasted of the fruits of his victory, and if he himself should ever manage to see Europe again he would at least be the first to have *returned* from Timbuktu; but this was poor consolation.

That night he tossed sleepless in his bed at the miserable inn. Glistening mosques with golden roofs danced before his eyes—he could only have missed them because it was already getting dark when he entered the city. The romantic bazaars, which housed all the world's treasures and where people from the strangest countries in the world could be found, together with the palaces of the Viziers, the monasteries and libraries of the Koran scholars from Fez and Cairo, were sure to lie in another quarter of the town. Again and again the old Arab saying went through his head: 'Gold cometh from the south, salt from the north, but words of wit and wisdom from Timbuktu.'

Our explorer did not suspect that this saying was anything but old, and that it was merely another example of Oriental exaggeration. It was probably due to the Moorish historian and geographer Hassan ibn Mohammed el-Wassan, a native of Granada, who after his, probably not quite voluntary, conversion to Christianity, had adopted the name of Leo Africanus at the Court of Pope Leo X, and had given the following description of Timbuktu in 1520:

> The town of Timbuktu presents a wonderful sight, merchants and artists live there in great numbers, and the inhabitants are very rich. . . . Numerous fountains provide fresh water and there is no lack of grain and livestock. . . . The king has a very distinguished and courtly bearing. Whenever he rides out, he mounts a camel and is preceded by nobles; all his warriors ride on horseback. He has three thousand mounted men and very many foot-soldiers, armed with poisoned arrows and constantly in readiness. . . . In Timbuktu there are also very many scholars, who are aided by the king. Countless manuscripts and books are imported from foreign lands, and not infrequently more money is spent on these than on all the other imports counted together.

Prisoners in hostile, or at least in foreign, lands usually see their own homes in the most glowing colours, since this helps to keep their spirits up. Furthermore, experience has taught us that those who are called upon to give information are particularly liable to exaggerate both the good and the evil. Thus the golden halo about Timbuktu is probably due to the influence of Leo Africanus. It was to lure travellers right up to the time of Heinrich Barth.

The glory of Timbuktu, which had undoubtedly been real at an earlier epoch, was probably due to the radiance of a unique personality. In 1493, the Negro state of Melli, which included this trading city on the Niger, fell under the sovereignty of Askia Mohammed Ture, king of Gao. The new ruler, who loved pomp and splendour as much as the Mandingu tribe, the owners of Timbuktu during the past hundred and fifty years, lavished the gold of the state treasury unstintingly on the town and its inhabitants. When Mansa Musa, the greatest king of the Mandingu, had gone on a pilgrimage to Mecca in 1324, his expenditure had been so magnificent that the price of gold had dropped to rock bottom in Egypt and Arabia. Askia Mohammed Ture did not wish to go down to history as less magnificent. Between 1495 and 1497 he too went to Mecca, and took three hundred thousand ducats for travelling expenses. But this did not suffice, and another hundred and fifty thousand ducats had to be added. The expenditure was well worth it, for just as Melli and Timbuktu had become famous throughout Arabia under the rule of Mansa Musa, so their glory was revived under Askia Mohammed Ture. Artists, merchants and scholars came in throngs to take up residence in the town, Askia Mohammed Ture himself was appointed the Caliph's plenipotentiary in the Sudan, and Leo Africanus wrote of his rule:

In his time the wealth of a man was assessed by the number of his books as well as by the horses in his stables.

Caillié, of course, had known nothing of this, and the following morning brought him a painful awakening. There was no 'Queen of the Desert'; Timbuktu was not in the least like the glamorous cities of *The Arabian Nights*. Deeply disappointed he noted in his journal:

When my first enthusiasm at reaching Timbuktu had died down, I had to admit that something quite different to my expectations lay before me. The town consisted of nothing but badly built houses of clay, surrounded by yellowish-white shifting sands. The streets were monotonous and melancholic like the desert. No birds could be heard singing from the roof-tops. Nevertheless it was a marvellous sight to see so large a city in the middle of the desert, and I had to admire the exertions of its founders to erect it.

This verdict is doubtless a little harsh and resembles that of a bachelor who discovers that his beloved is by no means as fair as she was in the photograph in the marriage bureau, but the description of Timbuktu in modern guide books is not much more encouraging. The writer usually stresses the cool shade of the narrow alleys, the small artificial lakes in the botanical gardens, and the buildings of the military and civil authorities—but that is all. If the great salt caravans with many thousands of camels did not pass Timbuktu twice yearly on their journeys to the south—*une vue très curieuse*—little more than 'the monotony and melancholy of the desert' would have remained.

Caillié could not have foreseen the subsequent importance of Timbuktu for the French, who sixty-six years later, under the command of a certain Major Joffre, were to conquer the town in bloody battle. Caillié stayed only fourteen days and on the 4th May 1828 he joined a large caravan of 1,400 camels going north. Its route lay across one of the most desolate parts of the Sahara, a region which was only opened up to motor transport in 1935, and where even today no tourist traffic of any kind is known. Only a few days after leaving Timbuktu, the last traces of vegetation ceased, yielding place to the desert which stretched fully twelve hundred miles to the north as far as the Mediterranean.

Caillié knelt down in reverence before the Almighty:

As soon as the desert began, I fell on my knees, following the example of the pious Muslims, but unlike them I prayed to the God of the Christians. My eyes were turned towards the north, my motherland, my family and my friends, and I besought God to lighten my burden. In the fervour of my desire, I imagined that my prayer had been heard and that I should be the first European to have crossed this ocean of sand from the south. This thought strengthened me. While all other faces showed signs of sorrow and sadness, mine was glowing with hope and joy. Heartened by these feelings, I swung up on my camel to overtake my companions and be the first to enter upon the desert separating the fertile Sudan from the North African regions.

Caillié had to pay for this privilege with terrible privations. Their rate of progress being slow—at best two and a half miles an hour—water soon became scarce. Since it was known that the alleged Egyptian was without any means, he was left to thirst like the slaves. His tongue swelled up, filling his parched mouth, and every gulp was agony to him. He was beset with hallucinations from the blinding sun and the scorching heat, and a persistent cough, herald of the tuberculosis which was to end his life ten years later, racked his emaciated body. Nevertheless, day after day he managed to make cryptic notes of his experiences and to draw sketches. Only those who have gone desperately short of water, not at sea, but in the desert, can know the full extent of René Caillié's tremendous achievement.

He did not give in, and on the 14th August 1828 he entered Fez, after seventy-five days of unspeakable torture. Full of gratitude and joy that he had won through, he went to see the French consular agent in Rabat, a rich native merchant. The agent did not have the slightest intention of bothering with the individual standing before his porch in the burning midday sun, 'covered in rags, burnt black by the sun, his body shaken by his incessant cough, and so aged that no one could have guessed that he was still young in years'. The coloured servants sent the beggar packing.

Once again Caillié's fortunes were at a low ebb, but again he did not give up. He hobbled and starved his way to the French consul in Tangier. After five hundred and thirty-eight days, having covered some three thousand miles, he was granted a respite. The consul enthusiastically embraced his compatriot, congratulating him on his great feat. He did everything in his power to help Caillié back to health and to the honours that awaited him in France. Proudly the consul reported to the Quai d'Orsay:

Caillié is the victor of Timbuktu. He has crossed Africa as a beggar. In this condition he threw himself upon the hospitality of my house. I took him in, and deem myself fortunate indeed that I was the first Frenchman to embrace him.

Hardly twenty-four hours after reaching Paris, the news of Caillié's exploit and safe return was in London, having been 'telegraphed' by semaphore, in all its details. The African Association, however, was much cooler in its praise of the courageous young Frenchman, for although it was very interesting that a European had finally managed to reach Timbuktu, and that he had returned alive, bringing fascinating details of life in the 'Queen of the Desert', little scientific knowledge had been won. Later the enthusiasm of Caillié's compatriots was even to be held against him. Moreover the Association was busy preparing another expedition to the Niger. It was led by the Scot, Hugh Clapperton, and managed to produce a fairly conclusive solution to the problem of the Niger.

Mungo Park's first journey had already shown that the Niger could not be a west-flowing branch of the Nile, since its course ran in the opposite direction, i.e. from west to east. Nevertheless, it might still be a tributary of the 'Father of Rivers', flowing right across the Black Continent and joining the headstream of the Nile or even the Congo, somewhere far to the east. The assumptions of antiquity, however, were quite obviously false, for no branch of the Nile flowing westwards existed.

But the above considerations still did not explain what really happened to the Niger. Although, three hundred years earlier, the Portuguese had discovered a mighty river in the Gulf of Guinea flowing through a vast delta into the ocean, and on more than one occasion had given it as their opinion that this was the mouth of the Niger, no conclusive evidence was obtained to settle the question until 1827, when one of Hugh Clapperton's men returned to Europe bringing the journals of the expedition. Clapperton, who had gone in search of the German Hornemann, had reached Lake Chad as early as 1823, and had then marched westwards. Not far from Sokoto, he had encountered a wide river, coming from the north-west and flowing south. His African and Arab advisers insisted that this was the Niger, but Clapperton, the wary Scot, had to see for himself before he was convinced.

No sooner had he arrived in London in 1824 to make his report for the African Association, than he booked a passage on a tea-clipper bound for India. With as much canvas as she could carry, the ship raced towards the south. In the spring of 1825, Clapperton was put ashore in the Bight of Benin, near Lagos. He had orders to make for Sokoto and Bornu, and from there to explore the headstream of the Niger. Since Clapperton had adequate funds at his disposal, his expedition was soon ready to leave. The first stage to the north was accomplished in forced marches and in the same year he and his companion Richard Lander entered Sokoto, the town that he had visited sixteen months earlier from the north.

Thus the western part of Africa had been crossed for the first time from north to south along a line running approximately at 10° East. Furthermore, Clapperton had established the important fact that the Niger did not run to the east as Mungo Park had stated but to the south. He still had no knowledge of the river's course through the Sahara from Timbuktu to Sokoto, and with Scottish tenacity he tried, for one and a half years, to obtain the Sultan of Sokoto's consent to continue his journey. The realization that he would never receive permission from the Arab ruler broke his heart; his health failed and he died on the 13th April 1827.

Under the circumstances it was not surprising that Caillié's exploits did not cause a greater sensation in London. France, as we have said, fêted and heaped honours upon him. The Parisian Geographical Society awarded him their prize and published his account of his travels; the government granted him a pension of 6,000 francs and dubbed him a knight of the Legion of Honour—honours such as rarely fall to the lot of a baker-assistant's son! But his glory was soon to pale. Voices were raised casting doubt on his achievements. Some of his enemies even went so far as to call him a liar and to state that he had never been to Timbuktu. This romantic young man, this fanatic, had something un-French about him, and the land of *raison* and *clarté*, having no sympathy with inspired enthusiasts, rejected him. It did not avail Caillié much to reply with proud modesty to his detractors that those who criticized his lack of scientific education were fully justified, he was no scientist, but he must defend himself against attacks on his integrity:

> I have done my deed despite poverty and my lack of science. I have told Europe what Timbuktu is. Truth is the only merit of my report. No one should try to deprive me of this achievement wrought with so much suffering. My imperfect style and my ignorance are open to criticism by all those who perfected their art and science instead of going to Timbuktu!

René Caillié retired to the country, a disappointed and embittered man. He never again appeared in public, and in the middle of May 1838, only ten years after his magnificent journey, he quietly passed away of tuberculosis—the doctors said, but we should like to add, of a broken heart also.

The greatest tribute to René Caillié came not from France itself, but from across the Rhine. Dr. Heinrich Barth, the great explorer from Hamburg, said on his own successful return from Africa, ten years after Caillié's death:

> It is a great pleasure for me to do justice to the name of a traveller who was the constant victim of attacks on his character and his integrity, and who died before the voices of calumny and malevolence could be silenced. I deem it my bounden duty to declare that René Caillié was one of the most reliable explorers of Africa. He was no scientist, it is true, but without instruments and with the minimum of means he achieved more than most other travellers would have done under the same circumstances.

This affidavit on behalf of a man who had followed the dreams of his youth, silenced the doubters and men of ill will. Caillié's magnificent achievement is now recognized everywhere. But in France they will never endorse the old Swedish saying: he goeth farthest who knoweth not where he goeth. This was surely the motto which René Caillié dedicated himself to prove.

7

One dismal October evening in the year 1849 a young man, dressed in what was then the latest fashion, was returning to his apartment in the Luisenstrasse in Berlin. He had a modest but cosy apartment on the first floor, filled with books and strange exotic bric-à-brac: silver-mounted Arabian pistols, wide-necked Roman *amphorae*, pointed African spears, copper coffee-mills from Morocco, Egyptian goldmasks, and Turkish carpets. On his front door there was a small brass plate, on which was engraved: Dr. phil. HEINRICH BARTH, and just a year ago the following words had been added: University lecturer.

Despite the fact that he was but twenty-eight years old, Dr. Barth had seen quite a bit of the world. He had been to North Africa, Egypt, Asia Minor and to Turkey, but it was not in those places that he had acquired his elegant habits. He just *had* to be well dressed. He was no dandy but whenever a man goes courting, or is in love—and Dr. Barth was deeply in love—he likes to shine for all the world to see. In addition, Dr. Barth was only trying to compensate for the reproaches that had dogged him since childhood and that had made him suffer so cruelly. It had continually been said of him that he was moody, obstinate and arrogant, a bad comrade and an unpredictable fellow.

He had enjoyed going to his primary school and had made friends there, but everything changed when in 1832, at the age of eleven, he went to the *Johanneum*, the most demanding of all the schools in Hamburg. The difficulties of his class-mates were child's play to him. He not only read Caesar, Virgil and Herodotus with ease, but at home delved into the ancient geographers and scientists such as Pausanias, Strabo and Pliny. Soon he was called a swot and a goody-goody by the other children. This was unjust for he did not want to curry favour with his teachers, but he was simply unable to make any sort of contact with his class-mates. While they were playing at Indians or other make-believe games, he preferred to pore over his Arab grammar, for Greek did not suffice him; since reading Mungo Park's own account of his travels he wanted to learn the language of Islam as well. He was learning English just by the way, and, at the age of fourteen, knew it so well that his teachers were chary of giving lessons to his class. Time after time the boy showed up gaps in their knowledge. They had noticed with astonishment out of the staff-room window that instead of playing with the other boys of his class, he would spend the play-times doing gymnastics to strengthen his body. They didn't quite know what to make of him!

Psychoanalysis was not known at that time, but if it had been, it would soon have been discovered that it was not his teachers and his class-mates that he wanted to impress, but his mother. He himself was quite ignorant of this, and he undoubtedly received his fair share of maternal love. His two sisters were perfectly normal, happy children, and he would have grown up equally happy, had not God endowed him with a hypersensitive soul. He sensed very early on how much his mother admired her husband. Johann Christoph Heinrich Barth had come to Hamburg a penniless orphan from Thuringia and had managed to make his own way to the top. He had become a rich merchant and a man of such honour and integrity that he was quickly accepted by the old Hamburg families as one of their own.

Young Heinrich was well aware that his father's achievements were considerable, and he, too, wanted to be heeded and admired. Love was not enough. He did not see much of his father—away at the office from early morning till late at night—but Mother was home all day and was the centre of his whole life. It was to her, and not to his father, that he looked for admiration, and thus, quite early on, the unconscious wish was born to outstrip his father. Year after year he came first at school, but that was not enough. If Mother was to admire him as much as she admired Father, then he would have to achieve something quite out of the ordinary.

Needless to say, Heinrich Barth's mother did not have any idea of what was going on in her son's mind. She came from Hanover of good middle-class stock, and valuing nothing more than bourgeois respectability, she was proud of the fact that her husband had gained wealth and respect through his own powers alone. She did not even realize that her son resented her admiration, and would have been upset and worried had she known that he felt slighted and that he was making desperate attempts to assert his own maturity, skill and worth. How could she have known this, when her son never allowed his fantasy to run away with himself, as is usual with young men, when he never boasted or showed any false pride? Thus Heinrich's mother was completely out of her depth when she was told that her son did not fit in, that he was sullen and obstinate.

Of course, it was quite evident that he was different from his school-fellows. Instead of joining his father's firm, he went to Berlin University as soon as he had matriculated. Instead of becoming a merchant, he sought after wisdom and learning. Instead of studying the fashionable subjects of his day—modern European languages, History of Art and Philosophy—he threw himself into the study of archaeology and geography. It was unheard of to study these young sciences, but he, after all, had to strive for the unusual with all his might.

Great intentions, even when they are not part of our conscious will, must be paid for. Just as Barth had no real childhood when at school, so as a young freshman he forwent his youth. On the 20th March 1843, at the age of twenty-two, he wrote an uncannily prophetic and perceptive letter to his parents:

To see how with every day and even with every hour one penetrates more deeply and more clearly into science, is an infinitely satisfying joy, but it can easily degenerate into supreme egotism, and bring a complete disregard for everything that happens outside oneself. One learns to find one's joy in one's own thoughts, one soon learns to make do without other people and almost to despise them. . . . I am only concerned with my own inner development, my own ability in order that I may best serve mankind, for which naturally I wish to get some recognition and a little glory.

To his father, his teachers and his friends it was clear from the very outset that this introspective, self-confident young man, who resisted every constraint, was completely unfitted to take a job as private tutor after he had finished his studies. This was the custom at the time and was not a bad custom either! Nowadays immature young pedagogues are sent into schools almost immediately after their final examinations. A hundred years ago they worked for some years as private tutors before going into the classroom, having gained a great deal of valuable practical experience beforehand. Heinrich Barth was not made for such a post. His father realized this with deep concern, but since he had money enough, he decided to send the newly graduated *Doctor Philosophiae et Magister Artium* on an extensive tour of North Africa, in the hope that the world would rub the corners off him and make him more sociable.

On the 31st January 1845, Heinrich Barth set out from Hamburg. He reached Tangier, travelling via London, Paris and Madrid in the summer of the same year. Much of this journey he accomplished on foot, carrying a rucksack on his back and a clumsy red box containing a daguerreotype. He travelled to Egypt along the southern coast of the Mediterranean, returning to Germany at the end of 1847 after an absence of almost three years via Palestine, Syria, Constantinople and Athens. He took back with him a store of new experiences, a bullet in his thigh—a memento of a fight with a band of predatory nomads in the African desert—and a pedantically exact account of his expenses which showed a final balance of 14,000 thalers.

Once again he went to Berlin in order to establish himself and began teaching at the university in the summer term of 1849. His first lecture was about the geological structure of North Africa, but he was not very successful. His students were much more concerned with politics, and in any case he was far from being a good speaker. Thus his lecture-hall, which even at the beginning had only contained a handful of students, emptied completely after the first two or three lectures. Dr. Heinrich Barth had to give up his course because of lack of interest.

This happens to a good many lecturers, who yet go on to become competent speakers and teachers. It is not easy to acquire the technique of lecturing and Rome has never been built in one day. Heinrich Barth was old enough to realize this and to profit from his mistakes, but he was a man who made enormous demands on himself and who expected success at the very first go. His failure was a fatal blow to him.

He would have taken it very tragically indeed, if at that very moment he had not met the woman of his life. We do not know who she was or what she was called. No letter from her hand, no forelock, or locket containing her picture has been preserved, but we can imagine that she must have been strongly attracted to this 'lone wolf', who was always grasping for the stars. To be *the* star of his life was a reward to tempt any woman; that is until she realized that there was yet a brighter star in his firmament—his mother; until she realized, too, that this man capable of such extraordinary things craved nothing so much as admiration and an attentive audience.

Obviously no woman would stand for such treatment for long. Thus, when on that 5th October 1849, Heinrich Barth returned to his apartment, he found a note on his desk. The paper was familiar to him and so was the handwriting; for some months now he had known it better even than his own. He opened the note and read its contents. For some moments his brain refused to take in what it said. At last the meaning of those words written in his beloved's hand forced itself upon him—she would never see him again. He sat down as if stunned, and it was some time before he noticed that he had another letter. It was in the handwriting of his revered colleague, friend and teacher, Karl Ritter, the founder of geographical science in Germany. In this official letter Ritter informed his friend that the name of Dr. Heinrich Barth had been put forward as an assistant for James Richardson on his second African expedition. Professor Ritter's letter stated that the British Government, which was financing Richardson's expedition to Kano, would almost certainly ask Dr. Heinrich Barth to participate.

He was highly excited and suddenly the image of an old Negro slave, met at Tunis four years before, flashed into his mind. The Negro had read his hand and stated: 'When it pleases God, you will set off to visit Kano.' Kano! the most important city of North Africa, lying south-west of Lake Chad! The other note was forgotten. Barth knew that fate had called him. He was *not* going to Africa because his heart was broken. He would have gone on this expedition even if the little note had sworn love eternal! Destiny had knocked on his door and Heinrich Barth was ready to follow its call.

8

Africa has a strong power to fascinate and charm and it never releases its hold over the traveller who has once succumbed to its wild, untamed beauty. Never again will he be able to forget the rumbling of the sandstorms in the infinite deserts, the hundred-throated choirs of the jungle, the indescribable play of sunset colours on the high mountain glaciers. The spell of Africa holds him enthralled.

Mungo Park renounced his profession and his safe bourgeois existence in order to travel in Africa once again. The magic of the dark continent had claimed Hornemann and Caillié when they were still children, and Hugh Clapperton, immediately on his return from his first expedition, took the first ship back again. Livingstone disappeared into Central Africa in 1841, to return to England fifteen years later for only a short stay. The rest of his life was devoted to the exploration of the Black Continent. Heinrich Barth was lost in Africa for five years and his presumed death was marked by solemn obituaries. Gustav Nachtigal, too, spent many years travelling in Africa and reappeared one day in 1879, hardly capable of speaking his own language, to confound the people who had long since given him up for lost. Henry Morton Stanley renounced a promising career as chief reporter on the *New York Herald* because Africa had cast its spell over him. He had left originally to go in search of Doctor Livingstone, but he was soon to be as bewitched as the former missionary. All his thoughts and activities were directed to completing the work of the other.

But the magic of Africa can be most clearly seen at work in the case of Heinrich Barth. Not only was he enticed back to Africa time after time, but a strange change took place in him. Many years later he was to write: 'I have become used to the desert and the infinite spaces, so that I have lost the sense for petty details which normally suffocate men.' As soon as he put foot on the soil of the Black Continent he was immediately transformed into a different man. Only there was his whole personality allowed to develop. His inhibitions, his complexes, fell off him like a discarded skin. His tender, sensitive soul no longer required a protective armour and the touchy, imperious outsider in Europe became a kind, fatherly friend to the natives in Africa. He called himself Abd-el-Kerim, servant of God, and even fifty years later the English traveller Lt. Hurst was advised to pretend he was the son of Abd-el-Kerim in Timbuktu. He was told that no better letter of recommendation could exist in the eyes of the wild Bedouins of the Sahara. It seemed that only in the desert could Barth find the missing half of his being, for once there, he became balanced and fully at one with himself. After the death of his last white comrade, the geologist Adolf Overweg—Richardson had died some days earlier—Barth found himself carrying the responsibility for the whole expedition and he wrote in a letter: 'Instead of feeling depressed at the death of my friend I felt that my forces were redoubled. There was a giant's strength in me!' With iron resolution he took the weight on his shoulders and carried on.

In the middle of December 1849, Barth and the German scientist Dr.

Adolf Overweg, also employed by the English Government, arrived in North Africa entrusted with the task of preparing the expedition and recruiting their coffle, their caravan. The expedition's stores, which included a small boat that could be dismantled into four parts, had not yet arrived from Europe and so they spent their time collecting together twenty camels, cowrie shells, which served as currency in large parts of Africa, goods for bartering and for presents, provisions, medicaments, tents, water-skins and arms, etc. Barth's personal luggage contained three books, a New Testament, an edition of the Koran and a copy of Herodotus. Many years after Barth's death this book was found in his library. The great explorer had inscribed on the fly-leaf: 'Herodotus, my daily companion, whom I revere deeply.'

By the end of March 1850 the other member of the party, James Richardson, had arrived, and the expedition was ready to leave. Richardson, a former missionary, had already explored the Sahara as far as the oases of Gat, about six hundred miles south-west of Tripoli. During his first trip Richardson had established connections with different Arab sheiks living in the desert, and also with the Sultan of Bornu, the black ruler of a state lying beyond the Sahara, west of Lake Chad, who was anxious to open diplomatic relations with Europe. In the spring of the previous year, he had sent his Foreign Minister, a Negro slave, together with a lengthy caravan heavily laden with presents, across the desert to Tripoli, with the express order to call on the Queen of England and make overtures of friendship to Britain. When the naked black minister arrived in Tripoli to pay an official visit to the British consulate, the consul was greatly surprised and in some embarrassment. What on earth was he to do with this 'nigger'? Fortunately the weather that spring was rather cool and His Excellency, the Foreign Minister of Bornu, was trembling like a leaf with cold. The British consul saw his chance, and told His Excellency that compared with the climate of Britain, that of Tripoli must be considered hot, and that His Excellency was sure to die of cold in England. He most strongly advised him to give up his visit to London and he, the consul, would transmit the greeting of the King of Bornu to Her Majesty. The Foreign Minister promptly accepted this and left at full speed.

The whole of Tripoli was still enjoying the joke, when Richardson, Barth and Overweg appeared on the scene. While the three joined in the laughter, they realized that here was a sudden stroke of fortune, for in case of need they could claim to be ambassadors from England. They left Tripoli on the 24th March 1848, in the happiest of moods, but five years later Barth was to be the only white man to return from the expedition.

Their first goal was the town of Murzuq in Fezzan, about five hundred miles from Tripoli by the most direct route, though no caravan had ever gone that way. It led for days straight across Hamada-el-Hamra, a high and stony desert without any trace of vegetation and completely without water. After fourteen days of travelling along a *Uëd*, a dry river valley, they came across the unmistakable signs of a former Roman settlement:

This *wadi* showed many traces of once having been cultivated, and soon afterwards other signs of Roman industry became visible which made it even clearer that once upon a time a Roman postal road, with milestones marking the distance, had run through this deserted central region. Unfortunately none of the inscriptions were preserved.

Although Barth had his copy of Herodotus in his pocket, he had left Pliny at home, otherwise he could have read that some two thousand years previously this desert region had in fact been conquered by Roman legions, and that Cornelius Balbus, a native of Cadiz, had penetrated as far as Garama in the year 20 B.C. Later on Barth's expedition found other great fields of ruins and graves in Djerma, north-east of Murzuq. Barth was certain that Garama, the 'famous capital of the Garamantes', had been situated here, as in fact Pliny had suggested, and as later investigations were to confirm. Had Barth been able to hire an aeroplane he could have seen even more. Everywhere, as far as his eye could reach, he would have seen the contours of meadows, fields, wells, cities and villages buried under the sand—traces of a rich civilization and of a highly developed culture.

Barth felt instinctively that he could not have been the first white man to have set foot in those parts. He had the greatest respect for the tremendous achievements of the Romans, but his astonishment was even greater when in the *Uëd* Telissarhe, the unexplored, uninhabited, sun-flooded mountain desert halfway between Murzuq and Gat, he discovered ancient rock-paintings, showing a watering-place with cattle, buffaloes, ostriches and many other kinds of animal. The only notable exception was the camel. Barth noted in his journal:

In view of the fact that these pictures were found at the gate of a watering-place along the great road leading to the interior of the continent, they must be taken as evidence to show not only that cattle were customary in those regions at that time, but also that they were used as beasts of burden instead of the camel. The camel, that indispensable means of transport across naked deserts, is not to be found among the animals shown in these pictures, nor in the rough drawings made at a much later date on the rocks in the vicinity.

Sixty years were to pass before these remains of an ancient past were investigated more closely. Barth's conclusions were fully confirmed: the people who had once lived here had not known the camel. Many more discoveries were made. Different stages in development and culture could be clearly distinguished. The oldest drawings on the rock walls represented long processions of animals, reminiscent of a nursery frieze. These painted outlines of animals, which were executed with great vitality, represented cattle, ostriches, giraffes, lions, elephants, rhinoceroses and hippopotami. All these tropical animals, which incidentally need a rich vegetation with lakes, rivers, swamps, extensive savannahs and great forests in order to exist, were drawn and painted so realistically, and are so true to life that the artists, who came from a tribe of hunters living in that area about the time of the early Stone Age, must have drawn them from life.

Later generations inconsiderately scratched *their* pictures over these paintings from the third millennium before Christ. These new pictures must have been the work of a pastoral people. They still show numerous large wild animals but these are overshadowed by cattle. Large herds, and very occasionally a horse, are shown. The horse appeared in Egypt about 1700 B.C., and was probably introduced there by the Hyksos who migrated from Asia to Egypt about that time. Hippopotami and elephants are missing from this second lot of drawings. Obviously the rich and fertile land had begun to dry up.

In the next phase, dated about 500 B.C., representations of rhinoceroses and giraffes became rarer, until they, too, disappeared completely. Eventually cattle gave way completely to horses, shown as drawing chariots with armed men. It was about this time that the kingdom of the Garamantes was founded here. The continual desiccation of the soil had by then destroyed the large grazing grounds needed for cattle, and the pastoral people had left the region, to be replaced by mounted nomadic tribes. Finally even horses disappeared, for now the barren soil bore nothing but coarse grasses and bushes, fit only for camels to eat. At last the 'ships of the desert', probably introduced into these regions by the Arabs, made their appearance on the rock walls. This last stage occurred as late as the first century A.D. when the fertile land of North Africa, rich in water, had become a barren desert.

Those inveterate enemies of Rome, the Carthaginians, did not make use of the camel, but brought elephants across the Mediterranean. Naturally, the Romans had met the camel during their campaigns in the Near East (the Semitic name *gamal* had, in fact, been borrowed by almost all European languages) but none of their officers had ever thought of introducing it into North Africa. At that time the Libyan province of the Roman Empire was still a fertile land, rich in water, but towards the end of the fourth century A.D., when it had long been desert, the means of governing it were simply no longer available. The power of Rome in North Africa had to give way to Arab warriors who, mounted on camels as they were, gradually took over the country as far as the Niger.

Naturally these changes did not take place overnight. For many centuries horses managed to coexist with these strange Asiatic beasts of burden, just as today the camel exists side by side with the motor-car. But just as, twenty-five years ago, the large-scale introduction of trucks led to a complete shifting of power relationships in North Africa, so, in its time, the camel produced an equally great revolution.

At first the introduction of the camel resulted in fairly simple changes in methods of transportation, but, as its use became more widespread, this new means of transport began to upset the political situation, until the whole structure came crashing to the ground. To begin with, the predatory Berbers of the coastal regions stuck to their own side of the Atlas Mountains, their motto being: 'I and my brother against our cousin. I and my cousin against the stranger', but soon they realized that the camel could be used for making raids deep into the immeasurable savannahs spreading south beyond the Atlas mountains. As the Berbers were not noted for their gentle manners, it can easily be understood why the peasants who lived around every water-hole, well and oasis in the Sahara migrated further south. The abandoned wells became filled with sand, irrigation schemes fell into decay, and the fertile patches were fertile no longer.

Perhaps the significance of this will become clearer if we add a few simple facts: a quart of water per second is sufficient to irrigate from five to eight acres of land and to change the sterile desert, as if by magic, into a fertile land. This quantity of water can support sixteen thousand sheep. Each well means not only a fortune for its owner, but also registers an important victory over the desiccation threatening the savannah. The Sahara is not, as it were, constitutionally barren; in fact only the ninth part of it is unable ever to support any vegetation. Today an area of some 750,000 square miles, i.e. an area equivalent to Germany, France, Spain and Italy put together, has been made fertile by artificial irrigation.

The black peasants who fled before the Berbers inevitably produced overcrowding in the southern forest regions, and so gradually the trees were cut down to make way for fields. As the trees disappeared, so the desert advanced and began to eat into the fertile landscapes. The process that had started in the north was continued in the south, and each year the desert advanced by about half a mile, driving the peasants before it.

Barth did not suspect anything of these former events. He did not even have the leisure to give a great deal of thought to the strange paintings in the *Uëd* Telissarhe. Though Hornemann had mentioned ancient petrified tree-trunks and extensive banks of fossilized shells in his accounts of the Egyptian desert, no one had inferred that those barren areas had once been fertile, growing crops, providing excellent pasture for cattle. Barth had no inkling that the remarkable pictures he was admiring gave the clue to the fate of that area, nor, indeed, did he have much time for reflection, as it was imperative to reach water quickly. As a rule, the coffle would start off at seven o'clock in the morning while it was still cool, and continue till the afternoon at an average speed of about two and a half miles per hour.

Thus the expedition covered some twenty-five to thirty miles per day. Hatita and Utaeti, the two native guides, would pitch camp in the late afternoon. The coffle travelled in the Arab manner, every camel going by itself, and though following the general direction it might wander off to the left or right of the path in search of a blade of grass or even a thin bush. The disadvantage of this method of travelling was that it was by no means easy to gather the animals together in the evening.

This was a constant source of irritation for Barth, and whenever possible he used horses. His journals give us full details of the technique of travelling with 'desert ships'. Many European explorers before Barth had travelled by camel, and all had had to contend with the attacks of 'sea-sickness' caused by the appalling swaying motion of the beast as it moves. But detailed reports of such matters had not been known before Barth published his journals, and the European public learnt with keen interest that one had to distinguish among three kinds of camel, i.e. the one-humped dromedary, the racing dromedary called the *méhari*, and the larger and more heavily built two-humped beast of burden, the Bactrian camel. All three kinds were surprisingly docile. They fed on any form of coarse vegetation and, whereas the elephant needed at least fifteen buckets of water with its meals, a camel could easily go without water for seven or eight days. The record time for a camel to go without water in the Sahara is seventeen days, and the camels used in building the telegraph line through the Australian bush are said to have gone without water for thirty-four days, though this was during the winter.

Bactrian camels can carry more than 300 pounds of cargo, while racing camels can only carry the rider and his personal luggage. Thus the fast Tuareg, the predatory and fanatical Bedouins of the central Sahara, did not have much difficulty in catching up with the caravans. They travelled in a completely different manner. Their camels were tied together head to tail, and they advanced like a long chain at the surprising speed of over sixty miles each day. Barth knew this and was certain that, in spite of Richardson's good connections, the expedition would be attacked. Armed with a double-barrelled gun and a revolver he would fuss around the caravan like a destroyer round a convoy. He seemed to be everywhere at once. He utilized this activity for taking compass readings, making rapid sketches of the landscape and jotting down brief notes. During the evening after the day's march he would enter his observations into his journal, writing on the desk which Mohammed, the servant who accompanied him from 1851 to 1855, would have produced from a plank and some boxes. Barth worked steadily on, well into the night, drawing the map of the caravan route from Tripoli to the south. In uncertain country he would order forced marches, sometimes of twenty-four to thirty hours at a stretch.

On the 24th March, death made its first attempt to seize Heinrich Barth. Strange turret-like mountain ruins could be seen rising above the sands, far from the route that the caravan was following. The ruins looked like the remains of forts or palaces. Against the advice of the guides Barth set out to investigate the strange rock formations. For safety, Overweg followed him some of the way at a distance, for the Arabs had refused to accompany the white explorers. They knew the 'haunted mountain', they knew that *djinns*, evil spirits, walked about there. Let the mad *giaours* risk their lives alone!

Barth took a small water-skin with him and a few dates, and advanced towards the ruins. Suddenly a deep ravine cut across his path. Barth climbed down with great difficulty and, a few hours later, stood on the opposite cliff not far from the 'haunted mountain'. No traces of buildings or pictures or inscriptions were to be discovered. The action of the weather had chiselled a huge piece of rock into the outlines of turrets and battlements. Night fell before Barth could return, and when the sun rose next morning he discovered he had lost his way. He could see or hear nothing of the caravan, or of Overweg.

His water was finished and the dried dates felt like pebbles in his mouth. As the sun rose, he felt the pangs of thirst and by noontide they were unbearable. He took his knife and with its point opened one of his veins and sucked his own blood. Dusk began to fall and he felt that he had no more hope of rejoining the caravan.

> Suddenly I heard the hoarse bleating sound of a camel. No music could have been sweeter to my ears at that moment. I raised myself a little from the ground and saw one of our men, some distance away, looking carefully around him. He had followed my footmarks in the sand but had lost the trace in the stony ground. With my parched throat and weakened voice I called, '*Aman*, *Aman*—water, water' and to my joy I heard him reply '*Iwua*, *Iwua*'. In a few moments he was sitting by my side washing and sprinkling my head, while I broke out involuntarily into an oft-repeated *el hamdu lillahi*, *el hamdu lillahi* . . ., Allah be praised! After my saviour had refreshed me thus, he gave me water to drink, but my mouth and throat were so dried up that I found it bitter as gall. Then he raised me onto his camel and hastened towards the tents. At first, I could speak but little and for three days I touched no food. Gradually, however, my strength came back to me.

At the beginning of May 1850, the caravan entered the town of Murzuq and on the 18th July, four months after leaving Tripoli, the three white men reached their first destination, the oasis of Gat. Richardson, who had been to Gat once before, tried unsuccessfully to win the favour of the Tuareg sheiks. Thus when, some days later, the caravan moved on to its next objective, the mountains of Aïr, it seemed more than likely that they would be attacked.

The desert south of Gat was completely unknown at the time, having never been entered by white men. Today it is crossed by highways with many rest-houses, wells and petrol pumps. The same Tuareg who sixty years ago were the rulers and the scourge of this region, now fill your car with petrol and water and expect a tip. They themselves are daring drivers who know the desert like the pockets of their overalls. As you switch on the engine they call out in husky French: '*Attention, monsieur*—look out! do not drown!' Strange though this warning might sound, the number of reckless tourists who have been drowned in the middle of the Sahara is surprising. The Aïr district in particular has claimed many victims. In September and October, when the clouds coming from the west pour out their burden of rain onto the mountain massif, tremendous masses of water rush down the many ravines and valleys carrying everything before them.

Fortunately Barth and his companions crossed this region shortly before the rainy season. After many dangerous adventures, they reached some sort of understanding with the Tuareg and were able to proceed unchallenged, and so could devote all their attention to surveying and mapping the route. When at last it did begin to rain, they were amazed to see how quickly the sterile desert became covered with grass. They saw it flourish and shine in the sun, and were filled with uncomprehending wonder.

As the expedition was proceeding through the Aïr mountains, one of the inhabitants of those parts informed Barth that the town of Agadès was not far away. Agadès, he said, was a great city in the middle of the desert and was far more beautiful than Timbuktu. This news thrilled Barth. Three hundred years earlier, Leo Africanus had written a long description of Agadès, but while Agadès is nowadays a favourite spot in the Sahara, at the time of Barth few had heard of it, and it is small wonder that our explorer was full of eagerness to make a small detour to visit it. He knew very well the dangers that might lie in wait for him and even the Tuareg tried to put him off, but Barth's resolution was unshakeable and, although his funds were almost exhausted, he managed to persuade some of the drivers and carriers to accompany him.

Contrary to all expectation, the detour was a great success. On Wednesday, the 15th October 1850, Barth entered Agadès at the head of a small coffle. The town was largely in ruins but it had obviously been much more important in the past. Although the town was but a shadow of its former greatness, it was still a strange experience to come upon a city that had once housed 50,000 inhabitants in the middle of the desert.

Naturally Barth was extremely interested in the origins of the place and in ascertaining who had once had the fantastic idea of founding a capital city in that deserted region, a city, moreover, which would have to be fully dependent on imports for its existence. Slowly he pieced together bits of information and learned that the town had been built by Berbers from

North Tripoli and that they had had very good reasons for doing so. By fair means and foul, by the beginning of the fifteenth century, they had made themselves masters of the mineral salt deposits on both sides of the Aïr mountains. This made them the rulers of North Africa, for salt was in short supply here and those who had none had to buy it either from the remote Sudan or from the Berbers with gold, ivory, slaves or other valuables. The Berbers soon realized that they could not control the ever-increasing volume of business from Tuat, Gadamès, and Aujila, which were too far away, so in 1460 the owners of the salt monopoly decided to found the city of Agadès as a kind of fortification, halfway between the two great salt deposits and in the immediate vicinity of the ancient caravan route. The town with its lofty battlements and towers, its fortifications and castles, had once been a centre of Islamic learning and had boasted a famous library. Its glory had lasted for about a century, during which time its population had risen to over 50,000 people.

But even in Africa, trade followed the flag. The might of the Berbers declined and Timbuktu came to the fore. Agadès began to fade in importance. The rich trading-houses abandoned the city, leaving behind at most an insignificant branch office. Eventually these too were given up as unproductive and too expensive and all that remained of the heyday of Agadès was old memories. Thus Barth noted:

> The picture of Agadès is that of an abandoned city. Everywhere one can find traces of a lost glory. Even in the centre of the town the houses are largely in ruins and only a few of the once numerous mosques remain. Hungry birds of prey perch on the decaying walls of the market-place, waiting to seize upon any kind of refuse.

Those who live in a world in decline, those who know that sooner or later they must give up their home that was once great but which is now inevitably lost, snatch at what moments of pleasure remain. Puritan morals are incomprehensible to them. We with our A-bombs and H-bombs and a whole alphabet of death know only too well these common truths, but Barth, coming from a safe world, lacked all understanding of the 'to-morrow we die' mentality. He made the following indignant little entry on the 23rd October 1850:

> This morning I had a striking proof of the easy morals of Agadès. Five or six girls or women came into our house to visit me, and with great simplicity they invited me to take my pleasure of them, since the Sultan was away hunting and there was no need for caution. Two of them were beautiful; their black hair hung down in plaits and they were well built without a superfluity of fat. Their eyes were lively and coquettish. These girls or women from Agadès went a little far in their wantonness; besides I was too convinced of the necessity for a European, who wished to travel unmolested through these lands, to behave with the utmost caution with regard to the feminine sex, for these women, who I repeat were by no means repellent, to make me waver in my resolution.

Not all European travellers in Africa have proved so virtuous and cautious; and many have entered into relations with native women. The

German nobleman Pückler-Muskau took back a brown slave-girl to Europe. 'Africa blackens' runs a proverb that covers such unions which have often led to severe conflicts. But obviously this formulation does not get to the bottom of the problem. Barth himself was aware of the deep complexity of the whole question, for he made the following entry in his journal after this visit from the noble ladies of Agadès:

> It would without doubt be better for a traveller in these lands if he could take a female companion with him, both in regard to his own convenience and also because of the respect in which he would then stand with the natives. In their simplicity they cannot understand how a man can live without female company. The Western Tuareg had nothing against me excepting the fact that I lived as a bachelor.

A new Sultan had just assumed office when Barth entered Agadès, and the German was able to attend his coronation. Barth presented the new potentate with a particularly elegant burnous, saying that it was a present from the Queen of England. He noted to his great pleasure that the Sultan was wearing his present at his Coronation. He was not the only one to notice it, for as the Sultan was carried in the ceremonial procession through the city, all the sheiks from near and afar could see that he was wearing the gift of the foreigner. This circumstance assured Barth of the favour of the local tribes and soon afterwards, when he left to rejoin the main caravan, Abd-el-Kerim was everywhere a well-known and respected figure.

At the end of October, he caught up with Richardson and Overweg, who had called a halt at the Tintellust oasis in the Aïr mountains. Equipped with impressive letters of recommendation from the Sultan of Agadès and certain of the effect of his personality and of ultimate success, Barth urged the immediate continuation of the journey. His two companions, however, decided to wait until the beginning of December in order to join a great salt caravan coming from the Bilma valley on its way to the Sudan. The delay was not to Barth's liking and this diversity of opinion was the beginning of differences between the leaders of the expedition that were to cause Barth to carry on later by himself, at his own risk.

The expected salt caravan arrived in Tintellust in December and the coffle of the three whites joined it. On the 6th January, after successfully crossing the desert, the expedition finally reached the fertile regions of the Sudan. The first cornfields appeared and prosperous native villages could be seen nestling among the valleys.

It was a rich land, but Barth's entry in his journal on Friday, the 10th January 1851, in which he gives his reasons for deciding to separate for the time being from Richardson, sounds most unconvincing:

> Here we had reached regions where it was possible for individual travellers to follow their own path. Overweg and myself decided to separate from Richardson owing to our lack of funds. Each one of us was to try what he could achieve by himself until extra supplies of money arrived from Europe.

While this argument strikes us as spurious, there must have been valid grounds for Barth and Overweg to leave Richardson, whose state of health was not particularly good and who was to die two months later of exhaustion. The real reasons, whatever they might have been, must remain secret, since Overweg was to die soon after Richardson, and our only source of information is Barth's journal.

On Saturday, the 11th January 1851, Barth started south towards Kano, the great Negro city. He had agreed with Richardson and Overweg to meet about the 1st April 1851, in Kuka, the capital of the kingdom of Burnu, west of Lake Chad. This was a long way from Kano, and Barth had to make great haste. But his journey proceeded smoothly and in under three weeks he had covered the incredible distance of about 375 miles. On the 1st February he entered the 'African London'. Probably he was the first white man to have achieved this feat, though not the first man from the Old World, since 300 years earlier, Leo Africanus had reported:

> The land of Kano lies about 500 miles east of the Niger. Its inhabitants live for the most part in villages and hamlets, breeding cattle and cultivating the soil. The land is fertile and much grain, rice and cotton are grown here, for the mountains are wooded and many springs emerge from them. The capital Kano is surrounded by firm walls. Its houses are built of light-coloured stone. Its inhabitants are wealthy and highly civilised.

Barth's coloured companions, particularly his servant Mohammed, were looking forward to the pleasures awaiting them in the glittering metropolis of the Sudan, and their master too was in a good mood. It was almost a year since he had set out on his first expedition. Time after time, during those twelve months, he had heard speak of Kano as the best starting-point for exploring Central Africa. Now he had reached it. Would he be able to continue? At first, this did not depend on himself but rather on his finances. True, he still possessed about 500,000 units of shell money, but during his entry into Kano he had been forced to pay 112,000 shells for duty, handling charges, etc., and he was faced with the necessity of having to make valuable presents to the *Serki*, the Governor of Kano and also to his First Minister, the *Galadima*. At the risk of becoming impoverished, he dipped deep into his presentation box and gave the *Serki* an elegant black burnous worth 60,000 shells and also a red cap, a white shawl, a large piece of muslin, two small bottles of rose oil, one pound of cloves, one pound of incense, a razor, scissors, a stiletto and a large mirror. The *Galadima* received a similar assortment of presents. Luckily both black statesmen were highly satisfied.

Thus Barth could visit the town without hindrance. Kano was a prosperous city, for caravans from strange lands called there and the shops sold all kinds of local and imported goods. There was a large roofed slave market where slaves of both sexes and of all ages could be bought. There were many gold- and silversmiths, dyers, and other tradesmen in this town. Great gentlemen in silken cloaks rode across the market, and close by were the lepers, the blind, the beggars and women of easy virtue. The peasants went out each day to till their fields outside the city, and groups of indolent loafers and gapers sprawled out in the mild sun of the early day. Fifty thousand people lived in Kano, and the whole province had a population of almost a million.

The town earned its livelihood mostly by manufacturing fine cotton materials which were exported to the whole of North Africa. The main centre for this trade was Timbuktu, which lay some one thousand miles to the north-west, but the direct route was so infested with robbers that the caravans from Kano had to make a long detour of some 2,500 miles, via the far more northerly oasis of Tuat and the most deserted parts of the desert, in order to reach their destination safely.

This delay was of relatively small importance. Time did not matter, and in any case, the profits from the trade in cotton materials were very good and the cost of living was low. Barth, who had left Europe at the beginning of the economic depression of the 'fifties, came to the conclusion that Kano was one of the most fortunate countries of the world.

> If we also take into consideration the fact that the inhabitants do not work, as in Europe, in tremendous factories which deprive human beings of their dignity, but that every family contributes to this prosperity without having to sacrifice the private lives of its members, we may well conclude that Kano is one of the happiest lands in the world.

This black city, which was hardly known in Europe, was rich enough to purchase Europe's goods. It imported cotton materials of all kinds from Manchester, silk and sugar from France, red woollen fabrics from Italy and Saxony, glass bowls from Venice, silk, writing-paper, mirrors, needles and fancy goods from Nuremberg, sword blades from Solingen and razor blades from Styria. Barth told his employers in London that this trade could be doubled if the lower Niger and its tributary, the Benuë, were explored more closely and if the travelling routes into the Sudan were used.

9

In order to reach Kuka at the appointed time, Barth had to leave Kano at the beginning of March. He travelled with three camels and one horse, and was only accompanied by his servant Mohammed. Although all the routes were infested by robber bands, he continued on his journey unmolested. In fact in the middle of the desert, he had the extraordinary good fortune to meet an Arab coming from Tripoli with letters for him. One of the letters contained two Spanish thalers, each one equal to about 5,000 shells—a fortune in that part of the world.

A few days' journey from Kuka, where he intended to join the two other white members of the expedition, he learnt that Richardson had died. He was deeply moved by this news and at first could not believe it. It was true that he had left Richardson suffering a little from the change of climate between the pure mountain air of Aïr and the heavy, damp climate of the Sudan, but he had not been dangerously ill. The news of Richardson's death *could not* be true, even though the natives insisted on it. They said he was buried in a grave under a large sycamore. Barth started off at once and late that same evening he arrived at the place. He could doubt no longer:

> The event had caused great excitement in the whole neighbourhood. Mr. Richardson had arrived on the 28th February in a debilitated state and had died early next morning. Night was far advanced when I returned to my tent. Reflecting upon my own fate and the excellent health I had enjoyed so far in spite of my many difficulties, I was filled with gratitude.

Now that Barth's task was doubled, he had no time for brooding. He hoped to be able to reach Kuka the following day at noon, and rather nervously he noted in his journal:

> This was to be a great day, which would decide the course of my activity in these regions. I had finally reached the capital of that King whom we had expressly been sent to find. The end of our journey was nigh, but the success of our enterprise depended on the outcome of my interview with the King. I had to request audience of him, with my clothes in a pitiful state and with no letter of recommendation.

It was only shortly before his audience with Omar, the Sheik and King of Bornu, that Barth fully realized how badly off he was. Despite the windfall of two Spanish thalers received in mid-desert, he was in debt to the tune of five million *kurdi* (shells). In addition he owed wages to Richardson's servants, carriers and camel drivers who after Richardson's death were eager to receive their money. This amounted to another 750,000 *kurdi*. Apart from this, he had to make King Omar a magnificent present. Anyone else would have been driven to despair by such a situation, but Barth was made of sterner mettle. Obviously he needed such difficulties in order to realize himself completely, to be quite 'himself'. He made his appearance as the proud ambassador of the Queen of England and he managed to charm both Omar and his Vizier with his gracious manner. Fortunately, he was able to carry the day, and the Vizier of Kano received the poor stranger with open arms and gave him full freedom of movement in Bornu.

His first wish was naturally to reach Lake Chad. It is possible that Hornemann had stood on its shores some fifty years before, but this was not certain and in any case could not be proved. Thirty years earlier, in

1822, Denham, Oudney and Clapperton had made a short stop on its shores, but no one had explored the vast lake lying in the middle of the desert and, during the rainy season, covering an area of more than 20,000 square miles. This task was to fall to Barth. It was fortunate that he had a collapsible boat among his baggage. He would get Overweg to sail around the lake and explore its whole circumference.

At the end of April 1851, Barth set out for Lake Chad. The King of Omar, who had received him as his guest, provided him with guides. With the eye of the experienced geographer he soon saw that, although it had shrunk in size within comparatively recent times, it had never been connected with the ocean. But the rumours of a fresh-water sea, situated in the interior of Africa and feeding all its rivers, which had been current in the Old World, were not entirely without foundation. Even in this region the gradual desiccation of the earth had affected the lake and the present-day shores had once been deep under water. Barth had the utmost difficulty in breaking through the gigantic swamps that surrounded it in order to reach its banks. Not many years later the German traveller Vogel could only see the open water of Lake Chad by means of binoculars, and today nothing remains of the one-time gigantic sweet-water lake but a few pools, not worthy of the name, and mile after mile of stinking swamps, the breeding ground of swarms of mosquitoes. Heinrich Barth's report of Lake Chad reads like a fairy tale to anyone who has seen it in its present state:

40. The faithful servant Mohammed.

Soon after sunrise I mounted and set off to visit the great lake in the interior of Africa, the main aim of our expedition, which we believed to be not far away. We travelled quickly over the endless grassy plain in which our eyes searched in vain for a resting place. Finally we reached a swamp which made our advance difficult. For a long time we tried in vain to get out of this swamp and I strained my eyes, equally in vain, for a glimpse of the open water. In the end I decided to return to Ngorno to find a guide familiar with the terrain. On my second visit to Lake Chad, during the winter of 1854, the landscape was to present a completely different aspect from the country I was now crossing. While the region around Ngorno was now dry, with only rare patches of swamp, three and a half years later the greater part of it was covered by water. A deep open lake, miles long, had formed around Ngorno and immeasurable areas of fertile land lay buried under the water. This is the great characteristic of Lake Chad! Its outline changes shape continuously according to the masses of water feeding it and the tremendous losses by evaporation, particularly during the hot season, so that it is quite impossible to fix the banks of the lake on a map.

The following day Barth was given guides who led him where he could see open water. Although he was only to see one of the bays of Lake Chad, the sight of so much fresh water extending before him after the weeks of travelling through desert regions, and after having been so long on the verge of dying thirst, was too much for him. In words betraying his deep emotion he praised the beauty of the great lake on whose banks he stood. It is not surprising that he considered this green landscape a veritable paradise after his earlier experiences of Africa, although a concern for truth makes us add that travellers here were constantly plagued by swarms of mosquitoes, and that crocodiles and hippopotami lay in wait by the dozen in the tall reeds bordering the lake. Moreover, the banks of the lake were extremely treacherous, for one false step would have precipitated horse and rider into deep quagmires. All these dangers were unimportant to Barth compared with the lake of fresh water; the horrible death by thirst has never been more eloquently described than between the lines of Barth's enthusiastic description of the infinite expanse of drinking water presented by Lake Chad.

However, he could not stay here indefinitely. Our explorer had been gripped by the tremendous appeal of the African landscape, and all the fibres of his being were drawn towards the blanks in the maps which stretched south of Lake Chad in what is today the North Cameroons. He awaited the arrival of his friend Dr. Overweg, so that he could instruct him in the work of sailing round Lake Chad and charting its banks. Then he himself immediately started south towards the Mandara mountains, whose ridges soar as high as 6,500 feet and form the watershed between the Niger-Benuë system and the rivers feeding Lake Chad. Today he could have taken a plane and arrived within only a few hours, but aeroplanes were unheard of in those days and it took Barth six weeks from Bornu to the Benuë. On the 18th June 1851, a youthful dream came true: he stood on the banks of this wide river. He had always considered the Benuë, which flows in majestic silence, as one of the gateways to Central Africa. In deep delight, he surveyed the wide rich landscape, and that evening he sat at his improvised desk and wrote a long and detailed report to the British Government. Three years later, when Barth was making his way back to Tripoli from the jungles of Nigeria, the British steamer *Pleiad*, on the basis of Barth's report, sailed up the Niger and the Benuë, and dropped anchor not far from the very spot where he had written it. The steamer had managed to sail right up to the granite walls of the Mandara mountains. Barth was very moved and impressed when he heard of this deed on his return into the civilized world.

Barth decided on another stay in Kuka even though he had solved the Benuë problem. This enforced delay was a great burden to him but he had no choice. In his journey to the Mandara mountains he had met a learned and widely travelled Arab, who had told him of the area around Lake Nyasa far in East Africa, and of the fiery mountains that towered high into the skies and which, despite the fact that they stood on the Equator, were covered winter and summer with snow and ice. The Arab also told him of a tremendous stream which flowed right across the entire continent towards the south-west, through jungles and steppes. This river was the Congo. Barth was sorely tempted to march to the east, but he had no money to equip himself for so great a journey. He sat down and wrote a long report to London asking for money and pointing out that the original plan of the expedition had been to cross Africa from Lake Chad to Zanzibar on the coast. The British Government, however, had other plans. In 1852 Barth received orders to explore the middle Niger and to proceed to Timbuktu. The same dispatch appointed him officially as Richardson's successor and contained a warrant for a considerable sum of money, provided in equal parts by English and German subscribers. At last his financial troubles were at an end; he paid off his debts and finally made those presents to his friends in Bornu which they expected of the representative of the Queen of England.

However, fate was to deal him a crushing blow. His friend and colleague Dr. Overweg died. Worn out by the strain of tramping through the swampy regions of Lake Chad he had no resistance to hold off an attack of fever. After days of dreadful delirium, he closed his eyes for the last time on the 27th September 1851.

> Thus died my former friend and companion in the thirtieth year of his life, in the very flower of manhood. It was not to be his fate to complete his journey, but to find a most honourable death in the service of science. He himself wished to be buried on the banks of that lake that made him famous as the first white man to have sailed around it. The feeling of approaching death guided him to the spot where he died, close to the boat in which he made his last voyage. The inhabitants of the village, who loved him as a friend, bitterly lamented his death and will certainly long remember the '*tahib*', as they called him.

Barth was deeply unhappy. He could not long bear to remain in Kuka, which reminded him constantly of his dead friend, and he decided to leave for Timbuktu as quickly as possible. This desert city was no longer unknown since Laing and Caillié had visited it twenty-five years ago, but neither of them had been able to stay there long. Thus Barth was the most important explorer of the trading centre on the Niger. It was he who dealt the final blow to the romantic illusions about Timbuktu, which were still current in Europe despite Caillié's reports.

Our explorer knew well the dangers facing him on his new journey. Not for nothing did trading caravans avoid the region he had to cross. Numerous bands of robbers infested the area, slave-traders held hunts for human game and the local tribes were constantly at war with one another.

To venture with only a small and very badly armed caravan into so precarious a region was taking a very great risk. Nevertheless Barth did not make the slightest changes in his usual mode of travelling. He left Kuka on the 25th November 1852, after having used it as his base camp for nearly two years. He travelled accompanied by Mohammed, his faithful servant, and six other companions. Half of the travellers were mounted

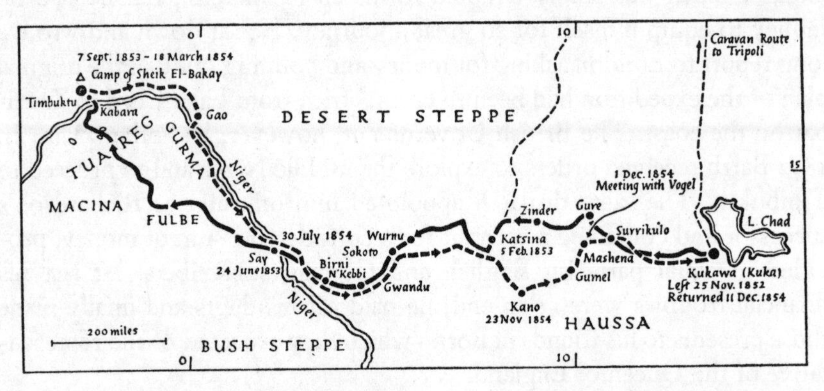

XXXVII. Heinrich Barth's journey from Kuka to Timbuktu.

on camels and half were on horseback. The next stage of his journey was to take him ten months, but Barth was firmly convinced that he would manage this new safari successfully. Furthermore, everyone was prepared to use his arms if necessary. To ensure that a good watch was kept, Barth played a slight practical joke on his men. He tells the story of it in his entry for the 27th November 1852:

> In order to test the vigilance of my people, since the major part of the security of a voyage in these regions depends on the look-out kept at night, I made a midnight round of inspection of my camp. I managed to disarm all my men unnoticed. The confusion next morning was most amusing. In this manner I gave them a much needed lesson and taught them to be more vigilant in future.

He travelled across the plains of Bornu reaching Sokoto, the capital of the Fulbe, in March 1853. There had been another blank space on the map west of the area, and Barth was the first white man to reach these regions. The expedition crossed the unknown territory keeping to the level ground, and on the 21st June they reached Say, an important junction and ferry-place on the *Joliba*, as the Negroes of West Africa call the Niger.

Everywhere Barth's caravan had aroused much more attention than was politic. As a precaution against attracting so much attention, the explorer described himself as a *Sherif*, a holy wise man, and pretended that he was to hand a number of pious old books from the Orient to the Sheik of Timbuktu. This disguise proved very successful and Barth was even taken for the *Mehedi*, the Messiah himself. In the middle of August he wrote in his journal:

> After leaving Say I was frequently asked about the *Mehedi*, the Messiah, whose second coming was eagerly awaited in those regions. The poor people, in particular, looked on me with wonder, believing me to be the sage coming from the East.

On the 7th September 1853, Barth entered Timbuktu, still disguised as a *Sherif*. Excitedly he examined the town, which was in the shape of a large triangle and was surrounded by walls of earth. Barth estimated the distance around these walls as about three or four miles. The town consisted mainly of single-storied houses, most of which were built of clay. Altogether there were about one thousand such houses. Occasionally a taller building was to be seen, but there was none of the glamour of Timbuktu's reputation. The town could boast only three mosques, and after Kano it cut a very poor figure! René Caillié had been completely right. The 'fantastic and truly incomprehensible descriptions' of the 'Queen of the Desert' current in Europe were altogether false and erroneous.

But Barth was not allowed much time for observation. The intelligence service of the rich merchants soon learned from Kuka and Kano that this alleged saint was no other than a Christian and an ambassador of the Queen of England. It also soon discovered that he was asking innumerable questions in the streets and market-places about the kinds and prices of the trading goods sold, about caravan routes, salt deposits and wells. Naturally he was taken for a spy. The authorities in Timbuktu had always had a great hatred for this type of person. The town, which was not very old, had originally been founded by the Tuareg, the predatory desert nomads, as a storing place for their booty and placed under the surveillance of the slave girl Tinboktu, 'the woman with the great navel'. In the middle of the nineteenth century it was ruled by an oligarchy of the leading families, who watched carefully lest one of their number should become more powerful than the others. Under these circumstances, a mysterious stranger like Abd-el-Kerim must have appeared most suspicious indeed!

At first Barth had no inkling of the trouble in store for him. Not long after his arrival he went down with a bout of fever, brought on by the strain of the journey, and was oblivious of the intrigue going on around him. More than once during those days his life hung by a thread, and perhaps he was only saved from Laing's fate by the fact that, one day before he fell ill, he had organized a shooting match before El Bakey, the Sheik of the city, with a Colt six-shooter.

> This had a tremendous effect on my future security. The people believed that I carried weapons everywhere on my body and that I could shoot as often as I pleased.

The pistol whose efficiency Barth had demonstrated was an entirely new weapon. Its inventor, the American mechanic Samuel Colt, had produced the first model twenty years earlier, but was only able to get it mass-produced during the Mexican war of 1847. From then on supply could never keep pace with demand. The conquest of the western prairies was only made possible through Colt, for although the muzzle-loading musket of the early farmers and trappers of North America had a greater range than the Indians' bow, it was clumsy and took so long to reload that very few of the settlers lived to fire a second shot once they were attacked. Like the Indians, the Arabs immediately understood the power of a man who could shoot six times in succession without reloading.

Nevertheless Barth's situation remained critical, and during the seven months which he spent in Timbuktu he was never certain of his life. Finally, on the 18th May 1854, he received permission to leave and to start his journey back. El Bakey, the Sheik, even accompanied him part of the way. At last he reached those familiar regions which he had already crossed on his way to Timbuktu. The natives greeted him with a great show of friendship and informed him of the rumour circulating in Europe that he was dead. In fact, the German newspapers had already published his obituary, and an expedition had been dispatched to attempt to discover some trace of him. Barth was even told the name of the leader of this expedition, a certain Dr. Vogel. Barth continued on his way, and by the end of November 1854, he had reached the jungles of Bundi, to the west of Kuka. Here the incredible happened: the two explorers met. Thus the famous meeting of Stanley and Livingstone had its parallel in this meeting of Barth and Vogel. We wish to give Barth's own account of this meeting, just as, later on, we shall quote that of Stanley.

'I was riding three miles in advance of the caravan, accompanied only by my faithful servant Mohammed, when I saw a person of most strange appearance approaching—a young man with a snow-white skin, which after these many years, seemed to me to be a sign of sickness. I saw that one of his black companions—it was a former servant of mine called Madi—suddenly rushed up to the young man and shouted a few words to him. Then the white man, who was none other than Dr. Vogel himself, who had been sent out to search for me, spurred his horse and galloped towards me. Our astonishment at this chance meeting can well be imagined; neither of us had even suspected that we might meet right here in the jungle. It was a most happy surprise. We dismounted in the middle of this inhospitable forest, greeted one another warmly and sat down. I took a small pack of supplies from my saddle bags and ordered coffee to be made, just as if we were at home. For more than two years now I had not heard a word of German or any other European language, and it was an infinite joy for me to be allowed once more to converse in my own language. But our conversation soon turned to subjects that were not so pleasant. To my great disappointment, I learned from Dr. Vogel that there was no money waiting for me in Kuka and that what funds he had brought with him had already been used up. This news did not affect me as much as the fact that Vogel did not even have one bottle of wine among his baggage. I had lived for more than three years without tasting a drop of wine or of any stimulant apart from coffee, and after my frequent bouts of fever and dysentery I felt an almost obsessional longing for the juice of the vine, of whose revitalising effect I had the most pleasant memories from my previous travels. After a conversation lasting almost two hours we had to separate again, Dr. Vogel to perform the other tasks allotted to him now that his main one of finding me had been accomplished, and I to catch up with my people, who had gone on in advance of me.

At the beginning of December 1854, Barth entered Kuka, the town which two years earlier had been the starting-point for his journey to the Niger. King Omar received him in his former friendly manner, and Barth made a Christmas present to the inhabitants of the Residence of fourteen head of cattle. Vogel, who had been carrying out explorations on a minor scale in the vicinity of Kuka, joined Barth at the end of December. A warm friendship soon sprang up between the hardened traveller and the young man of twenty-five who had previously been an assistant at Bishop's Observatory in London.

Edward Vogel, born in Krefeld in 1829, was the son of a grammar-school teacher. Like Overweg he was a scientist by training, with no previous experience of Africa and no familiarity with any of the native languages. But like him, he was full of the fire of idealism and enthusiasm. Barth and Vogel spent only twenty days together in Kuka, and then the latter set off towards the south. He would have been only too pleased if Barth could have accompanied him on his expedition into the unknown regions east of Lake Chad, but the older man was so exhausted from years of continual travel that he had to refuse. He had to let his friend go on alone, but noted his anxiety in his journal:

There were two circumstances with regard to Vogel that caused me great concern for his safety: first his complete lack of experience, as one would expect in a young man twenty-five years of age and straight out from Europe, and secondly, the weakness of his stomach; the sight of a meat dish made him vomit and he had to move where he could not see or smell it.

Many years later, when the mystery of Vogel's disappearance was finally solved, it was discovered that his aversion to meat had been one of the main reasons for his murder. Even when travelling in the jungle Vogel could not become accustomed to eating the diet of the inhabitants, and so he had mostly lived on eggs instead of meat. The natives of these regions considered his behaviour repellent and this, together with the fact that he was always asking questions and noting down the answers, had stamped him as a dangerous spy. On the 8th February 1856, he was assassinated on the orders of the Sultan of Wadai. Thus Barth's fears had unfortunately come true. Not long after Vogel's death, his companion, the British non-commissioned officer, McGuire, was also murdered, thus bringing the number of white men who lost their lives in the Barth-Richardson expedition to the Sahara and the Sudan to a total of four.

There is not much to report of Barth's return to Tripoli. This time he travelled by the ancient caravan route leading from the north-east bank of

Lake Chad through the Burnu valley to Murzuq, wending its way between the mountainous country of Tibesti in the east and the Aïr mountains in the west. The Tuareg made vast stretches of this 1,500-mile-long route, which even today is only passable by camel, their favourite hunting ground for loot. Many travellers before him and many after him have had to give up their lives as well as their money! Barth relied on his good fortune, and also took the precaution of travelling in forced marches from early morning until deep at night so that he had hardly any rest during the hot noon hours. At the end of May 1855, the caravan reached the desert proper, looking for all the world exactly like the layman's idea of the desert. Even Barth who had not yet experienced this 'classical form', so to speak, of the dry steppes was deeply impressed:

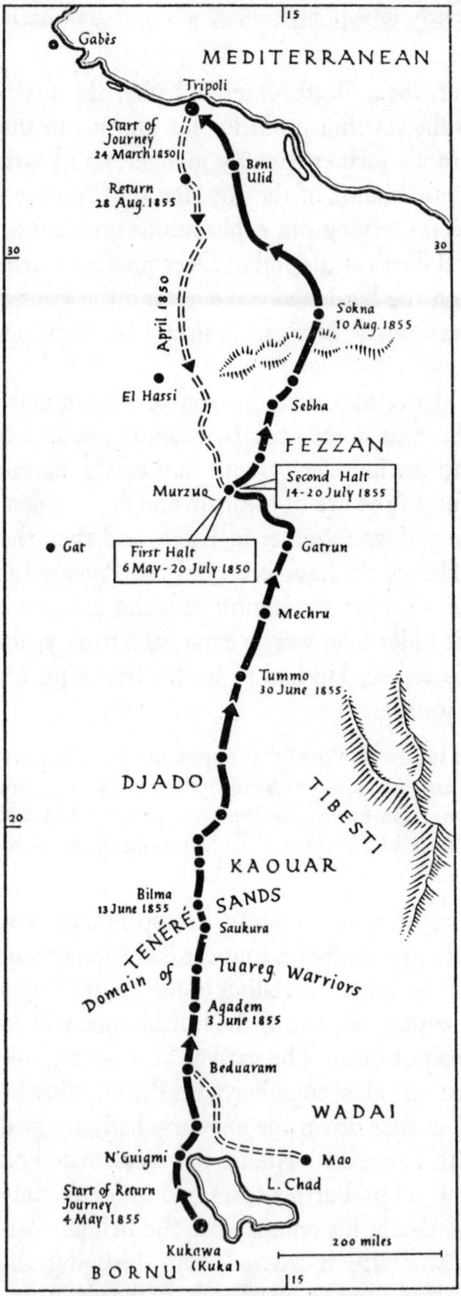

> After a march of six miles, we came upon a sea of sand. At last I had an opportunity to survey its immeasurable surface. Despite its uniformity the desert had something ineffably magnificent, and brought home to man the consciousness of his own insignificance.

XXXVIII. Heinrich Barth's return from Kuka to Tripoli.

Strangely enough even in the open sand-desert, where the dunes were occasionally so steep that steps had to be cut in the sand to allow the beasts of burden to advance, Barth continued to use a horse. In later times this was to become an almost impossible feat. Through the progressive desiccation of this area, wells dried up so quickly that horses could last out the longer stages only with great difficulty, and camels had to be used. This slight example gives us an idea of the speed at which vast regions of the earth have dried up in the last ten or twelve decades.

On Friday, the 14th July 1855, the travellers reached Murzuq. Barth was deeply moved as he recalled the day, five years earlier, when he and his comrades had first entered the town. His heart was heavy when he had to take his farewell from Mohammed his servant, who lived at the Gatrun oasis, south of Murzuq. Once this faithful man knew his white master out of danger, he was eager to get back to his wife and children. Three men who had served with Barth accompanied him to the coast. The English soldier, Church, who had come out with Dr. Vogel's expedition, but who had been left behind in Murzuq since he had proved completely unsuitable for the task both physically and mentally, accompanied Barth on his return journey. In addition to the above company, there were the two black men Dyreggu and Abbega. These men had been bought out of slavery three years before by Overweg and did not wish to leave Barth, once Overweg was dead. Dyreggu and Abbega not only went to Tripoli, they embarked for Europe and later settled down in the small Thuringian capital of Gotha. Some of the old people there can still remember these two friendly Negroes, the companions of one of the most eminent explorers of all time.

The road from Murzuq to Tripoli, which Barth had once considered excessively long, seemed to be nothing but a small jump now. On the 21st August 1855, our traveller finally returned to civilization after an absence of five and a half years during which he had covered more than 9,000 miles.

> My heart was filled with joy as we approached Tripoli, which I had left five and a half years before. The town seemed to me to be the gateway to peace and safety. After long years in barren desert regions, I was full of wonder at the flourishing plants in the gardens of the city. . . . When I came to the border of the ocean I felt such gratitude to God that I was tempted to dismount from my horse and to offer a prayer of thanks to the Almighty by the shores of the ocean. . . . Then I rode on moved to the very depths of my soul.

On the 6th September 1855, Barth landed in London, where he was received by Palmerston, who told him a few days later that the Queen had bestowed upon him the Order of the Bath. Three weeks after this he landed in Hamburg where his family awaited him. Hardly had he reached Europe than his old shyness took hold of him again, and in the midst of the noisy jubilance of the welcoming festivities he withdrew into his shell. Very soon he realized that in that climate he could not draw close to those about him.

Yet he longed for friendship as a child longs for its mother, and it is touching to read how Barth confessed in a letter to a relative that 'a companion, if I chose her well, could bring my whole life to fulfilment. I am longing for an exchange of hearts and love.' But this innermost wish was not to be granted to him, as it rarely is to men who suffer from the same mother-obsession. Barth remained a solitary figure and became more and more unapproachable. In 1857 the famous Berlin Academy of Sciences discussed the question of Barth's election as an ordinary member—he had already been appointed a corresponding member in 1855—but the idea was rejected. Among those who spoke against his election were the Egyptologist Lepsius, the historian Mommsen and even his former university teacher, the archaeologist Böckh.

Barth never recovered from this blow, and his appointment in 1863 as Professor of Geography at the University of Berlin did not lessen his disappointment. He knew full well that he had deserved better of his countrymen, and at the conclusion of the five thick volumes of his travel reports he wrote:

> When the original leader of our enterprise died, I did not become a prey to my despair but I continued to do my duty and explored extensive previously unknown regions, almost without any means. After the leadership was handed to me, I decided to make a journey to the far West. I managed to fulfil my resolution beyond my expectations and thus I investigated the land between Kano and Timbuktu which before had been unknown, even to Arabian merchants. Furthermore I established friendly relations with the chieftains along the Niger as far as the mysterious city of Timbuktu. All this I carried out, including payment of the debts left by the previous expedition, on approximately 10,000 thalers.

Heinrich Barth died in Berlin on the 25th November 1865, at the age of forty-four. A chronic stomach complaint which had troubled him in Africa had become more serious, and since, on his travels, he had become accustomed to treat himself, he did not consult any doctors. In any case the doctors of the time could not have helped him much. Rudolf Virchow, who performed a post-mortem, diagnosed a multiple perforation of the stomach walls caused by neglected ulcers. A hundred years ago doctors were not able to do anything for cases that had gone so far. Thus, Heinrich Barth, after less than four and a half decades of an unhappy life, rich in disappointments, left for another world. His grave lies forgotten in an old cemetery not far from the modern aerodrome of Tempelhof in Berlin. His successors have paid little tribute to his achievements, and yet Barth obtained far greater results than any traveller in Africa before him. In the words of the ninety-year-old Alexander von Humboldt: 'Barth opened up a new world.' This judgment, which puts him on a par with Columbus, is fully justified. Only Barth was able to give the Old World an adequate picture of Africa and the Sudan. Our knowledge of the life of the Berber and Negro peoples of the Sahara, of their history, culture and languages, dates from his travels. When today we cross the Sahara, throughout its length and breadth, in our trains and buses, we should spare a moment's thought for the man who was largely responsible for making our journey possible.

10

Deeply frightened, the young military surgeon saw the blood on the handkerchief he had just withdrawn from his mouth. A fit of coughing had racked his body and left him gasping for air. He knew exactly what these symptoms meant. Phthisis, or consumption, the disease which had carried off both his father and his brother, had staked a claim on him too! The first signs were loss of weight which continued until the body was quite emaciated; this process went on until death finally came for its victim. Sometimes only certain parts of the organism were attacked. When the lungs were affected, the sufferer would cough and spit blood and, as the disease reached the stage when it was called 'galloping consumption', there were frequent haemorrhages. The patient now had only another few weeks to live. Occasionally an isolated case could be cured, but no one knew why this was, or even the real cause of the disease. In any case when haemorrhages of the lung occurred, it was too late, much too late.

When in September 1862 the Prussian military surgeon Dr. Gustav Nachtigal found that he was dangerously ill, he was only twenty-eight years old. At the time he was garrisoned in Cologne on the Rhine. He liked Cologne and he loved the life of the town, the wine and the Rhenish maidens. It is not very agreeable to find out that you are a very sick man, but it is even worse to be a doctor and be able to predict almost exactly the course your illness will take, particularly when you know that the only possible outcome is a speedy death. This was the reason why Dr. Nachtigal's youthful face was white as chalk under his helmet when he reported to his superior officer, an hour after he had had to be helped from the parade ground, unable to control a terrible fit of coughing. His gaze did not flinch as he told the old staff surgeon that his death warrant was signed. He could see that the old man was deeply affected and was trying to hold back his tears, for he too knew what the tell-tale sign of blood in the handkerchief meant! There was however just one chance, a very small one it was true, but it was a chance. The old man explained to Nachtigal that French doctors had reported from Algeria, which had by then been a French colony for over thirty years, that they had had cases where patients suffering from consumption had recovered after spending a long period in the hot dry air of the desert. There were no grounds for believing that it was a cure which worked in every case, but he happened to have a relative in Algeria, a ne'er-do-well cousin, who had not made much of a success of his life in Europe but who seemed to have made good out there. The old surgeon offered to write to this cousin and ask him to receive Nachtigal.

A few weeks later the cousin's reply arrived, and at the end of 1862, the former military surgeon Gustav Nachtigal arrived in Algeria. He would have been the last person to suspect that he had reached a great turning-point in his life and that he was destined to become a famous explorer. He had never shown any aptitude or inclination for geography and the same applied to the study of foreign languages. In fact, some years later, as he was standing on the banks of Lake Chad, he remembered vaguely a lesson he had had in the grammar school in Stendal, a little town in the Old Electorate, in which the teacher had talked about this lake in the middle of North Africa and pointed to its position on the large school map. This was the sum total of Gustav Nachtigal's knowledge of the Black Continent.

Some time after his arrival in Algeria, Nachtigal went to live in Tunis. The hot, dry air seemed to have worked a miracle, and soon he felt well enough to begin to practise as a physician. By a stroke of fortune he quickly acquired a reputation and an official post. He managed to cure, and impress, the *Chasnadar*, the representative of the Bey of Tunis, who, out of gratitude, appointed him Court Physician. The Turkish dignitary had such faith in Nachtigal's ability that in 1864 he asked him to accompany the Tunisian army on a year's campaign against the predatory hordes of nomads who were infesting the desert regions.

It was during this year that Africa managed to cast its spell over the young man. He studied Arabic until he could speak it fluently, and he threw himself with passionate zeal into scientific studies. He read all the books to be had on Africa—and by this time the literature on Africa was quite considerable. Thus he became aware of what had been accomplished and what remained to be done. He learnt about the problems of exploration and even about the latest scientific theories. Although he was often to complain that his education had been inadequate and insufficient, he made up for any want in specific training by his practical sense, his great intelligence and his enthusiasm.

Nachtigal was most reluctant to return to Tunis once the campaign had been brought to a successful conclusion. He was bored with the life there and had almost decided to leave Africa for good, when a strange fellow brought him an even stranger commission. He was a certain Gerhard Rohlfs, a native of Vegesack near Bremen, who had started his career as a medical student and had served in the Austrian Army and in the French Foreign Legion. He was three years older than Nachtigal, who was born in 1834, and while the latter had been forced by illness to the shores of Africa, the former had chosen a life of adventure from inclination. In 1861, he had been discharged from the Foreign Legion after six years of service, but instead of returning to Germany, he had gone to live in Morocco even though the natives there were very suspicious of foreigners. He spoke Arabic fluently and knew the Koran, with its one hundred and fourteen *suras*, by heart. The knowledge he had gained during the few terms of his medical studies was sufficient to win him the appointment of Physician-General to the Sultan of Morocco's army and of Chief of Sanitation in the harem of the brown potentate. But Rohlfs was not content with these high positions, even though they gave him tremendous influence in the country. In 1862 he left his post, and from sheer love of adventure set out for the interior of the country. He travelled south from Meknès and managed to find a way over the Atlas mountains which were then completely unknown territory. Eventually he reached the oases of Tafilalet, the 'Land of the Dates'. Here he was attacked by a band of marauding Bedouins, stripped of his possessions and left for dead. By some miracle he recovered from his wounds and a few months later he was well enough to continue his journey. In addition, the former Foreign Legionnaire had come very near to dying of thirst on several occasions, but Africa had cast her spell over him and he was as if obsessed by the desert. Hardly waiting until he had properly regained his strength, Rohlfs had travelled to Agadir via Rabat and Casablanca. From Agadir, Rohlfs struck deep into the Sahara to the Tuat oases and thence to In-Salah. Both of these places were junctions of caravan routes. At this point Rohlfs turned east and some months later he appeared in Tripoli. This last journey had taken him along the future route of the railway linking Tunis to the coal deposits of Colomb-Béchar, the iron and lead mines of Erfoud and the harbour of Agadir. Although Rohlfs had had no training at all as an explorer or a surveyor and was working with a minimum of equipment, his journals and sketch maps are so detailed and accurate that even today they could still serve for planning roads and railway tracks.

This then was the man who in the late autumn of 1868 visited Nachtigal in Tunis. The exertions of his previous existence in the Legion and then his travels had marked his features. His face was frighteningly thin, with hollow cheeks and black shadows under his eyes. He seemed to be a prey to a feverish unrest that allowed him no peace, and looked as if he constantly responded to the clarion call of the Foreign Legion, '*Marche quand-même!*' ('Forward, regardless!'). He was anxious to start immediately for the oases between Tripoli and Alexandria, so that no other could get there before him. So far no *giaour* had visited these oases of the 'Pope of the Sahara', the mysterious Sidi el Hadj Mohammed Ibn Ali, chief of the fanatical Senussi. Six hundred miles of desert separated this area from Tripoli, but a fabulous country with great palm groves, cool blue lakes, ancient, mysterious, weatherbeaten buildings and glistening mosques awaited the man who could conquer the desert. These beauties lay, however, in a land filled with fanatical hatred of the Christian dogs. Even to this day the inhabitants mean business when they pray each day in their mosques and monasteries: 'O Allah, for the love of Thy prophet Mohammed, unite all Thy faithful throughout the world! Let us grow strong and fight against the foreign dogs, so to enter Thy eternal realm.'

The dangers of such an enterprise merely whetted Rohlfs's appetite, and he was all ready to start when he received unexpected instructions from the German Colonial Office which upset his plans. He was instructed to proceed to Kuka in Bornu and to visit Sultan Omar, as an ambassador of King William of Prussia, later to be the first emperor of a united Germany. It will be remembered that Omar was the ruler who had received Barth so hospitably. Rohlfs was furious at this order from distant Berlin, and even thought of ignoring it. The very air of Tripoli turned 'blue' with the stream of curses in Arabic, French and German which he let loose on to the head of Bismarck and the whole Colonial Office in Berlin. Bismarck was amused to learn from his secret agents in Tripoli of Rohlfs's distress and his extraordinary powers of invective, and wrote a second letter telling Herr Gerhard Rohlfs that he could go to Kufra by all means, provided only that he could find an acceptable substitute, as impressive and as reliable as Herr Rohlfs himself.

Bismarck knew that Rohlfs was proud of his capabilities and he was certain that his orders, however objectionable, would be obeyed. But Bismarck was wrong, for Rohlfs was not prepared to give up his expedition to Aujila and Kufra. He dashed around Tripoli, like Diogenes with his lantern, in order to find a replacement. At one point he played with the idea of sending Barth's old servant Mohammed, who was now in his pay, but then he heard of Dr. Gustav Nachtigal. At once he leapt on his horse and raced off to find him.

Nachtigal was highly amused at the prospect of trekking for several thousand miles through desert and jungle with a baggage train consisting of a velvet throne, life-size images of King William, Queen Augusta and the Crown Prince Frederick, in addition to numerous camel-loads of needle-guns and ammunition, pendulum clocks, pocket-watches, binoculars, tea services, heavy bales of silk and velvet, gallon bottles of rose oil, bracelets and necklaces, burnouses and tarbooshes, books, medicaments and, last but not least, a harmonium. But he too was passionately attracted by Africa and so in the end he accepted Rohlfs's proposition. A few weeks later Rohlfs and Nachtigal were on their separate ways; the one making for the east, the other across the desert to the south.

Rohlfs did not suspect that he would have to make three further attempts before he finally managed to reach Kufra. He had thought that he had seen the worst the desert could offer, but he had to revise his opinion. During his first attempt, which he made during the winter of 1873–4, he had to pass through a region where it had not rained for ten years. From the 26th January until the 12th February, a total of seventeen days, his caravan of one hundred camels had to go without water, and Rohlfs had no option but to return. The same thing happened again in 1878, four years later, but the former Foreign Legionnaire was not the man to give up easily. He made another attempt in the summer of 1879, and this time he was successful. By dint of making forced marches of nearly sixty miles a day, he eventually managed to reach his objective—Kufra; he saw the lakes, the castles, the mosques and the pleasure gardens—it was like a scene taken from *A Thousand and One Nights*. Owing to the hostile attitude of the fanatical Senussi he could only stay a very short time and on his return he confessed in his journal:

> For thousands I could not be persuaded to relive such days as I have experienced in Kufra, and yet I am glad to have been there. The journey and my stay there have aged me a great deal. My clothes are hanging from my body, but what is life without excitement!

The next time Kufra saw Europeans was to be forty years later, in 1920, and even then it was to be another ten years before the 'Rome of the Desert' became finally accessible. The Italian Marshals Graziani and Balbo made an expedition with 5,000 camels, 3,200 natives, 654 Italian soldiers and a corresponding number of bombers and saw to it that the region enjoyed the benefit of the 'Pax Romana' (new style). Thousands of Italians, descendants of the peasants of ancient Roman days, emigrated there, and as if by magic, villages and cultivated fields seemed to spring up from the barren sand. Not much of this peasant conquest of the desert is left today. The war in North Africa and the aftermath of the whole European conflict have more or less wiped out what advances in reclaiming the land had been made. To make a fresh start would require large capital funds and much idealism.

Our other traveller also had no idea what lay in wait for him on his journey to the south. He had neither the experience nor the self-confidence of Rohlfs, and he was assailed by doubts as to his fitness for the task on the very first day out of Tripoli. On the 18th February 1869, he wrote in his diary:

> Though fully aware of my lack of scientific training, I could not manage to resist the opportunity that was offered me. I had, in any case, already planned to leave Tunis, and I told myself that, at the worst, I would be making a memorable journey. I decided to seize my chance and to trust that my knowledge of Arabic, Mohammedan customs and my medical training would help to bring my task to a successful conclusion.

Ten years later, in May 1879, when Nachtigal was correcting the page-proofs of his three-volume account of his travels, *Sahara und Sudan*.

Ergebnisse sechsjähriger Reisen in Afrika ('Sahara and Sudan. Results of a six-year journey in Africa') he added in his own careful hand the following postscript, which reads quite differently from the quotation which we have just given:

Should I have had the courage to carry out my resolution if I had known that fate was to retain me in the unknown regions of that great continent for more than five years? During that time I lived in complete spiritual isolation, threatened by dangers and disease and suffering great hardships and privation. Even the most passionate enthusiast of Africa would have hesitated, if all the difficulties of the expedition had been known in advance, though once you are far from the feverish haste of European life and its diversity of pleasures and diversions, you quickly learn a new attitude to space and time. In a sense, you become more courageous in the face of adversity and more persistent in reaching your objectives.

An explorer must be physically strong, able to resist disease and fatigue, and also have a natural ability to make friendly contact with people of all kinds. He must be blessed with boundless patience, for this virtue bears within it the fruit of success. It was not easy to practise it always, and I was to have many hard struggles with my impetuous nature before I learnt how to accept the stupidity and unreliability of human beings.

II

Nachtigal and his caravan of seven camels did not choose the same southerly route to Murzuq that Barth and Rohlfs had taken; he travelled eastwards across the Tarhuna mountains and through Nefed, Bu Ngem, Sokna and Temenhint, roughly along the modern motor road from Misurata to Sebka. Although this was rather a roundabout way, it was safer since it had the advantage of being also the regular postal and caravan route, and since wells and inhabited intermediate stations were quite frequent along it. Nachtigal took some thirty days to cover the distance, advancing on an average eight to ten hours each day at a speed of two to three miles an hour. This leisurely pace soon taught Nachtigal the virtue of patience and he came to accept the fact that each evening, after noting the thermometer, barometer and anemometer, the wind and weather conditions, he could only record an advance of twenty or twenty-five miles.

After careful measurement I reckoned the speed of our caravan as a little over two miles per hour in regions where there was vegetation along the roadside for the camels to eat, and two and a half miles if there was no opportunity for this. With favourable ground conditions and no delays whatsoever the pace was a little faster still. I made such measurements on later journeys and always had the same results.

Nachtigal was frequently overtaken by the camel post which the Turkish government had introduced between Tripoli and Murzuq. This relay post which followed the eastern route covered the 550 miles to the capital of Fezzan in only eighteen days. Nachtigal was very impressed by its speed and efficiency:

> Fresh camels were held in readiness at fixed times at the main stations along the route. The District Chief would receive the locked bag and take out the letters destined for his region. Then he would lock the bag again and after a short rest the messenger would continue on a fresh camel. This service undertakes, against payments, to deliver parcels, and later in Murzuq I received some fairly large-sized packets from Tripoli.

The caravans which passed Nachtigal going in the opposite direction were almost all slave convoys. Nachtigal had been in the country long enough to know that slave-trading was still an active industry, despite all the efforts of humanitarian and charitable organizations to stop it. Nevertheless the profits to be made from this human cargo were showing a marked drop by 1870, and Nachtigal noted that those slaves who had successfully withstood the long march to the coast were treated far better than he had thought. Although he had been living in Africa for seven years now, Nachtigal still could not accept the idea of buying and selling human beings, and he was indignant that:

> trade with slaves was still very widespread and people enquired their price just as they would ask the price of grain, oil or butter.

On the 24th March, the second great Bairam festival, the Id-Ul-Kabir, was held. This Islamic feast commemorates Abraham's faith in the Lord, when, as Mohammedans generally believe, he was prepared to sacrifice his son Ishmael. Nachtigal and his people had hoped to celebrate this festival in Murzuq, but when the day came they were still some distance away, and so our German bought a fat ram, and a generous portion of *chrab*, palm wine, for each of his men.

> Since the Koran forbids the faithful to imbibe intoxicating drinks, this juice, drawn off from the palm tree, is drunk by true believers in its fresh state only, before fermentation takes place. The juice, when first drawn off, is whitish-blue in colour and is repulsively sweet. But the sugar of the date palm ferments very quickly, and by the second day the juice is already alcoholic, particularly if fermentation is accelerated by the addition of certain substances specially prepared for this purpose. The exact point where the liquid becomes alcoholic is very difficult to determine, and this is very fortunate indeed for the zealous votaries of the Prophet who, under the pretence of drinking date juice, manage to imbibe a fair quantity of good heady wine.

Thirty-five days after leaving Tripoli, the expedition entered Murzuq. Nachtigal would have liked to continue at once, but as there was no caravan leaving for Bornu, he was compelled to remain in Murzuq for a considerable time. During this enforced wait, he found it much more difficult to bear his bouts of malaria and dysentery, and above all the horrible plague of flies, than the strain of travelling through the desert. This is what he wrote:

Any activity during this season which fell at about the same time as our spring, was made almost impossible by the presence of unbelievable numbers of flies. In winter they are bearable, and also much reduced in number, though they never disappear completely, but in spring they are a veritable torture. They would settle on one's body and on everything one was using. At noon the torture reached its climax for they could not even be chased away, it was so hot. The ink-pot had to be shut tight, and when one was writing the pen had to be dipped quickly and the lid closed at once. To drink a cup of coffee or a glass of *laqbi*, the local brandy, was a difficult feat: the free hand had to be used incessantly to chase away the swarms of flies and if you were not careful, they even reached your throat. During the day I was reduced almost to despair, but the nights were peaceful and I could enjoy an untroubled sleep since desert cities are almost completely free from one of the greatest plagues of Africa, namely fleas. On the other hand the louse, the half-brother of the flea, finds exactly the conditions it likes and multiplies exceedingly rapidly. I was often asked by the Arabs if it were true that we Christians did not have to endure this plague. To my great astonishment I discovered that the Arabs do not consider the European's assumed freedom from lice as an advantage. They treat it as an intentional lapse on the part of the Creator.

Nachtigal might have added that as well as the stinging flies, the Sahara can boast four hundred different kinds of poisonous insects, and that Europeans were constantly troubled with stomach and intestinal complaints seeing that the water not only tasted of mineral springs, but even had the associated purgative effect. He did not wish to be taken for a moaner, and thus he kept silent on these matters and, like Hornemann and Barth, he related instead that he had successfully resisted many an 'attack' by the women of Fezzan. He considered flippant and immoral what was in fact nothing but the result of a recently terminated matriarchal state of society. With slight irony he noted in his journal:

That a child could sleep in his mother's womb for years, or even for ever, was not doubted by anybody, and since the men of Fezzan were frequently away on long voyages, this pious faith gave the abandoned women a convenient excuse for explaining an addition to the family during the husband's absence. The seed of the child, she would say, had been laid before his departure, but God had neglected to bring it to fruition at the right time. Many a husband might well have been sceptical, but he could not very well have argued against the well-known fact that birth had been postponed for a year or so.

In Murzuq, Nachtigal was able to renew his acquaintance with the Dutch lady, Alexandrina Petronella Francina Tinné, whom he had met some months previously in Tripoli. She and the Englishwoman Rosita Forbes, who in 1920 became the first European to reach Kufra after Rohlfs, are the only two women whose names deserve a place in the history of the exploration of Africa. It was rumoured that, like Heinrich Barth, she began her career as an explorer after the collapse of a great love-affair, though it is unlikely that the desire to forget a broken heart was her only incentive. She seemed to be possessed by the demon of exploration. This rather unusual pastime for a well-brought-up young lady caused a contemporary journalist to remark that: 'It does not happen every day that ladies from the best society go on adventurous voyages alone, without any other motive than their passion for unknown things and without any other protection than their courage.'

But the young Dutch woman had to pay severely for her love of adventure. In 1862, she set out on an expedition from Upper Egypt, but unfortunately her mother, her aunt and two of the scientists of the party died of fever and exhaustion in the Nile swamps. Depressed by the fact that she had been the cause of the loss of four human lives, Alexandrina Tinné returned to Cairo on the small fleet of Nile ships which she had hired.

However, the call of Africa was stronger than her feeling of guilt, and she read avidly about every new expedition into the Black Continent until finally she could stand her inactivity no longer. She suddenly turned up in Algeria in the middle of the 1860's and set out south to the Tuareg mountains in the Sahara. She failed in her attempt, and went to Tripoli shortly before Nachtigal's arrival, determined to make another try via Murzuq. The natives called her *Bent-el-Rè*, daughter of the King, and indeed she rode like a princess, followed by a large train of black and brown servants, of freed slaves, of Algerian women, Dutch seamen and a young German lad, who had run away from school and home in order to accompany Alexandrina Tinné into the African wilderness, as her page.

In Murzuq, too, Nachtigal found her every inch a queen. Even twenty years later she was still to be remembered there with affection. She distributed bread to the poor each day and often gave them money and clothing. Nachtigal paid her a visit one day, and the two travellers decided that if a large caravan did not appear before the end of the summer, they would join forces, hire an armed escort and make their own way to Bornu. Nachtigal was not completely happy about this plan. He was uneasy about her extremely odd assortment of companions, and also a little afraid that her reputation for carrying valuable treasures with her might encourage robber bands to attack them. Probably he also felt reluctant to travel with a person whose passion for exploration had had such fatal consequences for those in her company.

He was even slightly annoyed when Alexandrina Tinné told him that she intended to use the monotonous months of waiting for making a small detour to Tibesti, 'the mountain land of hunger' as the natives called it, for he had already thought of going there without her.

The most extravagant stories were told about this mountainous country, roughly 375 miles south-east of Murzuq, its many hot springs and its inhabitants, the savage Tibbu. No white man had ever been there and the Arabian experts in Murzuq, with whom Nachtigal had discussed his plan in detail, had tried repeatedly to dissuade him from an enterprise which was not to be repeated for over half a century. Nachtigal was not to be put off, and when Alexandrina Tinné mentioned her decision to go to Tibesti, he set off abruptly, on the 6th June 1869.

The loyal Mohammed, whose father came from Tibesti, was most unhappy about the recklessness of his master, and he warned him of the terrible risks he was taking. Nachtigal was well aware of the dangers and wanted to spare Mohammed, who was no longer young, so he suggested that he waited in his home in Gatrun for the expedition to return. Mohammed's reply was indignant:

'I have promised your friends in Tripoli to lead you safely to Bornu, just as I have guided your brothers Abd-el-Kerim (Heinrich Barth) and Mustapha Bey (Gerhard Rohlfs) to that place. With God's help we will reach that goal together. Until such time I will not leave you, and if the treacherous Tibbu should attack you, I wish to share your fate.'

Nachtigal was deeply moved by so much faithfulness, but he probably did not take Mohammed's warnings very seriously. It was only when Mohammed's wife, herself a Tibbu woman, turned up at the camp that he began to realize the critical time awaiting him. Mohammed's wife did not intend to leave her husband to face the perils of the journey alone. She wanted to be with him. It was a very serious sign indeed!

And things did become serious. At first it was the terrible heat which made travelling unbearable. On the very first day Nachtigal suffered such terrible sunburn on his thighs that he was hardly fit to sit in the saddle of the camel.

My legs felt like lumps of burning lead and every time my skin came in contact with the camel or with the sides of the cases I was sitting on, it caused me such pain that I almost lost consciousness.

Nachtigal adds that the weather had been extraordinarily hot, reaching temperatures of 120° F. in the shade. The chickens had lain half-dead or dead on the ground, their beaks wide open, and the dogs had tried desperately to scratch up the scorching sand to find somewhere cool to lie.

After a short rest at the Gatrun oasis south of Murzuq, their journey ran straight across the desert, away from the usual caravan routes. In this way Nachtigal hoped to avoid the attacks from robber bands which people in Murzuq had warned him were certain to occur, but the desert itself could present its own dangers. Even today this journey is no simple matter, and camels still remain the only reliable means of transport. Soon after leaving Gatrun both sides of the road presented their evidence of the mounting danger: human and animal skeletons, which spoke very clearly of the many who had collapsed and died of thirst there. Nachtigal alone remained unmoved. Soon, however, the inevitable stroke of bad luck happened. One of the smaller wells, which was essential for the caravan on its return journey, was found to have been sanded over, and the next one could not be found although it was not far away, since the guide had lost his sense of direction during the night march, made unavoidable by the scorching sun.

It was the middle of summer, when to go without water for two days means certain death. The heat had evaporated most of our already scant supply, despite the excellent condition of our water-skins. It was obvious that our water would be exhausted in the course of the following day, even with the strictest rationing. Although we still had a half-full skin containing three gallons of water, I had been told by Gerhard Rohlfs that, when travelling in the desert during the summer, he had allowed himself about two gallons of water a day; thus for six men we had little more than had sufficed for Rohlfs alone. We moved silently along, our noses and mouths masked by turbans to reduce the drying up of our mucous membranes and thus to lessen our thirst. Each one of us watched the guide, yet none dared to enquire directly if we were lost. In vain he searched for the well-known landmark, a heap of stones, but each time he spoke it was to utter: Mâ' zâl! Not yet! We travelled all that night and as morning came, we shared out the last of our water. Each one of us received a full glass of this precious liquid, and greedily we drank it down, fearing it would be our last. The last to drink was Kolokômi, my guide. He lifted his veil from his nose and mouth, took the glass, and drank one short draught. He rolled the liquid around his mouth and then squirted the water onto the sand through a gap in his teeth. He handed me the glass to finish, with the comment that he was not yet thirsty but that he could understand that we Europeans, people of the water, could not bear to be without water, even for a short time. This opinion that the whites on their swampy islands in the ocean lead a kind of amphibian life, is widespread among the Arabs. As the sun rose higher in the sky we began to be tormented by thirst. Our mouths were parched and our heads felt as if an iron band were tightening around them. When at last we came to a rock wall which afforded us some refuge from the sun's glare, all except Kolokômi, who had lost none of his energies, sank down at its foot. Saad began to say his prayers, preparing himself to enter Paradise. Ali just sat and stared in front of him without seeing anything. Mohammed began to expound his Panglossian belief that everything which Almighty God had predestined for us was good, and that we should resign ourselves to His will. Giuseppe, who had been brooding silently for some time, suddenly stood up, took his revolver and announced in a dazed manner that he was going to follow Kolokômi and shoot him down for having led us to this pass. None of us had the strength to restrain him from this senseless plan. When the afternoon came, without Kolokômi appearing, my hopes began to fade. There *was* no water here and my career in Central Africa was over. My mind instinctively refused to accept this sentence but my thoughts began to wander. I wondered how my friends would receive the news of my end. I found this pastime quite consoling and began to surrender to the thought of death. A veil seemed to be falling over my eyes, I no longer knew where I was, and then I must have fallen asleep and dreamed, for I saw quite clearly my parents' house and myself a child, playing in the garden. Then this vision faded and I must have lost consciousness completely.

Kolokômi managed to find the well just in the nick of time and race back with the precious fluid to revive the other members of the party. Soon the torture of the last two days was forgotten, and they were able to continue.

Not many hours later they could see massive walls of black rock rising from the sand. No plants grew on these walls, no bird ever made its nest among their worn stones, no desert fox barked there at night. The silence of the grave seemed to hang round them like a funeral shroud. Tremendous castles with fantastic roofs and gothic turrets had been cut in the rock by the corrosive force of timeless storms and winds. Sand trickled from empty window frames, and dripped like water from lofty beams in a castle which no man had ever inhabited. This was the kingdom of *Shaitan*! This was his hell and the dwelling-places of the djinns, the evil spirits. With shudders the coffle was travelling along the sky-high rocks. Even Nachtigal himself was affected by the superstitious fears of his men, but he took hold on himself and remembered that he was the first European here, the first white man to visit the devil in his own hide-out.

Day after day they continued to the south-east with relentless monotony. Anyone less determined than Nachtigal would have admitted defeat and turned back, but Nachtigal was made of sterner mettle. He had planned to see Tibesti and he meant to achieve his aim. Then one day, far away in the distance, they could make out the outline of some mountain peaks. Mohammed was beside himself with joy and rushed to Nachtigal shouting that he could see Tibesti, his father's birthplace. The peaks were part of the Tarso, a high mountain ridge. The highest is called Tusidde and rises to over 8,500 feet above sea-level. As soon as these tremendous masses became visible, Nachtigal decided he would have to climb them. He set off in the middle of August with a small party, chosen from the main caravan, and struggling over the jagged loose rock, eventually reached the main ridge. Even at a height of over 8,000 feet the temperature was still more than 100° F. during the day, but the nights were bitterly cold in comparison as the temperature dropped to 50° F. Even so the expedition was fortunate for temperatures of 120° F. during the day and 20° F. by night have frequently been recorded in those regions. When the year is wet, ice and deep snow cover the mountain. Nachtigal's native companions began to complain, and he too was finding the climate very uncomfortable. In addition to this, provisions were short and all that could be bought were a few sacks of ripe dates. Water too was hard to come by. Nachtigal, however, was determined to carry on and explore the ridge. At the base of the Tusidde peak was a gaping crater more than three miles across and 2,300 feet deep. The natives called it the 'Sodium Pit', and deep down there could be seen blinding-white, soft, loose masses. Nachtigal was highly excited but his companions had had enough for the time being.

I would have given almost anything to have stayed for a few days, in order to climb to the top of Tusidde and down into the crater. From the top of Tusidde I could have seen the whole wide panorama of Tibesti, and in the depths of the crater I could have studied the effects of the destructive and creative forces of Nature. I sat on the edge of the crater and gazed for the last time. Then I stood up and sadly followed my companions who were disappearing across the distant horizon. . . .

Today the *trou au natron* is visited by hundreds of tourists each year, and is referred to in the guide books as a 'peculiar and picturesque phenomenon'.

A few days later Nachtigal's expedition entered Bardai, the main town of the region. A bad harvest had reduced the inhabitants to the verge of starvation and so the white strangers, with their seemingly inexhaustible supplies, appeared to them like gifts of God. They crowded round Nachtigal and begged or wheedled food from him until his provisions were exhausted, whereupon he and his people were shut up in prison. The hatred of the whole population was directed against the *giaour*, and Nachtigal feared they would murder him at any minute. One night, however, he managed to escape. What little goods he still had were left behind and he could take nothing but a few stone-hard dates and his camel packs. He still had to face the apparently impossible 500-mile trek across the desert back to Murzuq. Even now Nachtigal's courage did not fail him, and the thought that he had been able to save all his notes and also the map which he had drawn of the 'mountainland of hunger', made him feel that all the hardships he had suffered had been worth it.

Forty years later this map was to be used by Jean Tilho, the second white man to reach these regions. The Frenchman Tilho spent the five years between 1907 and 1912 in this country and explored it thoroughly—nearly 40,000 square miles in all—from north to south and east to west. Nachtigal would have been proud to know this, but he had long been dead when Jean Tilho started out.

Cheered by the thought that his work had not been in vain Nachtigal struggled on, and at the beginning of October 1869 he limped into Murzuq, a pitiful figure, covered in sores and clad in rags. There he learnt to his great joy that all his men had managed to get back safely. He was also told of the fate which had befallen Alexandrina Tinné.

Instead of leaving for Tibesti as she had planned, the intrepid Dutch woman had accepted an invitation to visit the Tuareg, and was provided with letters of safe conduct from the Tuareg chieftain. However, as she was crossing a region considered to be safe, she met with a fate that could befall any traveller in Africa as recently as two generations ago. She was murdered for her assumed wealth by hired assassins.

Nachtigal was not able to leave for Bornu until six months later, in the April of 1870, when the Turkish governor of Tripoli sent a caravan bearing presents to King Omar. Nachtigal was allowed to join it. He realized that he would cut a poor figure in his ragged dress by the side of the Ottoman potentate, but this was his one opportunity to get away from Murzuq and carry out the expedition in safety from attacks. Nachtigal left Murzuq on the 18th April 1870, with nine camels and twenty-five Moroccans as his bodyguard. The caravan travelled almost due south, passing through the many oases in those regions. As far as Bilma, the southernmost oasis of the Hawa group, the going presented no difficulties, but then came the seventy-five-mile stretch of desert with pronounced dune formations which made tremendous demands on human beings and animals alike.

Once this uncommonly difficult stretch had been left behind, the part of the journey across desert was over. Patches of coarse grass appeared here and there, and this soon gave way to shrubs and bushes, marking the transition from desert into savannah. The sky, which for the last two weeks had been mercilessly clear, began to be covered with clouds and, while in the desert itself perspiration was unknown, here the whole body was bathed in sweat at the slightest movement. The sight of so much vegetation and of a variety of wild life cheered the traveller after the monotony of the desert. At one point the caravan found itself in a small forest, whose soil was covered with a thick carpet of blossoms of all colours. On the 28th June, Nachtigal stood on the banks of Lake Chad.

> The famous lake lay before our eyes flat and bare, surrounded by banks of thick reeds. Many years ago, during dull school lessons, I had often looked at its outlines on the map on the classroom wall. At that time it was the only place marked in the large blank space representing central Africa. At last I had reached this aim of my childhood dreams and of my later ambitions, but the reality did not measure up to my slightest expectations. Nothing but an infinite swamp lay before me.

A few days later the caravan reached its destination, the capital of King Omar. Kuka fully made up for the disappointment caused by Lake Chad. It made an impressive sight, especially when seen from a distance, with its one- and two-storied houses and its lofty walls, some twenty feet high. Nachtigal realized, on closer examination, that though the glory of earlier days had somewhat declined, the town could still boast a colourful, busy life, and was indeed one of the greatest and mightiest capitals of the whole of Africa.

As Nachtigal had expected, he was pushed very much into the background by the Ottoman ambassador, but his confident, decided appearance soon won him respect and his audience with Omar was a complete success. The presents from his 'brother' King William in distant Prussia filled the king with pride and emotion, and the needle-guns, which were the best that Europe could produce, delighted him more particularly. Nachtigal was asked countless times to dismantle and reassemble the guns and explain their mechanism. Nachtigal left the king confident that he could now count on his future support, and for the next three years he used Kuka as a base for all his expeditions, including a journey into the Wadai area. So far this region had proved inaccessible to white travellers. Vogel had attempted to reach it, but had had to pay for failure with his own life.

Although Nachtigal did not have the extensive scientific education of

Barth, he worked with such accuracy that he must be reckoned as one of the greatest German geographers. As well as simple geographical information supplemented by exact cartographic records, he gave meteorological, geological, economic, ethnological, social and political data of the utmost precision. His reports were always well presented and provided extremely rich material for all branches of scientific inquiry. Even today, a large part of our knowledge of Africa is based on the explorations of this traveller, who was so well suited by temperament and natural ability for this

41. *Audience of King Omar.*

activity. We wish to quote another short section of his journal in which he speaks about the slave market in Kuka:

The most valuable class of human goods is the so-called *Sedasi*, that is, a male slave measuring 6 spans from the ankle to the tip of his ears, and aged between 12 and 15 years. His price sets the scale for the whole range of these goods, and the foreign merchant who wishes to know the state of the market first asks the price of a *Sedasi*. Slaves older than fifteen are less desirable and therefore more difficult to sell than the *Sedasi*, particularly if they have not been slaves for long, for, it is argued, they can easily be enticed to run away and it is no longer so simple to train them for their duties. The price of a slave over twenty years old drops considerably, and there is little demand for them since they are past their best for heavy work and since women are more suited to domestic work. Ripe young girls are considerably more expensive than the *Sedasi*, as is natural, but here the prices are not standardised for obvious reasons; their value fluctuates according to the degree of their beauty and the subjective tastes of the merchants. Those girls fit to be concubines generally come off best out of all varieties of slaves. They fill the place of a housewife and often perform the task better than a real wife could, for they are always eager to gain the favours of their master by their diligence, in order not to go from one hand to another. In general the cost of their maintenance is much less than that of a legitimate wife, so that men without means, and all those who are forced to make long voyages, find it more convenient to buy a concubine than keep a wife, particularly since, according to the religious laws of the Bornu people, legitimate wives are not obliged to leave their clan and homeland and can never be forced to do so by any means. Furthermore, if the slave girl bears any children, her position with her master is almost as certain as that of a legitimate wife, for only unusual reasons would make the average Moslem sell the mother of his children.

An exceptional price is paid for eunuchs who, however, hardly ever appear in the public market. There is so great a demand from the dignitaries of the Mohammedan world of Europe, Asia and Africa that eunuchs are very quickly sold out of hand. Most of those who are sold in Bornu do not come from that country itself, yet many a mighty man of that land has not disdained to multiply their number. At times, hundreds of boys are gathered to be subjected to this mutilation, which even Islam condemns. The operating barbers, under the pretence of circumcising the boy, suddenly grasp the entire outer sexual parts of the unfortunate victim with their left hands and amputate them by a swift stroke with a very sharp knife. Boiling butter is held ready and is used to staunch the blood from the fresh wound. It is clear that very many do not survive this horrible operation.

At the beginning of 1874, Nachtigal decided to call a halt to his journey and return to Europe via Egypt, and on the 10th August of the same year he reached the southern borders of the immediate European sphere near El-Obeid in Kordofan. He was welcomed by the Sheik el-Beled, the Mayor of El-Obeid and Dr. Georgi, a Greek doctor and sanitary inspector for the Sudan, all of whom had long given him up for lost.

With the Sheik el-Beled, who spoke with me in Arabic, I felt completely at my ease, but the Greek doctor confused me utterly. He first spoke to me in French but changed to Italian when he saw that I could not follow him. It was only when he spoke Arabic that I managed to gather my wits again. I was unable to express myself in German, Italian or French for some time, for I had spoken only Arabic and the Sudanese languages during the past years, and I found the change back to European tongues difficult to manage.

That same evening the Pasha Ismail Eijub, Governor-General of the Egyptian Sudan, gave a banquet in honour of the explorer. Nachtigal felt extremely ill at ease among the resplendent uniforms and the elegant ladies in evening dresses. He stuttered and stammered, replied to questions in the Bornu language, and when he realized his mistake, blurted out his apologies in Arabic or a jumble of English, French, Italian and German words. It was long before he became accustomed to civilization again.

Like Heinrich Barth, Gustav Nachtigal did not live long to enjoy the fame brought by his successes, which had pulled the veil away from so many African deserts and steppes. He was elected President of the Geographical Society of Berlin and was able to continue his work of exploration indirectly by acting as adviser to many subsequent expeditions. In 1882 Bismarck appointed him Consul-General in Tunis, and when in

1884 Togo and the Cameroons became German colonies, he was granted the honour of acting as Germany's representative and hoisting the black, white and red flag. This ceremony was performed on the 14th July 1884, in rather a hurry. Nachtigal had learnt that an old friend of his, the British consul James Hewitt, whom his compatriots were later to call the *too-late consul*, was on his way to the Cameroons to claim them for England.

Nine months later, on the 19th April 1885, death put an end to a life rich in resolution, deed and achievement. Nachtigal died of his old complaint on his way back to Germany. In accordance with his own wishes he was buried in the Cameroons where a memorial stone still speaks of his former presence.

12

On the 18th January 1871, at the same noon hour when the Council in the Hall of Mirrors at Versailles was laying the foundations of the Second German Reich, and when roughly 4,500 miles further south the former Prussian military surgeon Dr. Gustav Nachtigal was leaving the capital of the King of Bornu to explore the regions north-east of Lake Chad, the Lieutenant of the Royal Prussian Reserve, Dr. Hans Suklow, had an unforgettable experience. In civil life he taught Latin, Greek, history and geography in a grammar school in Pomerania. Many a generation of sixth-formers were to pass through his hands and were to learn what had happened to him, when on that 18th January 1871, he had met the famous French explorer Henri Duveyrier, and had shaken him by the hand. At this point he always recited the following lines of Hölderlin:

> And armies surged like seething seas
> And like Poseidon many mighty minds
> Ordered the onslaught of this raging wrath.
> Brave blood flowed freely on this field of death
> And every wish and every human will
> Like lightning flashed and fused in one alone.

What had happened during his meeting with Duveyrier? How had Dr. Suklow, an obscure Pomeranian teacher, managed to meet the great man? The story can quickly be told. At the beginning of the war with France he had been called up, but because of a heart complaint he had not been sent to the front. Thus in the late autumn of 1870, Lieutenant Dr. Suklow found himself with the job of censor in the prisoner-of-war camp at Neisse, an old fortification in Silesia built by Frederick II of Prussia. This was a gigantic network of block-houses which had hardly been used for the last hundred years, but it was quickly made ready to house the prisoners captured near Sedan.

In our callous age, the task of censoring prisoner-of-war letters is considered a first-class sinecure in all armies of the world. Lieutenant Dr. Suklow was of a different opinion. He found it degrading to have to open and read letters which were not meant for him, just because he spoke French fluently. He made repeated requests to be sent to the Front, and to be relieved of his ignoble task, but he met with no success.

On that 18th January 1871, Suklow was performing his unwilling duty, taking letters from one pile, glancing through them and putting them on another pile, when his attention was attracted by a letter addressed to Captain Henri Duveyrier, Sixth Regiment of the Imperial Guard of Chasseurs. It had been sent by a highly esteemed professor of geography at the University of Leipzig.

Duveyrier, Suklow thought, Duveyrier? This surely could not be the famous explorer himself, the professor at the Sorbonne? He would be about thirty now and still liable to conscription, but they certainly could not have sent him to the Front! Perhaps it was his brother or his cousin. In any case Lieutenant Suklow sent his orderly across to the officers' camp to ask Captain Duveyrier to come and see him since he had a letter for him.

A little later he heard the soft jingling of spurs. The sentry posted outside Dr. Suklow's office clicked his heels smartly, an honour awarded even to captive enemy officers. Then the orderly opened the door to announce Captain Duveyrier. A tall, carelessly elegant figure with exceptionally bright eyes stood before Suklow, saluted him politely, and asked in impeccable German betraying an accent of slight surprise: 'You wished to speak to me?' The Prussian blushed. He had recognized his visitor as soon as he had appeared in the doorway. This was no cousin or brother, it was Duveyrier the famous traveller himself. Completely put out by the fame of his visitor he managed to stammer, 'Good God, Professor, how ever did you get here?' He discovered that the great scientist had rejected all attempts to use his services far from the scene of action, because he had believed it his duty to serve with his own regiment. Thus he was now a prisoner of war in the Neisse camp.

Suklow, still out of countenance, handed Duveyrier the letter from Leipzig. The Frenchman opened it, read it and with a slight smile handed it back to the censor, who read the following lines: 'We men of science are citizens of one world, and thanks to insoluble ties of liberty, fraternity and equality, we know no differences of nationality or race, and are totally disinterested in questions of political power!' Deeply moved, the Prussian officer handed the letter back. That single sentence became imprinted in his memory, and years later he would repeat it word for word to his sixth-formers as if it were the motto of his whole life.

When this scene happened, the Frenchman had not been to Africa for almost ten years and his career as an explorer was already over. Although, four years later in 1874, he went once more to the Sahara and in 1884, after innumerable petitions, he even managed to be allowed to accompany the Sultan of Morocco on a voyage from Tangier to Meknès, exploring the completely unknown Riff mountains, the mature man did not repeat the great deeds which it had been granted to the impatience of his young years to perform. In many respects he suffered the same fate that many decades later befell T. E. Lawrence, the uncrowned King of Arabia: politics destroyed his work.

And yet he had set off to a most promising start. He had managed to gain the friendship of the feared Tuareg, the robber barons of the Sahara, and had even become their blood-brother. He could speak and write their language, had lived in their tents, had accompanied them on their journeys of adventure, and had finally so won the respect of these fanatical sons of the desert that they had asked to be joined to France. If politicians had listened to Duveyrier it would probably have been easy to pacify the whole Sahara without removing the sword from its scabbard, and France might have avoided the tragic situation in North Africa.

But after all it is a well-known fact that a prophet is not without honour, save in his own country, especially when he has risen through his own powers and has no influential connections. The Duveyriers belonged to the small landed nobility and, furthermore, came from the Languedoc, a land which produced few lawyers and politicians but many poets and dreamers, crusaders and troubadours. Duveyrier's father was a typical example of these unusual people. As a young man he had been an ardent follower of Saint-Simon, and later he became an enthusiastic Socialist, ceaselessly working to cement the ties of brotherly love and striving for the removal of class differences. This was pure romanticism, and thus no one was astonished when in 1858 he sent his oldest son Henri, who was then fourteen, to Germany, the land of romanticism. At his boarding school in the Allgäu, the exceptionally talented young boy learnt Provençal and the middle high German, the languages of the crusaders and the troubadours.

But the lute and sword belong to the past, the modern knight has different emblems such as Stock Exchange prices, tax returns and profits, and so Duveyrier's father did not leave his son too long studying poems of medieval chivalry. In 1855, he sent him to a merchant school in Leipzig where the young student worked very hard for two years. It was here that the young man met the famous Orientalist Dr. Fleischer, a close friend of Heinrich Barth who at that time was on his way back from Africa.

The inevitable happened. Henri Duveyrier, who at the age of seventeen could already speak Arabic fluently, made his début not in Paris, London or Dresden but in Africa. It was not a very long or important journey. He went as far as one of the northernmost oases in the Sahara, just a stone's throw from the borders of the civilized world. But at this oasis he met a Tuareg noble and this nomad, wrapped in his dark blue cloak, his knightly lance in his fist and the tremendous two-edged sword hanging from the pommel of his saddle, made a deep impression on the young man. Despite his scientific training he was almost ready to believe the legend that the Tuareg were the descendants of some medieval knights who, during the Eighth Crusade, had penetrated as far as the Sahara in order to be invested with a fief there.

The romantic Henri Duveyrier was deeply struck by this meeting, particularly since he had always felt very proud to be French and a faithful son of his country, which some decades previously had made her entry on the African scene. In the middle of the summer of 1830 the French had landed with 37,000 men in North Africa and, by a rapid series of battles, had conquered the towns of Algiers, Bône and Oran. The reason for this invasion was that the coastal towns of Algeria had for long harboured nests of pirates, which had done much damage to French shipping, even in the northern waters of the Mediterranean.

The intentions of France in taking this action were highly moral. Admittedly the most beautiful corals in the world were to be found in the waters off Algiers, Bône and Tunis, and apart from this wheat grew abundantly in North Africa, but who knows whether these factors were taken into consideration when the government in Paris decided to undertake the heavy responsibility of acting as a Mediterranean police force and putting a stop to piracy. The whole of Europe looked on with admiration as these selfless sons of Gaul wiped out the pirates. Only the British were a little loath to applaud the action of the French. There is a malicious German proverb which says: 'Cotton and Christ are synonymous on the Thames', and thus London very cynically interpreted the French willingness to clean up the dens of pirates as the century-old interest of the merchants of Marseilles in wheat and corals. Whatever the truth of the matter may be, on the eve of the French excursion to Algiers Lord Stuart, the English ambassador in Paris, received orders to stress to the French government that England would resent any occupation of Algeria by France. When this official diplomatic step was taken, the French fleet had already sailed from Toulon. Baron d'Haussez, the French Minister of the Navy, was very abrupt with the English Lord and uttered words to the effect that France did not give a damn for England. The English ambassador could not believe his ears and thought he must have misheard, but d'Haussez made his meaning quite clear by shouting: '*Merde!* The times when you could dictate your will to Europe are gone for ever!'

Nevertheless at first Paris did not think of annexing Algeria. France, unlike England, was a peasant country, not an industrial state, and was self-supporting. She needed no colonies to sell her goods. In fact she had had very bad experiences with possessions overseas. She had lost Canada to the English after long and bloody warfare, and Louisiana had been sold to the United States. The possessions in the Senegal, annexed in the eighteenth century, and Madagascar, occupied by Richelieu in the seventeenth, had given nothing but trouble. In consequence, the French Ministerial Council deliberated for some time after Algiers had been plucked like a ripe fruit whether France might not restore this land to its nominal, if quite powerless, owners, the Turks. But soon it became clear that they were no longer free to act as they wished. If France marched out of Algeria, then not only would the pirates return, but other European powers, and England in particular, would not hesitate to annex this part of North Africa for themselves. Thus it was finally decided, albeit with sighs, to retain this distant land. Within ten years the profits from Algeria had been increased by some 600 per cent, having risen from eight million francs in 1831 to nearly sixty-one million in 1841. Today France boasts the greatest colonial empire on earth, covering an area of some four and a half million square miles, a good third of the Black Continent.

42. *A Targui in full battledress.*

Once the decision had been taken, North Africa became quite the fashion in the best sense of the word. The French were thrilled by the idea of bringing back into the European fold this old colony of Rome, the home of countless emperors, fathers of the church and great lawyers. The winning back of Algeria to western civilization appeared to nineteenth-century France as a noble, historical mission. At least, Henri Duveyrier, the son of a Socialist romantic from the Languedoc, could not help but see the African problem in this light. It was quite natural therefore that he should go to Africa. The same logic explains his special interest in the Tuareg.

Of course the legend of the Tuareg's descent from the Crusaders is nothing but a pious fable. It is within the realms of possibility that, at some time, a larger or smaller group of European people had reached the central Sahara. Since ancient times, Africa as far as the Niger and Lake Chad had been one of the large spheres of influence and power of the Old World, the continent being 'dark' only south of the Sahara. But the idea that crusaders were the ancestors of the Tuareg is completely out of the question, even though the latter are light-skinned, have no Semitic features and are generally just under six feet tall. Probably the Tuareg, 'the god-forsaken people of the sand', as the Arabs called them, are descended from that large family of peoples who inhabited vast regions of south and west Europe in the early Quaternary Period and who are possibly connected with Cro-Magnon man. Perhaps they are also dispersed remnants of the Hyksos, that mysterious people which probably came from the interior of Asia and about 1700 B.C. overran the land of Egypt.

Islam obviously considered the Tuareg an alien people, for they converted them to Mohammedanism in a most perfunctory manner. While the wild sons of the desert prayed in Arabic, they hardly understood what they were saying, having retained their original language, *tamasheq*. This isolation was made possible because the regions where they live, stretching from south Algeria to Lake Chad—an area equal to half the United States of America—include the most impenetrable parts of North Africa. Even to this day, the Northern Tuareg's home, the mountainous region of Hoggar, consisting of a crystalline primordial mountain ridge with tertiary volcanoes 10,000 feet high, has never been completely explored. The Arabs themselves call it 'The Land of the Spirits', and do not venture there. Wells and oases are non-existent and vegetation cannot survive. Duveyrier's Targui came from these regions and invited the young Frenchman to return with him. Duveyrier was deeply disappointed that he could not accept the Targui's invitation, but he had to return to Europe.

He first reported to Berlin, and it was a great honour for the beardless youth when the famous Oriental Society decided to publish his dictionary of the Berber dialect. One day Barth, who was living in London at the time, came across this dictionary and was so impressed that he invited the seventeen-year-old explorer to come and visit him in London. A few weeks later, at the end of 1857, the year of his visit to Africa, Duveyrier knocked at the door of the cosy cottage in St. John's Wood, London, where Heinrich Barth was living. Barth took him in and taught him all he knew.

> At first he tried to dissuade me from attempting such great enterprises while I was still so young, but when he saw that he could not shake my resolution he did not spare himself in his efforts to teach and guide me. . . . Later on, he watched over the success of my undertaking and sent me letters, full of cordial advice and the most valuable hints, which opened up new points of view and drew my attention to important facts that I might otherwise have missed. For my protection he gave me a letter in Arabic, addressed to all his friends in the Sahara and the Sudan. . . . I was a Frenchman but the narrow spirit of nationalism found no place in his great heart. . . .

All the knowledge that Heinrich Barth had been unable to pass on in Germany, where his lack of social graces had aroused resistance and antipathy, was now being bestowed in unstinting measure on this young explorer apprentice. He passed on the motto that had made him loved and respected in Africa: always to remain master of oneself and a gentleman, and to be scrupulously just towards black, brown and white. Duveyrier was fertile ground for such seed both by birth and by inclination. Thus equipped, he made a second journey to Africa in 1859, when he was just nineteen years old. This time it was not the gentleman's grand tour but a serious business with a scientific aim in view. He had prepared himself diligently for a full year. He had made himself familiar with the methods of orientation by the stars and had made excursions to distant goals until he was sure of himself and his abilities. He studied geography and the other sciences relative to his purpose with indefatigable zeal. His teacher for languages and ethnographical exploration was the most famous Orientalist of the day, Jean Ernest Renan, the man who fifty years later was to reach celebrity and notoriety through his *Vie de Jésus*. All the same, Henri Duveyrier was still a very young man and was lacking in experience. The other Africa explorers of his time had also been rather young. Hornemann had finished his travels at the age of twenty-five; Vogel, his compatriot, was only twenty-three at the end of his career; Caillié had reached the ripe old age of twenty-nine, and Heinrich Barth's work was over at the same age. Laing, who was murdered in Timbuktu, was thirty-two years old, and Gerhard Rohlfs and Alexandrina Tinné were in their early thirties. Nevertheless, Henri Duveyrier was considerably younger and the years covering the period of early manhood count for double, but still he had the advantage of being much better prepared and educated than many of the explorers who had preceded him. It is certain that on occasions he must have had doubts whether he would be able to master his task, but each time his natural optimism asserted itself. He wrote in a letter:

> I know only too well that the journey I wish to undertake is not without dangers, but I have full confidence in my own powers and I hope that by dint of great prudence and determination I shall manage to avoid all pitfalls and lead my expedition to a successful conclusion. Events will show whether I have deceived myself.

He did not deceive himself. Henri Duveyrier was one of the most successful and tenacious explorers ever to have worked in the Sahara. Next to Gerhard Rohlfs, he has the greatest claim on our gratitude, for it is thanks to his almost ceaseless activity during two years that we can drive our cars in safety across this gigantic ocean of sand.

It was as if fate had singled him out for this task. He started from Biskra, which today is the first station along the road from Constantine. Duveyrier naturally travelled by camel, so that he had none of the difficulties we experience in starting our cars after the cold night of the desert. From here he went south-west, leaving the old caravan route, which followed roughly the course of the modern railway to Tuggurt, then he bore due south making for Ghardaia, the capital of the Beni Mzab, a particularly orthodox tribe of Arabs. After a short stay, he went on to El Goléa, a fertile oasis inhabited by fanatically hostile nomads, who looked on irately as the Christian dog placed his sextant in the middle of the market-place, in order to make an accurate determination of his position. True, no one raised a hand against the almost childlike white youth with his bright, earnest eyes, but he was nevertheless a prisoner, and his return to the north coast was in the nature of an escape. That he had behaved a little injudiciously caused him some anxiety, and he wrote a little later:

> At first glance my voyage to El Goléa might be considered a defeat, since I was forced to leave the town at night under most inglorious circumstances, yet I consider it a success. . . . I have the impression that this route has now been opened up.

Today this is a fact, and drivers who understand something about their cars consider El Goléa a most pleasant and convenient halt. But still Duveyrier's optimism went a little far, for some years later France had to send General de Galiffet and a considerable contingent of troops to establish law and order there. In fact if we examine Duveyrier's first journey in a cold unemotional light, disregarding the evidence of his personal bravery, we are forced to the conclusion that it was not an unqualified success, for he did not carry out his plan of advancing as far as the Tuat oases.

Duveyrier did not allow this to discourage him, and a second expedition was ready to start in the following year. This time he managed to reach Tuareg country. Heinrich Barth had already studied the southern Tuareg tribes but their northern brothers in the Hoggar region, and also in the rugged mountainous country of Tassili, had never before been investigated by white men. Thus in 1860, with the financial backing of Napoleon III, Duveyrier travelled to Gadamès and Gat. Today both these places are connected with civilization by *pistes principales*, and although the words '*sables*', '*dunes*', '*Fech-Fech*' (deposits of pulverized sand dust) appear alongside these roads on the French maps of the area, the ordinary traveller has no difficulty in negotiating, within a few days, a stretch that took Duveyrier months to cover. His hopes to persuade the Tuareg to enter into economic relations with France seemed to be nearing fulfilment. He had established friendly relations with both Ikhenouken, the political head of the Tuareg, and Sheik Othman, their spiritual leader. He had also accompanied the Tuareg as they travelled through the length and breadth of the desert. The chivalrous bearing of the white youth had responded to their own knightly code. He was a crack shot, rode like a devil, fenced with charming elegance, and had been as devoted to the beautiful young Tuareg princesses as if he himself were by birth a knight of the desert. In 1927, seventy years later, the German explorer Conrad Kilian paid a visit to Gat and found that the people of the small oasis still sang heroic songs about the great deeds of this Frenchman.

Duveyrier's main political triumph was the magnificent reception given by Napoleon III to the eighty-year-old Ikhenouken in the Tuileries, but from then on he achieved little of importance. It is true he made other expeditions and returned safely from them, was made a member of the Légion d'Honneur at the age of twenty-one and was awarded the Gold Medal of the Geographical Society of France, but his life as a great explorer was over. He fell ill with typhus and lay at death's door for three months before pulling through. When he was finally cured he discovered to his deep horror that he had lost his memory. This dreadful state, which sometimes appears as a side effect of typhus, improved slowly, and three years after his return he managed to publish his great work, *The Tuareg of the North*. But he was never again to be the same man that had charmed and won the respect of the Tuareg. It was with deep sorrow that he had to stand by helpless while the friendship he had made possible between the Tuareg and France dribbled away like water in the sand. He had to look on while the stupidity of French colonial bureaucrats undid all the good work he had accomplished and when, some years later, an expedition led by the Englishman Flatters was cut down to the last man by his desert friends, the scales tipped heavily against the Tuareg and himself. He was blamed for having given a false picture of them. They were, people said, not noble knights, as the romantic Duveyrier believed, but treacherous lying robbers.

Perhaps this criticism was not entirely unfounded, but the Paris newspapers which spoke of the Tuareg as bandits, beasts and enemies of humanity, completely overlooked the fact that this strange people lived in a country which could not feed them. People who are forced to chew rough grasses and swallow the bitter sap of stunted acacias in order to deceive their empty stomachs and for whom grasshoppers, lizards and rats are rare delicacies, must either emigrate and conquer a new home with lance and sword, or else remain in their mountainous desert and demand a toll from the caravans passing through their barren, waterless country. Those who would not pay the price which the Tuareg demanded, and which they needed in order to exist, were murdered on the spot. Those who did were allowed to continue unmolested.

Today the problem has long been solved. Lance and sword, in these times of revolvers, have become collectors' objects or childish toys and even racing *méhara* cannot compete with French luxury buses, jeeps and aeroplanes. The Tuareg were the first to understand that. In the mining regions of Colomb-Béchar they are now mining coal; in Figuig, Erfoud, Aoufous, Beni Tadjit and Ougnat, they mine lead, copper, nickel, zinc, tungsten, cobalt and uranium. Thus they *have* evolved, at least the men, peacefully and without arms. Only time will show whether this lack of arms is not their strongest weapon. They are about to effect a complete change in the economic structure and the style of living of North Africa, and it seems that they are well aware of it.

Of course Henri Duveyrier could not possibly have had the slightest inkling of the fate awaiting his friends. It is doubtful indeed whether his romantic feelings would have allowed him to understand the difficult choice that faced his friends, and that by European standards they were undoubtedly highwaymen and thieves. But this partial blindness does not detract in the least from the scientific and even from the humanistic value of this great Frenchman's work. Even today, ninety years after its publication, his book is still considered one of the main sources of information about the people, the vegetation and the geographical conditions of the northern Sahara. This book stands alone in the literature on Africa: a happy mixture of youthful enthusiasm, idealism and strict scientific observation.

Duveyrier's own work was done, but he remained in the background, giving help and advice to others who were to continue the great task. Although highly esteemed and admired, he became more and more dissatisfied, feeling himself out-dated and no longer in harmony with the spirit of his times. Thus it came about that one fine spring morning in the year 1892, he took a pistol and blew out his brains in the Bois de Boulogne.

13

The price quoted by the travel agency was too steep. Seven hundred and fifty pounds for a trip to Tamanrasset in the Hoggar mountains in the central Sahara! Furthermore it could only be arranged if at least two other people would go as well. Twice £750 pounds is £1,500 and is an exorbitant amount for a round trip of less than 2,500 miles. In the end, we decided to trust to our luck and drive in our own 1½-litre car.

The trip was a great success. Any motorist who can do running repairs by himself, can nowadays venture across the Sahara. Naturally the car must be large enough to carry sufficient water, fuel and food. But during the winter, between November and February, when sandstorms are rare, hardly any serious difficulties arise. Apart from this, the two main highways—the western Tanezruft route, an all-weather road leading across the 'Land of Thirst', the literal translation of Tanezruft, to the Niger, and the somewhat more easterly Hoggar route which ends up in Zinder—are reasonably well supplied with repair and petrol stations and even with hotels. The French sectional commanders, to whom one reports both out of politeness and for safety's sake, and also the great oil firms in Algiers and their officials, receive one in the desert with touching care and assistance.

But despite the good roads and other services available for motorists, drives through the desert are not just Sunday afternoon trips, and if you have bad luck on such an excursion, it may well cost you your life. Those who do not feel quite sure of themselves should use the luxury coaches, run by the Compagnie Transsaharienne, or by the Société Algérienne des Transports Tropicaux, which have crossed the Sahara for many years on regular schedules; or else they should fly with one of those planes which hop from oasis to oasis. Perhaps better still, they would be advised to join one of the tours that travel via Biskra to Touggourt, a picturesque settlement in the middle of the desert, equipped with facilities for tourists and giving a good example of traditional oasis life.

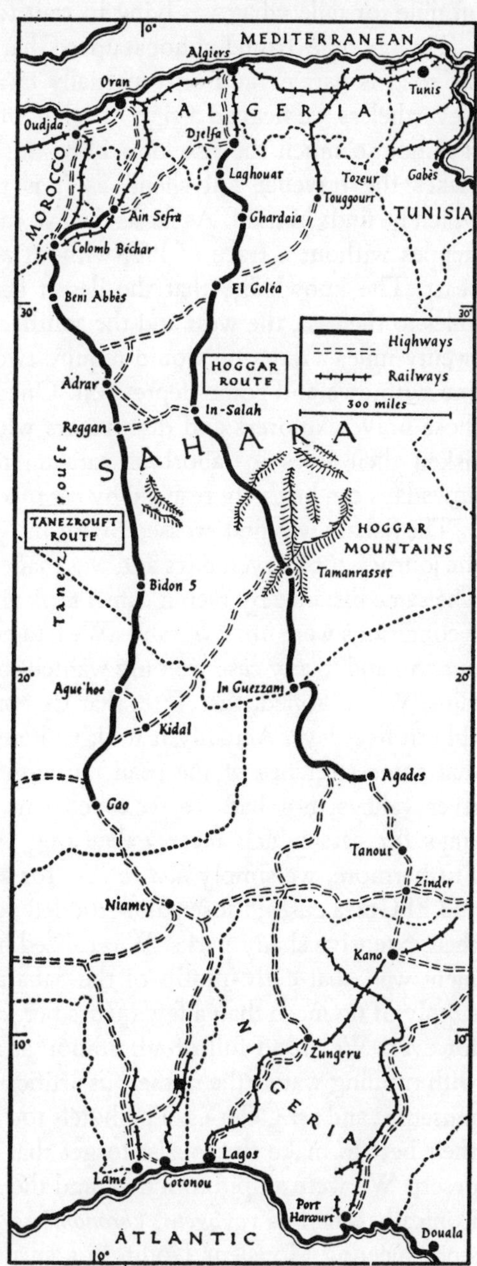

XXXIX. The Tanezruft and the Hoggar routes.

We began our trip from Laghouat, about 250 miles south of Algiers, the starting-point of the Hoggar route, which, although a little more difficult than the Tanezruft route, is very much more beautiful from the scenic point of view. The Shell Company in Algiers had provided us with one of their *Guides du Tourisme automobile et aérien au Sahara*, a magnificently illustrated little volume with numerous sectional maps and detailed descriptions of the 'sights' along the route, and we were always fully prepared and could, as it were, read off mile for mile what was lying in wait for us.

The 125 miles from Laghouat up to Ghardaia are on the level, and though the road is narrow and only partially tarred, high speeds were possible. Nevertheless we heaved a sigh of relief when the first day was behind us. It is not so much the fear of a blow-out that cannot be mended which makes the traveller fall silent, as it is the unimaginable loneliness in which he finds himself. As far as the eye can see there is nothing but stony steppes without a trace of life, without a tree or bush, without man or beast. The knowledge that the desert stretches for many thousands of miles to the east, the west and the south, and that marching at the rate of twenty miles a day one would require two hundred days to cover it, fills one with awe and some depression. One cannot help feeling respect for those brave explorers and discoverers who, until a few generations ago, risked their lives in laborious caravan trips to explore regions which nowadays can be easily reached by car in a few hours.

The Sahara was first crossed by car in 1924, more than thirty years ago; the journey took seven days and was made in stages of 350 miles each day. The same distance by racing camel took about forty-five days, and longer if conditions were unfavourable. We had no desire to break any records on our trip and in any case we only wanted to go as far as the Hoggar mountains. We reckoned, therefore, that we could cover the distance comfortably in five days. Actually it took us longer because we had not realized that some stretches of the road ran along *wadis*, those deep, steep, dry river valleys; nor had we reckoned with the *Fech-Fech* spots, veritable traps for cars which mean exhausting shovelling in order to get free. Furthermore, we simply *had* to stay for a few days at both the Ghardaia and El Goléa oases; those palm-studded dream islands in a sandy sea, with their extensive shady parks. We realized how right the oft-repeated statement was, that eight-ninths of the Sahara is fertile soil and that a water supply of no more than a few quarts per second would break the evil spell for ever. We stood full of admiration at the tiled swimming-pools filled with running water, the numerous artificial lakes and ponds, the mosques, museums and art galleries. The hotels too are generally fairly good and do their best to make the tourist forget that he is in the middle of the great desert. We were stupid to hurry, and the *Sahariens* quite right when they ironically called us *voyageurs chronomètres*, stop-watch travellers. But ever since meeting Monsieur Godin in a small village on the Moselle not far from Nancy—the kind old peasant had lent us his horses to pull our car out of a ditch—we had been filled with a burning zeal to visit Tamanrasset, and to see the final stages of the work of the Vicomte de Foucauld, of whom Monsieur Godin had told us so much.

One evening, the ninth day out from Laghouat, we were driving across the desert towards the Hoggar massif. Suddenly in the far distance we heard a strange roar of thunder, followed by a sudden resounding clap and then the din slowly rumbled into silence. It sounded for all the world as if the Heavenly Host were firing their cannons. Instinctively we tucked our heads down until the noise had stopped and all was quiet again. The

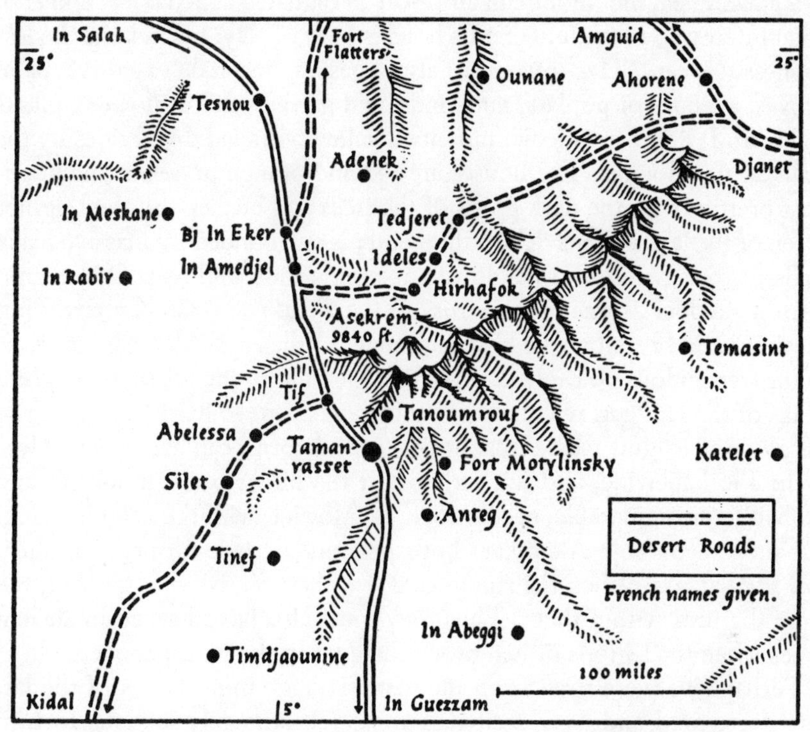

XL. The motor road to Tamanrasset in the Hoggar mountains.

next day we learned that it had been nothing but an avalanche of rocks, caused by the change in temperature between the scorching heat of the sun by day and the freezing cold by night.

Soon afterwards the road became flanked by jagged blue-black rock walls and began to climb, doubling back upon itself, in numerous difficult hairpin bends. We were in the former Tuareg mountain stronghold and we soon realized why the Tuareg, the rulers of the Hoggar, had managed to resist conquest for so long, despite the fact that their total fighting strength could not have been more than three to four hundred men. Even with the modern weapons of today it would still be a difficult task to block all means of access to their eagles'-nest hide-outs. Tamanrasset held out against the French until 1902, and even as late as 1919 two lieutenants were murdered not so far from where we were. Today, of course, law and order have long been established in this region, and not only because Tamanrasset has now become an outpost of the French army. This former hunting-ground of the Tuareg is an oasis just like the others and its reputation for being a dangerous spot slowly gave way before the glory of being one of the most beautiful and impressive tourist settlements in the whole desert.

Tamanrasset, the 'mountain air resort', is situated at 4,500 feet and is of great interest to rock climbers. Its hotel is built of clay, but is none the less spotlessly clean. The town can also boast a hospital, extensive palm groves, avenues of poplars, tamarinds, and gardens full of flowers, plants and fruit. It lies in a wide flat mountain valley bounded on all sides by the walls of the Hoggar. The houses are red and orange in colour, and contrast prettily with the dark green of the trees and bushes and the brighter green of the lawns. This delightful picture is surrounded by massive black walls of rock rising to a height of some nine thousand feet. One cannot resist a shudder as one looks across to the *Brèche de Roland*, a terrifying precipice and breach in the Hadrian range, to the east of Tamanrasset, or to the tremendous volcanic vents of the Asekrem to the north, the highest peaks of the Hoggar, real flues and chimneys burnt so hard by the heat of the glowing magma masses that not even sandstorms can harm them. Here is the Pic Laperrine, and not far from it the hitherto unconquered, and probably unconquerable, needle-rock, Le Mortier, with the neighbouring, but more accessible Akarakar: both primordial rock formations, alien, evil and satanic. When the sun goes down they can be seen glowing red from the fires within them. Thus they must also have looked in ancient times when the legions of hell raised them up in the world above.

Perhaps we were tired from the many strange impressions of the last few days, tired and over-excited, but we felt strangely anxious to turn round and run away.

And it was here that Père Foucauld had lived, the saintly hermit, revered and loved by priests, Tuareg princesses and French marshals alike. During the First World War he served his country as an information officer, and this holy man, who had once been a gambler, a seducer and the protagonist of countless scandals, fell here among the Tuareg far from the busy life of the great world.

14

Monsieur Godin of Pont-à-Mousson, a village eighteen miles from Nancy, could still recall the arrogant, dissolute young lieutenant of the 4th Chasseurs. At the time Father Godin had been a small boy in short trousers, but he could still clearly remember the squadrons of horsemen dressed in sky-blue tunics and scarlet breeches, clenching their curved cavalry sabres in their fists, as they rode past his home. France had based all her hopes on these units after the humiliation of 1870. Alas, Lieutenant Foucauld was not much of a military hope. He did his service, for worse rather than better, and as early in his career as his first appointment, in Pont-à-Mousson, immediately after passing out from the military academy, his superiors considered him an eccentric and reckless wastrel. He lived in a large, elegant mansion in the Rue du Manège and night after night the lights were only extinguished at dawn. People drank, gambled and made love, with charm, spirit and elegance, but also with deadly cynicism and abandon. During this epoch of his life, Foucauld's notoriety was based largely on the invention of a new way of preparing coffee. Since water was much too bourgeois he had his *café filtre* made with cherry brandy. This was a powerful brew and one needed a strong heart to take it, but *his* heart obviously could.

Quite suddenly, no one knew how, a woman entered into his life. Her name was Marie and she was the child of simple people. Foucauld had her dressed in velvet and silk and presented her with horses and carriages. At first she presided as *dame d'honneur* over the nightly orgies, and Foucauld's comments about her were as cynical as everything else that he said about women. But the delicate, fair girl, called Mimi by Foucauld, was one of those wonderful Frenchwomen who can subdue even a gambler, gourmand and drunkard. She saw the man who was keeping her for what he was: a spoilt and immature boy, and she acted accordingly. Imperceptibly Foucauld began to change. He still remained extravagant and wasteful but in a different way. There was more taste and style about his revelries. That winter was particularly cold and the Moselle became covered with thick ice. Foucauld had the brilliant idea of holding a banquet on the river itself. The scene would have delighted the eye of any painter and could not have been rivalled by any stage manager or Hollywood producer.

Chains of coloured lanterns, tied to the trees lining the two banks, hung across the river. Steaming bowls of punch were placed on small pedestals and servants in rich livery served it to the guests in silver goblets. Suddenly, from a group of trees, there emerged a gigantic swan, a sleigh in whose golden interior lay Mimi, covered with precious furs. It was a glorious spectacle, and even after so many years Father Godin's enthusiasm remained undiminished. He proudly gave us full details, as if some of the glory were reflected back on himself. The long tables were covered with the choicest delicacies that the world could offer, the orderlies, clad in furs, carried round bottles of champagne, and at the conclusion of festivities a gigantic bonfire was lit on the ice. The old gentleman became so excited by his own description that there was no holding him. He dragged us out to the Moselle to show us the very spot where it had all happened.

Thoughtfully we made our way back to our hotel. That celebration in honour of Mimi turned out to be Charles de Foucauld's farewell to France, and a farewell to all his previous life. A few days later his regiment was ordered to Africa and was stationed, under the name of the 4th Chasseurs d'Afrique, in Sétif, a small town in the district of Constantine. Thus in the mid-winter of 1880, Lieutenant Vicomte de Foucauld stepped on African soil for the first time. The dark continent was never to release its hold over him. At once it began to fashion him just as it had Rohlfs and Heinrich Barth.

In Africa, Foucauld struck up a friendship with two men who later became famous sons of France. The first was Lieutenant Laperrine, who was to found the famous Camel Corps, the Méharistes, and the other Lieutenant Lyautey who was later to become President-General of Morocco, and Minister of War during the difficult years of 1916 and 1917. These three managed to enact a thrilling last-minute rescue of a certain Captain Marquis de Castries and his beautiful wife from an ambush laid by rebellious Arabs. The Marquise was a brilliant horsewoman and a *grande dame* of the old school. The whole of North Africa was in love with her and admired her greatly, and Charles de Foucauld more than all the rest. Soon, however, he realized that the fascination she held for him did not come from her own personality but from Africa itself, and from her love and understanding of the country. The fever of Africa had claimed him and was to lead him to the little-known land of the Kabyles in Er Rif. It made him learn the language of the Kabyles and Arabic as well, and to delve deeply into the Koran.

Suddenly, things came to a head with his military superiors and Foucauld was dimissed the service. His family had also just added up the balance of his expenses and discovered in horrified amazement that the twenty-two-year-old had, in the two years of his ingloriously terminated military career, squandered over 110,000 francs. The family council then decided to put him on probation. He was given a small but adequate annuity and told to make his way in the world.

As soon as the embarrassing family conference, to which our ex-lieutenant had been summoned from Africa, was over, Charles de Foucauld took the first steamer back to Algiers and disappeared into the desert. Europe, France, his family—all that was past and done with. From now on it was Africa alone that counted. Nevertheless he had to wait a whole year before he could accomplish his great wish. He wanted to make for the interior of Morocco and chart that still widely-unknown territory, but in order to do that he first had to know how to handle a theodolite and as extant, and he needed astronomical, geographical, and cartographic knowledge and to speak the language of the land fluently and without accent.

At the beginning of June 1883, he set off from Oran towards the south.

He travelled disguised as a Jew, thus placing himself under the protection of the malicious contempt which the Arabs felt towards their Hebrew relatives. He explained his presence in the country by pretending to be busy collecting money for the sons of Abraham persecuted in Russia. He returned twelve months later with a wealth of material, completing Rohlf's rather sketchy reports. The largest part of Morocco, as far as the neighbourhood of Agadir, could now be considered fairly well known. In the early autumn of 1885, he started on a new expedition, planned as a preparatory exercise for his later journey right across the Sahara. In this second expedition he roughly followed the modern Hoggar route as far as El Goléa. Foucauld took almost eight weeks to cover a stretch which today means a three-hour drive by car! At the beginning of 1886 he was back on the coast and a week later in Paris. He wanted to rest for a few months, organize his notes and write a book on Morocco. He met Duveyrier, who took a keen interest in the young man, and the Geographical Society awarded him a Gold Medal for his expeditions. A little later his work on Morocco was published under the title *Reconnaissance au Maroc*, a volume of five hundred pages with numerous maps. But the man who one night wrote *Finis* to his manuscript was quite a different person from the one who had once begun it. He had decided to become a monk and to forsake the world, and so in the middle of January 1890 Charles de Foucauld entered the Trappist monastery Notre Dames des Neiges in the Cevennes Mountains, as Brother Alberic.

The reasons that impelled him to take this step were never divulged. As far as we know there was no sudden cause, no heavy disappointment, no illness. How God touched the heart of His servant, the Vicomte Charles de Foucauld, remains a closely guarded secret, though it seems likely that it took place in Africa and in the desert. He once wrote a letter to his friend the Marquis de Castries from Africa: 'Islam has wrought a deep transformation in me. Faced by the faith of these people who live constantly in the presence of God, I have begun to perceive things that stand above all earthly cares.' Even after taking his vows, Brother Alberic still felt so strongly drawn to the desert that he requested permission to work in the North African colonies of France. At the end of October 1901 this was granted and he settled as a hermit in Beni Abbès, today the second stop on the Tanezruft route. Contrary to all expectation he still preserved his dislike for conventional behaviour and refused to conform to it. When he first went to Beni Abbès, he was met on the outskirts of the settlement by a military guard of honour under the command of a young comrade from his former military academy. Father Alberic, his habit flying behind him, galloped towards the guard, saluted them smartly in the military fashion, and then rode to inspect the front of the troop.

This aroused much head-shaking, not so much on the part of the officers of the garrison of Beni Abbès, as in Algiers in the Maison Carrée, the headquarters of the Order of the White Fathers. This association of French missionaries in Africa had been founded in 1874, and had spread over the whole of French North Africa. The French government had expressly forbidden them active proselytizing, and thus they chose to serve as living examples of Christianity to the Arabs. Seeing that the White Fathers were inclined to the opinion that the honour of God and the glory of *La France* were identical, the political heads of the French Republic allowed this organization of patriotic missionaries to continue even after the laws disestablishing the church had been passed. The State worked hand in glove with them and the Intelligence Service had no more reliable and trustworthy agents.

Obviously Foucauld, the greenhorn who had a passion for making extended tours, was a thorn in the side of the veterans of the Maison Carrée. They decided to keep him in Beni Abbès where they could keep a close watch on him. Here they gave him a free hand and looked on with amusement as he began 'liberating' slaves, so to speak, on the conveyor-belt system. Men and women would queue up outside his hut and to each one he would give money, believing that these unhappy creatures could now buy their freedom, unaware that they were merely trading on his disingenuousness, later to disappear into the desert with what for them was a fortune. The White Fathers soon realized that as a 'fisher of men' Père Foucauld was a miserable failure. But there could be no doubt that trade between natives and French merchants in the coastal towns was considerably stimulated by his rich gifts, and in the final analysis every mirror, every necklace, every spade bought by a Bedouin in Algiers or Oran, was evidence of the blessings that the disciples of Jesus could bestow on the votaries of Mohammed, thus helping France in her mission.

Primitive and worldly-wise though this calculation might have been, it came off. It did not take very long for the Arab sheiks to find out what was happening. They were by no means pleased when they were suddenly confronted by numerous subjects who, through the generosity of the undoubtedly crazy new Father in Beni Abbès, had become rich overnight and were becoming correspondingly unruly. They pointed to Section V of the Franco-Arab Treaty which stated expressly: 'You will retain your old customs and usages as hitherto, nor shall we interfere in your internal affairs', and complained that this newcomer was undermining the social order. Foucauld's family in France also got wind of this new style of extravagance, and hastened to the banks, where they learnt to their sorrow and dismay that the earthly possessions of the pious Father Foucauld were disappearing at an even faster rate than had the fortunes of the former soldier. The family council took immediate action and the source of money pouring into Africa suddenly ran dry.

For a while he was able to borrow money from his old comrades in the Officers' Mess at Beni Abbès, but soon he was met with excuses and he had to give up his former practices.

Reckless though his philanthropic activities were, Foucauld proved himself an outstanding intelligence officer. His reports about Beni Abbès and the country around it were accurate and clear, and all the suggestions he made were excellent and to the point. The execution of those matters with which he was entrusted took place noiselessly, with the mechanical certainty of an experienced agent. In addition, Father Foucauld's personal integrity was undoubted. He lived more poorly than the poorest of beggars, allowing himself only two daily meals of unseasoned broth and dates. Even the Arabs held him in high esteem and overlooked his childish obsession with freeing people. These simple people of the desert had a sensitive perception of the force of his personality. Soon they were to call him *marabout*, saint, and as such he lives on in the memory of the older generations—from the Berbers of the coast to the Tuareg of the Hoggar region.

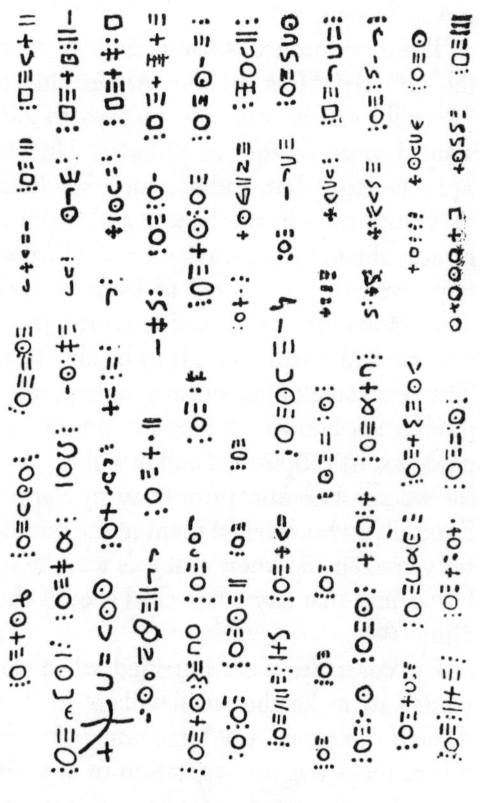

43. *An example of* tiffinar, *the writing of the Tuareg.*

Foucauld remained in Beni Abbès for two years, then one fine day an old friend arrived with a plan to travel to the Hoggar mountains across Tanezruft. This old acquaintance was Major Henri Laperrine, like Foucauld a former cadet from Saint-Cyr, the military school of the French army founded by Napoleon. Laperrine was now a divisional commander of the Méharistes, the Camel Corps of the Sahara which he himself had created. These Méharistes, so-called because they ride on *méhara*, fast racing dromedaries, are a crack troop consisting entirely of volunteers. It was a great honour to be allowed to serve in this unit and Foucauld was delighted when its leader asked him to accompany them. The two friends were vastly different in external appearance; the one lean and wiry from his ascetic way of life and the other an elegant yet burly army officer. But like all the other French explorers of Africa such as Caillié, Duveyrier, Lyautey and de Castries, they spoke the same language: the Sahara must belong to France. Laperrine, the free-thinker and atheist, would add, under his breath, that for all he cared it might even turn Catholic, provided only it was French.

The expedition was planned down to the last detail on the large map in the Officers' Mess in Beni Abbès, and in the middle of January 1904, Foucauld started out. He refused to ride on horse or camel back. He wanted to go on foot like Christ. Thus for eighteen days he trudged the 240 miles to Adrar, today a mere ten hours' drive by car. But time is not very important in the Sahara and it did not even matter much that Père Foucauld had to make a detour of a further 125 miles from Adrar to a very remote oasis. He wanted to learn *tamasheq*, the spoken language of the Tuareg, and *tiffinar*, its written form, from an Arab scribe there. He stayed until he had learnt enough to be able to translate and interpret with ease. The next stage of his journey, a desperate week-long race against death by thirst, took him to the Hoggar mountains. We, although of an age that is noted for its callousness and brutality, are obviously made of weaker fibre, for we shudder and turn away in alarm from these devilish mountains. Foucauld, who reached them in the middle of June 1904, at once felt himself attracted and knew that this was the spot where he wanted to make his home until that day when God should choose to call him to appear before Him.

His comrades were horrified when they found out that Foucauld intended to make the small village of Tamanrasset his future hermitage. Apart from some very large tamarisks and a few sparse patches of camelthorn, there was no vegetation of any kind. True, there were some deep wells, but the water supply was incomparably worse than that at Beni Abbès. In addition the village was in the heart of the Tuareg country, the home of the untamed robber-knights of the desert. Important though it was for the French Intelligence Service to have a reliable agent right in the centre of the Sahara and at the main junction of ancient caravan routes, they were loath to lose Foucauld, one of their best men, and he could be as good as written off if he were allowed to carry out his foolhardy plan.

While Algiers and Paris were still deliberating the matter, Charles de Foucauld had long cut the Gordian knot. Just as Henri Duveyrier had once befriended Ikhenouken, so the Vicomte de Foucauld was in contact with Musa ag Amastan, the uncrowned head of the Hoggar Tuareg. When the two men met, they discovered that both their lives had taken a similar course. Up to his thirtieth year, Musa had been a great warrior and a great lover, and even now the Arabs still sing of his romances and adventures round the camp-fire at night. But suddenly one day, this wild life came to a stop. Allah had laid His hand on him, and Musa had embraced Islam and decided to follow Mohammed. Thus he bade the Frenchman welcome, who like himself had left soldiering for earthly rulers to become a soldier of God. The two men must have approached each other with a certain amount of mistrust, but they were admirably placed for mutual understanding.

Probably the Princess Dassiné, Musa's close relative and perhaps his mistress, had some part in the decision to allow the French monk to live among the Tuareg. When, many months later, she first set eyes on this strange *marabout*, she became most devoted to him, and when she eventually died she was buried at her own request next to the grave holding the heart of her teacher and friend. From the very start she must have agreed with the judgement of the desert people: this strange white man, despite his monkish garb, was every bit of him a knight, full of understanding for the customs of other people, but springing up like a steel blade when his own nation or faith was doubted. The fact that even a European could be two things—noble knight *and* fighter for God—seemed to have aroused Dassiné's curiosity. She determined to make the acquaintance of this stranger and since the Tuareg had only recently abandoned the matriarchal forms of society, Dassiné's wishes were still in the nature of commands.

Thus in September 1905, Père Foucauld settled in Tamanrasset. With the exception of a few short trips, he was to remain there for the next eleven years until his death—without once baptizing, solemnizing a marriage, burying the dead or gaining a single soul. Once one of the sheiks fetched the Christian *marabout* to his mother's deathbed but Father Foucauld, in order to comfort the poor woman as she lay dying, read her passages from the Koran. He had one aim in life and he lived accordingly: 'May all men look upon me as their brother, Christians, Moslems and heathen alike!' This, however, is not the real crusading spirit, and as a missionary Foucauld must be written off as an utter failure. He was not the man to push his foot in the door and force his message of salvation like a commercial traveller. He was, and remained, an aristocrat and gave the Tuareg an aristocratic example of the Christian life, and it was just this which opened the hearts of his brown friends. The *Ihaggaren*, as the Tuareg call themselves, are not at all fanatical, and are rather lax Mohammedans. This was the loophole through which Foucauld had hoped to introduce himself, and Musa ag Amastan at once realized how well-founded were these hopes. He took immediate counter-measures. He made Tamanrasset his capital and the permanent residence of his family and their friends—an unprecedented step for a nomad—and at the same time he planned to erect a mosque and a *zaouia*, a Mohammedan monastery. When his sheiks heard of these plans, they rebelled at once. An *arrem*, a cultural centre with mosques and monasteries, cost money, *their* money, and they were very loath to part with it. Dassiné, too, was opposed to his idea and this probably explains why Musa's plans fell through. She feared that her European friend would not be able to compete with the Arab monks and priests and that he would be forced to leave Tamanrasset. This she could not allow to happen, for the white monk had become irreplaceable for the beautiful, clever and intelligent Tuareg princess. Together they began to collect and write down all the old Tuareg sagas and songs. Dassiné gave tea parties to which the sheiks were invited, there was dancing to the *imzad*, the one-stringed Tuareg instrument, there was singing and there was love-making, everything in the presence or with the knowledge of the hermit. Together they encouraged the mothers to have their children vaccinated, hygiene and physical culture were taught, and gardens and plantations began to spring up. In short, before Musa knew what had happened, Tamanrasset, once a miserable little village, had become an actual capital.

The Quai d'Orsay in Paris were highly interested when they learned that this Père Foucauld had wrought miracles. At the beginning of 1908, Major Laperrine was sent to Tamanrasset. He turned his old friend's hermitage into an imposing stronghold and built another small fortification nineteen miles further east in a commanding mountain position. At the conclusion of this official state visit, Musa ag Amastan presented his Tuareg warriors to the commander of the Méharistes. Foucauld, wearing sandals and his monk's habit, stood on the right of Laperrine as five hundred Tuareg, mounted on racing camels, thundered past at the gallop, lances in their fists, and with *takuba*, their gigantic double-edged swords, at their sides. Both Frenchmen's hearts were beating fast with excitement, and Duveyrier, who had so ardently desired the pacification of the Tuareg, their submission to France and their introduction into the Gallic Empire, saw that his hopes were now fulfilled. There still existed many blank spots in the map of the Sahara, rarely visited, unknown and unnamed, but those who had the Tuareg as their allies were masters of them all. The last stone of this tremendous superstructure of power had been laid. And it had been Charles de Foucauld who had brought it about.

Our hermit was to live for another eight years. When the First World War broke out, he, Père Foucauld, requested to be sent to the front immediately, either as a chaplain or as a hospital orderly. His request was refused and he received strict orders to remain where he was. Foucauld realized how important his advance post was for the intelligence service, but he insisted that this activity could be carried out equally well by any of the experienced missionaries of the White Fathers. Paris knew better. It was foreseen that if France used coloured troops at the front, the enemy would take retaliatory measures which were bound to be directed towards North Africa and the French Colonial Empire. This step was not long in coming: Turkey declared a Holy War, a political and religious measure which obliged all Mohammedans to take up arms against the infidels.

Now Foucauld understood why they had wanted him to stay in Tamanrasset. He warned the troops in Fort Laperrine to be on the alert, but he himself carried on with his normal peacetime tasks. He produced comprehensive studies in which railways, roads and irrigation installations were projected down to the last detail. The pious hermit knew only too well what he was doing. In one of his memoranda, he prefaced his remarks with the following statement which in the light of subsequent events has a tragically prophetic ring: 'If we do not manage to make Frenchmen out of the natives, they will drive us from their land. The only way, however, of turning them into Frenchmen, is by making them Christians first.'

While his former fellow students of Saint-Cyr, amongst them Pétain and Franchet d'Esperey, were installed at the front as staff officers, fighting for the immediate life of France, the hermit of Tamanrasset was looking after the future of his homeland. Thus he was not thinking of the war, when late at night on the 1st December 1916, there was a hard knocking at the gate of the fort. Thinking that a letter had arrived for him, he opened the door and put his hand out. Strong fists clamped down on it, he was thrown to the ground and tied up. A shock detachment of Senussi—xenophobic, fanatical Moslems from the northern Sahara oases—had attacked Fort Laperrine, and, since Musa ag Amastan and his warriors were away in far-distant parts of the Hoggar mountains, the Senussi warriors had an easy task. A shot from a carbine ended Foucauld's life.

Thirteen years later, in April 1929, the monk of the Sahara found a last resting-place in the oasis of El Goléa. While his heart, preserved in a casket, remained in Tamanrasset, where it belonged, his body was taken to the north in solemn procession. In a wide clearing under tall date palms, a grave was dug for him in the sand of the Sahara. And on the giant granite stone above it we can read:

In the expectation of the verdict of the Holy Church,
Here lie the mortal remains of God's servant
Charles de Jésus—Vicomte de Foucauld
1858–1916
He died in the service of God
On the 1st December, 1916, at Tamanrasset
Murdered by rebellious Senussi
Victim of his brotherly love and of his zealous faith.

15

On the way back we met Herr F. from Cologne in the bar of the hotel at El Goléa. He was highly interested when he learnt that we had been to Tamanrasset and plied us with questions. The night lingered on, it was pleasant to chat with a compatriot, and towards morning we knew Herr F.'s real business. Despite the political disturbances he was of the opinion that North Africa was *the* tourist attraction of the future, just as Switzerland had been a hundred years ago. He was there to have a good look round before settling down to the practical details of organizing tours and developing tourist sites and facilities. When we promised faithfully not to repeat anything, he became less reserved and what he had to say was extremely fascinating, though in the end we were quite overwhelmed by the figures he quoted. We learnt that flocks of tourists, like migrating birds, had already spent their holidays in Africa. Fräulein Müller, the shorthand-typist; Herr Lehmann, foreman of a factory, and his wife; Herr Meyer, the school teacher; Herr Schulz, the journalist, and hundreds of others like them, had all made up their minds to make a real tour once in their lives at least. Spain and Italy no longer attracted them, they simply *had* to see the Black Continent. They knew they would have to go in winter, and so they saved up their summer holidays and instead of talking about the Dolomites, Switzerland, and the Allgäu Alps, they now spoke of El Goléa, of Bidon 5, Ghardaia, Colomb-Béchar and Agadès. Most of them wanted to go by luxury coach in an organized tour, but there were some who wanted to take their own cars and a few even wanted to fly.

Herr F. was amused at our astonishment. He asked Monsieur Paul, the barman, a plump little Frenchman who had been to Germany with the armies of occupation and could speak the Saxon dialect like a native, to hand him the visitors' book. We read the names of those who had put up in the hotel during the last few weeks and months. It was like a directory of the big names in the tourist business. First and foremost, of course, there were the French, but there was also a score of American names, as well as English, Scandinavian and Dutch. A race was under way—a race to capture the North African tourist market. Only now did we understand why Herr F. was taking such a keen interest in us. We represented the typical tourist to him and he was doing a little market research, ahead of his rivals.

He gave us no peace with his questions: what did we know of *cerastes aegyptiacus*? Horn snakes? We had seen none and were scared stiff when we learnt what sort of snakes they were. Scorpions? Well! as a former member of the late *Wehrmacht* I knew something about this subject. It had become second nature to me to beat the sand and grass all around the spot where I wanted to sleep or have breakfast. But this was all I could tell him, for we had not encountered any of these unpleasant horrors on this trip. What about petrol? Were there enough fuel stations? Did they always have enough? Was there any rationing? We could not see what Herr F. was getting at, and we could only tell him that all the pumps had quite obviously been chock-a-block full of petrol.

That would be the main difficulty, said Herr F. If North Africa ever really became popular as a tourist country, with plane- and bus-loads of tourists arriving every day, what would the petrol situation be then? Didn't we realize that of the hundred tons sent, for instance, to Bidon 5, only seventy-five tons at most would arrive there in the summer? No, no, they had not been stolen on the way. The missing twenty-five tons had simply evaporated. At 122° F. in the shade that's how things were. Seventy-five per cent, if you were lucky! If more demands were made on the fuel stations in the desert the camels might have to be used for transporting petrol to them, but this would be next to futile. One of these animals could carry at most twenty-two gallons. Advancing at the rate of eighteen miles a day, it could cover the 800 miles between Colomb-Béchar and Bidon 5 in roughly forty-five days. It is not difficult to calculate how much fuel would be left in the canisters! This was one of the catches of the whole business. Much could be done within certain limits, and the French were past-masters in the art of improvisation, but even they were not magicians! Without a Trans-Sahara railway, the prospect was uncertain. Herr F. could not make up his mind whether to enter the Africa business or not.

Trans-Sahara railway! We had heard of it often enough, but only very vaguely. Obviously our Herr F. was expert on this subject. It was now our turn to ply *him* with questions.

Trans-Sahara railway, he replied, good God! The idea was as old as the hills. Ever since 1860 and Monsieur Duveyrier's return from the desert, the French had been talking of it. As early as 1875, the engineer Dupouchel had submitted a plan, and since then some eighty independent specialists had travelled throughout the length and breadth of the Sahara, surveying and investigating, and one thing had long been clear: if the line was ever built, it would have to run through Colomb-Béchar, Adrar, Bidon 5 and In-Tassit, i.e. along the Tanezruft route of the buses belonging to the SATT, the Société Algérienne des Transports Tropicaux. At Bidon 5 the railway line would fork with an eastern section running to Gao and Niamey where it would join the railway network from Lomé and Lagos, while the western section would go via Timbuktu and along the Niger to Ségou and join up with the railway connection from Dakar. It would not be much of a problem to build it, as not much excavating or many bridges would be required. It would take in all about two years to complete and the money to start could be found by exploiting the phosphate deposits of

In-Tassit. Furthermore, by means of quite simple irrigation measures it was possible to turn the land between Timbuktu and Ségou into cotton and rice plantations, and the money raised from selling the crops could be used to pay for the line. In short everything had been studied so carefully that no doubts about the technical problems remained.

But what would happen, we asked, if there was a *gibli*, one of those terrible sandstorms we had been warned about? Oh, that had been solved long ago! After all, in North Europe or America, snowstorms did not stop railway traffic. In the lower regions, protective walls would be constructed to stop the sand burying the line. Furthermore, the Italians, in their former Libyan colony, had shown how this could be done, and that with a little luck the gigantic wandering dunes could be anchored, if the trouble was taken to plant them with millions of deep-rooted grass plants that would hold the soil together. Quite apart from this, the line could be constructed far enough from the region of wandering dunes so that the danger of silting was not serious. Only one man would be needed for every six miles of track to keep it permanently clear. This had already been worked out in full.

But water, we interrupted, where are the locomotives to get the necessary water? There isn't an engine in the world capable of carrying enough water for crossing twelve hundred and fifty miles of desert, overloaded as it would be in any case by coal. Herr F. smiled and then apologized. Good Heavens, had we not heard of diesel engines needing hardly any water at all? Then he told us his theory that London was not interested in a line running from the Mediterranean to the Niger, since it would undermine the predominant position of Gibraltar. Just as England had done nothing to help develop the Danube into a truly great waterway between Hamburg and the Black Sea because it did not lie within her sphere of influence, so England had continued to put obstacles in the path of the Trans-Sahara railway. True, England had been unable to prevent the completion, in 1941, of the three-hundred-mile stretch of track from Oran to Colomb-Béchar because it was a connection of the utmost military importance, linking as it did the five thousand million tons of coal deposits in the basin of Colomb-Béchar with the Mediterranean. But that was all that had been accomplished. The argument about the lack of water for locomotives had been brought up time after time by the 'English lobby' in the French Chamber of Deputies, yet it was nothing but so much eye-wash!

Well, it sounded plausible enough, we thought, but, we asked, would the Trans-Sahara railway be able to carry such tremendous amounts of traffic that other nations would have to fear competition from it? We had hit Herr F.'s hobbyhorse bang on the rump, and he set off at a great pace. We discovered later that Herr F. had married a Frenchwoman and that his father-in-law was an old *Saharien* and a fanatical propagandist for the

Trans-Sahara railway. Herr F. calculated that a single local train, carrying fifty tons, would replace thirteen thousand bearers, or some seven thousand camels. And the Sahara railway did not intend to use the customary wagons carrying ten or at most fifteen tons each, but specially large wagons, so that each train could carry a cargo of about ten thousand tons, as much as an average freighter! The railway would in fact be just like a shipping line. All the most valuable goods would be transported on this line: copper, zinc, coal, phosphate, tungsten, manganese, nickel, iron, cobalt and bauxite. For, as Herr F. pointed out, one of the largest industrial areas in the world was in the process of being developed in the Sahara. The best indication of this is given by the figures showing the increase in the consumption of electrical energy. Whereas in 1938 only 500 million kilowatt hours had been used, the figure for the corresponding period in 1952 had already reached 2,000 million kilowatt hours. The same story was true of the exploitation of mineral deposits: ten times more phosphate, coal, lead, bog-iron ore, manganese, zinc, cobalt, etc., were being mined at the moment than before the war. Factories producing oxygen had suddenly sprung up, atomic research institutes and power stations for further hundreds of millions of kilowatt hours and gigantic coke works and benzol factories were being built. In short, these God-forsaken regions which until quite recently had claimed the body of every second explorer venturing to cross them, were in the process of becoming one of the largest industrial centres in world economy. This was just the snag, for the Trans-Sahara railway would also carry oil, fruit, rice, cotton, wheat and other produce grown in France herself, and this was one of the most thorny problems still to be solved. In Provence, in the Massif Central and other regions of the South of France, large areas of fertile soil were lying fallow, because in view of the prices of crops from Algeria, it did not pay to cultivate them. Thus the French farmers were the greatest enemies of the project for a railway across the Sahara and their opposition would continue unless the French government could find a way of safeguarding the French cultivator against competition from Africa. Of course, its eventual construction was inevitable, the pressure of events would force the hand of the French government, but should he, Herr F., put a lot of money into this business, given the risks? It might happen that owing to the sudden influx of tourists the desert would be left without the most essential supplies. And then where would he be?

Herr F. looked most perturbed. We ordered our last cocktail from Monsieur Paul and saw that dawn was breaking in the east behind the tall palms of the Parc Communal and the aerodrome control-tower, and the rising sun seemed appropriately symbolic of a new era breaking over the desert.

PART EIGHT

THE KINGDOM OF WATER AND FORESTS

Of the mule jenny and how a little boy learned Latin · Piecer Livingstone becomes a doctor and turns missionary · The Lord of the Kingdom of Water and Forests · Caterpillars make a delicious luncheon · The tsetse fly, or a losing battle · Hunger march to the sea · 'Mori oa tunya', thundering smoke · The first crossing of Africa · Two Roman centurions look for the Nile · The secret of the 'Lunar Mountains' · The results of damming Lake Tana · Triple discovery of the sources of the Nile · Of the 'Caravan Mountain' and 'njaro,' the evil spirit · Livingstone at Lake Nyasa · A tough job · The 'Bula-Matari' · The amorous women of Bagamoyo · How Paul Reichard discovered Katanga, and why Lt. Francqui became a rich man · Heads or tails in Nyangwe · Bo-bo-bo! Meat is coming downstream! · Recipes from the cannibals' cook-book, and of the delicious taste of white meat · The battle of the Aruwimi · Shakespeare intervenes to save Stanley's life · The revolting guinea-worm · Laurel-wreaths that smell of rum · A king reads a newspaper and has high-flown plans · Sweet water in the middle of the ocean · The Portuguese in the Congo · Four black princes in Lisbon · His Grace, Monsignor Henrique, the first black bishop · Dukes may come and dukes may go, but maize remains for ever · Iced beer in the jungle · The 'cités indigènes' · Of the western malaise, and of white primogeniture · Optimistic epilogue.

I

WELL! he had to face it, he wasn't doing any too well for himself, though he wasn't exactly a pauper, like so many thousands of his contemporaries. His father had sold his farm in the Hebrides at a good price and then had accepted a fairly well-paid job conveying large sums of money from Glasgow to the Blantyre works of Messrs. Monteith & Co. The old man had died some time ago and the money he had left had helped a lot. Also he, David Livingstone, travelling salesman in tea, had inherited his father's good name and so had managed to keep his head just above water, though it was a hard stuggle to support a family on what little he did manage to scrape together. Times were bad, and often he would return from making his rounds of Scotland without having sold as much as a pound of tea. Often the farmers' wives would slam the door in his face and some had even set their dogs on him. There was no denying it, his was not much of a life, all the insults and abuse he had to swallow and the shameless way they tried to beat down the price.

One evening in March 1823, the commercial traveller in tea felt that a part at least of his burden had been lifted; he thanked the Lord God that his eldest son, the ten-year-old Davy, would be starting work in Mr. Dale's cotton works the following morning, despite the terrible unemployment. True, he would only be an apprentice 'piecer', but he would bring in four shillings a week and this would relieve the strain on the family budget. He felt sorry that the small, thin, delicate lad should have to go to the factory instead of school: work began at six o'clock in the morning and stopped at eight o'clock at night—fourteen long hours—but Mr. Dale's child labourers were fed and cared for, they were not beaten or bullied, Mr. Dale saw to that. He personally exhorted his charges to be clean and to say their prayers regularly. At night, schooling was provided, free of charge, given by teachers paid by Mr. Dale himself.

Once little David had finished his apprenticeship, in six or seven years, he would be able to bring home twenty shillings a week! True, that day was still a long way off, but Davy was sure to get there. It was a pity the boy was so different from his brothers and sisters. Instead of reading elevating literature like that beautiful book *The Cloud of Witnesses*, or the Reverend William Wilberforce's magnificent *Practical Christianity*, he liked to pore over books of travel and all sorts of other scientific nonsense. Why, he had often had to thrash the boy to bring him to his senses! Davy had naturally complied, but David Livingstone senior was afraid lest the germ of evil had taken root. Still, he was sure that working in Mr. Dale's factory would knock the nonsense out of the lad's head. David Livingstone senior thanked God with renewed fervour in his prayers that night.

Young Davy had no idea of the anxiety he was causing his father. The next morning he rose early, and while it was still dark he left home and trotted off to Mr. Dale's textile mill. That night, just before nine, he returned home again. A few days later he was allowed to join the classes at the factory, which, needless to say, took place after working hours. Now Davy would only come home by about eleven o'clock, but even so he would continue to pore over his books, till his mother would spring up, take all his books away and chase him off to bed. With his first week's wages the boy had hastened to purchase Ruddiman's *Rudiments of Latin* and had begun to study Latin all by himself. At first he made slow progress —the poor child had so little time—but then he had the magnificent idea of propping up the book on a part of the spinning-jenny, that marvellous machine which, in a trice, could fill eighty spindles of yarn from one single bale of cotton. When he was promoted to a mule-jenny, a semi-automatic machine, things were even better. Here he had little else to do but pull a lever at regular intervals. One pull and the carriage travelled away from the rollers, another and it returned, another pull and the carriage started off again and so on, all day long. But as he pulled the lever David Livingstone was learning Latin.

His workmates thought he was being a bit superior, but apart from an occasional joke they dared not object to the boy. David Livingstone was the best cotton spinner in the factory, his machine never broke down, his yarn was even and elastic and his output considerably greater than that of any other worker. By the time he was nineteen, he could afford to work during the summer months only and spend the winter studying at the University of Glasgow in both the theological and medical faculties. There was no more diligent student than David Livingstone in the whole university.

For a student to read both theology *and* medicine is not very common, and those who decide to do so usually have quite a definite plan in mind. This was certainly the case with our young student-worker. One day, he had come across some tracts written by the Protestant missionary, Karl Friedrich August Gützlaff, a native of Pyritz in Pomerania, who had wanted to convert the Chinese to Christianity. Gützlaff had landed in Hong Kong in 1827 but did not know much Chinese. Thus his first missionary pamphlets were written in English. Since however those Chinese who could understand English were generally rich merchants, people who stood as much chance of entering the Kingdom of God as a camel did of passing through the eye of a needle, Karl Friedrich August Gützlaff discovered to his great sorrow that all his efforts had been in vain. He did not know, however, that not all his seed had fallen on barren soil. Although his pamphlets did not convert a single Chinese, they were responsible for David Livingstone's decision to become a missionary.

Blantyre is only eight miles from Glasgow. When the Scottish missionary Dr. Robert Moffat returned on leave from the Cape Colony, after many years of successful activity, his mission bade him seek out the gifted cotton spinner who had applied to become a missionary. Dr. Moffat himself came from the same sort of background as Livingstone and had started his career as a gardener's boy. Thus he had no difficulty in making contact with the shy student, and a few years later he received a letter at Kuruman, his mission station, in Bechuanaland announcing that his young protégé had graduated as a surgeon, that he had been ordained as a missionary on the 20th November 1840, and that he was coming to Africa.

Like Albert Schweitzer, Livingstone was both missionary *and* doctor, and his first desire, on arriving in South Africa early in 1841, was to build a hospital for the natives. Although he could not carry out this plan, he did all he could to heal the sick of Kuruman, as well as save their souls. He applied splints to broken bones, bandaged wounds, and operated as best he could under primitive conditions. He did not feel, however, that he was doing enough. He founded a mission station at Mabotsa, about a hundred and eighty miles north-east of Kuruman in the vicinity of the modern town of Mafeking. Then he went another forty miles farther north to Chonuane, and when Sechele, the chief of the Bakwena, the 'People of the Crocodile', decided to migrate to the north, thus avoiding the ever-increasing pressure of the Boers, Livingstone, who in the meantime had learnt the language of his black friend, went along with him. Towards the end of the 1840's he set up his third mission station on the Kolobeng river.

2

Dedicated first and foremost to the service of Christ, Livingstone's path in Africa unfolded, not under the tutelage of Aesculapius, the God of Medicine, but under that of Mercury, protector of wanderers and travellers. If Dr. Moffat had been more diligent in finding out the reasons why Livingstone had become a missionary, he might well have had second thoughts about giving him his daughter for his wife, for the favourite reading of the former cotton spinner was still, as it had always been, travel reports and geographical works. During his three months' voyage to South Africa, he had taken lessons from the captain on how to find one's exact position by the stars, and although during the first years in Africa he served his missionary society well, he simply could not bear to remain long in the same place. A stubborn thirst for knowledge had once driven little Davy to put up with the jeers of his comrades and fasten Ruddiman's Latin primer to his mule-jenny. A stubborn thirst for knowledge now forced the missionary to make longer and longer expeditions

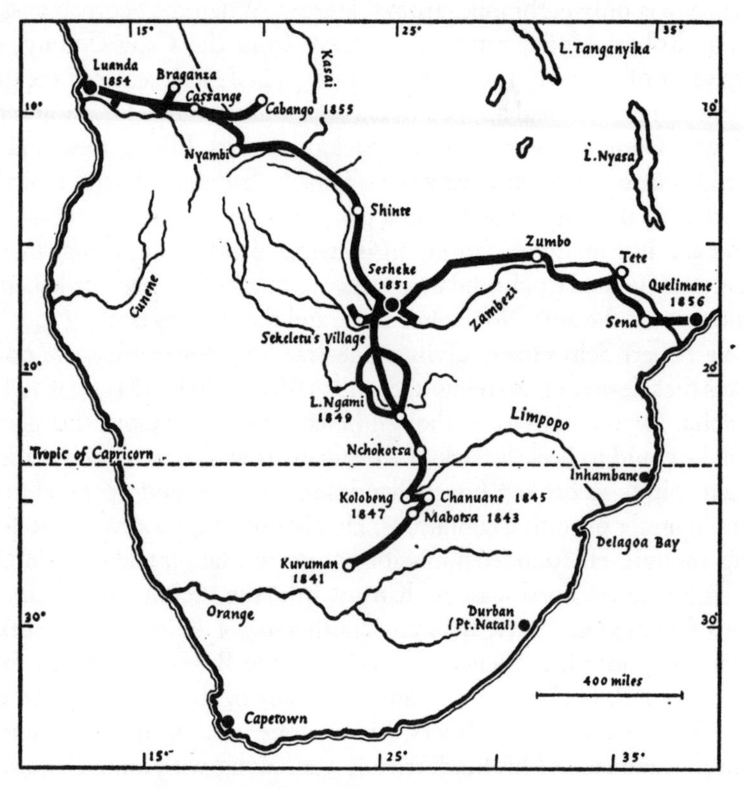

XLI. David Livingstone's journeys from 1841–56

into the environment of his station. Thirst for knowledge, but also stubbornness! Sechele, whom Livingstone held in high esteem, had told him that there was no path through the Kalahari to the north. He had to find out for himself. The Boers, under their commander Paul Kruger, placed every possible difficulty in the path of the hated English missionary, since, in their opinion, he was inciting the natives not to accept the benefits of Boer civilization. A lesser man would have given in, but such an idea never once entered his head. When his talks with 'Oom Paul' came to naught, he decided to take the unprecedented step of making for the north with his wife and three children.

Admittedly he did not take this step blindly. Livingstone's reputation as a wise, kindly man, able to heal the sick, had spread like wildfire amongst the natives, and this reputation had travelled even as far as Sebituane, a King living on the other side of the Kalahari, on the banks of the great Lake Ngami. Since Livingstone's friend Sechele knew this distant black ruler, 'the Lord of the Kingdom of Water and Forests', Livingstone soon had the thought of visiting him, with the aim of setting up a mission station in Linyanti, Sebituane's capital. A station in that neighbourhood would make it much easier for him to carry out his missionary activities than it would be from within Boer territory. Certainly, the Scot must have been astonished when he learnt that there were vast forests and a great lake instead of the barren, flat country he had expected, but for the time being exploration would have to yield to missionary work. Thus, when messengers came from the north to tell him that he would be received in friendship, Livingstone heard the news as if Sebituane were like a voice from the wilderness commanding him as once Jesus had commanded His disciples: 'Go ye into all the world, and preach the gospel to every creature!'

While he was making his preparations for the journey, two English elephant-hunters, Mungo Murray and Cotton Oswell, arrived in Kolobeng. They were intending to travel north, and when they heard that this was Livingstone's intention too, they suggested that they might all venture through the desert together. Naturally they did not plan to go straight across the Kalahari, an impossible task, but to skirt its eastern boundary, along the route of the modern railway line to Bulawayo. They planned to turn north-east, roughly in the neighbourhood of the modern Palapye Road, and go as far as Maun near the Okovango Swamp. Livingstone agreed and they all set out on the 1st June 1849. Eighty oxen pulled the four clumsy covered wagons through the sand; in addition they had twenty horses for explorations or for hunting. The two English sportsmen supplied the necessary meat, and David Livingstone carried among his luggage a thermo-barometer, an instrument that was used to measure altitude before the barometer proper was invented. To his great astonishment the missionary discovered that the Kalahari was a basin which dropped from 4,200 feet to 2,600 feet above sea-level.

Just as in the Sahara, ancient caravan routes crossed this large South African desert. Here too the native traders feared that the powerful white men would compete with them and take away their monopoly of the ivory and slave trade. Thus they obstructed the trek wherever they could—the little group of whites found the wells full of sand or bodies, the pygmy-like bushmen hostile; poisoned arrows whistled over their heads, cattle were stolen, in short, on more than one occasion it looked as if the expedition would never reach its aim. One evening, when according to their calculations they were near Nchokotsa, close to one of the Kalahari salt-pans, they saw a wide lake shimmering in the distance. It could only be the Ngami of which they had heard so much from the natives.

We had no idea that the long-looked-for lake was still more than three hundred miles distant. The mirage on these salinas was marvellous. The waves danced and the shadows of the trees were reflected in such a perfect manner, that the loose cattle, horses, dogs and even Hottentots hastened towards the distant pools. A herd of zebras looked in the mirage exactly like elephants, and Oswell began to saddle a horse in order to hunt them. A sort of break in the haze dispelled the illusion.

Once again they were facing nothing but the naked desert. The disappointment was terrible. They knew that fifteen years earlier, in 1834, another English traveller had set out to find Lake Ngami for the Cape Association for the Exploration of Central Africa but had been unsuccessful. Would they, after so much preparation, meet with the same fate? Fortunately the river which appeared one morning was no mirage. It flowed out from Lake Ngami, and wended its muddy, yellow way through the sterile land. The expedition marched along its banks, and on the 1st August 1849 Livingstone became the first white man to stand on the shores of the famous lake, which has long since silted over. It lay close to what is now the road from Windhoek to Livingstone, but modern maps or guide books fail to mention it at all.

... For the first time this fine-looking sheet of water was beheld by Europeans. The direction of the lake appeared to be north-north-east and south-south-west by compass. We could detect no horizon from where we stood nor could we form any idea of the extent of the lake except from the reports of local people; they professed to go round it in three days which would make it about 70 miles in circumference. It is shallow and can never be of much value as a commercial highway. In the months preceding the annual supply of water from the north it is with difficulty that cattle can approach to drink through the boggy reedy banks.

Even today, more than a hundred years later, we can sense the tremendous excitement which had gripped Livingstone. He had learnt from the natives that not far from the great lake there was a region full of rivers, streams and gigantic forests. Rainfall was plentiful and arid steppes and deserts were completely unknown. At once Livingstone conceived the idea of using Lake Ngami and its tributaries as a means of reaching those fertile, populated areas, unknown to Europeans. That he was the first white man to see the great lake now seemed to him rather insignificant. Half a century earlier, when rain had been heavier and more frequent in the Kalahari, the natives of the south had often travelled as far as the lake. Thus it was by no means unknown, although all attempts by Europeans to reach it had failed. The great forests north of Lake Ngami were completely different: nobody had any information about them, and if what the natives said was true, then geographers would have to change all their views about the nature of Central Africa.

Since the hot dry season was approaching, they could do nothing for the time being except return to Kolobeng. In April 1850, Livingstone started out a second time for Sebituane's domains, accompanied by his wife and children. However, the second attempt also failed. The children fell ill of malaria and Livingstone had to return. But a third attempt made in 1851 proved successful, though Livingstone and his wife had to pay the price of heart-rending anxiety before they reached their goal. One day they ran out of water and they had to watch their children suffering the agonies of death by thirst until, at the very last minute, water was found and the children were saved. Livingstone could never forget that day, and he decided to separate from his family and carry out his task of exploration alone. He had demanded much too much of his wife and children. A missionary's wife has no easy life, and Mary had always known that she might have to live just like the Negroes, eating roasted locusts, caterpillars and bull-frogs when there was nothing else. But, the thought ran through Livingstone's mind, it was unfair to expose wife and children to the most horrible kind of death in the world, death through thirst, simply because he had long ceased to be a good missionary and had become an explorer instead.

As well as thirst, there was another terrible danger to be faced—all the more frightful since it could not be seen or anticipated. Thirty years after Livingstone's first experience of it, the disease was to receive its scientific baptism: *Trypanosoma Brucei*, a name given it in memory of the English physician Dr. David Bruce who, in 1879, spent his honeymoon investigating the mysterious African cattle sickness called *nagana*. In the Zulu language *nagana* means decrepitude, weakness, or uselessness, and in fact no better term could be found, for the animals discovered by David Bruce to be infected by trypanosomes were in fact decrepit, weak and useless. The stomachs and legs of affected horses swell up and the poor beasts come to a quick, merciful end. Cattle begin to get thin and stagger about; raw patches suddenly appear on their bodies and then one morning they are dead. Dogs, sheep and other domestic animals are affected in the same way. The natives of the highlands of Africa believed that the disease was epidemic, and that if only they could prevent their cattle from feeding and drinking as they crossed the infected regions, the danger could be averted.

The tribes from the lowlands, however, placed all blame on the flies, tsetse flies in particular, apparently quite insignificant little creatures, mottled reddish-grey in colour, but otherwise hardly different from ordinary European house flies. Livingstone, who had obtained all his knowledge of the *nagana* from these natives of the lowlands, reasoned very ingeniously that the poison was introduced into the blood-stream when the insect punctured the skin with its proboscis to suck the animal's blood. And with strict logic—a sign of how much worry this terrible disease had given him, and of how carefully he had thought these things over—he continued that it was probable that as wild life gradually disappeared with the general adoption of guns for hunting, the tsetse flies, deprived of their food, would die out altogether.

This uncannily prophetic conclusion was to be proved right in the next few decades, but at the time nobody knew how to master the disease-bearing flies. At first an attempt was made to remove the natives from the infected areas into the tsetse-free mountain lands, but the grazing grounds of the highland mountains, which in any case were being forced to support too many cattle, were stripped completely bare within a few years and regressed to the position of steppes and barren desert. Then the authorities tried to drain the swamps and burn off the bush, as it was known that the tsetse fly could not exist in treeless and bushless savannahs. Sometimes it was sufficient to create bare strips of only a few hundred yards wide but often whole forests had to be pulled down, and although this exterminated the tsetse fly very efficiently, it made life impossible for men and beasts as well. Moreover, as regions are stripped bare of their vegetation, nature reacts immediately by causing less and less rain to fall, and the soil becomes drier from year to year.

Even the most fanatical of the microbe hunters did not go so far as to recommend that the whole of Africa be turned into a desert, and clearly less drastic means were needed for dealing with the pest. It was discovered that wild game, too, was attacked by the flies, and while here the disease took on a mild form, the animals themselves were turned into veritable germ depositories. Dr. Livingstone was the first to realize that the only thing to do in particularly dangerous regions was to kill off the wild life.

In 1954, Dr. Bernhard Grzimek, Director of the Zoological Gardens at Frankfurt-am-Main, published astounding figures on the decimation of wild game in the Black Continent in his *Flug ins Schimpansenland* ('Flight into the Land of the Chimpanzee'). He added that this butchery was not due to an exaggerated human lust to kill, but had taken place as a final desperate attempt to rid the country of the *nagana*. Today the disease still rages throughout the entire length and breadth of tropical Africa from the Sahara to Natal, a total area of about 4,500,000 square miles. More than half of this gigantic region—twice as large as the U.S.A.—is unsafe for cattle, and large areas are threatened by complete depopulation. We can now understand why the hunters were given a free hand, for since wild game cannot be resettled or fenced into reserves like human beings, it simply had to be eradicated. If Grzimek's figures are correct, the fauna of Africa will shortly be as extinct as its flora. The white rhinoceros, the gnu, the mountain gorilla, the blaubok and other animals infected by trypanosomes will then be found only in a few European and American Zoological Gardens, as is already the case with various species of antelope and zebras.

At first Livingstone obviously did not suspect that the tsetse fly attacked human beings also, nor that the cases of sleeping sickness, first observed by Winterbottom in 1803, had been caused in this way. In his *Missionary Travels*, from which we have been quoting, Livingstone stressed the fact that the tsetse fly had not harmed any of his people, although for months they had been in particularly infested regions.

In fact, the tsetse fly is one of the most remarkable creatures alive. By no means all kinds of tsetse fly are carriers of the disease. Some types live only in the forest, others keep to swamps and regions where there is plenty of water. One type bites only at night, and another only during the day. There are regions in which they exist by the billion, while a few hundred yards away they are completely unknown. Their breeding regions and seasons, too, have not yet been fully investigated.

Livingstone had observed all these things, but his idea that the tsetse fly was harmless to human beings was entirely false. True, Europeans were almost completely immune against sleeping sickness, and even among the natives the symptoms of sleeping sickness would often appear only some months after they had been bitten. But Livingstone, like every other traveller of his time, must have seen the many native villages depopulated through sleeping sickness. Everywhere he went he must have met its victims: people who had shrunken frames, with bloated bodies and limbs, and were subject to perpetual drowsiness. Thus it is strange that Livingstone failed to reach the obvious conclusion, that *nagana* and sleeping sickness were one and the same thing, even as early as at Lake Ngami. But obviously the explorer in him was not only stronger than the missionary, it also overshadowed the doctor and the father. Only a few days' journey separated him from Linyanti, the capital of Sebituane, and although the whole region was buzzing with tsetse flies, Livingstone did not falter.

Sebituane, the King of the Makololo, a tribe of the Bechuana, was at that time one of the 'strong men' of South Africa, like Chaka and Dingaan, the leaders of the Zulus, or Mosilikatse, the 'Napoleon' of the Matabele. Tall, well-built and with tremendous muscles he was an impressive figure of a man. He greeted Livingstone in a reserved, dignified but friendly manner. He had learned that the black man could only live with the whites, not without them, and above all not against them. This interview with the delegate of a far-distant, strange world meant to him the crowning stroke of his political life's work. He had won his position by his ability as a soldier, for he was not the son of a chief, although he came of noble birth. If he was to assure his rule, which rested on his two shoulders alone, then he would need lasting relations with England. For that reason he was happy when Livingstone told him that he wanted to found a station of the London Missionary Society in his land.

But before this could happen Sebituane suddenly died, a victim of swamp fever. Since the Makololo had never before had any contact with white men, Livingstone feared that the superstitious natives would lay the blame for Sebituane's death at his door. But the personality of the black ruler had been forceful enough for his faith in good relations with Europe to live on even after his death. Not one hair of the white man's head was harmed. The Makololo went much further; they provided him with bearers and provisions as soon as he expressed the desire to march to the north-east to find the great river of which they had spoken—the Leeambye, or Zambesi, as they called it. He wanted to find out if it was the same river that flowed into the Indian Ocean far to the east, or whether it belonged to the system of the Congo or perhaps connected with the Nile. He wanted to discover its source and the direction of its flow. At the end of June 1851, Livingstone stood on the banks of the Zambesi, at a point where the river is well over 2,000 feet wide. In his journal he made the following laconic note: 'This was a most important point, for the river was not previously known to exist there at all. The Portuguese maps had placed it much further east.' Livingstone did not hint that this discovery was the stimulus that made him say goodbye to life as a missionary and devote himself entirely to exploring.

3

While he was with the Makololo, Livingstone came across the first traces of the trade in slaves. These wretched creatures were exchanged for ancient Portuguese muskets and, to acquire slaves, tribes would make forays against weaker groups. They would never consent to sell any member of their own tribe, no matter how humble. The Makololo declared that at one time they had never heard of trade in human beings and that they had always held it in horror, but that the desire for guns had been stronger than their human feelings. Livingstone listened to this with dismay, but hope soon welled up in him again. The evil was not yet too deeply rooted, and perhaps it could still be eradicated. He discussed matters with his travelling companions, and they concluded that this unholy traffic would cease once the market was provided with honest European manufactures. Slaving could only be combated by devising a trade which could undersell it and make it an uneconomic proposition. Only by opening up the way from the coast to the centre of Africa could the profits of the slavers be undercut, and the sooner this was done the better.

Naturally there was only one person for the job, he, David Livingstone himself. He knew the way across the Kalahari, a route which no white man had travelled before him, but one which could be negotiated by trading caravans. Perhaps even the Zambesi could be used for carrying supplies, and Livingstone was keen to find out. If that were the case, then the bottom would be knocked out of the slave market, for European articles could flood the country and would be so cheap that nobody would need slaves to pay for them.

Livingstone's decision was made. He did not waste another word on the former plan of founding a mission station in the land of the Makololo. Hardly had he covered the 130 miles from the Zambesi to Linyanti, when he gave orders to pack and prepare for the march back. He had decided to send his family to England and return by himself. We do not know whether Mary, Livingstone's wife, knew of his plans, but probably she realized that she had lost her husband for ever. In any case in 1852, when the family appeared in Cape Town, Mary's mother spoke badly of David. She could not understand how any man could leave wife and children in order to chase after such wild dreams. Fervently she hoped that the leaders of the London Missionary Society to whom Livingstone would have to report would say no, but they had meanwhile learned about his voyage to Lake Ngami and had seen his excellent maps. The London Mission was sure of one thing, that whatever he did, he would do in the spirit of Christ and as the messenger and apostle of Jesus, and so they agreed to Livingstone's suggestions. On the 23rd April 1852, Mary and the children went to England while Livingstone prepared himself for a second great journey.

With Livingstone a new type of discoverer takes the stage for the first time: the missionary. There had been similar explorers before, but the Pope's legates—the Carpinis, Wilhelm van Ruysbrocks, Montecorvinos, John da Marignolas and the many others who half a millennium earlier had travelled to India and China—had, with a few exceptions, been diplomats and ambassadors rather than discoverers. It is true that they kept alight in Europe the flame of knowledge about distant lands and distant people in an otherwise dark era, but their significance in the history of exploration was slight.

Livingstone was the prototype of the new kind of explorer with a double personality. The explorer in his nature needed the inner incentive which flowed from the soul of the missionary, just as the missionary in him needed the explorer, his thirst for knowledge and his skills. Livingstone gave a great deal of thought to these problems, and he once confessed that the meaning of his geographical work lay only in the possibility of developing missionary activity. It was the possibility of opening new missions, of carrying the message of Christ to new regions, which alone made him capable of his tremendous achievements. The natives to whom he came, the countries through which he travelled, the plants and animals of the Black Continent, were not only objects of study, though he did study them carefully and diligently, they were the environment in which he and his successors would work as Christ's servants. 'Not guns and steam engines impress the natives but justice alone' was Livingstone's motto. But to be just one must know the land and its people, their customs and their habits. The work of the discoverer is a means to an end, not an end in itself. The missionary has an almost magical influence on the native because he speaks to him in *his* language, because he tries to be a living example of Christianity, because he knows no 'savages in Africa apart from those who have come there from Europe'. The confidence with which Livingstone and the two German missionaries Krapf and Retmann were met, and which alone made their explorations possible, was due to the trust the natives had in them.

A further example of this was given at the end of May 1853, when Livingstone reappeared in Linyanti amidst his Makololo. He told them that he planned to go up the Zambesi in order to search for a route to the ocean in the west. Sekeletu, the eighteen-year-old successor to Sebituane, was delighted with the idea. When one of the old diviners in the *picho*, the assembly, croaked out the gloomy prophecy: 'Where is he taking you? The white man is throwing you away. Your garments are already smelling of blood!', the young king laughed openly in the face of this Jonah. Thus the *picho* suddenly changed its mind and decided to support Livingstone's enterprise, to supply him with boats and twenty-seven oarsmen to man them, and also with provisions and a stock of ivory, the 'small change' of Central Africa.

There is no doubt that Livingstone received such help because the Makololo had faith in him and because Sebituane's personal attitude had lived on after his death. Sebituane's point of view was based on a simple but shrewd commercial calculation; he knew that the way to the Cape was far and difficult and that black merchants incurred large expenses and often suffered unforeseen losses on the journey, and this made their articles disproportionately dear. If a shorter route to the coast could be found then things would be different. European goods would be cheaper, and then it would pay his people to collect ivory and other local products to barter with. Livingstone was a member of a nation of export merchants, and it pleased him to know that the Makololo were so keen to trade with Europeans. He knew full well that without such trade their future was uncertain, seeing that the Arab merchants, by charging exorbitant prices, were robbing them at every turn.

On the 11th November 1853, they started off. Livingstone knew he was undertaking a dangerous enterprise, and so he wrote to his brother, asking the latter to look after his little daughter, for, come what may, he was determined to open up that part of Africa.

The route of the expedition seemed to court disaster. It led through regions which even today are almost inaccessible to the ordinary traveller.

For example Barotseland, in the extreme west of North Rhodesia, has been almost completely ignored by road-makers. Nowadays, Livingstone would be able to go by a truck of the Zambesi River Transport Service up to Mongu on the Zambesi, but from there he would have to walk the next 250 miles before being able to take another truck. It was only his native dourness that carried the enterprise to a successful end. By the end of February 1854, Lake Dilolo and the mountain chain forming the watershed between the Congo and Zambesi systems had been reached. *Dilolo* in the language of the natives means roughly the same as despair, and in fact, while camping on the edge of the lake, our explorer became subject to terrible fits of depression. Together with many of the natives in his party he was attacked by a bout of malaria which he found difficult to throw off. A great apathy fell upon him and he neither took his bearings nor explored the lake very closely. Moreover, the local natives, incited by the slave-traders, were so hostile that Livingstone had to summon up his entire moral courage in order to deal with them without bloodshed. His faithful Makololo were slowly wasting away with fever, and Livingstone noted this with sorrow. He was no longer surprised that expeditions to the coast had generally failed to reach their objective. Most of his men wanted to turn back, and Livingstone was greatly upset at the thought of having to give up here, on the very threshold of the Portuguese settlement. Using all his powers of persuasion, he told them that, if need be, he would carry on alone. Then he went into his tent to pray.

At last, however, a brighter day dawned, the melancholia disappeared and the expedition set off again in a westerly direction, through the country in which lie the sources of the Kasai and the Kwango, both tributaries of the Congo. To repeat this trek as Livingstone made it would be an exhausting experience even in modern times, for the 375 miles between Lake Dilolo and Cassange are not spanned by any highway. Thus not even a hitchhiking vagabond, without a penny in his pocket, can have any idea of the difficulties which Livingstone had to overcome, and of the privation which he suffered without complaint. On the 13th April 1854 he entered Cassange, the last Portuguese station of West Africa. From far away he had been able to see the high grassy plain and the thirty or forty houses belonging to the Portuguese merchants. Livingstone's heart leapt for joy. He was thin as a rake and his face, despite his sun tan, was a greenish-yellow, but he had fought his way forward to his goal.

I made my entrance among our Portuguese allies in a somewhat forlorn state as to clothing. The first gentleman I met asked me for my passport and said he must take me to the authorities. Like the people who commit petty depredations in order to be given food and shelter in a prison, in the hope of a meal I went with him gladly to the house of the Commandant, Senhor de Silva Rego, who politely asked me to supper. As we had eaten nothing but farina since the Kwango I expect I appeared particularly ravenous to the other gentlemen around the table.

The Portuguese received the English traveller, who claimed to be a missionary, politely but not without a certain suspicion. At first they took him for an agent of the British government sent across Africa to gather evidence for the suppression of the slave trade, but obviously they soon came to regard him as a harmless and rather dotty Englishman. Livingstone, for his part, considered his malaria-stricken hosts as distinctly odd, and, in this atmosphere of mutual condescension, friendship soon flourished. Livingstone was showered with invitations from the Portuguese merchants who were also, without exception, officers in the Portuguese army. That evening he noted:

> None of these gentlemen had Portuguese wives. They usually come to Africa to make a little money and then return to Lisbon. Hence they seldom bring their wives with them and never can make successful colonists in consequence. It is common for them to have families by native women. It was particularly gratifying to me, who have been familiar with the stupid prejudice against colour entertained by those who are themselves becoming tawny, to view the liberality with which the people of colour were treated by the Portuguese. Instances so common in the south of half-caste children being abandoned are here extremely rare. They are acknowledged at table and provided for by their fathers. The coloured clerks of the merchants sit at the same table as their employers without embarrassment. Nowhere in Africa is there so much goodwill between Europeans and natives as here.

Since Livingstone had to restock his expedition, he sold, making sure that some of the Makololo were present at the transaction, an elephant tooth. The news soon flew round amongst the Makololo bearers that their leader had received two guns, three barrels of gunpowder, sufficient calico to dress them all and a large quantity of beans, in return for one elephant tooth. They were convinced that Sebituane had been right and that it was most important to find a shorter way to the outside world than that across the Kalahari to the Cape. However, the route up the Zambesi to Luanda did not seem to be particularly suitable as there were numerous rapids, preventing the passage of shipping. Livingstone, with the enthusiastic support of the Makololo, decided to attempt to go down the river to the east. Linyanti, the 'capital' of the Makololo, lay almost in the centre of the South African triangle, and the Indian Ocean was probably just as near as the Atlantic.

On the 31st May 1854, Livingstone and his small band arrived in Luanda, the old Portuguese port. Four months later on the 20th September he started on the return journey and reached Linyanti one year later, in the autumn of 1855. The explorers were given a welcome fit for kings, especially as the tribal witch doctors and wise men had long since given up the missionary and his men for dead. Now they had returned loaded with goods of all kinds which the merchants of Luanda had given them as presents. Sekeletu was particularly happy: the Junta da Facenda Pública, the government of Luanda, had sent the King of the Makololo a complete colonel's uniform. On the Sunday after the return of the expedition, Sekeletu wore it for the first time, and Livingstone was forced to the melancholy conclusion that the gold braid and tassels excited much more interest than his sermon. The general delight was so great that in the *picho*, which was held soon after their return, the suggestion was voiced that the tribe should abandon their old country and should settle further west, to be closer to the sea and to civilization. When this counsel was rejected, the Makololo themselves suggested that an expedition go east to determine whether the path to the Indian Ocean was not more negotiable than that to Luanda. The missionary spoke in favour of this plan of action, and soon volunteers reported to him, while the rest of the tribe began to collect elephant and rhinoceros teeth for the new enterprise. Livingstone, too, was highly satisfied with the fortunate outcome of his journey, and his self-satisfaction left him no doubts about the advisability of allowing the natives to come into contact with white civilization. Livingstone was perfectly aware that the old social structure of the tribes would be affected and that new classes would arise; he foresaw that customs, traditions, and the entire moral code of the natives would be changed radically, but he welcomed this prospect, for he was a child of an epoch which had unbounded optimism and complete faith in itself.

While the missionary in him was happy, the explorer had been wounded in his pride. He had received letters from England and one had contained a reprint of a lecture given three years earlier by Sir Roderick Murchison to the Royal Geographical Society in London. In this lecture, Murchison had suggested that in all probability Africa was not the high plateau which it had long been considered to be, but rather a kind of flat bowl, bounded in the east and west by mountain ranges. If this idea was correct—and Murchison left no doubt that according to the maps at his disposal this was indeed the case—then Central Africa could not consist of desert or dry steppe land but must be fertile country, irrigated by many rivers and lakes.

Livingstone had seen this with his own eyes, but someone in London had gone no further than his own back garden and had reached the same results. Livingstone had hoped that the information he had would be new, but there it was written down in black and white. Naturally he was more than a little piqued.

4

This chagrin was one of the main reasons for Livingstone's second great Zambesi expedition, though naturally he did not admit this, and undoubtedly he was honestly convinced that the decision to march to the east was due to his missionary zeal. On the eve of his departure, one of the Makololo chiefs came to him to warn him of the dangers of the journey.

He reminded Livingstone of his mission and said he must remember that he was going among people who had never heard the message of Christ and whom he could not trust. The chief prayed that Jesus would help him and guide him back safely. Livingstone himself believed that God was with him, and the strength he derived from this inner conviction enabled him to overcome hardships and exertions beyond normal human endurance.

Again the first stages of the journey were accomplished smoothly and without difficulty. The expedition had left by boat from Linyanti, proceeding up the Chobe into the Zambesi. On the 14th November 1855, they were within sight of the Victoria Falls. Many years before, when Livingstone had met Sebituane for the first time, the black ruler had told him of this natural wonder, referring to the Falls as *mosi oa tunya*, thundering smoke. Sebituane had asked Livingstone whether there was also thundering smoke in his home country but Livingstone had been completely nonplussed by the expression and had said no, merely to satisfy the King with an answer. When, on that November day, he saw, on the eastern horizon, the lofty towers of foam and vapour which since time immemorial have risen into the sky above the Falls of the Zambesi, he remembered Sebituane's question and he felt that there could be no better description of the miraculous effect. It seemed as if large tracts of grass were being burnt in the distance and as if the smoke was rising up in thick clouds to the sky. Five columns, the missionary counted, white at the base but darkening towards the top so that they closely resembled pillars of smoke. The air was still, he was too far away to catch even a murmur of the thundering wall of water. He drank in the silent beauty of the landscape, the majestic flow of the river, the sky, like a great canopy of blue silk, reflected in its waters, and the tall trees clad in dark green foliage enlivened by colourful patches of blossom. It was early morning and the dew was still on the grass. Livingstone offered up a prayer of thanksgiving to his Maker for so much loveliness.

Gradually the sound of the waterfalls became audible and as they drew closer it developed from a pianissimo note to the full-throated music of a mighty organ, in which were blended triumphant fanfares of trumpets, the clash of giant cymbals and the thunder of tremendous drums. At last Livingstone stood at the head of the Falls, roughly at the point where today the magnificent bridge of the Rhodesian Railways swings out across the water. At this point the river is about one mile broad and it makes a sudden leap of 120 feet down into a slender ravine, a mere crack in the basaltic rock, so narrow that the bottom of it is invisible. Standing there one is deafened by the roar, and half-blinded by the whirling clouds of spray which rise up from the abyss. One feels that here the primordial forces of the cosmos have been unleashed. And yet these same forces have been harnessed by man and provide him with two million horse power of electrical energy, sufficient for all the copper mines of Northern Rhodesia. His younger brother Charles had told Livingstone about the great Niagara Falls, but he felt that these were an even greater spectacle—more imposing and also more beautiful. For once he made an exception to his general rule of keeping the native name for places or rivers, and he called the cataracts after his Queen—the Victoria Falls. For hour after hour he stood on the brink of the roaring abyss unable to tear himself away. He drew a strange comfort from the rainbows that appeared in the spray. *Motse oa carimo*, divine staffs, the natives called them, and he too found confirmation in them of the bond between God and man. This feeling of oneness with the natives in a common admiration of the beauty of God's earth touched Livingstone very deeply. He felt strong in the love of God and able to face any dangers and hardships: 'Yea, though I walk through the valley of the shadow of death, I will fear no evil: for thou *art* with me; thy rod and thy staff they comfort me.'

Although Livingstone had much better equipment this time, was much more experienced, and not plagued by fever as much as before, he still had plenty of difficult moments to live through. His provisions were soon exhausted and as he frequently had to make detours in order not to be involved in one of the many tribal feuds, he often had to live on what he could gather himself in the way of wild berries, wild honey and fruit. The country through which the expedition was passing was an animal paradise with gigantic herds of buffalo, elephants, zebras and antelopes. These animals had never been frightened by men and were unsuspecting and friendly towards Livingstone, but as the explorer had had his right arm damaged in an encounter with a lion early on in his African career, he was only able to shoot with his left hand and that badly, and so the expedition went short of meat. Livingstone knew full well that to kill big game with spears was a very risky business and better not attempted. As they advanced further towards the east, Livingstone found the natives rather hostile and occasionally he had to take out his revolver, but he was never forced to fire even a warning shot. As on his earlier journeys the force of his personality proved sufficient to avoid any serious hostilities.

On the 14th January 1856, after a march of two months over a stretch of country which nowadays can be covered at ease by car, railway or aeroplane in a fraction of the time taken by Livingstone, the expedition reached the point where the Loangwa flows into the Zambesi. To his great surprise, Livingstone found here, near the village of Zumbo, the ruins of an old Christian church. He discovered fragments of the bell, and everywhere there were broken crosses on which the inscription IHS was still legible. Some distance away were the ruins of a small fort and of eight or nine stone houses. This was unmistakable evidence that a white man had once lived here in the middle of Africa. The natives could give him no further information about it and the station had been forgotten even in Europe, though it was only abandoned as late as 1780. The settlement had once belonged to the Portuguese who, some centuries before, had decided to make the 'backbone of Africa' Portuguese territory.

There were good reasons for that decision. The Portuguese needed 'Vitamin Stations' for reviving their scurvy-stricken sailors, supply bases stocked with everything for voyages across the Indian Ocean, and visible tokens of Portuguese power for keeping in check Arabs and natives alike. To do all this they had been forced to take an interest even in the interior of Africa. Then a new factor had appeared—gold. One day the Arabs near Sofala had offered the Portuguese large bags of a glittering reddish substance in exchange for muskets. When the Portuguese discovered that this metal was gold, and furthermore, gold in such a pure state that it no longer needed to be refined with quicksilver, there was no holding them back. Individually and in groups they set out to seek the African El Dorado where, as the Arabs told them, gold could simply be picked up by the roadside.

This was the true reason why East Africa had become Portuguese, and why it had remained so for such a long time. This was the reason why expeditions had forced their way up the Zambesi and its tributaries and in the final analysis why that mission station had been built whose ruins Livingstone discovered in the wildest bush. A German missionary, Dr. Johann Ludwig Krapf, who was working in Africa roughly at the same time as Livingstone, had also come across these ruins. He decided to follow up the history of the station, delved into archives, and searched systematically through dusty papers and faded manuscripts. In his book *Reisen in Ostafrika während der Jahre 1837 bis 1853* ('Travels in Africa during the years 1837 to 1853') he gives a full account of the Portuguese work of exploration in East Africa.

All this happened while Livingstone was still in the African forests, and when he returned to England Krapf's first report about his discoveries in East Africa had just appeared. Once again somebody had anticipated him. While searching through the ruins of Zumbo he had in fact had a presentiment that someone had been there before him. After taking his bearings he discovered that he was still six hundred miles away from the sea, and he began to wonder if he could cover the distance. Would his health last? Would the extremely hostile tribes let him pass? Would he be the first, this time, to report that the healthy and fertile mountain regions had been crossed, that they were, so to speak, made for the white man, and that centuries ago white people had in fact lived there?

Evening. Felt some turmoil of spirit in view of having all my efforts for the welfare of this great region and its teeming population knocked on the head by savages tomorrow. . . . It seems a pity that the important facts about two healthy ridges should not be known to Christendom.

Livingstone felt that failure now was certain to be interpreted at home as evidence that Africa was nòt ready to receive the Gospel. But then he picked up his Bible and read that Jesus came and said: 'Go ye into all the world, and preach the gospel to every creature. . . . Lo, I am with you alway, *even* unto the end of the world.' As he read this he received new assurance that the Lord would not desert him.

Once again the missionary had helped the explorer. But next morning Livingstone was to discover that his anxiety about the natives had been only too well founded. The natives had sent their women and children into the forest, had taken up their weapons, and the situation looked serious indeed. Once more his strength of character won the day, all misunderstandings were cleared up, and he could go on his way unchallenged. His Makololo were none too happy about the way events had turned out. They felt themselves infinitely superior to the local natives in feats of arms, and were certain that they would have been victorious had it come to a skirmish. They had already looked forward to acquiring concubines and slaves to carry the baggage of the expedition, but Livingstone held their bellicose exuberance in check and a few days later they marched into Tete, then an old Portuguese settlement on the Zambesi, but today a main junction on the Cape to Cairo road.

Livingstone was received enthusiastically. The English government had officially notified Lisbon that a member of the London Missionary Society planned to cross the Black Continent and all Portuguese stations in the area had been notified. At first the Portuguese colonists had looked forward to his arrival, but finally they had given up all hope of ever seeing him alive, for bloody tribal wars were in progress at the time and the natives were known to stop their own hostilities to massacre any whites they could lay their hands on. It was hopeless for a single white man to attempt to pass through the trouble spots. Then suddenly, shortly before Livingstone's entry into Tete, some natives living up-stream arrived in the settlement with a strange report that the Son of God had descended on earth. They had heard say that he would point at the sun with a strange tube, fetching it down and taking it under his arm. The Portuguese commander of Tete who was on friendly terms with the natives asked question after question until he was certain that the 'Son of God who fetched down the sun' could only be a white man taking bearings with a sextant. He concluded that it was probably none other than the Scottish missionary. As the son of an enlightened age it did not even dawn upon him that a miracle had taken place and that so simple an object as the sextant had saved the white man's life. Livingstone himself had not realized this, but then he had had little time for reflection. Overjoyed at having reached his goal, he now calmly accepted the fact that the natives had taken the sextant for an object of great magic power and had considered that under no circumstances must the master of such an object come to any harm. This time, the scientist had saved the missionary.

Livingstone had reached Tete at the beginning of March 1856, and he remained in the interior until the bad weather preceding the season of the South-east Trades was over. He asked that his Makololo bearers be given land, and saw to it that they settled there. Then he started alone for the coast: on the 20th May 1856 he was in Quelimane, the great harbour north of the Zambesi estuary, and on the 12th December he stepped out of the train in London. Mary, whom he had last seen in Cape Town five years earlier, was waiting on the platform. With tears of joy she rushed to embrace him. The other travellers stopped and recognized the modestly dressed man in his worn-out suit and soon loud hurrahs rang out in the station. The small unknown missionary who had left England fifteen years before had, in the meantime, become widely acclaimed as the first white man to have crossed the dark continent from west to east.

The British have ever been sports enthusiasts interested in records and their breaking, and Livingstone's was a most important achievement. The Scotsman Mungo Park had begun the business of exploring Africa with his expedition to the Niger. Then the French and the Germans had appeared on the scene and the latter's best man, Dr. Heinrich Barth from Hamburg, had recently taken up residence in London. Now Dr. Livingstone had followed him and gone one better. He was the first white man to have crossed Africa from coast to coast.

So far Livingstone's contribution to geography had been to confirm theoretical conclusions drawn from the existing map of Africa, i.e. that Central Africa was a basin bordered by oceanic mountain formations. In addition he had established the exact location of a large number of places and their altitudes above sea-level and had brought back important information of interest to ethnologists. Thanks to him the course of the Zambesi was no longer a mystery, and he had established that it was independent of the Congo and Nile systems. Finally he had added to the store of knowledge about caravan routes and travelling conditions in the Kalahari and he had also sent in detailed reports on the mountainous country known today as Southern Rhodesia.

His reports opened up new avenues of development for both scientist and politician. He had made it clear that sugar-cane, cotton and other local products could be cultivated on a large enough scale to warrant a considerable investment of capital in Central Africa. The rich variety of English articles already exported to Africa enjoyed great favour with the natives and could be bartered for ivory. The opening up of the dark continent to the English merchant required only the building of roads and the setting up of good relations with the tribes of the interior.

The politicians were seized by Livingstone's enthusiasm and began to see Africa as another theatre of British predominance like India. It was of paramount importance to secure control of the sea-routes to the few negotiable harbours by means of a mighty fleet, and then the rest would automatically follow. Germany was divided into some thirty small states and was incapable of taking any decisive action. France had her hands full with her interests in North Africa and on the southern coastal borders of the Mediterranean. Apart from this, Napoleon III had not long become emperor and was not yet sufficiently established in power to take part in such races. Finally, the North and South of America were so much at loggerheads, and the New World was so infinitely vast, that Uncle Sam could not be considered as a serious competitor. Thus the missionary from Blantyre in Scotland had placed an empire at the feet of his Queen. And how did David Livingstone view his own achievement? He expressed himself clearly and unequivocally on the subject, when he said that as far as he himself was concerned he looked upon the opening up of Central Africa as an event that gave much cause for congratulation, since it led one to hope that the natives might in this way be elevated.

After this basic observation his report went into details. He suggested that flat-bottomed steamers be sent up the Zambesi, thus using the great river as a supply route. There would be no difficulties as far as Tete. After that there was a stretch of rapids to be negotiated, but once over this obstacle, a steamer could proceed without difficulty for another 300 miles up to the foot of an eastern mountain range. At that point the steamer would be deeper into Central Africa than any white man had reached. It is significant that the Scottish missionary continued by suggesting that 'it was hoped that by encouraging the natives to occupy themselves with the development of the resources of their country, a considerable advance might be made towards the extinction of the slave trade'.

5

When Livingstone arrived in London on that December day of 1856, he was welcomed as a famous discoverer *and* missionary, but when he left England again on the 10th March 1858, his missionary aspirations were of secondary importance. This time he left at the invitation of the British government to perform a clearly outlined task. Obviously some of the reasons why Livingstone changed the direction of his activity can be found in his own nature, but we shall never know exactly all the factors involved, as indeed we can never know all the workings of the mind of a great man. It is therefore a waste of time to ask for a detailed account of how Livingstone lived in England after his return, and whether he had the same experiences as Heinrich Barth and other explorers, who never felt at home again in the civilized narrowness of the Old World. Such questions are of little interest when compared with the larger issues we shall discuss now. Therefore, before we accompany our Scot on his next voyage to Africa, let us allow him a well-earned rest of one and a quarter years in Europe while we, like spectators in a cinema, fill up the interlude with a flash-back into history.

We begin with Nero, the mad Roman dictator, the lock of hair over his forehead and the emerald monocle before his short-sighted eye. He wanted to show the Roman upper classes that he was more than a brutal overlord. Thus when he became emperor he organized *conversationes*, the Roman equivalent of a *salon*. Among the topics discussed by the literate was the Nile and its mysterious sources. Nero off-handedly ordered two officers of the Imperial Guard to go and discover the sources of the Nile. For all his faults he was no fool and he had obviously 'got up' the subject from some of the Roman professors of geography—a custom not unknown among present-day monarchs. Nero had probably been informed that both the Egyptian Pharaohs and the Persian overlords had tried time after time to solve the problem of the Nile. He was convinced that where they had failed, *he* would succeed. All that was needed was to deal with one's men energetically. Man is naturally a coward and lazy, but if one instils sufficient fear in him, he can be made to do anything.

In fact, his two officers, who started sixty years after the birth of Christ, tried their best. We have reports of their madcap adventure which show clearly that they reached the Sudd, the vast plains covered with thick grass and plants near Bahr el Ghazal. Their expedition was a magnificent achievement not to be overshadowed by white men until as late as 1841. Although the officers did not reach the actual sources of the Nile, their geographical knowledge obviously stretched further south than the Sudd, situated at about 5° North. Seneca, their contemporary who died in 65 A.D., knew that the White Nile was fed by two lakes, the 'Lake of the Crocodiles' and the 'Lake of the Waterfalls'—we do not need to use our imagination much to realize that these names refer to Lake Victoria and the Ripon Falls. Furthermore, Seneca knew that the waters of these lakes came from gigantic snow-capped mountains. Ptolemy, who lived in Alexandria one hundred years after Seneca, also stated that the snow masses of the 'Lunar Mountains' were the real sources of the Nile.

It was only in 1863 that the lakes feeding the Nile were discovered by the British explorers Speke and Grant, and another twenty-five years were to pass before the snow-capped mountains mentioned by Seneca were finally explored. We stand amazed, and a little shamefaced, before these magnificent early achievements. How small and modest are our own efforts in comparison!

Seneca and Ptolemy were obviously referring to the mountainous country round Lakes Kivu and Albert, and in particular to the Ruwenzori, a glacier situated at almost 16,800 feet, which Ptolemy could only have learnt about by hearsay. The whole of this knowledge was lost soon after, and even in 1854 the English geographer William Cooley expressed the opinion that Ptolemy had made a terrible mistake, for glaciers could not possibly exist in tropical Africa. This point is discussed at length in Cooley's book *Claudius Ptolemy and the Nile*. Cooley was of the opinion that the snow-caps consisted of a thick fall of hail, or more probably even thick layers of quartz or salt. But apparently Ptolemy was much less the victim of prejudice than Cooley, and the ancient geographer was to be fully vindicated when Stanley later discovered the Ruwenzori.

Long before Ptolemy, another Greek, the historian and geographer Strabo (63 B.C.–A.D. 20), had reported that the Nile issued from large lakes lying far to the south, and that one of these lakes was called Lake Psebo. Since Strabo's report undoubtedly referred to the Blue Nile, the great eastern tributary which flows into the White Nile, the main stream, near Khartoum, Lake Psebo is obviously our Lake Tana. This interpretation has been generally accepted, and we may assume that quite large areas of Abyssinia were already known by the beginning of our times. We are no longer impressed by the fact that today we can fly from Cairo to Addis Ababa and spend the week-end away from the insufferable heat of the capital of Egypt, but we find it difficult to swallow the fact that two thousand years before our era, some nameless travellers covered the 1,500-mile stretch to Lake Tana, a journey that must have been made many times for news of it to have reached as far as Rome.

Admittedly we must not imagine that the driving force behind this unknown discovery of Abyssinia was an urge for geographical knowledge. Our earlier travellers had much more practical reasons: they were looking for ivory, a much sought-after material in ancient times. Jewellery and ear-rings of ivory have been discovered in Egypt of the pre-Dynastic times, in Crete, Troy and the Hall district in Upper Austria and even in northern countries of Europe. Although some of these pieces may be of fossilized mammoth teeth, by far the largest part is of ivory coming from southern countries. The gigantic thick-skinned animals, the African as well as the Indian elephant, were far more widespread two and a half thousand years ago than they are today. Elephants were common in Syria, in Mesopotamia, Iran and in the whole of North and North-west Africa, and it was only in the fourth century B.C. that they began to disappear from these regions. As they became rarer their value mounted not merely by virtue of the ivory they provided, but also because their usefulness in battle had been realized. They were used by the Persians against Alexander, and by the Carthaginians against Rome, much in the way that modern generals use tanks. All the kings of the earth wanted to have elephants in their army. The Egyptian kings sent out elephant hunters to the south, and it is probable that Abyssinia was discovered during one of these expeditions. When Egypt became a Roman province after the death of Cleopatra, the Romans, too, began to take an interest in the southern highland. Although elephants had by then been superseded as a means of aggression by the development of heavy, long-range catapults, and were only used in punitive expeditions against the primitive natives, the demand for them did not decrease, for they were now required for the many circuses that were growing in popularity not only in Rome but also in Byzantium and in every other great capital of the Empire. Thus we can understand the lively interest taken by the Romans in Abyssinia.

Numerous hunting expeditions were sent out, and these were invariably followed by surveyors, making cartographical reports about the strange country, with merchants and traders coming in their wake. Outposts and then colonies were set up, and as the traders went deeper into the south they must eventually have come across Lake Tana, the 'inland sea', covering some 1,400 square miles and lying at an altitude of 6,000 feet.

Although we have no documentary evidence on which to base our conclusions, it is obvious that the Romans, like the Egyptians before them, soon recognized the importance of Lake Psebo for Egypt. The fertility of this granary of the Latin empire was based entirely on the yearly floodings of the Nile. What would happen, they must have asked themselves in Rome, if these floodings did not take place? The answer was quite clear. The land round the Nile would become a barren desert and Rome would be threatened with famine. The Romans were unable to measure that the Blue Nile, thundering down from the 'roof of East Africa', provided up to 175,000 cubic feet of water per second while the main stream, the White Nile, only supplied less than 30,000 cubic feet. Even though people might not yet have realized that the Nile, the sole river of North Africa, crossing as it did vast expanses of desert, would dry up and evaporate in these arid regions without the tremendous addition from the Abyssinian Alps, nevertheless the Roman geographers must very soon have perceived that the main water masses came via the Blue Nile from Lake Tana. Thus the Roman colonists in Egypt must have become aware that they must either have possession of Lake Tana or else prevent any strong concentration of power developing in Abyssinia, and when, under Constantine the Great, Christianity became the official religion of the Roman Empire, the politicians on the Tiber and the Bosphorus must have been grateful to know that Abyssinia, the tremendous state of Axum, was being converted too, and that the water reservoir of Egypt would no longer be in the hands of heathen barbarians.

These reflections may sound very fanciful on our part, and since we cannot produce any documentary proof, we may well be accused of applying our own shrewd mentality to centuries that were blissfully incapable of such a calculating policy. But events are on our side, for some 1,200 years after the Romans had marched into Egypt there happened exactly what the clever politicians of the Empire had once feared. Lake Tana was dammed off!

The man responsible was called Lalibala. He was the ruler of the Coptic Christian kingdom of Shoa in Abyssinia, and since he was also lord of Lake Tana and the Blue Nile, he believed that he could play the part of destiny. During the sixth Crusade, Saint Louis and all his knights had been beaten in battle and captured. To avenge this shame on the fair name of Christendom, Lalibala, in the year 1250, collected a gigantic army of slaves and built tremendous dams not far from Lake Tana, so that its waters no longer ran away to the north but flowed south into Lake Zwai. The consequences for Egypt were terrible: the Nile floods ceased, the harvests dried up, hunger and plagues depopulated the country. The Negus had achieved his aim of punishing the Mohammedans for their sacrilege, and of securing himself from attack from Egypt.

But the cup of victory soon tasted bitter. The waters of the diverted Lake Tana produced in the dry unfertile regions such unheard-of harvests that the rulers residing there became mighty and correspondingly impertinent. Unless the Emperor of Shoa wanted to endanger his own supremacy and his whole empire, he had no option but to destroy the dam on Lake Tana. When he did so, fertility returned to the Nile valley and in South Abyssinia the dukes of Mara, Hadae and Adal once again became rulers of a poor and arid country.

This gigantic enterprise must have made a tremendous impression on the Old World, or at least on Italy, where relations between the Vatican and the *Abuna* of Abyssinia, the head of the Ethiopian Church, were very close in the years around 1230. The German geographer Richard Hennig, in his well-known book *Terrae Incognitae*, has dealt with this contact between Abyssinia and Rome and has made out a good case for saying that it was much more significant than had been previously assumed.

Leaving aside now the question whether the Middle Ages knew of the threat to Egypt's life-line or not, in 1522, Rodrigo de Lima, the Portuguese ambassador to Abyssinia, reported that he had seen the tremendous remains of Lalibala's dams. Once again the sword of Damocles hung over the Land of the Nile. Albuquerque, the Portuguese Viceroy of India, whose name has appeared earlier in this book, made the suggestion to Lisbon that the waters of Lake Tana should be diverted in order to bring Egypt to her knees. Napoleon Bonaparte, too, knew this, and immediately upon landing in Africa he sent rich presents and a treaty of friendship to the Negus. The British also were to consider using the advantage over Egypt afforded by Lake Tana.

In 1902, England made a treaty with King Menelik II, according to which none but the British were allowed to erect dams on Lake Tana. During the Second World War the Allies did their best to drive the Italians out of Abyssinia as quickly as possible in order to get hold of this water reservoir for themselves. At the beginning of February 1941, roughly half a year after Italy had entered the war, Great Britain went over to the attack in East Africa. On the 6th April 1941, hardly eight weeks later, the first British troops marched into Addis Ababa, long before anyone had so much as heard of Rommel. Had the Germans overrun Egypt, then England would undoubtedly have met them with the same terrible blow inflicted on the enemies of Christ by the Negus Lalibala in 1250. Fortunately these desperate measures were not required, but at the same time the English offensive in East Africa made it clear that Egypt's fate was not to be decided on the Nile but on Lake Tana, and that the British had been well aware of this.

Such geopolitical considerations are much more quickly *felt* by people than *consciously recognized*. It is for this reason that the Strait of Gibraltar, the Channel, the Strait of Malacca, the Nile, have since time immemorial been the stages for the unfolding of history, while other more spacious regions have been spared this fate. This is the reason why the search for the sources of the Nile, the *quaerere caput Nili,* had begun so early on. This Latin expression, used as a tag to imply that somebody is trying the impossible, was no exaggeration, for even after John Hanning Speke had sent his famous telegram in 1863 from Gondokoro: 'The Nile is settled!', the source of the Nile was to be discovered twice more: in 1898 by the German doctor Richard Kandt who penetrated to the source of the Kagera, the so-called 'Alexandria Nile', and in 1937 by the Belgian Dr. Burkhard Waldecker who believed that he had discovered the southern source of the Nile in the source of the Kasumo not far from Kitega, east of Lake Tanganyika. Today we can go there by car and the *Guide du Voyageur au Congo Belge et au Ruanda-Urundi*, 1954, after giving a detailed description of the route from Usumbura to Mount Kikizi, states:

> From here you get the first glimpse of the pyramid erected on the peak of the mountain. After another three kilometres, leave the car and mount the peak up a narrow path rising to 200 metres and to the southernmost end of the 6,700-kilometre-long waterway to the Mediterranean. . . .
>
> Dr. B. Waldecker erected a stone pyramid at this spot with the following inscription in Latin: 'Pyramid on the southernmost source of the Nile, showing that the river springs from here.'

The search for the sources of the Nile had begun at the mouth of the great river, where it is an easily negotiable water route. Ships could sail up it so easily that the explorer Alexandrina Tinné, whom we have already met in the Sahara on her great Nile expedition of 1862, took her Bechstein grand piano on board one of her ships. Alexandrina Tinné was surrounded by twenty white stewardesses and chambermaids and by two hundred coloured servants. She travelled as far as the Austrian Mission Station Gondokoro in the Mongalla mountains which had been erected a dozen years before at the point where navigation becomes more difficult. But Alexandrina Tinné met neither the pious fathers, of whom the majority had already died of the murderous climate during their first years, nor Speke and Grant, who had disappeared into the interior in 1860 and to whom she wanted to bring help. Thus in September 1862 she turned back again, six months before the two explorers finally reached Gondokoro, to 'settle the Nile'.

Their laconic report aroused tremendous excitement throughout the world, but nowhere did it create the same deep impression as in the small village of Korntal in Wurtemburg, where lived the missionary and traveller Dr. Ludwig Krapf, who had returned from Africa some few years earlier in order to recover his health. After a rather unfortunate attempt to work as a missionary in Abyssinia, he had spent seven years in East Africa not far from the port of Mombasa, and had founded the mission station of Neu-Rabai. He had mastered Swahili, spoken along the whole East African coast, and had soon gained the confidence of the natives. Now his real work could begin. He had planned to found a whole chain of mission stations, nine or ten in number, right across the Dark Continent from Mombasa in the east to Gaboo in the west, thus to put a stop to slave trading. Before, however, any steps towards this work could be taken, the interior had to be explored more closely. This had been his, Dr. Ludwig Krapf's, task.

Never before, as far as he knew, had a white man even attempted to venture into the interior, nor did any white man understand and speak the African languages as well as he did, and this was of prime importance. One had to speak to the natives in their own language, one had to understand their customs and habits, one had to be able to think like them. Thus Dr. Krapf had started travelling up and down the coast listening to the natives' stories, and one day he had learned from an Arab trader that not far from the interior there lay the gigantic 'caravan mountain', whose lofty silvery peaks had since earliest times served as a landmark to columns of bearers, pointing the way to the vast lake lying to the west of them. This silver mountain was said to be quite inaccessible and moreover was guarded by the *njaro*, the evil spirit, so that no one had ever dared to climb it. He himself, the Arab said, had always been curious to find out whether the peak of this unusual mountain was in fact made of silver. Many years ago he had once sent a slave up on it to see what was there, but the mountain spirit had worked a spell. The slave had placed handfuls of the strange, cold, white substance into a bamboo reed and had brought it down, but it had all been changed to water.

Dr. Krapf's heart had beaten faster when he had heard this. Had the ancient geographers been right after all? The 'silver' could not have been anything but snow and ice, but could these exist so close to the Equator? If this was so, then the story of the freshwater lake which the Arab had told him need not have been a fable, and this lake formed from the melting snow and ice might perhaps be the source of the Nile! Dr. Krapf had difficulty in recalling that he was a missionary and not an explorer. He had been sorely tempted to start at once for the Silver Mountain, but he could not be spared from his work on the station and soon after he had fallen ill with malaria. Thus it had not been he but his mission brother Johannes Rebmann who had set out on the 11th April 1846 to see the miracle. Eventually, after days of marching through the jungle, he had come upon a tremendous mountain massif towering high in the sky, and one of its peaks was glistening silver in the bright sunshine.

> During the rainy season the mountains are constantly hidden by clouds, but in the hot season I could clearly distinguish all the different peaks of the range. There are two main peaks separated by a ridge, running east to west and about nine miles long. The eastern peak (Mawensi) is lower and more pointed in shape than the western (Kibo) which even in the hot season, when its lower neighbour exhibits its bare rocks, is still covered with a mantle of glistening snow. . . . This snow cap supplies the many rivers which have their source here (at least twenty) and causes rain to fall even during the hot months.
>
> The Swahilis of the coast call this snow-capped mountain Kilimanjaro (mountain of the caravans), because caravans could see it from afar and use it as a landmark. The local natives call it Kibo, which refers to the snow itself. . . . I asked them expressly about it and from the many tales which they told me, for instance that if you put Kibo into the fire it turned into water, I could see that they understood the nature of snow. They also informed me that the river which flowed past had its source in the Kibo.
>
> I told the Swahilis that the white substance could not be silver since they could see with their own eyes how it appeared on the peak in greater or smaller quantities according to the seasons, and that if it had been silver, it would not have done this. I pointed out that some people had climbed up and down the mountain without harm and that those who had perished in the attempt had done so because they had chosen an unfavourable time for the ascent. . . .

Johannes Rebmann had been moved to the depths of his soul. Many years before, when the Basle Missionary Society had accepted him, the son of a peasant from Wurtemburg, into their school he had grown familiar with a landscape of ice, snow and high mountains.

Dr. Krapf too had been a pupil of the Basle Mission School and he had been greatly impressed by the story brought back by his assistant. As soon as he could leave the station, he had marched to the mountain and, proceeding roughly along the site of the modern railway line, he came to Nairobi and Mount Kenya. Here, too, there were ice-covered peaks towering high into the sky. Streamers of fine snow blown by the wind decorated the mountain ridges. He could hear the roar as the snow-cliffs crashed, melted by the blaze of the equatorial noonday sun. Krapf's suspicions had been confirmed when the natives had told him that not far away there was a lake and that a mighty river flowed out from it to the north to the 'Land of the Turks', where it entered a large 'salt lake', whose opposite shores washed the 'Land of the Whites'.

Ludwig Krapf had immediately understood what his discovery implied: *Caput quaerere Nili.* Now the ancient question had been solved. Somewhere in that region must be the sources of the Nile, and the Congo could not be very far away. Bana Cheri, his black guide, had told him that there was a large river fifty days' journey to the west and if he sailed down it, he would come to the western coast of Africa and to the *wasungu*, the Europeans. Krapf had been full of excitement and made the following prophetic entry in his journal:

> Who knows but in centuries to come, and even perhaps within decades, a railway may run across this plateau, from one side of Africa to the other. Since it is possible to reach Mount Kenya in a march of about 200 hours along this plateau, by railway it would be possible to reach the sources of the Nile, which are situated in the vicinity of Mount Kenya, in a few days. This high plateau will be studded with towns and villages and no savage tribes will endanger these regions.

This vision was written down in 1851 and fifty-one years later, in 1902, it became a reality. A railway line almost 600 miles long runs from Mombasa to Nairobi, the capital of Kenya, and to Kisumu, until recently one of the most important aerodromes and markets on Lake Victoria. The journey to Nairobi takes twenty hours, a tenth of the time needed by Ludwig Krapf. The small tent in which he sat when he wrote down his prophecies stood not far away from the very spot where the line passes. This region, which was so heavily overgrown that an army of 36,000 Indian coolies was needed to clear it and level it for the railway track, is today strangely reminiscent of the English countryside with fields of crops, rich pasture land for cattle and horses, and farmhouses with roses and dahlias growing in their gardens. Towns and villages follow one another in rapid succession and the European traveller can feast his eye on the strikingly familiar pastoral scene.

Only in one aspect did the missionary's prophecy not come true. When the guests of Torr's Hotel in Nairobi come in for their five o'clock tea, they take off their hats and coats but not their revolvers. Even the ladies' handbags seem strangely bulky, until you realize there is a ·35 inside. 'No savage tribes will endanger these regions!' yet Mau-Mau is in the neighbourhood and that is a thousand times worse, for the Mau-Mau leaders have largely been to English schools, and the process has often turned them out as unfortunate products of a mixture between African and European cultures. Before the building of the Kenya Railway the transport price for a ton of cargo from Mombasa to Nairobi and Lake Victoria was £180. Moreover it was no easy task to navigate Lake Victoria owing to the strong currents and large breakers. With the laying of the railway, transport costs dropped considerably and it became possible to carry the dismantled sections of large-sized steamers to Kisumu on Lake Victoria where they were mounted and launched. These steamers had no difficulty in overcoming the currents of Lake Victoria and transport costs could be reduced even further. But many a lonely farmer must have thought during the last few years that he would prefer to pay the £180 per ton of cargo and make do without the railway and without the steamers, but also be without the fear of Mau-Mau.

Naturally a hundred years ago nobody had foreseen that such a problem could arise. Ludwig Krapf himself, like Livingstone, had been deeply convinced that his message of salvation could bring nothing but good to the natives and he had spent much time planning to establish a chain of missionary stations throughout the whole of Africa. In 1855 he had published a map drawn by himself and his collaborators in the journal of the London Missionary Society, in order to show the world how much had already been achieved. His map was astonishingly accurate and cleared up many of the misconceptions about this strange land. Some time later Krapf had fallen severely ill and returned to Europe where he had followed up his map with a two-volume report on his travels.

A storm of protest had set in. Scientists and professional geographers were quick to point out that Krapf had had no geographical training or education whatsoever, and that without an elaborate scientific preparation travellers were only too easily deceived and were bound to bring back fanciful tales. Ice and snow on the Equator indeed! It was utterly ridiculous! So fantastic did Krapf's report seem to his contemporaries that even a man such as Alexander von Humboldt only withdrew his criticisms after he had spoken to Krapf himself some years later. In fact these disbelievers were only convinced in 1899, when the Leipzig Professor Hans Meyer climbed to the summit of Kilimanjaro and brought back a series of photographs to Europe. The scepticism of Krapf's opponents is surprising, since reports that there were high mountains covered with snow and ice in Central Africa had been made as early as two hundred years earlier. Dr. Olivier Dapper had written in his *Umbständliche Beschreibung* of Africa:

The Lunar Mountains, which lie between the tropic of Capricorn and the Cape of Good Hope, surpass all the other mountains of the African continent in height. They are quite uninhabitable for human beings, since they consist of nothing but bare rock incessantly covered with snow and ice.

But then who was this Dr. Olivier Dapper? He had studied medicine and not geography: that in itself was sufficient to rule him out of court!

But whatever the rest of the world had to say about Krapf's report, England, in view of her interest in Egypt, was deeply interested in it, for anything connected with the Nile was considered of major importance in London. Although the white substance seen by the two German missionaries on the top of Kilimanjaro and Mount Kenya might be quartz or salt, the possibility that it was snow could not be ruled out and the reports, based on hearsay, of the existence of large lakes in Central Africa might be true after all. In this case, it would be easier to reach the source of the Nile from East Africa. A British expedition would have to start at once before any other nation could get there.

The Foreign Office enlisted the support of its best people. One of the leaders of the expedition which started in 1856, one year after Krapf had published his map, was Richard Burton. Burton, who was Irish by birth and had served as an officer in the Indian army, was an exceptionally gifted linguist. In 1853 he had made a journey disguised as a Persian to the holy cities of Mecca and Medina which were forbidden to every infidel on pain of death. The second leader of the expedition was John Hanning Speke, a lieutenant in the East India Company's army, who had already proved himself in the Himalayas. This team of keen and able men was entrusted with the task of solving the 2,000-year-old riddle of the Nile.

But Rome was not built in a day. The two travellers reached Tanganyika at the beginning of 1858, but as Burton fell seriously ill with fever, Speke went on alone. At the end of July he reached Lake Ukerewe, which he renamed Lake Victoria in honour of the Queen. He saw nothing, however, of the Nile which he had been sent to find. He questioned the natives and they confirmed the report made by the German missionaries that a large river flowed out of Lake Victoria towards the north; but Speke could not find it. When he returned to Burton the latter was unwilling to accept his story outright, for he believed that scientific knowledge must be based on what one has seen oneself and not on what the natives have said. Speke was met with the same argument when he returned to London some weeks in advance of Burton. Sir Roderick Murchison, the President of the Geographical Society, received him and questioned him eagerly about the maps of Lake Victoria which Speke had submitted, but he was as little satisfied as Burton himself. At the end of April 1860, Speke, accompanied by the Scotsman, James Augustus Grant, also of the Indian army, left England determined to succeed this time. Two years later, on the 27th July 1862, the two men reached the place where the fabulous great river leaves Lake Victoria by way of plunging cataracts.

We were well rewarded for . . . [this] . . . was by far the most interesting sight I had seen in Africa. Everybody ran to see the falls at once, though the march had been long and fatiguing . . . the falls, about 12 feet deep and 400 to 500 feet broad, were broken by rocks. . . . It was a sight that attracted one to it for hours—the roar of the waters, the thousands of passenger-fish, leaping at the falls with all their might . . . made, in all, with the pretty nature of the country—small hills, grassy topped with trees in the folds, and gardens on the lower slopes—as interesting a picture as one could wish to see. The expedition had now performed its function. I saw that old father Nile without any doubt rises in the Victoria N'yanza and, as I had foretold, that lake is the great source of the holy river. . . .

As one reads this entry, and also the account Speke gave of the difficulties an explorer had to face in Africa in the 1860's, one understands why he came to the conclusion that the Nile had its origin in Lake Victoria. We, seated in our comfortable arm-chairs under the restful light of an electric reading-lamp can easily object that if Mr. Speke had thought a little more about the lakes of Europe, he would have seen that as a rule large lakes are merely gathering basins for rivers and only very rarely true sources. In the wilds of Africa everything looked quite different. We must add that the Kagera also, a 400-mile-long western tributary of Lake Victoria, excited Speke's interest considerably. Possibly this was the true source of the Nile, but to investigate all the regions feeding a large river is an enormous task and it would have to be left to a later expedition to discover the southernmost trickle of water. These were the thoughts running through Speke's mind when he sent the London Geographical Society his famous telegram: 'The Nile is settled.'

Less than fifty years later, another Englishman stood at the head of the rapids where Lake Victoria bids goodbye to the Nile. He looked at them carefully, and when he reached the Owen Falls, some miles to the north where the tremendous river crams its bulk through a narrow fissure some 460 feet wide, he took the cigar out of his mouth and announced that it might be fun to let the old Nile begin its course with a jump through a turbine. Winston Churchill, when he said this, was no longer an unknown person, though he was still a very young man. Today the Owen Falls hydro-electric dam is nearing completion. This tremendous achievement is one of the results of the building of the Kenya railway, and of the enormous economic development which has taken place in East Africa in the last decades. Lack of energy proved a serious handicap to progress in the area, and since the cost of transporting coal and oil from Mombasa by rail was much too high, it became more and more imperative to exploit the natural resources of water power. But probably the main factor in the decision to start work on the surveying engineer's project was the knowledge that the dam would only have to be some sixty feet high and the building costs small. The dam will be ready by 1960 and will provide 150,000 kilowatts. This supply of energy will open up the phosphate deposits of

Torocora and the copper deposits near Kilembe. Cotton mills, iron and steel foundries, sugar refineries, cement works, and other industries can grow up in the district, and those already existing can double and triple their output. The first five generators are already working and the little town of Jinja, the headquarters of the engineers, is feverish with life and activity.

6

We had taken our leave of Livingstone on that March day of 1858, when, together with his wife and a party of scientists and doctors, he had embarked for Africa once more. His contract with the London Missionary Society had been dissolved and, although he remained ever faithful to the Christian faith, he was never again to be a missionary. He set out, no longer the servant of God, but the servant of the state, which, speaking through the mouth of Lord Clarendon, the then British Foreign Minister, had expressed quite clearly what was expected of Livingstone. According to the prosaic instructions of the English Government he was

> to extend the knowledge already obtained of the geography and mineral and agricultural resources of eastern and central Africa; to improve our acquaintance with the inhabitants and endeavour to engage them to apply themselves to industrial pursuits and to the cultivation of their lands, with a view to the production of raw material to be exported to England in return for British manufactures.

In the same breath Her Majesty's Government also stressed that it attached much importance to the moral influence that could be exerted on the minds of the natives by a well-regulated and orderly household of Europeans. The most important question, however, was whether cotton, tea, indigo, tobacco and sugar-cane could be planted in Africa and exported from there. Livingstone himself expected to find a navigable river route by which trade into the interior could be opened. His expedition was magnificently equipped. He even received a small steam launch whose ten horse-power, though insufficient by itself, meant a considerable help in negotiating the Zambesi.

At the beginning of September 1858, Livingstone, after crossing the swamps of the Zambesi delta, entered Tete again, happy to be back in Africa and rejoicing in the power and glory of the untouched continent.

> When a native of the temperate north first lands in the tropics, his feelings resemble in some respects those which the first man may have had on his entrance to the Garden of Eden. He has set his foot in a new world; another state of existence is before him. Everything he sees, every sound that falls upon his ear, has all the freshness and charm of novelty. The trees and the plants are new, the flowers and the fruits, the beasts, the birds, and the insects are curious and strange. The very sky itself is new, glowing with colours and sparkling with constellations never seen in northern climes.

He was equally happy when he saw that the Makololo, whom he had left in Tete, had settled down well in their new surroundings. They, for their part, were overjoyed to see him again and most of them were eager to accompany their white friend and guide up the Zambesi to their old home, though there were many who wanted to remain in Tete, for 'civilization' had cast its spell upon them. They could obtain anything they wanted for ivory, and the forests around Tete were rich in elephants. It is said that approximately thirty thousand of these giant beasts were shot yearly at that time. Although this figure is somewhat exaggerated, elephants were certainly massacred on a large scale. Incidentally, the official exchange for a hundred pounds of ivory was two pounds of glass beads. Nevertheless, the simple natives felt this was progress indeed!

In the middle of November 1858, Livingstone left Tete, accompanied by a party of his Makololo friends. Neither he nor they suspected that a two-year trek lay before them. The expedition started off with a great disappointment, for Livingstone soon discovered that none of the four mouths of the Zambesi, the assumed 'Gate to the Continent', was navigable for larger ships. While the sandbanks and reedy swamps did not present an insuperable obstacle for flat-bottomed vessels, the Kebrabasa rapids, roughly fifty-five miles above Tete and slightly more than three hundred and fifty miles from the sea, proved impassable. The situation remains unaltered today. All steamers starting from the mouth of the Zambesi can get no further than these rapids, and, to all intents and purposes, no further than Tete. Livingstone could not have known that, less than a hundred years later, people would fly over these obstacles, landing at Tete aerodrome, and that a stream of cars would pour through this small village. All he knew was that his hopes of using the Zambesi as a highway to the fertile highlands of Central Africa had been dashed. It might be possible, he reflected, to get past during the rainy season when the river was several feet deeper, but in that case a steamer with more powerful engines would be needed. Livingstone reported this to England without attempting to conceal his lack of faith in the latter possibility. He added that he would explore the Shire River, which flowed from the north into the lower Zambesi. He did not state outright that this might prove the answer to the demand for a navigable waterway into the interior of the dark continent, but we may assume that this was indeed his hope. Again disappointment awaited him, for after almost two hundred miles his steamer was brought to a stop by a series of waterfalls.

Today express trains of the Trans-Zambesi Railway thunder through the Shire valley, and regions once the home of hostile natives who smeared their arrow-heads with deadly poison are now covered with neatly planned camping sites. Larger and smaller settlements follow one another with monotonous regularity: everywhere there are hotels, cinemas, banks and post offices—in short, it is difficult for us to imagine that, only a few generations ago, this land was a dangerous wilderness.

'Our Government has ordered us to assist and protect you,' complained the local Portuguese official when Livingstone told him he intended to follow the Shire to the north. 'You will be travelling in a region into which we dare not follow you. How shall we protect you there?' If we read the report published in 1865 by David Livingstone and his brother Charles under the title *The Zambezi and its Tributaries*, then we can sympathize with that Portuguese major. No white man had ever returned

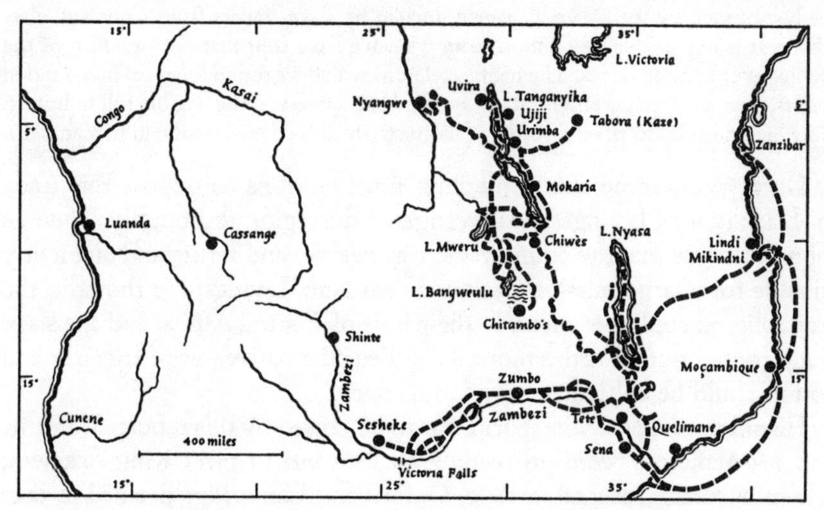

XLII. Livingstone's last journeys between the Zambesi and the Congo.

alive from that green hell, and it was nothing short of a miracle that Livingstone managed to survive, and that, time after time, he was able to pacify the natives.

On the 18th April 1859, two months after leaving the Zambesi, the expedition discovered Lake Shirwa, 'a considerable body of bitter water containing leeches, fishes, crocodiles and hippopotami'. Here Livingstone heard of a much larger lake further north, Lake Nyasa, separated only by a narrow strip of land from Lake Shirwa. Without hesitation he decided to make for it, and on the 16th September 1859, he stood on the shores of that vast expanse of water, a lake about thirty miles wide and three hundred miles long. He was not the first white man to reach Lake Nyasa. Long before him the Portuguese had reached it, but their feat had remained unknown, and thus Livingstone was fully entitled to claim that he was the first to discover it. His joy in this was ruined by the discovery that the Shire too would not serve as the longed-for waterway to the interior. He made this point very firmly in his official report to the British Government. Then, he asked himself, was he compelled to go to Central Africa?

Were not his tasks here in the east, within the sphere of influence of the Arab slave-traders, much more important?

The British Consul in Zanzibar had calculated that nineteen thousand slaves were taken each year across Lake Nyasa to be sold in the markets of Ibo or Kilwa, and Livingstone added some very unpleasant details to the bare figures.

> Those taken out of the country are but a small section of the sufferers. Thousands are killed and die of their wounds and famine, driven from their villages by the slave-trade proper. Thousands perish in internecine war, waged for slaves, and are slain for the lust of gain by their own clansmen, incited by slave-traders from Cuba and elsewhere. It is our deliberate opinion from what we have seen that not one-fifth of the victims ever become slaves. The many skeletons which we found lying on rocks and in forests, near small pools and by the wayside, bear witness to the terrible toll in human life which must be ascribed directly or indirectly to this devilish traffic in human flesh.

Deeply convinced that something must be done to oppose this trade in 'black ivory', Livingstone investigated the region thoroughly. Then he reported home that the countryside was healthy and fertile and eminently suitable for a large mission station. From here, Livingstone thought, the true religion could be spread to the whole of Central Africa, and the slave trade rooted out. Furthermore, he added, the natives were friendly and cotton could be cultivated on a large scale.

He did not suspect what harm was to be caused by this report. While he and his Makololo were proceeding to Linyanti to meet King Sekeletu, whom he finally reached in 1860, Oxford and Cambridge decided to take up Livingstone's suggestions, and the Universities' Mission to Central Africa sent an expedition to the upper Shire valley. The members of this enterprise, led by Bishop Mackenzie, landed at the beginning of 1861 on the east coast of Africa, a cotton-stripping machine in their baggage. A few days later they started on a journey across the wild country to Lake Nyasa, some four hundred and twenty-five miles away, though none of the members had any previous experience of Africa. Deeply worried at what might happen to them, Livingstone hastened to meet the pious expedition, but was too late to avert their fate. The reverend gentlemen had encountered a slave convoy, driven away the slave-traders and freed the victims of their shackles. Livingstone had wanted to warn them not to proceed too forcefully, for he had foreseen that neither the slave-traders nor the natives themselves would understand the intentions of the expedition, and that all of them would merely view Bishop Mackenzie and his young men as undesirable competition. This is exactly what happened. While Livingstone and his Makololo were still far away, the Universities' Mission became involved in skirmishes with the very Negroes that Livingstone had described as being so peaceful. The outcome was that the missionaries were forced to turn and flee back to the coast. Mackenzie and the majority of his party had to pay for their over-zealous behaviour with their lives.

In England people were horrified, and, as always in such cases, questions were asked, not about the real reason for the failure, but rather to discover who was responsible for the unfortunate enterprise. Although Livingstone had had no hand in the Universities' Mission, he was made the scapegoat. Public opinion, which had but recently acclaimed him as a hero, changed overnight. The Government could do nothing to stem the tide, and for want of results from Livingstone the Foreign Office sent an open telegram to him in which it told him coldly that all payments to him would be suspended as from the 31st December 1863.

This was a terrible blow for Livingstone. He had spent every penny he possessed on Africa. His wife, whom he had left at the coast, had died of malaria in 1862. He had not seen his children for five years, and in the meanwhile they had grown up and become completely estranged from him. All his savings had been invested in the launch, *Lady Nyasa*, with which he had explored all the bays of the great lake. The great adventure was over. Remittances stopped promptly on the 31st December 1863, and seeing that he was now completely without any means, he had no option but to call a halt to his work of exploration. The dispatch from the Foreign Office had not breathed a word about the *Lady Nyasa*; the British Government obviously had not the slightest intention either of buying the launch or of giving Livingstone any compensation whatsoever. He was left entirely to his own devices. True, the slave-traders of Lake Nyasa and the East African coast were only too willing to pay any price he might ask for the trim little ship, since such a flat-bottomed, fast watercraft was just what they needed. But although the Scot was at his wits' end, he could not bring himself to *that*. He refused all offers and once again he tried the impossible—resolutely he crossed the Indian Ocean from East Africa to Bombay on the *Lady Nyasa* and sold his 'cockleshell' there, but the bank into which he put the money failed. A broken man, infamously neglected by his Government and his nation, Livingstone returned to England on the 30th April 1864. He was fully convinced that his career was now ended and that all that remained for him to do was to write his memoirs. When these were published in 1864, the Government and the public suddenly changed their minds and the veteran explorer was sent on yet another expedition, this time a search for the ultimate sources of the Nile, proposed by Sir Roderick Murchison, President of the Royal Geographical Society. Although Livingstone was no more than fifty-three, he had become an almost legendary figure. The Foreign Office retracted its former hostile attitude and conferred upon him the rather vague title of 'Consul-at-large to the heart of Africa'. On the 3rd January 1866, he started on his last expedition to Africa. He was never to see his home again but this enterprise, though he was never to learn it himself, made him one of the most famous men in the world. While the last act of the explorer's life was being played out, the stage was being set in Madrid, in New York and in Paris for a most dramatic development.

Livingstone started on his march west from near the mouth of the Ruvuma, north of Cape Delgado. His path led him through swamps and thorn-bush and the going was hard and slow. Even today it is no easy matter to cross this district, since it has no good roads at all. At last Lake Nyasa was reached, but the densely populated and fertile land had by now become depopulated. Slave-traders had carried off the native inhabitants, and those who had escaped were hiding in the bush. Livingstone found it impossible to hire boats to cross the lake, and he was forced to make a detour of four hundred and fifty miles round the southern banks. This proved too much for his bearers, who deserted at the end of September 1866, and marched back to the coast. Thus Livingstone was left stranded with all the baggage. When the bearers reached the coast, they spread the rumour that Livingstone had fallen into the hands of the savage Mazitu tribe, and was certain to have been murdered. This story had important consequences. It caused an American newspaper reporter to sail for Africa and make a series of expeditions which were to change the face of the world, for out of them grew the great industrial state of the Belgian Congo with the largest copper mines, uranium deposits and hydro-electric plants in the world.

7

'Buy my fine ribbons, ladies! Who'll buy my fine ribbons?'

The narrow streets of Calton, Bridgeton and Camlachie, the working-class districts of Glasgow, were ringing with the pedlar's cry. Up and down the streets and narrow alleys, in courtyards and passages, the shrill voice reverberated. The pedlar had been up and down the streets with his box of ribbons and laces, threads and cottons and knick-knacks of all kinds, as the menfolk were on their way to the factories and shipyards. Now it was late afternoon and in all the houses the kettle was singing on the hob, but still the cry continued: 'Who'll buy my fine ribbons?'

Of course they all knew him, this young red-haired lad, James Gordon Bennett by name, who would trudge through the streets of Glasgow with his box of laces, ribbons and other fancy goods towards the end of each week. What he sold was of good quality and he knew his business well. From Mondays to Thursdays he travelled round the Highlands buying embroidery and lacework from the farmers' wives for a few pence, and at the week-end, when the men had been paid and there was money again in town, he would reappear in Glasgow. His wares were good and not very expensive, and many a worker's wife had become his customer. The lad was a great charmer and could talk most persuasively, so that the women's hearts went out to him. Most of them came from the country and were pining away in the great city. They longed to meet someone who could conjure up for them memories of their childhood and of their first loves.

James Gordon Bennett could do this to perfection, and more important still—he gave credit. He had patience and left the womenfolk sufficient time to put the few pence by, for he had instinctively grasped the fact that a new era had dawned, the age of the masses. The worker could not afford to throw away pounds or even shillings, but he could spend by the penny. James Gordon Bennett had seen that the *modern* business man must aim at diverting this stream of pennies into his pocket. Naturally his wares were of good quality, but he also coaxed the good housewives of Glasgow to buy from him by singing them Highland songs and telling them stories.

It is extremely unlikely that Livingstone knew Bennett, for, when the latter emigrated to America in 1819, the former was a boy of six, though he might well have heard the shrill voice of the pedlar during occasional visits to Glasgow, while Bennett might equally well have set eyes upon the thin, pale child, tightly clasping his father's hand as they walked through the streets of the town. Fifty years later neither of them remembered having ever seen the other. By that time James Gordon Bennett had become the millionaire owner of the *New York Herald*, and David Livingstone the most famous explorer and traveller of his time.

Mr. James Gordon Bennett never learnt whether the rescue expedition financed by his newspaper to find Mr. Livingstone was successful or not. He died on the 1st June 1872, and it was only four weeks later, on the 1st July 1872, that the *New York Herald* received the now famous telegram from its London correspondent stating that the leader of the expedition had found Livingstone and that the latter was well.

It is difficult for us, who live in a much more callous age, to imagine the tremendous excitement caused by this telegram and the subsequent publication of Stanley's letter relating his meeting with Livingstone. Africa was the topic of the moment and people searched through their newspapers over breakfast to find some new account from the dark continent. With one stroke Henry Morton Stanley had achieved fame on a par with the great Dr. Livingstone.

Livingstone! Everybody knew who he was! His name had appeared in the newspapers on numerous occasions during the last twenty years. But who on earth was this chap Stanley? It was not discovered until much later that this correspondent of the *New York Herald* had not been christened Henry Morton Stanley, but James Rowlands, and that he was not an

American but a Welshman. In 1858, while still a boy, he had run away from the St. Asaph Orphanage in Denbigh and, crossing to America, he had eventually reached the town of New Orleans, where he was adopted by the wealthy merchant Stanley whose name he took. Some years later he became a journalist on the *New York Herald*. In each of these events chance had played a leading part, and it was chance again that made him famous. In 1867 a British force had entered Abyssinia to establish order in that troubled country. Stanley had staked his entire savings of three thousand dollars on one throw to go as a correspondent with the British troops. He had been the first to cable reports about the decisive defeat of Theodore, the megalomaniac 'Emperor' of Abyssinia, and, because the cable had snapped immediately after he had sent his dispatch, the *New York Herald* had been the only paper to publish the news. As a result his name became well known in the world of journalism and he was showered under by commissions. Stanley was the automatic choice for the trouble spots of the world, and in 1869 he was sent to Spain to report on the revolution which had just broken out there.

It was at this point that the chain of events began which was to make his name famous throughout the world. The first link of this chain was a very commonplace journalistic commission. Stanley, who had been to Valencia in the south to report on the fierce battles taking place there, arrived back in Madrid in the early hours of the morning of the 16th October 1869. He took his reports to the telegraph office, and then went to his hotel to take a nap after the long night journey. At about 10 a.m. he was awakened by the porter with an urgent dispatch from Paris. The telegram was signed by Mr. James Gordon Bennett Jr., European managing director of the *New York Herald*, and asked Stanley to 'come to Paris on important business'. Stanley was surprised. It was unusual for the parsimonious Mr. Bennett Jr. to send telegrams—things must indeed have been most urgent. Five hours later, at 3 p.m., our correspondent was sitting in the Madrid–Hendaye express. He arrived in Paris in the middle of the night, and at dawn he reported to Mr. Bennett in the Grand Hotel.

Mr. Bennett was still fast asleep, but, when woken, immediately asked Stanley if he thought Livingstone was alive and if so where did he think he was. Before Stanley could even stammer out that he had not the slightest idea, James Gordon Bennett Jr. announced that he, Henry Morton Stanley, was going to Africa to find Livingstone:

> ... the old man may be in want:—take enough with you to help him, should he require it. Of course you will act according to your own plans, and do what you think best—BUT FIND LIVINGSTONE!

Stanley stood speechless. This was the last thing he had expected, and the last thing he wanted. It was the devil of a job, and quite futile, since

Livingstone had probably long been dead. If he should fail to find him and return with nothing better to report than that the missionary had disappeared, and that no one knew anything about him, his own career would be at an end and he would once more be a small-town journalist. In an attempt to dissuade his chief from the rash enterprise, he pointed out the tremendous costs involved but it availed him nothing.

'Well,' Bennett said, 'I will tell you what you will do. Draw a thousand pounds now; and when you have gone through that, draw another thousand, and when that is spent, draw another thousand, and when you have finished that, draw another thousand, and so on; but FIND LIVINGSTONE.'

Now Stanley was really frightened. He had never seen Bennett so determined. But he had not yet abandoned all hope and so he asked: 'Do you mean me to go straight on to Africa to search for Dr. Livingstone?' To his relief Stanley learned that he was to go first to the Suez Canal to witness the opening ceremonies, then to Jerusalem, Constantinople and to the old battlegrounds of the Crimean War, then via the Caucasus to the Caspian Sea, thence to Baghdad, the Euphrates Valley and to India, and only then was he to organize the rescue expedition of the *New York Herald*. Stanley quietly calculated that he had gained eighteen months' grace, and discreetly heaved a sigh of relief. A great deal could happen in eighteen months, but Bennett could read his thoughts and continued: '. . . Probably you will hear by that time that Livingstone is on his way to Zanzibar; but if not, go into the interior and find him, if alive. Get what news of his discoveries you can; and if you find he is dead, bring all possible proofs of his being dead. That is all. Good night, and God be with you.'

Stanley carried out his orders to perfection. He wrote a brilliant account of the opening of the Suez Canal, and moving letters from the Crimea, evoking the glory and the suffering of the war between the Western Allies and Russia which had come to an end some fifteen years before. He travelled from the Caucasus via the Euphrates to Baghdad and on to India, dutifully sending articles, letters and cables to his newspaper. During these eighteen months not a word was received from Livingstone. It was as if Africa had swallowed him up. At the beginning of October 1870, a very unwilling Stanley bought a passage to the Dark Continent, and eighty days later, on the 26th January 1871, he was put ashore in Zanzibar.

The British consul there was a certain Dr. John Kirk, who had accompanied Livingstone on one of his last expeditions. Stanley called on him at once. He asked the British official whether in his opinion Dr. Livingstone was still alive. Kirk was fairly certain that he was. 'We are continually sending something up for him,' he said, by way of proof. 'What kind of a man was Livingstone to get along with?' Stanley asked. Kirk said with a laugh: 'He is not quite an angel,' adding that, in his opinion, if the explorer should come to hear anything about a rescue operation, he 'would put a hundred miles of swamp in a very short time between him and them'. All things considered, he was not an easy customer to deal with.

This was not exactly encouraging and we can understand Stanley's mood when he wrote that, although eighteen months had now gone by since he first received his orders, no one in Zanzibar had had any news of Livingstone. While some took him for dead and some for lost, others again said that he had married an African princess and had settled down with her. Stanley had not heard from Mr. Bennett, and was left with precisely eighty dollars.

This was not a princely sum, and although the American consul at Zanzibar advanced the money needed, Stanley was far from happy while equipping his expedition. His worst difficulty was the terrible confusion over currency. Just as the American who comes to Europe has to distinguish between pesos, French, Belgian and Swiss francs, West and East German marks, Austrian and English shillings, Turkish, English and Egyptian pounds, Polish zloties, Italian liras, Russian roubles, Danish and Swedish crowns, etc., so Stanley had to distinguish between the numerous currencies in use in East Africa. While some districts used only glass beads and made a difference between white, black, blue, green or red ones, and some used materials, others again would accept nothing but brass wire, scorning both fabrics and beads. Stanley reported that he had to determine in advance the length of his stay in the different regions, so as to be able to calculate his financial needs in the different currencies. Needless to say, the whole of Zanzibar did its best to swindle Stanley as he equipped his expedition. The Arab merchants reckoned that the crazy white man, like Livingstone and many others before him, would never come out of the bush alive and that therefore it was safe to fleece him. Stanley was no fool and he soon realized what the merchants were up to. He did not stop to argue, but took a good stick and belaboured the rogues until the price fell. Thus even during the very first weeks of his stay in Africa, Stanley began to qualify for the name the natives later gave him: *Bula-Matari*, the Breaker of Stones. He was in fact a real martinet, driving others as he drove himself, and his reports speak frequently of the 'encouraging' effects of his whip.

On the 21st March 1871, only two months after his arrival in Africa, the main body of Stanley's expedition set out. It consisted of a hundred and eighty-seven men, twenty-seven donkeys and two horses. The whole troop did not start out together, but was divided into five sections, the first of which had been sent on ahead in the middle of February. He aimed to reach Ujiji, an important caravan station on the eastern shores of Lake

Tanganyika which, as London had reported, was also the destination of Livingstone. Stanley had had no experience of this style of travelling. Fortunately the going was easy for the first few days. It gave him the opportunity of gathering some experience, and so he was not altogether unprepared when three weeks later he was put to the crucial test of marching through jungle.

The next weeks were hard, terribly hard. Time and again in his journal Stanley speaks of forests, swamps, gorges and mountains, of demands for tribute by hostile chiefs, of mutinies, illnesses and losses. Although he overcame all difficulties, his pace was so reduced that his average daily speed was rarely more than ten or eleven miles. His march took him roughly along the site of the modern railway line from Dar-es-Salaam to Tabora and Ujiji. Those who have made the journey by rail will scarcely be able to believe that, eighty years ago, Stanley took six months to cover the distance.

At the beginning of November 1871, Stanley had his first news of Livingstone. He met a caravan coming from Lake Tanganyika and learnt that, only recently, a white man had arrived in Ujiji. Could this be Livingstone? 'He is old,' the natives reported, 'he has white hair on his face, and is sick.' Stanley had to hurry now. It was essential to find Livingstone before the rumours of a search party could reach him, and rumour has an uncanny habit of outstripping human messengers in Africa. If Livingstone were to hear that a rescue expedition was on its way, he might perhaps disappear and hide himself in an inaccessible swamp. Thus Stanley drove both man and beast to the limits of their strength.

Yet there was no need to hurry. Livingstone was tired to death. He had left Lake Nyasa in 1866, and had turned north through fever-infested valleys between inaccessible mountains. All but three of his bearers had deserted him, and, believing Livingstone to have gone mad, they had disappeared into the jungle, taking the medicine chest with them. Without quinine, a defenceless victim of malaria, our explorer dragged himself along. He managed to reach Lake Mweru and the Luapula, a river which flows into the upper Congo, but he was not certain whether it was part of the Nile whose source he was seeking, or of the Congo system, and nobody could tell him. The natives could tell him no more than that the Luapula came from Lake Bangweulu, further south. On hearing this, Livingstone followed the river to the south, but because of his lack of medical supplies, he was soon reduced to a lamentable state. An Arab slave-trader saved him from death by starvation and also gave him sufficient articles for barter to continue his investigations of Lake Bangweulu. From there Livingstone returned to Ujiji, but was so exhausted that he had to be carried in a *kitanda*, a kind of litter. Even so he would never have reached Ujiji alive, had not the slave-trader again come to his rescue.

The missionary in him was deeply ashamed, but the traveller and explorer retained the upper hand. He had seen and experienced so much that he wanted to bring these experiences to the notice of the scientific world whatever the cost. But then, he asked himself, what did he really know?

He did not remain long in Ujiji for he was anxious to find the River Lualaba which the natives had told him lay to the north-west. In the middle of March 1871, Livingstone entered Nyangwe, an ancient trading centre on the Lualaba, the upper Congo, which had been conquered by the Arabs ten years before. All Livingstone could learn from the Arabs was that the great stream rushed through a narrow gully in the north-west (the Stanley Falls) and disappeared into impenetrable forests.

Shrunk to a mere skeleton and covered like Job from head to foot with ulcers and boils, the white man tried to obtain boats from the natives in order to explore the river. When they heard, however, that he was also interested in Katanga, they refused all his requests, since they feared he would tell the *wasungu* of the great copper deposits there and they would come and take the copper away!

Thus Livingstone had no option but to return to Ujiji, where he found, to his delight, that supplies had arrived for him from England during his absence. The quinine, tea and other essentials would soon put him on his legs again, and then he would be able to solve the riddle of the Lualaba. He proceeded at a snail's pace, and was only too happy if he could make two to three miles a day. For long stretches he had to be carried. Dangerously ill, and nothing but skin and bones, he would still not give up. Obviously he must have suspected that the Lualaba and the Congo were one and the same river and that this was the answer to the problem of a waterway to the heart of the African continent. Should another steal this palm from him? No, that must never happen! So he dragged his tired body along to the east. After an absence of months Livingstone returned to Ujiji in the middle of October 1871.

In the meantime, Stanley had approached his goal by forced marches. Time after time he had been delayed by greedy chiefs who demanded tribute. The lengthy discussions nearly drove the American mad with fury. In order not to lose time, he forced the expedition to march even during the night across wilderness and uninhabited parts. On the 10th November, 236 days after leaving the coast, he had his first view of Lake Tanganyika, and nearly wept with excitement and joy as he saw the huge shining silver mirror surrounded by palms and in the west bordered by imposing blue-black mountains.

On the 10th August 1872, the *New York Herald* came out in banner headlines, giving the gist of the following entry in Stanley's journal, written ten months earlier:

... While I write my diary of this day's proceedings, I tell Selim to lay out my new flannel suit, to oil my boots, to chalk my helmet, and fold a new puggaree around it, that I may make as presentable an appearance as possible before the white man with the grey beard, and before the Arabs of Ujiji; for the clothes I have worn through jungle and forest are in tatters. ... We are descending the western slope of the mountain ... we push on rapidly, lest the news of our coming might reach the people of Ujiji before we come in sight. ... At last the sublime hour has arrived! — our dreams, our hopes and anticipations are now about to be realised!

'Unfurl the flags and load your guns!'

'Ay Wallah, ay Wallah, bana!' respond the men eagerly.

'One two three — fire!'

A volley from nearly fifty guns roars like a salute from a battery of artillery: we shall note its effect presently on the peaceful-looking village below.

'Now, kirangozi, hold the white man's flag up high, and let the Zanzibar flag bring up the rear. And you men keep close together, and keep firing until we halt in the market-place, or before the white man's house. ...'

Before we had gone a hundred yards our repeated volleys had the effect desired. We had awakened Ujiji to the knowledge that a caravan was coming, and the people were witnessed rushing up in hundreds to meet us. The mere sight of the flags informed every one immediately that we were a caravan, but the American flag borne aloft by gigantic Asmani, whose face was one vast smile on this day, rather staggered them at first. However, many of the people who now approached us remembered the flag. They had seen it float above the American Consulate and from the masthead of many a ship in the harbor of Zanzibar, and they were soon heard welcoming the beautiful flag with cries of 'Bindera Kisungu' — a white man's flag! 'Bindera Amerikani!' — the American flag!

Then we were surrounded by them: by Wajiji, Wanyamwezi, Wangwana, Warundi, Waguhha, Wamanyuema and Arabs, and were almost deafened with the shouts of 'Yambo, yambo, bana! Yambo, bana! Yambo, bana!' To all and each of my men the welcome was given.

We were now about three hundred yards from the village of Ujiji, and the crowds are dense about me. Suddenly I hear a voice on my right say,

'Good morning, sir!'

Startled at hearing this greeting in the midst of such a crowd of black people, I turn sharply around in search of the man, and see him at my side, with the blackest of faces, but animated and joyous — a man dressed in a long white shirt, with a turban of American sheeting around his woolly head, and I ask:

'Who the mischief are you?'

'I am Susi, the servant of Dr. Livingstone,' said he, smiling, and showing a gleaming row of teeth.

'What! Is Dr. Livingstone here?'

'Yes, sir.'

'In this village?'

'Yes, sir.'

'Are you sure?'

'Sure, sure, sir. Why, I leave him just now.' ...

And I — what would I not have given for a bit of friendly wilderness, where, unseen, I might vent my joy in some mad freak, such as idiotically biting my hand, turning a somersault, or slashing at trees, in order to allay those exciting feelings that were well-nigh uncontrollable. My heart beats fast, but I must not let my face betray my emotions, lest it shall detract from the dignity of a white man appearing under such extraordinary circumstances.

So I did that which I thought was most dignified. I pushed back the crowds, and, passing from the rear, walked down a living avenue of people, until I came in front of the semicircle of Arabs, in the front of which stood the white man with the grey beard. As I advanced slowly towards him I noticed he was pale, looked wearied, had a grey beard, wore a bluish cap with a faded gold band round it, had on a red-sleeved waist-coat, and a pair of grey tweed trousers. I would have run to him, only I was a coward in the presence of such a mob—would have embraced him, only, he being an Englishman, I did not know how he would receive me; so I did what cowardice and false pride suggested was the best thing—walked deliberately to him, took off my hat, and said: 'Dr. Livingstone, I presume?'

'YES,' said he, with a kind smile, lifting his cap slightly. . . .

A deep friendship grew up between the young reporter and the former missionary. Together they explored the northern part of Lake Tanganyika and found that the Rusizi River flowed into the lake at the northernmost tip and not out of it, as might have been expected. Worried about his friend's failing health, Stanley asked Livingstone if he did not want to return to England to recover his strength, but Livingstone replied:

'No, I should like to see my family very much indeed. My children's letters affect me intensely; but I must not go home; I must finish my task. It is only the want of supplies that has detained me. I should have finished the discovery of the Nile by this, by tracing it to its connection with either Baker's Lake [Lake Albert], or Peterick's branch of the Nile [the White Nile]. If I had only gone one month further, I could have said, "the work is done".'

This may sound as if Livingstone had in fact mistaken the Lualaba for the upper course of the Nile, and as if he had felt quite sure of himself, but this was by no means the case. It is true that Livingstone was an honest, upright man, but why on earth should he have told the young American journalist of the doubts which assailed him? The Arabs in Nyangwe had said that the Lualaba disappeared in the north-east into impenetrable jungles, and that that was all they knew. Only by seeing for himself could he tell whether the Lualaba was part of the Nile system or not. Why should he, now fifty-eight years old, tell his young partner all this? Stanley was at the beginning of his life as an explorer and Livingstone could feel that all his activities would be devoted to Africa. His own life was reaching its end, but the remaining task to be accomplished on the watershed between the Nile and the Congo was *his* alone. It was *his* duty to see it through. It was simply for this reason that he stated so emphatically that he had nearly discovered the sources of the Nile. This was the reason that made him refuse to return to England and led him to say that in six or seven months' time, at the most, his work would be finished.

Stanley believed him and decided to return to the coast alone, leaving his fellow explorer to follow in a few months' time. All Livingstone needed was some new equipment which could easily be collected from Stanley's supply base in Tabora where there were plentiful supplies of everything. Livingstone accompanied Stanley as far as Tabora, today an important railway junction, but then famous as a flourishing slave market. Once again, in February 1872, Stanley tried to persuade the great British explorer to return home, but he refused absolutely. Neither of them suspected that almost at the same time, a British search party, including Livingstone's son Oswald, had landed in Bagamoyo, some five hundred miles to the east. As Livingstone would not hear of returning to England, Stanley re-equipped him for his new expedition and took his leave. We can read the following laconic note in Livingstone's diary, dated 14th March 1872: 'Mr. Stanley leaves.'

The American was very generous and supplied Livingstone with forty loads consisting of three thousand yards of cloth, sixteen bags of beads and two hundredweight of brass wire. Together with his own supplies amounting to thirty loads, Livingstone, according to Stanley's calculations, now had enough to last him and sixty men for seven hundred days. Livingstone had been deeply moved by this gesture, though he had also calculated that within fifty days the *Bula-Matari*, the Breaker of Stones, would be at the coast and ready for new deeds. He might even decide to turn round and seek out the sources of the Nile himself. He had tried to persuade Stanley to wait until the rainy season was over before returning to the coast. 'You had better stop until the rains, which are now near, are over,' Dr. Livingstone had said. But Stanley would not even listen to this.

He had to be back at the coast with his journalistic sensation—Livingstone had been found. Of course he could not tell this to the venerable old gentleman, and so he had replied: 'I would to God I could, my dear Doctor, but every day I stop here, now that there is no necessity for me to stay longer, keeps you from your work and home.' Livingstone was not to be put off so easily: 'I know,' he said, 'but consider your health—you are not fit to travel. What is it? Only a few weeks longer. You will travel to the coast just as quickly when the rains are over as you will by going now. The plains will be inundated between here and the coast.' Stanley knew that the other was right, but he was not to be detained. He marched to the coast, while Livingstone returned to Ujiji, oppressed with deep anxiety. Was another to outstrip him again? He did not suspect that the worst blow had not yet been struck.

This blow arrived in the form of Livingstone's second son, Oswald. Stanley met him on the 6th May 1872, in Bagamoyo, where the members of the British search party were awaiting the end of the rainy season. Of course they received the American with warm congratulations on his 'marvellous success', but they could not hide their disappointment that Stanley had rather taken the wind out of their sails. He understood this well enough, but Livingstone's condition worried him a great deal, and he could not allow the party to turn back. He stated that in his opinion Oswald should hasten to his father as quickly as possible, to take him the supplies and help he needed. At first Oswald agreed to this course of action, but on the 19th May he had changed his mind and surprised Stanley with a note stating that he had decided not to proceed 'for reasons he thought just and sufficient'.

Thus the British search party was re-formed by Stanley. Oswald Livingstone's place in it was taken by Jacob Wainwright, a Negro brought up in an Indian missionary school. Wainwright, who became the leader of the caravan, was later to accompany the explorer on his last journey. Livingstone had undoubtedly heard that his son had been in Bagamoyo and had refused at the last moment to meet his father. We have no record of how he received this news but we can safely assume that he was deeply hurt. This was a fitting punishment for his sin of many years ago when he had renounced his vocation, had abandoned his wife and children in order to become an explorer, a decision in which personal ambition had played no small part. His son had renounced him just as he had once renounced his family. Livingstone must have felt the bitter irony of his sentence. Somewhere amongst his papers there must be a copy of the letter, which he had written to his daughter Agnes in the middle of May 1852, when his family was on its way back to England. It was nearly twenty years since he had sent it but there was no need to search, he knew it by heart. 'This letter is meant for you alone. Mother will read it out to you and then it will seem as if I were talking to you.' Then he had added: 'It will be a long time before I see you again. Farewell, my darling Nannie.' Tears welled up in the lonely man's eyes. How happy he had been! He stumbled across to the hut which the natives had given him, and to the box with his few poor personal belongings. He hardly had the strength to open the lid. The letter from Agnes, received a few months before, was lying on top. 'Much as I wish you to come home, I would rather have you finish your work to your own satisfaction, than to return merely to gratify me,' she had written. Did she, too, not want to see him, like her brother Oswald? Despite the sincerity of his religious convictions, Livingstone did not realize that all great deeds in this world must be paid for with loneliness, suffering and tears, and that all heroism means renunciation. All he could see was the offended and avenging God—an eye for an eye, a tooth for a tooth.

Thus he accepted his fate in silence, and his journals give no hint of the physical pain and the mental anguish of the months he spent in that miserable hut in Ujiji. All we know is that on the 25th August 1872,

Livingstone started on yet another journey. This time he travelled south to the regions of Lake Bangweulu. It is true that at that time there were bitter wars in progress between the natives in the north-west and that the Zambesi and the Luapula, the two great rivers south of Ujiji, which Livingstone had once crossed on his march from Laka Nyasa to Lake Tanganyika, might still have proved to be the headstreams of the Nile, but by far the most important task lay to the north-west—Nyangwe and the Lualaba.

Should not Livingstone have waited until the war between the tribes was over and the road clear? Should he not have waited in Ujiji until the rainy season had come to an end, for he had never before travelled during this time of the year? Such questions, though interesting, could be continued *ad infinitum*. The bare fact remains: Livingstone marched south and marched to his death. The German author Jakob Wassermann wrote that this last journey was a conscious sacrifice of himself, and perhaps he is right. Perhaps Livingstone deliberately gave back his life and existence into the hands of God who once had led him to Africa and whose service he had rejected when he became an explorer.

But this is nothing but a plausible assumption. Livingstone never gave the slightest hint that on that 25th August 1872 he had started on a journey from which he knew there would be no return. On the contrary, we have evidence that even during his last days, when his spent body could no longer perform the demands of his unbroken spirit, he asked repeatedly with feverish anxiety: 'How much further is it to the Lualaba?' Someone who is on the point of taking leave does not ask after the morrow, and the final entry in his journal, made three days before his death on the shores of Lake Bangweulu, shows that even at the last his spirit was indomitable: 'Knocked up quite and remain . . . [to] recover. . . .' But the Lord of all had decided otherwise. When on the 1st May 1873, towards four o'clock in the morning, Jacob Wainwright and Susi, the faithful servant who had taken part in most of Livingstone's expeditions, came to see to the sick man, they found him dead. Their friend and master was kneeling before his bed as if in prayer, his head buried in his hands. On the ground next to him lay his journal.

Livingstone, with his mixture of deep religious feelings, honesty and fairness, was the ideal type of British colonizer, and the epitaph on his tomb in Westminster Abbey is a memorial, not only to one of the greatest sons of Britain, but also to the land that made him:

BROUGHT BY FAITHFUL HANDS
OVER LAND AND SEA
HERE LIES
DAVID LIVINGSTONE
MISSIONARY,

TRAVELLER,
PHILANTHROPIST,
BORN MARCH 19, 1813,
AT BLANTYRE, LANARKSHIRE,
DIED MAY 1, 1873
AT CHITAMBO'S VILLAGE, ULALA.

FOR 30 YEARS HIS LIFE WAS SPENT
IN AN UNWEARIED EFFORT
TO EVANGELIZE THE NATIVE RACES,
TO EXPLORE THE UNDISCOVERED SECRETS,
TO ABOLISH THE DESOLATING SLAVE TRADE
OF CENTRAL AFRICA,
WHERE WITH HIS LAST WORDS HE WROTE,
'MAY HEAVEN'S RICH BLESSING COME DOWN
ON EVERYONE, AMERICAN, ENGLISH, OR TURK,
WHO WILL HELP TO HEAL
THIS OPEN SORE OF THE WORLD'.

8

Livingstone's death near Lake Bangweulu was a terrible loss to scientific exploration in Central Africa. Nevertheless it is doubtful that he could have achieved what his successor Stanley, the discoverer and conqueror of the Congo, later carried out, even had he felt inclined to attempt it. Stanley, who was made of tougher and less sensitive fibre than Livingstone, appeared on the stage of history in the rôle of a pitiless taskmaster and driver of men. His own countrymen, in particular, were to reproach him for every lash of the whip and every shot fired at a hostile cannibal, and everyone was agreed that by no stretch of the imagination could Stanley's methods be called humane. He himself was fully conscious of this and, when taking leave of his Negroes in Zanzibar in May 1872, he told them: 'You are now about to return to Unyanyeme, to the "Great Master". You know him; you know he is a good man, and has a kind heart. He is different from me; he will not beat you, as I have done. But you know I have rewarded you all—how I have made you all rich in cloth and money. You know how, when you behaved yourselves well, I was your friend. I gave you plenty to eat and plenty to wear. When you were sick I looked after you.' All his critics should have borne in mind that Stanley would never have achieved what he did by coaxing and praying alone, and also that unlike Livingstone, who often travelled through comparatively open country, he traversed one of the most nightmarish regions of the world—the jungles of the Congo. The one trump card he held was his unshakeable determination to succeed.

Stanley was urged by a very different spirit from Livingstone. He cared little for religious considerations and had no ambition to go out and preach Christ's message of salvation, and yet clearly providence had decreed that *Bula-Matari*, the Breaker of Stones, was to be the gentle missionary's successor and that the herald of western civilization was to complete what the ambassador of western religion had not been permitted to finish. And the result, as we have already said, is the Belgian Congo, one of the largest industrial areas in the world, where white men work side by side with black and brown, without any of the social and political tensions which make life a veritable hell on earth in so many parts of the dark continent. This state of social equilibrium, which so far has never been seriously disturbed, exists, of course, for very obvious reasons. The Union Minière du Haut Katanga, for instance, has done everything in its power both for its black and for its white workers, and the Belgian State has followed suit. However, the same has been done elsewhere in Africa, without like results. We, for our part, like to believe that the blessing of Livingstone rests on a country that had been almost within his grasp.

Two complete strangers, men diametrically opposed by temperament, were responsible for the fact that Stanley took over Livingstone's heritage. The first of these was Lieutenant Verney Lovett Cameron, a member of a party sent to take aid to Livingstone. In 1874 Cameron had advanced up to the Lualaba. His thermo-barometer had shown him that this mysterious river had an altitude of more than 1,600 feet above sea-level. Cameron at once concluded that the Lualaba could not be part of the Nile system, since six hundred miles further north, near Lake Albert, the Nile flowed at a height of more than 2,000 feet. Obviously water cannot climb a mountain, and so this ruled out the possibility that the Lualaba was connected to the Nile. Cameron also calculated that, near Nyangwe, this mighty jungle river raced past at the rate of more than one hundred thousand cubic feet of water per second, five times the amount carried by the Nile in its upper course. What happened to this water? Cameron asked himself. It was not possible to explain away such an enormous difference by talking of evaporation. Did it run away in the desert sands? That, too, was out of the question since the desert belt only began much further north. Again the same conclusion was forced on him; the mysterious Central African river must be independent of the Nile. The question still remained: where did it go? It might belong to the Niger system whose sources were, after all, still unknown—they were only discovered in 1879—but more likely it was a tributary of the Congo.

Quite impossible, declared the greatest English geographical authority, W. D. Cooley, the same man who had ridiculed the reports sent by Krapf and Rebmann about the existence of snow-capped mountains on the Equator. About the same time, however, another geographer, the German Ernst Behm who, like Cooley, had hardly ever been further than his back garden, wrote an article agreeing with Cameron's assumption, stating categorically that the Lualaba was the upper course of the Congo.

Livingstone had died before Cameron made his discovery, and it is unlikely that Stanley read Behm's *Beweise für die Identität des Lualaba mit dem Kongo* ('Proof of the Identity of the Lualaba with the Congo') but he had no need of any prompting to go beyond Nyangwe, where Livingstone had turned back. Strangely enough, even Lieutenant Cameron had gone no further along the Lualaba-Congo than this town. Was it mere coincidence or had the Arab slave hunters, the lords of Nyangwe, been responsible for his turning back? Had they known that the natives spoke the truth when they said that the Lualaba could be followed as far as the western ocean? Were they merely trying to preserve their control of the whole area and so had fobbed him off with stories calculated to discourage him?

Stanley was convinced that the natives knew what they were talking about. He told the directors of the London *Daily Telegraph* of his conviction, and they immediately smelled a sensation. They declared that they were ready, in principle, to send the American reporter to find the Congo, but they remembered a little uneasily the scandal that arose in 1872, when Stanley published his book *How I Found Livingstone in Central Africa*, a scandal that only died down when the American had a private audience of Queen Victoria. Thus the London paper looked for another backer for their agreement with this 'charlatan and liar'. The *Daily Telegraph* approached the *New York Herald*. A lengthy cable was sent to Mr. James Gordon Bennett asking for his collaboration. A few hours later his reply arrived in Fleet Street. The chief, and after the recent death of his father, the sole owner of the greatest New York paper, and one of the richest men in America, had remained as parsimonious as ever, and his cable is a masterpiece of concision. It read: 'Yes; Bennett.'

These two words were enough. The expedition was assured, and Stanley drew up a comprehensive programme for his employers. Everything was to proceed systematically. He would avoid any possibility of being called a swindler and liar in future. Lake Victoria, the position of which had so far only been determined by a few geographic points, was to be explored in greater detail and charted. The 'Lunar Mountain' of Ptolemy and the Arab geographers, he told his listeners in the conference hall of the *Daily Telegraph* building, would be his next objective; furthermore, he would sail round Lake Tanganyika to determine whether there was an outflow which could belong to the Nile and which therefore might be considered its source; finally from here he would proceed westwards across the vast blank space which stretched on contemporary maps to the Atlantic coast.

A few days after this memorable discussion, the plans of the new expedition were splashed across the headlines. Stanley was showered with applications from people offering their services. 'I might have led 5,000 Englishmen, 5,000 Americans, 2,000 Frenchmen 2,000 Germans, 500 Italians, 250 Swiss, 200 Belgians, 50 Spaniards and 5 Greeks, or 15,005 Europeans, to Africa.' The list consisted by no means entirely of retired colonial officers. All sorts and conditions of men were represented, including managers of hotels, mechanics, seamen, bank clerks, market gardeners and rat catchers. He even had applications from clairvoyants, mediums and magnetizers who promised to guide the expedition to success, or make it invisible through their magic. Some claimed that they could put to sleep all those natives who had no desire to be discovered and who would otherwise be hostile. Stanley made no use of their arts, and chose instead two fishermen from the county of Kent who were already known to him. These two men, the brothers Pocock, gave him valuable service during his passage through the African lake regions.

In the middle of November 1874, he set off from Bagamoyo into the jungle at the head of 224 men, many of whom had served under Livingstone. The most important piece of his very considerable luggage was the *Lady Alice*, a launch built in England, which was to prove worth its weight in gold. It was so constructed that it could be rapidly dismantled into a number of sections, each weighing about 60 pounds, roughly the normal load carried by a porter. At the beginning things went none too smoothly, for many of the porters had never been on a caravan journey before and found the pace too much.

On the second day there was a rebellion. We shall give a brief report of this because such trouble often arose on undertakings of this kind, usually for similar reasons. When he was some miles away from Bagamoyo, Stanley discovered that certain young ladies had attached themselves to the caravan as a means of escape from their lords and masters. Suddenly the expedition was stopped by black soldiers, armed to the teeth, who showed him a written order from the Governor to the effect that the fugitive women were to be returned at once. This demand infuriated Stanley's porters, who loaded their guns and were about to massacre the soldiers when Stanley managed to make his authority felt. Amid murmurs of dissatisfaction and disapproval the porters handed back the women and set off again. Stanley knew what he was up against, and this first bad experience which could so easily have resulted in serious bloodshed was probably the cause of many a later harsh act. He had to be constantly on his guard, and so he remained throughout the whole expedition, thus averting many a serious incident but gaining himself the reputation of a slave-driver.

Despite all these unwanted halts, the march proceeded with extraordinary speed; Stanley kept roughly to a north-westerly direction and on the morning of the 27th February 1875, after only a hundred and three days, he sighted Lake Victoria. One week later, the *Lady Alice* began her maiden voyage. Stanley had been unable to find a single volunteer from the porters to accompany him on the perilous exploration of the mighty lake. All his questions were answered by a tense silence, until finally one of the caravan leaders advised him: 'Master, have done with these questions. Command your party. All your people are your children, and they will not disobey you. While you ask them as a friend, no one will offer his services.' Finally a crew was assembled and the launch set off. The voyage demanded many sacrifices in lives and material, but it reached its objective —it was discovered that the northern outflow of Lake Victoria was one of the main sources of the Nile. Thus one of the questions which Stanley had posed himself was answered.

From Lake Victoria he turned south along the East African rift valley via Lake Kivu to Lake Tanganyika. Again the *Lady Alice* was assembled to complete the circumnavigation, begun in the company of Livingstone. Fifty-one days were required for this task. Stanley wanted to find out whether there was any connection between Lake Tanganyika and Lake Victoria, and whether the Nile, as Livingstone had assumed, drew on Lake Tanganyika also. This was shown not to be the case and the Victoria-Nile, as Stanley had called the northerly efflux of Lake Victoria, proved to be the southernmost influx of the Nile. On the other hand, there was a very wide river flowing west, called the Lukuga, in the region of the modern Albertville. This river only flowed when the lake was full, but as Stanley was soon to discover, when that was the case it flowed to the west into the Lualaba.

Stanley very nearly investigated the highland of Katanga, which he had seen from Lake Tanganyika. Obviously the headstreams of the Lualaba were bound to be situated there, since the heavy rain clouds coming from the west broke up on these heights. However, he had not time enough to seek out these headstreams one by one. His employers, the *Daily Telegraph* and the *New York Herald*, would think he was making fun of them if his reports contained nothing else but the unpronounceable names of tiny trickles of water. He too, like Livingstone, would be nicknamed 'River Seeker' and even his black companions would one day charge him with madness, as they had his friend. So Stanley decided to march west along the Lukuga—and missed an opportunity without equal.

Six years later another explorer, the German traveller and geographer, Paul Reichard, was to reap the benefits of this discovery. He was not a journalist like Stanley, but a scientist and explorer. In 1882, he left Uganda, with the backing of the German Africa Society, and travelled south to Katanga. Reichard did not suspect that he would make a sensational discovery, nor was he interested in making one. However, his thirst for knowledge and his curiosity were aroused when he noticed that the local natives were covered from head to toe with copper ornaments. He began to search around in the area, and was astonished one day to come upon the ruins of ancient settlements where he unearthed what were obviously prehistoric bronze implements. He began to excavate seriously and so made

44. A collapsible steel boat, which Stanley took with him to Africa.

his sensational discovery: he found copper deposits containing 25 per cent of metal, and so near the surface that they could be worked in open mines.

Dr. Reichard was no mining expert. He had no idea that ore deposits with a metal content of 25 per cent are extremely rare. He did not know that the American copper deposits of Utah, considered to be so rich, contain only 2 to 3 per cent of metal. Above all he could not realize that the geological properties of the Katanga deposits were such that they involved the minimum maintenance costs for mining, so that years later, during the depression of 1929 to 1933, the Central African workings could continue to work even when most other copper mines had to suspend activities. Nor could he have known that the Katanga fields are the greatest concentration of metal deposits in the whole world, with their width of sixty miles and length of more than two hundred and fifty miles.

All this, as we have said, was still unknown. But, of course, Paul Reichard was not slow in realizing that here were tremendous treasures, simply waiting to be lifted. Thus he returned to the coast and to Germany. His two German comrades succumbed to the exertions of the journey, yet he managed to get back because he *had* to. The information he was carrying was too important to be lost. However, the German Foreign and

Colonial Offices hesitated and came to no decision, and Belgium and Britain stepped in first. At the beginning of the 1890's, after reading Paul Reichard's reports published in the *Mitteilungen der Afrikanischen Gesellschaft in Deutschland*, both these powers sent expeditions to annex the area containing the copper deposits. The Belgian Lieutenant Émile Francqui arrived on the spot some weeks earlier than the British, and so the latter had to content themselves with Northern Rhodesia, while Belgium, which claimed Katanga itself, laid hands not only on the copper mines, but also on vast deposits of uranium. Needless to say, the real extent of these deposits and the amount of uranium extracted each year remains a closely guarded secret.

Some decades later, Lieutenant Émile Francqui became Belgian Minister of Finance, sole ruler of the copper market and the richest man of the small country lying between the estuary of the Schelde and the Ardennes. All that he wanted the world to know about him can be found in *Who's Who*, but Dr. Paul Reichard, born in 1854 in Neuwied in the Rhineland, died in 1938, as poor and unnoticed as he came into the world.

Stanley, too, would probably not have become rich and mighty, even had he turned south instead of west from Lake Tanganyika. In 1899 he was granted a title by the Queen, was elected to the House of Commons and became one of the founder members of the International Association of the Congo. But his bank balance could never have been compared with that of Monsieur Francqui. In the course of the many years that he stayed in Africa he succumbed completely to its magical powers, just as all his predecessors had done. He had only *one* thought, *one* aim, *one* will: Africa. It was never his ambition to grow rich out of Africa, and thus he never became an Émile Francqui or a Cecil Rhodes. He strove neither for power nor for wealth. It is for this reason that fate reserved for him the glory of the discovery of the Congo, and with it the solution of the last geographical puzzle of the Black Continent.

This was a task requiring an almost superhuman resistance to fatigue and exertion, and glancing through the pages of Stanley's travel reports, we are puzzled about what it was in Stanley's make-up that enabled him to bear all these dangers, rigours and deprivations. Time and time again we have asked similar questions, and although the name of the protagonist changes from Columbus to Vasco da Gama or Magellán, Mungo Park, Caillié, Barth, etc., the question remains each time in the same form. Within certain limits, we can offer a partial solution of the motives that urged these men on, such as incentives of trade, glory or religious convictions, but the core of the question remains untouched. We can glibly state that all these men were endowed with exceptional natures and that they marched towards their goal as if under a spell, insensitive of all suffering, but this facile answer brings us no nearer the crux of the problem.

With Stanley, too, the real driving force behind his stupendous achievements remains a mystery.

Although Stanley had been repeatedly warned against turning west at Lake Tanganyika and marching through the country of the Manyuema, a notorious cannibal tribe, he was not to be dissuaded. When his porters learnt where the *Bula-Matari* intended to lead them, thirty-eight of them deserted on the spot, and the American had to keep a strict watch over the particularly faithful remainder in order to stop them taking fright and leaving as well. This was hardly a favourable beginning, but it made not the slightest impression on Stanley. He did not hesitate for a single moment, but marched along the banks of the Lualaba. At the end of October, 1876, two years after leaving Bagamoyo, he finally reached Nyangwe, that mysterious place which had held Livingstone and Cameron in its grip and not allowed them to proceed beyond it. For days he consulted with his sole surviving white companion, Frank Pocock, whether he should attempt to sail down the Lualaba. Even if this river were indeed the Congo, even if it did suddenly alter course from the north towards the west, he would still be more than 1,250 miles from the nearest Portuguese stations in West Africa, and this was a tremendous distance. All these objections were nothing but the last impotent rebellion of human reason against the tremendous temptation of the dark unknown distance. Finally the two white men tossed a coin. Heads to the north, down the Lualaba: tails to the south—and though Stanley did not know it—to the copper deposits of Katanga. Six times the coin flipped in the air and six times it came down tails. The oracle pointed to the south. Then the two drew lots with long and short blades of grass and again six times fate pointed to the south. But what did Stanley do? He ordered the march to the north, down the Lualaba! Since his bearers refused to traverse such dangerous country without an armed escort, Stanley made an agreement with Sheik Hamed ben Mohammed, or Tippu Tib as he was better known, the most influential Arab trader of Central Africa, whereby he would accompany them for sixty days with his private army of 140 riflemen and 70 spearmen for 5,000 dollars. But on the 16th November, twelve days after leaving Nyangwe, the Arab refused to fulfil his contract. He declared that he had never before been in such hellish regions and that he had not had the slightest suspicion that such places existed on earth. A further cheque for 2,600 dollars finally persuaded him to add another twenty to the twelve marching days already behind them. But when these were over Tippu Tib had had enough. He took his formal leave from the white men and turned back.

Stanley's account of this terrible journey in his journal makes Tippu Tib's decision to return perfectly understandable. At first the American had underestimated the malevolence of the jungle, and after all, he argued, it was not the first jungle that he had had to cross in his life. But when from the high banks of the Lualaba nothing could be seen as far as the eye could reach but this single, silent, unbroken mass of blackish-green forest, dark and horrible, then for a moment his courage sank. For that one brief instant he even played with the idea of turning back, but then with a quick decided step he placed himself at the head of his 149 men and was the first to enter the green hell. At once the sky was blotted out. A gloomy darkness pervaded everything and at times Stanley could not see to make an entry in his journal. The atmosphere was oppressively humid and heavy drops fell from the leaves to the ground, which squelched underfoot and seemed reluctant to release the shoe that had pressed into it.

The terrible undergrowth that here engrossed all the space under the shade of the pillared bombax and mast-like mvulé was a miracle of vegetation. It consisted of ferns, spear-grass, water-cane, and orchidaceous plants mixed with wild vines, cable thicknesses of the *Ficus elastica*, and a sprinkling of mimosas, acacias, tamarinds; llianes, palms of various species, wild date, *Raphia vinifera*, the elais, the fan, rattans, and a hundred other varieties, all struggling for every inch of space, and swarming upward with a luxuriance and density that only this extraordinary hothouse atmosphere could nourish. We had certainly seen forests before but this scene was an epoch in our lives ever to be remembered for its bitterness; the gloom enhanced the dismal misery of our life; the slopping moisture, the unhealthy reeking atmosphere, and the monotony of the scenes; nothing but the eternal interlaced branches, the tall aspiring stems, rising from a tangle through which we had to burrow and crawl like wild animals, on hands and feet. . . . We saw a python 10 feet long, a green viper, and a monstrous puff-adder on this march, besides scores of monkeys, of the white-necked or glossy black species, as also the small grey, and the large howling baboons. We heard also the 'soko' or chimpanzee, and saw one 'nest' belonging to it in the fork of a tall bombax. A lemur was also observed; its loud harsh cries made each night hideous.

The path presented myriapedes, black and brown, 6 inches in length, while beetles were innumerable, and armies of the deep brown 'hot-water' ants compelled us to be cautious how we stepped.

It was also at about this time that Stanley had an extraordinary experience:

. . . a native was found in the bushes close to the town with a small bow and a quiver of miniature arrows in his hand, and, it being a suspicious circumstance, he was secured and brought to me. He was a most remarkable specimen for a warrior, I thought, as I looked at the trembling diminutive figure. He stood, when measured, 4 feet 6½ inches, round the chest 30 inches and at the waist 24 inches. His head was large, his face decked with a scraggy fringe of whiskers, and his complexion light chocolate. . . . Everybody seemed to be particularly careful, as they examined the arrows, not to touch the points, and, as many of them were folded in leaves, it appeared to me that the native had some reason for this precaution. In order to verify this opinion, I uncovered one of the leaf-guarded points, and taking hold of one of his arms I gravely pretended to be about to inoculate the muscle with the dark substance on the arrow. His loud screams, visible terror, and cries of 'Mabi! Mabi!' ('Bad, bad') with a persuasive eloquence of gesture, left no doubt in my mind that the arrows were poisoned.

Apart from this they saw little of the natives. Every village along the river showed signs that it had been hurriedly abandoned. It was clear that the Arab slave-hunts had even penetrated the jungle, and that the local tribes had mistaken Stanley's enterprise for a slave-hunting expedition. Occasionally there was a threatening call from the jungle, but generally the natives announced their presence by the whizz of foot-long poison arrows or else by a spear thrown with tremendous force. What happened to their victims was clear, for the natives did not bury the dead but used their bones and skulls as macabre ornaments for their huts and for lining the streets in the villages. On one occasion Stanley came near to establishing peaceful relations with the natives. Wadu, his drummer, was a virtuoso performer and his skill on the great drum of the expedition aroused the greatest delight amongst the local population who listened enthusiastically to his easy mastery, as only an expert audience could. When Stanley tried to exploit this sudden contact, the natives disappeared like lightning and again the menacing calls were heard from all sides. 'I had to admit to myself,' Stanley noted in his journal, 'that I was not capable of charming the natives.' Finally even the unshakeable *Bula-Matari* realized that it was impossible to continue through the jungle, and that he had better travel down the Lualaba itself. The *Lady Alice*, the launch which had already given such good service to the expedition, was unpacked and assembled. In addition Stanley had managed to buy twenty-three canoes from the natives. But the river journey, which began in January 1877, proved just as difficult as had the march through the jungle. The natives, cannibals to the last man, made everything as difficult as possible. Stanley had his interpreters stand in the bows and shout, *senneneh, senneneh*! peace, peace, but invariably the echo came back from the banks *Bo-bo-bo-bo*! Meat! meat! Ah! ha! we shall have plenty of meat! *Bo-bo-bo-boo*!

At first Stanley felt as if he was dreaming. It seemed too fantastic that any human beings on God's earth could look upon their fellow men with feelings akin to those of a gourmet at the sight of a *châteaubriant saignant*. The guns of the expedition spat fire, but things might have been worse had the American realized that the howls of the cannibals were particularly directed at him, for the flesh of Europeans was considered to be a special delicacy, more succulent and juicy than the rather stringy meat of natives. These details were brought back in 1906 by the German missionary Father Josef Fräszle who spent twenty years among the cannibals of the Congo. When he first arrived among them, he had been welcomed with dance and song:

> We have slaughtered men,
> Bombongo is picking the bones,
> We have eaten their brains,

Bombongo is sucking the bones,
We have roasted their hearts,
Bombongo is crunching the bones.

And this festive madrigal culminated in a general whoop of delight as the leader yelled:

Welcome white stranger
To our cooking-pot!

Father Fräszle's hair must have stood on end but he survived somehow to add the following dry little comment:

They knew very well what they were talking about for only recently they had eaten the English Lt. Bell and another soldier. All night long they had danced round them chanting monotonously 'White men, tomorrow we shall devour you!'

Bula-Matari, as we have said, had no true appreciation of his own culinary attractions. 'Meat! *We?* Heavens! What an atrocious idea!' he wrote, and saw to it that he got away. For this reason he did not see what Fräszle had had to see, namely that the shallow banks of the river were lined with heavy poles driven deep into the mud, and that people were tied to them, young and old alike, men and women, slaves and prisoners of war. For four days they would remain there, alive and conscious, up to their necks in water, so that their flesh would lose its dark colour and become soft and ready for slaughtering. They were only tied loosely so that the ropes did not prevent the body fluids from circulating, but they could not escape: their ankle joints had been broken.

This and many similar stories can be found in Father Fräszle's fascinating book *Meiner Urwald Neger Denken und Handeln* ('The Deeds and Thoughts of my Jungle Natives'). Moreover, it is certain that the missionary only wrote down a part of what he had seen. At first, this knowledge that there were people on the banks waiting to eat them, affected the nerves of the travellers, though later they became inured to it. The cannibals, for their part, did their utmost to get their roast. Showers of arrows fell on the launch and among the little fleet of canoes, and Stanley's guns would answer, sending bullets whining across to the forest. The situation became more critical at the mouth of the Aruwimi, a large river fed by the limpid waters of the Ruwenzori glacier which flowed into the muddy waters of the Lualaba from the east. News of the arrival of the foreigners had been telegraphed by drum from village to village and, although the jungle which advanced down to the river-banks hid everything, the travellers knew that hundreds of eyes were watching them from between the trees and that at any minute a hail of arrows might be loosed against them.

Still, the expedition managed to get past safely, a few volleys having sufficed to discourage the local natives from attempting to board the flotilla. But the drums continued to reverberate incessantly, and to Stanley it seemed that they had become more urgent in their call than before. If he had understood the language of the drum, he might have been less anxious, for their message read: 'A man is on the river, he has white flesh like a drowned man, he comes in a large swift canoe.' The drums were silent. Then they started again. 'He is coming down the Lualaba, he looks like a dead man. In the water from which all life has sprung, he has found life. Now he is returning to us.' And again the drums beat out: 'He is white as the first man whom God created. God created man in the water. Thus he was white. The man with the white flesh is very near. He is coming, he is coming, he is coming!'

All the American could hear was the insistent rhythm of the drums. He did not understand what they said, and he had never observed that, after four days, the skin of drowned Negroes takes on a yellowish-white hue. He did not suspect that native babies are not black but reddish in colour and that the dark pigment in their skin begins to form only a few days later. He knew nothing of the mythology of the Basoko, the 'People of the Water', which tells that the creator formed the first man in the water, and that when he left it to step on dry land, his skin was white in colour. All Stanley could hear was the thud and rumble of the drums, and when suddenly, round a bend in the river, he caught sight of fifty large canoes racing in formation towards him, each impelled by the rhythmic stroke of forty paddles, the drums starting to roar with unaccustomed savagery, the ivory war-horns screaming and two thousand Basoko beginning to yell at the top of their voices, he believed he was being attacked and that it was a question of life and death. He gave the order to fire. The Basoko seemed bewildered, and were seized by panic, but they quickly rallied and it came to a bitter battle. Stanley's nerves were tensed to breaking point and he reported:

> The monster canoe aimed straight for my boat, as though it would run us down; but, when within fifty yards off, swerves aside, and, when nearly opposite, the warriors above the manned prow let fly their spears, and on either side there is a noise of rushing bodies. But every sound is soon lost in the ripping crackling musketry.... Our blood is now up. It is a murderous world, and we felt for the first time that we hate the filthy, vulturous ghouls who inhabit it. We therefore lift our anchors, and pursue them up-stream along the right bank, until rounding a point we see their villages. We make straight for the banks, and continue the fight in the village streets with those who have landed, hunt them out into the woods, and there only sound the retreat, having returned the daring cannibals the compliment of a visit.

Thirty years later the missionary Father Josef Fräszle, of whom we have already heard, became the first white man to establish friendly relations with the Basoko. Their King Muyimba, by then a shrivelled old man, had, when a young chief, taken part in the fight against Stanley.

Since that first encounter with a white man, he had come into contact with them many times and had felt the tremendous cultural superiority of the strangers. He received the missionary benevolently, and it was not long before he told the German clergyman of his battle against Stanley.

> When we heard that a man of white flesh was coming down the Lualaba, we were dumbfounded. All night the tree-drum brought us the strange news. . . . We wanted to hold a feast and receive our brother ceremoniously and accompany him into the village. We adorned ourselves, we manned our great canoes, we listened to the drums of our brothers from the Lualaba. 'He is approaching you,' they said. This was the signal. We started out, my canoe in the front, the others behind us, with jubilant song, our drums sounding, towards the first white man we had ever set eyes on, to pay him homage.
>
> But when we approached his canoe, it began to make loud sharp noises. Fire sticks began to spit iron against us. We stood stiff with fright, unable to close our mouths at the unseen, unheard, unsuspected work of evil spirits!
>
> This was no brother. This was the worst enemy our country had ever seen.
>
> And still his sticks were spitting fire. The water was hissing from the flying iron which whistled round our heads. Many of our brothers fell. We fled into the village, they followed us. We escaped into the forest, and lay down on the ground. When we returned at evening, then our eyes beheld a terrible sight: dead people, dying people, bleeding brothers, a plundered and burnt-down village and the river full of blood.

The man who told this story, Muyimba, King of the Basoko, was not a very pleasant character. A cannibal, at least in secret, he made Father Fräszle's spine chill with fear. 'I was terrified of this tattooed cannibal', writes the pious missionary, but he has given us Muyimba's account and does not hint at all that he considered the story untrue. On the contrary, Father Fräszle concluded his account of this conversation with the comment: 'The reception that Stanley encountered, and which he thought to be hostile in intention, is even today the customary form of honour with which I myself have been met on many occasions.'

If everything had in fact been as Muyimba recounted, then Stanley's 'twenty-eighth encounter', as he himself called this battle on the Aruwimi in a careful enumeration of all his engagements, must have been due to a terrible misunderstanding. And since history is usually written by the conquerors and rarely by the conquered, it is likely that what took place between Muyimba and Stanley on the Aruwimi was quite different from the report published by the *New York Herald*. In any case, Stanley now had peace for a few days. The horror instilled in the natives by the expedition's fire-arms must have persuaded them that it was better not to come near the white man at all.

In the meantime the Lualaba had carried its travellers further and further towards the north. On the 1st December 1876, Stanley established his position as roughly 3° south of the Equator, and two months later at the beginning of February 1877, the expedition was almost at 2° north and still the course of the river ran northwards. But during his entire stay in the jungle, Stanley had covered only 5° towards the west and he very much doubted that this river could be the Congo.

One day, however, the stream did take a sharp westward turn and continued in that direction. Stanley had won out; he knew now that the river could be none other than the Congo and that it was only a question of luck and time until he reached the Atlantic Ocean. We can imagine what were the feelings of joy which flooded his heart, particularly since the last four weeks had seen some very tense moments, culminating in the difficult passage of the Stanley Falls. The natives had been certain that it was quite impossible to negotiate the falls in any way, except by going round by land. Stanley soon discovered that these reports were only too well founded: the river poured wildly over the edge, swirling and eddying. There was indeed no possibility of passing there, but the way by land round the falls had proved almost as dangerous. The tall warriors of the Bakomo had been the most fearless fighters that Stanley had so far encountered. The expedition had been forced to fight its way through the forest yard by yard, under murderous fire from invisible sharpshooters. Every eight hundred yards small camps protected by brushwood called *bomas* had been set up against hostile attacks. Only then had they been able to tackle the arduous task of pulling the canoes along a hastily erected slipway of logs, and so they had continued for twenty-one days under constant fire from the Bakomo. But the falls had been by-passed, and on the 8th February Stanley's belief that he had reached the Congo had been fully confirmed when the chief of the Rubunga had replied to a question about the name of the river: 'Ikutu ya Kongo!'—'It is called the Congo!'

It is certain that several times during these weeks Stanley had almost decided to give up, but each time his obstinacy and perseverance had won the day. In England, at the time, they used the term 'Tuckey disaster' to signify a total collapse, an absolute failure. Its history is briefly this: at the beginning of the century a certain Captain James H. Tuckey and a party of seventeen men had perished through fever or poison arrows, 120 miles from the coast, in an attempt to sail up the lower course of the Congo already discovered by the Portuguese Diego Cão. Not at any price should England and America speak of a Stanley disaster. Stanley had sworn to himself and to the world that he would have the will to carry on and conquer.

And this sheer presumption, this over-weening self-confidence, had succeeded. The expedition had had to travel sixty miles by land to by-pass the falls and, on the 28th January 1877, Stanley heaved a sigh of relief as the seventh and last cataract was left behind. He re-embarked in all probability at the site of the large modern city of Stanleyville. But even the modern world has been unable to surmount the rapids: the railway line, beginning near Ponthierville, makes a wide detour until such time as the river settles down again to its broad, majestic course.

The river slowly widened until the average distance from bank to bank was about 13,000 feet. At one point the river-banks retreated so much that the width increased to nearly nine miles. Such wide expanses of water can be whipped up with even the slightest winds into considerable waves, and great care had to be taken that the canoes as well as the launch did not capsize. As if to make up for this additional danger, the local natives remained almost exclusively friendly. The war drums were silent, and nobody thought of taking a pot-shot at the passing canoes with their cargo of delicacies. Instead of wild howls, the interested natives would frequently sing out the happy word '*senneneh!*'—peace! All those whom Stanley approached replied with friendship and without shyness. As much food as was wanted could be obtained by barter, and it was obvious that more civilized regions were not far distant. But the ceremonies of blood-brothership, which Stanley had met up-stream, were still widespread even here. Apparently white people were so unusual that the natives were anxious to enter into blood-brothership with them. But this excess of brotherly zeal on their part, pleasant and gratifying though it was, had its disadvantages too. An incident that might have caused an irreparable loss took place one evening in the region of Babwende. The local natives, who wandered freely about the camp, noticed the great *mundelé*, the European, sitting in his tent and writing on *tara tara*—white paper with small black signs. This was a great mystery to them, but they were certain that it could be nothing else but some terrible magic. Surely the white man wanted to bewitch them. It would never rain again, their fields would dry up and their women become barren. Thus one day Stanley was confronted by six hundred excited natives, armed to the teeth. They looked as if they were going to storm his tents, and only with great difficulty did he manage to pacify them sufficiently to learn what it was that they wanted. They asked him to burn his journal, so that the magic which he had exerted over them would become ineffective. They added that they were deeply disappointed in the *mundelé*, who had repaid their kindness by laying a terrible curse on them. Then they added that they would forget everything and there would be friendship again, if only he would throw the *tara tara* into the fire.

The American was thunderstruck. Burn his journal! The fruit of almost nine hundred days of travelling, containing countless determinations of places, altitudes and ethnological notes, thousands of barometric readings, meteorological and hydrographic observations, as well as maps, sketches and plans! It would be an irreplaceable loss. Suddenly Stanley remembered that his journal was just like the *Works of Shakespeare* that he carried with him. Would he be able to deceive the natives? Stanley felt his heart pounding in his breast. He turned, went to his tent and came back with a volume of Shakespeare under his arm. The chief of the Babwende, a tall chap with a mass of fuzzy hair, who had parleyed with the white man, stretched out his hands as if to ward off the evil spell. Yes! this was the red-covered *tara tara* in which the *mundelé* had painted his magical signs. A giant fire was kindled, and Stanley threw his Shakespeare into it. The natives watched the flames curl round the binding while Stanley took his stick and forced the covers apart so that the flames could reach the pages. Anxiously the natives saw the white pages char, turn black and flare up. But even when the book had turned to ashes, it retained its form, proof positive that a terrible danger had been averted.

Stanley too heaved a sigh of relief and took care not to write up his journal in public again. He noted, with amusement, that he was probably the first and only admirer of the great English dramatist who had to thank him for saving his life, since the Babwende would certainly have killed him if he had not handed over the book for burning. But all things considered he would have preferred death to giving up his journal of his own free will. Stanley was neither a professional geographer nor a scientist, and the world had already once treated him as an outsider, an imposter, and a liar. Without his journals all his wanderings in Africa would have been in vain.

Such reflections made Stanley realize that the whole expedition depended on his own person, and that he must move on as quickly as possible to place his notes into the hands of Europeans. With the Babwende in and out of the camp the journalist in Stanley was being completely stifled and this frustration wrought a change in his outlook, for it taught him that, though as before he was the leader of the whole undertaking, a new duty had devolved upon him. Up to now he had been concerned with coming through alive with a good scoop for his paper, but the episode of the journal had clearly shown him that he was the only man of the party capable of carrying back the details of the exploration of the Congo to Europe.

At once, steps were taken to get the expedition under way again. Stanley ordered the men to complete the canoe which they were building for him as quickly as possible. This was the main reason why he had stopped there, though he had also wanted to allow himself and his people a well-earned rest after the strain of the earlier part of the voyage. His concern about the poor state of health of Frank Pocock, his last white companion, was pushed into the background. Stanley ordered the voyage to continue.

For many days everything went well. The great river flowed smoothly to the south-west. On the 12th March 1877, the flotilla lay in the regions of Stanley Pool, where the great river opens out like a lake some twenty-five miles wide. (Today the modern French town of Brazzaville stands on one bank and the Belgian town of Leopoldville on the other.) But four days later there came more rapids and waterfalls, which had to be passed by land. Even today these areas present such difficult problems that the two railway lines, to Brazzaville and to Leopoldville, have to make a wide detour to by-pass them. This time the going was very much more difficult than it had been around the Stanley Falls in the upper course of the Congo. The river plunged in stages almost 1,300 feet between vertical rock walls, and Stanley and his bearers had to scramble perilously down over steep escarpments, covered with loose rock. Before the boats could be dragged along, a rough-and-ready slipway had to be laid, for they were a little more than sixty-five feet in length and weighed nearly three tons. To cap it all the rains had started and the work had to be performed under torrential downpours, to the accompaniment of tropical thunder and lightning which, although not particularly dangerous, can seem terrifyingly powerful, particularly to nerves already strained to breaking point. Moreover, as the expedition drew nearer to more civilized regions, the prices of all foodstuffs rose rapidly. Stanley's financial resources, fabrics, brass wire, beads and shells, dwindled so rapidly that finally the day came when meat was declared to be too expensive to have except on rare occasions. Tea, coffee, tobacco, spices, all these were almost forgotten things and Stanley had no option but to live exactly like his porters.

Worst of all, their boots had completely disintegrated. Frank Pocock, despite the warnings of his master, generally went barefoot; Stanley himself wore a kind of light slipper, which he had sewn together from remnants of all kinds. This footgear was not much use as a protection against the stones and splinters of the rocky mountain cliffs, but it proved adequate against the bites of snakes, insects and ants, present in countless millions. The worst danger for the feet, apart from snakes, was the guinea worm. This loathsome parasite would inject its eggs under the skin and soon afterwards the foot would be afflicted with evil-looking sores full of short, fat worms.

Dr. Olivier Dapper had already spoken of this terrible tropical disease 200 years previously.

He told his astonished contemporaries:

> Strangers who come to Guinea are horribly plagued by worms which grow in their bodies. These worms are of different sizes. Some are two ells long and others a little shorter. Some are as thick as the lowest string of a fiddle and like a common earth worm, others are as slender as a fine silk fibre. There is no recognised cure for these worms, except to wait until the worm shows its head; which is then seized between the fingers and held fast so that it cannot retreat back into the body. Then the worm must be gently pulled by the head until there is enough to wind round a twig. The twig should be slowly rotated until all the worm is free of the body. The hole through which the worm has been pulled must be kept covered and above all protected

against cold, for if one does not pay much care the area will swell up and become inflamed.

Pocock, too, was covered by such sores and the previously happy lad was soon turned by the pain and perpetual itching into a complaining and prematurely old man. Pocock's health was completely undermined and he reached a point where he could only proceed by crawling along or by being carried. He became so ashamed of this that one day, despite all warnings, he tried to shoot some particularly fierce rapids in a canoe and was drowned. Stanley was now the only white man left. The loss of Pocock, the last of the white companions with whom he had set out in 1874 and who had shared his life for the last three years, oppressed Stanley so much that he hardly found the strength to pull himself together and continue his voyage. Furthermore, Pocock's death caused the deepest confusion even amongst the porters, and mutiny broke out in the caravan, which required Stanley's last strength to suppress. On the 10th June his spirits were very low, and he made the following despairing entry:

. . . Oh! Frank, Frank, you are happy, my friend. Nothing can now harrow your mind or fatigue your body. You are at rest for ever and for ever. Would that I were also!

New cataracts had to be surmounted and navigation became more difficult as the masses of water from the recent storms swelled the river. But a hundred and twenty-five days after setting out, on the 1st August 1877, the last rapid lay behind them, the cataract of Isangila, which the luckless Captain Tuckey had once reached. The purpose of the voyage was fulfilled and the Congo was explored. Stanley obtained a new lease of courage, and even his porters believed that at last they were nearing the sea. When their beloved *mundelé*, their lord and master, told them that they would cover the last stretch by marching over land their joy was unbounded. The jungle had now given way to fertile, undulating highland, across which it was a pleasure to march. Despite the many sick, they made quick progress and, on the 4th August, the local natives told them that the sea was only a few days' march away. As inspiring as this news was at first, it produced the complete collapse of master and men alike; as so often happens after an arduous journey when the end is in sight, their courage suddenly abandoned them. Emaciated forms with gaunt faces lay on the ground, unable to take another step. Even Stanley was completely finished. He sent a native courier from Nsanda, his last halt, to the trading town of Boma with a written request for help. The letter, addressed 'to any gentleman who speaks English at Embomma', had the following postscript by Stanley: 'You may not know me by name; I therefore add that I am the person that discovered Livingstone.' This letter reached the hands of the manager of the English firm of Hatton and

Cookson, who, deeply moved by Stanley's plight, immediately sent off a caravan of porters with everything that he considered essential.

The American had not placed too many hopes on this call for help. So far, fate had given him no presents and from the beginning he had had to fight for everything himself. But now Dame Fortune gave him the laurel wreath even before victory had been achieved, and to Stanley's great delight, this laurel wreath smelt noticeably of rum. Hardly four days after having dispatched his letter, four black porters climbed down the steep cliff. They were, as was soon discovered, heavily laden with foodstuffs. The rear of the caravan was made up of a few particularly strong men who were picking their way carefully among the stones. These latter were carrying bulging kegs of rum and were immensely proud that no accident had befallen their load. They laid their greeting of victory before the *Bula-Matari.* A frenzy of joy broke out in the camp of the half-starved when the porters were seen approaching. History does not record the effect of the rum on empty stomachs but we may hazard a shrewd guess.

At long last the expedition was approaching its goal. On the 9th August 1877, exactly 999 days after leaving Zanzibar, Stanley encountered white men again for the first time. With a shaky hand he wrote in his journal:

> As I looked into their faces, I blushed to find that I was wondering at their paleness. ... The pale colour, after so long gazing on rich black and richer bronze, had something of an unaccountable ghastliness. I could not divest myself of the feeling that they must be sick.

His first contact with an outpost of Europe after three years of bush-ranging was very confusing. He imagined himself belonging to an intermediate race, halfway between Africans and Europeans, and was touched to see how elegant and intelligent were the remarks of the whites. He had to force himself to realize that he too was one of these remarkable people.

This he was indeed. True, there were much better-educated and cultured Europeans than Henry Morton Stanley, but compared with his remarkable achievement, such things weighed lightly in the balance. And the scales hang more in his favour still, if we consider how this alleged slave-driver treated the natives who had accompanied him across Africa. He could have paid them off, and returned by the next steamer to England. No man could have reproached him, not even his coloured travelling companions, for the reward which each one of them received for their three years of service was enough to make them rich for life.

But when the reception committee in Boma made this suggestion to him, he rejected it out of hand: he wanted to accompany his black men back to Zanzibar. When he was then told that the steamer *Kabinda* was leaving in two days' time, on the 11th August, and that he would have to travel the day after next if he insisted on his decision, Stanley became polite but remained firm. He understood only too well the motives of his hosts. Boma had made the headlines. The Morse telegraph was spluttering out, hour after hour, foot-long telegrams. New York and London were plying the handful of white men in this remote outpost with a stream of unending questions. Messages of congratulation were arriving from every part of the world. Something had happened in Boma to interrupt the deadly monotony, and then the eccentric Yankee declared that he wanted to leave the next day! He even had the nerve to stress that he had to leave because he had to take his blacks back to Zanzibar! Stanley reflected how he himself had suffered from loneliness after the death of his white companions. He understood that, for the eighteen Europeans in Boma, he was a kind of elixir, a miraculous cure against the spiritual scurvy to which they had fallen victims. Thus he mellowed. He would insist on sailing with the *Kabinda*, but he allowed the whole rigmarole of receptions, banquets, dinners, and toasts to be showered upon him. He even replied to toasts and made some himself. He participated in champagne breakfasts and club functions; he drew on his last reserves of strength to appear excited and gay.

But nevertheless he breathed a deep sigh of relief when, on the afternoon of the 11th August 1877, his steamer weighed anchor with the receding tide. He stood on the foredeck with his natives, amused at their excitement at travelling on such a 'fat iron canoe' which moved by itself across the ocean. He was deeply happy. Again and again it was suggested to him that now he could return to England. His men would be able to get to Zanzibar without him, but Stanley was not to be shaken. He refused to be separated from his people and led them to Luanda, where they changed ship for the *Industry*, which was sailing for Cape Town. He saw to it that his black comrades could cover even the last stage of the journey home by ship, and on the 26th November 1877, three months after his departure from Boma, he landed in the harbour of Zanzibar.

9

Stanley did not waste his time on his voyage. Immediately he arrived in Cape Town, he cabled many columns of preliminary reports and announced his return to London. On the 12th November 1877, while the American was still sailing with his natives to Zanzibar on board an English gunboat, the *Daily Telegraph* printed the first instalment of Stanley's report.

Twenty-four hours later, the *Daily Telegraph* of Friday, 12th November, was lying on the desk in the study of a country house at Laeken, near Brussels in Belgium. The stocky, well-dressed owner of the estate had just finished his breakfast and had retired to his study to devote himself to the business of the day. Despite his correct appearance, which made him look like a successful company director, he gave an obvious start as he scanned the headlines of the *Daily Telegraph*. Then he sat down and devoured the whole of Stanley's report. He was visibly excited and began to pace rapidly up and down his study. This gentleman was none other than Leopold II, King of Belgium, scion of the house of Coburg and cousin of the Prince Consort Albert of England. At once Leopold saw that Stanley's discoveries had altered all his plans and that he would have to abandon the idea of starting from East Africa, and begin at the mouth of the Congo. The King had announced his plans to the world in an impressive congress convened at Brussels, at the beginning of September 1876, to which Cameron from England, Duveyrier from France, and Nachtigal, Rohlfs and Schweinfurth from Germany, had been invited. Before them all and before a host of scientists, bankers, technicians and journalists, the King had declared his idealistic intentions of initiating a magnificent development programme for Africa, in the name of international co-operation. Slavery was to be abolished, the incessant tribal wars between the various chiefs were to be prevented and arbitration courts were to be set up. Medical stations and scientific laboratories were to be erected everywhere, streets, bridges and railways were to be built, great plantations were to be laid: in short, it was his royal will, Leopold II declared, to raise the Black Continent from its state of barbarism through the common effort of all the civilized peoples of the world, and to lay the foundations of progress. For this purpose an association called the International African Society was founded, which had the duties of studying the relevant economic, scientific and humanitarian problems.

Thus it came about that when, on his return from Africa at the end of 1877, Stanley landed in Marseilles, he was greeted by two gentlemen, who on the orders of Leopold II of Belgium submitted 'The Great Plan' to him. But the Anglo-American was unwilling to commit himself at once. Before the thought of international efforts on behalf of Africa were given any fixed form, he, Henry Morton Stanley, a Welshman born, had the obvious duty of informing his motherland of the tremendous possibilities offered by the economic exploitation of Africa and particularly of the Congo regions. He hastened to London, where he threw himself into a whirl of discussions, lectures and conferences. Articles, pamphlets, reports flowed from his pen. He spoke at ladies' teas and gentlemen's clubs, he lobbied Members of Parliament, appealed to bankers and merchants and did everything in his power to interest England in the Congo.

And what happened? Again he earned nothing but scorn and derision.

Those who called him a Don Quixote used perhaps the mildest insult. Stanley did not let himself be put out by this, and carried on for almost a year. He was called a hot-headed reporter, a newspaper hack grown wild, a dreamer who had lost all sense of proportion. In November 1877, Stanley had had enough, and together with a number of Belgian business men, he founded the Comité d'Études du Haut Congo in Brussels. A few months later he was back in the Congo ready to start the tremendous work. After a year of incessant efforts, a road some fifty miles long had been forced through swamp, forest and rock. Not very much, if we remember that the total length of the Congo is three thousand miles, but this was only the beginning. Leopold II had proclaimed the motto: '*Coloniser c'est transporter*' and there was nobody who agreed more strongly than Stanley. Soon more than five hundred chiefs recognized the agreements which *Bula-Matari* submitted to them in the name of the Association Internationale du Congo, this being the designation which his society had now adopted.

Four hundred years before Stanley, in 1482, a similar project had already been attempted by the Portuguese Admiral Diego Cão, who in the course of the Portuguese exploitation of Africa had reached as far as Cape Santa Maria, south of modern Benguela. Thus he had come across the mouth of a tremendous river which the natives called *Nzadi*, the great water. The royal cartographers on the Portuguese caravels corrupted this to *Zahira*, but even this did not last long, for the natives with whom the interpreters managed to hold a broken conversation let it be known that the stream came from far within the interior, from the realm of the mighty king Mani Kongo. Thus the name Congo appeared for the first time on contemporary maps alongside the designation *Zahira*.

All this might easily have come to nothing, but for the fact that Diego Cão decided to send four of his best and wisest companions on a diplomatic mission to Mani Kongo, offering His Black Majesty a treaty of peace and friendship with the King of Portugal. From a faded, but still readable, inscription on one of the rock walls near Matadi, today one of the most important inland ports on the Congo, we can read that the Portuguese used the time of waiting for the return of their four ambassadors in making distant voyages of exploration and that they had made a careful study of the land and the people. In the end, however, the main body grew tired of waiting and started on their return voyage, taking back to Lisbon with them four black men, obviously of royal blood and closely related to Mani Kongo.

Not all trips 'into the blue' finished as happily as this one. Neither the four white men who had gone to King Mani nor the four black princes who had gone to Lisbon came to any harm. The four white men saw with astonishment that there, deep in the jungle, everything went on just as it did at the Court in Lisbon. Missions came and went to the Court of His Black Majesty, there were great receptions and gala dinners, wars were waged and peace negotiated, armourers saw to it that the arsenal was always furnished with weapons, that swords were kept sharp and keen; customs stations along the state road through the jungle relieved passers-by of some of their wealth for tolls and taxes, cowrie shells were used as coin and were carried in full bags by the tax collectors from the provinces to the capital where they were laboriously counted out. There was also the island Luanda, belonging to the King himself, where these gastropods flourished, forming a kind of natural mint. Just as at home, the high and mighty were well off and the small man fared badly.

Thus the four Portuguese met with conditions which in many ways resembled those at home and on the whole they felt quite at their ease. Of course it was frightening that weeks and months went by without the four black princes or a single Portuguese appearing. Had Diego Cão perhaps forgotten his four comrades in the Congo jungles? They felt their life was hanging by a thread.

Meanwhile the four black princes had reached Portugal in good health. They had there been looked after and pampered, and just like their four white counterparts in the Congo, the four black gentlemen at Lisbon realized that life at the Court of the King of Portugal was not so very much different from life in Mbaji, the residence of King Mani Kongo. They learnt to speak Portuguese with remarkable ease and when a few years later they returned to Mbaji they were quite Europeanized. The four Portuguese hostages of King Mani Kongo thanked God on their knees that they were free at last. The princes who had arrived from Portugal told of the many wonderful things that they had experienced, and they returned bearing the most valuable presents from the white to the black king. The compliment was returned and in the following years many of the princes of the Congo went to visit the Court of Portugal. Portugal replied by sending artisans, edible plants, domestic animals and tools to Africa. Occasionally there was intermarriage, since the difference in skin colour counted for naught beside the common Christian faith.

Priests and missionaries arrived in Africa, and in 1491 Mbaji was re-christened San Salvador. Soon a cathedral rose up there, followed by ten Christian churches and a chapel. A Jesuit college and a Dominican monastery were built, and in 1522 Prince Henrique, grandson of Mani Kongo, returned after a long stay in Lisbon and Rome as the first solemnly ordained black Bishop of the Congo. This was a significant event, not-withstanding the comic side of the proceedings. When his Grace entered San Salvador, the town of the Holy Saviour, he was received by black dukes, earls, princes and barons. The King of Portugal had been as generous with titles as he had been with glass beads and mirrors. Anyone of any standing at the Court of Mani Kongo or of his successor Alphonso I was received into the Portuguese nobility and given a resplendent uniform and solemn letters patent.

This sounds like a music-hall joke, but it was meant seriously. The Congo had never been considered a subject colony by Portugal, and these early beginnings only came to a standstill because the small land on the Tagus did not have sufficient financial or manpower resources to fulfil the great task that fate had given it. Obviously Portugal sent its best men to East Africa and to India, and could only spare mediocre men for the Congo. These quickly undid all the efforts that had been made. Missionaries had gone as far as Stanley Pool and the Kwango, and in 1582 another group of them landed in Africa, but that was the end. No supplies or funds or replacements were ever sent again, and, in the course of the great African migration of peoples which took place at the beginning of the seventeenth century, the Chaggas wiped out the Europeans in the Congo with a few strokes of the sword. What they did not destroy were the many edible plants which the Portuguese had imported themselves from South America and then introduced into Africa, such as maize, the batata, beans, peas, onions, manioc and yams, tomatoes, chilli peppers, lemons, oranges and pineapples, and also cocoa and tobacco. All of these, as also the pig, the dog and the cat, were gifts of the Portuguese to the Black Continent.

In 1879, Henry Morton Stanley appeared at the mouth of the Congo as the delegate of a European King, like Diego Cão some four hundred years before him. The Belgian King, however, did not appoint dukes, earls and barons. Instead, his representatives today promote the black railway worker to foreman; the blast furnace engineer, whose grandfather had been a cannibal, is fetched to the drawing-board and works with a slide rule, logarithms and calculating machines, just like his white colleague. The black fireman of a modern locomotive becomes a locomotive driver; former slaves become petrol-station attendants and car mechanics; others serve on radar equipment on the one hundred and seventy-five aerodromes of the Congo basins; others again have advanced from being simple unskilled labourers on the incessantly advancing road constructions to the status of divisional leaders, concrete mixers or foremen. Negroes steer the Congo steamers, are stationmasters on the railways, teachers, doctors and precision engineers, in short, the letters patent bestowed by monarchs of earlier centuries have become degrees and diplomas, and the master of the order is called progress.

We sceptical people of the west feel satisfied when we hear such things. Within the space of seventy-five years, developments have taken place which needed five hundred years in Europe and which have not yet been fully assimilated technically or spiritually. How will the black man react to this forcible feeding? How can he assimilate himself to this strange foreign world? How will he fit into it?

One thing is certain: the external successes are breathtaking. Africa is seething with discontent but there is peace in the Congo. In many respects the native is the equal of the white man. The two races do not fight each other but pull together with the same fanatical optimism. Here nobody tries to stem the development of the Negro. He has possibilities of making his way in the world such as do not exist for him in the Union of South Africa and Rhodesia or in Kenya. On the other hand, no attempts are made to force the emancipation of the coloured people; thus, for instance, it has been decreed that only black men have the right to plant cotton. For this reason, most of the Negroes live in the forests like their fathers as peasants, hunters and fishermen, divided among themselves by two hundred and eighty different languages and some five hundred dialects. Many a chief, however, rides in a super-modern American road cruiser, listens to the latest hits on the radio and tells his servant to get him a tin of German export beer or a bottle of Coca-Cola from the Frigidaire. But these are exceptions, and it is only a newly created thin upper crust which participates in directly progressive or intellectual occupations. Nevertheless the black professors, bishops, bank directors and mayors in the *Cités indigènes*, the coloured quarters of Leopoldville, Stanleyville or Elisabethville have very much more work to do than their white colleagues in the less crowded European quarters.

We must remember that in 1881, when Stanley pitched his camp at the foot of the modern Mount Leopold, the town consisted only of a few miserable reed huts, while today it is the capital of the Belgian Congo and is inhabited by about 265,000 people. We must also bear in mind that, a few decades ago, Stanleyville, Elisabethville, Matadi, Fort Francqui, Bukama, Jadotville, and all other great industrial cities and harbours were merely a number of black lines on the drawing-boards of European engineers. All these tremendous achievements could only have been brought about because of the co-operative attitude of the Negro.

We do not detract from the Belgian 'wonder' on the Congo with its skyscrapers, its mines, uranium deposits, chemical factories, highroads and aerodromes, when we stress that in the climate of Equatorial Africa the co-operation of the black man is essential, and that one of the main problems of the Congo is the question how the already 950,000 strong Negro labour force can be increased to cope with all the proposed projects.

That is the problem. Earlier centuries would not have hesitated in such a situation. They would have 'made slaves' or else have set up recruiting offices using forcible methods. But this approach is out of date, particularly since the rational techniques of modern industry require highly trained workers with initiative of their own. Moreover any considerable exploitation of human labour forces is at once opposed by weighty ethical and humanitarian protests. Thus in the Congo there are only two roads open, to rationalize work by the increasing use of machines and to improve living conditions, even in the deepest bush, so that the mortality rate of the native population will fall. Both presuppose that the Congo native should be brought into contact with civilization in an ever-increasing measure, and that the white man renounces his claim to supremacy and offers his coloured co-operator all the economic and social possibilities that he needs for his well-being. It is obvious that there are many problems to be solved, and it is understandable that Kenya, and particularly South Africa, regard the way things are developing in the Congo with a certain anxiety. But the course of history cannot be stopped nor can the hands of the world clock be turned back. In our technological age it is quite irrelevant whether machines are served by red, black or yellow hands; the important person is he who invents and builds them. The real task of the white man is to serve as teacher and guide in those regions of the world discovered by him, and as long as he has the courage and perspicacity to continue in this path he will preserve his rights of primogeniture.

We have arrived at the end of our story. It began with Columbus's discovery of a new world and ends with the hope of the dawn of a new day. An American by choice, as it were, Cristoforo Colombo, from the Mediterranean port of Genoa, stood at its beginning, an American by choice, the Welshman James Rowlands, who later called himself Henry Morton Stanley, stands at its end. Needless to say it is not by virtue of this convenient rhetorical figure that our books ends with the discovery of the Congo, but rather because this achievement marks the end of the classical period of the history of discovery. Though blank spaces still exist on our maps, the outlines of the continents and their general characteristics are now essentially known. True, voyages of exploration still continue. True, new peoples, rivers, lands and mountains are still being discovered, as the Poles of the earth are visited by aeroplane. But this is merely routine scientific work of investigating small details, or areas that are not inhabitable. As in his previous work,[1] the writer has not been able to join the chorus of the prophets of doom. We must cut our suit according to the cloth. Let us recognize by all means that we are, as it were, living in tents, and that new storms could easily blow away everything we consider valuable, that here on earth there is no security and that each one of us can tomorrow be a new Job, without the happy ending.

But that is no reason for singing dirges and lamentations nor for sitting

[1] *Conquest by Man* (Harper & Brothers).

patiently, our hands neatly folded in our laps, waiting for the blow to fall. The end of man's rôle on earth is still very far away and probably it looks further away than ever in the history of humanity—we are all frightened by nightmarish dreams of a morrow in the last minutes before awakening. Perhaps none of us alive now will ever witness the dawn of this bright day, but that it will come, and will shine more brilliantly and more wonderfully than at any time since the creation of the universe, is certain. True, this is a matter of faith, but whoever recognizes that there is a mysterious order in the course of events, must agree also that a time-worn race waiting for final extinction would never have been granted those miraculous discoveries that science has made in the last three decades. All in all it is very much more probable that *homo sapiens* is ready to cast off his childhood apparel.

We have accompanied him as he groped his way uncertainly across the earth in order to learn the limits of his earthly home. As we take leave of him, for the time being, large parts of his universe are still unknown and unexplored. But just as brave men in the twenties and thirties of our century went out to those far spaces covered by limitless sand or eternal ice to measure and survey, so the first rockets are already being prepared which will carry the men of the near future into infinite space and infinite time. 'It is a great joy to be alive,' proclaimed the German humanist Ulrich von Hutten, during a period which had many things in common with our own. Should we not join him in his exhilaration and gratitude? True, our existence is full of need and worry, but despite our heavy burdens, *this* is not a time of decline, of complaint and distress. For the bars of our earthbound finality have been broken, and a new era is beginning in which we must live our lives and perform our daily tasks on earth, *sub specie aeternitatis*, in the light of eternity. . . .

BIBLIOGRAPHY

W. D. ALEXANDER: 'The origin of the Polynesian race', in: *Journ. Race Development*, I, Worcester, Mass., 1910–11.

PETRUS ALLIACUS: *Ymago mundi, Ed. Buron*, Paris, 1930.

FELIPE HUAMAN POMA AYALA: *El primer Cronicon y Buen Gobierno*, Paris, 1936.

S. W. BAKER: *The Albert Nyanza. Great basin of the Nile*, 2 vols., London, 1867.

HEINRICH BARTH: *Wanderungen durch die Küstenländer des Mittelmeeres, ausgeführt in den Jahren 1845–47*, Berlin, 1849.

Reisen und Entdeckungen in Nord- und Zentralafrika in den Jahren 1849–55, 5 vols., Gotha, 1857–9.

SARA WARE BASSETT: *The story of Vasco da Gama*, Philadelphia, 1927.

RUDOLF BAUMGARDT: *Fernando Magellán. Die Geschichte der ersten Weltumseglung*, Mainz, 1949.

C. F. BEHRENS: *Der wohlversuchte Südländer*, Leipzig, 1923.

RUTH BENEDICT: *Patterns of culture*, Boston, 1934.

E. BENSON: *Ferdinand Magellán*, London, 1929.

DOROTHEA BERLIN: *Erinnerungen an Gustav Nachtigal*, Berlin, 1887.

H. A. BERNATZIK: *Südsee. Ein Reisebuch*, Innsbruck, 1949.

A. BERTHELO: *L'Afrique Saharienne et soudanaise ce qu'ont connu les anciens*, Paris, 1927.

IWAN BLOCH: *Der Ursprung der Syphilis*, vols. I and II, Jena, 1901–11.

E. V. C. BODLEY: *The warrior saint*, Boston, 1952.

HANS GEORG BONTE: *Francisco Pizarro. Der Sturz des Inkareiches*, Leipzig, 1925.

J. BOULENGER: *Le voyage de René Caillié à Tombouctou*, Paris, 1932.

OLIVIER DE BOUVEIGNES: *Les anciens rois de Congo*, Namur, 1948.

W. C. BOYD: 'Blood groups', in: *Tabul. Biol.*, vol. XVIII, New York, 1939.

D. BRINTON (Ed.): *Cantares de Los Mexicanos*, Washington, 1887.

R. BROWN: *The Story of Africa and its Explorers*, 4 vols., London, 1892–4.

H. H. BRÜNING: 'Balkenflösse an der Küste von Peru', in: *Der Erdball*, Year 5, No. 10, Stuttgart, 1930.

MAX BÜDINGER: 'Akten zur Kolumbus-Geschichte von 1473 bis 1492', in: *Sitzungsbericht der Wiener Akademie der Wissenschaften, Phil.-Hist. Kl., No. II*, Vienna, 1886.

OTTO BUNZENDAHL, *Tahiti und Europa*, Leipzig, 1935.
R. F. BURTON: *The lake regions of Central Africa*, 2 vols., London, 1860.
V. L. CAMERON: *Across Africa*, 2 vols., London, 1877.
GASPAR DE CARJAVAL, ALONSO DE ROJAS and CHRISTOBAL DE ARUNA: *Descobrimentos do Rio das Amazonas*, São Paulo, 1928.
L. CARL and J. PETIT: *Geheimnisvoller Tefedest. Auf den Spuren einer alten Kultur*, Hamburg, 1955.
ALFONSO CASO: *The religion of the Aztecs*, Mexico, 1937.
FRANZ CASPAR: *Tupari. Unter Indios im Urwald Brasiliens*, Brunswick, 1952.
BERNAL DIAZ DEL CASTILLO: *The True History of the Conquest of New Spain*, translated by A. P. Maudsley (Hakluyt Soc., London, 1908–1916), 5 vols.
ADALBERT VON CHAMISSO: *Reise um die Welt in den Jahren 1815–1818*, Leipzig, 1842.
G. B. CHARCOT: *Christophe Colomb. Vu par un marin*, Paris, 1928.
HUGH CLAPPERTON: *Journal of a second expedition into the interior of Africa*, London, 1829.
MAURICE COLLIS: *Cortes and Montezuma*, London, 1954.
JAMES COOK: *Captain Cook's third voyage in the Pacific and towards the North Pole in the years 1776–1780.*
A voyage towards the South Pole and round the world, performed in His Majesty's ships 'The Resolution' and 'Adventure' in the years 1772–1775, London, 1777.
Captain Cook's journal during his first voyage round the world made in H.M. bark 'Endeavour' in the years 1768–1771, London, 1893.
W. D. COOLEY: *Claudius Ptolemy and the Nile*, London, 1854.
HERNAN CORTÉS: *Testamento de Hernan Cortés. I[a] edicion facsimile*, Mexico, 1930.
C. CRAMER: *Ulrich Schmiedel. Abenteuer in Südamerika 1535 bis 1554*, Leipzig, 1922.
CREUTZ-STEUDEL: *Einführung in die Geschichte der Medizin*, Iserlohn, 1948.
HEINRICH CUNOW: *Geschichte und Kultur des Inkareiches*, Amsterdam, 1927.
OLIVIER DAPPER: *Umbständliche und Eigentliche Beschreibung von Africa und denen dazu gehörigen Königreichen und Landschaften*, Amsterdam, 1670; *Die Welt*, Munich, 26th September 1953.
HANS DIETRICH DISSELHOFF: *Geschichte der altamerikanischen Kulturen*, Munich, 1953.
KEIZO DOHI: *Beiträge zur Geschichte der Syphilis in Ostasien*, Leipzig, 1923.
HENRI DUVEYRIER: *Exploration du Sahara*, 2 vols., Paris, 1864–81.

JEANETTE EATON: *Dr. Livingstone*, Aarau, 1951.
GORDON F. EKHOLM: 'Wheeled toys in Mexico', in: *American Antiquity*, vol. XI, No. 4, New York, 1946.
HENRI PAUL EYDOUX: *L'exploration du Sahara*, Paris, 1938.
P. H. FAWCETT: *Exploration Fawcett*, London, 1953.
ARNOLD FEDERMANN: *Deutsche Konquistadoren in Südamerika*, Berlin, 1938.
JOHN FISKE: *The discovery of America*, Boston, 1892.
FOLKE-HENSCHEN: 'Die älteste Geschichte der Syphilis in der Beleuchtung neuerer Skelettfunde', in: *Europäischer Wissenschafts-Dienst*, 3 Year, No. 10, Berlin, October 1943.
A. FORNANDER: *An account of the Polynesian race, its origin and migrations*, London, 1878.
G. FORSTER: *J. R. Forsters Reise um die Welt*, vols. I and II, Berlin, 1779–80.
CHARLES-EUGÈNE, VICOMTE DE FOUCAULD: *Reconnaissance au Maroc*, Paris, 1888.
Lettres à Henri de Castries, Paris, 1938.
JOSEPH FRÄSZLE: *Meiner Urwaldneger Denken und Handeln*, Freiburg, 1923.
FR. FREISE: *Bergbauliche Unternehmungen in Afrika während des Altertums*, Brunswick (1907?).
GUSTAV FREYTAG: *Bilder aus der deutschen Vergangenheit*, 6 vols., Leipzig, 1928.
GEORG FRIDERICI: *Malayo-polynesische Wanderungen*, Leipzig, 1914.
ROGER FRISON-ROCHE: *La piste oubliée*, Paris, 1953.
LEO FROBENIUS: *Kulturgeschichte Afrikas*, Neue Ausgabe, Cologne, 1954.
H. GEISELER: *Die Osterinsel. Eine Stätte prähistorischer Kulturen der Südsee*, Berlin, 1883.
EUGEN GELCICH: 'Die Route des Kolumbus auf der ersten Hinreise', in: *Zeitschrift der Gesellschaft für Erdkunde*, Berlin, 1885.
OSWALD GERHARDT: *Mikroben im Weltgeschehen. Sieg über die Seuchen*, Munich, 1954.
PAUL GRAETZ: *Im Auto quer durch Afrika*, Berlin, 1926.
A. GRIMBLE: *A Pattern of Islands*, London, 1952.
BERNHARD GRZIMEK: *Flug ins Schimpansenland*, Stuttgart, 1954.
Kein Platz für wilde Tiere, Munich, 1954.
Guide du Tourisme automobile et aérienne au Sahara, Shell, Algiers, 1951.
Guide du voyageur au Congo belge et au Ruanda-Urundi, Brussels, 1954.
K. GÜNTHER: *Gerhard Rohlfs*, Freiburg, 1912.
S. GÜNTHER: *Heinrich Barth. Biographische Blätter*, Leipzig, 1896.
Die Beteiligung der Deutschen am Zeitalter der Entdeckungen, Berlin, 1908.

STEPHEN GWYNN: *A Hermit of the Sahara*, London, 1929.
M. G. HAARDT and L. AUDOUIN-DUBREUIL: *Die erste Durchquerung der Sahara im Automobil*, Berlin, 1924.
A. C. HADDON: *The races of man and their distribution*, New York, 1924.
CONRAD HAEBLER: 'Die Columbus-Literatur der Jubiläumszeit', in: *Histor. Zeitschrift*, vol. LXXVI Berlin, 1895.
Die überseeischen Unternehmungen der Welser und ihrer Gesellschafter, Leipzig, 1903.
ARNOLD HEIM: *Wunderland Peru*, Berne, 1948.
R. HEINE-GELDERN: 'Einige Wanderungsprobleme im Pazifik', in: *Kultur und Sprache*, Vienna, 1952.
HANS HELFRITZ: *Die Osterinsel*, Zürich, 1953.
EDWIN HENNIG: *Die Weltumseglungsfahrten des Kapitäns James Cook*, Hamburg, 1908.
R. HENNIG: *Kolumbus und seine Tat. Eine kritische Studie über die Vorgeschichte der Fahrt von 1492*, Bremen, 1940.
'Das Christentum im mittelalterlichen Asien', in: *Histor. Vierteljahrsschrift*, vol. 29, 1935.
FRANZ HERWIG: *Fernando de Magellãn*, Munich, 1942.
W. HEYD: *Geschichte des Levantehandels*, vols. I and II, Stuttgart, 1879.
THOR HEYERDAHL: *American Indians in the Pacific. The theory behind the Kon-Tiki Expedition*, London, 1952.
FRIEDRICH HORNEMANN: *Tagebuch seiner Reise von Cairo nach Murzuk, der Hauptstadt des Königreichs Fessan in Africa in den Jahren 1797 und 1798. Aus der Teutschen Handschrift desselben herausgegeben von Carl Konig*, Weimar, 1802. Also published in the *Proceedings of the Association for promoting the discovery of the Interior Parts of Africa*, vol. II, London, 1810.
SIEGFRIED HUBER: *Im Reich der Inkas. Geschichte, Götter und Gestalten der peruanischen Indianer*, Olten, 1951.
FRANZ HÜMMERICH: *Vasco da Gama und die Entdeckung des Seewegs nach Ostindien*, Munich, 1898.
J. B. HUTCHINSON, R. A. SILOW and S. G. STEPHENS: *The evolution of gossypium and the differentiation of the cultivated cottons*, London and New York, 1947.
ULRICH VON HUTTEN: *De Guaiaci medicina et morbo Gallico*, Nuremberg, 1519.
A. IHLE: *Das alte Königreich Kongo*, Leipzig, 1929.
RUY DIEZ DE ISLA: *Tractado contra el Mal Serpentino: que vulgarmente en España es llamado Bubas*, Seville, 1539.
Jahrbuch der Görresgesellschaft, vol. XXIX, Cologne, 1908.
G. JANSELME: *Traité de la syphilis. Son origine, son expansion*, Paris, 1931.

M. JOMARD: *Notice historique sur la vie et les ouvrages de René Caillié*, Paris, 1839.

Journal d'un voyage à Tombouctou et à Jenne dans l'Afrique centrale, 3 vols., Paris, 1830.

A. J. JUAN DE ULLOA: *Relación historica del viaje a la America meridional*, I–IV, Madrid, 1748.

R. KANDT: *Caput Nili. Eine empfindsame Reise zu den Quellen des Nils*, Berlin, 1904.

RAFAEL KARSTEN: *Das altperuanische Inkareich*, Leipzig, 1949.

RICHARD KATZ: *Auf dem Amazonas*, Zürich, 1946.

Zickzack durch Südamerika, Zürich, 1935.

C. M. KAUFMANN: *Amerika und das Urchristentum*, Munich, 1924.

F. A. KIRKPATRICK: *The Spanish conquistadores*, London, 1934.

KURT KLEIN-SCHONNEFELD: 'Cortez und Marina', in: *Berliner Hefte für geistiges Leben*, Berlin, 3rd Year, 1948, I, No. 5.

F. KLETTKE: *Eduard Vogels Reise in Zentralafrika*, Berlin (1860?).

KARL KLUNZINGER: *Der Anteil der Deutschen an der Entdeckung von Südamerika durch die Abenteuer des Ambrosius Dalfinger und des Nikolaus Federmann*, Stuttgart, 1857.

W. KNOCHE: *Die Osterinsel*, Concepción, 1925.

W. KONER: 'Heinrich Barth', in: *Zeitschrift der Gesellschaft für Erdkunde*, vol. I, Berlin, 1866.

LUDWIG KRAPF: *Reisen in Ostafrika in den Jahren 1837–1855*, 2 vols., Stuttgart, 1858.

K. KRAUSE: *Die Portugiesen in Abessinien. Mitteilungen des Vereine für Erdkunde*, Dresden, 1912.

KONRAD KRETSCHMER: *Die Entdeckung Amerikas in ihrer Bedeutung für die Geschichte des Weltbildes*, Berlin, 1892.

WERNER G. KRUG: *Südlich der Sahara*, Hamburg, 1954.

KARL KRÜGER: *Afrika*, Berlin, 1952.

H. KÜHN: *Auf den Spuren des Eiszeitmenschen*, Wiesbaden, 1950.

JOSEPH KULISCHER: *Allgemeine Wirtschaftsgeschichte des Mittelalters und der Neuzeit*, Munich, 1929.

GERD KUTSCHER: *Chimu. Eine altindianische Hochkultur*, Berlin, 1950.

ALEXANDER GORDON LAING: *Travels in Timannee, Kooranko and Soolima, countries in Western Africa*, London, 1825.

RICHARD LANDER: *Records of Captain Clapperton's last expedition to Africa and the subsequent adventures of the author*, 2 vols., London, 1830.

Journal of an expedition to explore the course and termination of the Niger, 3 vols., London, 1832.

BARTHOLOMÉ DE LAS CASAS: 'Historia de las Indias', in: *Coleccion de documentos meditos para la historia de España*, Madrid, 1875–6.

LEO AFRICANUS: *History and description of Africa*, 3 vols., London, 1896.

HENRI LHOTE: *Les Touareg du Hoggar*, Paris, 1944.

DAVID LIVINGSTONE: *Missionary travels and researches in South Africa*, London, 1856.

Narrative of an expedition to the Zambesi, London, 1865.

A. GRANT MACCURDY: 'Human skeletal remains from the highlands of Peru', in: *American Journal of Physical Anthropology*, VI, 3, Washington, 1923.

PIO LUIGI MARINI: *Vasco da Gama*, Turin, 1929.

CLEMENT R. MARKHAM: *The Incas of Peru*, London, 1912.

HECTOR PEREZ MARTINEZ: *Cuauht émoc. La vie et la mort de la Culture aztèque*, Paris, 1952.

OTTO MENGHIN: *Las pinturas rupestres de la Patagonia*, Buenos Aires, 1952.

A. METRAUX: *Easter Island*, London, 1917.

Ethnology of Easter Island, Honolulu, 1940.

L'île de Pâques, Paris, 1941.

HANS MEYER: *Der Kilimandscharo*, Leipzig, 1902.

O. MEYNIER: *La pacification du Sahara et la pénétration saharienne*, Algiers, 1930.

G. MORI: *L'esplorazione geografica della Libia*, Florence, 1927.

S. E. MORISON: *Admiral of the Ocean Sea. A life of Christopher Columbus*, Boston, 1942.

E. H. MORRIS, J. CHARLOT and A. A. MORRIS: 'The temple of the warriors at Chichen Itza, Yucatan', in: *Carnegie Inst. Wash. Publ.*, No. 406, Washington, 1931.

MORUS: *Eine Geschichte der Tiere*, Hamburg, 1952.

GUSTAV NACHTIGAL: *Sahara und Sudan*, 3 vols., Berlin, 1879–89.

C. NIGG: 'A study of the blood group distribution among Polynesians', in: *Journ. Immunology*, vol. XIX, 2, Washington, 1930.

R. NITSCHE: *Uralte Wege, ewige Fahrt. Handel entdeckt die Welt*, Munich, 1953.

E. NORDENSKIÖLD: *Origin of the Indian civilisations in South America. Ethnogr. Stud.*, vol. IX, Gothenburg, 1931.

DORÉ OGRIZEK: *L'Afrique du nord*, Paris, 1952.

ADOLF PAHDE: *Der erste deutsche Afrikaforscher Friedrich K. Hornemann*, Hamburg, 1895.

F. E. PARIS: *Essai sur la construction navale des peuples extraeuropéens*, Paris, 1843.

MUNGO PARK: *Travels in the interior districts of Africa*, London, 1799.

S. PASSARGE: *Die Kalahari, Versuch einer physisch-geogr. Darstellung der Sandfelder des südafrikanischen Beckens*, Berlin, 1904.

Die Kalahari, Berlin, 1904.

OSKAR PESCHEL: *Geschichte des Zeitalters der Entdeckungen*, Leipzig, 1858, and Meersburg, 1930.

A. PIGAFETTA: *Relation du premier voyage autour du monde par Magellán, 1519–1522* Paris, 1923.

PEDRO PIZARRO: *Descubrimiento y conquista de los Reinos del Peru*, Lima, 1917.

H. PLETICHA: *Der Weg ins Unbekannte, Drei Jahrtausende Afrikaforschung in Augenzeugenberichten*, Rimpar, 1953.

HANS PLISCHKE: *Tahiti und Göttingen um 1780* (*Geschichtsverein für Göttingen und Umgebung*), Göttingen, 1938.

Christoph Columbus und die Entdeckung Amerikas, Leipzig, 1923.

Vasco da Gama, Leipzig, 1924.

'Thor Heyerdahls Kon-Tiki-Theorie und ihre Problematik', in: *Zeitschrift für Wissenschaft, Kunst und Literatur*, 8th year, No. 8, Stuttgart, 1953.

ELISE POCKO: *Erinnerungen an einen Verschollenen*, Leipzig, 1863.

W. PRESCOTT: *History of the Conquest of Peru*, London, 1892.

E. PRESTAGE: *The Portuguese Pioneers*, London, 1933.

J. PRINGLE: *A discourse upon some improvements of the means for preserving the health of mariners*, London, 1776.

J. K. PROKOSCH: *Die Literatur über die venerischen Krankheiten*, vols. I, II and III, Bonn, 1889–91.

PAUL REICHARD: *Stanley*, Berlin, 1897.

ERICH REIMERS: *Die Welser landen in Venezuela*, Leipzig, 1938.

RAOLO RIVELLI: *Christophoro Colombo a la scuola cartografica Genovese*, Genoa, 1937.

G. ROBERTSON: *The discovery of Tahiti. A journal of the second voyage of H.M.S. 'Dolphin' round the world under the command of Captain Wallis in the years 1766–1768*. London, 1948.

HENRY MORTON ROBINSON: *Stout Cortez. A biography of the Spanish conquest*, New York, 1931.

GERHARD ROHLFS: *Quer durch Africa, Reise vom Mittelmeer nach dem Tschadsee zum Golf von Guinea*, 2 vols., Leipzig, 1874–5.

Reise durch Marokko, Bremen, 1868.

Reise von Tripolis nach der Oase Kufra, Leipzig, 1881.

CHARLES DE LA RONCIÈRE: *La Découverte de l'Afrique au moyen âge*, 3 vols., Cairo, 1929.

SOPHUS RUGE: 'Was kostete die Entdeckung Amerikas?', in: *Globus*, vol. LXIII, Brunswick, 1893.

C. O. SAUER: 'A geographic sketch of early man in America , in: *Geogr. Revue*, vol. XXXIV, New York, 1944.

HEINRICH SCHIFFERS: *Die grosse Reise. Dr. H. Barths Forschungen und Abenteuer 1850–55*, Minden.

Wilder Erdteil Afrika. Das Abenteuer der grossen Forschungsreisen, Bonn, 1954.

Die Sahara, Stuttgart, 1950.

HERBERT L. SCHRADER :*Und dennoch siegte das Leben, Roman der grossen Krankheiten*, Stuttgart, 1954.

PERCY E. SCHRAMM: *Deutschland und Übersee. Der deutsche Handel mit den anderen Kontinenten, insbesondere Afrika, von Karl V bis zu Bismarck*, Brunswick, 1950.

GUSTAV VON SCHUBERTH: *Heinrich Barth, der Bahnbrecher der deutschen Afrikaforschung*, Berlin, 1897.

F. SCHULZE-MAIZIER: *Die Osterinsel*, Leipzig (probably 1927).

ARTHUR SCHURIG: *Die Eroberung von Mexiko durch Ferdinand Cortés*, Leipzig, 1918.

GEORG SCHUSTER: *Die Entdeckung Amerikas und ihre Folgen*, Basel, 1892.

JURI SEMJONOW: *Glanz und Elend des französischen Kolonialreiches*, Berlin, 1942.

H. J. SHAPIRO: 'The physical relationship of the Easter Islanders', in: *B. P. Bishop Mus. Bull.*, No. 160, Honolulu, 1940.

J. H. SPEKE: *Journal of the discovery of the source of the Nile*, 2 vols., London, 1863.

H. M. STANLEY: *In darkest Africa*, 2 vols., London, 1890.

Autobiography, edited by Dorothy Stanley, London, 1909.

How I found Livingstone, London, 1872.

Through the dark continent, 2 vols., London, 1878.

JULIAN H. STEWARD: *Handbook of South American Indians*, Washington, 1946.

KARL SUDHOFF: *Graphische und typographische Erstlinge der Syphilis-Literatur aus den Jahren 1495 und 1496*, Munich, 1912.

ARII TAIMAI: *Memoirs of Arii Taimai, E. Marama of Eimeo, Terriirere of Tooarai, Teriinui of Tahiti, Tauraatua i Amo*, Paris, 1901.

JULIO C. TELLO: *Prehistoric trephining among the Yauyos of Peru. International Congress of Americanists. Proceedings of the XVIIIth Session*, London, 1913.

FRANZ TERMER (Ed.): *Durch Urwälder und Sümpfe Mittelamerikas.* Cortés's fifth report to the Emperor Charles V. German translation and commentary, Hamburg, 1941.

JEAN TILHO: *Du lac Tchad aux montagnes de Tibesti*, Paris, 1926.

Une mission scientifique en Afrique Centrale, 2 vols., Paris, 1910–14.

LUIS TORRES: *Hernan Cortés*, Saragossa, 1939.

Transafrican Highways, Cape Town, 1949.

B. L. TRAPIER: *Les voyages Arabes au moyen âge*, Paris, 1937.

E. TREGEAR: *The Maori-Polynesian Comparative Dictionary*, Wellington, New Zealand, 1891.

Segelhandbuch für den Stillen Ozean Deutsche Seewarte, Hamburg, 1897.

JOHN W. VANDERCOOK: *Great sailor. A life of the discoverer Captain James Cook*, New York, 1950.

W. VOLZ: *Beiträge zur Anthropologie der Südsee. Arch. f. Anthropologie*, vol. 23, Berlin, 1895

HERMANN WAGNER: 'Die Reproduktion der Toscanelli-Karte vom Jahre 1474', in: *Göttingische Gelehrte Nachrichten* No. 3, Göttingen, 1894.

P. WAGNER: *James Cooks erste Entdeckungsreise in die Südsee und ihre Beziehung zu Winden und Strömungen*, Emsdetten, 1934.

H. WALLER: *The last journals of David Livingstone in Central Africa from 1865 to his death*, London, 1874.

J. WASSERMANN: *Das Leben Stanleys*, Zürich, 1949.

FRANCISCO DE XEREZ: *Verdadera Relación de la Conquista del Peru*, Madrid, 1891.

M. YANTOK: 'Das Geheimnis des Sargasso-Meeres', in: *Exponente, São Paulo*, March, 1953.

Year Book and Guide to Southern Africa, edited by A. Gordon-Brown, London, 1955.

HENRY YULE: *Cathay and the way thither*, London, 1866.

HEINRICH ZIMMERMANN: *Die Reise um die Welt mit Kapitän Cook*, Mannheim, 1781.

Revised edition by *Hans Franke*, Heidelberg, 1948.

ANTON ZISCHKA: *Afrika, Europas Gemeinschaftausgabe,* No. 1, Oldenburg, 1951.

STEFAN ZWEIG: *Magellán. Der Mann und seine Tat*, Vienna, 1938.

INDEX